CW01203721

ISBN 978-0-331-32236-1
PIBN 11105236

YEAR BOOK

of the

STATE OF COLORADO

1924

DETAILED INFORMATION REGARDING THE STATE, ITS RESOURCES, OPPORTUNITIES AND ATTRACTIONS, COMPILED FROM OFFICIAL AND SEMI-OFFICIAL SOURCES AND PUBLISHED UNDER THE AUTHORITY VESTED BY THE STATE LEGISLATURE IN THE STATE BOARD OF IMMIGRATION

Compiled and Edited by Howard D. Sullivan

STATE BOARD OF IMMIGRATION

GOV. WILLIAM E. SWEET, President

L. Wirt Markham, Lamar — Arthur H. King, Sterling

Allison Stocker, Denver

Edward D. Foster, Commissioner of Immigration

*Howard D. Sullivan, Deputy and Statistician

*Died May 10, 1924. Tolbert R. Ingram appointed Deputy Commissioner and Statistician.

Denver, Colorado. Eames Brothers, Printers
1924

SS

Table of Contents

Foreword

HE first Year Book of the State of Colorado, issued in 1918 by the Colorado Immigration Bureau, was received with favor by those who are interested in having statistical information relating to the state and its political subdivisions carefully tabulated and published so as to be easily available for the use of those who need it, and conveniently preserved as a permanent state record. Realizing the value of such a record and the necessity for maintaining its continuity, the Twenty-second General Assembly enacted a law requiring the Immigration Bureau to compile and publish the Colorado Year Book annually in the future. The second Year Book was published in compliance with this law in 1919, and it has been published annually since.

In order to make room for the large amount of statistical information now available for the Year Book it became necessary, beginning with 1921, to omit the descriptive county stories which had been included in previous issues. These county stories are now available in other publications issued by the Immigration Bureau. The additional statistical information available is obtained largely under an act passed by the Twenty-second General Assembly, clothing the Immigration Bureau with authority to collect much information it had been unable to obtain before the law was enacted. Additions to and improvements in the Year Book will be made from time to time as the funds available for the Bureau permit.

The Bureau acknowledges with thanks the willing assistance of state, county and city authorities and commercial club executives, to whose co-operation much of the success of this work is to be attributed.

THE COLORADO STATE BOARD OF IMMIGRATION.

Denver, Colorado, June 1, 1924.

Appreciation

Howard D. Sullivan, deputy commissioner and statistician of the Colorado State Board of Immigration, died May 10, 1924, only a few days before this edition of the Colorado Year Book came from the press. Until a short time prior to his death he remained steadfastly at his desk, despite a degree of physical weakness which would have justified him in abandoning all thought of work.

Because of his exceptional personal qualities and the splendid service which he rendered the State, the officers and members of the Immigration Bureau feel that some expression of appreciation of his work in this volume is eminently fitting.

The Colorado Year Book, now accepted and quoted as authority throughout the state, constitutes a veritable monument to his memory. From the first edition, published in 1918, down to the present edition it has been the product of his energy and intelligence. Gifted to an unusual degree with an understanding of the importance of preserving from year to year the outstanding statistical facts which tend to sketch the growth and development of a State and its industries, he developed sources of information which, combined with his insistence upon accuracy, made his work of exceptional value.

It is a privilege, therefore, for the officers and members of the Board of Immigration to give this public expression of their appreciation of the high class of service which Mr. Sullivan gave the State, his devotion to his work and the conscientious manner in which he enlarged and broadened its scope.

The Colorado State Board of Immigration

THE work carried on by the Colorado State Board of Immigration is best described by the statute creating the board, enacted in 1909, which provides that the duties shall be:

"To collect reliable information and statistics regarding agriculture, stock-growing and feeding, horticulture, mining, manufacturing, climate and health in Colorado, and to publish the same with a view to attracting health-seekers, tourists, investors and prospective settlers to the state; to prepare and cause to be circulated books, pamphlets, leaflets and other literature, illustrated or otherwise, regarding Colorado and the various localities of the state; to personally visit the various localities of the state, investigate the resources and possibilities thereof, and stimulate their proper advertising and exploitation; to personally and by deputies and employes visit other states and there distribute advertising matter, call personally upon intending investors, visitors or immigrants, install exhibits of Colorado views and prodncts, give lectures on Colorado and in general further the advertising of Colorado."

Much difficulty has been experienced in the past in obtaining the "reliable information and statistics" referred to in this act, for the reason that the Immigration Bureau was not clothed with any authority to collect them or require their collection. To correct this condition the Twenty-Second General Assembly enacted a law, supplementary to that of 1909, giving the bureau authority to require state, county, city, town, precinct and school district officers, owners, operators and managers of manufacturing, mining and other business establishments and certain other persons to furnish "such information as may be required for properly setting forth the resources of the state and their development." This law also provides for co-operation between the State Board of Immigration and the Division of Crop Estimates of the United States Bureau of Agricultural Economics in the collection and publication of information regarding livestock and acreage, condition and production of all crops, and requires county assessors, when making the annual property assessment, to collect for the bureau a wide variety of information regarding "farm operations, the principal farm products, agricultural resources and livestock."

Under the authority vested in the board by this act blanks have been furnished annually to all county assessors, and reports have been made for all counties where agriculture is followed. Complete reports for 1923 are published elsewhere in this volume. In the Year Books for 1919 and 1920 acreage figures collected by county assessors for the current year were published, but the volume is now published before assessors' reports are complete and only figures for the past year are used. Acreage figures for 1924 will be published in the monthly crop bulletin as soon as they are available and will be published complete in the 1925 Year Book.

The State Board of Immigration, acting under the authority granted in the act of 1919, has also entered into a contract with the United States Department of Agriculture prescribing the conditions under which the board shall co-operate with the Bureau of Crop Estimates in the publication of agricultural statistics for the state and the several counties. The contract provides for the organization of the Colorado Co-operative Crop Reporting Service, which is now in operation, and which publishes a crop bulletin monthly, using the acreage information collected through county assessors and statistics on condition and production of crops collected through the regular reporters of the Bureau of Crop Estimates and through other channels.

The corrected acreages as reported by assessors for 1923 are found in this volume, together with the production of the principal crops by counties, as determined by the Co-operative Crop Reporting Service. It has been found impracticable to give the production of all crops by counties, but a table will be found in this volume giving the total production of all crops for the state, as determined by the Crop Reporting Service, together with the values of these crops at prices prevailing on or about December 1, 1923. Beginning with the 1921 edition of the Year Book statistics of the acreage and production of all crops are published annually, providing a permanent record of the agricultural development of the state and the various counties, which will be of great value to all who are interested in Colorado's growth.

Colorado—General Description

COLORADO lies in the east-central part of the Rocky Mountain region and contains the most elevated portions of the Rocky mountains in the United States, though there are higher altitudes in both California and Washington, in the Cascade mountains, than are found in Colorado. The United States geological survey, in its latest published reports, assigns to two peaks in Lake county the honor of being the highest points in the state. These are Mount Elbert and Mount Massive, each with an altitude of 14,402 feet. The United States coast and geodetic survey, however, fixes the altitude of Mount Massive at 14,419 and that of Mount Elbert at 14,404 feet. The highest point in the United States is Mount Whitney, California, 14,501 feet. Colorado has the highest mean altitude of any state, only about one-fourth of its area being below 5,000 feet, while approximately two-thirds of it ranges from 6,000 feet to 14,000 feet. It has at least 43 peaks that tower 14,000 feet or higher above sea level, and approximately 1,000 having altitudes of more than 10,000 feet. The eastern two-fifths of the state lies in the Great Plains, and is a level or broken prairie, crossed by the valleys of the Arkansas and South Platte rivers and their numerous tributaries, and rising gradually from the state line westward to the foothills of the Rockies. The main range of the Rocky mountains passes north and south through the central part of the state, with numerous secondary ranges and spurs running in all directions, giving Colorado the greatest extent and widest variety of mountain scenery found in any state. The western part lies in the Pacific water-shed and contains the largest streams in the state. Its surface is much more broken than that of the eastern part, embracing numerous high mesas and fertile, narrow agricultural valleys, and rising to the rugged and wonderfully picturesque San Juan mountains in the southwest. In outline the state is almost a perfect rectangle, having the most regular form of any state in the Union. It ranks seventh in size, with a land area of 66,341,120 acres or 103,656 square miles. Its water area is 290 square miles, making the total area 103,948 square miles. It is more than twelve times as large as the state of Massachusetts, nearly twice as large as Iowa, and about the same size as New York, Ohio, Connecticut and New Hampshire combined. Its extreme length east and west is about 387 miles, or 37 miles more than the distance from New York City to Portland, Maine, and its width approximately 276 miles, about the same as the distance from Chicago to St. Louis.

Natural Divisions—As a result of its large size and the extreme irregularity of its surface, the state is divided into a number of districts that show considerable variation in topography, soil, climatic conditions, industries and products. The most important of these are the following: The non-irrigated prairie section in the eastern part of the state, popularly referred to as "Eastern Colorado;" the South Platte valley, in the north and northeast; the Arkansas valley, extending through the southern part of the eastern half of the state; the San Luis valley, a vast basin, the bed of an ancient lake, lying in the south-central part of the state, almost wholly surrounded by mountain ranges; the San Juan basin in the southwest; the valleys of the Colorado river and numerous tributary streams in the central-western part; the rugged plateau districts drained by the White and Yampa (Bear) rivers, in the northwest; the mountainous, mineral-bearing districts, extending in a broad, irregular belt across the central part of the state from the Wyoming to the New Mexico line; and the mountain park districts, chief of which are North park, in Jackson county; Middle park, in Grand county; and South park, in Park county. These last are very similar to the San Luis valley, but all have higher average altitudes and consequently enjoy less intensive agricultural development. In topography and climatic conditions the South Platte and Arkansas valleys are very similar to the non-irrigated sections of eastern Colorado, but by reason of the fact that a large supply of water is available in these valleys for irrigation, they enjoy the most extensive agricultural development found in the state and produce a wider range and greater yield of crops than the non-irrigated districts. The San Luis valley has very light rainfall, but an abundant water supply for irrigation is derived from the Rio Grande del Norte and its tributaries. The average altitude is more than 7,500 feet, which limits the range of crops grown;

but the fertile soil, abundant water supply and good climate make this valley one of the finest general farming and stockraising districts in the state. The San Juan basin is a region of from moderate to heavy rainfall, having a considerable area of irrigated land in the river valleys and much good non-irrigated agricultural land on the higher mesas. This is also an excellent stock-raising district. The valleys of the Colorado, Gunnison, Uncompahgre and other rivers and smaller streams of the Colorado river basin contain the principal fruit-growing areas of the state, as well as a large amount of the fine general agricultural land. The rainfall in this area is generally inadequate for farming without irrigation, but the water supply is adequate for all land that can be irrigated, and recently farming without irrigation has been undertaken successfully on some of the higher mesa lands, where rainfall is somewhat heavier than in the valleys. The northwest part of the state is less developed than any other district, chiefly because of lack of transportation facilities, but it contains some of the best agricultural and grazing land in Colorado. The mineral area is very extensive, but the principal producing areas are somewhat restricted and are outlined in tables published elsewhere in this volume.

Early History—That part of Colorado lying east of the Rocky mountains was included in the territory acquired by purchase from France in 1803, usually referred to as the Louisiana Purchase. All the southeastern part of the state, lying south of the Arkansas river, and a narrow strip extending north through the mountain district into Wyoming, was claimed by the state of Texas and became a part of the United States when Texas was annexed in 1845. This included a considerable amount of the territory belonging to the Louisiana Purchase, but the controversy regarding the northern boundary of Texas was settled long before Colorado became a state. The western part of what is now Colorado and an additional strip lying west and south of the Rio Grande del Norte was ceded to the United States by Mexico in 1848, following the war with Mexico. The actual settlement of Colorado began with the discovery of gold in the summer of 1858, at which time most of the eastern half of the state was included in Kansas territory under the name of Arapahoe county. The boundaries of this county were very imperfectly defined, and the settlers in the new gold camps, moreover, objected to being governed by a set of territorial officials 400 miles away. They appealed to the federal government for the organization of a new state or territorial government, and finally, in February, 1861, the territory of Colorado was organized, about a month after statehood had been conferred upon the territory of Kansas. The boundaries of the territory were substantially the same as are those of the state at present. In 1876 Colorado was admitted to the Union as the thirty-eighth state.

Population—The population of Colorado has increased steadily and rapidly since its actual settlement began immediately following the discovery of gold in 1858. The following table shows its growth from 1860 to the present time, as compared with the growth for the entire country, all figures being taken from census reports:

Year	Population	Pct. of Increase Over Previous Census	Pct. of Increase For United States
1860	34,277	....	....
1870	39,864	16.3	22.6
1880	194,327	387.5	30.1
1890	413,249	112.7	25.5
1900	539,700	30.6	20.7
1910	799,024	48.0	21.0
1920	939,629	17.6	14.9

During the two decades following 1860, the population was confined largely to the mining districts and to the city of Denver. The cities of Pueblo, Colorado Springs and Trinidad did not make their appearance in the census population statistics until 1880, when the three had a combined population of less than 10,000. During the early 80's the period of agricultural development began and the decade ending with 1890 was in many ways the most important in the history of the state. During that period 24 new counties were organized and scores of new towns were laid out in the agricultural districts. The percentage of increase in population dropped off materially in the succeeding decades, but remained considerably greater than the percentage of increase for the country at large. In 1910 the density of population for the state was 7.7 per square mile, as compared with 30.9 for the United States. Denver county ranked first in this respect, with 3,679, and Dolores and Jackson counties were tied for last place, with 0.6. The 1920 census showed the density of population for the state to be 9.06 per square mile. Denver still holds first place in this respect, with 4,422.26, and Jackson county ranks last, with 0.81. The rural population in 1910, including all people except those living in incorporated places of 2,500 population or more each, was 394,184, or 49.3 per cent of the total. The rural population as shown by the 1920 census was 486,370, or 51.76 per cent of the total. In 1910 the foreign-born white population was 15.9 per cent of the total, the principal foreign nationalities then being, in the order named, as follows: German, Italian, Russian, Austrian, English, Swedish, Canadian, Irish and Scotch. In 1920 the foreign-born white population was 12.4 per cent of the total, the principal foreign nationalities being Russian, Italian, German, Mexican and Swedish.

Land Classification—A table published elsewhere in this volume gives a classification of the 66,341,120 acres of land in the state as far as is practicable from available records. It is divided into 63 counties, of which Denver county is the smallest, with an area of 37,120 acres, and Las Animas county is the largest, with 3,077,760 acres. The records of the several county assessors showed a total of 33,347,491 acres of patented land on the tax rolls in 1923, including railroad rights of way and town and city lots and not including state land that has been sold but for which patent has not yet been issued. The records of the federal and state governments at the same time showed a total of 24,339,611.18 acres of non-patented land included in the national forests, homestead areas, national parks and monuments, Indian lands and state lands. From these records it is apparent that 50.26 per cent of the state's area consists of patented land, 36.84 per cent of state, federal and Indian land, and the remainder, amounting to 12.9 per cent, is principally unclassified as to ownership. This includes about 750,000 acres of state land that has been sold but not yet fully paid for, and approximately 1,500,000 acres of government land temporarily withdrawn from homestead entry for various reasons. The remaining unclassified area consists principally of homestead land that has been filed upon but not yet proved up and therefore not yet appearing on the tax rolls. In the five years ending with July 1, 1923, something more than 5,500,000 acres of homestead land has been filed upon under the various public land acts, comparatively little of which has been patented. In addition to this some of the land originally entered more than five years ago has not yet been patented, for the reason that it has been relinquished one or more times and the present holders have not had it long enough to obtain patents. In the mining counties there is some mineral land that has been filed upon under the mineral land laws but not yet patented. In three counties, Archuleta, Hinsdale and Lake, the amount of land shown in the various classifications is slightly more than the areas of these counties, as reported from government surveys. These discrepancies are perhaps due chiefly to inaccuracies in surveys, as considerable portions of the mountainous areas of the state have not yet been accurately surveyed, and all these counties contain mountainous areas. Of the land in private ownership in 1923 over 31,000,000 acres is classified as agricultural land. Of this amount 30,129 acres is producing fruit land, 2,286,592 acres is being farmed under irrigation and 271,988 acres is natural hay land. As all the orchards and most of the natural hay land are irrigated, the total amount of land classified for taxation purposes as irrigated amounts to something more than 2,585,000 acres, though the amount of land in the state for which water is actually available is considerably more than 3,000,000 acres. The non-irrigated farming area of the state is placed by the assessors at 11,167,030 acres, and 18,008,349 acres is classified as grazing land, much of which will eventually be placed under cultivation. These classifications include some waste and desert areas of no real value for agricultural purposes. The remaining privately owned area is principally patented mineral land, railroad rights of way, and town and city lots.

Drainage and Water Supply—Containing, as it does, the most elevated portions of the Rocky mountains, Colorado is quite naturally the source of many of the important streams in the west. The continental divide crosses the west-central part of the state, and the streams in the western part flow to the Pacific, while those in the east find their way to the Gulf of Mexico. The streams of the western slope are all tributaries of the Colorado river, from which this state derives its name. The Colorado (Grand) river, the largest stream in the state, has its source in Grand county. The Green river, which was regarded as one of the two streams forming the Colorado when the upper course of the Colorado was called the Grand river, flows through the northwestern corner of Moffat county. The northwestern corner of the state is drained by tributaries of the Green river, chief of which are the Yampa (Bear) and White rivers. The principal tributary of the Colorado river is the Gunnison, which has its source in Gunnison county and enters the Colorado at the city of Grand Junction. The southwestern corner of the state is drained by the San Juan and Dolores rivers, both tributaries of the Colorado. The south-central part of the state, including the San Luis valley, is drained by the Rio Grande del Norte. The southeastern part is drained by the Arkansas river and its tributaries, and the northeastern part by the South Platte river. The North Platte river has its headwaters in Jackson county and unites with the South Platte in Nebraska to form the Platte river. The Republican river, a tributary of the Kansas, drains a considerable area in the eastern part of the state. These streams have hundreds of small tributaries, most of which have their sources in the mountains where the snowfall is heavy. They furnish the principal water supply for irrigation and for the development of hydro-electric power. Water for domestic purposes is obtained principally from these streams, but in most agricultural sections wells are utilized as a secondary source of domestic water supply. Most of these wells are pumped, but there is a well-defined artesian belt in the San Luis valley, and artesian water is found in numerous other places. There are more than 8,000 artesian wells in the state, fully two-thirds of which are in the San Luis valley.

National Parks and Monuments—There are two national parks and three national monuments in Colorado. Rocky Mountain national park, with an approximate area of 254,327 acres, lies in Larimer, Boulder and Grand counties, and includes some of the most picturesque portions of the Rocky mountains. It is one of the newest of the national parks, having been created by an act of congress, approved January 26, 1915. Its highest point is Longs peak, 14,225 feet, and there are within its boundaries thirteen other mountain peaks more than 13,000 feet above sea level. It is the most accessible of the large western parks, and this fact, together with its wide range of picturesque mountain scenery and its delightful climate, has made it the most popular of the nation's great public playgrounds. The report of the secretary of the interior places the number of visitors to this park in 1915 at 31,000. The following year the number had increased to 51,000, and in 1917 it was 117,186. The nearest approach to this was recorded at the Mount Ranier national park, which had 35,568 visitors in 1917. In 1923 the number of visitors in the Rocky Mountain national park was about 218,000. Mesa Verde national park is located in Montezuma county and is especially noted for the ruins of homes and villages of the ancient Cliff Dwellers, supposed to have been the earliest inhabitants of this part of the continent. Travel to this park has increased very materially in the past few years, as the result of the construction of good highways leading to it. It was established by an act of congress June 29, 1906. Its area is 48,966 acres. The Colorado national monument, in Mesa county, near Grand Junction, was established by presidential proclamation on May 24, 1911. Its area is 13,883 acres. The site is in a picturesque canon which has long been a popular scenic feature of that part of Colorado. The formation is similar to that of the Garden of the Gods at Colorado Springs, but it is generally conceded to be much more picturesque. There are many caverns in the monument, several of which have not yet been explored. Wheeler national monument, located in Mineral county, northeast of Creede, was established by presidential proclamation on December 7, 1908. Its area is approximately 490 acres. It is especially noted for its weird and very picturesque rock formation, unlike anything found elsewhere in Colorado. Hovenweep, an Indian name meaning "Deserted Valley," is the third of Colorado's national monuments. It was established by presidential proclamation on March 2, 1923, and is situated on the Colorado-Utah line in western Montezuma county, its area of 285 acres lying partly in Colorado and partly in Utah. It contains four remarkable groups of ruins similar to those found in Mesa Verde park.

Industries—The principal industries of the state are agriculture, stock-raising in its various branches, dairying, bee-keeping, manufacturing, mining, quarrying, lumbering and commerce. These are treated in detail elsewhere.

Climatological Data — As a result of its great size and the extreme irregularity of its surface, the climate of Colorado is wonderfully varied and cannot be described in detail here. Various tables contained in this publication show the most important climatic data for different sections of the state. The mean annual temperature for the entire state is 44.3 degrees, but it varies from about 31 degrees in some of the higher mountain districts to 52 degrees in parts of the Arkansas valley. The average annual precipitation for the state is 17.54 inches, but there is also a very wide range here in the different sections of the state. The lowest average precipitation is about 6.5 inches, in the San Luis Valley, and the highest above 40 inches, in the San Juan mountains and a few other mountain districts of restricted areas. The delightful and wonderfully healthful qualities of Colorado's climate are well known throughout the country. The tables before referred to show that the rainfall is comparatively light in all sections of the state and the percentage of sunshine is very high. The range of temperature is wide. The amount of moisture in the air is always low, and as a result the unpleasant effects of extremely low or high temperatures are greatly modified. The normal relative humidity ranges from 45 to 60 per cent, being lower than in any other state except Arizona. The high altitude is another important factor in governing climatic conditions in the state. As a result of this high altitude and the correspondingly low atmospheric pressure, impurities in the air are quickly dissipated and the depressing effects common at low altitudes, especially during periods of warm, damp weather, are entirely foreign to this state.

Railroads, Telegraph and Telephone Facilities—There are 31 railroad companies represented in Colorado, operating an aggregate of 5,088.69 miles of main line track. Every county in the state except Baca county has some railroad mileage, though the railroad facilities of some other counties, particularly in the northwestern and southwestern parts of the state, are inadequate. The total value of railroad property in the state, as returned by the state tax commission for the year 1923, was $160,693,730. The following table shows the main line tracks owned by the several railroad companies:

Road	Mileage
Atchison, Topeka & Santa Fe Railway Company	505.62
Chicago, Burlington & Quincy Railroad Company	395.39
Chicago, Rock Island & Pacific Railroad Company	165.83
Colorado Railway Company	108.49
Colorado-Kansas Railroad Co.	22.20
Colorado, Wyoming & Eastern Railway Company	43.88
Colorado & Southern Railroad Co.	729.15
Colorado & Southeastern Railroad Company	6.27
Colorado & Wyoming Railroad Company	42.65
Crystal River Railroad Company	20.66
Crystal River & San Juan Co.	7.32
Denver & Inter-Mountain Railroad Company	15.10
Denver & Interurban Railroad Co.	9.48
Denver & Rio Grande Western Railroad Company	1,504.33
Denver & Salt Lake Railroad Co.	252.00
Great Western Railway Company	86.84
Greeley Terminal Railway Co.	1.60
Manitou & Pikes Peak Railway Company	8.70
Midland Terminal Railroad Co.	56.30
Missouri Pacific Railroad Co.	152.11
Northwestern Terminal Railway Company	3.18
Rio Grande Junction Railway Co.	62.08
Rio Grande Southern Railroad Company	171.16
San Luis Central Railroad Co.	12.21
San Luis Southern Railway Co.	31.53
Silverton Railroad Company	10.50
Silverton, Gladstone & Northerly Railroad Company	7.30
Silverton Northern Railroad Co.	8.00
Treasury Mountain Railroad Co.	4.00
Uintah Railway Company	50.80
Union Pacific Railroad Company	582.51

Several of the companies above named operate extensively under leasing arrangements over tracks owned by other companies.

Ninety-seven telephone companies operate in the state, owning an aggregate total of 371,700.52 miles of telephone line. This is an increase of more than 38,000 miles over the amount reported to the tax commission for 1922. The valuation of all property owned by these companies, as returned by the state tax commission for the purposes of taxation in 1923, was $13,544,500. Most of these companies are small and operate in but one or two counties. The Colorado and Eastern Telephone and Telegraph company operates in fifteen counties in the eastern part of the state, and the Mountain States Telephone and Telegraph company operates its own lines in all but two counties in the state, Baca and Dolores, and has a total of 361,330 miles of line in Colorado. Four telegraph companies operate a total of 27,723.59 miles of line in the state. Five counties, Baca, Hinsdale, Jackson, Moffat and Rio Blanco, had no telegraph lines in operation when reports were made to the tax commission for 1923. A table published elsewhere in this volume shows the mileage of railroad, telephone and telegraph lines in the various counties of the state as returned to the state tax commission for 1923.

Colorado State Land

WHAT is popularly known as state land in Colorado and other western public land states comprises the various areas turned over by the federal government to the state governments under general acts of congress and sundry special statutory grants, to be administered for the particular state interests in those states for which the grants were made. The most important of these grants were made under an act of congress passed in 1875, the year before Colorado became a state, by which the United States gave to each of the public land states an amount of land equal to one-eighteenth of the area of the state, for the benefit of the public schools. This is known as school land and quite generally in public land states all state land is referred to as school land, though various grants were made to the states for purposes in no way connected with the schools. The various grants made to Colorado, with the purposes for which made and the area acquired under each, are as follows:

	Acres
Public Schools	3,757,224.19
Agricultural College	89,991.18
Internal Improvements	499,789.96
Penitentiary	31,345.49
Public buildings	31,904.62
University	45,844.43
Reformatory	520.00
Saline lands	18,830.22
Total	4,475,450.09

The original school land grant gave to the state sections 16 and 36 in every township. As there were large Indian reservations and extensive private land holdings in Colorado at the time the grant was made, the state was permitted to select other public lands in lieu of those within these reservations and private holdings. As a result, the state acquired large blocks of land in various localities, sometimes almost entire townships. When the national forests were created the state also exchanged considerable areas of state land within the forest boundaries for government land in other localities. By the terms of the grants from the government the funds derived from the sale of school land constitute a permanent school fund, only the interest and the revenue derived from the administration of unsold land being available for use. The total amount of state land sold up to December 1, 1923, excluding all cancellations, was 1,483,760.91 acres, leaving 2,991,689.18 acres of state land unsold. Because of the low prices of farm products during the past year or so, the acreage of state land unapropriated is but a little less this year than last, due to cancellations of sales previously made.

The state lands are administered by the state board of land commissioners. State lands are leased and sold under regulations made by the board, which may be obtained from that body upon application. Leases are made for grazing purposes, for agriculture, for oils, minerals, etc. Before state lands can be sold, they must be appraised by representatives of the board and the applicant must agree to pay the price fixed by the appraiser. The land is then sold at public auction, selling at or above the appraised price. No state lands may be sold at less than $3.50 an acre. Leases are made much in the same way, minimum prices being fixed at which state lands may be leased for various purposes.

Of the 2,991,689.18 acres of state land in Colorado, approximately 473,732 acres is coal land, according to estimates made by the mineral superintendent of the state land board. This is the most valuable asset owned by the state, practically all of which was granted to Colorado by the federal government for the benefit of the public school system. The value of this land is estimated at approximately $100,000,000. It is distributed through nearly every coal-bearing district in the state as follows:

	Total Acres
Canon City District	
Fremont county	1,960
Northern Coal Fields	
Adams county	9,600
Arapahoe county	9,080
Boulder county	760
Denver county	1,920
Douglas county	13,180
Elbert county	30,020
El Paso county	44,700
Jefferson county	1,820
Weld county	75,560
Southern Coal Fields	
Huerfano county	11,400
Las Animas county	33,360
Yampa Coal Fields	
Moffat county	120,400
Routt county	69,720
Miscellaneous	
Archuleta county	732
Grand county	2,960
Gunnison county	3,440
Jackson county	25,080
La Plata county	9,960
Montezuma county	4,160
Park county	3,880
Total coal area	473,732

The estimates of the acreage and distribution of state coal lands are based on the reports of the United States geological survey. It is assumed that a very large percentage of the coal acreage will not be found to contain workable coal, and the estimates of value are based on this assumption. Government appraisers have placed the value of public coal land in Colorado at from $100 to $400 per acre, depending on the character of the deposits and their accessibility. The value of state coal land has been estimated at a little more than $200 per acre, which is generally conceded to be very conservative.

Only a small amount of state coal land has ever been sold as such by the state board of land commissioners. When state land is sold for agricultural purposes the state reserves all coal that may underlie it. The revenue derived by the school fund from this land comes from rentals on non-operative coal leases and from royalties on producing leases. During the biennial period ending November 30, 1922, there was a total of 17,114.45 acres of coal land leased by the state, the revenue from which during the period was $141,306.73. For the purpose of illustrating the development that is being made of state coal lands it may be stated that the revenue derived by the state from rental of and royalties on state coal land during the biennial period ending November 30, 1916, was $89,865.30, and for the preceding biennial period $81,088.56. The coal leases are granted for a period of five years and require a minimum royalty of 10 cents a ton run of mine upon at least 1,000 tons annually, whether any coal is mined at all or not, and 10 cents a ton on all coal in excess of an amount sufficient to produce the minimum annual rental.

From the figures given above it will be seen that only a very small percentage of the coal land owned by the state is under lease. This, of course, is due to the fact that most of it lies at a considerable distance from any railroad and cannot be worked profitably under existing conditions. The most important producing leases are located in the Canon City, Northern and Southern coal fields, in Fremont, Las Animas, Huerfano and Weld counties.

Homestead Land

ON JULY 1, 1923, there was 7,753,129 acres of unappropriated homestead land in Colorado, of which 6,131,339 acres was surveyed and opened to immediate entry. Four years previous the area of homestead land unappropriated was 10,062,078 acres. There was a small amount of withdrawn land restored to entry during the twelve months ending July 1, 1923, and a considerable amount of land applied for in tracts larger than 320 acres under the grazing homestead act, which applications were not allowed. This resulted in a considerable apparent increase in the amount of homestead land during the twelve months, and in a measure accounts for the comparatively small decrease in the amount of homestead land available on July 1, 1923, as compared with July 1, 1922, the actual decrease being only about 200,000 acres. The amount of land actually filed upon during the past twelve months was approximately 500,000 acres, which is considerably less than that filed upon during the preceding year. A considerable amount of land has been restored to entry since July 1, 1920, and a larger amount which was filed upon in tracts larger than 320 acres has not been classified as open to entry under the grazing homestead act, with the result that filings in excess of 320 acres have been restored to entry.

Nearly one-third of this homestead land lies in two counties in the northwestern part of the state, Moffat and Rio Blanco counties. It is in the Glenwood Springs land district and is classed by the officials of the land office as farming, grazing and mineral land, with no information given as to what portions belong to each of the three classifications. Practically all of it is from 25 to 90 miles from any railroad. Somewhat more than one-third of the homestead land of the state, approximately 3,000,000 acres, lies in the mountainous or semi-mountainous counties, at an altitude above 7,000 feet. Most of this is primarily useful for grazing purposes or for minerals it may contain. Small areas of agricultural land are to be found in the large homestead areas of these mountain counties, but practically all the land suitable for farming that lies within a reasonable distance from a railroad has been filed upon. About 200,000 acres of homestead land is to be found in the 25 counties lying east of the mountains. Perhaps not to exceed 10 per cent of this amount is suitable for farming, and nearly all of it is very small tracts, much below the size of a government homestead. It is safe to say that a dozen desirable full 320-acre government homesteads could not be found in this section of the state. The remainder of the available homestead land, somewhat less than 3,000,000 acres, is widely scattered over the western part of the state. A considerable amount of it is good farming area, but nearly all of it lies from 15 to 40 miles from any railroad. The rainfall in some sections is not sufficient to produce good crops without irrigation, and no definite plans for its reclamation by the government have been announced.

In addition to these withdrawals, there are a few comparatively small tracts withdrawn under what is known as the Carey act. These tracts are turned over by the federal government to the state and are administered by the state land board pending the construction of irrigation systems. But one Carey act irrigation system has been completed in Colorado, that being a small system watering about 15,000 acres in the neighborhood of Two Buttes, in northern Baca county. The accompanying table shows the amount of homestead land, by counties, open to entry in the various land districts of the state on July 1, 1923:

HOMESTEAD LAND OPEN TO ENTRY JULY 1, 1923

Del Norte Land District

County	Surveyed	Unsurveyed	Total
Alamosa	25,647	3,840	29,487
Chaffee	2,597	....	2,597
Conejos	135,760	....	135,760
Huerfano	3,900	3,840	7,740
Las Animas	....	28,640	28,640
Rio Grande	54,446	....	54,446
Saguache	214,276	....	214,276
Total	436,626	36,320	472,946

Denver Land District

County	Surveyed	Unsurveyed	Total
Adams	40	....	40
Arapahoe	40	....	40
Boulder	880	....	880
Clear Creek	2,350	11,600	13,950
Douglas	680	....	680
Eagle	17,820	....	17,820
Gilpin	560	3,480	4,040
Grand	94,020	25,040	119,060
Jackson	171,400	....	171,400
Jefferson	2,200	....	2,200
Larimer	28,480	4,141	32,620
Morgan	480	....	480
Routt	....	7,680	7,680
Summit	5,660	4,630	10,290
Weld	480	....	480
Total	325,090	56,570	381,660

Durango Land District

County	Surveyed	Unsurveyed	Total
Archuleta	83,498	35,303	118,801
Dolores	9,734	19,058	28,792
La Plata	51,317	6,415	57,732
Montezuma	155,968	58,160	214,128
Total	300,517	118,936	419,453

Glenwood Springs Land District

County	Surveyed	Unsurveyed	Total
Eagle	79,718	153,080	232,798
Garfield	564,695	139,164	703,769
Gunnison	....	5,760	5,760
Mesa	180,355	25,440	205,795
Moffat	999,035	304,200	1,303,235
Pitkin	23,430	9,000	32,430
Rio Blanco	780,354	323,403	1,103,757
Routt	116,583	4,560	121,143
Total	2,744,080	964,607	3,708,687

Lamar Land District

County	Surveyed	Unsurveyed	Total
Baca	1,007	....	1,007
Bent	1,521	....	1,521
Cheyenne	77	....	77
Kiowa	280	....	280
Las Animas	443	....	443
Prowers	200	....	200
Total	3,528	....	3,528

Leadville Land District

County	Surveyed	Unsurveyed	Total
Chaffee	62,191	....	62,191
Fremont	26,840	....	26,840
Lake	7,238	....	7,238
Park	62,830	4,000	66,830
Summit	465	....	465
Teller	2,480	....	2,480
Total	162,044	4,000	166,044

Montrose Land District

County	Surveyed	Unsurveyed	Total
Delta	130,635	32,520	163,155
Dolores	18,872	3,780	22,652
Gunnison	351,221	52,095	403,316
Hinsdale	98,541	11,200	109,741
Mesa	534,267	92,361	626,628
Montrose	388,466	153,636	542,102
Ouray	13,300	....	13,300
Saguache	110,564	....	110,564
San Miguel	110,559	70,447	181,006
Total	1,756,425	416,039	2,172,464

Pueblo Land District

County	Surveyed	Unsurveyed	Total
Alamosa	11,235	....	11,235
Bent	453	....	453
Crowley	668	7,326	7,994
Custer	6,201	....	6,201
El Paso	2,220	1,160	3,380
Fremont	264,101	7,116	271,217
Huerfano	28,686	....	28,686
Kiowa	....	2,438	2,438
Kit Carson	169	....	169
Las Animas	25,460	40	25,500
Lincoln	954	6,642	7,596
Otero	1,080	596	1,676
Pueblo	4,026	....	4,026
Saguache	20,223	....	20,223
Teller	29,969	....	29,969
Total	395,445	25,318	420,763

Sterling Land District

County	Surveyed	Unsurveyed	Total
Logan	1,040	....	1,040
Morgan	1,081	....	1,081
Phillips	160	....	160
Sedgwick	120	....	120
Washington	440	....	440
Weld	3,823	....	3,823
Yuma	919	....	919
Total	7,583	....	7,583
State Total	6,131,339	1,621,790	7,753,129

Colorado Water Power

ONE of the most valuable of Colorado's natural resources is water power. Although the volume of water carried in the streams of the state is generally comparatively small, most of these streams have their sources at high altitudes and a vast amount of power is developed as they descend over precipitous courses from the mountain sides to the plains below. The principal river systems having their origin in the state and developing sufficient water power to be utilized commercially are: The Colorado, on the western slope, the principal tributaries of which are the Yampa, White, Grand, Gunnison, Dolores and San Juan; the Rio Grande, in the south, draining the San Luis valley; the Arkansas, in the southeast, and the Platte, in the northeast. These streams have scores of comparatively small tributaries rising in the mountains, which drop from 1,000 to 6,000 feet in their courses. There is considerable variation in the amount of power available in these streams, due to the fact that the volume of water they carry differs widely at different seasons of the year. A maximum development could be obtained only through the storage of water in reservoirs during the flood seasons, so that a uniform flow of water could be obtained through the year. The following figures, taken from reports of the United States geological survey, furnish a good idea of the immense amount of water power available for commercial use in the state:

Minimum horsepower available from direct stream flow	828,500
Horsepower available from storage of water	2,568,200
Minimum horsepower from direct flow and storage	3,396,700
Maximum horsepower available during flood seasons	4,241,300

According to the report of the National Conservation commission, made in 1908, the total hydro-electric energy developed in the entire country at the time was 5,356,680 horsepower, and the total development in Colorado was 78,878 horsepower. Since that time the development in some parts of the country has been very marked, but the total horsepower now in use is less than three times the maximum amount available in the state of Colorado. Water power development in this state since 1908 has been slow, due largely to the withdrawal from entry of many of the best power sites, which are on government land. After working for several years in perfecting it Congress has now passed an act regulating the leasing of government power sites, and development of water power in all sections of the country has been given renewed impetus through the definite settlement of questions of policy relating to the development of water power in navigable streams and interstate streams. In Colorado several new power enterprises have been undertaken since the new law became effective and permits have been granted for a number that have done nothing so far in the way of construction. Further development of water power on the Colorado river, the largest stream in the state, is delayed to some extent by the fact that the compact between the several states interested and the federal government regulating the development of water power and irrigation on this stream, which has been in process of formation for some years, has not yet been fully ratified.

In 1919, when the latest detailed inquiry of the census bureau into manufacturing development was made, the factories of Colorado were using but 194,634 horsepower of energy in their operations. Of this amount only about 60,000 horsepower was electric and not all of this was hydro-electric. The total development of hydro-electric energy in the state at this time is probably not in excess of 125,000 horsepower, much of which is being utilized in operating street lighting systems, street railways and traction lines and in furnishing power for the operation of mining machinery in metal and coal mines. Figures from the partial census of manufacturing for 1921 are not yet available.

Much of the electric energy for street lighting in Denver is generated nearly 200 miles from the city, at the town of Shoshone, Garfield county, and is carried across the range by high voltage transmission lines. This example is cited to show the possibilities for the distribution of hydro-electric energy, and should be conclusive evidence that the power generated from the streams in the most remote parts of the state can be utilized profitably in the development of manufacturing and other industries in the cities and more thickly populated rural districts.

The need for further development of water power occasioned by the war demand for greatly increased production from the country's factories has emphasized anew the manufacturing possibilities of the Rocky Mountain west, where raw materials of nearly all kinds are abundant, and where hydro-electric energy can be developed in large volume, at comparatively small expense. The people of Colorado are keenly alive to the wonderful possibilities in this direction offered in the Centennial state, and there is every indication that considerable investments in the development of water power in the state may be expected in the immediate future.

Irrigation in Colorado

FARMING under irrigation began in Colorado almost as soon as gold mining. Its development was not very rapid in the beginning but it was steady and persistent, and today the value of the annual output of the state's irrigated farms is more than ten times as great as that of its gold mines.

David K. Wall, one of the pioneer agriculturists of the state, farmed a two-acre tract of land at Golden in 1859, which he irrigated by direct flow from one of the small tributaries of Clear creek. His experiment proved so successful that he increased his irrigated area to eight acres the following year. Again he was very successful and the story of his success spread rapidly.

It was not until about 1870, however, that large community irrigation enterprises began to be undertaken. Up to this time only short ditches had been in operation, carrying water directly from the streams to the low lands lying in the narrow creek and river valleys. Most of these pioneer irrigation systems were individual enterprises, watering from 10 to 100 acres each. With the new era of development, large community enterprises were undertaken and ditches were constructed that carried water to the fertile uplands, far back from the narrow valleys. Irrigation on a large scale was first undertaken in the Greeley district, in northern Colorado, the water being taken from the South Platte river and its tributaries. The undertakings were generally successful and other districts immediately followed the example of northern Colorado. In 1889, when the United States census bureau made its first detailed report on irrigation enterprises, Colorado ranked second among the states in irrigation development, with 890,775 acres of land under ditch. California was first at that time, with 1,004,223 acres irrigated.

The two decades following 1889 witnessed Colorado's greatest irrigation development. In 1899 the census bureau found that this state had taken first rank, with 1,611,271 acres of irrigated land, an increase of 80.9 per cent over the acreage irrigated in 1889. California, in the meantime, had shown an increase of but 44 per cent, having a total irrigated area of 1,445,872 acres. In 1909 Colorado still ranked first with 2,792,032 acres under irrigation, and California second, with 2,664,104 acres. In 1919 Colorado ranked second and California first.

Completed irrigation enterprises in this state at present are capable of watering approximately 3,900,000 acres of land, and the total amount spent on all irrigation enterprises to the beginning of 1920 was in excess of $88,000,000. The accompanying table gives important irrigation statistics as compiled by the United States census bureau for 1919 and 1920:

Irrigation in 1919

Number of farms irrigated in 1919	28,756
Acreage irrigated in 1919	3 348,385
Acreage enterprises were capable of irrigating in 1920	3,855,348
Acreage included in irrigation projects in 1920	5,220,588
Main ditches—number, 1920	8,867
Length, miles	19,022
Laterals—Number, 1920	6,185
Length, miles	8,571
Reservoirs—Number, 1920	979
Capacity, acre-feet	2,406,372
Flowing wells—Number, 1920	476
Capacity, gallons per minute	20,139
Pumped wells—Number, 1920	527
Capacity, gallons per minute	210,094
Pumping plants — Number, 1920	406
Capacity, gallons per minute	299,726
Average lift, feet	23
Cost of irrigation enterprises up to January 1, 1920	$88,302,442
Estimated final cost of existing irrigation enterprises	$95,198,423

In 1909 62.7 per cent of the area cultivated in Colorado was irrigated. Since that time there has been a comparatively small increase in the irrigated acreage, but a very large increase in the cultivated acreage of non-irrigated land. In 1919 the irrigated acreage was about 38 per cent of the entire acreage cultivated, and in 1921 it was only about 30 per cent. The percentage is decreasing each year as the acreage of non irrigated land under cultivation in the state increases. In 1909 the value of crops grown on irrigated land was 79.6 per cent of the value of all crops grown in the state, while in 1919 it was only a little more than 50 per cent.

It will be noted from a comparison of the reports of the census bureau for 1909-10 and for 1919-20 that there was an increase of 19.9 per cent in the acreage of land actually irrigated in the decade between the two reports, but a loss of 3.4 per cent in the acreage completed enterprises were capable of irrigating and a loss of 11.8 per cent in the acreage included in irrigation enterprises. The report for 1910 showed 3,990,166 acres capable of being irrigated in 1910, compared with 3,855,348 acres capable of being irrigated in 1920. This apparent decrease is due very largely to a discovery after irrigation systems had been put into operation that they would not irrigate as many acres of land as they were intended to irrigate when first constructed. In some cases this was due to the fact that less water was available than preliminary estimates indicated and in other cases more water was required for the irrigation of a given acreage than it was thought would be required. It was found that several irrigation enterprises completed before the beginning of 1910 did not have nearly as much water as it was thought they had, this being especially true of enterprises on the east side of the mountains that were built to use flood waters. The same facts account to a certain extent for the decrease in acreage included in irrigation enterprises in 1920 as compared with 1910. The report for 1910 showed 5,917,457 acres of land included in all irrigation enterprises in the state, while that for 1920 showed but 5,220,588 acres. A part of this decrease also was due to the facts that many small enterprises have been abandoned since 1910 and parts of a considerable number of large enterprises have been given up for one reason or another. The period between 1910 and 1920 was very unfavorable for large irrigation development in Colorado and few new enterprises were undertaken, while many of the older ones were partly or wholly abandoned. A great many enterprises already under way were completed, however, which accounts for the substantial increase in irrigated acreage in 1920 as compared with 1910.

But the acreage irrigated in 1919 was considerably more than the acreage cultivated under irrigation, as shown by the report of the census bureau on cultivated areas in Colorado. This report showed 1,923,950 acres cultivated under irrigation in 1919, exclusive of orchards. Of course there was a considerable amount of irrigated land previously cultivated that was lying fallow that year and a considerable acreage devoted to pasture, which is not listed in the crop acreage report. It is evident, however, that the irrigated acreage reported includes a considerable amount of land that has never been under cultivation. The census bureau reported 1,581,394 acres of land cultivated under irrigation in the state in 1909, exclusive of orchards, and such information as is available indicates that very little more than 2,000,000 acres of irrigated land has ever been cultivated in the state in any one year.

An inquiry made by the immigration department early in 1919 indicated that there is in the state a very considerable acreage of land for which water is available that has never been under cultivation and the census figures bear out this indication. According to the census report there is more than 500,000 acres capable of being irrigated by existing systems to which water has never been supplied, and there also is nearly as large an acreage reported as irrigated that has never been actually placed under cultivation. It also appears that a full development of irrigation in the state, with the use of all available water that can be applied to land without prohibitive expense, will bring the irrigation of practically twice as much land as has ever been actually watered.

A special committee appointed at the suggestion of the Colorado Council of Defense in 1918 reported to the members of the Twenty-second General Assembly that there was special need for some sort of supervision over the financial affairs of many of the irrigation districts organized under the state irrigation laws. As a result of this report a law was enacted providing for the creation of a commission to co-operate with those financially interested in the various irrigation districts, including bondholders as well as landholders, in an effort to straighten out some of the financial tangles that have interfered with the completion of the irrigation systems undertaken in many of these districts. This commission was appointed and during 1919 and 1920 framed a bill for an amended irrigation district law, which was enacted with some amendments by the Twenty-third General Assembly in 1921. A number of other important irrigation measures were enacted in 1921, among them a series of laws providing for co operation between Colorado and other states of the Colorado river basin in settling controversies among the states of this basin over the use of its waters for both power and irrigation. Such laws were passed by the other states of the basin and commissioners were appointed to represent each state and the federal government. The commission thus created was organized and has practically completed its work with the submission of an agreement or compact between the states interested and the federal government. The compact has now been ratified by all the states except Arizona. Present indications are that Arizona will persist in its refusal to ratify and it may become necessary to modify the compact somewhat before complete ratification can be obtained.

For the purpose of making it possible to secure comparative statistics of any value concerning the development of irrigation in Colorado, the law relating to the administration of the public waters of the state is in need of material amendment. Under the law as it now stands the state engineer has no authority by which he can compel the commissioners of the various districts to render accurate reports each year on the various phases of irrigation development which are of vital interest to the state and the country at large.

By reason of that condition it is impossible to secure from the biennial reports of the state engineer any authoritative comparative data by which the development of irrigation may be traced. The amount of irrigation and storage water used on the irrigable land of the state varies materially from year to year, being governed largely by precipitation and other climatic conditions. This information, together with the capacity of ditches and reservoirs, the number of acres irrigated and the number of miles of main and lateral ditches, should be prepared each year by the commissioners and submitted to the state engineer for compilation.

For the purpose of administering the waters, the state is divided into six divisions, each in charge of a division engineer; the divisions in turn are divided into districts, of which there are 69 in the state, each in charge of a water commissioner. The state engineer is appointed by the governor, subject to civil service regulations; the division engineers are appointed by the governor, with the approval of the senate, and the water commissioners are appointed by the governor upon the recommendation of the county commissioners of the counties included in each district, all subject, of course, to civil service regulations prescribed by constitutional amendment and by statute, after the acts designating methods of appointing these officials were passed. As will be seen, the system confers upon the state engineer no authority which he can enforce. Partly as a consequence of this condition the records in the office of the state engineer are of less value than they would be had that official authority to require the collection and compilation of accurate information by each commissioner each year.

Reports of all county assessors for 1923 showed a total of 2,286,592 acres of irrigated farm land in the state and 30,129 acres of orchards, practically all of which are irrigated. In addition to this the same records showed 271,988 acres of natural hay land, a very large percentage of which is irrigated. These figures include approximately all the land that is actually being cultivated under irrigation, though not all for which irrigation water is available. Competent authorities estimate that there has been close to 1,000,000 acres of irrigated land in the state so damaged from over-irrigation, combined with lack of proper drainage, that it is not now producing to anything like its former capacity and much of it is not now being cultivated at all.

Agriculture

FOR more than a quarter of a century following the discovery of gold in the mountains west of where Denver now stands Colorado was known to the industrial world almost exclusively through its metal mines. It was a leader among the states in the production of gold and silver, but its agricultural output was almost negligible. The eastern part of the state was classed as desert land, and the reclamation of the river valleys by means of irrigation was just begun. The natural result is that Colorado is still best known in other parts of the country as a mining state, though the annual value of the output of its farms today, including livestock, poultry and dairy products, is nearly four times that of its mines and quarries.

It is not the purpose of this volume to enter into any extended discussion of the development of agriculture or of any other industry that has grown up in the state. A few figures will be given from census reports, however, for the purpose of illustrating the rapidity with which farming developed in Colorado after it was demonstrated that it could be carried on profitably. The principal crops grown in the state on which acreage reports have been returned to the census bureau each decade, beginning with 1879, are corn, oats, wheat, barley, hay, forage and potatoes. The following table shows the acreage devoted to these crops as returned to the census bureau in five census reports:

Year	Acres
1879	211,936
1889	859,429
1899	1,519,395
1909	2,388,749
1919	4,701,524

From this tabulation it will be seen that the acreage devoted to these crops was more than twenty times as great in 1919 as it was in 1879. In 1923 the area devoted to these same crops was considerably greater than that in 1919. In the past decade, which has been the period of greatest agricultural development in the state's history, the area devoted to these crops has doubled. In addition to this there has been a very substantial increase in the acreage devoted to field peas, sugar beets, field beans, melons, truck and seed crops and a few other crops not included in the above acreage figures.

Under a law enacted by the Twenty-second General Assembly early in 1919 county assessors are required to collect annually for the state immigration department a large amount of information regarding agricultural operation, including the acreage cultivated to all crops each year. The work was first undertaken in 1919, assessors being furnished blanks for obtaining reports on the acreage of all crops planted for the 1919 harvest. These blanks are prepared jointly by the state immigration department, the agricultural statistician for Colorado of the division of livestock and crop estimates of the United States bureau of agricultural economics and the Colorado Agricultural college. All county assessors obtained remarkably complete reports on these schedules in 1919, considering the short time available for preparation, as the law was signed less than a week before the annual property assessment was begun and it requires that all agricultural data be gathered when the property assessment is being made. The reports have shown an improvement each year since 1919.

Tables printed elsewhere in this volume show the acreage devoted to all important crops grown in the state in 1923, by counties, as reported by county assessors, and the production by counties for the most important crops, as calculated by the immigration department for the State Co-operative Crop Reporting Service. It is believed that this information will be found especially valuable to all interested in the production, movement and marketing of farm crops, since it has never before been available by counties except for census years, and then not until more than a year after the crop reported upon had been harvested.

The same law referred to above provides for co-operation between the state immigration department and the division of livestock and crop estimates of the United States bureau of agricultural economics in collecting, compiling and publishing information relating to acreage, condition and production of all crops. Under the authority thus granted the immigration department has entered into a contract with the United States department of agriculture specifying the manner in which this work shall be done and authorizing the establishment of the Colorado

Co operative Crop Reporting Service, which publishes monthly bulletins showing the progress and development of all crops from planting time to harvest.

Through this service accurate information is available showing the production of all important crops by counties and of all farm and orchard crops for the state as a whole. Elsewhere in this volume will be found, in addition to the agricultural tables mentioned above, a table showing the acreage and production of all crops for 1923 and 1922, and the values of these crops, according to prices prevailing on or about December 1 of each year. It is the purpose of the Crop Reporting Service to maintain a uniform set of statistical agricultural production tables from year to year, so that it will be possible in the future to trace the agricultural development of the state and of each county in the state, a thing which has not before been possible in Colorado with available records. In the past accurate statistics of agricultural production were collected only once in ten years, by the census bureau. Reference to these figures will give some idea of the rapidity with which agriculture has been developed in Colorado. The federal census bureau found the value of all crops grown in the state in 1899 to be $16,970,588. In 1909 the same bureau found the value of all crops grown in the state to be $50,974,958. The value of all crops grown in the state in 1919, according to reports of the census bureau, was $181,065,239. The Co-operative Crop Reporting Service estimated the value of crops grown in the state in 1920 at about $157,000,000, that of 1921 crops at about $91,000,000, of 1922 crops about $102,000,000, and that of 1923 crops at about $130,000,000. These large increases in the value of crops grown in the state in the past two decades are partly the result of increases in prices, but primarily they are due to increases in production. The large decrease for 1921 and 1922 was due chiefly to decreases in prices.

There has been a remarkably rapid increase in the value of farm property in Colorado in the past 40 years, as well as in the number of farms and the acreage of land in farms. The acreage of land cultivated has increased very rapidly in this period, but it is still far below the available area that can be farmed. In past years the immigration department has collected through county assessors figures by counties showing the acreage of privately owned land capable of cultivation that had not yet been broken. These figures were never complete and for that reason their collection has been discontinued, so they do not appear in the Year Book this year. It is safe to say, however, that less than 40 per cent of the patented land in this state that is capable of being farmed profitably has been broken. There is also a considerable acreage of homestead land and state land in the state capable of producing crops that has never been placed under cultivation.

Complete reports on the results of the agricultural census for 1919 and 1920 are now available. Some of the data were published in the 1921 Year Book and a few census tables were included in the 1922 volume.

The following tabulations, compiled from the census reports for 1890, 1900, 1910 and 1920, show how rapid the increase in farm area and value of farm property has been:

Number of farms: 1890, 16,289; 1900, 24,700; 1910, 46,170; 1920, 59,934.

Land in farms, acres: 1890, 4,598,941; 1900, 9,474,588; 1910, 13,532,113; 1920, 24,462,014.

Average size of farms, acres: 1890, 281; 1900, 384; 1910, 293; 1920, 408.

Value of farm property: 1890, $110,358,040; 1900, $161,045,101; 1910, $491,471,806; 1920, $1,076,794,749.

The number of farms reported by the census bureau for 1920 is somewhat greater than the number reported by county assessors, the principal reason for this being that county assessors generally report only farms on which land is actually being cultivated, while the census bureau reports all farms. The acreage in farms reported by the census bureau also is much greater than the acreage reported to the state immigration department, chiefly for the same reason. County assessors report for purposes of taxation, however, about 7,000,000 acres more of farm land in the state than is reported by the census bureau for 1920. The average size of farms as reported by the census bureau is much larger than the average size of the farms reported to the immigration department by county assessors. This is due to the fact that most of the pasture and other unimproved farms reported by the census bureau and not reported by the county assessors are much above the average size of improved farms reported. The increase in the average size of farms in the past ten years has been due chiefly to the fact that much homestead land has been entered during that period, chiefly in tracts of 320 acres or more. A large number of small farms also have been consolidated in the past decade into larger farms, principally in the fruit-raising districts. The value of farm property has grown very rapidly in the past decade, as will be seen from the figures given, but the 1920 census was taken at a time when farm values were at about their highest. There has been a decrease in prices of nearly all classes of farm property since that time, so that the value of farm property in the state today is considerably lower than that reported by the census bureau.

Stockraising

STOCKRAISING is, next to mining, Colorado's oldest industry. In the territorial days, when perhaps not one person in one hundred who knew anything about Colorado had any confidence in its agricultural possibilities, the stockmen were already establishing themselves on the free range and were pasturing thousands of cattle and sheep on the rich native meadows of the mountain parks and the more favored lowlands. Almost the entire state was open range then and cattle and sheep were pastured at very small expense during the summer and shipped east to be finished for the packers' markets. At first stockraising was confined largely to the mountain valleys and the lowlands near the foothills, but gradually the herds overran the plains of eastern Colorado, where government land was abundant and there was almost no farming.

In the late 70's and early 80's homesteaders began to take up the free range and to restrict somewhat the activities of the stockmen. There was really plenty of land for all, however, and open range stockraising continued to thrive in all parts of the state until far into the 90's. Since that time the settlement of farming lands has been very rapid, and at the present time range pasture is confined largely to the national forests and the government land in the northwestern part of the state. Range regulations within the national forest are strict and are carefully enforced, while the remaining homestead land is being filed upon so rapidly under the grazing homestead act that free government range will become obsolete in Colorado within a very few years.

But the passing of the range has proved a blessing to the stockraising industry in this state. While it has greatly diminished the number of stock cattle marketed, it has made Colorado one of the leading states in the production of high grade fat cattle, hogs and lambs. The production of feeder stock has given place largely to a more intensive industry, that of producing finished animals of the best grades, ready for selling to the packers at the highest market price. There has also been a very substantial development of the dairying industry in the past two decades. In 1910 74.1 per cent of the farms in the state reported cattle of some kind, and 70.7 per cent of them reported dairy cattle. On January 1, 1920, the census bureau found cattle on 84.3 per cent of the farms in the state, and dairy cattle on 61.9 per cent. Most of the farms which have no cattle at present belong to homesteaders who have not yet found the means to stock them.

A table published elsewhere in this volume gives the number of domestic animals of all kinds in the state, as reported to the county assessors for assessment purposes in 1923. These figures are considerably below the actual number of domestic animals in the state, but they are of great value in showing the distribution of these animals by counties. The following tabulation, taken from reports published by the United States department of agriculture, shows the estimated number of domestic animals in the state on January 1, 1924, and January 1, 1923:

	1923	1924
Horses	408,000	400,000
Mules	33,000	33,000
Milch cows	253,000	261,000
Other cattle	1,361,000	1,279,000
Sheep	2,444,000	2,360,000
Swine	523,000	622,000

The census bureau found the value of all domestic animals sold in the state in 1909 to be $22,453,959. The value of those slaughtered on farms was placed at $1,754,216, making a total value of $24,208,175. This figure includes horses and mules sold, as well as food animals. The census bureau did not collect this information for 1919, but the value of the livestock sold from the farms and ranches of the state that year was close to $50.-000,000, or more than twice as great as that for 1909. While this increase is due partly to increased prices for food animals as well as for horses and mules, a large part of it resulted from a substantial increase in the number of animals produced and a very pronounced improvement in the quality of the stock marketed.

There has been a substantial increase in the numbers of each class of livestock on farms in the state in the past decade, as shown by the census reports for 1920 and 1910. The following table shows the numbers of each of the principal classes of livestock as reported by the census bureau for the two years:

	1920	1910
Horses	420,704	284,647
Mules	31,125	14,000
Cattle	1,756,616	1,041,536
Sheep	1,813,255	1,305,596
Swine	449,866	179,294

In 1920 and 1921 conditions in the livestock industry were generally unfavorable, and the increase in numbers of livestock in the state did not continue. There was a material decrease in the number of beef cattle and some decrease in the number of sheep, while horses and mules have remained about the same, and milch cows and swine increased somewhat. The temporary depression is apparently passing, and every class of livestock shows a tendency toward price recovery in the early part of 1924, though the advance is very slow.

Detailed information regarding the localities where the various branches of the livestock industry are being followed most extensively cannot be given in this volume, but such information will be found in district booklets published by this department describing the several sections of the state.

In a general way it may be stated here that very large numbers of feeder cattle still are produced on the excellent grazing lands in the national forests, in the mountain park districts and on the open range in the northwestern, western and southwestern parts of the state, while stock-feeding is most extensively developed in the irrigated districts of the South Platte watershed, the Arkansas valley, the San Luis valley, the western slope and southwest Colorado. Sheep are still kept in large numbers for shearing, principally in southern Colorado, while lambs are fattened for market principally in the South Platte valley, the Arkansas valley and the San Luis valley. The total wool clip for 1919 was found by the federal census bureau to be 9,755,312 pounds, Colorado ranking twelfth among the states in wool production. The following table shows the rank of the state in the number of domestic animals on farms January 1, 1924:

	Rank
Horses	18
Mules	22
Milch cows	28
Other cattle	8
Sheep	8
Hogs	27

Colorado undoubtedly ranks considerably higher in the value of livestock and livestock products marketed annually than these figures would indicate. It is difficult to obtain anything like accurate data showing actual returns from the sale of livestock and livestock products, there being no state department and no single commercial or shipping organization which gathers all the information. The act passed by the Twenty-second General Assembly giving the state board of immigration authority to demand this information from those having it in their possession and providing a penalty for failure to supply such information when it is properly requested will eventually make it possible for the immigration department to collect these statistics annually. At the present time, however, the funds available for the use of the department are not sufficient to meet the expense of gathering and tabulating them, in addition to the other duties imposed by law upon the board.

Dairying

THERE has been very rapid development in the dairying industry in Colorado during the past decades, but the output of dairy products in the state is still considerably short of consumption and there is excellent opportunity in nearly all agricultural districts for further development.

The number of dairy cattle still is increasing steadily each year, especially in the non-irrigated districts, where agricultural development at present is much more rapid than in the irrigated areas. During the past four years, while there was a decrease in nearly every class of livestock in the state, dairy cattle continued to increase slightly in numbers and the character of dairy stock improved even more rapidly than during more prosperous periods.

The United States department of agriculture estimated the number of dairy cows over one year old in Colorado on January 1, 1924, at 261,000, compared with 253,000 for 1923. The census bureau found the number of milch cows on farms in the state April 1, 1910, to be 144,734. The number of milch cows not on farms at that time was 11,722, making a total for the state of 156,506. Census reports of the 1920 census showed 233,747 dairy cows on the farms of the state on January 1, 1920.

The following statistics, compiled under the direction of the state dairy commissioner, show the number of commercial establishments in the various branches of the dairying industry in the state on July 1, 1923:

Creameries making butter	80
Condenseries	5
Cheese factories	7
Ice cream plants	69
Goat cheese factories	21
Dried milk plants	1

The latest data available showing the amount and value of dairy products manufactured in the state is from the same source. The following figures show the amount and value of dairy products manufactured in the state and certain data on farm production and consumption of dairy products for the year ending July 1, 1923:

	Quantity	Value
Butter, lbs.	15,319,765	$ 6,587,498.95
Ice cream, gals.	1,768,168	2,033,393.20
Condensed milk, cases	435,848	1,841,028.00
Cheese, lbs.	1,407,073	267,343.87
Ice cream mix, gals.	149,919	151,418.19
Condensed skim	....	27,486.00
Powdered and malted milk	....	261,320.44
Condensed and dried buttermilk, lbs.	602,340	30,919.38
Goat cheese, lbs.	250,00	75,000.00
Buttermilk, gals.	487,767	24,388.35
Other dairy products manufactured	....	54,680.52
Total value of factory products	....	$11,354,476.90
Estimated value of milk consumed, gals.	48,390,900	$ 9,238,790.63
Estimated value of farm butter, lbs.	6,406,952	2,754,989.89
Total value of all dairy products	....	$23,348,256.89

At the present time the production of butter in the state is slightly in excess of consumption and some butter is being shipped into surrounding districts where consumption exceeds production. The production of cheese is much below consumption and this branch of the industry offers good opportunities for further development.

There is no strictly authentic record available showing the present distribution of dairy cattle by counties, there having been considerable change since January, 1920, when the latest census figures were compiled. The reports of the various county assessors on livestock assessed, published elsewhere in this volume, show but 143,163 dairy cows in the state in 1923, as compared with 253,000 reported by the United States department of agriculture, and 233,747 reported by the census bureau for 1920. In this report Weld county leads in the number of milch cows, with El Paso county second, Elbert county third, Logan county fourth, and Adams county fifth. In a general way it may be stated that the most rapid development in the dairy industry during the past decade has been in the non irrigated districts of eastern Colorado. This has been largely the result of a very general change in farming methods in these districts. Forage crops are now being grown extensively and nearly all farmers are keeping a few dairy cattle to consume this forage. Few sections of the country have shown more rapid increase in the number of silos during the last five years than eastern Colorado, and they are being built rather rapidly in all sections of the state, principally to preserve winter feed for dairy cattle. The number of silos in the state is above 4,000. During the past year the increase has been much less rapid than it would have been normally, because of the high cost of construction, the difficulties in obtaining necessary materials and the low prices prevailing for farm products. It is generally conceded that no branch of agriculture offers better opportunities in the state than dairy farming.

The following figures, taken from the reports of county assessors before referred to, are given here, not because they show accurately the number of dairy cattle on hand in the leading dairying counties, but as an indication of where the industry is most extensively developed:

County	Number of Dairy Cows	Value
Weld	15,785	$663,320
Logan	7,020	280,970
El Paso	6,155	254,330
Adams	6,065	273,690
Elbert	5,872	239,023
Larimer	5,764	299,780
Boulder	5,536	239,620
Mesa	5,338	236,153
Douglas	5,050	260,665
Delta	4,886	199,445
Pueblo	4,481	219,625
Jefferson	4,415	180,700
Arapahoe	4,247	206,615
Morgan	3,999	170,860
Garfield	3,493	152,255
Otero	3,480	134,825
Kit Carson	3,320	133,726
Routt	3,254	138,050

Horticulture

SOIL and climatic conditions in certain sections of Colorado are especially suited for the production of nearly all orchard and small fruits adapted to this latitude. In 1919 the Centennial state ranked twenty-first among the states in the production of apples, eighth in the production of peaches, and twelfth in the production of pears. Other fruits grown rather extensively are cherries, plums, apricots, grapes, strawberries, blackberries, raspberries, loganberries, gooseberries and currants.

While Colorado does not yet rank among the leaders in the amount of fruit produced annually, for the reason that the fruitgrowing districts are of restricted area, it is among the first in the production of high-grade fruits, which always command the best market price. High altitude, an abundance of sunshine, cool nights, and water for irrigation just when it is needed, are the principal conditions that unite to make Colorado fruit of the highest quality in form, color and flavor. The following table shows approximately the amount of fruit produced in the state in 1923 and its market value:

Kind	Quantity	Value
Apples, bu.	3,010,000	$2,799,300
Peaches, bu.	792,000	1,354,320
Pears, bu.	400,000	624,000
Cherries, tons	5,500	660,000
Other fruits	....	550,000
		$5,987,620

The most important fruitgrowing districts are the western slope, in the valleys of the Grand and Gunnison rivers and tributary streams, comprising parts of Garfield, Mesa, Delta and Montrose counties; the Canon City district, comprising a part of Fremont county; the Arkansas valley, comprising parts of Crowley, Otero, Pueblo, Bent and Prowers counties; southwestern Colorado, comprising parts of La Plata and Montezuma counties, and comparatively small areas near the foothills along the eastern side of the mountains. The western slope area ranks first in importance from the standpoint of production, with the Canon City district second. Apples, peaches and pears are principal fruit crops in the Grand valley and in the valleys of tributary streams, though practically all fruits grown in the state are produced here. This district produces nearly all the commercial peach crop of the state and a very large proportion of the apple crop. Southwest Colorado produces as fine a variety of all kinds of fruit as is grown in any part of the state, but lack of adequate transportation facilities has retarded development of the fruitgrowing industry in this district. In the Canon City district, the principal crop is apples, with a considerable production of cherries and small fruits. Some apples, cherries and small fruits are grown in the Arkansas valley, especially in Crowley and Otero counties, and cherries are grown rather extensively in several of the counties just east of the mountains, particularly in Larimer county. Apples have been grown to a considerable extent in this same area for a good many years, but the yield is not so dependable as on the western slope and the quality of the fruit is not so high. In the irrigated district immediately north of Denver, including parts of Boulder, Adams, Larimer and Weld counties, berries and other small fruits are grown successfully and always find a good market in Denver. Routt county is especially famous for its strawberries, which come into market late in the summer, after the berries from most other districts are gone, and for that reason command exceptionally high prices.

In 1919 the federal census bureau found the total production of fruits and nuts in the state to be worth $8,751,678, compared with $5,078,978 in 1909. Practically all this is fruits, as nuts are not grown commercially in Colorado. The total production of apples was 3,417,682 bushels, compared with 3,559,094 bushels reported for 1909. Mesa county was the leader, with 969,200 bushels, and other leading counties followed in this order: Delta county, 937,220 bushels; Fremont county, 416,403 bushels; Jefferson county, 195,554 bushels; Larimer county, 175,164 bushels; Garfield county, 125,335 bushels; Crowley county, 110,194 bushels; Otero county, 95,519 bushels; Montezuma county, 89,692 bushels, Boulder county, 73,781 bushels; Montrose county, 67,432 bushels. Montrose county is ordinarily one of the most important apple producing counties in the state, but its crop was almost totally destroyed by the late frosts in 1919. It ranked fourth among the counties in the state in 1909, with a production of 264,769 bushels.

The production of peaches in 1919 was 721,480 bushels, of which Mesa county produced more than one-half, or 486,234 bushels. Other leading peach producing counties that year were: Delta, 204,597 bushels; Montrose, 7,-154 bushels; Garfield, 5,996 bushels; Montezuma, 4,439 bushels. The season that year was unfavorable for peaches in Delta and Montrose counties, but especially favorable in Mesa county.

The production of pears in the state in 1919 was 269,465 bushels, of which Mesa county produced 251,924 bushels. Other counties producing more than 1,000 bushels were: Delta, 8,756 bushels; Fremont, 3,029 bushels; Montezuma, 1,560 bushels; Garfield, 1,188 bushels.

There has been little change in the number of fruit trees of bearing age in the various counties since 1919, though the number for the state is increasing gradually. Production in the several counties varies considerably each year, but Mesa county generally leads all in the combined production of all classes of orchard fruits, with Delta county second and Fremont county third.

Some attention has been paid in the past few years to the growing of orchards in the non-irrigated districts of eastern Colorado, and a few small trees of hardy varieties are being grown on many of the farms. In the irrigated sections of eastern Colorado apples and some other tree fruits are grown successfully. Late spring frosts frequently damage fruits in all sections of the state, but the organization of community forces in the principal fruit-producing districts to heat orchards with specially devised heaters on nights when the temperature falls below the frost point has in a large measure eliminated the danger of loss from this source.

The total number of mature apple trees in the state, as reported by the census bureau for January, 1920, was 1,777,737, compared with 1,688,425 in 1910; peach trees, 446,946, compared with 793,372 in 1910; pear trees, 136,-117, compared with 99,989 in 1910; plums and prune trees, 80,027, compared with 143,921 in 1910; cherry trees, 348,832, compared with 203,806 in 1910. It should be noted that the number of young trees indicates a continued increase in bearing apple trees, pear trees and cherry trees, while in the case of peaches the number of young trees is perhaps not more than enough to replace the old trees that are constantly becoming unproductive.

Poultry

CLIMATIC conditions are especially favorable for poultry raising in Colorado. Comparatively little rain and an abundance of sunshine make it possible for fowls to spend much of the time out of doors, with the result that disease is less prevalent than in most sections of the country, and young fowls make quick and vigorous growth. Since Colorado is a comparatively new state, however, the poultry interest is not yet extensively developed, and offers exceptional opportunities for good profits in nearly all sections of the state, except the mountain counties, where the climate is too severe. In 1920, when the latest detailed survey of the poultry industry for the entire country was made by the census bureau, Colorado ranked thirtieth in the number of fowls of all kinds on farms reported, with 2,-994,347, compared with 1,721,445 in 1910. Of the 59,934 farms in the state at that time, 51,884 reported fowls of some kind on hand, and by far the largest part of fowls reported were found on farms. At that time the leading poultry-raising counties, with the number of fowls reported in each, were as follows:

Weld	294,948
Yuma	160,114
Washington	137,772
Logan	126,418
El Paso	97,996
Boulder	95,899
Kit Carson	95,279
Pueblo	95,057
Larimer	92,400
Morgan	91,276
Adams	90,062
Mesa	86,643
Baca	86,191
Jefferson	85,841

Reports from the census for 1919 and 1920 give the number of chickens on the farms of the state on January 1, 1920, at 2,874,721, compared with 1,-644,471 on April 1, 1910. The number of chickens raised in 1919, according to this report, was 3,880,873, compared with 2,706,945 in 1919. The number of eggs sold during 1919 was 14,172,375 dozen. It will be seen from the figures given above, that there were about 74 per cent more chickens on the farms of the state in 1920 than in 1910, that about 44 per cent more chickens were raised in 1919 than in 1909, and about 33 per cent more eggs were sold.

Elsewhere in this volume will be found reports by county assessors of the number of poultry assessed in the various counties in 1923, and the number of hens on farms when assessments were made in 1923. The assessment figures are evidently far below the actual number of poultry in the state and the figures showing the number of hens on farms last year are undoubtedly 20 per cent below the actual number. They are of much value, however, as showing the comparative importance of the poultry industry by counties, but are not entirely reliable in this respect, as the reports for some counties are far more nearly complete than for others. It is estimated that the total number of domestic fowls of all kinds on farms at this time is more than 4,000,000, and that the value of poultry and eggs marketed in 1923 was approximately $7,000,000, or perhaps more. Well informed poultry dealers estimate that at least $5,000,000 worth of poultry and eggs still are brought into the state annually to supply the local demand.

It will be seen from the tables above referred to that most of the poultry in Colorado is raised in the important agricultural counties. Poultry raising as a separate industry has not been developed extensively, though it is followed to some extent in the neighborhoods of Denver, Colorado Springs and Pueblo. In recent years, special attention has been given to poultry raising in and around Lamar, Prowers county. This locality is now one of the leading poultry raising sections of the state. In all the counties of the non-irrigated section of eastern Colorado, poultry raising is developing very rapidly in connection with farming. In all the irrigated districts considerable poultry has been raised for a good many years, and within the past four or five years the poultry industry has made rapid advances in the northeastern part of the state, where formerly cattle raising was about the only industry followed.

Bees and Honey

IN 1920 Colorado ranked twenty-fifth among the states in the number of colonies of bees reported by the census bureau, compared with a rank of twenty-third in both 1910 and 1900. Since that time there has been an increase in the production of honey per hive of bees, and perhaps in the total production of honey for the state, and a slight increase in the number of colonies of bees.

Final reports of the census for 1920 show that the number of colonies of bees on the farms in the state on January 1 of that year was 63,253, compared with 71,434 on April 1, 1910. The aggregate production of honey reported by the census bureau for 1909 was 2,306,492 pounds, or a little less than 36 pounds for each stand of bees that produced honey. Not all colonies of bees reported in 1910 were producing honey in 1909. In 1919 the production of honey was 2,493,950 pounds, or a little more than 39 pounds per stand reported. While there was a decrease in the number of stands of bees kept by farmers in nearly all sections of the state in the decade from 1910 to 1920, there has been an increase in the number kept by many of the professioual honey producers, so that a much larger percentage of the bees in the state are now in the hands of expert bee keepers than in 1910.

No report is available showing the number of colonies of bees in the state not on farms. In many of the smaller cities and towns bee keeping is followed to a considerable extent and the number of stands of bees in such localities is perhaps much larger than in 1910, so that the total number of stands of bees in the state at the present time is about the same as in 1910. The average amount of honey produced per stand of bees is increasing each year, as the number of stands of bees held by professional honey producers increases in proportion to the total number.

Perhaps 60 per cent of the bees in the state today are in the hands of professional bee keepers, and the percentage is increasing, though a few colonies of bees are being introduced by other than regular commercial producers in the newer agricultural districts. The acreage of alfalfa raised in Colorado has increased very rapidly in the past decade, while sweet clover, field beans and other crops from which bees feed have been introduced in the past ten years. Though there has been a considerable decrease in the number of colonies of bees kept in the orchard districts since 1910, due chiefly to difficulties arising from the spraying of fruit trees, this loss could have been much more than compensated for in the agricultural districts, where the area of honey producing crops has been greatly increased. The area now devoted to alfalfa in Colorado is in excess of 780,000 acres, compared with 508,892 acres in 1909.

The bee keeping industry is confined largely to the principal alfalfa producing districts and the fruit growing districts, where the bees find an abundance of honey-bearing blossoms from which to harvest their honey. The statistics furnished by reports of county assessors on the number of colonies of bees in the various counties of the state are published elsewhere in this volume. While they are of comparatively little value as showing the actual number of stands of bees in the several counties, they are of much value as showing the distribution. The following figures, taken from the reports of county assessors for 1923, show the relative importance of the leading honey producing counties:

County	Stands of Bees
Weld	6,846
Delta	5,555
Larimer	4,620
Boulder	4,170
Mesa	4,116
Montrose	3,993
Otero	3,961
Jefferson	3,872
Garfield	3,734
La Plata	2,277
Prowers	2,021

The total number of stands of bees assessed in 1923 was 59,334, compared with 55,582 in 1922. The number assessed in 1920 was considerably below the number reported by the census bureau on farms alone, and inquiries have shown that the census enumeration was in some cases at least 10 per cent too low. During 1921 more than 60 cars of honey was shipped out of the state, and about the same amount in 1922. There is every indication that the number of stands of bees in the state will increase from now on, as the farming districts are more fully developed.

The Co-operative Crop Reporting Service estimated the average surplus production of honey per stand for 1921 at approximately 58 pounds, compared with an average of about 44.2 pounds for the country at large. In 1922 it was estimated at 55 pounds to the stand, but in 1923 it dropped to only 31 pounds on account of the exceptionally heavy rainfall throughout the season. The average surplus production of honey per stand for Colorado is almost always considerably above that for the entire United States, this state ranking well up among the leaders in this respect. No figures are available showing the production of honey in the state by counties, but the Co-operative Crop Reporting Service hopes to begin the collection of statistics of this character in the near future.

Mineral Resources

NO state except California has so wide a variety of mineral resources as Colorado. Nearly every useful mineral produced in the United States is found in the Centennial state and most of them have been mined to some extent. About 250 useful metallic and non-metallic minerals and compounds have been reported in the state, and undoubtedly numerous others are yet to be found. The extreme irregularity of the state's surface and the wide range of geological formations exposed for examination present excellent opportunities for the production of valuable minerals.

METALS

Mining is Colorado's oldest industry. Gold was the first metal produced and has surpassed all others in the total value of its output.. The first important discovery of gold was made in the summer of 1858, and since that time the value of the state's gold output has been more than $685,000,000. The production of silver began soon after that of gold and the white metal ranks second, the total value of the state's output to date being more than $515,000,000. At the present time zinc ranks second in the annual volume of its output, only a little way behind gold. The zinc production, on a commercial scale, did not begin, however, until 1902. Copper has been produced steadily since 1870 and lead since 1872. The total value of gold, silver, lead, copper and zinc marketed in Colorado to the beginning of 1924 is approximately $1,570,000,000.

While these are the principal metals being produced in Colorado, almost every useful metal found in the United States exists here. Tungsten has been produced commercially since 1904, and uranium, vanadium and radium have been produced since 1906. Colorado ranks first in the production of these metals. Molybdenum is also being produced in considerable quantities at the present time and promises soon to take an important place in the statistics of the state's metal output.

There was considerable falling off of metal production in Colorado in 1919 and a further decrease in production in 1920, 1921 and 1922, due very largely to unsatisfactory markets for practically all metals. The total value of gold, silver, copper, lead and zinc produced in the state in 1922 was about $15,230,000, compared with about $14,005,500 in 1921. These two years show the lowest values in the production of these five metals since 1899. The output of other metals also was lower in 1921 and 1922 than during the years immediately previous. There has been some increase in the production of silver in certain sections of the state, and a consequent increase in the output of lead and zinc from ores in which silver is found. This increase has been due to the increased price of silver, but the high cost of operation has largely counteracted the increase in the market value of silver and prevented the reopening of many silver properties that might have been opened if production costs had been lower. The price of silver has been decreased again, but prices of zinc and lead have been advanced materially, and there was a substantial increase in the total value of metals produced in the state in 1923 and indications point to further increases in 1924.

The production of metals in Colorado is confined largely to the mountainous counties in the central and western parts of the state. The metals occur usually in compound ores found in well-defined veins or lodes. Up to the present time approximately thirty metals have been produced in commercial quantities. The most important of these, in the order of their annual output at the present time, are gold, zinc, silver, lead and copper.

Free gold is found in numerous widely separated districts and has been mined in the following counties: Chaffee, Clear Creek, Costilla, Eagle, Jefferson, Moffat, Park, Routt, San Miguel and Summit. Free gold is the principal output of the placer mines, and Summit county has led all other counties in the state for fifty years in the output of its placer mines. There is a wide variety in the gold ores found in Colorado. Among the compound ores from which gold is obtained are amalgam, calverite, petzite and sylvanite.

Zinc is the predominant metal in many of the ores which carry gold. The principal compound ores carrying zinc are aurichalcite, calamine, chalcophanite, hetaerolite, hydrozincite, nicholsonite, smithsonite and sphalerite.

Silver is found very commonly associated with both zinc and gold as well as with lead. Native silver has been mined in the following counties: Boulder, Clear Creek, Dolores, Gunnison, Hinsdale, Lake, La Plata, Montrose, Pitkin and Teller. The principal compound ores in which silver is found are acanthite, amalgam, calaverite, cosalite, galena, massicot, mimehessite, krennerite, pearceite, petzite, polybasite, proustite, pyrargyrite, stephenite, stromeyerite and sylvanite.

Lead is perhaps more widely distributed than any other metal found in the state, and is often associated with both gold and silver. The principal compound ores from which lead is produced are altaite, anglesite, cerusite, cosalite, galena, massicot, mimetite, minium, plumbojarsite and pyromorphite.

Copper is very widely distributed, but usually occurs in comparatively small quantities. Native copper has been reported in the following counties: Dolores, Jefferson, Mesa, Montrose, Park and Routt. The principal compound ores containing copper are azurite, bornite, brochantite, chalcanthite, chalcocite, chalcopyrite, chrysocolla, covellite, cuprite, enargite, malachite, melaconite, stromeyerite, tennantite and tetrahedrite.

The following tabulation gives the principal metals found in Colorado and the counties in which they occur:

Aluminum (alunite, bauxite, cryolite) --Chaffee, Conejos, Custer, El Paso, Fremont, Gunnison, Hinsdale, Lake, Mineral, Ouray, Rio Grande, Saguache.

Antimony (bournonite, polybasite, stibnite) — Boulder, Clear Creek, Dolores, Grand, Gunnison, Ouray, Pitkin, San Juan, San Miguel, Teller.

Arsenic (arsenopyrite)—Gilpin, Gunnison, Pitkin, San Juan, San Miguel.

Barium (barite) — Boulder, Mineral, Pitkin, San Miguel.

Bismuth (beegerite, bismuthinite, bismutite, cosalite, tetradymite) — Boulder, Chaffee, Fremont, Grand, Gunnison, Jefferson, Lake, La Plata, Larimer, Montezuma, Ouray, Park, San Miguel.

Cadmium (greenockite)—Lake.

Cerium (allanite, gadolinite, monazite) — Boulder, Chaffee, Costilla, Douglas, Routt, Washington.

Cobalt (erythrite, smaltite)—Gunnison.

Copper — Archuleta, Baca, Boulder, Chaffee, Clear Creek, Conejos, Custer, Dolores, Eagle, Fremont, Garfield, Gilpin, Grand, Gunnison, Hinsdale, Huerfano, Jackson, Jefferson, Lake, La Plata, Larimer, Mesa, Mineral, Moffat, Montezuma, Montrose, Ouray, Park, Pitkin, Rio Grande, Routt, Saguache, San Juan, San Miguel, Summit, Teller.

Gold—Archuleta, Boulder, Chaffee, Clear Creek, Conejos, Costilla, Custer, Dolores, Douglas, Eagle, Fremont, Garfield, Gilpin, Grand, Gunnison, Hinsdale, Huerfano, Jackson, Jefferson, Lake, La Plata, Mineral, Moffat, Montezuma, Montrose, Ouray, Park, Pitkin, Rio Grande, Routt, Saguache, San Juan, San Miguel, Summit, Teller.

Iron (brown iron ore, hematite, magnetite, marasite, pyrite, pyrrhotite, siderite)—Chaffee, Costilla, Dolores, Fremont, Gunnison, Hinsdale, Jefferson, Lake, Ouray, Pitkin, Routt, Saguache, San Juan, San Miguel, Summit, Teller.

Pyrite is found in nearly every metal producing county in the state.

Lead—Archuleta, Boulder, Chaffee, Clear Creek, Custer, Dolores, Eagle, Fremont, Gilpin, Gunnison, Hinsdale, Lake, La Plata, Mineral, Montezuma, Ouray, Park, Pitkin, Routt, Saguache, San Juan, San Miguel, Summit, Teller.

Lithium (amblygonite)—Fremont.

Manganese (alabandite, chalcophanite, psilomelane, pyrolusite, rhodochrosite) — Boulder, Chaffee, Custer, Dolores, Eagle, Gunnison, Hinsdale, Lake, Park, Saguache, San Juan, Summit.

Mercury (amalgam, cinnabar, quicksilver)—Boulder, La Plata.

Molybdenum (molybdenite) — Boulder, Chaffee, Clear Creek, Grand, Gunnison, Lake, San Juan, Summit, Teller.

Nickel (annabergite, nicolite)—Custer, Fremont, Gunnison.

Platinum—Clear Creek, Chaffee, Gunnison, Pitkin, Saguache, San Miguel.

Silver—Archuleta, Baca, Boulder, Chaffee, Clear Creek, Conejos, Costilla, Custer, Dolores, Douglas, Eagle, Fremont, Garfield, Gilpin, Grand, Gunnison, Hinsdale, Jackson, Lake, La Plata, Mineral, Moffat, Montezuma, Montrose, Ouray, Park, Pitkin, Rio Grande, Routt, Saguache, San Juan, San Miguel, Summit, Teller.

Tantalum (columbite) — Fremont, Jefferson, Teller.

Tellurium—Boulder, Teller.

Tin (cassiterite)—Garfield.

Titanium (ilmenite, rutile, perofskite) —El Paso, Gunnison.

Tungsten (ferberite, hubernite, scheelite)—Boulder, Chaffee, Clear Creek, Gilpin, Gunnison, Lake, Ouray, San Juan, San Miguel, Summit.

Radium, Uranium, Vanadium (carnotite, pitchblend, volborthite) — Clear Creek, Custer, Dolores, Eagle, Garfield, Huerfano, Jefferson, La Plata, Mesa, Moffat, Montrose, Park, Rio Blanco, San Miguel.

Yttrium (allanite, gadolinite) — Boulder, Douglas, Washington.

Zinc—Archuleta, Chaffee, Clear Creek, Conejos, Dolores, Eagle, Fremont, Gilpin, Hinsdale, Lake, Mineral, Ouray, Park, Pitkin, Saguache, San Juan, San Miguel, Summit.

Zircon—El Paso.

NONMETALS

The range of useful nonmetals found in Colorado is almost as wide as that of the metals, but their production has not been so extensive up to the present time. Coal ranks first among the nonmetals in value of output and, perhaps, in the total value of known deposits. Colorado ranks fourth among the states in available coal supply, and eighth in annual output. According to the United States geological survey, the coal fields of the state cover approximately 19,750,000 acres, and the available coal supply is about 317,500,000,000 short tons. The only states surpassing Colorado in total available coal are North Dakota, Wyoming and Montana. The Colorado state geological survey estimates the area of Colorado's coal fields somewhat below the estimates of the United States geological survey, but places estimated tonnage considerably higher. The following tabulation shows the area of the various fields and the estimated tonnage, accord- to this authority:

	Area (Square Miles)	Estimated Tonnage
Denver region	4,300	13,590,000,000
Durango field	1,900	21,428,000,000
North Park	500	453,000,000
Trinidad	1,080	24,462,000,000
Uinta region	6,000	271,810,000,000
Yampa field	3,700	39,639,000,000
Scattered fields	350	388,000,000
	17,830	371,770,000,000

Colorado coal ranges in quality from black lignite and sub bituminous varieties through various grades of bituminous to true anthracite. The bituminous varieties include high-grade coking coal found in the Trinidad district, in the Glenwood Springs area, and in Gunnison county. High-grade bituminous coal is also found in Jackson, Routt, Moffat, Rio Blanco, Mesa, Delta, Montezuma, La Plata, Fremont and Huerfano counties. True anthracite coal is found near Crested Butte, in Gunnison county, and is found in several localities in Routt and Moffat counties.

Although Colorado has never ranked high in petroleum output, it has produced crude oil steadily since 1887. The maximum annual output was recorded in 1892, being 824,000 barrels. The total output of the state to the end of 1923 was in excess of 12,000,000 barrels. The most important producing fields are in Fremont county, in and about the city of Florence, and in Boulder county, near the city of Boulder. There has been some production from Rio Blanco county, near the town of Rangely; Garfield county, near the Colorado-Utah line, and Mesa county, near DeBeque. Late in 1923 a gas well having a daily capacity of more than 80,000,000 cubic feet of gas was brought in at Wellington, in Larimer county, at a depth a little greater than 4,000 feet. The well began spraying oil before it could be capped, and since it was drilled almost at the peak of the structure in which it was lolated, oil experts generally were convinced that a strong flow of oil would be encountered lower down on the structure in the same sand. Further drilling of this structure is now under way, and as a result of the discovery in this structure many other structures in Larimer, Weld and Boulder counties are being tested with deep wells, since the Wellington well is the first ever drilled below 4,000 feet in this section of Colorado. Early in 1924 an oil well was brought in near Hamilton, Moffat county, the flow being estimated at about 3,000 barrels daily. This discovery has given an impetus to prospecting in that section of the state and several other wells will be drilled in 1924. The oil sand here was also reached at near the 4,000-foot level. These successes in deep drilling operations have given rise to much deep drilling activity in other parts of the state, and many structures that have been tested previously to moderate depths are now being drilled deeper. Several of the strongest of the operating oil companies are engaged during 1924 in making thorough drilling tests of all structures upon which their geologists have reported favorably and it is confidently expected that important new fields will be opened in the state before the end of the year.

Colorado has immense deposits of oil shale, which promise in the near future to become one of the most important sources of petroleum production in this country. The constantly increasing demand for petroleum products during the past few years has caused both the federal and state governments to make special investigations of the economic possibilities of these shale deposits, and reports have been made which promise much in the direction of speedy and extensive development. Several private compauies have been organized for the purpose of extracting petroleum and other valuable products from the Colorado oil shales, but so far as the public is at present informed there is no process developed which will handle the Colorado shale at sufficiently low cost to justify extensive commercial development.

Colorado's oil shales are found in what is known as the Green River formation, in the western part of the state, chiefly in Mesa, Garfield, Rio Blanco and Moffat counties. They cover an area of perhaps 2,000 square miles, and the various shale strata sometimes attain an aggregate thickness of 100 feet or more. Tests made by the United States geological survey have shown a recovery of from 10 to 68 gallons of petroleum from a ton of shale, and in one case the recovery was 90 gallons per ton. Experts from the geological survey have estimated the amount of petroleum available in Colorado shale at 20,000,000,000 barrels and the amount of ammonium sulphate which should be recovered from the same shales by the same processes, at 300,000,000 tons. The process of distillation by which oil is recovered may also result in the recovery of large quantities of producer gas, dyes and other valuable by-products.

Perhaps no state has a wider variety or greater deposits of high-grade stone than Colorado. Sandstones, granites and basalts are perhaps most abundant, but marbles, lavas, abrasives, limestone, slates and shale are common. Onyx and various gem stones are found in several localities.

Sandstone, granite and marble have been extensively quarried for building purposes and marble and granite have been produced rather extensively for interior decorating and monumental purposes. The most extensive marble deposits are in Gunnison county near the town of Marble. Along the course of Yule creek, in this neighborhood, are said to be the largest deposits of pure white marble in the world. These deposits have been worked extensively, but the company working them is now in the hands of a receiver and it is understood that a reorganization is under way.

Brick clay is found in practically every county in the state and has been dug to some extent in perhaps two-thirds of the counties. Fire clay, plastic clay and kaolin are also rather widely distributed. Many varieties of high-grade pottery are being manufactured at Golden, chiefly from clays mined in Jefferson county, near that city. Colorado pottery is rapidly making for itself a wide reputation, and there are several known deposits of good pottery clay that have not yet been developed

The accompanying tabulation shows the principal valuable nonmetals found in the state, together with the counties where they have been reported:

Abrasive Stone—Gunnison.
Amber—Boulder.
Asbestos — Boulder, Chaffee, Fremont, Rio Grande.
Asphalt — Garfield, Grand, Jefferson, Mesa, Routt, Rio Blanco.
Basalt—Boulder, Delta, Eagle, Garfield, Grand, Huerfano, Jefferson, Las Animas, Mesa, Rio Blanco.
Cement Materials — Boulder, Chaffee, Fremont and many others.
Corundum—Chaffee, Clear Creek.
Coal — Adams, Arapahoe, Archuleta, Boulder, Delta, Dolores, Douglas, Elbert, El Paso, Fremont, Garfield, Gunnison, Huerfano, Jackson, Jefferson, La Plata, Las Animas, Larimer, Mesa, Moffat, Montezuma, Montrose, Ouray, Park, Pitkin, Rio Blanco, Routt, Weld.
Feldspar—El Paso.
Fire Clay — Bent, Boulder, Custer, Douglas, El Paso, Fremont, Garfield, Gunnison, Huerfano, Jefferson, Larimer, Las Animas, Pueblo.
Fluorspar — Boulder, Chaffee, Clear Creek, Custer, Dolores, Douglas, El Paso, Fremont, Gilpin, Jefferson, Lake, Larimer, Mineral, Montezuma, Montrose, Park, San Juan, Saguache, San Miguel, Teller.
Fuller's Earth—Chaffee, Washington
Gem Stones — Chaffee, Clear Creek, Eagle, El Paso, Fremont, Hinsdale, Jefferson, Lake, Larimer, Moffat, Park, Saguache, Teller.
Glass Sand — Bent, Fremont, Prowers, Pueblo.
Granite — Archuleta, Boulder, Chaffee, Clear Creek, Conejos, Costilla, Custer, Delta, Dolores, Douglas, Eagle, El Paso, Fremont, Garfield, Gunnison, Jackson, Jefferson, La Plata, Larimer, Las Animas, Mineral, Moffat, Ouray, Park, Pueblo, Rio Blanco, Rio Grande.
Graphite — Chaffee, Gunnison, Las Animas.
Gypsum—Custer, Delta, Dolores, Eagle, El Paso, Fremont, Garfield, Jefferson, Larimer, Montrose.
Kaolin — Boulder, El Paso, Fremont, Huerfano, Jefferson, La Plata, Morgan, Pueblo.
Limestone—Boulder, Chaffee, Douglas, Fremont, Gunnison, Jefferson, La Plata, Larimer, Las Animas, Mesa, Mineral, Ouray, Park, Pueblo, Rio Blanco.
Marble — Boulder, Chaffee, Gunnison, Larimer, Pueblo.
Mica—Clear Creek, Fremont, Larimer, Mesa.
Oil Shale — Garfield, Gunnison, Mesa, Moffat, Montrose, Rio Blanco.
Onyx—Gunnison.
Petroleum — Boulder, Delta, Fremont, Mesa, Montrose, Pueblo, Rio Blanco.
Potash—Costilla, Delta.
Sandstone — Archuleta, Boulder, Chaffee, Conejos, Costilla, Custer, Delta, Dolores, Douglas, Eagle, Elbert, El Paso, Fremont, Garfield, Gunnison, Jackson, La Plata, Larimer, Las Animas, Mesa, Mineral, Ouray, Park, Pueblo, Rio Blanco.
Salts of Sodium—Alamosa, Saguache.
Slate—Gunnison.
Sulphur—Gunnison, Mineral.

Manufacturing in Colorado

THE manufacturing industry in Colorado has developed rapidly in the past 20 years. In the five years ending with 1919 there was a rapid increase in the value of goods manufactured, in the value added by the manufacturing process and in the amount paid for wages and salaries in the industry. From 1914 to 1919, according to reports of the census bureau, the number of factories in the state increased 23.8 per cent, the number of persons engaged in the industry increased 32.7 per cent, the total value of goods manufactured increased 101.3 per cent, value added by the manufacturing processes increased 109.8 per cent and the amount paid as wages in the industry increased 104.4 per cent. In the 20 years ending with 1919, the number of factories in the state just about doubled, capital invested increased about 320 per cent, the number of persons engaged in the industry about doubled, the value of goods manufactured annually increased more than 250 per cent. The value added by manufacturing increased more than 250 per cent. The following table, compiled from final reports of the United States census bureau for 1899, 1909, 1914 and 1919, gives a good idea of the growth of the industry in the past 20 years:

	1919	1914	1909	1899
Number of establishments	2,631	2,126	2,034	1,323
Persons engaged	44,731	33,715	34,115	*...... ...
Proprietors and firm members	2,234	1,716	1,722	*.........
Salaried employes	7,241	4,721	4,326	1,870
Wage earners (average number)	35,256	27,278	28,067	19,498
Primary horsepower	194,634	162,828	154,615	43,434
Capital invested	$243,827,000	$181,776,339	$162,667,801	$58,172,865
Salaries paid	13,049,000	6,367,863	5,647,684	2,058,798
Wages paid	41,280,000	20,199,754	19,912,342	11,707,566
Cost of raw materials	176,600,000	89,756,302	80,490,904	60,750,784
Value of products	275,391,000	136,839,321	130,044,312	89,067,879
Value added by manufacturing	98,791,000	47,083,019	49,553,408	28,317,095

* Figures not available.

The increase in value of goods manufactured was much greater during the period from 1914 to 1919, than during any corresponding period in the state's history and the percentage of increase has been greater than for any period of the same length in the past 20 years. The large increase in value of output was due partly to increased output, but very largely to higher prices that prevailed then on account of the World war. The census for 1919 covered the period of highest prices, and the value of the output for 1920 was considerably less than that for the previous year, while that for 1921, though perhaps greater than the 1920 output, fell short of that for 1919 in both volume and value. The census bureau's report on manufacturing for 1921 is not yet complete, but partial reports show rather large decreases in the value of manufactured products for Colorado, as well as for nearly all other states. The total value of manufactured products for this state for 1921 is given in the preliminary figures at $221,324,285, compared with $275,622,335 for 1919. The figures for the two years are not strictly comparable, however, since those for 1921 do not include manufacturing establishments with products less than $5,000 in value, or establishments engaged in automobile repairing, while those for 1919 include such establishments. The value of goods manufactured in the state for 1922 was undoubtedly slightly above that for 1921, while 1923 perhaps showed a slight decrease as compared with 1922.

But Colorado, in spite of the rapid growth as a manufacturing state, still holds only a low rank in manufacturing activity. In 1914 it ranked thirty-second among the states in the value of manufactured products, thirty-sixth in the number of wage earners, and thirty-third in the value added by manufacture. The value of goods manufactured in Colorado in 1914 represented only six-tenths of one per cent of the total value of goods manufactured in the United States. While the increase in the value of goods manufactured here since 1914 has been very substantial, it has not kept pace with the increase in other states where the production of goods needed for the prosecution of the war was carried on more extensively, consequently Colorado ranks perhaps no higher as a manufacturing state now than it did in 1914, and the value of its manufactured goods is no doubt smaller in comparison with the total value produced in the United States than it was at that time, though exact data are not available. In 1921 the value of goods manufactured in Colorado was five-tenths of one per cent of the total value of goods manufactured in the United States.

The 1914 census showed that the manufacture of beet sugar ranked first among the various branches of the manufacturing industry, the value of the output being $17,635,556, or 12.9 per cent of the value of all goods manufactured in the state. In the manufacturing census for 1919 the census bureau included the figures for the manufacture of beet sugar with "All other industries," presumably to avoid disclosing individual operations. That branch of the industry apparently still led most others then, however, with an output valued at about $28,000,000. In 1921 it still took first rank, with an output valued at above $35,000,000. Production of beet sugar reached a record figure in 1921, though the price of sugar was much below that of 1919. In 1922 the output decreased materially and the price showed a substantial increase. In 1923 the output increased above the 1922 figure, and price also showed some increase.

Slaughtering and meat packing ranked second among the state's manufacturing industries in 1914, the total value of the output being $12,726,127. Since 1914 there has been some increase in the price of packinghouse products, and a very substantial increase in the output, so that the value of all packinghouse products for the state in 1919, as shown by the census report, was $41,007,531, this industry holding first rank. The output for 1923 was about the same in value as that for 1919.

Flour and gristmill products ranked third in 1914, with an output valued at $7,535,633. Since that time there has been a slight increase in the output and a large increase in the market price of the products. The value of flour and gristmill products for 1919 was $19,954,119. The output for 1923 was greater than that for 1919, but prices were somewhat lower, so that the total value of the output was perhaps about the same.

Among the other manufacturing industries which have shown large increases in the value of their output since 1914 are iron and steel works, rolling mills, and makers of chemicals and explosives. The Colorado Fuel & Iron company, which is the largest steel manufacturing establishment in the west, was until the latter part of 1920 operating at full capacity and turning out a much larger production than at any time in its history. Since that time it has been almost entirely closed down much of the time, or has operated at far below its normal capacity. In 1923, however, most of the company's several mills operated nearly at capacity, and the output has been large. The price of all steel products increased materially as a result of the heavy demand caused by the war, in consequence of which the annual value of the state's steel products for 1919 was perhaps 100 per cent above that for 1914. Prices have been reduced materially, however, since 1919. Several new chemical factories have been put in operation and old factories are greatly increasing the output as a result of the demands caused by the war, and the needs of the reconstruction period, especially those engaged in the production of acids and dyes.

The census bureau does not segregate manufacturing output completely by counties and it is impossible under present conditions to supply accurate data on these industries showing the comparative ranks of the various counties in all respects. In 1914 there were seven cities in the state having a population of more than 10,000 each, which reported 40.1 per cent of the value of the state's manufactured products. These cities are Boulder, Colorado Springs, Denver, Fort Collins, Greeley, Pueblo and Trinidad. The same cities reported 53 per cent of the total manufactured output of the state in 1919, due principally to the large increase in the city of Denver. From these figures it may be seen that the manufacturing industry is being developed very substantially in the smaller cities and rural districts since they produce about the same percentage of the total manufactured output that is produced in the larger cities. All of the state's 16 sugar factories are located in places having less than 15,000 population and the big steel mills of the Colorado Fuel & Iron company, usually credited to the city of Pueblo, are not located in the city's limits and their output is not assigned by the census bureau to that city.

The butter, cheese and condensed milk industries are growing very rapidly in the rural districts. All of the condenseries and most of the creameries and cheese factories are located in small communities. In 1914 the value of butter, cheese and condensed milk manufactured in the state was $3,596,565, while in 1919 it had risen to $11,906,140. It has shown further increases since 1919.

The Twenty-second General Assembly enacted a law giving the state immigration department authority to call upon manufacturers for data regarding their operations and providing a penalty for refusal to furnish such data when properly requested. The appropriation made to the department, however, was not sufficient to meet the expense of a general manufacturing survey of the state. A partial survey was begun early in 1920, chiefly for the purpose of putting the department in a position to co-operate with the census bureau of the United States department of commerce in future surveys of the industry. Since that time, however, the department of commerce has apparently adopted a permanent policy of making a survey of the manufacturing industry biennially instead of every five years, so that apparently all data regarding output that this department might reasonably expect to collect is now being furnished by the census bureau, though it is not always completed as promptly as might be wished. In the future it is hoped that some plan can be worked out so that, through co-operation between the state and the census bureau, information on manufacturing in Colorado may be obtained somewhat more promptly than is now possible.

Colorado offers exceptional opportunities for the development of manufacturing in a wide variety of lines. It has a great wealth of raw material. Its supply of coal is practically inexhaustible and is so distributed as to be conveniently located to furnish fuel for all of the manufacturing centers of the state.

It has been the hope of this department for the past five years to furnish annually statistics of the manufacturing industries by counties, as a proper basis for aiding the further development of the manufacturing industry in the state. The experienced manufacturer who contemplates entering a new territory always wants a very considerable amount of information regarding this new territory, not the least important of which is accurate data regarding the amount of manufacturing in the line he proposes to establish that is already being done in the territory and something of the success that is attending the operations of those already in the field. It is not difficult to supply information regarding the raw materials available for manufacturers in this state, but up to the present time it has been difficult to tell what was being done in the manufacturing line in the variou counties in the state.

In order to be able to furnish this and other information regarding manufacturing development in Colorado by counties, which this department believes is necessary in connection with any campaign to develop the manufacturing industry here, the department will require considerably more money than it has ever had available for the collection of statistical information.

Some data regarding the manufacturing development in the various counties and the raw materials available for further development are given in other publications issued by this department. The following list contains some of the most important raw materials available here for manufacturing purposes: Apples, apricots, alfalfa, asbestos, asphaltum, asphaltic rock, arsenic, aquamarine, aluminum, agate, alunite, anthracite coal, antimony, amethyst, amber, abrasive stone, basalt, barite, bauxite, building sand. beans, bismuth, barley, bitumen, bituminous coal, brick and tile clay, broomcorn, beets, berries, cadmium, cattle, celery, cement materials, chalcedony, chalk, copper, cherries, corn, cobalt, coal, coke, clays, corundum, carnotite, cucumbers, diatomaceous earth, dolomite, eggs, elaterite, emmer, earthenware materials. fuller's earth, feldspar, flaxseed, fluorspar, feterita, fire clay, glass sand, graphite, grain sorghum, granite, gold, gypsum, garnet, gilsonite, honey, hogs, horses, hides, hay (many varieties), iron ore, kaolin, kafir corn, lava, lead, limestone, mica, mineral paint, moulding sand, molybdenum, mercury, melons, marble, milo maize, manganese, magnesium, millet, mineral waters, milk, oats, oil shale, opal, onyx, petroleum, potash, plastic clay, producer gas, pyrite, platinum, potatoes, peaches, pears, plums, pumpkins, quartz, radium salts, rutile, rye, road metal, sandstone, salts of sodium, salts of potassium. speltz, shale, slate, silver, sand, sulphur, sheep, sugar beets, tellurium. tantalum, tungsten, timber (pine, cedar, spruce, hemlock, aspen, pinon, cottonwood, etc.), turnips, topaz, tourmaline, trona, turquoise, uranium,, vanadium, volcanic ash, vegetables, wheat, wool, wood (see timber), water power (more than 2,000,000 horsepower), wurtzilite, zinc, zircon.

National Forests

(By H. N. Wheeler, Chief of Public Relations District 2, U. S. Forest Service.)

THE act of congress under which the national forests of the country were created was passed March 3, 1891. The following provision, Section 24 of the act, shows how and for what purpose the forests were created:

"The President of the United States may from time to time set apart and reserve in any state or territory having public land bearing forests, any part of the public lands wholly or in part covered with timber or undergrowth, whether of commercial value or not, as public reservations, and the President shall, by public proclamation, declare the establishment of such reservations and the limits thereof."

The first national forest was created by President Harrison in 1891, under the name of the Yellowstone Park Timberland reserve. Originally all forests established under this act were known as forest reserves, but in 1907 congress changed the official designation to "national forests."

There are at present 146 national forests in the United States, of which 15 lie wholly and two partly within the state of Colorado. The total area within these forests and within the borders of the state is 14,743,283 acres. A considerable amount of land within the forest boundaries has passed into private ownership or has been otherwise withdrawn from the forest area under provisions of the various acts of congress relating to the national forests, leaving a total net national forest area for the state of 13,277,038 acres.

The administrative headquarters for Colorado national forests is located at Denver, the national forests of the state, except the very small part of the La Sal forest located in the extreme western part, being in what is known as the Rocky Mountain district. The chief executive officer of the district is the district forester, and each forest is in charge of a forest supervisor, whose chief headquarters is at some central place within or near the forest area. The total number of national forest officers in the state at present is about 304. The accompanying table gives the name of each national forest wholly or partly in this state, together with its net area within this state, and the headquarters of the supervisor.

Nat'l Forest	Headquarters	Acres
Arapahoe	Hot Sulphur Springs	635,900
Cochetopa	Salida	908,335
Colorado	Fort Collins	853,641
Grand Mesa	Grand Junction	659,863
Gunnison	Gunnison	905,303
*Hayden	Encampment, Wyo.	65,769
Holy Cross	Glenwood Spgs	1,124,369
–La Sal	Moab, Utah	26,631
Leadville	Leadville	927,388
Montezuma	Mancos	697,141
Pike	Colorado Spgs	1,084,338
Rio Grande	Monte Vista	1,135,778
Routt	Steamboat Spgs.	742,827
San Isabel	Pueblo	598,936
San Juan	Durango	1,240,112
Uncompahgre	Delta	778,291
White River	Glenwood Spgs.	892,416

*Lies principally in Wyoming.
–Lies principally in Utah.

These forests lie almost exclusively in the mountainous districts of the central and western parts of the state. Their boundaries are very irregular and most of them lie in two or more counties, while some of them are made up of two or more separated tracts. The location of the various forests wholly or partly in the state by counties is as follows:

Arapahoe Forest: Grand and Jackson counties.

Cochetopa Forest: Chaffee, Gunnison, Hinsdale and Saguache counties.

Colorado Forest: Boulder, Gilpin, Jackson, Jefferson and Larimer counties.

Grand Mesa Forest: Delta, Garfield, Gunnison and Mesa counties.

Gunnison Forest: Delta, Gunnison and Montrose counties.

Hayden Forest: Jackson county.

Holy Cross Forest: Eagle, Garfield, Gunnison and Pitkin counties.

La Sal Forest: Mesa and Montrose counties.

Leadville Forest: Chaffee, Lake, Park and Summit counties.

Montezuma Forest: Dolores, La Plata, Montezuma and San Miguel counties.

Pike Forest: Park, Clear Creek, Douglas, El Paso, Teller and Jefferson counties.

Rio Grande Forest: Conejos, Hinsdale, La Plata, Mineral, Rio Grande, Saguache and San Juan counties.

Routt Forest: Grand, Jackson, Moffat and Routt counties.

San Isabel Forest: Alamosa, Chaffee, Custer, Fremont, Huerfano, Las Animas, Pueblo and Saguache counties.

San Juan Forest: Archuleta, Conejos, Hinsdale, La Plata, Mineral, Rio Grande and San Juan counties.

Uncompahgre Forest: Gunnison, Hinsdale, Mesa, Montrose, Ouray, San Juan and San Miguel counties.

White River Forest: Eagle, Garfield, Moffat, Rio Blanco and Routt counties.

The national forests are administered by the secretary of the department of agriculture through an official created by act of congress and known as the national forester. The secretary of agriculture is authorized by act of congress to issue from time to time regulations governing the use and occupancy of national forest lands and the use of timber and other national forest resources. These regulations are published in what is known as the "Use Book," which may be obtained by actual or prospective users of the national forests from the national forester at Washington, or from any district forester or forest supervisor.

"National forests have for their objects to insure a perpetual supply of timber, to preserve the forest cover which regulates the flow of streams, and to provide for the use of all resources which the forests contain, in the ways which will make them of largest service. Largest service means greatest good to the greatest number during the longest period of time."

Timber—Colorado has a tremendous resource in her timber. There are over 22½ billion board feet of timber within the national forests of Colorado. The U. S. forest service protects these forests from fires in co-operation with local people and is encouraging their development. With the rapid depletion of other sources of timber, lumbering within the national forests of Colorado promises to become one of her large industries and there are many undeveloped tracts waiting the initiation of the industry. This development, although in its infancy, is already taking place as is witnessed by the sale by the U. S. forest service of some 300 million feet of timber in one body in the southern part of the state. All timber cutting is done under forestry principles and the industry in the state will be permanent rather than transitory, and on account of increased growth obtained through the practice of forestry will increase in size. During the year 1923,

32,557,000 feet, board measure, were cut by commercial operators within the national forests of the state, for which the government received $85,862. Twenty-five per cent of this amount is given the state by the federal government. Eight hundred ninety thousand feet were sold to homesteaders and settlers at a nominal cost for the development of their ranches. In addition, free use to homesteaders, ranchers, miners and settlers of dead material was granted. This alone amounted to better than 11 million feet of timber. Three thousand five hundred and four permittees took advantage of the free dead timber that is available to homesteaders and ranchers, etc., by request of the U. S. forest service. The availability of a perpetual supply of timber within the boundaries of the state is becoming increasingly important, and with increased transportation charges Colorado is indeed in a fortunate position in this respect.

Reforestation—During 1923, a total of 908 acres was planted in the state of Colorado. This consisted mostly of Douglas fir and Engelmann spruce, with small quantities of yellow and bristlecone pine. The greater part of the planting was done on the Pike national forest on Ruxton creek above Manitou and adjacent to the Pikes Peak cog road. A small area was planted on the Uncompahgre plateau west of Montrose. During the year a reconnaissance was made of areas in need of reforestation throughout the state and it was found that there are 891,000 acres either treeless or covered with worthless brush or small tree growth that has no commercial value. Of this amount 463,000 acres is in the Englemann spruce type, 214,000 acres in the Douglas fir type, 119,000 acres in the lodgepole pine type and the remainder in the yellow and bristlecone pine types. The largest areas of land not producing commercial timber are located on Grand mesa in the forest of that name; in the Cochetopa forest west of the San Luis valley; on the Routt forest east and north of Steamboat Springs; on the San Juan forest north of Durango, and on the White River forest. Most of these areas were burned over from 40 to 70 years ago and the denudation was so complete that valuable coniferous forests have not replaced the former stand. Instead there are large areas covered with oak brush or aspen, the greater part of which has no commercial value. In time, as funds are made available by congress, the amount of planting in this state will be greatly increased. Following is a statement showing the investments for logging and manufacturing national forest timber, number of mills drawing all or an important part of timber supply from forests, and number of employes engaged in such work, made up in response to a request from the forester, for the state of Colorado only:

Forest	Estimated Investment	No. of Mills	No. of Employes
Arapahoe	$132,000	6	125
Cochetopa	170,000	19	140
Colorado	161,250	29	257
Grand Mesa	7,500	6	44
Gunnison	49,000	14	160
Holy Cross	50,000	15	100
Leadville	20,000	2	72
Montezuma	60,000	11	110
Pike	86,150	6	70
Rio Grande	49,550	15	60
Routt	9,000	14	60
San Isabel	16,400	7	60
San Juan	15,000	4	40
Uncompahgre	30,000	6	80
White River	25,000	14	75
Totals for Colorado	$880,850	168	1,453

Protection—Fifty-nine forest fires occurred during the year 1923 and burned 33 acres of timber land and 57 acres of open and brush land in the national forests. The damage to timber and forage is estimated at $47. It cost $1,039 to suppress the fires, though only two covered larger areas than 10 acres each. Twenty-three of these fires were man-caused and, therefore, preventable. The other 36 were set by lightning. Campers still constitute one of the greatest menaces with which the forest officers have to deal. There is need for extreme care on the part of everyone camping in the open and all camp fires must be drowned out with water if the forests art to be properly safeguarded. Careless smokers were responsible for nine of the fires which occurred. There is too little realization of the danger from tossing away a lighted match or live cigarette butt while traveling by auto, or in emptying pipe ashes, if precaution has not been taken to see that they are dead and, therefore, harmless. The local forest officers take care of the fire problem on most of the forests without the aid of lookout observers. For a number of reasons, however, there are certain parts of the forested region given additional protection in this way. Two such lookout stations are maintained in Colorado, one on Twin Sisters peak, near Estes Park, on the Colorado forest, and the other on the Devils Head, south of Denver, on the Pike forest. These stations are manned during the dry season and much damage is eliminated by the fact that fires are picked up quickly from these points. The greatest asset in fire protection in Colorado is the wonderfully fine spirit of co-operation shown by the large percentage of the resident population. In general, due care and diligence are used in preventive measures. There are many cases where initial action has been taken to suppress fires and no longer is there a delay in promptly reporting fires to forest officers. That there were fewer fires and less damage and cost in 1923 than ever before in the history of the forest service in Colorado is attributed largely to the fact that there was a great excess in precipitation amounting to frequent cloudbursts. The fire record for 1923 is an enviable one and affords a new mark to strive for. With the exercise of proper precaution and care on the part of everyone in the national forests, there is no reason why this record should not be maintained even in years when there is little rain.

Other Resources: Forage—Intermixed with the stands of timber on the forests are many parks or open places covered with a heavy growth of forage. There is also much grass and other forage plant growth in the timber where the tree growth is not too heavy. Most of this forage can be grazed by stock without injury to the timber. Some areas are closed to grazing in order to protect the slopes of streams, which furnish municipal water supplies, and other areas, rock slides, etc., are barren of any forage growth. About ten million acres of the thirteen and one-quarter million acres in the national forests of Colorado is used for pasturage, and feeds for the summer over 25 per cent of the cattle and 40 per cent of the sheep owned in the state. During 1923, this area supported 332,210 cattle, 6,634 horses and 845,446 sheep grazed under paid permits. The average grazing season for cattle and horses is about five months and the fee for this period is 50 cents per head for cattle and 62 cents for horses. The average season for sheep is about three months and the fee is 8¼ cents per head. Up to the present time, and for the year 1925, the fees have been based on a flat annual rate regardless of variations in character of individual ranges. Intensive appraisal has been conducted which is being considered as a basis for revision of the grazing fees beginning in 1926. This, if put into effect, will result in the revision fees being based upon the worth of the various individual ranges rather than on a flat rate for all ranges. Sheep are grazed in the extremely high portions of the forests, where the snow stays until the latter part of June and begins falling again in September. About 3,400 cattle and 4,400 horses were grazed free under a regulation which provides for grazing free not to exceed ten head of work and milk stock in actual use by settlers, prospectors, etc.

Larkspur Eradication—Certain poisonous plants on the range kill stock, but it has been found that about 90 per cent of this loss can be prevented by digging or grubbing the principal poisonous plant, which is larkspur. During the latter part of 1915 definite grubbing of larkspur was begun in Colorado. Since that time about 5,346 acres has been grubbed, at a cost of approximately $3.81 per acre. It is estimated that this work effected a saving of $21,300 to the livestock industry of the state during the past year. Past experience has shown that it can be expected that this amount will be saved annually on the areas where grubbing has been carried on.

Range Improvements—The construction of range improvements that are at present in use on the national forests of Colorado consists of: Fences, 428 miles, value $57,469; corrals, 46, value $2,639; improved stock driveways, 653 miles, value $19,831; stock bridges, 5, value $1,313; water developments (improved springs), 157, value $4,637.

Range Reconnaissance — Intensive range reconnaissance to determine just what forage the forests are growing has been carried on in several places, in order that the range may be stocked to the full carrying capacity without damage. Over 1,397,000 acres has been covered by this intensive investigation.

Game—Game animals are always interesting and the forest service game census for 1923 shows there are in the national forests of the state approximately 20,914 black-tailed or mule deer and 51 white-tailed deer, 5,610 mountain sheep and 5,837 elk, 507 mountain lions, 103 wolves and 29,585 coyotes, 2,592 black and brown bear, 5,346 lynx and wildcats, 3,467 foxes, 41,594 beaver, 8,450 weasels, 25,460 muskrats, 8,068 marten, 5,907 mink and 3,418 badger. 4,198,000 fish fry were planted by the forest officers in the state in 1923. Twelve of the state game refuges have been established within the national forests of the state, under the following names. The forest service co-operates with the state authorities in the protection of these areas.

Name	Counties where located in whole or part
Cochetopa	Saguache
Colorado	Larimer and Boulder
Denver Mountain Parks	Clear Creek, Jefferson, Park
Gunnison	Gunnison
North Park	Jackson
Ouray	Ouray
Pikes Peak	Teller and El Paso
Poncha Pass	Chaffee, Gunnison, Saguache
Royal Gorge	Fremont
Snowmass	Pitkin
Spanish Peaks	Huerfano and Las Animas
Williams Fork	Grand

Agricultural Land—When the boundaries of the national forests originally were established, it was inevitable that some agricultural and non-forest land should be included. The boundaries, however, since have been readjusted from time to time until within the state of Colorado approximately 1,830,722 acres, or about 11 per cent of the original area, has been released; partly because of the agricultural possibilities of the lands and partly because it was not suitable or needed for timber production or other national forest purposes. In addition to this general contraction of the boundaries by eliminations from the outer edges, a total area of 269,642 acres, mostly in small tracts scattered throughout the interior of the forests, has been made available for entry under the forest homestead act of June 11, 1906, which authorized the secretary of agriculture to list with the interior department for entry under the homestead laws such lands in the national forests as in his opinion were chiefly valuable for agriculture and not needed for public purposes. By an act of congress passed August 10, 1912, the secretary of agriculture was directed to "select, classify and segregate, as soon as practicable, all lands within the boundaries of national forests that may be open to entry under the homestead law." This general classification now has been completed in the national forests of Colorado, and all the lands therein found to be chiefly valuable for agriculture have been listed for entry. The remaining lands were classified as permanently more valuable for national forest purposes, and no further applications for examination and listing are accepted by the forest service. Many of the areas already listed, however, still are vacant and where this is so may be entered by qualified persons upon application to the local land office concerned as in ordinary cases.

Land Exchange—There are 1,466,245 acres of privately owned lands within the exterior boundaries of the Colorado national forests, acquired under the various land laws. Much of this is permanently adapted to the production of timber and is not desired by the owner; in some cases because it was taken up for the merchantable timber which has now been removed; in other cases it was taken up in the hope of making a successful farm and proved to be worthless; in still other cases it is mineral ground which has been worked out or proved to be valueless. Some of it is used for grazing; some not at all. Often a single owner has acquired a number of widely separated tracts. On March 20, 1922, the president approved the land exchange act, which authorizes in general language the exchange of private lands for government lands in the national forests, or authorizes the exchange of private lands for timber of equivalent value. This will make it possible for private owners to consolidate their holdings and to exchange timber producing land for land of greater value for grazing, and will at the same time, permit the government to consolidate its holdings in more compact bodies of timber land, which will be easier of administration and less expensive to protect. Both the private land offered and the government land or timber to be selected must be within the same state and within the exterior boundaries of a national forest. Exchanges not conforming to these requirements cannot be made except where additional authority by special act of congress is secured. Private land which contains a relatively large proportion of agricultural soils or is distinctly mineral in character will not be accepted in exchange; only lands primarily adapted to timber growing are desired as a rule. Persons interested in making such exchanges should apply to the forest supervisor of the forest concerned or to the nearest forest officer for detailed information as to procedure.

Recreation—Primarily the forests of the United States should be protected and perpetuated because they are the source of the nation's future wood supply, but the forests have other values which justify the interest of the public in their protection. More and more people realize the value of the recreation center as a mighty factor in the development of both the youth and the adult of cities. Recreation grounds grow in importance as population increases. In 1923, 1,580,-483 people visited the national forests of the state. There are under license 63 hotels, resorts and club houses and 590 summer residences within the forests of Colorado. Areas intensively used as camping and picnic grounds have been reserved from appropriation for an exclusive use and the convenience and pleasure of the public thereby provided for.

Roads—The forest service participates in building roads in and near the forests. Some roads it builds alone or in co-operation with the counties, using its own enginering organization, road-building machinery and government funds. During 1923 a total of 123 miles of new road was constructed by the expenditure of $406,773. The large projects required $285,765, and the small projects $121,008. Trails cost $5,236, 176 miles having been constructed. In constructing roads, the counties and the forest service choose the roads and provide the funds, and the bureau of public roads does the engineering and construction work on the large projects. Trails in the forests are necessary to protect the areas against fire by making it possible to get in with pack train loads of supplies.

Finances—The receipts from the sale of timber, grazing permits, special use permits, etc., during 1923, amounted to $464,945.74. Of this amount, 35 per cent, or $162,736.05 was used in the state for roads and schools, 25 per cent being sent the counties in which national forests are located, and 10 per cent spent directly by the forest service for roads. The total spent in operating the district office in Denver, the experiment stations, and the administration of the 15 forests in Colorado, including the amount spent by the forest service on roads, trails, telephone lines, ranger stations, etc., was $678,492.94.

Tourist Attractions

FOR a good many years there has been a decrease in the value of the output from Colorado's metal mines. Expert mining engineers familiar with mining conditions and operations and with ore supplies in Colorado are agreed that the state's metal supplies are far from exhausted, but the fact remains that less gold and silver and associated metals is being marketed from our mountains than they produced twenty years ago.

But whatever may be the condition of Colorado's metal supplies, there can be no doubt that the state has in its incomparable climate and its wonderful mountain scenery a resource which is returning a larger revenue each succeeding year and which promises more than to offset any further losses that may be suffered from curtailment of metal mining operations. The number of tourists and vacationists from other states and countries who come to Colorado annually is larger now than it has ever been before and each year is showing a substantial increase over the previous year. Our climate and scenery are permanent resources and the game of our hills and mountain fastnesses and the fish of our streams and lakes are being so replenished and protected that fishing and hunting are now and will continue to be among the state's greatest attractions for visitors.

Switzerland has been more successful than perhaps any other country in capitalizing its mountain scenery for profit. Circumstances have aided nature and the energy and enterprise of the Swiss people in making the scenery of that country return a substantial revenue every year. Before the war Switzerland was for many years on nearly all the direct routes of tourist travel through Europe and few persons who visited the continent failed to spend some time in the Alps and to visit the cities and lakes of

Switzerland that are so familiar to all European travelers. Before the war estimates placed the revenue derived by the Swiss people from tourist travel as high as $35,000,000 annually.

Yet Colorado is nearly seven times as large as Switzerland, and its mountain area is fully six times as great. Colorado has at least 43 peaks that tower more than 14,000 feet above sea level, while Switzerland has but eight, Colorado has fully 1,000 peaks 10,000 feet high and over, while Switzerland has fewer than one-eighteenth as many. Every peak in Colorado is accessible for any careful and reasonably strong mountain climber entirely to its summit, while the highest peaks in Switzerland are accessible to their summits only for hardy and expert climbers and then only under the direction of experienced guides.

There are thousands of beautiful lakes in the mountains of Colorado, many of them of large size and all of them of wonderful beauty. Some of Colorado's lakes, though far less famous than Lake Lucerne, are not surpassed by it in certain characteristics of natural beauty. If they were surrounded by beautiful villas and hotels scores of Colorado's lakes might soon have almost as many admirers as have the lakes of Switzerland. Some of the more easily accessible of our mountain lakes are beginning to be surrounded by the modern conveniences that many tourists and travelers demand, but there will always be in Colorado hundreds of picturesque lakes where fishing is good and where natural beauty is not too much marred by the art of man.

It is not the purpose of this volume to enumerate, even partially, the important tourist atractions of the state. A much larger volume than this would be required to treat the subject adequately. The intention here is only to give such data as are available regarding the importance of the tourist trade to the state and to show something of its growth in recent years and its prospects for much greater growth in the future. The railroads serving Colorado, the Commerciai clubs of the various cities and towns, the Denver tourist bureau and other similar corporations and organizations publish annually hundreds of booklets and leaflets descriptive of the state's tourist attractions, and such literature may be obtained upon application to the various railroads and organizations.

The national parks and monuments located in the state are named and briefly described elsewhere in this volume. Some idea of the rapidly growing importance of the tourist industry in Colorado may be gathered from figures showing the increase in the number of visitors to these parks annually. The Rocky Mountain national park was created by act of congress in 1915. That year the secretary of the department of interior estimated the number of visitors to the park at 31,000. In 1916 the number of visitors was about 51,000 and in 1922 the number of visitors, according to the official records of the secretary of the department of interior, was 219,164. These visitors came from 45 states. During the season 51,112 automobiles were driven into the parks, coming from 40 states. The number of visitors in 1923 was about the same as in 1922. Detailed figures are not available showing the number of visitors annually in the Mesa Verde national park, but within the past four years the number has much more than doubled, due partly to the construction of new automobile highways leading across the state and into the park and partly to the extensive advertising recently given to the remains of habitations of the pre-historic Cliff Dwellers which are found here.

Fifteen national forests lie wholly within Colorado and two lie partly in the state. These forests have an aggregate area of about 13,270,000 acres. They include nearly all the higher mountain peaks not within the national parks and a very large part of the most beautiful scenery in the state lies within their boundaries. The forest service is devoting more attention each year to popularizing these forests as national playgrounds and to improving them with roads, trails, shelter houses and other conveniences for travelers. The forest service estimates that about 1,580,000 people visited the national forests of the state in 1923, some of them remaining in the forest limits only a few hours, some remaining several weeks and some of them making several visits. The average time spent by each of the visitors within the forest limits, according to the records of the forest service, was three days. Most of them spent much more time than this in the state. Of course, a very considerable number of these forest visitors were Colorado people, but some idea of the vast and growing importance of the state's tourist business may be gathered from the figures here given. A great many of the visitors to the state do not enter the national forest limits except on railroad trains and hence are not counted in the forest service's enumeration. Many of the visitors to Rocky Mountain national park never enter the national forests. If the number of visitors to the state each tourist season is not more than 500,000, and they spend an average of three days each in the state they must leave in Colorado not less than $15,000,000 annually. The actual number of visitors annually now is perhaps nearly 500,000, but the time these visitors spend in the state averages much more than three days each, so that the actual amount of money spent by tourists and sightseers annually in Colorado is no doubt more than the present annual value of the output of the state's metal mines.

Big game still is found rather abundantly in Colorado, including deer, antelope, bear, elk, mountain lion, gray wolf and coyote. In an article in this book devoted to the national forests of the state will be found approximate estimates of the numbers of various kinds of big game found within the national forests. The numbers found outside the forest boundaries bring the totals considerably above the figures there given, but no accurate survey has been made except within the forests. There is also much small game, including sage hen, grouse, pheasant, dove, wild duck, rabbit, squirrel and other varieties. In recent years the state has exercised strict supervision over the killing of game, and such protective measures as have been adopted and enforced have had the effect of increasing the supply of many kinds of the larger game birds and animals which were in danger of extinction. There is open season on practically all game, and the regulations under which game may be killed may be obtained from the state game and fish commissioner at the state capitol. There are now within the state protected areas in which game may not be killed at any time, except certain predatory animals, which may be trapped or hunted under special permits granted by the state game and fish commissioner. These are known as game refuges, the following having been created by the state legislature in 1921:

The Colorado State game refuge, in Larimer and Boulder counties, surrounding the Rocky Mountain national park on the north, east and south. Restrictions on hunting and trapping within the national park are even more rigid than in the game refuge. This refuge lies within the borders of the Colorado national forest.

The Pikes Peak game refuge, in El Paso and Teller counties, including much of the area about Pikes peak, and being within the Pike national forest.

The Spanish Peaks game refuge, in the southwestern part of Huerfano county and extending into western Las Animas county, in the San Isabel national forest.

The Denver Mountain Parks game refuge, west of the city of Denver, in Jefferson, Clear Creek and Park counties, including the Denver mountain parks.

The Colorado Antelope refuge, comprising four townships in Larimer and Weld counties, north of Wellington.

Seven additional game refuges were created by the legislature in 1923, the acts creating them not becoming effective until some time in August.

Nothing more important has been done to increase tourist travel to Colorado than the construction of good highways reaching nearly all parts of the state. A decade ago nearly all visitors to Colorado came by rail. It was next to impossible then for an automobile to make a trip across the state east and west, for there were no roads worthy of the name across the mountains. When occasionally an automobile guided by some daring driver made such trip without mishap over such roads as there were his accomplishment was looked upon in the nature of an extraordinary achievement and newspapers gave him something of the same sort of notice they give today to airplane pilots who fly across the continent without stopping.

But in recent years excellent highways have been built into many of the most beautiful mountain districts and many of our most magnificent mountain peaks which were unknown even to most of the people of Colorado are now coming to be almost as well known as Pikes peak, which in the past was practically the only mountain in Colorado known outside the state. Today there are five or more automobile routes across the state east and west and travel is heavy on all of them. More tourists visit Colorado today by automobile than visit it by rail, and automobile travel to the state is increasing much more rapidly than travel by railroad. The amount of money available for highway construction in the state is increasing each year, and it is fair to assume that the progress made in this direction in the next decade will be more rapid than that of the past decade. Some of the mountain areas that are yet inaccessible because of lack of highways are of exceptional beauty and grandeur and Colorado will for many years be offering each season some new scenic attraction to its visitors. People no longer come to Colorado year after year to see Pikes peak alone, but each year they may visit some new peak, lake or mountain park and none of our visitors of today will live long enough to see all that is worth while in the Colorado Rockies by making one visit to the state each year.

The characteristics of the Colorado climate that make it so attractive to tourists and healthseekers are its dryness, high percentage of sunshine, moderate air movements, and moderate and equable temperatures. The high altitude affects the climate favorably for persons afflicted with pulmonary and similar diseases, the air being rarer, less humid and generally purer than the air in lower altitudes. The average annual precipitation for the state is about 17 inches, ranging from as low as 6 inches in some localities in the San Luis valley to above 30 inches in parts of the San Juan mountains. The humidity of the atmosphere is generally very low in all parts of the state, which renders the climate much less oppressive during periods of high temperature than in districts of lower altitude and higher precipitation. Average humidity is lower in Colorado than in any other state except Arizona. Air movements are moderate in all parts of the state, though there is frequently considerable wind in some seasons of the year, cyclones are unknown, and the hot winds that cause great damage to crops in states immediately east and south of Colorado seldom reach into this state.

Colorado is rich in mineral waters, some of them acknowledged to be of high curative qualities. More than 250 mineral springs and wells in the state have been carefully studied and their waters analyzed by the state geological survey, and there are perhaps as many which have not been analyzed. The largest single group of mineral springs in Colorado is found in and about the city of Steamboat Springs, in Routt county. Among other well known groups of mineral springs are those at Glenwood Springs, Idaho Springs, Pagosa Springs, Hot Sulphur Springs, Manitou and Canon City. Many of these places are well known health and tourist resorts, some of them having large bathing pools, sanitoria, hotels and other conveniences. One of the springs at Pagosa Springs has an average flow of about 700 gallons per minute, being one of the largest mineral springs in the United States. The waters of many of the Colorado mineral springs are highly radio-active, comparing favorably with the most notable springs in the world in this respect. Temperatures of the waters vary greatly, the highest being that of the Hortense hot springs, near Mt. Princeton, in Chaffee county.

Colorado Highways

HIGHWAY construction has proceeded more rapidly in Colorado in the past decade than in any other state of the Rocky Mountain group, but not quite so rapidly as in some of the more densely populated states of the east and on the Pacific coast. Survey of highway mileage in the state made by the United States bureau of public roads in 1921 and carefully revised in 1923 shows a total of 67,608 miles of public highways, not including streets and alleys in incorporated cities and towns, and 2,445 miles of streets and alleys in such incorporated places. This is the most complete survey of road mileage ever made in Colorado, showing 28,000 more miles of public roads in the state than was shown by the survey made by the state highway department in 1916. The increase over the 1916 survey is partly due to an extensive increase in highway mileage since that time, and partly to the fact that the recent survey was much more nearly complete. The total road mileage is divided into 8,923 miles of state highways and 58,685 miles of county roads. The most notable feature in the survey is the rapid increase in improved roads in the state since 1916. At that time there was not a mile of hard surfaced road in Colorado outside the larger cities, while at the present time there is about 170 miles of hard surfaced road, 3,200 miles of gravel and sand-clay state roads, and 5,013 miles of gravel and sand-clay county roads, 5,303 miles of graded state roads, and 28,606 miles of graded county roads. Practically all of the surfacing and a large part of the grading has been completed since 1916. Every important city and town in the state at the present time may be reached over good automobile roads, while excellent mountain highways make it possible for the tourist and sightseer to visit the most attractive scenic districts in the state and even to drive to the summits of some of the best known mountain peaks. Las Animas county ranks first in total road mileage with 6,000 miles, it being also the largest county in the state. Weld county, which ranks third in area, ranks second in road mileage and first in mileage of improved roads. Hard surfaced roads have been built chiefly near the larger cities in Adams, Arapahoe, Jefferson, Boulder, Larimer, Weld, El Paso, Pueblo, Otero and Mesa counties.

Figures compiled by the United States bureau of roads show that approximately $11,000,000 was spent for highway construction and maintenance in 1923, exclusive of expenditures for streets and alleys in incorporated cities and towns. Of this amount, $5,453,466 was spent under the direction of the state highway department and $4,934,449 by the several counties. The United States forest service during the same period spent approximately $523,448 on roads within the national forests.

State road funds include contributions to the state from the federal government, which are spent on what is known as federal aid projects, being mainly highway projects approved by the United States bureau of roads. On such approved projects the government pays 56.12 per cent of the cost and the state the remainder. Total expenditures on federal aid projects in the state in 1923 were $3,407,004. The state also supervises the construction of what is known as state projects, in the cost of which the state and the several counties interested cooperate. On such state projects the expenditures in 1923 were $1,262,247. The state is also spending more money each year for maintenance, annual expenditures now running close to $1,000,000.

It is impossible to determine accurately the amount of money available from all sources for highway construction and maintenance in Colorado in 1924. Indications are that state funds will amount to close to $3,500,000, county funds to about $4,000,000 and federal funds including federal aid, forest service appropriation and national park expenditures, something over $2,000,000. The total will be considerably less than that available in 1923, but will be increased by a balance of more than $2,500,000, left over at the end of 1923 from the funds available that year. This large balance was due in a measure to the fact that unfavorable weather in 1923 prevented the construction of much highway for which contracts were let and appropriations made. The state fund for the year 1924 includes $1,500,000 of bonds from the $6,000,000 bond issue approved in 1922. Beginning August 1, 1923, all money due the state highway fund from the registration and licensing of motor vehicles, which is one-half the license and registration fees, must be paid into the fund to meet the interest and amortization charges on these bonds. The state highway department's share of all motor license fees, which have been used in the past for highway construction and maintenance, must now be used to meet fixed charges on the bonds until they are retired.

A law enacted by the Twenty-third General Assembly provided for a tax of one cent a gallon on gasoline and other petroleum products, the proceeds of which are to be divided equally between the state highway department and the several counties and to be used exclusively on highway work. The Twenty-fourth General Assembly amended the law to make this tax two cents a gallon, the proceeds to be divided as before. It also repealed the half-mill tax levy for road purposes levied by an act of the General Assembly in 1919, the theory being that the additional one cent per gallon tax on gasoline will provide the revenue lost to the road funds through the repeal of the half-mill levy and will place the tax directly upon the people who make use of the roads. However, the amount of money collected under the additional one cent gasoline tax, though increasing each year, is not yet so large as that formerly collected under the one-half mill levy.

The Twenty-third General Assembly enacted a new law for the managing and regulation of the state highway department, providing for an advisory commission of seven members, and a chief highway executive, to be appointed by the governor, and known as the state highway engineer. Under this act the highway department has been entirely reorganized, being now composed of four main divisions, known as the accounting, engineering, maintenance, and purchase and traffic divisions. The four men at the head of these divisions, acting under the direction of the state highway engineer and the assistant highway engineer, are the executive officers of the department.

Certain main trunk highways, designed to connect all sections of the state and to reach all county seats and important cities, laid out by the state highway engineer with the advice of the commission and the concurrence of the governor, are designated as state highways and state funds are expended only on such highways. The state highway budget is made up annually in the same way the state highways are designated. The law provides that no state highway funds may be used within the limits of any incorporated city or town, with certain exceptions affecting smaller towns.

The boards of county commissioners of the several counties have general supervision over the construction and maintenance of roads and bridges within their respective counties. They have absolute jurisdiction over county roads, and they co-operate with the state highway department in all work on highways within their respective counties. All work on county roads and bridges is paid for from county funds, derived from special tax levies and from other less important sources. Federal aid money is now expended upon a definite system of federal aid highways, equal to seven per cent of the total highway mileage of the state.

The state highway fund, the expenditure of which is directed by the state highway department upon state highways exclusively, is derived: (1) From a special half-mill tax levy authorized by vote of the people in the general election in November, 1914, and until 1924 from an additional half mill levy authorized by the Twenty-second General Assembly, but repealed by the Twenty-fourth. (2) From such funds as may be appropriated by the state legislature to the state highway fund. (3) From all funds now in and hereafter to be paid into the internal improvement income fund, derived from the sale and administration of land granted by the federal government to the state for internal improvements. (4) One-half the revenue arising from the licensing of motor vehicles, from chauffeurs' licenses and from fines and penalties for violation of vehicle and road regulations. (This revenue, as above stated, must be used to pay interest and sinking fund on the $6,000,000 road bond issue of 1923 until the issue is retired.) (5) One-half the revenue arising from a tax of two cents a gallon on gasoline and other petroleum products authorized by the Twenty-fourth General Assembly. (6) All public donations, including allotments made by the federal government to the state for highway purposes. Such federal allotments, however, are administered partly under the direction of the federal government and cannot be paid out until federal highway engineers have approved preliminary engineering on the project on which they are to be expended, and cannot be paid over until government agents approve the work done. (7) The proceeds of the sale of the $6,000,000 bond issue authorized by the vote of the people in November, 1922, such bonds to be sold at the rate of $1,500,000 annually for four years, beginning with 1923. (8) Interest from the investment of highway funds.

The national forest service does considerable road construction work within the national forests or near their borders, partly in co-operation with the state highway department and partly in co-operation with the several counties. The federal bureau of roads also co-operates with the forest service in some of this work and furnishes a part of the funds. The amount being spent on roads and trails within the forest boundaries is being increased each year and some of the state's finest highways are in the national forests.

It is only within recent years that Colorado's highway program has been financed in such a way that a definite plan of road construction and maintenance could be established and carried into effect, but since highway finances have been put on a sound basis and large federal funds have been made available a greal program of improvement has been put under way and is being pushed rapidly. Before many years the principal roads leading through the state from north to south and east to west will be paved for the greater part of their distance if not in their entirety, and while that work is being done all other main roads are being surfaced and maintained with the joint aid of federal, state and county funds.

Colorado's Educational System

COLORADO'S public school system compares favorably with the best state public school systems in the country. It is being enlarged and expanded rather rapidly to meet the needs of a growing population, there being few states in which the percentage of increase in the number of school buildings and in the number of teachers employed has been greater in the past decade. In recent years the number of schools has been decreasing instead of increasing, however, due to the large number of Consolidated schools, which provide much better educational facilities than the smaller schools they replaced. At present there are 1,944 school districts in the state, according to the records of the state superintendent of schools, with 3,230 schools, including 3,622 school buildings. In these there were employed during the school year ending June 30, 1923, 8,599 teachers, of whom 7,263 were females and 1,336 males. Tabulations found elsewhere in this volume show the number of school buildings and school teachers employed in the various counties of the state for the school year ending June 30, 1923, the figures being taken from the records of the state superintendent of schools.

There are approximately 80 consolidated schools in the state and the number is increasing gradually each year. There are more than 50 centralized schools and many joint schools, in which two or more counties are interested. The school population of the state for the school year ending June 30, 1923, was 287,318, compared with 272,693 for the previous year. The total enrollment in the public schools of the state during the same school year, including enrollment in the county high schools, was 249,813, and the average daily attendance, including attendance in county high schools, was 174,484. Enrollment during the previous school year was 243,004, while the average daily attendance that year was 170,426. Total public school revenues for the year ending June 30, 1923, including special revenues of county high schools, were $27,070,684, compared with $22,151,541 for the preceding year. Public school revenues in Colorado have increased very rapidly in recent years, due chiefly to the levying of higher school district taxes. A considerable part of the increase for the past three years has been called for to pay increased salaries of teachers, due to the fact that the legislature in 1921 enacted a law providing for a minimum salary of $75 per month for all public school teachers in Colorado. The fund necessary to provide this increase has been provided partly by increased district levies and partly by increased county levies. The law was revised by the legislature in 1923, but the minimum salary remains the same. Average salaries paid teachers in all classes of public schools have increased substantially, as may be seen by consulting tables published elsewhere in this volume and in previous issues of the Colorado Year Book. For the school year ending June 30, 1923, the average monthly salary paid women teachers in high schools of the state was $136.11, and men teachers, $177.87. These averages are slightly lower than the averages for the previous year, but the general average of salaries paid all teachers in the state is perhaps higher now than ever before. The lowest average salary now paid is to women teachers in schools employing only one teacher, being $94.32.

The state has a large and growing permanent school fund derived from the sale of land granted by the federal government for the benefit of the public schools and popularly known as state school land. On November 30,1922, acording to the state board of land commissioners, there was $7,235,268.78 in the permanent school fund. The increase since that time has been considerable, but the exact figures at the present time are not available. This permanent fund is invested in farm mortgages, state bonds, state warrants and other securities, and the interest is turned into the public school income fund, which is distributed semi-annually among the various counties of the state for the benefit of their schools in proportion to the school population of the several counties. On November 30, 1922, deferred payments and accrued interest on all state land sold and not fully paid for amounted to $7,207,406.77. This total has decreased somewhat since that date, on account of the fact that sales of public land have been few and cancellations of previous sales have been rather large. A small amount of the total does not belong to the school fund, being due for the payment of other state land, but the amount due the school fund from this fund is only a little short of $7,000,000. Payments on the purchase price of this land are all turned into the permanent school fund, while payments of interest go into the income fund and are distributed among the counties. Income derived from the administration of the unsold school lands and the mineral rights reserved on school lands that have been sold also is turned into the school income fund, which fund now provides more than $8,000 annually for distribution among the various public schools of the state. This amount is increasing steadily, both as a result of the increased interest accruing from the permanent fund each year and the increased revenue derived from the administration of the unsold land and the mineral rights. On November 30, 1923, there was 2,991,689 acres of state land remaining unsold, nearly all of which is school land and most of which is under lease and bringing in a revenue to the school fund. This land is valued at approximately $33,000,000. while the mineral rights on school land, which are always retained for the benefit of the school fund, are conservatively valued at $100,000,000.

By far the largest part of the revenue of the public schools is from direct taxation. Special county tax levies are made for school purposes, these levies having increased materially in 1921 and succeeding years to meet the requirements of the teachers' minimum wage law. In addition to the county levies each school district has its own tax levy, these district levies producing considerably more than one-half of the revenue of the public schools. The following table, compiled from the records of the state superintendent of schools, gives the total revenue of the public schools from all sources for the school year ending June 30, 1923:

County	Total Receipts
Adams	$ 441,927.74
Alamosa	170,180.48
Arapahoe	315,545.55
Archuleta	65,203.99
Baca	203,075.73
Bent	158,420.44
Boulder	700,128.50
Chaffee	249,394.23
Cheyenne	198,480.49
Clear Creek	64,501.46
Conejos	164,231.25
Costilla	86,909.92
Crowley	219,508.49
Custer	25,259.21
Delta	291,576.25
Denver	774,798.90
Dolores	
Douglas	80,204.25
Eagle	87,566.72
Elbert	206,326.67
El Paso	1,438,908.64
Fremont	408,109.34
Garfield	222,725.30
Gilpin	38,457.99
Grand	43,541.58
Gunnison	102,818.45
Hinsdale	13,609.73
Huerfano	317,219.80
Jackson	20,091.15
Jefferson	425,521.21
Kiowa	214,534.22
Kit Carson	349,864.83
Lake	120,179.03
La Plata	286,821.00
Larimer	738,530.11
Las Animas	912,569.52
Lincoln	300,121.92
Logan	503,926.44
Mesa	492,646.24
Mineral	16,324.08
Moffat	110,581.64
Montezuma	152,334.75
Montrose	220,812.81
Morgan	439,393.59
Otero	579,322.54
Ouray	34,042.26
Park	51,060.24
Phillips	168,862.71
Pitkin	52,421.72
Prowers	345,937.67
Pueblo	1,353,177.98
Rio Blanco	60,230.40
Rio Grande	231,598.48
Routt	262,048.34
Saguache	132,621.64
San Juan	33,012.54
San Miguel	102,033.85
Sedgwick	107,585.74
Summit	47,387.03
Teller	123,697.69
Washington	380,134.21
Weld	1.597,973.36
Yuma	349,415.81
Total	$ 25,078,633.85
County High Schools	992,050.24
Grand Total	$ 26,070,684.09

The expense of administering the state public school system has been increased substantially in the past eight years by the issuance of large amounts of bonds, chiefly for the construction of new school buildings. On January 1, 1924, there was outstanding $20,373,120 in bonds issued by school districts, in addition to over $700,000 issued by counties for the purpose of county high schools. The interest on this large bonded debt amounts to more than $1,000,000 annually, while sinking fund charges are increasing gradually each year. A very large amount of the proceeds of bond issues in rural districts has been used for the construction and equipment of consolidated and centralized schools, furnishing greatly improved school facilities for nearly all counties in the state.

Institutions of higher education supported by the state are: State Agricultural college at Fort Collins, with a branch school at Fort Lewis, near Hesperus, La Plata county; Western State college, formerly State Normal school, at Gunnison; State Teachers' college, at Greeley; State School of Mines, at

Golden, and University of Colorado, at Boulder. All these are practically supported by legislative appropriations and by substantial tax levies. The Agricultural college and the University also derive some revenue from the sale and administration of special grants of land made by the federal government for their benefit, these lands being administered through the State Board of Land Commissioners in the same manner as the public school lands.

Besides the educational institutions previously mentioned there are the State Industrial School for Boys, at Golden; the State Industrial School for Girls, at Morrison; the State School for Deaf and Blind, at Colorado Springs; the State Home and School for Dependent and Neglected Children, at Denver, and the State Home and School for Mental Defectives, at Grand Junction. These institutions are supported by special legislative appropriations from general revenue.

In addition to the public schools and institutions of higher learning supported by the state there are numerous private and sectarian schools and colleges and many business, trade and professional schools, which cannot be described or enumerated in this volume.

Colorado—Brief Land History

THE territory now included in the state of Colorado did not all become the property of the United States at the same time, nor was it all conveyed in the same manner or by the same nation. Parts of it have at times belonged to the territories of Kansas, Nebraska, New Mexico and Utah, and a very considerable section of it was claimed by the Republic of Texas when that enterprising little nation won its freedom from Mexico.

The Louisiana Purchase, a vast tract of land acquired by the United States from France in 1803, extended, in a general way, westward from the Mississippi river to the Rocky mountains. About half of the land now comprising the state of Colorado was included in this purchase, the entire cost of which was about $27,250,000.

The area south of the Arkansas river and west of the Rocky mountains was first claimed by Spain and later by Mexico. When Texas, after winning its independence from Mexico, was admitted to the Union in 1845, it claimed that part of what is now Colorado lying south of the Arkansas river, and in addition a rectangular strip extending north through the mountains into Wyoming, lying between the 106th and the 108th meridians. By reference to the map it will be seen that a considerable part of this territory claimed by Texas was included in the Louisiana Purchase, but the controversy over the northern boundary of Texas was amicably settled before Colorado territory was organized.

The western part of Colorado and the territory in the south lying west and south of the Rio Grande del Norte was included in the immense tract of land ceded to the United States by Mexico in 1848 following the war with that country. The eastern boundary of this ceded land was at about the 108th meridian, except on the south, where its boundary, as before stated, was the Rio Grande del Norte.

The territory of Utah was organized in 1850. It extended east to the main range of the Rocky mountains, including nearly one-half of what is now Colorado. In 1854 the territories of Kansas and Nebraska were created by the famous Kansas-Nebraska act. Kansas territory then extended west to the territory of Utah, the southern boundary being the territory of New Mexico, which at that time extended north to the Arkansas river, and the northern boundary being at the 40th parallel, which passes near the present site of the city of Brighton. That part of what is now Colorado, lying north of this parallel and extending west to the boundary of Utah territory, was included in Nebraska territory.

In 1855 that part of Colorado then included in Kansas territory was organized into Arapahoe county, and Allen P. Tibbitts, Levi Mitchell and Jonathan Atwood were named as commissioners to locate the county-seat of the new county, which was to be called Mountain City. They were likewise to act as commissioners for the new county, but there is no record available showing that they ever assumed their duties. In 1856 an election was held in Arapahoe county, K. T., and Benjamin F. Simmons was chosen as the first representative from this county in the Kansas territorial legislature.

But the people in the new towns and mining camps, dissatisfied with a government the seat of which was several hundred miles away, and could be reached only after a week's hard travel, soon started a movement for the organization of a new territory, to include that part of Kansas territory known as Arapahoe county. This movement gained strength rapidly, and some of the more ambitious conceived the idea that the creation of a new state was the proper procedure. They spent some months working on the plan and finally agreed that the new state should be called Jefferson and should extend north far into what is now Wyoming. An election held late in 1859 showed that a majority of the voters were in favor of trying a territorial government before attempting statehood, and Robert W. Steele was elected as the first governor of "Jefferson Territory." The following counties were provided for in the organization of the so-called "Jefferson Territory:" Arapahoe, Cheyenne, El Paso, Fountain, Jackson, Jefferson, Mountain, North Park, Saratoga, Steele and St. Vrain.

In the meantime, however, steps were being taken at Washington to bring about the organization of a territory through the regularly constituted legislative channels. In February, 1861, Colorado Territory was regularly organized, its boundaries being substantially the same as those of the state today. On June 6, 1861, Mr. Steele formally abdicated as governor of "Jefferson Territory," and that unique political subdivision passed into history.

The organization of Colorado territory did not settle the numerous controversies regarding land titles that existed when the territory was organized. Within the area formerly claimed by the state of Texas, as well as that ceded by Mexico, there were numerous land grants, made by the Spanish and Mexican governments, all of which were confirmed by the United States when this area became a part of the Union. A special land court was created for the examination and adjudication of these titles, and in all cases where the records showed that the grants were properly made they were formally approved by this court. In addition to these old grants there were large tracts of land which had been set apart for Indian tribes who had long claimed this territory as their own. Those who are familiar with the early history of the state will know that the controversies with these Indians were not settled without many bloody battles, which resulted in heavy loss of life among both the Indians and the pioneer settlers. In 1861 the federal government entered into a treaty with the Cheyenne and Arapahoe Indians, under which the Indians ceded to the government their lands in eastern Colorado. The Indians did not abide by this treaty, however, and they waged vigorous warfare against the white settlers for several years with a view to driving them from the plains of eastern Colorado. On October 28, 1867, they signed another treaty with the United States, ceding all their lands between the Platte and Arkansas rivers, and agreeing to their removal to Indian Territory.

In the western part of the state settlers came in contact with the Ute Indians. In 1868 a treaty had been made between these Indians and the government by which the government confirmed their title to a large tract of land in the southern and western parts of the state. After the discovery of rich metal deposits in the San Juan district, white settlers began to come in rapidly, and steps were taken to recover the land that had been confirmed by the government as the property of the Utes. The Indians were strongly opposed to giving it up, but in 1873, largely through the influence of Chief Ouray, one of the most illustrious leaders of the red men in Colorado, a treaty was signed by which the Utes ceded to the government the mineral lands in the San Juan district.

They still retained, however, more than 15,500,000 acres of land on the western slope. Numerous encounters occurred between these Indians and the white men during the early settlement of the agricultural lands in this territory, and it was not until 1881 that the Indians in this region, usually known as the Uncompahgre Utes, were removed to the Uintah reservation, in eastern Utah.

An Indian reservation also was established in southwestern Colorado and northwestern New Mexico, to which most of the southern Utes were removed. This is the only Indian reservation in Colorado at present, though there is some Indian land in La Plata county, belonging to Ute Indians.

Statistical Tables

THE statistical tables and charts found on pages 50 to 175, inclusive, have been compiled from various official sources, the authority for the data usually being given in connection with the title of the table. The agricultural tables and charts found on pages 50 to 145, inclusive, have been compiled chiefly from reports of the county assessors to the State Immigration department in compliance with the law enacted in 1919, with the exception of the tables showing average yields, assessment figures and some other data, which have been compiled from the reports of the division of crop and livestock estimates of the United States department of agriculture and other sources. Other tables contain information from various other official sources, both state and federal, proper credit being given in each instance. All reports by counties on acreage of crops, number of farms, farm tenure, farms reporting various crops and the like are from assessors' reports and are given by counties just as reported by the several assessors, though total acreage for the state as used in the table on page 52 has been increased somewhat for each crop because of the incompleteness of some of the assessors' reports.

Average yields per acre of the principal crops for 1923, as determined by the Co-Operative Crop Reporting Service, are given for each county, and the total production by counties, based on the acreages reported by the county assessors and these yields, have been calculated for corn, winter wheat, spring wheat, oats, barley and potatoes, and are found on pages 53, 59, 60, 65, 66, 67 and 70. Average yields by counties have not been computed for other crops because of lack of sufficient information from some counties. The average yields per acre of the principal crops above referred to, by counties, are found in the table on page 85, while on page 86 are found the average yields of the same crops for the five years ending with 1923, which is the entire period in which the Co-Operative Crop Reporting Service has been making estimates of average yields by counties.

On page 52 is a table giving the estimated acreage and production and the value of all crops for 1922 and 1923. In the preparation of this table the total acreage planted to each crop was first arrived at, the process in most cases involving the addition of a slight percentage to the acreage reported by county assessors, the additions being made because of the incompleteness of assessors' reports from some of the counties. Only the estimated acreage harvested is given in this report, which was arrived at by deducting from the acreage planted in each a certain acreage that was abandoned on account of crop failure, change of plans by individual farmers after reporting their acreage in April or for other reasons. The acreage so abandoned was determined by the bureau of livestock and crop estimates from reports received from its several hundred volunteer reporters. In the case of barley and oats much of the acreage that matures is harvested for hay instead of for grain, and the estimated acreage so harvested is deducted from the acreage planted in determining the acreage harvested for grain, but is used in the acreage of small grains cut for hay. The entire acreage of corn and grain sorghum except that abandoned or cut for silage is treated as harvested for grain, though much of it is in reality harvested for forage or pastured in the field. In the case of field beans and sweet sorghums only that actually harvested for beans in the one case or for seed in the other is used in calculating the production of beans and sorghum seed, the remaining acreage being included in dry forage and crops pastured. These facts are given here to explain the several seeming discrepancies to be found between the acreage and production figures as shown in this table and in the several county tables on pages 53, 59, 60, 65, 66, 67 and 70, and in the table of crop values shown on pages 50 and 51.

County assessors reported on 51,589 farms in 1923, which is perhaps slightly below the actual number of farms operated during the 1923 crop season, and it is because of this apparent shortage in reports that additions were made to the assessors' figures. The census bureau reported 59,934 farms in the state in 1920, but a very considerable number of these farms were homesteads and pasture farms, on which no crops ever had been raised. The county assessors in 1922 reported on 54,664 farms, approximately 3,000 more than the number reported for 1923. While the 1923 total probably is not wholly accurate, there was considerable abandonment of farms in some of the non-irrigated sections, due to the low prices paid for farm products and the exceptionally unfavorable season for small grains and some other crops in 1922, and the total number of farms operated in 1923 was probably somewhat below the total operated in the preceding year.

The charts showing distribution of acreage of the various crops by counties, found on pages 55, 61, 68, 71, 77, 79, 80, 81 and 82, are based upon reports of county assessors to the State Immigration department. They are not at all comparable with one another, for the reason that the same unit of comparison has not been used in all. The number of acres represented by each symbol is given in connection with the title of each of the charts. The maps showing the distribution of livestock, found on pages 102 and 103, are based wholly upon the reports of the county assessors.

While it has been found impracticable to make corrections in the acreage and production of the leading crops by counties, some idea of the completeness or incompleteness of the reports from the several counties may be obtained by comparing the total number of farms reported by each county assessor, found in the table on page 93 of this *Year Book*, with the total number reported for the same county by the census bureau, found on page 76 of the *Year* Book for 1921 and found in the census reports. It will be noted that in a few counties assessors reported more farms than were found by the census bureau, while in a few other counties the numbers reported by the two agencies are approximately the same. In most counties, however, the census bureau reported considerably more farms than were found by the assessors, and while these discrepancies may be accounted for in part by the fact that the farms reported by the census bureau are not all being farmed, this will not account for all of the shortages. While the larger number of the agricultural counties of the state are reported very fully by the assessors, there are still a number in which agricultural activity and progress are not adequately reported. The failure of an assessor in such a county to do justice to the agricultural industry reflects seriously on the county, as his report does not show the true progress which agriculture is making.

Special attention is again called to the tables showing the percentages of the various crops grown with irrigation and without, as shown in the tables on pages 91 and 92, and the tables showing average yields of the leading crops, both irrigated and non-irrigated, shown on pages 85 and 86. The rapid increase in the acreage of non-irrigated land cultivated in Colorado in recent years has been the most important factor in reducing general average yields per acre of wheat, oats, barley, corn, rye and similar crops. In 1909 more than 50 per cent of the wheat grown in Colorado was irrigated, but in 1923, as will be seen from the table on page 64, only 15.45 per cent of it was irrigated. Yields on irrigated land in this state are as high now as they were a decade ago, and in many cases higher, but yields on non-irrigated land are much lower than on the irrigated lands, so a lowering of the general average yield per acre has been inevitable. A rapid increase in the acreage of crops grown without irrigation and a relatively small increase in the acreage of crops grown under irrigation has resulted in an apparent lowering of the average yield for the entire state, despite the fact that irrigated yields are as high as ever, if not higher. It will be noted from the county tables that counties where most of the crops are grown under irrigation will show high average yields.

From the tables of values shown on pages 50 and 51 and on page 52 (the discrepancies in which have been explained in this introduction) it will be seen that the total value of farm crops for 1923 was considerably above the total for 1922, which in turn was above the 1921 total. This was due in some instances to a larger acreage in 1923 than was harvested in the two years preceding, but in more instances it was due to a more favorable farming season and to a general increase in the prices paid for farm products. In this connection it must be noted that the values given in these tables do not represent the actual receipts from the sale of these crops, but that they reflect the hypothetical values of the various crops, based upon the prices commanded by such crops as were actually sold.

FARM VALUE OF CROPS FOR 1923

COUNTY	Corn	Wheat	Oats	Barley	Rye	Potatoes	Beans	Sorghums	Sugar Beets	Hay	Fruits	Miscellaneous Crops	Total
Adams	$ 532,350	$ 817,177	$ 82,717	$ 75,195	$ 19,824	$ 41,580	$ 101,004	$ 152,800	$ 502,975	$ 718,750	$ 37,500	$ 250,000	$ 3,331,872
Alamosa	...	51,204	45,976	19,726	...	233,740	...	...	...	859,100	...	75,150	1,284,896
Arapahoe	327,600	317,391	20,456	34,216	8,006	2,100	188,100	61,100	21,258	370,300	59,500	42,150	1,452,177
Archuleta	2,100	8,829	30,375	8,122	...	6,370	...	...	...	201,687	100	500	258,083
Baca	476,520	186,031	1,296	30,129	3,000	...	6,143	1,050,000	...	49,875	3,500	515,200	2,321,694
Bent	511,500	201,262	14,515	14,000	1,200	...	14,040	285,350	347,288	621,600	7,500	95,650	2,113,905
Boulder	212,550	525,000	82,720	64,350	360	13,277	1,900	3,500	682,000	826,500	68,000	45,250	2,525,407
Chaffee	294	25,272	35,944	16,494	...	20,592	...	...	...	223,440	250	242,500	564,786
Cheyenne	652,860	126,000	4,432	56,786	2,610	13,491	4,095	262,150	...	121,923	425	6,750	1,251,522
Clear Creek	385	160	1,203	...	...	1,040	...	...	...	12,250	...	400	15,438
Conejos	1,086	137,600	63,360	158,340	...	341,600	20,140	...	...	532,950	...	252,000	1,507,076
Costilla	979	56,133	30,800	53,248	...	20,865	17,325	...	...	215,118	...	235,000	629,468
Crowley	277,200	22,858	36,630	13,500	...	...	55,825	100,000	292,600	303,450	99,800	215,250	1,417,113
Custer	18,090	27,702	58,995	20,750	941	26,650	...	550	...	337,995	...	165,350	657,023
Delta	102,920	128,000	64,715	12,266	...	248,040	4,680	...	333,300	894,300	1,695,000	98,250	3,581,471
Dolores	52,800	15,088	10,395	2,657	660	4,270	3,160	15,000	...	24,150	250	1,500	129,930
Douglas	252,525	59,894	69,000	5,962	13,400	16,500	11,970	28,950	...	310,750	1,450	2,350	772,791
Eagle	...	23,240	42,320	4,719	...	255,310	...	...	...	204,720	500	78,500	609,309
Elbert	867,100	238,000	104,650	20,909	51,408	45,084	972,800	105,000	...	291,879	675	10,500	2,708,005
El Paso	780,000	49,800	151,892	6,480	24,640	52,500	851,200	81,000	16,170	427,140	11,500	53,250	2,505,572
Fremont	82,170	13,702	27,152	12,190	1,482	16,900	1,975	1,250	...	215,688	695,200	108,950	1,176,659
Garfield	53,504	96,768	55,546	12,960	...	559,033	...	...	222,200	888,720	635,900	22,500	2,547,131
Gilpin	...	119	8,208	700	...	4,200	...	...	...	12,520	...	2,150	27,897
Grand	1,360	3,715	13,478	3,053	1,150	8,760	...	...	...	504,000	...	126,250	661,766
Gunnison	...	6,499	13,041	5,616	...	30,128	...	...	...	568,320	...	21,000	644,604
Hinsdale	...	...	702	583	...	3,900	...	...	...	43,900	...	550	49,635
Huerfano	91,287	14,400	29,040	14,580	1,344	2,760	47,424	12,500	...	282,150	6,800	15,750	518,035
Jackson	...	323	2,880	1,089	134	1,500	...	...	...	1,055,808	...	14,500	1,076,234
Jefferson	109,200	221,444	61,456	37,368	784	17,556	1,560	...	43,450	41,055	465,250	385,500	1,384,623
Kiowa	649,440	110,880	...	16,065	336	...	3,040	415,000	...	98,762	1,000	5,650	1,300,173
Kit Carson	2,073,600	830,830	29,560	317,520	38,808	44,200	12,000	402,000	...	211,680	850	12,500	[illegible]

Lake	....	....	....	690	....	....	....	....	....	53,612	....	3,500	57,802
La Plata	64,260	117,040	71,632	25,928	560	54,332	4,860	2,750	....	572,250	15,500	12,350	941,462
Larimer	247,455	431,609	160,301	86,978	1,680	74,750	27,360	1,250	1,320,880	1,254,000	510,250	89,350	4,205,863
Las Animas	332,800	120,309	31,202	10,303	3,326	7,254	228,000	71,500	12,120	368,832	2,500	12,350	1,200,496
Lincoln	1,244,160	544,148	17,986	113,022	34,496	44,785	332,500	310,500	....	282,240	950	7,350	2,932,137
Logan	2,160,000	1,844,675	156,630	248,184	56,213	50,320	143,640	298,600	1,520,750	1,233,960	4,750	12,750	7,730,472
Mesa	199,485	113,280	62,744	9,677	2,100	335,544	42,180	7,650	479,325	1,213,960	2,345,000	194,250	5,005,195
Mineral	....	....	1,366	837	....	650	....	....	....	40,824	....	26,800	70,477
Moffat	63,360	48,057	89,856	12,788	24,640	40,455	7,600	12,350	....	579,810	1,500	10,250	890,666
Montezuma	99,840	48,572	37,463	24,180	1,026	14,911	2,432	4,150	....	302,148	135,500	750	670,972
Montrose	117,180	214,245	111,320	6,720	....	966,735	27,360	....	306,075	923,884	750,000	94,500	3,518,019
Morgan	1,201,200	339,702	71,144	164,317	26,936	152,000	225,720	225,500	1,936,000	1,059,940	4,850	42,500	5,449,809
Otero	390,000	128,858	64,690	22,453	504	....	114,000	78,500	1,144,275	922,080	180,000	1,175,200	4,220,560
Ouray	660	32,643	20,007	8,223	280	38,675	....	....	2,222	106,275	....	1,000	209,985
Park	....	1,075	47,760	18,144	2,240	42,900	....	....	....	525,600	....	28,000	665,719
Phillips	1,170,000	842,450	102,341	46,305	23,778	6,930	4,560	120,500	....	411,600	500	800	2,729,764
Pitkin	....	7,282	29,250	3,850	....	189,100	....	....	....	155,325	500	2,500	387,807
Prowers	482,300	526,635	26,790	42,136	3,276	....	18,240	595,100	435,600	1,278,595	10,000	101,250	3,519,922
Pueblo	565,500	66,732	47,969	29,128	4,004	....	282,150	95,950	444,400	956,319	39,500	115,250	2,646,902
Rio Blanco	2,600	68,880	39,396	12,522	2,059	5,590	....	....	....	294,816	750	650	427,263
Rio Grande	....	113,400	73,788	40,664	....	1,461,600	....	....	....	379,620	....	475,500	2,544,572
Routt	585	168,059	119,790	84,291	1,210	57,660	....	....	....	588,600	6,560	68,500	1,095,255
Saguache	....	65,491	51,867	22,253	....	468,720	....	....	....	578,790	500	180,000	1,367,621
San Miguel	21,946	23,408	19,228	89,991	540	72,540	....	3,500	....	164,920	800	10,500	407,373
Sedgwick	712,725	364,536	74,727	43,697	12,012	43,160	6,840	67,520	504,900	284,760	950	16,250	2,132,077
Summit	....	1,050	2,961	1,540	....	7,085	....	....	....	99,440	....	1,500	113,576
Teller	....	....	120,000	13,780	....	102,375	....	....	....	63,936	....	51,500	351,591
Washington	1,883,700	1,266,580	59,409	428,868	87,360	13,650	91,200	410,500	67,375	344,085	3,000	28,500	4,684,227
Weld	1,404,000	1,726,400	364,320	484,704	82,634	2,163,200	1,056,400	210,150	4,365,900	2,847,600	52,500	1,140,200	15,898,008
Yuma	2,983,500	642,420	39,675	210,600	98,560	16,632	18,240	425,100	....	257,640	8,000	32,600	4,732,967
State	$23,476,676	$14,182,857	$3,309,066	$3,346,346	$ 639,561	$8,463,499	$4,951,663	$5,917,220	$15,001,063	$29,615,941	$7,865,310	$7,037,200	$123,806,402

The crop values found in this table are based upon acreage reports by county assessors, average yields as estimated by the Co-operative Crop Reporting Service or the Immigration Department, and average prices prevailing about December 1 or at market time, as reported by competent authorities in the various counties. The total values for the various crops differ materially from the values of the same crops given in the production table found on page 52, being less in nearly all cases. The total value for all crops in the state in this table is more than $6,000,000 less than that in the general table on page 52. These discrepancies are due to different methods used in arriving at the values given in the two tables. In the general production table acreages reported by county assessors have been increased materially because of incompleteness of assessors' returns, while in this table only comparatively small increases are made from assessors' reports. The result is that values for nearly all crops and total values for all crops in nearly all counties in this table are slightly below actual values.

CROP ACREAGE PRODUCTION AND VALUE, 1923 AND 1922

KIND OF CROPS	1923			1922		
	Acreage	Production	Value	Acreage	Production	Value
Winter Wheat	1,060,000	12,720,000 Bu.	$ 10,557,600	1,262,000	16,406,000 Bu.	$ 14,601,340
Spring Wheat	330,000	5,280,000 Bu.	4,382,400	358,000	5,370,000 Bu.	4,779,200
Corn*	1,490,000	37,250,000 Bu.	24,212,500	1,145,000	18,320,000 Bu.	12,091,200
Oats for Grain.........	198,000	6,336,000 Bu.	2,914,560	185,000	4,625,000 Bu.	2,081,240
Barley for Grain.......	221,000	6,409,000 Bu.	3,460,860	186,000	3,534,000 Bu.	2,085,060
Rye for Grain..........	73,000	876,000 Bu.	490,560	97,000	873,000 Bu.	576,180
Emmer	4,500	135,000 Bu.	81,000	9,400	188,000 Bu.	116,560
Grain Sorghum for Grain.	336,000	6,720,000 Bu.	5,376,000	247,000	3,705,000 Bu.	2,593,500
Sweet Sorghum for Seed..	5,700	74,100 Bu.	59,280	3,800	38,000 Bu.	30,400
Broom Corn	48,000	7,200 T.	1,044,000	10,000	1,800 T.	341,250
Field Peas for Grain....	17,000	225,000 Bu.	270,000	18,000	216,000 Bu.	259,200
Dry Beans	170,000	1,360,000 Bu.	4,488,000	81,000	405,000 Bu.	1,782,000
Potatoes	110,000	13,530,000 Bu.	8,794,500	142,000	18,460,000 Bu.	6,830,200
Sugar Beets	165,453	1,962,177 T.	15,304,980	148,000	1,466,000 T.	11,420,140
Root Crops for Stock Feed.	1,200	16,800 T.	84,000	1,200	14,400 T.	57,600
Cabbage	5,270	58,000 T.	429,000	5,240	62,900 T.	269,000
Onions, Dry	2,360	590,000 Bu.	637,000	1,900	532,000 Bu.	277,000
Tomatoes	3,860	19,300 T.	193,000	1,940	15,900 T.	138,000
Cantaloupes and Honey Dew Melons	8,620	....	862,000	14,000	....	1,162,000
Cucumbers for Pickles....	4,250	332,000 Bu.	515,000	3,080	200,000 Bu.	290,000
Cucumbers for Seed......	2,350	....	164,500	2,740	....	178,000
Peas for Canning and Mkt.	3,200	....	240,000	2,900	....	188,500
Beans for Seed.........	9,300	55,800 Bu.	149,660	9,000	72,000 Bu.	172,800
Lettuce	6,710	560,000 C.	728,000	6,000	192,000 C.	249,600
Celery	670	137,000 C.	290,000	600	127,000 C.	364,000
Flax Seed	500	3,500 Bu.	6,650	360	1,620 Bu.	2,754
Millet Seed	38,000	532,000 Bu.	266,000	16,000	160,000 Bu.	96,000
Alfalfa Seed	1,800	7,200 Bu.	82,800	2,900	11,600 Bu.	104,400
Other Garden and Seed Crops	10,000	....	1,000,000	10,000	....	1,000,000
Tame Hay, All Varieties†.	1,203,000	2,406,000 T.	27,187,800	1,191,000	2,263,000 T.	25,345,600
Wild Hay	373,000	391,600 T.	4,111,800	366,000	355,020 T.	3,195,180
Silage	44,000	308,000 T.	2,156,000	76,500	306,000 T.	2,142,000
Dry Forage	92,000	....	2,300,000	255,600	....	2,556,000
Crops Pastured	286,000	....	1,072,500	297,100	....	940,000
Farm Gardens	**33,500	....	1,340,000	**33,500	....	1,005,000
Apples	......	3,010,000 Bu.	2,799,300	......	4,250,000 Bu.	3,187,500
Peaches	......	792,000 Bu.	1,354,320	......	960,000 Bu.	960,000
Pears	......	400,000 Bu.	624,000	......	519,000 Bu.	389,250
Cherries	......	5,500 T.	660,000	......	5,200 T.	624,000
Miscellaneous Fruits	4,400	....	550,000	4,400	....	550,000
Sugar Beet Tops........	‡165,000	....	742,500	‡150,000	....	975,000
	6,289,143		$130,022,070	5,771,660		$102,370,314

*This includes the entire acreage of corn harvested in every way and the value estimated as if it were all harvested for grain. For purposes of information corn for silage, forage and pasture are included under those items in the table, but their acreages and values are not included in the totals. See text for details.

†The varieties of tame hay with the estimated acreage of each variety for 1923 are as followws: Alfalfa, 780,000 timothy, 44,000; red clover, 5,000; timothy and clover mixed, 122,000; sweet clover, 18,000; sudan grass, 25,000; millet, 75,000; other tame grasses, 22,000; field peas, 9,000; grains cut green, 103,000; total, 1,203,000 acres. For 1922: Alfalfa, 765,000; timothy, 45,000; red clover, 5,000; timothy and clover mixed, 124,000; sweet clover, 16,000; sudan grass, 19,000; millet, 47,000; other tame grasses, 21,000; field peas, 14,000; grains cut green, 135,000; total, 1,191,000 acres.

**The estimated number of farm gardens is here given instead of the acreage. This figure is not included in the totals.

‡This acreage is all accounted for in the acreage of sugar beets harvested and is not included in the total acreage figure. See also for reconciliation with preceding table footnote on page 51.

ACREAGE AND PRODUCTION OF CORN, 1923

COUNTY	IRRIGATED			NON-IRRIGATED			TOTALS	
	Acreage Irrigated	Average Yield	Production Bushels	Acreage Non-Irrigated	Average Yield	Production Bushels	Total Acreage	Total Production
Adams	2,356	38	89,528	32,140	20	642,800	34,496	732,328
Alamosa	10	25	250	......	....	....	10	250
Arapahoe	753	34	25,602	20,536	20	410,720	21,289	436,322
Archuleta	145	27	3,915	186	15	2,790	331	6,705
Baca	432	35	15,120	33,538	19	637,222	33,970	652,342
Bent	11,800	42	495,600	10,014	19	190,266	21,814	685,866
Boulder	5,776	38	219,488	3,160	23	72,680	8,936	292,168
Chaffee	10	30	300	3	20	60	13	360
Cheyenne	......	....	......	33,266	27	898,182	33,266	898,182
Clear Creek ...	......	....	......	31	18	558	31	558
Conejos	47	26	1,222	6	21	126	53	1,348
Costilla	53	25	1,325	5	18	90	58	1,415
Crowley	7,421	40	296,840	5,082	16	81,312	12,503	378,152
Custer	23	26	598	1,241	20	24,820	1,264	25,418
Delta	3,723	40	148,920	10	16	160	3,733	149,080
Dolores	......	....	......	4,750	16	76,000	4,750	76,000
Douglas	55	32	1,760	17,089	21	358,869	17,144	360,629
Eagle	......	....	......	......	....	....	......	......
Elbert	......	....	......	51,579	23	1,186,317	51,579	1,186,317
El Paso	978	35	34,230	55,084	20	1,101,680	56,062	1,135,910
Fremont	1,601	40	64,040	1,621	20	32,420	3,222	96,460
Garfield	1,640	40	65,600	213	23	4,899	1,853	70,499
Gilpin	......	....	......	1	18	18	1	18
Grand	99	20	1,980	......	....	....	99	1,980
Gunnison	......	....	......	1	16	16	1	16
Hinsdale	......	....	......	......	....	....	......	......
Huerfano	193	28	5,404	5,460	23	125,580	5,653	130,984
Jackson	2	20	40	1	18	18	3	58
Jefferson	2,687	40	107,480	1,265	25	31,625	3,952	139,105
Kiowa	......	....	......	36,657	24	879,768	36,657	879,768
Kit Carson ...	......	....	......	109,196	27	2,948,292	109,196	2,948,292
Lake	......	....	......	......	....	....	......	......
La Plata	1,505	33	49,665	1,328	20	26,560	2,833	76,225
Larimer	5,601	35	196,035	6,951	21	145,971	12,552	342,006
Las Animas ...	2,219	34	75,446	20,102	18	361,836	22,321	437,282
Lincoln	......	....	......	65,759	27	1,775,493	65,759	1,775,493
Logan	5,260	40	210,400	105,523	26	2,743,598	110,783	2,953,998
Mesa	6,606	42	277,452	854	15	12,810	7,460	290,262
Mineral	......	....	......	......	....	....	......	......
Moffat	36	30	1,080	6,905	12	82,860	6,941	83,940
Montezuma ...	1,034	32	33,088	4,221	22	92,862	5,255	125,950
Montrose	3,837	42	161,154	35	22	770	3,872	161,924
Morgan	9,067	40	362,680	61,479	22	1,352,538	70,546	1,715,218
Otero	12,084	42	507,528	2,605	17	44,285	14,689	551,813
Ouray	5	30	150	18	17	306	23	456
Park	3	20	60	3	18	54	6	114
Phillips	......	....	......	68,711	24	1,649,064	68,711	1,649,064
Pitkin	1	30	30	......	....	....	1	30
Prowers	13,531	37	500,647	10,994	18	197,892	24,525	698,539
Pueblo	12,022	42	504,924	16,378	20	327,560	28,400	832,484
Rio Blanco...	4	30	120	120	20	2,400	124	2,520
Rio Grande ..	......	....	......	......	....	....	......	......
Routt	......	....	......	43	18	774	43	774
Saguache	......	....	......	......	....	....	......	......
San Miguel ..	67	34	2,278	1,286	25	32,150	1,353	34,428
Sedgwick	1,303	39	50,817	38,437	25	960,925	39,740	1,011,742
Summit	......	....	......	......	....	....	......	......
Teller	......	....	......	......	....	....	......	......
Washington ..	645	40	25,800	123,003	20	2,460,000	123,648	2,485,800
Weld	18,149	40	725,960	62,896	19	1,195,024	81,045	1,920,984
Yuma	......	....	......	154,123	27	4,161,321	154,123	4,161,321
State.....	132,783	39.64	5,264,556	1,173,909	23.28	27,334,341	1,306,692	32,598,897

ACREAGE OF CORN AND RYE AS REPORTED BY COUNTY ASSESSORS

COUNTY	CORN				RYE			
	1923	1922	1921	1920	1923	1922	1921	1920
Adams	34,496	30,590	27,866	30,136	2,948	4,432	4,118	4,077
Alamosa	10	......	......	......	....	....	....	....
Arapahoe	21,289	13,738	10,230	22,491	1,112	1,270	848	1,984
Archuleta	331	11	85	188	....	3	....	7
Baca	33,970	41,198	31,814	11,774	460	1,410	3,838	1,556
Bent	21,814	22,322	18,325	11,296	193	230	908	433
Boulder	8,936	8,358	5,089	9,396	60	14	39	128
Chaffee	13	9	27	8	4	5	5	....
Cheyenne	33,266	29,627	32,043	24,876	....	1,127	661	771
Clear Creek	31	22	2	28	10	16	20	28
Conejos	53	50	501	109	....	....	....	....
Costilla	58	168	38	17	....	24	36	237
Crowley	12,503	12,364	11,546	16,031	....	25	693	87
Custer	1,264	967	1,007	1,219	133	143	453	296
Delta	3,733	2,760	2,789	3,351	8	23	46	33
Dolores	4,750	3,459	3,185	3,251	57	148	155	52
Douglas	17,144	14,200	16,952	16,436	1,938	2,107	2,200	2,097
Eagle	......	......	......	3	....	12	20	4
Elbert	51,579	44,247	51,203	55,044	7,644	15,221	12,882	9,979
El Paso	56,062	51,377	54,314	55,866	3,891	8,765	9,065	8,049
Fremont	3,222	2,846	2,842	3,878	174	325	299	286
Garfield	1,853	1,488	987	1,326	34	178	184	228
Gilpin	1	......	......	......	24	14	42	49
Grand	99	......	1	2	224	478	382	274
Gunnison	1	3	1	1	20	....	18	36
Hinsdale	......	......	......	......	....	....	....	....
Huerfano	5,653	6,461	4,671	11,716	166	287	251	486
Jackson	3	......	......	......	26	21	15	18
Jefferson	3,952	5,668	3,376	2,649	82	568	250	595
Kiowa	36,657	28,865	26,069	14,938	37	392	686	341
Kit Carson	109,196	67,944	79,622	67,030	6,267	13,814	10,146	8,135
Lake	......	......	......	......	2	10	10	14
La Plata	2,833	2,164	2,029	1,975	40	78	47	37
Larimer	12,552	8,680	8,122	7,273	164	309	315	290
Las Animas	22,321	22,301	22,677	17,384	533	546	1,119	1,055
Lincoln	65,759	61,984	61,287	61,833	5,586	10,857	11,191	10,776
Logan	110,783	98,330	93,462	94,860	7,171	11,871	5,936	8,331
Mesa	7,460	6,925	6,294	5,796	233	388	246	499
Mineral	......	......	......	......	....	....	15	....
Moffat	6,941	3,377	5,002	5,213	4,338	7,483	5,893	5,774
Montezuma	5,255	5,601	5,400	8,107	114	171	205	165
Montrose	3,872	2,275	2,221	3,170	....	....	8	56
Morgan	70,546	54,314	57,234	61,505	3,654	6,648	4,065	3,786
Otero	14,689	14,419	12,539	13,345	58	152	212	244
Ouray	23	20	16	23	22	27	48	8
Park	6	3	14	6	408	297	296	373
Phillips	68,711	51,499	51,976	51,438	3,856	5,579	3,390	3,491
Pitkin	1	......	......	1	....	16	18	144
Prowers	24,525	29,702	24,618	14,916	384	582	1,488	1,434
Pueblo	28,400	32,919	25,811	25,341	544	1,342	733	3,113
Rio Blanco	124	109	91	114	353	497	445	804
Rio Grande	......	......	......	......	....	....	4	36
Routt	43	14	178	159	163	266	243	518
Saguache	......	3	8	62	....	....	1	....
San Miguel	1,353	694	326	323	67	69	55	55
Sedgwick	39,740	31,070	28,883	23,776	1,046	2,993	1,478	2,979
Summit	......	......	......	......	61	25	....	117
Teller	......	......	10	6	27	128	121	356
Washington	123,648	81,747	69,625	85,933	12,261	15,985	10,595	16,077
Weld	81,045	76,926	67,504	101,198	10,539	11,335	8,103	7,783
Yuma	154,123	127,160	119,998	127,997	15,630	26,270	22,526	17,640
State	1,306,692	1,100,978	1,049,910	1,074,814	93,366	154,976	127,066	126,221

ACREAGE OF CORN, 1923

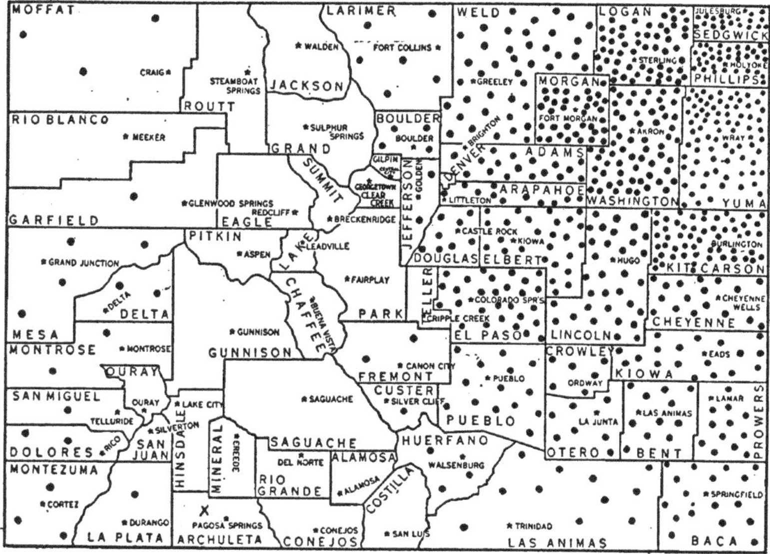

Each dot represents 2,000 acres. The cross (X) is used in counties reporting less than 1,000 acres.

ACREAGE OF SORGHUMS, 1923

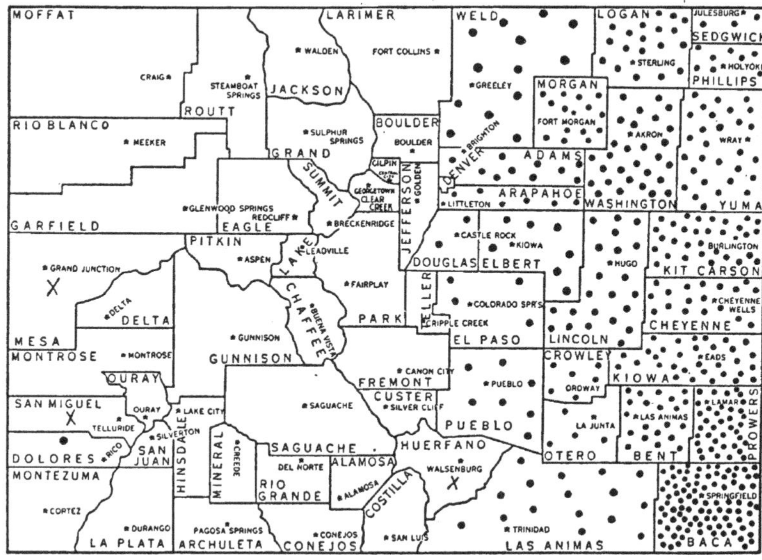

Each dot represents 1,000 acres. The cross (X) is used in counties reporting less than 500 acres.

ACREAGE OF GRAIN AND SWEET SORGHUMS REPORTED BY COUNTY ASSESSORS, 1923

COUNTY	GRAIN SORGHUMS			SWEET SORGHUMS		
	Irrigated	Non-Irrigated	All Grain Sorghums	Irrigated	Non-Irrigated	All Sweet Sorghums
Adams	104	314	418	70	9,153	9,223
Alamosa	....	......	......	....	......	......
Arapahoe	85	1,470	1,555	135	4,153	4,288
Archuleta	....	......	......	....	......	......
Baca	380	83,902	84,282	....	7,115	7,115
Bent	508	19,554	20,062	735	374	1,109
Boulder	8	......	8	20	......	20
Chaffee	....	......	......	....	......	......
Cheyenne	....	15,954	15,954	....	2,018	2,018
Clear Creek	....	......	......	....	......	......
Conejos	....	......	......	3	......	3
Costilla	....	......	......	....	......	......
Crowley	252	4,366	4,618	33	972	1,005
Custer	....	20	20	....	12	12
Delta	2	......	2	4	......	4
Dolores	....	1,219	1,219	....	42	42
Douglas	....	1,624	1,624	47	152	199
Eagle	....	......	......	....	......	......
Elbert	....	2,755	2,755	....	4,479	4,479
El Paso	20	2,169	2,189	15	1,950	1,965
Fremont	71	6	77	....	2	2
Garfield	2	......	2	....	......	......
Gilpin	....	......	......	....	......	......
Grand	....	......	......	....	......	......
Gunnison	....	......	......	....	......	......
Hinsdale	....	......	......	....	......	......
Huerfano	....	298	298	....	240	240
Jackson	....	......	......	....	......	......
Jefferson	5	......	5	....	......	......
Kiowa	....	23,860	23,860	....	8,491	8,491
Kit Carson	1	24,097	24,098	....	6,876	6,876
Lake	....	......	......	....	......	......
La Plata	....	28	28	10	20	30
Larimer	....	9	9	17	4	21
Las Animas	219	12,948	13,167	45	2,647	2,692
Lincoln	....	16,343	16,343	....	5,557	5,557
Logan	126	12,516	12,642	172	5,892	6,064
Mesa	69	327	396	20	......	20
Mineral	....	......	......	....	......	......
Moffat	70	130	200	5	749	754
Montezuma	25	192	217	4	......	4
Montrose	1	......	1	....	......	......
Morgan	184	6,839	7,023	....	7,342	7,342
Otero	758	3,138	3,896	224	140	364
Ouray	....	......	......	....	......	......
Park	....	......	......	....	......	......
Phillips	....	5,952	5,952	....	2,196	2,196
Pitkin	....	......	......	....	......	......
Prowers	4,455	30,917	35,372	378	2,559	2,937
Pueblo	916	6,318	7,234	8	264	272
Rio Blanco	....	......	......	....	......	......
Rio Grande	....	......	......	....	......	......
Routt	....	7	7	....	......	......
Saguache	....	......	......	....	......	......
San Miguel	....	......	......	....	258	258
Sedgwick	10	110	120	92	2,986	3,078
Summit	....	......	......	....	......	......
Teller	....	......	......	....	......	......
Washington	45	15,886	15,931	20	13,051	13,071
Weld	24	9,525	9,549	113	3,259	3,372
Yuma	6	19,587	19,593	....	8,056	8,056
State	8,346	322,380	330,726	2,170	101,009	103,179

ACREAGE OF GRAIN AND SWEET SORGHUMS IN COLORADO AS REPORTED BY COUNTY ASSESSORS

COUNTY	GRAIN SORGHUMS				SWEET SORGHUMS			
	1923	1922	1921	1920	1923	1922	1921	1920
Adams	418	4,361	5,602	2,557	9,223	2,590	1,443	5,279
Alamosa	....	....	....	....	....	....	....	....
Arapahoe	1,555	1,598	477	4,880	4,288	1,378	1,961	1,726
Archuleta	....	....	....	....	....	....	....	....
Baca	84,282	71,791	51,300	43,083	7,115	20	7,962	3,424
Bent	20,062	16,526	19,917	22,759	1,109	1,861	146	388
Boulder	8	32	10	57	20	22	....	46
Chaffee	....	....	....	....	....	....	....	....
Cheyenne	15,954	12,883	14,413	15,892	2,018	50	375	39
Clear Creek	....	....	....	....	....	....	....	....
Conejos	....	....	....	....	3	....	....	....
Costilla	....	....	....	....	....	....	....	1
Crowley	4,618	3,807	4,004	5,772	1,005	685	1,062	832
Custer	20	....	56	....	12	....	....	....
Delta	2	118	38	19	4	....	5	17
Dolores	1,219	593	46	38	42	42	376	305
Douglas	1,624	1,242	1,400	1,609	199	....	73	41
Eagle	....	....	....	....	....	....	....	....
Elbert	2,755	1,948	2,278	2,408	4.479	1,955	2,688	2,690
El Paso	2,189	2,433	3,154	3,578	1,965	1,917	1,433	683
Fremont	77	29	37	166	2	9	8	10
Garfield	2	21	2	42	....	....	40	136
Gilpin	....	....	....	....	....	....	....	....
Grand	....	....	....	....	....	....	....	....
Gunnison	....	....	1	....	....	....	....	....
Hinsdale	....	....	....	....	....	....	....	....
Huerfano	298	444	428	500	240	274	176	746
Jackson	....	....	....	....	....	....	....	....
Jefferson	5	20	36	10	....	10	14	3
Kiowa	23,860	7,759	8,918	13,567	8,491	6,010	7,561	142
Kit Carson	24,098	22,792	23,788	18,235	6,876	1,630	2,179	6.945
Lake	....	....	....	....	....	....	....	....
La Plata	28	16	28	48	30	10	52	27
Larimer	9	5	4	46	21	....	45	37
Las Animas	13,167	13,715	16,849	20,726	2,692	2,825	3,647	4,750
Lincoln	16,343	13,245	16,810	16,247	5.557	4.148	3,485	4.460
Logan	12,642	6,971	10,421	12,369	6,064	9,421	3,627	7,287
Mesa	396	250	66	440	20	65	284	20
Mineral	....	....	....	....	....	....	....	....
Moffat	200	162	12	214	754	454	374	183
Montezuma	217	305	124	40	4	167	20	216
Montrose	1	....	1	32	....	....	1	1
Morgan	7,023	4,955	5,929	5,942	7,342	3,770	3,835	6,247
Otero	3,896	4,364	5,307	8,162	364	678	370	1,084
Ouray	....	....	....	....	....	....	....	....
Park	....	....	2	2	....	....	....	....
Philips	5,952	7,128	335	7,244	2,196	....	5,209	10
Pitkin	....	....	....	....	....	....	....	....
Prowers	35,372	29,065	22,794	33,521	3,937	2,721	1,182	2,719
Pueblo	7,234	5,827	5,902	3,182	272	1,491	780	2,281
Rio Blanco	....	....	....	2	....	....	....	11
Rio Grande	....	....	....	....	....	....	....	....
Routt	7	....	100	....	....	....	....	....
Saguache	....	....	....	....	....	....	....	....
San Miguel	....	....	10	....	258	70	47	....
Sedgwick	120	35	12	6	3,078	2,211	2,036	2,180
Summit	....	....	....	....	....	....	....	....
Teller	....	....	....	....	....	....	....	....
Washington	15,931	12,112	6,750	8,404	13,071	7,953	9,953	20,963
Weld	9,549	5,023	5,397	6,396	3,372	7,587	8,504	16,171
Yuma	19,593	16,019	11,985	9,113	8,056	10,969	9,204	17,541
State	330,726	267,594	244,743	266,768	103,179	73,002	80,157	109,641

GRAIN AND SWEET SORGHUM IN COLORADO, 1923

COUNTY	Grain Sorghums Acres	Sweet Sorghums Acres	Total Acres	Percent Grain Sorghums	Percent Sweet Sorghums
Adams	418	9,223	9,641	4.34	95.66
Alamosa	......	......	......	....	....
Arapahoe	1,555	4,288	5,843	26.44	73.56
Archuleta	......	......	......	....	....
Baca	84,282	7,115	91,397	92.21	7.79
Bent	20,062	1,109	21,171	94.76	5.24
Boulder	8	20	28	28.57	71.43
Chaffee	......	......	......	....	....
Cheyenne	15,954	2,018	17,972	88.77	11.23
Clear Creek	......	......	......	....	....
Conejos	......	3	3	....	100.00
Costilla	......	......	......	....	....
Crowley	4,618	1,005	5,623	82.13	17.87
Custer	20	12	32	62.50	37.50
Delta	2	4	6	33.33	66.67
Dolores	1,219	42	1,261	96.67	3.33
Douglas	1,624	199	1,823	89.08	10.92
Eagle	......	......	......	....	....
Elbert	2,755	4,479	7,234	38.08	61.92
El Paso	2,189	1,965	4,154	52.70	47.30
Fremont	77	2	79	97.47	2.53
Garfield	2	......	2	100.00	....
Gilpin	......	......	......	....	....
Grand	......	......	......	....	....
Gunnison	......	......	......	....	....
Hinsdale	......	......	......	....	....
Huerfano	298	240	538	55.39	44.61
Jackson	......	......	......	....	....
Jefferson	5	......	5	100.00	....
Kiowa	23,860	8,491	32,351	73.75	26.25
Kit Carson	24,098	6,876	30,974	77.80	22.20
Lake	......	......	......	....	....
La Plata	28	30	58	48.27	51.73
Larimer	9	21	30	30.00	70.00
Las Animas	13,167	2,692	15,859	83.02	16.98
Lincoln	16,343	5,557	21,900	74.62	25.38
Logan	12,642	6,064	18,706	67.58	32.42
Mesa	396	20	416	95.19	4.81
Mineral	......	......	......	....	....
Moffat	200	754	954	21.08	78.92
Montezuma	217	4	221	98.19	1.81
Montrose	1	......	1	100.00	....
Morgan	7,023	7,342	14,365	48.88	51.12
Otero	3,896	364	4,260	91.46	8.54
Ouray	......	......	......	....	....
Park	......	......	......	....	....
Phillips	5,952	2,196	8,148	73.05	26.95
Pitkin	......	......	......	....	....
Prowers	35,372	2,937	38,309	92.33	7.67
Pueblo	7,234	272	7,506	96.38	3.62
Rio Blanco	......	......	......	....	....
Rio Grande	......	......	......	....	....
Routt	7	......	7	100.00	....
Saguache	......	......	......	....	....
San Miguel	......	258	258	....	100.00
Sedgwick	120	3,078	3,198	3.75	96.25
Summit	......	......	......	....	....
Teller	......	......	......	....	....
Washington	15,931	13,071	29,002	54.93	45.07
Weld	9,549	3,372	12,921	73.91	26.09
Yuma	19,593	8,056	27,649	70.86	29.14
State	330,736	103,179	433,905	76.22	23.78

ACREAGE AND PRODUCTION OF WINTER WHEAT, 1923

COUNTY	IRRIGATED			NON-IRRIGATED			TOTALS	
	Acreage Irrigated	Average Yields	Production Bushels	Acreage Non-Irrigated	Average Yields	Production Bushels	Total Acreage	Total Production
Adams	6,477	25	161,925	48,055	12	576,660	54,532	738,585
Alamosa	....	....	......	......	...	......	......	......
Arapahoe	1,041	33	34,353	24,029	12	288,348	25,070	322,701
Archuleta	8	25	200	......	...	......	8	200
Baca	525	15	7,875	26,563	6	159,378	27,088	167,253
Bent	6,810	24	163,440	3,480	8	27,840	10,290	191,280
Boulder	8,733	29	253,257	4,012	20	80,240	12,745	333,497
Chaffee	....	....	......	......	...	......	......	......
Cheyenne	....	....	......	24,199	6	145,194	24,199	145,194
Clear Creek	....	....	......	......	...	......	......	......
Conejos	10	25	250	......	...	......	10	250
Costilla	55	25	1,375	......	...	......	55	1,375
Crowley	253	25	6,325	763	12	9,156	1,016	15,481
Custer	204	25	5,100	109	19	2,071	313	7,171
Delta	449	30	13,470	11	13	143	460	13,613
Dolores	12	24	288	241	18	4,338	253	4,626
Douglas	62	26	1,612	4,742	11	52,162	4,804	53,774
Eagle	....	....	......	10	20	200	10	200
Elbert	80	24	1,920	20,984	10	209,840	21,064	211,760
El Paso	1	25	25	2,557	12	30,684	2,558	30,709
Fremont	142	31	4,402	90	15	1,350	232	5,752
Garfield	348	32	11,136	142	19	2,698	490	13,834
Gilpin	....	....	......	6	14	84	6	84
Grand	141	25	3,525	27	16	432	168	3,957
Gunnison	20	29	580	100	16	1,600	120	2,180
Hinsdale	....	....	......	......	...	......	......	......
Huerfano	127	30	3,810	324	11	3,564	451	7,374
Jackson	7	24	168	11	16	176	18	344
Jefferson	3,215	33	106,095	1,722	21	36,162	4,937	142,257
Kiowa	....	....	......	12,933	10	129,330	12,933	129,330
Kit Carson	....	....	......	136,155	7	953,085	136,155	953,085
Lake	....	....	......	......	...	......	......	......
La Plata	236	25	5,900	339	18	6,102	575	12,002
Larimer	1,956	32	62,592	5,554	19	105,526	7,510	168,118
Las Animas	349	25	8,725	18,245	6	109,470	18,594	118,195
Lincoln	....	....	......	46,075	11	506,825	46,075	506,825
Logan	5,360	25	134,000	124,309	13	1,616,017	129,669	1,750,017
Mesa	1,876	31	58,156	377	11	4,147	2,253	62,303
Mineral	....	....	......	......	...	......	......	......
Moffat	70	28	1,960	2,047	13	26,611	2,117	28,571
Montezuma	48	25	1,200	496	13	6,448	544	7,648
Montrose	687	31	21,297	21	17	357	708	21,654
Morgan	960	29	27,840	19,437	15	291,555	20,397	319,395
Otero	3,970	29	115,130	375	10	3,750	4,345	118,880
Ouray	....	....	......	164	16	2,624	164	2,624
Park	....	....	......	7	14	98	7	98
Phillips	....	....	......	97,725	10	977,250	97,725	977,250
Pitkin	38	33	1,254	......	...	......	38	1,254
Prowers	15,670	28	438,760	24,045	6	144,270	39,715	583,030
Pueblo	1,278	25	31,950	6,396	12	8,352	7,674	40,302
Rio Blanco	....	33	......	505	23	11,615	505	11,615
Rio Grande	....	....	......	......	...	......	......	......
Routt	30	30	900	2,408	25	60,200	2,438	61,100
Saguache	....	....	......	......	...	......	......	......
San Miguel	53	25	1,325	583	18	10,494	636	11,819
Sedgwick	422	22	9,284	30,840	8	246,720	31,262	256,004
Summit	40	26	1,040	......	...	......	40	1,040
Teller	....	....	......	......	...	......	......	......
Washington	736	26	19,136	202,835	7	1,419,845	203,571	1,438,981
Weld	16,130	28	451,640	49,868	11	548,548	65,998	1,000,188
Yuma	....	....	......	120,856	8	966,848	120,856	966,848
State	78,629	27.63	2,173,220	1,064,772	9.19	9,788,407	1,143,401	11,961,627

ACREAGE AND PRODUCTION OF SPRING WHEAT, 1923

COUNTY	IRRIGATED			NON-IRRIGATED			TOTALS	
	Acreage Irrigated	Average Yields	Production Bushels	Acreage Non-Irrigated	Average Yields	Production Bushels	Total Acreage	Total Production
Adams	10,274	,20	205,480	3,128	14	43,792	13,402	249,272
Alamosa	2,510	20	50,200	......	...	......	2,510	50,200
Arapahoe	1,977	25	49,425	535	12	6,420	2,512	55,845
Archuleta	175	24	4,200	428	14	5,992	603	10,192
Baca	....	....	......	8,198	6	49,188	8,198	49,188
Bent	1,910	20	38,200	443	10	4,430	2,353	42,630
Boulder	10,864	24	260,736	486	15	7,290	11,350	268,026
Chaffee	1,297	24	31,128	......	...	......	1,297	31,128
Cheyenne	....	....	......	783	5	3,915	783	3,915
Clear Creek	4	24	96	5	15	75	9	171
Conejos	8,559	20	171,180	......	...	......	8,559	171,180
Costilla	3,856	17	65,552	206	6	1,236	4,062	66,788
Crowley	470	22	10,340	135	10	1,350	605	11,690
Custer	557	23	12,811	923	15	13,845	1,480	26,656
Delta	4,374	28	122,472	......	...	......	4,374	122,472
Dolores	....	....	......	891	15	13,365	891	13,365
Douglas	243	23	5,589	1,284	10	12,840	1,527	18,429
Eagle	877	32	28,064	......	...	......	877	28,064
Elbert	70	24	1,680	7,026	10	70,260	7,096	71,940
El Paso	189	26	4,914	2,055	12	24,660	2,244	29,574
Fremont	263	31	8,153	118	18	2,124	381	10,277
Garfield	5,134	28	143,752	140	15	2,100	5,274	145,852
Gilpin	....	....	......	......	...	......	......	......
Grand	9	25	225	10	16	160	19	385
Gunnison	104	26	2,704	45	16	720	149	3,424
Hinsdale	2	25	50	......	...	......	2	50
Huerfano	99	20	1,980	1,201	6	7,206	1,300	9,186
Jackson	....	....	......	......	...	......	......	......
Jefferson	3,876	30	116,280	441	18	7,938	4,317	124,218
Kiowa	....	....	......	208	8	1,664	208	1,664
Kit Carson	....	....	......	6,738	4	26,952	6,738	26,952
Lake	....	....	......	......	...	......	......	......
La Plata	4,922	24	118,128	1,153	14	16,142	6,075	134,270
Larimer	12,646	25	316,150	2,182	12	26,184	14,828	342,334
Las Animas	560	20	11,200	3,092	5	15,460	3,652	26,660
Lincoln	69	20	1,380	13,459	10	134,590	13.528	135,970
Logan	4,380	26	113,880	40,864	9	367,776	45,244	481,656
Mesa	2,378	31	73,718	85	10	850	2,463	74,568
Mineral	....	....	......	......	...	......	......	......
Moffat	498	25	12,450	7,034	16	12,544	7,532	24,994
Montezuma	1,854	22	40,788	674	13	8,762	2,528	49,550
Montrose	10,662	30	319,860	138	15	2,070	10,800	321,930
Morgan	1,349	28	37,772	3,833	12	45,996	5,182	83,768
Otero	1,800	20	36,000	67	8	536	1,867	36,536
Ouray	721	28	20,188	411	17	6,987	1,132	27,175
Park	5	23	115	69	16	1,104	74	1,219
Phillips	....	....	......	3,831	5	19,155	3,831	19,155
Pitkin	338	31	10,478	......	...	......	338	10,478
Prowers	1,344	18	24,192	1,303	5	6,515	2,647	30,707
Pueblo	834	30	25,020	1,544	8	12,352	2,378	37,372
Rio Blanco	841	29	24,389	2,749	18	49,482	3,590	73,871
Rio Grande	4,851	28	135,828	......	8	......	4,851	135,828
Routt	30	25	750	7,407	20	148,140	7,437	148,890
Saguache	3,790	27	102,330	......	8	......	3,790	102,330
San Miguel	481	25	12,025	422	12	5,064	903	17,089
Sedgwick	2,584	20	51,680	14,961	9	134,649	17,545	186,329
Summit	8	22	176	......	...	......	8	176
Teller	....	....	......	......	...	......	......	......
Washington	55	18	990	15,796	5	78,980	15,851	79,970
Weld	36,240	22	797,280	27,556	10	275,560	63,796	1,072,840
Yuma	....	....	......	8,469	5	42,345	8,469	42,345
State	150,933	23.99	3,621,978	192,526	8.92	1,718,765	343,459	5,340,743

ACREAGE OF WINTER WHEAT, 1923

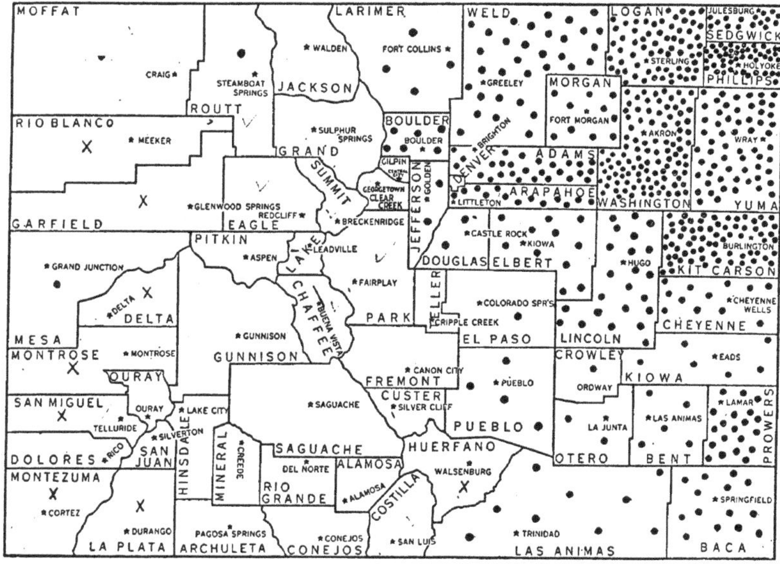

Each dot represents 2,000 acres. The cross (X) is used in counties reporting less than 1,000 acres.

ACREAGE OF SPRING WHEAT, 1923

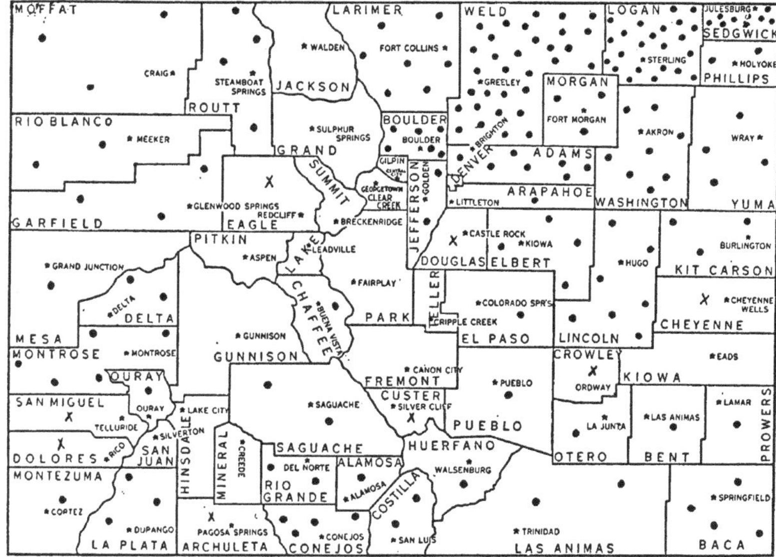

Each dot represents 2,000 acres. The cross (X) is used in counties reporting less than 1,000 acres.

ACREAGE OF SPRING AND WINTER WHEAT PLANTED IN COLORADO AS REPORTED BY COUNTY ASSESSORS

COUNTY	SPRING WHEAT				WINTER WHEAT			
	1923	1922	1921	1920	1923	1922	1921	1920
Adams	13,402	21,934	13,832	13,249	54,532	58,736	54,123	44,500
Alamosa	2,510	2,370	470	997	......	......	......	94
Arapahoe	2,512	5,387	3,240	4,140	25,070	29,382	15,174	22,530
Archuleta	603	211	737	1,119	8	670	174	33
Baca	8,198	30,052	10,881	2,485	27,088	80,069	69,250	14,783
Bent	2,353	4,144	3,502	1,156	10,290	17,331	13,411	5,579
Boulder	11,350	17,715	9,205	11,286	12,754	14,379	13,666	18,219
Chaffee	1,297	1,258	1,456	1,622	......	23	......	1
Cheyenne	783	1,799	948	1,101	24,199	48,345	28,854	1,945
Clear Creek	9	10	25	....	......	......	......	......
Conejos	8,559	11,191	7,956	6,255	10	89	7	26
Costilla	4,062	6,995	8,740	5,775	55	257	39	36
Crowley	605	1,103	3,480	2,110	1,016	1,077	1,820	300
Custer	1,480	1,825	1,194	601	313	146	502	552
Delta	4,374	5,878	6,512	4,639	460	646	800	825
Dolores	891	1,562	1,586	690	253	409	392	59
Douglas	1,527	1,823	2,064	2,214	4,804	6,851	5,624	3,652
Eagle	877	923	1,047	863	10	70	60	18
Elbert	7,096	11,831	12,314	11,446	21,064	27,644	19,691	12,188
El Paso	2,244	4,760	4,484	6,824	2,558	2,535	2,591	1,197
Fremont	381	794	582	633	232	502	602	658
Garfield	5,274	5,810	7,146	6,363	490	1,018	492	730
Gilpin	....	....	10	23	6	5	......	......
Grand	19	63	52	91	168	96	187	100
Gunnison	149	94	119	92	120	121	200	22
Hinsdale	2	....	....	17	......	......	......	......
Huerfano	1,300	2,235	1,872	5,705	451	1,578	731	2,342
Jackson	....	11	5	....	18	56	11	......
Jefferson	4,317	5,957	5,310	2,917	4,937	7,334	6,203	3,439
Kiowa	208	1,070	1,731	687	12,933	39,849	18,980	2,210
Kit Carson	6,738	7,890	14,754	10,608	136,155	141,045	126,072	26,283
Lake	....	....	....	....	......	......	......	......
La Plata	6,075	7,278	11,448	10,184	575	921	907	690
Larimer	14,828	20,152	14,559	9,594	7,510	11,739	14,211	18,400
Las Animas	3,652	7,533	4,267	2,894	18,594	28,906	22,879	10,870
Lincoln	13,528	13,593	21,611	14,716	46,075	43,172	31,988	17,634
Logan	45,244	34,454	16,819	18,525	129,669	170,275	209,735	177,743
Mesa	2,463	3,609	3,396	2,464	2,253	3,245	2,861	1,181
Mineral	....	....	....	....	......	......	......	1
Moffat	7,532	11,340	13,753	14,378	2,117	5,377	4,335	6,172
Montezuma	2,528	4,479	5,357	6,404	544	1,174	505	831
Montrose	10,800	9,507	12,101	11,288	708	1,499	1,452	1,368
Morgan	5,182	8,038	5,283	3,025	20,397	30,083	33,833	27,793
Otero	1,867	5,143	4,030	1,440	4,345	6,373	5,466	3,402
Ouray	1,132	1,162	999	994	164	160	447	170
Park	74	82	97	135	7	3	27	26
Phillips	3,831	2,920	3,324	2,082	97,725	124,559	109,551	87,141
Pitkin	338	426	448	506	38	17	9	54
Prowers	2,647	11,330	21,908	3,418	39,715	52,058	30,865	16,397
Pueblo	2,378	5,201	5,010	4,332	7,674	10,983	10,951	10,365
Rio Blanco	3,590	5,366	5,655	5,025	505	1,265	1,313	2,093
Rio Grande	4,851	7,679	8,984	8,842	......	......	10	......
Routt	7,437	9,804	10,116	9,300	2,438	2,763	2,995	4,578
Saguache	3,790	3,872	3,411	3,375	......	......	119	70
San Miguel	903	744	980	745	636	460	573	796
Sedgwick	17,545	8,264	6,757	5,785	31,262	49,758	53,404	41,401
Summit	8	42	29	77	40	39	12	109
Teller	....	....	13	86	......	......	1	10
Washington	15,851	13,442	7,435	10,873	202,771	218,117	192,077	164,530
Weld	63,796	73,082	59,037	67,995	65,998	101,741	121,559	124,108
Yuma	8,469	4,590	5,729	10,676	120,856	196,875	176,539	138,886
State	343,459	429,827	377,810	334,866	1,142,601	1,541,825	1,408,260	1,019,142

SPRING AND WINTER WHEAT IN COLORADO, 1923

COUNTY	Winter Wheat Acres	Spring Wheat Acres	Total Acres	Percent Winter Wheat	Percent Spring Wheat
Adams	54,532	13,402	67,934	80.27	19.73
Alamosa	....	2,510	2,510	....	100.00
Arapahoe	25,070	2,512	27,582	90.89	9.11
Archuleta	8	603	611	1.31	98.69
Baca	27,088	8,198	35,286	76.77	23.23
Bent	10,290	2,353	12,643	81.38	18.62
Boulder	12,745	11,350	24,095	52.89	47.11
Chaffee	....	1,297	1,297	....	100.00
Cheyenne	24,199	783	24,982	96.87	3.13
Clear Creek	....	9	9	....	100.00
Conejos	10	8,559	8,569	.12	99.88
Costilla	55	4,062	4,117	1.34	98.66
Crowley	1,016	605	1,621	62.68	37.32
Custer	313	1,480	1,793	17.46	82.54
Delta	460	4,374	4,834	9.51	90.49
Dolores	253	891	1,144	22.11	77.89
Douglas	4,804	1,527	6,331	75.87	24.13
Eagle	10	877	887	1.13	98.87
Elbert	21,064	7,096	28,160	74.80	25.20
El Paso	2,558	2,244	4,802	53.27	46.73
Fremont	232	381	613	37.85	62.15
Garfield	490	5,274	5,764	8.50	91.50
Gilpin	6	......	6	100.00	....
Grand	168	19	187	89.84	10.16
Gunnison	120	149	269	44.61	55.39
Hinsdale	....	2	2	....	100.00
Huerfano	451	1,300	1,751	25.75	74.25
Jackson	18	......	18	100.00	....
Jefferson	4,937	4,317	9,254	53.35	46.65
Kiowa	12,933	208	13,141	98.41	1.59
Kit Carson	136,155	6,738	142,893	95.28	4.72
Lake	....	......	....	....	....
La Plata	575	6,075	6,650	8.63	91.37
Larimer	7,510	14,828	22,338	33.62	66.38
Las Animas	18,594	3,652	22,246	83.58	16.42
Lincoln	46,075	13,528	59,603	77.30	22.70
Logan	129,669	45,244	174,913	74.13	25.87
Mesa	2,253	2,463	4,716	47.77	52.23
Mineral	....	......	....	....	....
Moffat	2,117	7,532	9,649	21.94	78.06
Montezuma	544	2,528	3,072	17.71	82.29
Montrose	708	10,800	11,508	6.15	93.85
Morgan	20,397	5,182	25,579	79.74	20.26
Otero	4,345	1,867	6,212	69.79	30.21
Ouray	164	1,132	1,296	12.65	87.35
Park	7	74	81	8.64	91.36
Phillips	97,725	3,831	101,556	96.23	3.77
Pitkin	38	338	376	10.10	89.90
Prowers	39,715	2,647	42,362	93.75	6.25
Pueblo	7,674	2,378	10,052	76.34	23.66
Rio Blanco	505	3,590	4,095	12.33	87.67
Rio Grande	....	4,851	4,851	....	100.00
Routt	2,438	7,437	9,875	24.69	75.31
Saguache	....	3,790	3,790	....	100.00
San Miguel	636	903	1,539	41.33	58.67
Sedgwick	31,262	17,545	48,807	62.00	38.00
Summit	40	8	48	83.33	16.67
Teller	....	......	....	....	....
Washington	202,771	15,851	218,622	92.75	7.25
Weld	65,998	63,796	129,794	50.85	49.15
Yuma	120,856	8,469	129,325	93.45	6.55
State	1,142,601	343,459	1,486,060	76.88	23.12

IRRIGATED AND NON-IRRIGATED WHEAT IN COLORADO, 1923

COUNTY	Irrigated Acres	Non-Irrigated Acres	Total Acres	Percent Irrigated	Percent Non-Irrigated
Adams	16,751	51,183	67,934	24.66	75.34
Alamosa	2,510	....	2,510	100.00	....
Arapahoe	3,018	24,564	27,582	10.94	89.06
Archuleta	183	428	611	29.95	70.05
Baca	525	34,761	35,286	1.48	98.52
Bent	8,720	3,923	12,643	68.97	31.03
Boulder	19,597	4,498	24,095	81.33	18.67
Chaffee	1,297	....	1,297	100.00	....
Cheyenne	......	24,982	24,982	....	100.00
Clear Creek	4	5	9	44.44	55.56
Conejos	8,569	....	8,569	100.00	....
Costilla	3,911	206	4,117	95.00	5.00
Crowley	723	898	1,621	44.60	55.40
Custer	761	1,032	1,793	42.44	57.56
Delta	4,823	11	4,834	98.72	1.28
Dolores	12	1,132	1,144	1.05	98.95
Douglas	305	6,026	6,331	4.82	95.18
Eagle	877	10	887	98.87	1.13
Elbert	150	28,010	28,160	.54	99.46
El Paso	190	4,612	4,802	3.77	96.23
Fremont	405	208	613	66.07	33.93
Garfield	5,482	282	5,764	95.11	4 89
Gilpin	......	6	6	....	100.00
Grand	150	37	187	80.21	19.79
Gunnison	124	145	269	46.09	53.91
Hinsdale	2	....	2	100.00	....
Huerfano	226	1,525	1,751	12.90	87.10
Jackson	7	11	18	38.89	61.11
Jefferson	7,091	2,163	9,254	76.62	23.38
Kiowa	......	13,141	13,141	....	100.00
Kit Carson	......	142,893	142,893	....	100.00
Lake	......	....	....	....	....
La Plata	5,158	1,492	6,650	77.56	22.44
Larimer	14,602	7,737	22,338	65.36	34.64
Las Animas	909	21,337	22,246	4.08	95.92
Lincoln	69	59,534	59,603	99.88	.12
Logan	9,740	165,173	174,913	5.56	94.44
Mesa	4,254	462	4,716	87.87	12.13
Mineral	......	....	....	....	....
Moffat	568	9,081	9,649	5.88	94.12
Montezuma	1,902	1,170	3,072	61.91	38.09
Montrose	11,349	159	11,508	98.62	1.38
Morgan	2,309	23,270	25,579	9.03	90.97
Otero	5,770	442	6,212	92.88	7.12
Ouray	721	575	1,296	55.63	44.37
Park	5	76	81	6.17	93.83
Phillips	......	101,556	101,556	....	100.00
Pitkin	376	....	376	100.00	....
Prowers	17,014	25,348	42,362	40.17	59.83
Pueblo	2,112	7,940	10,052	21.01	78.99
Rio Blanco	841	3,254	4,095	20.54	79.46
Rio Grande	4,851	....	4,851	100.00	....
Routt	60	9,815	9,875	.82	99.18
Saguache	3,790	....	3,790	100.00	....
San Miguel	534	1,005	1,539	34.69	65.31
Sedgwick	3,006	45,801	48,807	6.16	93.84
Summit	48	....	48	100.00	....
Teller	......	....	....	....	....
Washington	791	217,831	218,622	.36	99.64
Weld	52,370	77,424	129,794	40.35	59.65
Yuma	......	129,325	129,325	....	100.00
State	229,562	1,256,498	1,486,060	15.45	84.55

ACREAGE AND PRODUCTION OF WHEAT AND ACREAGE OF RYE, 1923

COUNTY	WHEAT			RYE		
	Acreage	Avg. Yield	Production	Spring	Winter	All Rye
Adams	67,934	14.54	987,857	356	2,592	2,948
Alamosa	2,510	20.00	50,200	.....	.....	.....
Arapahoe	27,582	13.72	378,546	333	779	1,112
Archuleta	611	17.00	10,392	.....	.....	.....
Baca	35,286	6.13	216,441	.....	460	460
Bent	12,643	18.50	233,910	38	155	193
Boulder	24,095	24.96	601,523	9	51	60
Chaffee	1,297	24.00	31,128	4	.....	4
Cheyenne	24,982	5.96	149,109	8	356	364
Clear Creek	9	19.00	171	10	.....	10
Conejos	8,569	20.00	171,430	.....	.....	.....
Costilla	4,117	16.55	68,163	.....	.....	.....
Crowley	1,621	16.76	27,171	.....	.....	.....
Custer	1,793	18.86	33,827	38	95	133
Delta	4,834	28.15	136,085	4	4	8
Dolores	1,144	15.72	17,991	.....	57	57
Douglas	6,331	11.40	72,203	143	1,795	1,938
Eagle	887	31.86	28,264	.....	.....	.....
Elbert	28,160	10.07	283,700	2,180	5,464	7,644
El Paso	4,802	12.55	60,283	1,463	2,428	3,891
Fremont	613	26.14	16,029	101	73	174
Garfield	5,764	27.70	159,686	31	3	34
Gilpin	6	14.00	84	21	3	24
Grand	187	23.21	4,342	178	46	224
Gunnison	269	20.83	5,604	17	3	20
Hinsdale	2	25.00	50	.....	.....	.....
Huerfano	1,751	28.00	16,560	48	118	166
Jackson	18	19.11	344	11	15	26
Jefferson	9,254	28.79	266,475	31	51	82
Kiowa	13,141	9.96	130,994	.....	37	37
Kit Carson	142,893	6.85	980,037	409	5,858	6,267
Lake	....	....	....	2	.....	2
La Plata	6,650	21.99	146,272	20	20	40
Larimer	22,338	22.85	510,452	108	56	164
Las Animas	22,246	6.51	144,855	46	487	533
Lincoln	59,603	10.78	642,795	594	4,992	5 586
Logan	174,913	12.75	2,231,673	1,137	6,034	7,171
Mesa	4,716	29.02	136,871	90	143	233
Mineral	....	....	....	.....	.....	.....
Moffat	9,649	5.55	53,565	502	3,836	4,338
Montezuma	3,072	18.61	57,198	22	92	114
Montrose	11,508	29.85	343,584	.....	.....	.....
Morgan	25,579	15.76	403,163	577	3,077	3,654
Otero	6,212	25.01	155,416	25	33	58
Ouray	1,296	22.99	29,799	.....	22	22
Park	81	16.25	1,317	252	156	408
Phillips	101,556	9.81	996,405	161	3,695	3,856
Pitkin	376	31.20	11,732	.....	.....	.....
Prowers	42,362	14.48	613,737	57	327	384
Pueblo	10,052	7.72	77,674	90	454	544
Rio Blanco	4,095	20.87	85,486	.....	353	353
Rio Grande	4,851	28.00	135,828	.....	.....	.....
Routt	9,875	21.26	209,990	146	17	163
Saguache	3,790	27.00	102,330	.....	.....	.....
San Miguel	1,539	18.78	28,908	.....	67	67
Sedgwick	48,807	9.06	442,333	155	1,491	1,646
Summit	48	25.33	1,216	61	.....	61
Teller	....	....	....	2	25	27
Washington	219,422	6.92	1,518,951	569	11,692	12,261
Weld	129,794	15.97	2,073,028	5,115	5,424	10,539
Yuma	129,325	7.80	1,009,193	132	15,498	15,630
State	1,486,860	11.63	17,302,370	15,296	78,434	93,730

ACREAGE AND PRODUCTION OF OATS, 1923

COUNTY	IRRIGATED			NON-IRRIGATED			TOTALS	
	Acreage Irrigated	Average Yields	Production Bushels	Acreage Non-Irrigated	Average Yields	Production Bushels	Total Acreage	Total Production
Adams	3,300	45	148,500	1,566	20	31,320	4,866	179,820
Alamosa	3,240	33	106,920	......	23	......	3,240	106,920
Arapahoe	545	50	27,250	1,013	16	16,208	1,558	43,458
Archuleta	195	40	7,800	2,247	26	58,422	2,442	66,222
Baca	......	....	......	179	15	2,685	179	2,685
Bent	670	44	29,480	49	10	490	719	29,970
Boulder	3,734	45	168,030	238	26	6,188	3,972	174,218
Chaffee	1,772	45	79,740	......	25	......	1,772	79,740
Cheyenne	......	....	......	407	23	9,361	407	9,361
Clear Creek	22	45	990	122	28	3,416	144	4,406
Conejos	3,922	36	141,192	......	20	......	3,922	141,192
Costilla	1,980	35	69,300	3	23	69	1,983	69,369
Crowley	1,908	39	74,412	268	20	5,360	2,176	79,772
Custer	1,696	40	67,840	2,031	30	60,930	3,727	128,770
Delta	3,334	43	143,362	8	14	112	3,342	143,474
Dolores	36	38	1,368	1,042	20	20,840	1,078	22,208
Douglas	55	44	2,420	5,914	25	147,850	5,969	150,270
Eagle	1,831	50	91,550	8	22	176	1,839	91,726
Elbert	......	....	......	8,741	26	227,266	8,741	227,266
El Paso	223	44	9,812	11,467	26	298,142	11,690	307,954
Fremont	587	50	29,350	1,286	25	32,150	1,873	61,500
Garfield	2,590	48	124,320	34	20	680	2,624	125,000
Gilpin	......	....	......	571	30	17,130	571	17,130
Grand	486	43	20,898	228	30	6,840	714	27,738
Gunnison	587	35	20,545	466	17	7,922	1,053	28,467
Hinsdale	16	40	640	38	20	760	54	1,400
Huerfano	445	42	18,690	1,498	30	44,940	1,943	63,630
Jackson	127	40	5,080	3	28	84	130	5,164
Jefferson	2,007	46	92,322	1,330	30	39,900	3,337	132,222
Kiowa	......	....	......	14	22	308	14	308
Kit Carson	15	42	630	3,552	18	63,936	3,567	64,566
Lake	......	....	......	......	....	......	......	......
La Plata	3,586	40	143,440	816	21	17,136	4,402	160,576
Larimer	6,676	50	333,800	588	25	14,700	7,264	348,500
Las Animas	1,007	40	40,280	2,222	12	26,664	3,229	66,944
Lincoln	......	....	......	1,705	23	39,215	1,705	39,215
Logan	5,142	42	215,964	6,207	21	130,347	11,349	346,311
Mesa	3,166	42	132,972	248	12	2,976	3,414	135,948
Mineral	73	35	2,555	17	24	408	90	2,963
Moffat	1,090	45	49,050	6,109	22	134,398	7,199	183,448
Montezuma	1,742	42	73,164	506	20	10,120	2,248	83,284
Montrose	5,481	45	246,645	261	19	4,959	5,742	251,604
Morgan	3,126	43	134,418	948	20	18,960	4,074	153,378
Otero	3,375	41	138,375	58	20	1,160	3,433	139,535
Ouray	862	45	38,790	278	20	5,560	1,140	44,350
Park	......	....	......	3,977	25	99,425	3,977	99,425
Phillips	......	....	......	8,239	27	222,453	8,239	222,453
Pitkin	1,305	50	65,250	......	....	......	1,305	65,250
Prowers	1,449	35	50,715	371	20	7,420	1,820	58,135
Pueblo	1,465	45	65,925	1,698	23	39,054	3,163	104,979
Rio Blanco	914	50	45,700	1,760	27	47,520	2,674	93,220
Rio Grande	4,221	39	164,619	......	....	......	4,221	164,619
Routt	128	52	6,656	8,122	33	268,026	8,250	274,682
Saguache	3,389	34	115,226	......	....	......	3,389	115,226
San Miguel	577	40	23,080	1,319	23	30,337	1,896	53,417
Sedgwick	732	45	32,940	4,962	26	129,012	5,694	161,952
Summit	193	30	5,790	16	24	384	209	6,174
Teller	......	....	......	15,995	25	399,875	15,995	399,875
Washington	327	43	14,061	5,822	20	116,440	6,149	130,501
Weld	15,278	43	656,954	6,562	21	137,802	21,840	794,756
Yuma	15	43	645	3,736	23	85,928	3,751	86,573
State	100,642	42.52	4,279,455	126,865	24.38	3,093,764	227,507	7,373 219

ACREAGE AND PRODUCTION OF BARLEY, 1923

COUNTY	IRRIGATED			NON-IRRIGATED			TOTALS	
	Acreage Irrigated	Average Yields	Production Bushels	Acreage Non-Irrigated	Average Yields	Production Bushels	Total Acreage	Total Production
Adams	1,817	36	65,412	3,756	20	75,120	5,573	140.532
Alamosa	1,405	27	37,935	......	....	......	1,405	37,935
Arapahoe	348	45	15,660	2,317	20	46,340	2,665	62.000
Archuleta	......	....	......	707	22	15,554	707	15,554
Baca	345	30	10,350	2,973	15	44,595	3,318	54,945
Bent	634	32	20,288	362	12	4,344	996	24,632
Boulder	2,721	40	108,840	200	28	5,600	2,921	114,440
Chaffee	1,203	26	31,278	10	19	190	1,213	31.468
Cheyenne	......	....	......	4,764	22	104,808	4,764	104,808
Clear Creek	4	32	128	......	....	......	4	128
Conejos	8,627	35	301,945	......	....	......	8,627	301,945
Costilla	3,184	32	101,888	2	18	36	3,186	101,924
Crowley	644	31	19,964	292	13	3,796	936	23,760
Custer	515	34	17,510	937	23	21,551	1,452	39,061
Delta	614	37	22,718	11	16	176	625	22,894
Dolores	......	....	......	226	21	4,746	226	4,746
Douglas	......	....	......	475	23	10,925	475	10,925
Eagle	224	35	7,840	35	21	735	259	8.575
Elbert	8	33	264	1,756	22	38,632	1,764	38.896
El Paso	70	34	2,380	429	22	9,438	499	11,818
Fremont	183	35	6,405	796	20	15,920	979	22,325
Garfield	573	41	23,493	23	25	575	596	24.068
Gilpin	......	....	......	50	25	1,250	50	1,250
Grand	106	43	4,558	40	22	880	146	5.438
Gunnison	228	32	7,296	162	18	2,916	390	10,212
Hinsdale	20	37	740	2	25	50	22	790
Huerfano	200	35	7,000	472	23	10,856	672	17,856
Jackson	39	35	1,365	13	25	325	52	1.690
Jefferson	1,333	45	59,985	397	25	9,925	1,730	69,910
Kiowa	......	....	......	1,747	17	29,699	1,747	29.699
Kit Carson	92	40	3,680	27,604	21	579,684	27,696	583,364
Lake	......	....	......	51	23	1,173	51	1.173
La Plata	1,254	38	47.652	384	24	9.216	1.638	56,868
Larimer	3,508	42	147,336	622	22	13,684	4,130	161,020
Las Animas	362	33	11,946	701	10	7,010	1,063	18,956
Lincoln	48	41	1,968	9,016	23	207,368	9,064	209.336
Logan	3,207	43	137,901	12,114	27	327,078	15,321	464,979
Mesa	542	32	17,344	13	15	195	555	17,539
Mineral	34	35	1,190	18	22	396	52	1.586
Moffat	92	40	3,680	839	23	19,297	931	22,977
Montezuma	1,015	36	36,540	528	18	9.504	1,543	46.044
Montrose	274	33	9,042	200	15	3,000	474	12.042
Morgan	5,004	44	220,176	3,816	22	83,952	8,820	304,128
Otero	1,022	40	40,880	61	13	793	1,083	41,673
Ouray	68	35	2,380	580	22	12,760	648	15,140
Park	9	42	378	1,338	24	32,112	1,347	32,490
Phillips	40	42	1,680	3,386	25	84,650	3,426	86,330
Pitkin	204	35	7,140	......	....	......	204	7,140
Prowers	1,606	35	56,210	1,456	15	21,840	3,062	78,050
Pueblo	998	41	40,918	864	15	12,960	1,862	53,878
Rio Blanco	54	43	2,322	803	27	21,681	857	24,003
Rio Grande	2,311	34	78,574	......	18	......	2,311	78,574
Routt	96	40	3,840	4,044	36	145,584	4,140	149,424
Saguache	1.184	34	40,256	......	17	......	1,184	40,256
San Miguel	561	31	17,391	4,530	21	95,130	5,091	112,521
Sedgwick	750	41	30,750	2,136	24	51,264	2,886	82,014
Summit	64	28	1,792	......	20	......	64	1,792
Teller	......	30	......	1,304	20	26,080	1,304	26,080
Washington	635	42	26,670	35,470	22	780,340	36,105	807,010
Weld	14,642	42	614,964	11,761	23	270,508	26,403	885.472
Yuma	......	....	......	14,649	26	380,874	14,649	380,874
State	64,721	38.31	2,479,842	161,242	22.68	3,657,115	225,963	6,136,957

ACREAGE OF OATS, 1923

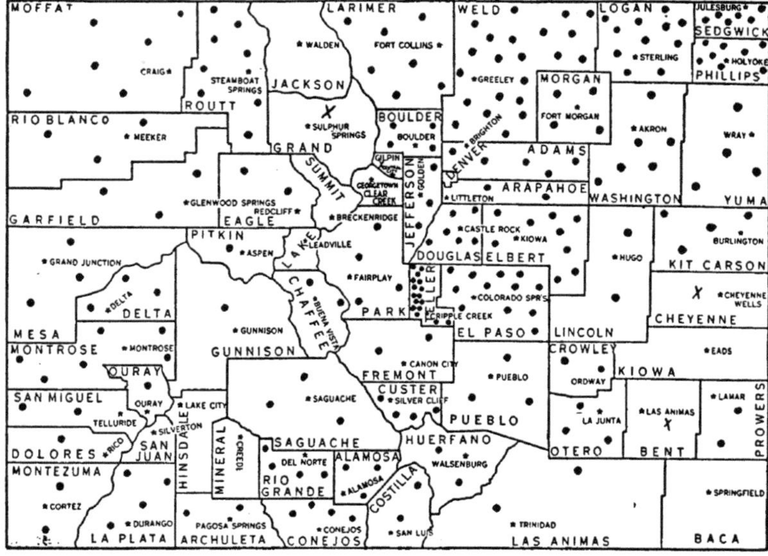

Each dot represents 1,000 acres. The cross (X) is used in counties reporting less than 500 acres.

ACREAGE OF BARLEY, 1923

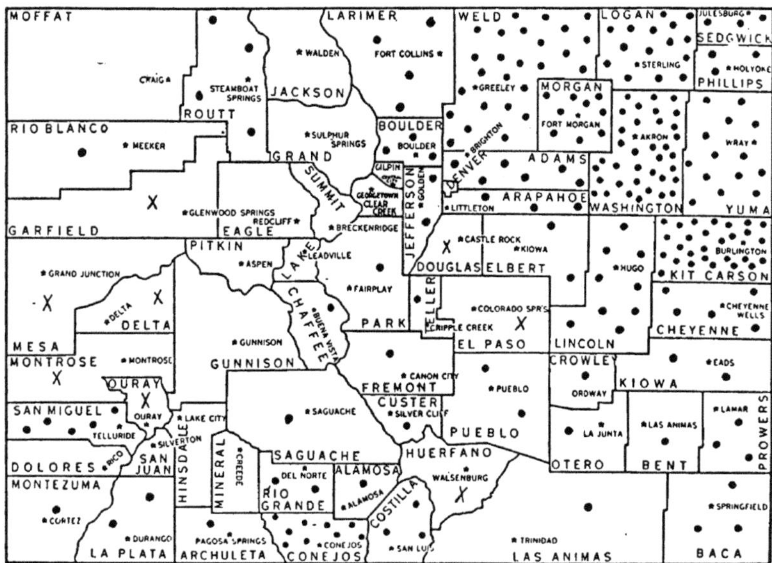

Each dot represents 1,000 acres. The cross (X) is used in counties reporting less than 500 acres.

ACREAGE OF OATS AND BARLEY IN COLORADO AS REPORTED BY COUNTY ASSESSORS

COUNTY	OATS				BARLEY			
	1923	1922	1921	1920	1923	1922	1921	1920
Adams	4,866	5,350	4,286	4,978	5,573	7,230	5,465	4,181
Alamosa	3,240	2,990	2,305	2,207	1,405	2,760	2,003	1,606
Arapahoe	1,558	1,820	1,244	2,221	2,665	2,266	1,238	2,269
Archuleta	2,442	2,686	2,976	2,993	707	816	760	1,477
Baca	179	392	957	658	3,318	8,962	9,595	2,691
Bent	719	937	1,035	961	996	1,752	1,974	2,163
Boulder	3,972	3,520	2,553	3,988	2,921	3,325	3,143	4,203
Chaffee	1,772	1,353	1,813	1,733	1,213	1,089	851	966
Cheyenne	407	581	485	434	4,767	6,299	6,364	5,101
Clear Creek	144	224	253	198	4	4	18	32
Conejos	3,922	4,214	6,600	2,372	8,627	8,718	8,163	5,541
Costilla	1,983	2,680	2,506	2,164	3,186	2,851	3,596	3,183
Crowley	2,176	858	3,760	2,037	936	1,020	1,683	2,682
Custer	3,727	3,829	4,731	4,581	1,452	1,758	1,642	1,213
Delta	3,342	3,911	4,876	5,154	625	316	419	332
Dolores	1,078	2,762	1,997	926	226	685	167	194
Douglas	5,969	6,363	8,804	5,787	475	786	761	608
Eagle	1,839	2,292	3,155	2,131	259	454	553	333
Elbert	8,741	8,758	12,022	10,005	1,764	1,684	1,755	2,437
El Paso	11,690	14,948	21,405	13,146	499	942	848	641
Fremont	1,873	2,754	2,706	2,018	979	959	852	1,212
Garfield	2,624	2,812	3,581	4,136	596	846	1,122	1,056
Gilpin	571	450	467	428	50	91	131	115
Grand	714	960	1,106	892	146	255	490	217
Gunnison	1,053	966	777	797	390	382	352	388
Hinsdale	54	11	2	3	22	5	....	30
Huerfano	1,943	2,204	1,872	3,344	672	1,327	1,047	2,081
Jackson	130	270	137	56	52	50	177	16
Jefferson	3,337	5,803	3,749	3,672	1,730	3,199	1,385	1,218
Kiowa	14	342	324	99	1,747	1,828	1,641	815
Kit Carson	3,567	3,725	4,076	2,478	27,696	27,546	41,054	44,033
Lake	....	49	40	30	51	58	40	92
La Plata	4,402	4,495	5,511	4,978	1,638	2,839	2,403	2,555
Larimer	7,264	6,338	7,914	6,894	4,130	4,178	6,054	5,134
Las Animas	3,229	4,527	4,375	4,040	1,063	1,371	1,010	1,017
Lincoln	1,705	2,817	2,776	2,219	9,064	8,694	10,848	13,285
Logan	11,349	15,929	17,626	11,888	15,321	17,395	11,544	8,879
Mesa	3,414	4,070	5,315	3,192	555	742	843	707
Mineral	90	63	125	162	52	64	285	248
Moffat	7,199	9,341	7,413	7,441	931	917	650	736
Montezuma	2,248	3,659	3,320	4,584	1,543	2,974	1,792	2,132
Montrose	5,742	4,865	6,243	7,012	474	210	302	548
Morgan	4,074	5,669	6,601	5,028	8,820	7,783	8,546	5,736
Otero	3,433	3,196	4,960	5,212	1,083	940	1,283	1,349
Ouray	1,140	1,091	905	699	648	644	540	273
Park	3,977	3,386	3,553	3,485	1,347	1,325	1,162	1,260
Phillips	8,239	8,397	7,277	3,383	3,426	2,416	1,227	533
Pitkin	1,305	1,633	1,862	1,683	204	199	246	217
Prowers	1,820	2,266	3,208	4,280	3,062	4,343	4,237	4,482
Pueblo	3,163	7,309	4,127	4,263	1,862	3,080	2,370	2,360
Rio Blanco	2,674	2,925	4,222	3,613	857	975	850	1,394
Rio Grande	4,221	5,586	6,341	7,607	2,311	2,848	3,917	3,402
Routt	8,250	8,433	8,956	8,502	4,140	4,580	4,846	6,344
Saguache	3,389	3,657	5,104	4,349	1,184	1,393	2,231	2,219
San Miguel	1,896	1,789	2,518	2,350	5,091	2,779	4,573	5,914
Sedgwick	5,694	5,255	5,104	2,795	2,886	2,071	1,355	1,649
Summit	209	203	212	257	64	120	92	103
Teller	15,995	10,867	5,350	5,074	1,304	1,232	402	927
Washington	6,149	4,811	6,582	5,840	36,105	24,674	24,484	26,418
Weld	21,840	25,317	25,685	25,580	26,403	28,918	30,884	32,607
Yuma	3,751	5,250	5,236	4,319	14,649	11,957	12,016	11,103
State	227,507	253,958	275,021	237,356	225,966	231,924	240,281	236,657

ACREAGE AND PRODUCTION OF POTATOES, 1923

COUNTY	IRRIGATED			NON-IRRIGATED			TOTALS	
	Acreage Irrigated	Average Yields	Production Bushels	Acreage Non-Irrigated	Average Yields	Production Bushels	Total Acreage	Total Production
Adams	877	60	52,620	111	20	2,220	988	54,840
Alamosa	2,812	130	365,560	......	....	......	2,812	365,560
Arapahoe	32	70	2,240	24	20	480	56	2,720
Archuleta	......	......	......	126	70	8,820	126	8,820
Baca	......	......	......	......	....	......	......	......
Bent	......	......	......	......	....	......	......	......
Boulder	185	90	16,650	70	20	1,400	255	18,050
Chaffee	339	90	30,510	14	40	560	353	31,070
Cheyenne	42	90	3,780	264	60	15,840	306	19,620
Clear Creek	......	......	......	39	60	2,340	39	2,340
Conejos	3,419	140	478,660	......	....	......	3,419	478,660
Costilla	216	110	23,760	7	30	210	223	23,970
Crowley	......	......	......	......	....	......	......	......
Custer	5	90	450	961	40	38,440	966	38,890
Delta	2,379	160	380,640	21	60	1,260	2,400	381,900
Dolores	1	150	150	94	60	5,640	95	5,790
Douglas	223	100	22,300	......	....	......	223	22,300
Eagle	2,002	190	380,380	5	75	375	2,007	380,755
Elbert	19	110	2,090	1,193	50	59,650	1,212	61,740
El Paso	......	......	......	920	60	55,200	920	55,200
Fremont	23	90	2,070	434	50	21,700	457	23,770
Garfield	4,136	170	703,120	107	65	6,955	4,243	710,075
Gilpin	......	......	......	123	40	4,920	123	4,920
Grand	47	100	4,700	95	60	5,700	142	10,400
Gunnison	161	150	24,150	232	70	16,240	393	40,390
Hinsdale	34	140	4,760	6	70	420	40	5,180
Huerfano	2	140	280	72	35	2,520	74	2,800
Jackson	13	100	1,300	......	....	......	13	1,300
Jefferson	82	90	7,380	198	70	13,860	280	21,240
Kiowa	......	......	......	14	40	560	14	560
Kit Carson	1	90	90	730	65	47,450	731	47,540
Lake	3	100	300	......	....	......	3	300
La Plata	378	120	45,360	284	60	17,040	662	62,400
Larimer	798	120	95,760	65	50	3,250	863	99,010
Las Animas	20	125	2,500	110	50	5,500	130	8,000
Lincoln	60	100	6,000	1,130	50	56,500	1,190	62,500
Logan	197	130	25,610	803	60	48,180	1,000	73,790
Mesa	3,438	140	481,320	364	55	20,020	3,802	501,340
Mineral	3	130	390	2	60	120	5	510
Moffat	54	165	8,910	620	80	49,600	674	58,510
Montezuma	197	90	17,730	69	30	2,070	266	19,800
Montrose	8,573	165	1,414,545	10	65	650	8,583	1,415,195
Morgan	1,770	110	194,700	378	27	10,206	2,148	204,906
Otero	8	100	800	1	40	40	9	840
Ouray	242	155	37,510	197	75	14,775	439	52,285
Park	5	100	500	1,048	60	62,880	1,053	63,380
Phillips	......	......	......	274	35	9,590	274	9,590
Pitkin	1,438	200	287,600	......	75	......	1,438	287,600
Prowers	3	95	285	9	35	315	12	600
Pueblo	1	90	90	8	40	320	9	410
Rio Blanco	8	170	1,360	79	80	6,320	87	7,680
Rio Grande	12,129	160	1,940,640	......	....	......	12,129	1,940,640
Routt	35	160	5,600	894	90	80,460	929	86,060
Saguache	4,118	155	638,290	......	....	......	4,118	638,290
San Miguel	35	160	5,600	891	115	102,465	926	108,065
Sedgwick	596	90	53,640	158	55	8,690	754	62,330
Summit	57	110	6,270	3	90	270	60	6,540
Teller	......	110	......	1,617	90	145,530	1,617	145,530
Washington	......	......	......	541	35	18,935	541	18,935
Weld	22,259	135	3,004,965	1,098	35	38,430	23,357	3,043,395
Yuma	31	130	4,030	523	37	19,351	554	23,381
State	73,506	146.8	10,787,945	17,036	60.7	1,034,267	90,542	11,822,212

ACREAGE OF POTATOES, 1923

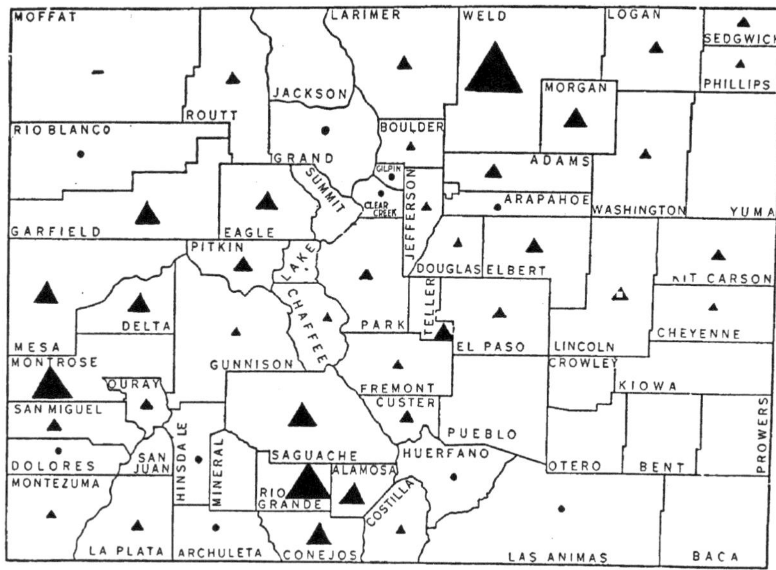

The largest triangle represents 23,357 acres. The dot represents less than 200 acres.

ACREAGE OF BEANS, 1923

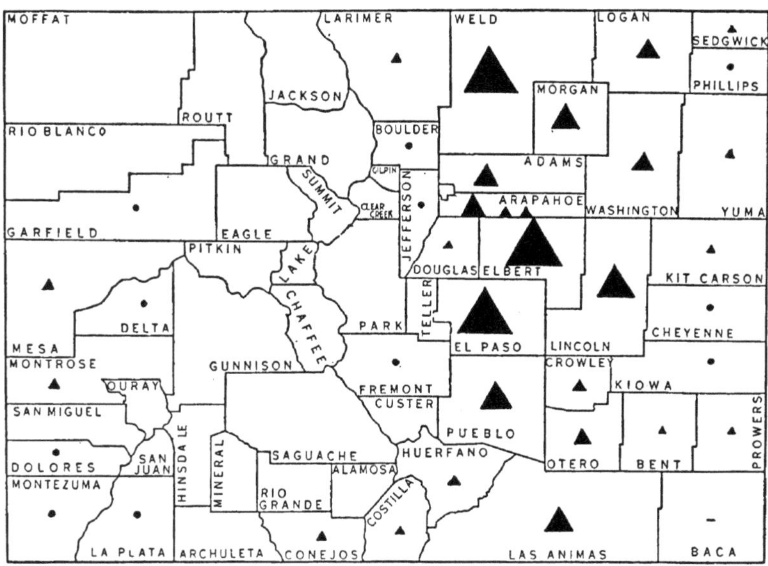

The largest triangle represents 23,917 acres. The dot represents less than 200 acres.

ACREAGE OF POTATOES AND BEANS IN COLORADO AS REPORTED BY COUNTY ASSESSORS

COUNTY	POTATOES				BEANS			
	1923	1922	1921	1920	1923	1922	1921	1920
Adams	988	1,826	1,171	1,081	4,428	2,652	1,659	1,748
Alamosa	2,812	5,396	1,201	1,074	....	....	....	....
Arapahoe	56	388	158	286	6,493	2,433	946	1,683
Archuleta	126	83	111	205	12	....	....	76
Baca	....	16	13	6	225	47	272	....
Bent	....	14	8	38	413	1,372	323	381
Boulder	255	446	307	385	37	37	....	62
Chaffee	353	777	585	451	....	21	....	....
Cheyenne	306	376	361	269	150	47	17	78
Clear Creek	39	51	47	40	....	3	....	....
Conejos	3,419	5,710	3,121	1,730	529	84	169	512
Costilla	223	436	295	187	448	206	282	237
Crowley	....	24	234	191	1,340	1,216	612	768
Custer	966	1,409	1,046	579	....	19	21	11
Delta	2,400	4,428	3,331	2,150	98	58	44	124
Dolores	95	148	94	108	83	12	33	35
Douglas	223	257	316	252	313	92	9	1
Eagle	2,007	3,006	2,601	1,443	....	....	....	....
Elbert	1,212	2,593	2,531	2,232	28,295	19,705	10,155	10,686
El Paso	920	2,545	2,713	2,219	24,639	20,742	9,046	8,324
Fremont	457	690	500	403	25	49	19	51
Garfield	4,243	6,772	4,917	2,954	28	39	4	63
Gilpin	123	131	134	112	....	....	....	....
Grand	142	206	95	64	....	....	....	....
Gunnison	393	349	382	324	....	....	1	....
Hinsdale	40	13	8	19	....	....	....	....
Huerfano	74	193	183	418	1,142	903	724	....
Jackson	13	29	18	19	....	....	....	....
Jefferson	280	1,483	604	755	11	....	1	3
Kiowa	14	46	25	11	97	1,630	51	18
Kit Carson	731	929	908	571	295	227	98	292
Lake	3	....	....	....	....	....	....	....
La Plata	662	683	833	405	105	174	129	109
Larimer	863	1,536	728	412	456	177	58	199
Las Animas	130	134	188	188	6,082	5,146	2,068	5,415
Lincoln	1,190	1,755	1,824	1,082	10,410	6,862	2,974	3,132
Logan	1,000	1,570	1,692	916	3,474	1,461	593	338
Mesa	3,802	4,077	2,232	1,479	733	450	49	90
Mineral	5	4	6	7	....	....	....	....
Moffat	674	964	938	799	177	223	176	145
Montezuma	266	655	486	565	49	46	9	232
Montrose	8,583	15,087	10,823	6,822	513	132	43	37
Morgan	2,148	3,468	1,531	788	5,961	3,842	863	1,521
Otero	9	150	52	53	2,010	836	496	688
Ouray	439	741	318	177	15	2	1	....
Park	1,053	1,918	1,501	1,069	....	....	....	....
Phillips	274	173	241	148	132	....	307	75
Pitkin	1,438	1,242	1,249	1,118	....	....	....	....
Prowers	12	33	4	4	344	277	123	198
Pueblo	9	37	51	143	7,433	8,953	2,896	4,318
Rio Blanco	87	189	219	200	5	....	1	7
Rio Grande	12,129	18,669	16,339	9,559	....	....	....	....
Routt	929	1,065	749	646	....	1	65	2
Saguache	4,118	5,875	3,540	2,120	....	....	4	....
San Miguel	926	130	142	152	12	12	4	....
Sedgwick	754	911	862	546	176	33	30	1
Summit	60	40	25	65	....	....	....	....
Teller	1,617	1,422	1,147	884	....	....	....	....
Washington	541	630	542	575	2,626	535	326	369
Weld	23,357	38,011	24,097	16,939	23,917	23,090	7,829	14,487
Yuma	554	673	782	903	451	31	88	31
State	90,542	142,612	101,159	69,320	134,182	103,878	43,618	56,548

ACREAGE OF CROPS REPORTED BY COUNTY ASSESSORS, 1923

COUNTY	Rye	Sugar Beets	Root Crops for Stock Feed	Field Peas	Winter Emmer	Spring Emmer	Flax	Alfalfa Seed, 1922	Broom Corn	Early Cabbage	Late Cabbage
lams	2,948	5,396	89	17	....	371	...	53	5	841	562
lamosa	....	....	....	4,710	....	....	...	....	.....	....	2
apahoe	1,112	228	9	....	....	81	...	12	5	28	56
chuleta	....	....	5	46	....	....	...	....	.....	1	....
ica	460	....	....	....	....	....	...	....	29,441	....	....
ent	193	2,756	28	5	....	70	...	30	484	....	....
oulder	60	7,170	6	305	....	12	...	....	.....	129	190
haffee	4	....	13	2,312	....	....	...	....	.....	10	3
heyenne	364	....	171	....	....	....	3	1	462	....	....
ear Creek	10	....	8	2	....	....	...	....	.....	....	....
nejos	....	....	3	11,135	....	....	...	....	.....	....	....
stilla	....	....	66	11,626	....	....	...	....	.....	....	....
owley	....	2,526	....	5	....	....	...	....	100	....	....
ister	133	....	....	134	....	....	16	10	.....	1	1
elta	8	2,710	2	7	....	....	10	....	22	....	....
olores	57	....	2	....	....	....	...	....	.....	....	....
ouglas	1,938	....	....	....	32	20	...	....	.....	....	....
igle	....	....	....	7	....	....	...	2	.....	....	....
bert	7,644	....	2	....	....	435	...	....	3	....	....
Paso	3,891	124	....	55	....	19	...	....	.....	....	3
emont	174	....	27	49	7	....	...	4	6	15	16
arfield	34	1,410	14	9	....	....	..*	5	2	4	2
lpin	24	....	2	10	....	....	...	....	.....	....	....
and	224	1	....	....	....	....	...	....	.....	....	....
innison	20	....	2	26	....	....	...	....	.....	....	2
insdale	....	....	....	....	....	....	...	....	.....	....	1
ierfano	166	3	9	259	2	....	...	39	3	3	2
ckson	26	....	1	23	....	....	1	....	.....	....	....
fferson	82	384	10	....	....	10	...	43	3	61	79
owa	37	....	....	....	....	....	20	....	537	....	....
t Carson	6,267	....	....	....	....	87	...	....	10	....	....
ke	2	....	....	....	....	....	...	....	.....	....	....
Plata	40	5	10	....	....	....	...	21	.....	....	....
rimer	164	13,018	131	152	....	50	...	....	14	14	59
s Animas	533	98	23	41	....	....	35	115	328	6	3
ncoln	5,586	....	....	7	147	697	36	28	.....	....	....
gan	7,171	15,340	2	....	....	180	10	101	7	5	31
sa	233	3,582	66	12	....	6	...	762	16	8	7
neral	....	....	....	2	....	....	...	....	.....	....	....
ffat	4,338	41	42	26	....	57	27	37	10	....	....
ntezuma	114	....	5	15	....	....	...	....	.....	....	....
ntrose	....	2,287	6	41	....	....	...	156	.....	1	6
rgan	3,654	22,089	57	....	....	65	...	72	125	25	70
ero	58	10,426	10	16	....	21	8	492	148	5	5
ay	22	17	....	3	....	....	...	....	.....	....	1
k	408	1	24	74	....	6	...	....	.....	....	1
llips	3,856	....	....	....	....	48	...	22	.....	....	....
kin	....	8	....	....	....	....	...	....	.....	....	....
wers	384	3,586	7	1	20	42	...	386	8,317	....	....
eblo	544	3,387	60	37	....	....	40	15	16	11	44
Blanco	353	1	10	....	....	....	...	1	.....	....	....
Grande	....	....	....	23,133	....	....	...	....	.....	....	....
itt	163	....	8	....	....	....	6	5	.....	....	....
uache	....	....	....	8,798	....	....	...	....	.....	....	....
Miguel	67	....	....	2	....	....	...	....	7	....	....
gwick	1,646	5,181	....	....	....	63	...	20	5	....	....
imit	61	....	....	....	....	....	...	....	.....	....	....
er	27	....	....	....	....	....	...	....	.....	....	....
hington	12,261	640	....	....	....	136	...	5	4	....	12
d	10,539	45,305	217	381	61	1,467	17	187	31	1,027	2,264
ia	15,630	....	....	....	....	32	...	....	2	....	....
State	93,730	147,720	1,147	63,483	269	3,975	229	2,624	40,113	2,195	3,422

ACREAGE OF CROPS REPORTED BY COUNTY ASSESSORS, 1923

COUNTY	Cauli-flower	Cucum-bers, Pickles	Cucum-bers, Seed	Toma-toes	Garden Peas	Beans for Market	Snap Beans	Beans for Seed	Sweet Corn	Sun-flowers	Lettuce
Adams	112	253	16	266	79	4,428	219	723	156	1	97
Alamosa	...	....	....	....	....	......	....	....	...	...	....
Arapahoe	2	7	3	5	6	6,493	51	....	4	...	13
Archuleta	...	....	....	....	....	12	....	5	...	...	....
Baca	...	....	....	....	60	225	....	....	...	...	....
Bent	...	7	13	2	....	413	18	133	...	3	....
Boulder	...	99	3	129	527	37	106	27	3	...	8
Chaffee	34	....	....	....	242	......	1	....	...	...	474
Cheyenne	...	....	....	....	....	150	....	....	2	3	....
Clear Creek	2	....	....	....	....	......	....	....	...	...	26
Conejos	...	....	....	....	....	529	2	....	1	...	42
Costilla	...	....	....	....	....	448	....	....	...	...	3
Crowley	...	53	10	3	2	1,340	....	110	...	...	....
Custer	55	....	....	....	44	......	....	5	...	...	824
Delta	...	....	....	7	....	98	17	79	15	7	12
Dolores	...	....	....	....	....	83	8	4	...	...	....
Douglas	...	....	....	....	....	313	....	....	...	...	6
Eagle	14	...	....	....	....	......	....	....	...	...	741
Elbert	...	...	....	....	....	28,295	....	....	...	...	....
El Paso	1	....	1	....	2	24,639	....	30	15	...	....
Fremont	65	12	4	15	34	25	57	40	28	...	171
Garfield	...	4	....	6	2	28	10	1	33	...	5
Gilpin	...	....	....	....	15	......	....	....	...	...	11
Grand	6	....	....	....	6	......	....	....	...	...	1,507
Gunnison	1	....	....	....	....	......	3	....	...	...	200
Hinsdale	1	....	....	....	....	......	....	....	...	...	2
Huerfano	...	....	1	....	1	1,142	4	10	...	1	10
Jackson	...	....	....	....	....	......	....	....	...	...	139
Jefferson	67	39	3	62	41	11	3	3	122	...	56
Kiowa	...	....	....	....	....	97	....	....	...	...	....
Kit Carson	...	....	....	....	....	295	....	8	...	...	....
Lake	...	....	....	....	....	......	....	....	...	...	20
La Plata	...	....	....	....	....	105	....	201	4	...	....
Larimer	3	21	....	13	44	456	12	128	56	2	2
Las Animas	...	....	....	15	3	6,082	....	73	...	88	9
Lincoln	...	....	....	1	....	10,410	....	....	...	...	....
Logan	...	175	....	6	....	3,474	13	580	...	10	....
Mesa	2	2	8	537	133	733	187	83	15	16	3
Mineral	...	....	....	....	....	......	....	....	...	...	281
Moffat	...	....	....	....	....	177	....	57	2	47	....
Montezuma	...	....	....	3	6	49	....	29	3	1	....
Montrose	...	....	....	1	14	513	38	12	8	4	1
Morgan	...	80	....	11	....	5,961	....	290	...	22	....
Otero	4	107	1,836	688	39	2,010	45	262	13	...	2
Ouray	...	....	....	....	....	15	2	....	...	...	....
Park	...	....	....	....	3	......	....	....	...	...	[illegible]
Phillips	...	....	....	....	....	132	....	....	...	...	....
Pitkin	3	....	....	....	....	......	....	....	...	...	32
Prowers	11	1	16	10	....	344	....	121	...	1	....
Pueblo	28	27	294	41	7	7,433	74	158	25	17	79
Rio Blanco	...	....	....	....	....	5	....	3	...	...	....
Rio Grande	...	....	....	....	....	......	....	....	...	...	50
Routt	...	1	....	....	....	......	....	1	...	45	521
Saguache	...	....	....	....	....	......	....	....	...	...	49
San Miguel	...	....	....	....	....	12	....	5	...	...	66
Sedgwick	...	....	....	....	....	176	12	....	...	...	....
Summit	...	....	....	....	....	......	....	....	...	...	5
Teller	...	....	....	....	....	......	....	....	...	...	448
Washington	...	....	....	....	....	2,626	....	....	...	...	....
Weld	23	318	22	451	1,289	23,917	468	3,107	22	57	8
Yuma	...	....	1	....	....	451	....	1	1	...	....
State	434	1,206	2,231	2,272	2,599	134,182	1,350	6,289	528	325	6,163

ACREAGE OF CROPS REPORTED BY COUNTY ASSESSORS, 1923

COUNTY	Canta-loupes for Market	Canta-loupes for Seed	Honey-dew Melons	Water-melons	Pump-kins, etc.	Dry Onions	Green Onions	Onion Seed	Celery	Farm Garden
Adams	109	3	19	83	40	146	31	6	212	310
Alamosa	....	....	....	....	....	....	....	....	....	....
Arapahoe	1	....	....	40	3	4	16	20	25	102
Archuleta	....	....	....	....	21	....	....	....	....	....
Baca	....	....	5	5	50	....	....	....	....	....
Bent	1,286	29	93	16	....	4	....	....	....	51
Boulder	14	....	5	9	109	2	....	....	1	153
Chaffee	....	....	....	....	....	....	....	....	8	57
Cheyenne	2	....	....	7	2	....	....	....	....	....
Clear Creek	....	....	....	....	....	....	....	....	....	9
Conejos	....	....	....	....	....	....	....	....	....	....
Costilla	....	....	....	....	....	....	....	....	....	38
Crowley	1,758	221	5	84	33	2	....	....	....	9
Custer	....	....	....	....	....	....	....	....	....	7
Delta	....	....	2	37	11	838	4	3	....	447
Dolores	....	....	....	....	3	....	....	3	....	88
Douglas	....	....	....	....	20	....	....	....	....	9
Eagle	....	....	....	....	....	....	....	....	....	69
Elbert	....	....	2	....	6	....	....	....	....	69
El Paso	....	....	....	....	2	....	....	....	2	26
Fremont	6	23	....	3	76	6	4	2	25	743
Garfield	1	....	....	4	17	4	1	....	2	312
Gilpin	....	....	....	....	....	....	....	....	....	9
Grand	....	....	....	....	....	....	....	....	....	9
Gunnison	....	....	....	....	....	....	....	....	....	134
Hinsdale	....	....	....	....	....	....	....	....	....	11
Huerfano	2	1	....	2	17	2	....	....	....	75
Jackson	....	....	....	....	....	....	....	....	....	34
Jefferson	....	....	....	5	4	13	6	2	146	812
Kiowa	....	....	....	35	55	....	....	....	....	53
Kit Carson	....	....	....	16	1	....	....	....	....	179
Lake	....	....	....	....	....	....	....	....	....	1
La Plata	....	....	....	....	59	....	2	....	....	18
Larimer	3	....	1	3	6	14	9	2	12	5
Las Animas	37	1	41	18	23	2	....	....	....	186
Lincoln	....	....	2	25	....	....	....	....	....	67
Logan	2	....	1	8	....	17	5	....	....	172
Mesa	81	2	1	40	44	1	14	2	34	370
Mineral	....	....	....	....	....	....	....	....	....	8
Moffat	....	....	....	5	4	....	....	....	....	556
Montezuma	6	1	3	14	....	1	....	....	1	114
Montrose	....	....	....	....	48	919	28	2	....	84
Morgan	2	1	1	5	1	7	1	....	....	74
Otero	3,653	875	662	269	33	54	9	4	13	282
Ouray	....	....	....	....	....	....	....	....	....	60
Park	....	....	....	....	....	1	....	....	....	....
Phillips	....	....	7	3	3	....	....	....	....	19
Pitkin	....	....	....	....	....	....	....	....	....	35
Prowers	29	3	2	24	3	4	....	....	1	808
Pueblo	59	27	....	272	43	6	4	1	50	308
Rio Blanco	....	....	....	....	....	....	....	....	....	30
Rio Grande	....	....	....	....	....	....	....	....	....	....
Routt	....	....	....	1	2	....	....	....	....	48
Saguache	....	....	....	....	....	....	....	....	....	....
San Miguel	....	....	....	....	....	....	....	....	....	72
Sedgwick	4	....	....	2	....	....	....	....	....	....
Summit	....	....	....	....	....	....	....	....	....	18
Teller	....	....	....	....	....	....	....	....	....	....
Washington	1	....	....	4	....	....	....	....	....	115
Weld	84	5	8	86	83	244	23	18	15	225
Yuma	7	....	....	64	6	....	....	....	....	41
State	7,147	1,192	860	1,189	828	2,291	157	65	547	7,631

ACREAGE OF HAY CROPS REPORTED BY COUNTY ASSESSORS, 1923

COUNTY	Alfalfa	Sweet Clover	Other Clover	Timothy	Timothy and Clover Mixed	Millet	Sudan Grass	Other Tame Grass	Wild Grass Cut for Hay	All Hay
Adams	21,248	42	14	8	20	1,049	340	4	1,436	24,161
Alamosa	19,323	....	...	....	....	....	....	....	14,820	34,143
Arapahoe	12,603	37	...	15	22	326	97	....	18	13,118
Archuleta	2,504	....	...	127	3,412	34	....	249	843	7,169
Baca	810	20	...	....	....	20	650	....	....	1,500
Bent	15,436	231	...	6	....	37	635	3	....	16,348
Boulder	17,803	160	2	514	400	8	12	93	1,447	20,439
Chaffee	5,146	....	8	522	2,453	2	....	159	654	8,944
Cheyenne	495	335	16	....	11	2,240	1,115	....	....	4,212
Clear Creek ...	56	....	...	4	272	....	....	64	120	516
Conejos	10,110	1,160	...	100	....	10	4	10	11,462	22,856
Costilla	5,440	134	...	8	319	28	....	78	3,078	9,085
Crowley	7,728	....	...	....	....	....	25	....	....	7,753
Custer	1,826	....	...	....	....	13	....	296	10,962	13,097
Delta	25,375	96	14	77	52	71	31	24	32	25,772
Dolores	288	24	...	15	70	34	100	1	....	532
Douglas	7,391	24	6	46	2,262	591	289	208	827	11,644
Eagle	7,136	....	...	58	2,808	....	....	2	60	10,064
Elbert	6,787	129	5	....	....	3,270	219	20	864	11,294
El Paso	4,100	168	...	162	....	6,885	221	175	3,379	15,090
Fremont	5,842	3	12	303	603	106	27	82	552	7,530
Garfield	29,475	26	...	545	322	2	6	27	600	31,003
Gilpin	25	....	10	123	115	....	2	20	309	604
Grand	554	....	...	20	13,102	25	....	539	10,749	24,989
Gunnison	2,207	....	...	724	4,979	....	....	773	20,587	29,270
Hinsdale	54	....	2	51	1,639	....	....	....	918	2,664
Huerfano	7,026	100	8	110	362	444	70	280	1,194	9,594
Jackson	13	1	...	40	30	1	....	....	68,848	68,933
Jefferson	13,906	67	10	100	733	13	....	21	227	15,077
Kiowa	1,862	216	...	....	10	363	552	....	....	3,003
Kit Carson ...	1,157	353	...	20	25	4,341	1,296	....	1,233	8,425
Lake	....	....	7	25	70	....	....	....	3,137	3,239
La Plata	17,791	182	220	392	362	10	14	361	977	20,309
Larimer	39,558	33	12	160	94	109	10	661	2,600	43,237
Las Animas ..	9,934	90	10	758	378	463	619	63	545	12,860
Lincoln	2,254	414	...	....	....	6,060	1,337	....	570	10,635
Logan	20,859	517	40	2	55	6,270	1,556	268	11,751	41,318
Mesa	32,397	23	5	128	129	54	51	35	15	32,837
Mineral	11	....	...	25	37	....	....	....	2,285	2,358
Moffat	11,616	192	1	761	1,632	455	1,054	1,695	3,752	21,158
Montezuma ...	10,405	89	...	120	57	2	46	183	553	11,455
Montrose	28,741	967	11	689	760	1	18	133	95	31,415
Morgan	23,391	304	...	5	5	6,410	738	....	1,072	31,925
Otero	21,651	144	116	....	....	91	321	49	256	22,628
Ouray	2,284	....	10	66	2,969	2	....	7	1,338	6,676
Park	25	11	...	57	77	3	....	....	28,627	28,800
Phillips	1,889	936	...	....	....	11,279	1,903	....	8	16,015
Pitkin	1,605	....	...	382	6,421	....	....	....	....	8,408
Prowers	31,937	113	...	....	5	220	1,162	52	467	33,956
Pueblo	22,024	31	8	651	383	140	129	16	1,052	24,434
Rio Blanco ...	10,035	609	2	241	2,203	109	6	725	1,704	15,634
Rio Grande ..	9,061	27	...	....	....	....	....	....	6,685	15,773
Routt	3,596	64	64	591	21,730	4	54	1,200	348	27,651
Saguache	3,962	....	...	....	....	....	....	....	22,740	26,702
San Miguel ...	5,132	24	...	1,498	1,522	36	....	....	....	8,212
Sedgwick	3,991	308	...	....	....	2,842	1,156	70	95	8,462
Summit	9	....	...	....	4,712	....	....	....	152	4,873
Teller	....	....	...	775	....	....	....	....	1,374	2,149
Washington ..	4,018	289	11	....	54	5,762	2,375	594	698	13,801
Weld	95,841	1,311	11	....	70	13,353	297	5,952	1,053	117,888
Yuma	2,358	253	19	....	55	5,772	977	44	1,796	11,274
State......	650,101	10,257	654	11,024	77,801	79,360	19,514	15,236	250,964	1,114,911

ACREAGE OF SUGAR BEETS, 1923

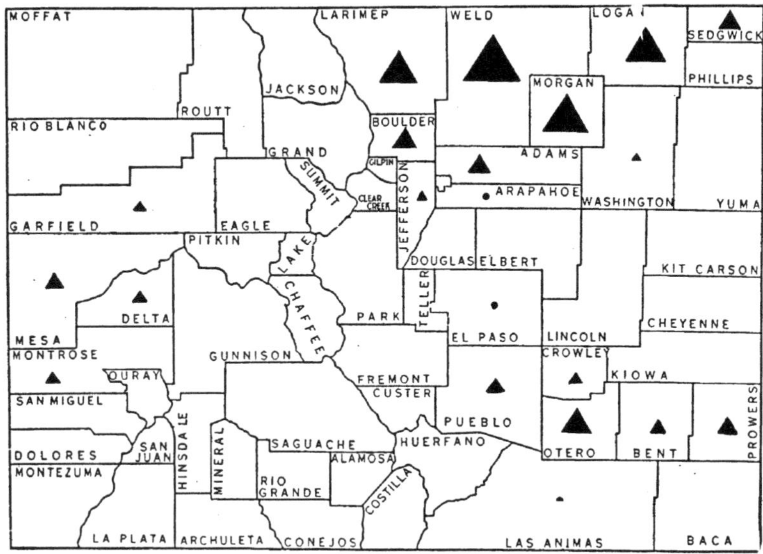

The largest triangle represents 45,305 acres. The dot represents less than 450 acres.

ACREAGE OF ALFALFA, 1923

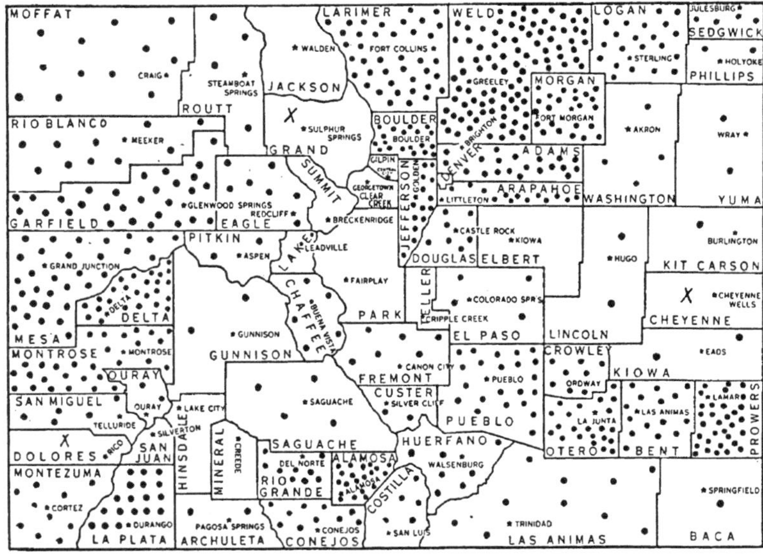

Each dot represents 1,000 acres. The cross (X) is used in counties reporting less than 500 acres.

ACREAGE OF ALFALFA AND WILD GRASS CUT FOR HAY IN COLORADO AS REPORTED BY COUNTY ASSESSORS

COUNTY	ALFALFA				WILD GRASS CUT FOR HAY			
	1923	1922	1921	1920	1923	1922	1921	1920
Adams	21,248	21,176	17,589	19,245	1,436	744	105	714
Alamosa	19,323	17,975	17,670	12,387	14,820	10,670	13,275	6,410
Arapahoe	12.603	8,625	5,744	11,580	18	1	259	356
Archuleta	2,504	2,593	2,398	3,656	843	626	1,159	1,147
Baca	810	412	1,178	694	....	....	....	....
Bent	15,436	16,001	15,895	10,933	....	10	....	....
Boulder	17,803	18,901	14,903	21,517	1,447	2,110	1,266	1,989
Chaffee	5,146	4,640	4,944	4,929	654	431	879	1,137
Cheyenne	495	595	498	382	....	40	30	....
Clear Creek	56	46	38	44	120	113	325	385
Conejos	10,110	10,906	7,928	4,203	11,462	11.950	7.602	3.897
Costilla	5,440	5,335	5,421	5,206	3,078	4,325	3,705	317
Crowley	7,728	8,978	9,462	13,888	....	....	220	17
Custer	1,826	1,925	1,872	1,848	10,962	10,733	11,579	3,740
Delta	25,375	31,309	32,042	28,735	32	....	28	13
Dolores	288	246	264	590	....	133	25	50
Douglas	7,391	7,854	8,520	7,544	827	1,556	2,236	2.025
Eagle	7.136	8,208	8,205	7,681	60	29	335	133
Elbert	6,787	6,726	6.213	6.315	864	1.440	1,896	2.365
El Paso	4,100	4,568	4,340	1,720	3,379	2,567	2,658	2,989
Fremont	5,842	5,511	4,514	5,768	552	1,727	1,264	1,177
Garfield	29,475	30,770	31,344	32,135	600	141	308	109
Gilpin	25	6	6	3	309	517	527	538
Grand	554	217	389	116	10,749	12,011	13,183	6,962
Gunnison	2,207	1,681	1,803	1,987	20,587	15,596	20,718	22,566
Hinsdale	54	....	....	42	918	1,992	1,962	1,130
Huerfano	7,026	6,326	6,776	14,535	1,194	1,364	297	1,981
Jackson	13	13	....	....	68,848	54,921	71,176	73,045
Jefferson	13,906	15,784	14,531	11,325	227	134	729	631
Kiowa	1,862	979	760	18	....	....	170	....
Kit Carson	1,157	2,415	1,237	1,187	1,233	379	1,084	625
Lake	....	1	1	....	3.137	2,408	4.130	3,402
La Plata	17,791	20.282	19,142	16.306	977	528	685	438
Larimer	39,558	41,075	41,695	36,281	2,600	692	3,930	907
Las Animas	9,934	9,070	8,001	7,501	545	398	482	369
Lincoln	2,254	2,938	1,968	1,603	570	559	651	422
Logan	20,859	21,431	20,923	19,577	11,751	12,604	12.513	13,488
Mesa	32,397	34,848	34,910	27,061	15	41	152	241
Mineral	11	....	7	12	2,285	2,422	2.118	2,199
Moffat	11,616	9,941	7,235	5.566	3,752	3,587	2,278	2.005
Montezuma	10,405	13,004	14,981	20,258	553	....	30	60
Montrose	28,741	24,679	27,028	31,380	95	20	25	171
Morgan	23,391	23,117	22,353	21,444	1,072	1,186	880	1,219
Otero	21,651	23,465	20,415	25,419	256	40	81	34
Ouray	2,284	2,101	1,537	2,477	1,338	1,175	20	155
Park	25	40	26	34	28,627	29.973	34.459	24.522
Phillips	1,889	2,129	1,717	1,330	8	287	281	219
Pitkin	1,605	2,483	2,634	2,532	....	405	879	28
Prowers	31,937	31,523	29,005	32,039	467	905	260	210
Pueblo	22,024	25,478	23,613	24,891	1.052	941	903	1,431
Rio Blanco	10,035	11,426	11,199	8,837	1.704	1,491	1.288	1,819
Rio Grande	9.061	7,355	8.225	5.688	6.685	5.916	6.560	7.168
Routt	3,596	3,622	3,250	3,056	348	636	678	2,833
Saguache	3,962	3,519	5.037	3,194	22.740	22,251	23,555	11,770
San Miguel	5,132	4.760	5.707	4,749	....	....	90	....
Sedgwick	3,991	3,801	4,189	3,913	95	1,154	1,774	2,871
Summit	9	14	10	20	152	215	4,732	1,372
Teller	....	....	1	15	1,374	375	40	727
Washington	4,018	2,833	4,245	4,422	698	237	1,371	4,275
Weld	95,841	100,424	89,696	103,409	1,053	2,399	3,266	3,644
Yuma	2,358	2,887	3,236	4,030	1,796	2,827	2,300	1,820
State	650,101	668,967	638,470	646,757	250,964	231,932	269,411	226,270

ACREAGE OF FIELD PEAS, 1923

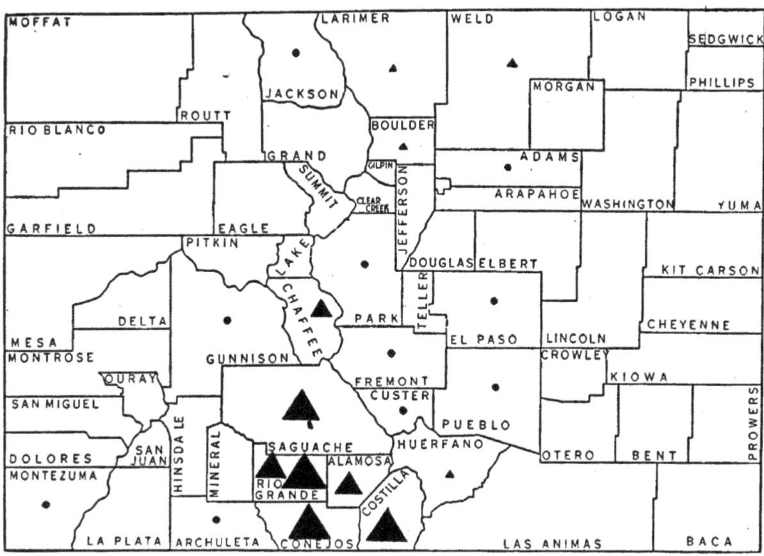

The largest triangle represents 23,133 acres. The dot represents less than 200 acres.

ACREAGE OF ONIONS, 1923

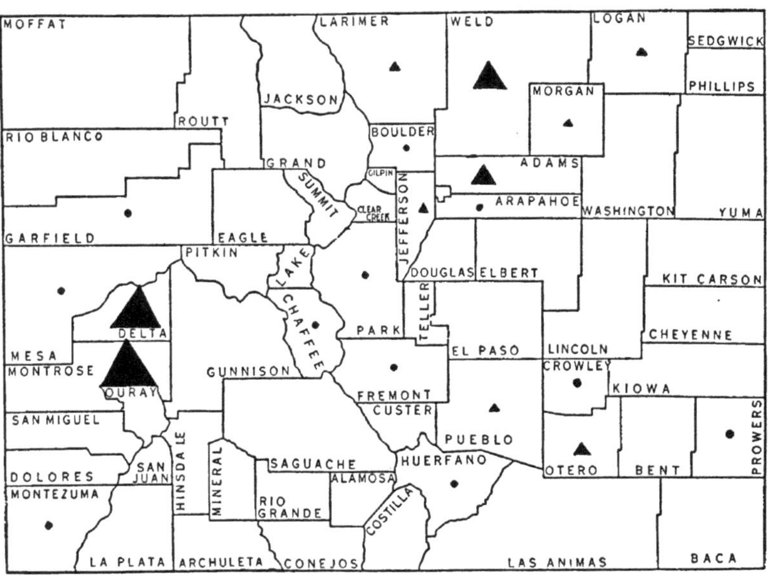

The largest triangle represents 919 acres. The dot represents less than 9 acres.

ACREAGE OF CABBAGE, 1923

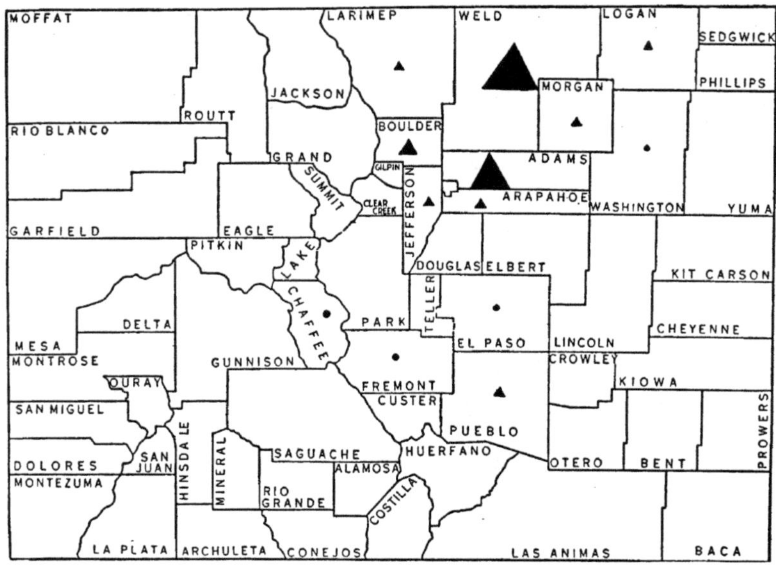

The largest triangle represents 3,291 acres. The dot represents less than 25 acres.

ACREAGE OF LETTUCE, 1923

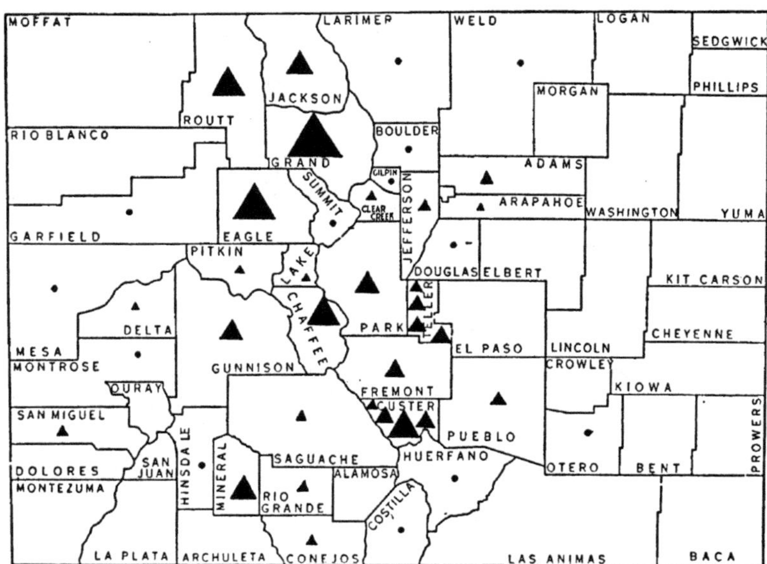

The largest triangle represents 1,507 acres. The dot represents less than 10 acres.

DISTRIBUTION OF APPLE TREES AS REPORTED BY THE CENSUS BUREAU

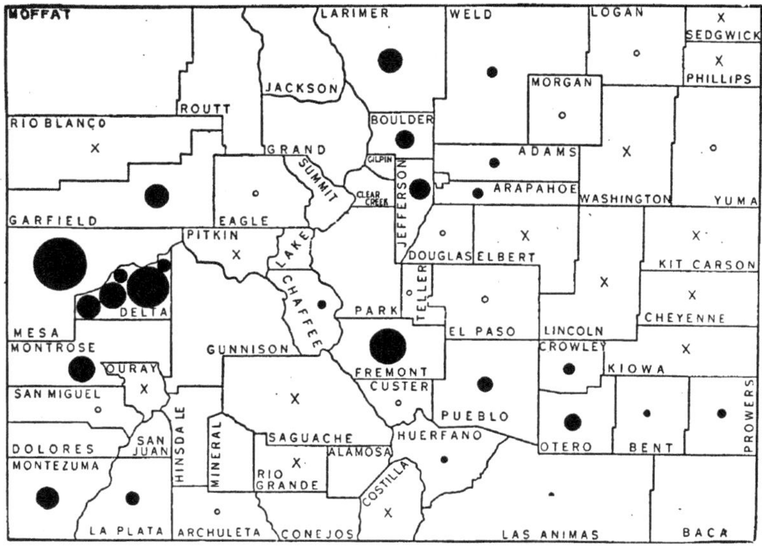

The largest circle represents 447,800 trees. The cross (X) represents fewer than 2,500 trees.

DISTRIBUTION OF PEACH TREES AS REPORTED BY THE CENSUS BUREAU

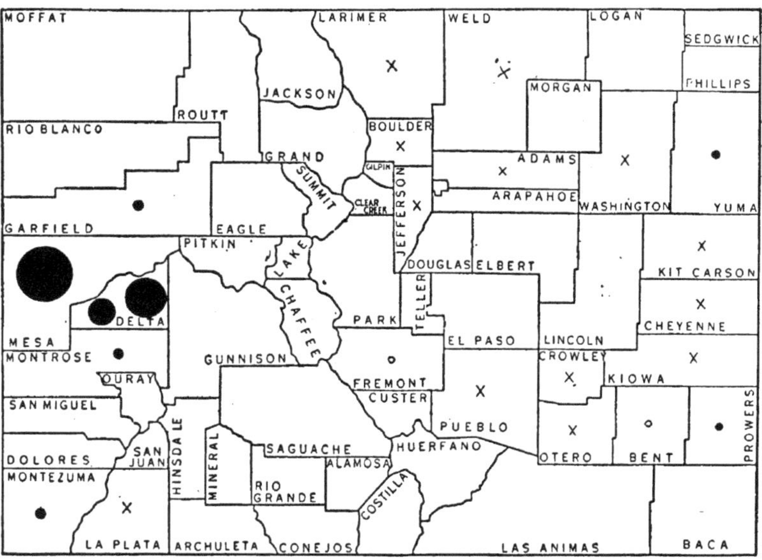

The largest circle represents 242,200 trees. The cross (X) represents fewer than 1,000 trees.

DISTRIBUTION OF PEAR TREES AS REPORTED BY THE CENSUS BUREAU

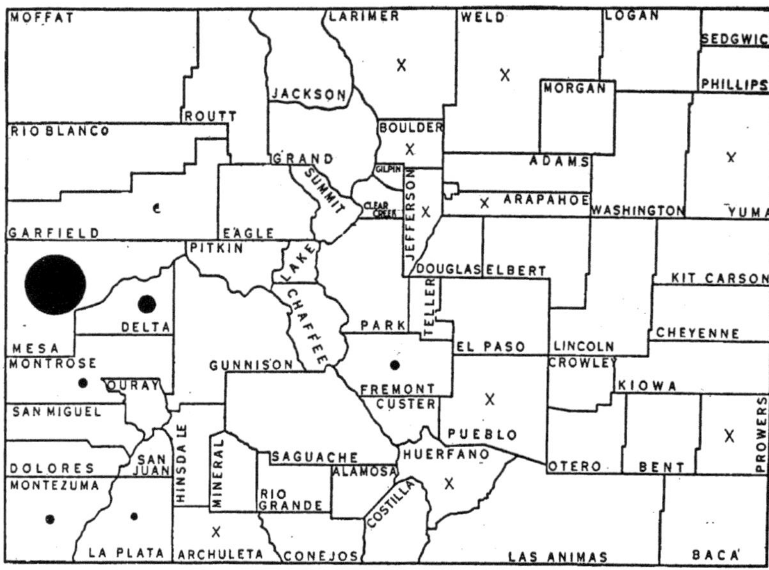

The largest circle represents 115,525 trees. The cross (X) represents fewer than 500 trees.

DISTRIBUTION OF CHERRY TREES AS REPORTED BY THE CENSUS BUREAU

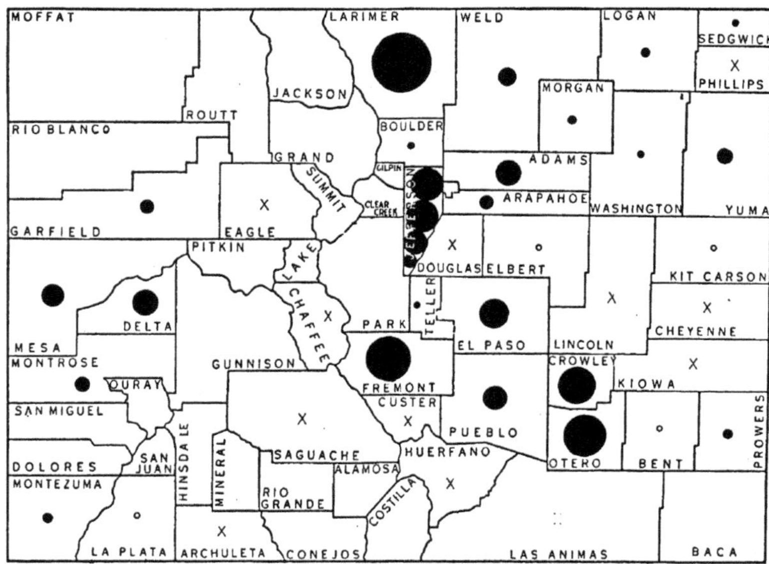

The largest circle represents 73,169 trees. The cross (X) represents fewer than 500 trees.

PER CENT CULTIVATED AREA DEVOTED TO PRINCIPAL CROPS, 1923

COUNTY	Corn	Winter Wheat	Spring Wheat	Oats	Barley	Rye	Sorghums	Alfalfa	Sugar Beets
Adams	20.87	32.99	8.11	2.94	3.37	1.78	5.83	12.85	3.26
Alamosa	.02	....	5.45	7.04	3.05	....	....	41.98	....
Arapahoe	26.47	31.17	3.12	1.93	3.31	1.38	7.27	15.67	.28
Archuleta	2.89	.06	5.28	21.36	6.18	....	....	21.90	....
Baca	17.33	13.82	4.18	.09	1.69	.23	46.63	.41	....
Bent	27.50	12.97	2.96	.91	1.25	.24	26.69	19.46	3.47
Boulder	12.76	18.27	16.27	5.69	4.18	.08	.04	25.52	10.28
Chaffee	.07	....	7.74	10.57	7.24	.02	....	30.72	....
Cheyenne	38.36	27.90	.90	.47	5.48	....	20.72	.56	....
Clear Creek	3.86	....	1.12	17.91	.50	1.24	....	6.96	....
Conejos	.09	.02	14.40	6.62	14.56	....	.01	17.06	....
Costilla	.19	.18	13.17	6.43	10.33	....	....	17.64	....
Crowley	33.88	2.75	1.63	5.89	2.53	....	15.22	20.94	6.84
Custer	5.36	1.32	6.28	15.81	6.16	.55	.14	7.75	....
Delta	8.28	1.02	9.64	7.41	1.37	.02	.02	56.32	6.01
Dolores	50.88	2.71	9.55	11.55	2.42	.61	13.51	3.08	....
Douglas	37.31	10.46	3.32	12.99	1.03	4.21	3.97	16.09	....
Eagle	....	4.60	5.51	11.57	1.63	....	....	44.91	....
Elbert	35.77	14.38	4.85	5.96	1.20	5.21	4.93	4.63	....
El Paso	45.93	2.09	1.83	9.57	.41	3.18	3.40	3.35	.10
Fremont	19.65	1.41	2.32	11.42	5.97	1.06	.48	35.64	....
Garfield	3.86	1.02	10.98	5.47	1.24	.07	.04	61.41	2.94
Gilpin	.07	.42	....	40.04	3.50	1.68	....	1.75	....
Grand	.35	.59	.06	2.54	.52	.79	....	1.97	.01
Gunnison	.01	.37	.47	3.32	1.23	.06	....	6.97	....
Hinsdale	....	....	.01	1.93	.78	....	....	1.93	....
Huerfano	25.72	2.05	5.91	8.84	3.05	.75	2.44	31.96	.01
Jackson	.01	.03	....	.19	.07	.03	....	.02	....
Jefferson	11.06	13.82	12.09	9.34	4.84	.22	.01	38.95	1.07
Kiowa	41.77	14.73	.24	.16	1.99	.04	36.86	2.12	....
Kit Carson	33.05	41.21	2.03	1.07	8.37	1.89	9.37	.35	....
Lake	....	....	....	....	1.53	.06	....	....	....
La Plata	7.65	1.55	16.41	11.89	4.42	.11	.16	48.06	.01
Larimer	11.97	7.16	14.14	6.93	3.93	.15	.02	37.74	12.42
Las Animas	26.11	21.76	4.27	3.76	1.24	.62	18.55	11.62	.11
Lincoln	35.19	24.65	7.23	.91	4.85	2.98	11.71	1.20	....
Logan	27.57	32.28	11.26	2.82	3.78	1.78	4.66	5.19	3.81
Mesa	12.39	3.74	4.09	5.67	.90	.39	.69	53.81	5.95
Mineral	....	....	....	3.21	....	....	....	.39	....
Moffat	13.11	3.99	14.23	1.75	1.76	8.19	1.80	21.94	.08
Montezuma	21.51	2.22	10.35	9.20	6.31	.47	.90	42.59	....
Montrose	5.88	1.08	16.42	8.57	.71	....	.01	43.70	3.47
Morgan	37.11	10.73	2.72	2.14	4.64	1.92	7.55	12.31	11.62
Otero	19.74	5.82	2.51	4.61	1.46	.08	5.69	29.11	14.02
Ouray	.22	1.58	10.94	11.02	6.26	.21	....	22.08	.16
Park	.01	.02	.20	11.04	3.74	1.13	....	.06	.01
Phillips	32.64	46.43	1.82	3.91	1.62	1.83	3.87	.89	....
Pitkin	....	.31	2.77	10.70	1.67	....	....	13.16	.06
Prowers	15.50	25.11	1.67	1.15	1.93	.24	24.22	20.17	2.26
Pueblo	32.08	8.87	2.68	3.57	2.10	.61	8.48	24.88	3.83
Rio Blanco	.51	2.11	15.03	11.20	3.58	1.47	....	42.03	.01
Rio Grande	....	....	7.77	6.76	3.70	....	....	14.52	....
Routt	.08	4.71	14.39	15.97	8.01	.32	.01	6.96	....
Saguache	....	....	7.89	7.05	2.46	....	....	8.24	....
San Miguel	6.93	3.26	4.63	9.72	26.09	.34	1.32	26.30	....
Sedgwick	34.06	26.79	15.04	4.88	2.47	1.41	2.74	3.42	4.44
Summit	....	.75	.15	3.91	1.20	1.14	....	.16	....
Teller	....	....	....	74.25	6.05	.12	....	....	....
Washington	27.87	45.70	3.57	1.37	8.12	2.76	6.53	.81	.14
Weld	16.04	13.06	12.62	4.32	5.22	2.08	2.55	18.96	8.96
Yuma	43.10	33.80	2.36	1.05	4.09	4.37	7.73	.65	....
State	24.09	19.62	6.33	4.20	4.17	1.99	7.98	11.99	2.72

ACREAGE UNDER CULTIVATION AS REPORTED BY COUNTY ASSESSORS

COUNTY	Acreage in Cultivation				Percent of Total Area in Cultivation			
	1923	1922	1921	1920	1923	1922	1921	1920
Adams	165,250	174,264	148,302	144,927	20.45	21.58	18.34	17.94
Alamosa	46,020	45,623	40,174	28,757	9.80	9.81	8.63	6.23
Arapahoe	80,414	69,904	43,148	78,731	14.91	12.97	8.01	14.61
Archuleta	11,430	10,103	14,683	15,413	1.46	1.29	1.88	1.97
Baca	195,996	245,914	197,336	85,740	12.00	15.06	12.08	5.24
Bent	79,325	89,192	81,280	60,687	8.11	9.14	8.33	6.22
Boulder	69,750	76,774	57,470	82,774	14.26	15.70	11.75	16.93
Chaffee	16,750	15,880	16,375	14,536	2.41	2.29	2.63	2.09
Cheyenne	86,715	115,500	88,701	55,093	7.62	10.16	7.79	4.84
Clear Creek	804	865	965	968	.32	.34	.39	.39
Conejos	59,265	65,723	56,789	38,734	7.40	8.20	7.08	4.83
Costilla	30,833	44,625	40,426	34,316	4.07	5.88	5.33	4.52
Crowley	36,903	37,674	47,045	51,893	7.14	7.29	9.10	10.04
Custer	23,561	24,745	25,946	20,704	4.93	5.18	5.43	4.33
Delta	45,048	53,723	53,309	50,232	5.81	6.99	6.94	6.54
Dolores	9,334	10,962	8,671	6,549	1.40	1.64	1.30	.98
Douglas	45,947	45,817	51,209	45,100	8.49	8.47	9.47	8.23
Eagle	15,889	22,197	21,226	16,525	1.53	3.05	2.05	1.59
Elbert	146,440	149,461	142,486	135,113	12.32	12.57	11.99	11.36
El Paso	122,027	118,627	128,453	116,479	8.98	8.74	9.46	8.58
Fremont	16,390	17,346	15,872	17,571	1.64	1.74	1.59	1.76
Garfield	47,995	54,206	52,056	52,143	2.41	2.73	2.62	2.62
Gilpin	1,426	1,257	1,349	1,283	1.69	1.49	1.59	1.52
Grand	28,030	30,277	27,646	24,987	2.34	2.54	2.32	2.09
Gunnison	31,657	33,069	32,592	34,215	1.55	1.63	1.60	1.68
Hinsdale	2,797	2,141	2,163	2,293	.45	.34	.34	.37
Huerfano	21,979	27,165	21,717	48,291	2.29	2.82	2.26	5.03
Jackson	69,373	55,399	71,559	73,220	6.64	5.30	6.85	7.01
Jefferson	35,702	48,932	40,303	30,678	6.90	9.46	7.79	5.93
Kiowa	77,761	89,928	68,172	33,554	7.63	7.81	5.92	2.92
Kit Carson	330,345	296,273	312,540	210,820	23.90	21.44	22.62	15.26
Lake	3,316	2,902	4,605	3,643	1.40	1.22	1.94	1.53
La Plata	37,017	41,432	45,708	40,022	3.12	3.50	3.85	3.37
Larimer	104,808	109,594	115,883	103,473	6.23	6.51	6.89	6.15
Las Animas	85,468	100,573	91,208	81,013	2.77	3.26	2.96	2.63
Lincoln	186,862	178,972	176,490	156,106	6.07	10.88	10.73	9.49
Logan	401,678	425,057	432,110	403,428	34.44	36.45	37.05	34.59
Mesa	60,200	63,336	62,512	46,791	2.97	3.13	3.08	2.31
Mineral	2,796	2,957	2,863	3,106	.50	.53	.52	.56
Moffat	52,932	60,159	52,112	53,687	1.77	2.01	1.74	1.80
Montezuma	24,425	33,713	33,116	45,442	1.86	2.57	2.52	3.46
Montrose	65,764	62,340	62,845	67,808	4.54	4.30	4.34	4.67
Morgan	190,070	181,957	179,825	170,001	23.09	22.11	21.85	20.66
Otero	74,363	84,345	78,972	88,894	9.23	10.47	9.80	11.03
Ouray	10,343	11,369	9,508	9,668	3.11	3.42	2.86	2.91
Park	36,002	38,326	41,329	31,091	2.50	2.66	2.87	2.16
Phillips	210,459	212,244	190,494	182,067	47.79	48.20	43.26	41.35
Pitkin	12,192	13,499	14,820	12,770	1.87	2.07	2.27	1.96
Prowers	158,157	171,825	149,585	127,916	15.16	16.47	14.34	12.26
Pueblo	88,533	111,240	90,320	93,114	5.69	7.14	5.80	5.97
Rio Blanco	23,874	30,336	33,538	30,941	1.15	1.47	1.63	1.50
Rio Grande	62,418	72,706	76,489	68,540	10.86	12.65	13.31	11.92
Routt	51,653	56,783	59.744	64,817	3.49	3.84	4.14	4.37
Saguache	48,030	49,357	52,691	36,387	2.39	2.46	2.63	1.81
San Miguel	19,506	12,985	17,613	17,745	2.37	1.57	2.14	2.15
Sedgwick	116,650	117,043	114,863	102,069	34.32	34.44	33.80	30.03
Summit	5,338	6,724	5,164	5,842	1.28	1.61	1.24	1.41
Teller	21,540	15,965	7,078	8,226	6.15	4.56	2.02	2.34
Washington	443,672	391,588	341,196	361,071	27.49	24.27	21.14	22.37
Weld	505,317	569,176	530,803	630,663	19.63	22.11	20.62	24.62
Yuma	357,562	411,582	374,337	351,154	23.60	27.16	24.71	23.18
State	5,422,100	5,713,651	5,357,784	5,009,821	8.17	8.61	8.08	7.55

AVERAGE YIELD OF PRINCIPAL CROPS PER ACRE, 1923

COUNTY	Winter Wheat Bu.	Spring Wheat Bu.	All Wheat Bu.	Corn Bu.	Oats Bu.	Barley Bu.	Potatoes Bu.
Adams	13.54	18.59	14.54	21.22	36.95	25.21	55.50
Alamosa	....	20.00	20.00	25.00	33.00	27.00	130.00
Arapahoe	12.87	22.23	13.72	20.49	27.89	23.26	48.57
Archuleta	25.00	16.90	17.00	20.25	27.11	22.00	70.00
Baca	6.17	6.00	6.13	19.20	15.00	16.55	.....
Bent	18.58	18.11	18.50	31.44	41.68	24.73	.....
Boulder	26.16	23.61	24.96	32.69	43.86	39.17	70.78
Chaffee	....	24.00	24.00	27.69	45.00	25.94	88.01
Cheyenne	6.00	5.00	5.96	27.00	23.00	22.00	64.11
Clear Creek	....	19.00	19.00	18.00	30.59	32.00	60.00
Conejos	25.00	20.00	20.00	25.43	36.00	35.00	140.00
Costilla	25.00	16.44	16.55	24.39	34.98	31.99	107.48
Crowley	15.23	19.32	16.76	30.24	36.65	25.38	.....
Custer	22.91	18.01	18.86	20.10	34.55	26.90	40.25
Delta	29.59	28.00	28.15	39.93	42.93	36.63	159.12
Dolores	18.28	15.00	15.72	16.00	20.60	21.00	60.94
Douglas	11.19	12.06	11.40	21.03	25.17	23.00	100.00
Eagle	20 00	32.00	31.86	....	49.87	33.10	189.71
Elbert	10.05	10.13	10.07	23.00	26.00	22.04	50.94
El Paso	12.00	13.17	12.55	20.26	26.34	23.68	60.00
Fremont	24.79	26.97	26.14	29.93	32.83	22.80	52.01
Garfield	28.23	27.65	27.20	38.04	47.63	40.38	167.35
Gilpin	14.00	....	14.00	18.00	30.00	25.00	40.00
Grand	23.55	20.26	23.21	20.00	38.84	37.24	73.23
Gunnison	18.16	22.97	20.83	16.00	27.03	26 18	102.77
Hinsdale	....	25.00	25.00	....	25.92	35.90	129.50
Huerfano	16.35	7.06	9.45	23.17	32.74	26.57	37.83
Jackson	19.11	....	19.11	19.33	39.72	32.50	100.00
Jefferson	28.81	28.77	28.79	35.19	39.62	40.41	75.85
Kiowa	10.00	8.00	9.96	24.00	22.00	17.00	40.00
Kit Carson	7.00	4.00	6.85	27.00	18.10	21.06	65.03
Lake	....	....	....	....	....	23.00	100.00
La Plata	20.87	22.10	21.99	26.90	36.47	34.71	94.25
Larimer	22.38	23.08	22.85	27.24	47.97	38.98	114.72
Las Animas	6.35	7.30	6.51	19.59	20.73	17.83	61.53
Lincoln	11.00	10.05	10.78	27.00	23.00	23.09	52.52
Logan	13.49	10.64	12.75	26.66	30.51	30.34	73.79
Mesa	27.65	30.27	29.02	38.90	39.82	31.60	131.86
Mineral	....	....	....	....	32.92	30.50	102.00
Moffat	13.49	3.31	5.55	12.09	25.48	24.67	86.81
Montezuma	14.05	19.60	18.61	23.96	37.04	29.84	74.43
Montrose	30 58	29.80	29.85	41.81	43.81	25.40	164.88
Morgan	15.65	16.16	15.76	24.31	37.64	34.48	95.39
Otero	27.36	19.56	25.01	37.56	40.64	38.47	93.33
Ouray	16.00	24.00	22.99	19.82	38.90	23.36	119.10
Park	14.00	16.47	16.25	19.00	25.00	24.12	60.18
Phillips	10.00	5.00	9.81	24.00	27.00	25.19	35.00
Pitkin	33.00	31.00	31.20	30.00	50 00	35.00	200.00
Prowers	14.68	11.60	14.48	28.48	31.94	25.48	50.00
Pueblo	5.25	15.71	7.72	29.31	33.18	28.93	45.55
Rio Blanco	23.00	20.57	20.87	20.32	34.86	28.00	88.27
Rio Grande	....	28.00	28.00	....	39.00	34.00	160.00
Routt	25.06	20.02	21.26	18.00	33.29	36.09	92.6?
Saguache	....	27.00	27.00	....	34.00	34.00	155.00
San Miguel	18.58	18.92	18.78	25.44	28.17	22.10	116.70
Sedgwick	8.18	10.62	9.06	25.45	28.44	28.41	82.66
Summit	26.00	22.00	25.33	....	29.54	28.00	109.00
Teller	....	....	....	....	25.00	20.00	90.00
Washington	7.06	5.04	6.92	20.10	21.22	22.35	35.00
Weld	15.15	16.81	15.97	23.70	36.38	33.53	130.29
Yuma	8.00	5.00	7.80	27 00	23.07	26.00	42.20
State	10.46	15 54	11.63	24.94	32.40	27.15	130.57

AVERAGE YIELD OF PRINCIPAL CROPS PER ACRE FOR FIVE YEARS ENDING WITH 1923

COUNTY	Winter Wheat Bushel	Spring Wheat Bushel	All Wheat Bushel	Corn Bushel	Oats Bushel	Barley Bushel	Potatoes Bushel
Adams	11.10	19.78	12.95	16.40	28.75	18.88	74.57
Alamosa	27.73	21.04	21.17	25.00	31.64	25.89	131.96
Arapahoe	9.16	15.06	10.10	16.24	21.64	17.31	54.54
Archuleta	16.82	14.63	15.10	20.12	24.77	19.78	58.74
Baca	9.69	6.40	9.00	15.48	16.88	12.61	51.26
Bent	21.06	17.55	20.44	25.23	36.83	23.69	46.36
Boulder	23.72	23.91	23.80	25.86	38.56	32.58	88.25
Chaffee	16.45	24.46	24.44	26.68	35.18	28.62	99.57
Cheyenne	12.54	9.19	12.38	20.03	18.16	15.61	48.41
Clear Creek	25.00	14.21	14.21	15.45	22.13	19.03	64.12
Conejos	22.52	20.87	20.88	24.16	32.04	29.53	130.41
Costilla	23.65	21.15	21.20	20.05	33.00	29.13	114.52
Crowley	13.77	20.42	18.11	22.21	35.08	29.25	33.65
Custer	18.06	14.85	15.62	17.62	25.90	21.89	60.06
Delta	25.92	28.00	27.76	35.15	40.11	30.99	157.42
Dolores	13.05	10.82	11.28	15.76	20.23	15.72	57.77
Douglas	11.60	10.25	11.23	17.48	18.62	16.04	60.12
Eagle	25.72	31.13	30.87	8.45	48.29	31.13	205.19
Elbert	12.35	10.02	11.46	18.12	19.28	17.64	50.22
El Paso	12.43	10.84	11.33	17.71	20.12	17.55	47.20
Fremont	11.78	22.69	15.29	23.96	26.11	20.69	51.62
Garfield	21.93	25.78	25.41	32.78	41.25	28.91	166.11
Gilpin	11.27	12.02	11.86	18.00	18.14	13.84	53.89
Grand	22.40	18.10	21.21	20.01	30.57	25.82	72.17
Gunnison	18.68	20.39	19.68	27.16	30.49	25.30	121.97
Hinsdale	.....	23.00	23.00	.....	26.86	30.59	111.08
Huerfano	14.21	11.73	12.38	16.75	26.73	25.13	78.42
Jackson	10.99	6.25	10.11	19.33	27.35	22.04	84.30
Jefferson	23.28	25.17	24.14	22.04	26.47	27.36	64.57
Kiowa	11.91	10.96	11.85	19.18	17.00	15.00	28.85
Kit Carson	10.89	9.08	10.71	19.16	16.83	17.94	42.47
Lake	.....	.....	.....	.....	34.62	24.95	100.00
La Plata	22.91	23.72	23.66	23.47	35.79	29.93	96.96
Larimer	19.91	24.58	22.34	22.06	38.29	31.37	98.62
Las Animas	9.25	12.27	9.84	17.68	24.11	18.71	44.92
Lincoln	12.41	10.35	11.71	19.60	18.70	17.58	47.42
Logan	13.48	11.05	13.15	19.11	25.26	21.60	57.13
Mesa	23.08	27.37	25.40	33.79	37.24	28.46	124.15
Mineral	28.00	.....	28.00	.....	34.94	28.20	107.03
Moffat	12.38	10.37	10.88	14.00	22.37	19.97	67.54
Montezuma	14.50	20.05	19.46	21.00	34.67	26.82	99.00
Montrose	26.62	29.07	28.76	35.48	40.26	26.09	172.64
Morgan	10.45	14.56	11.04	16.57	30.24	22.49	79.62
Otero	29.46	24.16	27.65	31.61	42.03	33.89	43.55
Ouray	19.12	24.21	23.35	20.55	37.27	21.07	120.85
Park	11.88	11.28	11.38	17.86	17.69	15.49	65.11
Phillips	12.14	8.35	12.03	18.40	19.54	17.25	38.28
Pitkin	27.05	30.53	30.25	31.50	45.94	32.25	201.59
Prowers	17.46	15.68	17.08	24.96	33.76	24.14	59.92
Pueblo	12.07	19.21	14.05	23.97	30.46	23.58	40.20
Rio Blanco	13.50	15.62	15.19	17.23	32.65	21.84	89.22
Rio Grande	26.00	25.98	25.98	.....	36.75	29.08	169.96
Routt	20.58	15.29	16.69	19.95	30.54	25.53	112.96
Saguache	21.91	24.48	24.44	21.95	32.73	27.71	150.87
San Miguel	15.64	20.27	18.23	24.47	28.43	19.45	114.52
Sedgwick	12.39	12.15	12.35	18.19	23.03	23.54	117.06
Summit	20.72	23.90	22.26	.....	29.51	25.30	99.24
Teller	13.00	9.96	10.23	18.07	18.77	16.39	73.83
Washington	10.21	7.40	10.03	16.10	17.68	16.67	34.22
Weld	15.58	17.75	16.42	17.83	31.03	26.60	126.42
Yuma	12.01	9.04	11.86	18.96	18.77	18.04	36.38
State	12.64	16.68	13.58	19.00	28.23	21.71	127.01

NUMBER OF FARMS REPORTING PRINCIPAL CROPS IN 1923

COUNTY	Corn	Oats	Barley	Winter Wheat	Spring Wheat	All Wheat	Rye	Pota-toes	Grain Sor-ghums	Sweet Sor-ghums	Alfalfa	Sugar Beets
Adams	893	360	318	537	528	815	126	187	20	379	720	249
Alamosa	1	190	86	....	170	170	...	208	....	....	301	....
Arapahoe	415	111	117	229	85	291	39	29	59	161	320	8
Archuleta	45	178	57	1	90	91	...	138	....	....	108	....
Baca	1,022	8	101	220	125	313	11	10	1,193	1	20	....
Bent	641	42	49	230	47	264	11	....	448	31	321	94
Boulder	558	419	295	408	527	658	13	83	....	1	789	332
Chaffee	4	113	91	....	117	117	1	128	....	....	149	....
Cheyenne	518	29	133	196	14	204	18	68	476	77	38	....
Clear Creek	2	15	1	....	2	2	...	28	....	....	12	....
Conejos	15	131	248	....	264	264	...	252	....	....	281	....
Costilla	13	68	177	6	210	211	...	61	....	....	204	....
Crowley	328	51	73	26	10	36	...	....	169	48	269	131
Custer	85	231	147	22	131	141	16	266	2	1	62	....
Delta	787	448	82	49	549	586	1	648	....	....	1,162	208
Dolores	201	73	21	12	43	52	6	111	105	4	25	....
Douglas	387	254	40	117	98	194	95	78	93	9	257	....
Eagle	....	111	43	1	105	106	...	160	....	....	169	....
Elbert	1,065	386	86	351	219	491	285	551	98	302	273	....
El Paso	1,065	373	35	37	128	164	159	279	161	145	124	3
Fremont	341	208	126	23	83	121	50	117	4	3	629	....
Garfield	313	380	96	29	412	430	4	494	....	....	669	88
Gilpin	....	35	8	2	....	2	7	36	....	....	8	....
Grand	....	59	25	9	7	16	13	107	....	....	27	....
Gunnison	1	121	79	5	37	42	5	235	....	....	93	....
Hinsdale	....	7	8	1	1	2	1	23	....	....	8	....
Huerfano	305	132	59	22	91	110	20	17	10	26	198	....
Jackson	2	14	10	4	....	4	3	17	....	....	1	....
Jefferson	239	257	88	135	221	284	12	104	1	....	578	31
Kiowa	503	2	52	71	6	75	2	9	462	341	19	....
Kit Carson	1,251	184	691	863	123	891	148	909	913	58	39	....
Lake	....	....	6	....	....	....	1	1	....	....	....	....
La Plata	278	334	177	29	349	364	7	387	4	2	466	....
Larimer	526	571	317	145	619	687	15	131	1	4	946	575
Las Animas	1,048	258	85	328	186	450	36	46	577	177	281	....
Lincoln	1,034	103	321	414	262	477	175	634	619	314	139	....
Logan	1,587	626	561	1,074	740	1,434	215	587	695	300	653	395
Mesa	962	447	100	210	408	565	28	841	47	7	1,307	182
Mineral	....	7	6	....	....	....	...	2	....	....	2	....
Moffat	397	310	55	77	282	327	322	414	25	90	333	....
Montezuma	282	199	131	25	194	218	9	225	14	....	324	....
Montrose	607	660	93	67	805	823	...	953	1	....	1,069	224
Morgan	1,125	274	486	242	178	392	127	261	340	180	683	462
Otero	753	303	107	198	133	295	11	9	202	30	735	457
Ouray	7	101	36	12	102	110	3	129	....	....	99	3
Park	....	219	131	2	23	25	51	229	....	....	1	....
Phillips	667	367	144	587	72	597	125	317	451	115	174	....
Pitkin	1	101	25	3	53	56	...	139	....	....	61	....
Prowers	922	113	190	553	132	608	17	6	757	151	557	150
Pueblo	763	239	168	210	190	341	47	14	300	20	761	273
Rio Blanco	35	152	64	37	86	91	17	151	....	....	139	....
Rio Grande	....	264	235	....	235	235	...	340	....	....	317	....
Routt	9	395	248	93	199	276	4	357	....	....	196	....
Saguache	....	144	93	7	128	135	...	113	....	....	113	....
San Miguel	89	137	187	34	70	100	7	101	....	30	110	....
Sedgwick	394	236	120	261	264	394	44	57	10	219	176	127
Summit	....	25	19	7	3	10	13	44	....	....	2	....
Teller	....	339	269	....	....	....	3	336	....	....	....	....
Washington	1,650	274	1,004	1,443	265	1,507	418	685	701	587	223	26
Weld	2,187	1,546	1,478	913	1,839	2,240	252	1,544	452	185	2,426	1,752
Yuma	1,506	198	434	931	126	964	325	711	823	452	123	5
State	27,829	13,932	10,732	11,508	12,386	20,868	3,318	15,117	10,233	4,450	20,287	5,775

PERCENTAGE OF TOTAL NUMBER OF FARMS REPORTING PRINCIPAL CROPS FOR 1923

COUNTY	Corn	Oats	Barley	Winter Wheat	Spring Wheat	All Wheat	Rye	Potatoes	Grain Sorghums	Sweet Sorghums	Alfalfa	Sugar Beets
Adams	58.17	23.45	20.72	34.98	34.39	53.09	8.21	12.18	1.30	24.69	46.90	16.22
Alamosa	.27	52.92	23.95	....	47.35	47.35	...	57.94	....	....	83.84	....
Arapahoe	66.51	17.79	18.75	36.70	13.62	46.63	625	4.71	9.45	25.80	51.26	1.28
Archuleta	14.95	59.13	18.93	.33	29.90	30.23	...	45.84	....	....	35.88	....
Baca	80.72	.63	7.97	17.37	9.87	24.72	.86	.78	94.23	.07	1.57	....
Bent	74.61	4.85	5.67	26.77	5.47	30.73	1.28	....	52.15	3.61	37.37	10.96
Boulder	70.10	52.64	37.06	51.24	66.21	82.69	1.62	10.43	....	.13	98.86	41.70
Chaffee	1.62	45.93	36.99	....	47.56	47.56	.40	33.74	....	....	60.56	....
Cheyenne	92.48	5.18	23.79	35.06	2.50	36.49	3.22	12.16	84.72	13.77	6.79	....
Clear Creek	5.55	41.66	2.77	....	5.55	5.55	...	77.77	....	....	33.33	....
Conejos	2.67	12.38	32.23	....	48.08	48.08	...	45.90	....	....	51.18	....
Costilla	3.10	16.23	42.24	1.43	50.11	50.36	...	14.56	....	....	48.68	....
Crowley	61.77	9.60	13.75	4.90	1.88	6.77	...	....	31.82	9.04	50.66	24.66
Custer	22.19	60.31	38.38	5.74	34.20	36.81	4.17	69.45	.52	.26	16.18	....
Delta	52.46	29.86	5.46	3.26	36.60	39.07	.06	43.20	....	....	77.46	13.86
Dolores	72.56	26.35	7.58	4.33	15.52	18.77	2.16	40.06	37.90	1.44	9.02	....
Douglas	90.85	59.62	9.38	27.46	23.00	45.53	22.30	18.31	21.83	2.11	60.33	....
Eagle	....	51.15	19.81	.46	48.37	48.84	...	73.73	....	....	77.87	....
Elbert	94.66	34.31	7.64	31.20	19.48	43.64	25.33	48.97	8.71	26.84	24.26	....
El Paso	89.57	31.37	2.94	3.11	10.76	13.79	13.37	23.46	13.54	12.19	10.42	.25
Fremont	33.07	20.17	12.22	2.23	8.05	11.73	4.85	11.35	.39	.29	61.01	....
Garfield	37.09	45.02	11.37	3.62	48.80	50.94	.47	58.53	....	....	79.25	10.43
Gilpin	....	89.74	20.51	5.12	....	5.12	17.92	92.30	....	....	20.51	....
Grand	....	12.42	5.26	1.89	1.47	3.37	2.73	22.53	....	....	5.68	....
Gunnison	.30	35.86	23.44	1.48	10.98	12.46	1.48	69.73	....	....	22.59	....
Hinsdale	....	16.27	18.60	2.32	2.32	4.65	2.32	53.49	....	....	18.60	....
Huerfano	44.52	19.27	8.61	13.28	13.28	2.88	2.92	2.48	1.46	3.79	28.90	....
Jackson	.72	5.07	3.62	1.44	....	1.44	1.08	6.15	....	....	.36	....
Jefferson	23.22	24.97	8.55	13.11	21.47	27.56	1.16	10.10	.09	....	56.17	3.01
Kiowa	89.18	.35	9.22	12.58	1.06	13.29	.35	1.59	81.87	60.46	1.77	....
Kit Carson	92.46	13.59	51.07	63.78	9.09	65.85	10.94	67.18	67.47	4.28	2.88	....
Lake	....	....	24.00	....	....	....	4.00	4.00	....	....	....	....
La Plata	36.63	44.01	23.32	3.82	45.96	47.96	.91	37.81	.53	.26	61.39	....
Larimer	48.34	52.48	29.13	13.32	56.88	63.14	1.37	12.04	.09	.18	86.95	52.84
Las Animas	57.58	14.17	4.67	18.02	10.21	24.72	1.97	2.52	20.71	9.72	15.48	....
Lincoln	91.42	9.10	28.38	36.60	23.16	42.17	15.47	56.05	54.73	27.76	12.29	....
Logan	71.61	28.24	25.31	48.46	33.39	64.71	9.70	26.48	31.36	13.53	29.46	17.82
Mesa	36.13	16.79	3.76	7.89	15.32	21.22	1.05	31.59	1.76	.26	49.09	6.83
Mineral	....	24.13	20.68	....	....	....	...	6.90	....	....	6.90	....
Moffat	18.08	14.12	2.50	3.50	12.84	14.89	14.67	18.86	1.13	4.10	15.17	....
Montezuma	46.61	32.89	21.65	4.13	32.07	36.03	1.49	37.19	2.31	....	53.55	....
Montrose	49.91	54.27	7.64	5.50	66.20	67.68	...	78.37	.08	....	87.91	18.42
Morgan	78.56	19.13	33.93	16.90	12.43	27.37	8.86	18.22	23.74	12.56	47.69	32.26
Otero	63.43	25.52	9.01	16.68	11.20	24.85	.92	75	17.01	2.57	61.92	38.92
Ouray	4.11	59.41	21.17	7.05	6.00	64.70	1.76	75.88	....	....	58.23	1.76
Park	....	73.74	44.11	.67	7.74	8.42	17.17	77.10	....	....	.33	....
Phillips	93.93	51.69	20.28	82.68	10.14	84.08	17.61	44.65	63.52	16.20	24.51	....
Pitkin	.64	64.74	16.02	1.92	33.97	35.90	...	89.10	....	....	39.10	....
Prowers	77.02	9.44	15.87	46.19	11.02	50.79	1.42	.50	63.24	12.61	46.53	12.53
Pueblo	49.60	15.53	10.92	13.65	12.35	22.17	3.05	.91	19.50	1.30	49.47	17.75
Rio Blanco	7.64	33.18	13.97	8.08	18.77	19.86	3.71	32.98	....	....	30.34	....
Rio Grande	....	54.65	48.65	....	48.65	48.65	...	70.39	....	....	65.63	....
Routt	1.30	57.16	35.81	13.46	28.79	39.94	.58	51.66	....	....	28.36	....
Saguache	....	62.07	40.08	3.01	55.17	58.18	...	48.70	....	....	48.70	....
San Miguel	13.79	21.24	28.99	5.27	10.85	15.50	1.09	15.66	....	4.65	17.05	....
Sedgwick	73.78	44.19	22.47	48.87	49.43	73.78	8.24	10.67	1.87	41.01	32.95	23.78
Summit	....	50.00	38.00	14.00	6.00	20.00	26.00	88.00	....	....	4.00	....
Teller	....	108.78	69.50	....	....	....	.78	107.75	....	....	....	....
Washington	86.61	14.38	52.70	75.74	13.91	79.10	21.94	35.95	36.79	30.81	11.70	1.36
Weld	52.37	37.02	35.39	21.86	44.04	53.63	6.03	36.97	10.82	4.43	58.09	41.95
Yuma	87.45	11.49	25.20	54.06	7.31	55.98	18.87	41.28	47.79	26.24	7.14	.29
State	53.94	27.16	20.80	22.31	24.01	40.45	6.43	29.45	19.84	8.62	39.32	11.19

AVERAGE NUMBER OF ACRES OF PRINCIPAL CROPS GROWN PER FARM IN 1923, AS REPORTED BY COUNTY ASSESSORS

COUNTY	Corn	Winter Wheat	Spring Wheat	Oats	Barley	Rye	Sorghums	Sugar Beets	Potatoes	Alfalfa
Adams	22.47	35.52	8.73	3.17	3.63	1.92	6.28	3.52	.64	13.84
Alamosa	.03	....	6.99	9.02	3.91	3.91	....	....	7.83	53.82
Arapahoe ...	34.11	40.17	4.02	2.50	4.27	1.77	9.36	.37	.09	20.20
Archuleta ...	1.09	.02	2.00	8.11	2.34	....	....	....	.41	8.32
Baca	26.83	21.38	6.47	.14	2.6	.36	72.19	....	....	.64
Bent	25.39	11.98	2.74	.83	1.12	.22	24.65	3.21	....	17.97
Boulder	11.21	15.89	14.26	4.98	3.6[illegible]	.08	.04	9.01	.32	22.37
Chaffee	.05	....	5.27	7.20	4.93	.01	....	....	1.43	20.92
Cheyenne	59.33	43.29	1.40	.72	8.53	....	32.15	....	.55	.88
Clear Creek ..	.86	....	.25	4.00	.11	.27	....	....	1.08	1.55
Conejos	.09	.02	15.57	7.14	15.71	....	.01	....	6.22	18.41
Costilla	.14	.13	9.69	4.72	7.60	....	....	....	.53	12.98
Crowley	23.54	1.91	1.13	4.10	1.78	....	10.59	4.75	....	14.55
Custer	3.30	.82	3.86	9.70	3.71	.35	.07	....	2.52	4.76
Delta	2.48	.30	2.91	2.23	.42	.01	.01	1.81	1.60	16.91
Dolores	17.14	.91	3.21	3.86	.82	.21	4.55	....	.34	1.04
Douglas	40.24	11.27	3.58	14.01	1.11	4.54	4.27	....	.52	17.35
Eagle	....	.05	4.04	8.47	1.19	....	....	....	9.24	32.88
Elbert	45.85	18.72	6.31	7.76	1.56	6.79	6.43	....	1.07	6.03
El Paso	47.95	2.18	1.91	10.00	.43	3.32	3.55	.11	.78	3.50
Fremont	3.13	.22	.36	1.81	.94	.16	.07	....	.44	5.66
Garfield	2.19	.58	5.88	3.11	.67	.40	.01	1.67	5.02	34.92
Gilpin	.02	.15	....	14.64	1.28	.61	....	....	3.15	.64
Grand	.21	.35	.04	1.50	.31	.27	....	.01	.29	1.16
Gunnison ...	.01	.35	.44	3.12	1.15	.06	....	....	1.16	6.54
Hinsdale	....	....	.04	1.26	.51	....	....	....	.93	1.26
Huerfano	8.25	.60	1.88	2.82	.96	.24	.75	.01	.11	10.26
Jackson	.01	.06	....	.47	.18	.09	....	....	.05	.05
Jefferson	3.84	4.79	4.19	3.24	1.68	.08	.01	.37	.27	13.51
Kiowa	64.50	22.86	.36	.02	3.09	.06	57.35	....	.02	3.30
Kit Carson ..	80.70	100.63	4.98	2.63	20.47	4.63	32.89	....	.54	.85
Lake	....	....	....	....	2.04	.08	....	....	.12	....
La Plata ...	3.73	.76	8.00	5.79	2.16	.05	.07	.01	.87	23.44
Larimer	11.54	6.90	13.63	6	3.79	.15	.02	11.97	.79	36.35
Las Animas..	12.26	10.21	2.01	6.78	.58	.29	8.71	.05	.07	5.46
Lincoln	58.14	40.74	11.96	[illegible].51	8.01	4.93	19.36	....	1.05	1.99
Logan	49.99	58.51	20.41	6.12	6.91	3.24	8.44	6.92	.45	9.41
Mesa	2.80	.84	.92	1.27	.20	.08	.15	1.34	1.42	12.17
Mineral	....	....	....	3.10	1.79	....	....	....	.16	.37
Moffat	3.16	.96	3.43	3.27	.42	1.97	.43	.01	.31	5.29
Montezuma ..	8.69	.90	4.18	3.72	2.55	.19	.37	....	.44	17.19
Montrose	3.18	.58	8.88	4.72	.38	....	.01	1.88	7.05	23.64
Morgan	49.26	14.24	3.61	2.84	6.15	2.55	10.03	15.74	1.50	16.33
Otero	12.37	3.66	1.57	2.89	.91	.04	3.58	8.78	.01	18.24
Ouray	.13	.96	6.65	6.70	3.81	.12	....	.10	2.58	13.43
Park	.02	.03	.25	13.39	4.53	1.37	....	.01	3.54	.08
Phillips	96.77	137.64	5.40	11.60	4.82	5.43	8.24	....	.38	2.66
Pitkin	.01	.24	2.16	8.36	1.30	....	....	.05	9.21	10.28
Prowers	20.48	33.17	2.21	1.52	2.55	.32	32.00	2.99	.01	26.62
Pueblo	18.46	4.98	1.54	2.05	1.21	.35	4.88	2.20	.05	14.31
Rio Blanco...	.27	1.10	7.82	5.84	1.87	.78	....	.01	.19	21.91
Rio Grande ..	....	....	10.42	8.51	4.68	....	....	....	25.11	18.35
Routt	.06	3.52	10.76	12.38	5.99	.24	.01	....	1.34	5.05
Saguache ...	....	....	16.33	14.60	5.10	....	....	....	17.75	17.07
San Miguel ..	2.10	.98	1.40	2.93	7.87	.10	.40	....	1.43	7.95
Sedgwick ...	74.42	58.50	32.86	10.66	5.40	3.08	5.98	9.70	1.41	7.47
Summit	....	.80	.16	4.18	1.28	1.22	....	....	1.20	.18
Teller	....	....	....	41.33	3.36	.06	....	....	4.17	....
Washington ..	64.90	106.44	8.32	3.22	18.95	6.43	15.22	.33	.29	2.11
Weld	19.40	15.80	15.27	5.22	2.52	6.32	3.09	10.84	5.59	22.95
Yuma	89.44	70.16	4.91	2.15	8.50	9.07	16.05	....	.32	1.36
State....	25.32	22.15	6.66	4.41	4.38	2.01	8.38	2.86	1.76	12.60

AVERAGE NUMBER OF ACRES OF PRINCIPAL CROPS FOR EACH FARM REPORTING SUCH CROPS IN 1923

COUNTY	Corn	Oats	Barley	Winter Wheat	Spring Wheat	All Wheat	Rye	Potatoes	Grain Sorghums	Sweet Sorghums	Alfalfa
Adams	38.62	13.51	17.52	101.54	25.38	83.35	23.39	5.28	20.90	24.33	29.51
Alamosa	10.00	17.05	16.33	....	14.76	14.76	....	13.51	....	....	64.19
Arapahoe	51.29	14.03	22.77	109.47	29.55	94.78	28.51	1.93	26.35	26.63	39.38
Archuleta	7.35	13.71	12.40	8.00	6.70	6.71	....	0.91	....	....	23.18
Baca	33.23	22.37	32.85	123.12	65.58	112.73	41.81	....	70.64	....	40.60
Bent	34.03	17.11	20.32	44.73	50.06	47.89	17.54	....	44.78	35.77	48.08
Boulder	16.01	9.47	9.90	31.23	21.53	36.61	4.61	3.07	....	20.00	22.56
Chaffee	3.25	15.68	13.32	....	11.08	11.08	4.00	2.75	....	....	34.53
Cheyenne	64.22	14.03	35.84	123.46	55.92	122.46	20.22	4.50	33.51	26.20	13.02
Clear Creek	15.50	9.60	4.00	....	4.50	4.50	....	1.39	....	....	4.66
Conejos	3.53	29.93	34.78	....	32.42	32.45	....	13.56	....	....	35.97
Costilla	4.46	29.16	18.00	9.16	19.34	19.51	....	3.65	....	....	26.66
Crowley	38.11	42.66	12.82	39.07	60.50	45.02	....	....	27.32	20.93	28.72
Custer	14.87	16.13	9.87	14.22	11.29	12.71	8.31	3.63	10.00	12.00	29.45
Delta	4.74	7.45	7.62	9.38	7.96	8.24	8.00	3.70	....	....	21.83
Dolores	23.63	14.76	10.76	21.08	20.72	22.00	9.50	.85	11.60	10.50	11.52
Douglas	44.29	23.50	11.87	41.05	15.58	32.63	20.40	2.85	17.46	22.11	28.75
Eagle	....	16.56	6.02	10.00	8.35	8.36	....	12.54	....	....	42 22
Elbert	48.43	22.64	20.51	60.01	32.40	57.35	26.82	2.19	28.11	14.83	24.86
El Paso	52.64	31.34	14.25	69.13	17.53	29.28	24.47	3.29	13.59	13.55	33.06
Fremont	9.44	9.00	7.76	10.08	4.59	5.06	3.48	3.90	19.25	0.66	9.28
Garfield	5.92	6.90	6.20	16.89	12.80	13.40	8.50	8.58	....	....	44.05
Gilpin	....	16.31	6.25	3.00	....	3.00	3.42	3.41	....	....	3.12
Grand	....	12.10	5.84	18.66	2.71	11.68	17.23	1.32	....	....	20.51
Gunnison	1.00	8.70	4.93	24.00	4.02	6.40	4.00	1.67	....	....	23.73
Hinsdale	....	7.71	2.75	....	2.00	1.00	....	1.73	....	....	6.75
Huerfano	18.53	14.71	11.38	20.50	14.28	15.91	8.30	4.35	29.80	9.23	35.48
Jackson	1.50	9.28	5.20	4.50	....	4.50	8.66	0.76	....	....	13.00
Jefferson	16.53	12.98	19.65	36.57	19.53	32.58	6.83	2.69	5.00	....	23.68
Kiowa	72.87	7.00	33.59	182.15	34.66	175.21	18.50	1.55	51.64	24.90	98.00
Kit Carson	87.28	19.38	40.08	157.76	54.78	160.37	42.34	0.80	26.39	18.19	29.66
Lake	....	....	8.50	....	....	....	2.00	3.00	....	....	....
La Plata	10.19	13.17	9.25	19.80	17.40	18.26	5.71	1.71	7.00	15.00	38.17
Larimer	23.86	12.72	13.02	51.79	23.95	32.51	10.93	6.58	9.00	5.25	41.81
Las Animas	21.29	12.51	12.50	56.68	19.63	49.43	14.80	2.82	22.81	15.20	35.35
Lincoln	63.59	16.55	28.23	111.29	51.63	124.95	31.92	1.87	26.40	17.69	16.21
Logan	69.80	18.12	27.31	120.73	61.14	121.97	33.35	1.70	18.18	20.21	31.94
Mesa	7.75	7.63	5.55	10.72	6.03	8.34	8.32	4.52	8.42	2.85	24.78
Mineral	....	12.85	8.66	....	....	....	....	2.50	....	....	5.50
Moffat	17.48	23.22	16.92	27.49	26.70	29.50	18.61	1.62	8.00	8.37	34.88
Montezuma	18.63	11.29	11.77	21.76	13.03	14.09	12.66	1.18	15.50	....	32.11
Montrose	6.37	8.70	5.09	10.56	13.41	13.98	....	9.00	1.00	....	26.88
Morgan	62.70	14.86	18.14	84.28	29.11	65.25	28.77	8.22	20.65	40.78	34.24
Otero	19.50	11.33	10.12	21.94	14.03	21.05	5.27	1.00	19.28	12.13	29.45
Ouray	3.28	11.28	18.00	13.66	11.09	11.78	7.33	3.40	....	....	23.07
Park	....	18.15	10.28	3.50	3.21	3.24	8.00	4.59	....	....	25.00
Phillips	103.01	22.44	23.79	166.48	53.20	170.11	30.84	0.86	13.19	19.09	10.85
Pitkin	1.00	12.92	8.16	12.66	6.37	6.71	....	10.34	....	....	26.31
Prowers	26.59	16.10	16.11	71.81	20.05	69.67	22.58	2.00	46.72	19.45	57.33
Pueblo	37.22	13.23	11.08	36.54	12.51	29.47	11.57	0.64	24.11	13.60	28.94
Rio Blanco	3.54	17.59	13.39	13.28	41.74	45.00	20.76	0.57	....	....	72.19
Rio Grande	....	15.98	9.83	....	20.64	20.64	....	35.67	....	....	28.58
Routt	4.77	20.88	16.69	26.21	37.37	35.77	40.75	2.60	....	....	18.34
Saguache	....	23.53	12.73	....	29.60	28.07	....	36.44	....	....	35.06
San Miguel	15.20	13.83	27.22	18.70	12.90	15.39	9.57	9.16	....	8.60	46.65
Sedgwick	100.86	24.12	24.05	119.77	66.45	123.87	37.40	13.22	12.00	14.05	22.67
Summit	....	8.36	3.36	5.71	2.66	4.80	4.69	1.36	....	....	4.50
Teller	....	47.18	5.69	....	....	....	9.00	4.81	....	....	....
Washington	74.93	22.44	35.96	140.52	59.81	145.07	29.33	0.78	22.72	22.26	18.01
Weld	37.05	14.12	17.86	72.28	34.69	57.94	41.82	15.12	21.12	18.22	39.50
Yuma	102.33	18.94	33.75	129.81	67.21	134.15	48.09	0.77	23.80	17.82	19.17
State......	46.95	16.33	21.05	99.28	27.73	71.21	28.13	5.98	32.34	23.18	32.04

PERCENTAGE OF CROPS GROWN WITH AND WITHOUT IRRIGATION

COUNTY	WINTER WHEAT		SPRING WHEAT		POTATOES		CORN	
	Percent Irrigated	Percent Non-irrigated	Percent Irrigated	Percent Non-irrigated	Percent Irrigated	Percent Non-irrigated	Percent Irrigated	Percent Non-irrigated
Adams	11.89	88.11	76.66	23.34	88.77	11.23	6.82	93.18
Alamosa	....	....	100.00	....	100.00	....	100.00	....
Arapahoe	4.15	95.85	78.71	21.29	57.14	42.86	3.54	96.46
Archuleta	100.00	....	30.68	69.32	....	100.00	43.81	56.19
Baca	1.94	98.06	....	100.00	....	....	1.27	98.73
Bent	66.18	33.82	81.18	18.82	....	....	54.09	45.91
Boulder	68.52	31.48	95.72	4.28	72.55	27.45	62.40	37.60
Chaffee	....	....	100.00	....	96.03	3.97	76.92	23.08
Cheyenne	....	100.00	....	100.00	13.73	86.27	....	100.00
Clear Creek	....	....	44.44	55.56	....	100.00	....	100.00
Conejos	100.00	....	100.00	....	100.00	....	88.68	11.32
Costilla	100.00	....	94.93	5.07	96.86	3.14	91.38	8.62
Crowley	24.90	75.10	77.69	22.31	....	....	59.35	40.65
Custer	65.17	34.83	37.64	62.36	.51	99.49	1.82	98.18
Delta	97.60	2.40	100.00	....	99.13	.87	97.05	2.95
Dolores	4.74	95.26	....	100.00	.01	99.99	....	100.00
Douglas	1.29	98.71	15.91	84.09	100.00	....	.32	99.68
Eagle	....	100.00	100.00	....	99.75	.25	....	....
Elbert	.37	99.63	.98	99.02	1.56	98.44	....	100.00
El Paso	.01	99.99	8.42	91.58	.11	99.89	1.74	98.26
Fremont	61.21	38.79	69.03	30.97	5.03	94.97	49.69	50.32
Garfield	71.02	28.98	97.34	2.66	97.48	2.52	88.50	11.50
Gilpin	....	100.00	....	....	....	100.00	....	100.00
Grand	83.92	16.08	47.37	52.63	33.03	66.97	100.00	....
Gunnison	16.66	83.34	69.79	30.21	40.97	59.03	....	100.00
Hinsdale	....	....	....	100.00	85.00	15.00	....	....
Huerfano	28.16	71.84	7.62	92.38	2.70	97.30	3.41	96.59
Jackson	38.89	61.11	....	....	100.00	....	66.67	33.33
Jefferson	65.12	34.88	89.08	10.92	29.29	70.71	67.99	32.01
Kiowa	....	100.00	....	100.00	....	100.00	....	100.00
Kit Carson	....	100.00	....	100.00	.14	99.86	....	100.00
Lake	....	....	....	....	100.00	....	....	....
La Plata	41.04	58.96	77.73	22.27	57.10	42.90	53.14	46.86
Larimer	26.05	73.95	85.28	14.72	92.46	7.54	44.62	55.38
Las Animas	1.87	98.13	15.33	84.67	15.38	84.62	9.94	90.06
Lincoln	....	100.00	.51	99.49	5.04	94.96	....	100.00
Logan	4.13	95.87	9.68	90.32	16.03	83.97	4.98	95.02
Mesa	83.27	16.73	96.54	3.46	84.45	15.55	84.53	15.47
Mineral	....	....	....	....	60.00	40.00	....	....
Moffat	3.31	96.69	6.61	93.39	8.01	91.99	.52	99.48
Montezuma	8.82	91.18	73.33	26.67	74.06	25.94	18.83	81.17
Montrose	97.02	2.98	98.72	1.28	99.88	.12	91.35	8.65
Morgan	4.71	95.29	26.03	73.97	82.40	17.60	12.85	87.15
Otero	91.36	8.64	96.41	3.59	88.89	11.11	82.26	17.74
Ouray	....	100.00	63.63	36.37	55.13	44.87	21.74	78.26
Park	....	100.00	6.76	93.24	.47	99.53	50.00	50.00
Phillips	....	100.00	....	100.00	....	100.00	....	100.00
Pitkin	100.00	....	100.00	....	100.00	....	100.00	....
Prowers	39.46	60.54	50.77	49.23	25.00	75.00	55.17	44.83
Pueblo	16.65	83.35	35.07	64.93	11.11	88.89	42.33	57.67
Rio Blanco	....	100.00	23.43	76.57	9.31	90.69	3.23	96.77
Rio Grande	....	....	100.00	....	100.00	....	....	....
Routt	1.23	98.77	.40	99.60	3.77	96.23	....	100.00
Saguache	....	....	100.00	....	100.00	....	....	....
San Miguel	8.33	91.67	53.26	46.74	3.78	96.22	4.95	95.05
Sedgwick	1.35	98.65	14.73	85.27	78.90	21.10	3.28	96.72
Summit	100.00	....	100.00	....	95.00	5.00	....	....
Teller	....	....	....	....	....	100.00	....	....
Washington	.36	99.64	.35	99.65	....	100.00	.52	99.48
Weld	24.44	75.56	56.81	43.19	95.29	4.71	22.39	77.61
Yuma	....	100.00	....	100.00	5.59	94.41	....	100.00
State	6.88	93.12	43.94	56.06	81.18	18.82	10.16	89.84

PERCENTAGE OF CROPS GROWN WITH AND WITHOUT IRRIGATION

COUNTY	OATS		BARLEY		BEANS		SORGHUMS	
	Percent Irrigated	Percent Non-irrigated	Percent Irrigated	Percent Non-irrigated	Percent Irrigated	Percent Non-irrigated	Percent Irrigated	Percent Non-irrigated
Adams	67.82	32.18	32.60	67.40	2.69	97.31	1.80	98.20
Alamosa	100.00	....	100.00	....	....	....	....	....
Arapahoe	34.98	65.02	13.06	86.94	.12	99.88	3.75	96.25
Archuleta	7.98	92.02	....	100.00	....	100.00	....	....
Baca	....	100.00	10.40	89.60	....	100.00	.38	99.62
Bent	87.06	12.94	63.59	36.41	63.92	36.08	5.87	94.13
Boulder	92.65	7.35	93.15	6.85	....	100.00	100.00	....
Chaffee	100.00	....	99.18	.82	....	....	....	....
Cheyenne	....	100.00	....	100.00	3.33	96.67	....	100.00
Clear Creek	15.28	84.72	100.00	....	....	....	....	....
Conejos	100.00	....	100.00	....	98.49	1.51	100.00	....
Costilla	99.85	.15	99.94	.06	97.10	2.90	....	....
Crowley	87.68	12.32	68.80	31.20	1.19	98.81	5.06	94.94
Custer	45.51	54.49	35.47	64.53	....	....	....	100.00
Delta	99.76	.24	98.24	1.76	87.76	12.24	100.00	....
Dolores	3.33	96.67	....	100.00	....	100.00	....	100.00
Douglas	.92	99.08	....	100.00	....	100.00	2.58	97.42
Eagle	99.56	.44	86.48	13.52	....	....	....	....
Elbert	....	100.00	.45	99.55	.05	99.95	....	100.00
El Paso	1.91	98.09	14.03	85.97	.11	99.89	.82	99.18
Fremont	31.34	68.66	18.69	81.31	84.00	16.00	87.96	12.04
Garfield	98.70	1.30	96.12	3.88	100.00	....	100.00	....
Gilpin	....	100.00	....	100.00	....	....	....	....
Grand	68.07	31.93	72.60	27.40	....	....	....	....
Gunnison	55.75	44.25	58.46	41.54	....	....	....	....
Hinsdale	29.62	70.38	90.91	9.09	....	....	....	....
Huerfano	22.90	77.10	29.46	70.54	3.23	96.77	....	100.00
Jackson	97.69	2.31	75.00	25.00	....	....	....	....
Jefferson	60.14	39.86	77.05	22.95	90.90	9.10	100.00	....
Kiowa	....	100.00	....	100.00	....	100.00	....	100.00
Kit Carson	.42	99.58	.33	99.67	2.03	97.97	.01	99.99
Lake	....	....	....	100.00	....	....	....	....
La Plata	81.46	18.54	76.55	23.45	28.57	71.43	17.24	82.76
Larimer	91.76	8.24	84.94	15.06	42.54	57.46	56.66	43.34
Las Animas	31.19	68.81	34.05	65.95	18.56	81.44	1.66	98.34
Lincoln	....	100.00	.52	99.48	.19	99.81	....	100.00
Logan	45.31	54.69	20.93	79.07	16.03	83.97	1.59	98.41
Mesa	89.22	10.78	97.66	2.34	84.45	15.55	21.39	78.61
Mineral	81.11	18.89	65.38	34.62	....	....	....	....
Moffat	15.14	84.86	9.88	90.12	2.82	97.18	7.86	92.14
Montezuma	77.49	22.51	65.78	34.22	2.04	97.96	13.12	86.88
Montrose	93.71	6.29	57.81	42.19	91.23	8.77	100.00	....
Morgan	76.73	23.27	56.73	43.27	10.17	89.83	6.08	93.92
Otero	95.39	4.61	94.37	5.63	88.86	11.14	23.05	76.95
Ouray	75.61	24.39	10.49	89.51	....	100.00	....	....
Park	....	100.00	.67	99.33	....	....	....	....
Phillips	....	100.00	1.17	98.83	....	100.00	....	100.00
Pitkin	100.00	....	100.00	....	....	....	....	....
Prowers	79.61	20.39	52.44	47.56	85.17	14.83	12.61	87.39
Pueblo	46.32	53.68	53.59	46.41	17.21	82.79	12.31	87.69
Rio Blanco	33.93	66.07	6.30	93.70	....	100.00	....	....
Rio Grande	100.00	....	100.00	....	....	....	....	....
Routt	1.55	98.45	2.32	97.68	....	....	....	100.00
Saguache	100.00	....	100.00	....	....	....	....	....
San Miguel	30.93	69.07	11.01	88.99	....	100.00	....	100.00
Sedgwick	12.86	87.14	25.98	74.02	....	100.00	3.19	96.81
Summit	92.34	7.66	100.00	....	....	....	....	....
Teller	....	100.00	....	100.00	....	....	....	....
Washington	5.32	94.68	1.76	98.24	1.41	98.59	.22	99.78
Weld	69.95	30.05	55.45	44.55	.36	99.64	1.06	98.94
Yuma	.39	99.61	....	100.00	....	100.00	.22	99.78
State	44.23	55.77	28.64	71.36	12.94	87.06	2.57	97.43

FARM TENURE, NUMBER AND SIZE OF FARMS, 1923

COUNTY	Owners	Renters	Owners and Renters	Home-steaders	Tenure not Specified	Total No. of Farms	Average Size of Farms Acres	Farms not Reporting Acreage
Adams	929	470	27	1	108	1,535	206.71	32
Alamosa	258	88	....	....	13	359	323.40	9
Arapahoe	424	145	26	....	29	624	271.15	14
Archuleta	272	22	....	7	....	301	262.66	2
Baca	892	196	....	47	131	1,266	365.02	240
Bent	478	268	10	99	4	859	269.00	24
Boulder	393	246	13	1	143	796	131.02	28
Chaffee	204	41	....	1	....	246	245.06	2
Cheyenne	402	150	....	5	2	559	418.72	5
Clear Creek	21	8	3	4	....	36	326.81	....
Conejos	430	101	17	1	....	549	180.67	....
Costilla	258	136	25	....	....	419	166.63	....
Crowley	301	203	10	15	2	531	184.29	4
Custer	256	45	19	63	....	383	473.70	....
Delta	1,120	345	15	10	10	1,500	80.18	8
Dolores	171	40	....	65	1	277	269.48	3
Douglas	316	110	....	....	....	426	683.93	....
Eagle	183	26	....	7	1	217	251.32	2
Elbert	823	285	5	4	8	1,125	583.22	9
El Paso	701	322	9	21	136	1,189	437.19	45
Fremont	782	172	24	46	7	1,031	50.30	19
Garfield	623	191	1	16	13	844	174.73	20
Gilpin	26	8	....	5	....	39	297.41	....
Grand	386	42	....	35	12	475	355.61	1
Gunnison	277	27	....	32	1	337	309.11	4
Hinsdale	33	7	....	3	....	43	281.00	....
Huerfano	581	84	....	9	11	685	356.76	14
Jackson	232	22	....	21	1	276	806.64	1
Jefferson	824	166	14	6	19	1,029	81.09	10
Kiowa	444	105	....	6	9	564	429.43	13
Kit Carson	712	444	93	3	101	1,353	426.26	34
Lake	18	6	1	....	....	25	554.68	....
La Plata	563	154	26	7	9	759	212.62	24
Larimer	575	486	14	2	11	1,088	162.71	89
Las Animas	1,260	204	36	188	132	1,820	336.04	68
Lincoln	843	259	3	16	10	1,131	424.24	42
Logan	1,043	1,163	....	10	....	2,216	311.43	10
Mesa	2,044	399	56	109	54	2,662	88.26	10
Mineral	28	1	....	....	....	29	650.17	....
Moffat	1,359	63	59	707	7	2,195	401.64	7
Montezuma	427	150	....	24	4	605	166.29	5
Montrose	773	352	40	17	34	1,216	109.93	164
Morgan	774	637	8	8	5	1,432	258.54	6
Otero	610	498	51	14	14	1,187	103.99	25
Ouray	122	47	....	1	....	170	191.44	1
Park	181	27	....	87	2	297	704.62	2
Phillips	254	277	177	....	2	710	423.84	2
Pitkin	130	18	....	8	....	156	281.17	....
Prowers	563	439	96	76	23	1,197	280.23	21
Pueblo	1,212	299	14	13	....	1,538	417.23	10
Rio Blanco	346	34	1	77	....	458	384.20	....
Rio Grande	336	147	....	....	....	483	277.27	1
Routt	501	96	4	83	7	691	348.21	9
Saguache	149	78	....	5	....	232	441.22	....
San Miguel	431	31	....	183	....	645	331.12	1
Sedgwick	202	234	97	....	1	534	235.84	3
Summit	49	1	....	....	....	50	361.82	....
Teller	283	65	....	39	....	387	268.85	1
Washington	1,091	603	172	7	32	1,905	443.19	75
Weld	2,132	1,759	89	10	186	4,176	204.05	140
Yuma	1,186	458	60	8	10	1,722	461.62	13
State	33,237	13,500	1,315	2,232	1,305	51,589	290.36	1,272

FARM TENURE AS REPORTED BY COUNTY ASSESSORS, 1923

COUNTY	Percentage of Farm Land Farmed by Owners	Percentage of Farms Operated by Owners	Percentage of Farm Land Farmed by Renters	Percentage of Farms Operated by Renters	Percentage of Farm Land Farmed by Owners and Renters	Percentage of Farms Operated by Owners and Renters	Percentage of Farm Land Farmed by Homesteaders	Percentage of Farms Operated by Homesteaders
Adams	60.52	56.54	30.59	34.12	1.75	4.65	.06	.01
Alamosa	71.86	79.03	24.51	17.53	....	....	....	....
Arapahoe	67.94	63.50	23.24	28.92	4.16	4.66	....	....
Archuleta	90.36	92.28	7.30	5.82	....	....	2.32	1.24
Baca	70.45	67.81	15.45	8.50	....	....	3.71	1.87
Bent	55.65	56.36	31.19	27.32	1.16	2.77	11.52	9.99
Boulder	49.24	44.85	30.90	33.29	1.63	1.69	.12	1.99
Chaffee	82.92	84.23	16.66	14.69	....	....	.40	.27
Cheyenne	71.91	70.25	26.83	28.16	....	....	1.24	2.70
Clear Creek	58.33	80.40	22.22	14.35	8.33	.45	11.11	4.77
Conejos	76.50	77.72	18.39	17.71	3.09	4.41	.18	.16
Costilla	61.57	62.14	32.45	29.23	5.96	8.63	....	....
Crowley	56.65	60.34	38.22	31.13	1.88	1.62	2.82	4.86
Custer	66.82	64.85	11.76	11.08	4.97	8.26	16.45	15.78
Delta	74.67	71.06	23.00	25.08	1.00	2.23	.66	.43
Dolores	61.73	56.89	14.44	37.05	....	....	23.46	4.70
Douglas	74.17	75.94	25.83	24.00	....	....	....	....
Eagle	84.33	80.74	11.98	14.72	....	....	3.22	3.22
Elbert	73.15	75.41	25.33	23.11	.44	.42	.36	.17
El Paso	58.95	57.23	27.08	27.65	.75	1.07	1.76	.26
Fremont	75.84	63.83	16.68	18.54	2.90	1.73	4.46	14.02
Garfield	72.63	76.65	22.63	18.04	.11	.04	1.89	2.87
Gilpin	66.66	76.04	20.51	9.38	....	....	12.82	14.61
Grand	81.26	81.51	8.85	9.33	....	....	9.09	6.87
Gunnison	82.19	83.06	8.01	6.47	....	....	9.49	8.96
Hinsdale	76.74	85.21	16.27	8.10	....	....	6.97	6.61
Huerfano	84.81	87.97	12.26	9.64	....	....	1.35	.33
Jackson	84.05	89.67	7.96	7.22	....	....	7.60	1.38
Jefferson	80.07	75.68	16.13	18.23	1.36	4.51	.58	1.42
Kiowa	78.68	78.61	18.07	18.29	...	....	1.06	.79
Kit Carson	52.62	49.83	32.81	29.45	6.87	12.10	.22	.07
Lake	72.00	54.32	24.00	44.52	4.00	1.15	....	....
La Plata	74.17	69.58	20.28	19.86	3.42	5.94	.92	1.16
Larimer	52.84	50.83	44.66	38.57	1.27	1.71	.18	.18
Las Animas	69.23	63.69	11.20	8.31	1.98	4.09	10.32	13.63
Lincoln	74.53	72.07	22.90	22.84	.26	.62	1.41	.71
Logan	47.06	51.69	52.47	47.50	....	....	.45	.35
Mesa	76.78	76.78	14.98	13.34	2.10	1.73	4.09	5.32
Mineral	96.54	99.12	3.45	.87	....	....	....	....
Moffat	61.91	55.90	2.87	4.67	2.68	5.77	32.20	33.24
Montezuma	70.57	52.78	24.79	18.31	....	....	30.97	4.53
Montrose	63.56	57.01	28.94	24.27	3.28	3.41	1.39	1.25
Morgan	54.04	55.94	44.48	42.42	.56	.41	.56	.52
Otero	51.39	50.95	41.95	38.04	4.29	.89	1.17	7.29
Ouray	71.76	74.28	27.64	24.88	....	....	.58	.24
Park	60.94	70.71	9.09	5.54	....	....	29.29	23.07
Phillips	35.77	34.92	38.87	35.43	24.91	29.14	....	....
Pitkin	83.33	87.60	11.53	9.78	....	....	5.13	2.61
Prowers	47.03	53.01	36.67	26.93	8.02	9.79	6.34	8.46
Pueblo	78.80	87.63	19.44	10.39	.91	.75	.84	.64
Rio Blanco	75.54	74.96	7.42	7.17	.22	.17	16.81	17.11
Rio Grande	69.56	73.45	30.44	26.33	....	....	....	....
Routt	72.50	78.18	13.89	14.04	.58	.68	12.01	5.18
Saguache	64.23	76.54	33.62	20.76	....	....	2.15	2.69
San Miguel	66.82	63.83	4.81	24.85	....	....	28.37	11.15
Sedgwick	37.81	32.14	43.81	38.06	18.16	29.22	....	....
Summit	98.00	99.11	2.00	.89	....	....	....	....
Teller	73.13	82.44	16.78	9.81	....	....	10.09	7.47
Washington	57.27	53.16	31.65	26.22	9.02	15.48	.36	.09
Weld	51.05	53.89	42.12	36.89	2.13	4.13	.24	.32
Yuma	68.86	69.38	26.59	25.21	3.48	4.14	.68	.19
State	64.43	64.72	26.17	22.76	2.55	4.06	4.32	4.69

FARM ACREAGE REPORTED UNDER VARIOUS TENURES AND TOTAL FARM ACREAGES, 1923

COUNTY	Acreage Owners	Acreage Renters	Acreage Owners and Renters	Acreage Home-steaders	Acreage Tenure Not Specified	Total Farm Acreage*
Adams	179,427	108,312	14,767	40	8,153	317,304
Alamosa	91,751	20,360	......	......	1,080	116,102
Arapahoe	107,443	48,943	7,891	......	1,125	169,198
Archuleta	72,956	4,600	......	980	......	79,061
Baca	313,353	39,290	......	8,620	13,252	462,120
Bent	130,237	63,133	6,395	23,094	1,760	231,075
Boulder	46,788	34,727	1,763	2,080	15,271	104,298
Chaffee	50,777	8,858	......	160	......	60,285
Cheyenne	164,445	65,934	......	633	960	234,066
Clear Creek	9,460	1,689	54	562	......	11,765
Conejos	77,093	17,565	4,376	160	......	99,194
Costilla	43,376	20,419	6,025	......	......	69,820
Crowley	59,751	30,661	1,590	4,800	320	97,859
Custer	117,658	20,117	15,021	28,633	......	181,429
Delta	85,477	30,176	2,686	520	776	120,276
Dolores	42,669	27,658	......	3,512	......	74,647
Douglas	221,270	70,086	......	......	......	291,356
Eagle	44,439	8,103	......	1,774	221	55,040
Elbert	494,817	151,663	2,796	1,120	480	656,125
El Paso	292,522	141,301	5,470	1,320	51,798	511,085
Fremont	33,105	9,616	899	7,273	5	51,864
Garfield	113,047	26,616	70	4,247	......	147,475
Gilpin	8,816	1,088	......	1,695	......	11,599
Grand	137,974	15,798	......	11,635	3,509	169,272
Gunnison	86,533	6,740	......	9,340	320	104,169
Hinsdale	10,303	980	......	800	......	12,083
Huerfano	215,864	23,666	......	800	55	245,380
Jackson	199,651	16,089	......	6,088	......	222,635
Jefferson	63,158	15,214	3,760	1,184	324	83,451
Kiowa	190,481	44,320	......	1,920	......	242,304
Kit Carson	285,086	168,476	69,220	410	34,351	572,036
Lake	7,533	6,174	160	......	......	13,867
La Plata	112,322	32,060	9,590	1,880	426	161,381
Larimer	90,005	68,287	3,045	320	898	177,036
Las Animas	395,985	51,665	25,477	84,718	40,987	621,683
Lincoln	345,031	109,366	2,946	3,411	160	478,732
Logan	356,719	327,865	......	2,440	......	690,138
Mesa	180,413	31,356	4,083	12,511	5,718	234,964
Mineral	18,695	160	......	......	......	18,855
Moffat	492,887	41,183	50,903	293,055	779	881,618
Montezuma	70,573	24,480	......	4,558	160	100,602
Montrose	76,221	32,457	4,562	1,673	741	133,683
Morgan	207,122	157,093	1,516	1,960	1,000	370,242
Otero	62,899	46,965	1,109	9,028	836	123,437
Ouray	24,176	8,099	......	80	......	32,546
Park	147,972	11,603	......	48,290	......	209,274
Phillips	105,107	106,636	87,696	......	640	300,927
Pitkin	38,427	4,294	......	1,143	......	43,864
Prowers	174,478	90,350	32,842	28,401	3,485	335,441
Pueblo	561,880	66,681	4,847	4,122	......	641,170
Rio Blanco	131,924	12,632	300	31,108	......	175,964
Rio Grande	98,377	35,270	......	......	......	133,924
Routt	188,130	33,791	1,634	12,478	1,443	240,610
Saguache	78,354	21,260	......	2,750	......	102,364
San Miguel	136,339	53,087	......	23,819	......	213,576
Sedgwick	40,491	47,940	36,801	......	......	125,940
Summit	17,931	160	......	......	......	18,091
Teller	86,005	10,240	......	7,800	......	104,314
Washington	448,844	221,417	130,678	800	9,308	844,286
Weld	459,259	314,391	35,212	2,712	11,956	852,097
Yuma	551,249	200,293	32,835	1,540	2,540	794,459
State	9,695,075	3,409,453	609,019	703,997	214,837	14,979,458

* The figures in this column include the estimated acreage of farms for which acreages were not reported.

DISTRIBUTION OF FARMS ACCORDING TO SIZE, 1923

COUNTY	Less Than 3 Acres	3 to 10 Acres	10 to 20 Acres	20 to 50 Acres	50 to 100 Acres	100 to 175 Acres	175 to 260 Acres	260 to 500 Acres	500 to 1,000 Acres	1,000 Acres & Over
Adams	6	138	145	166	170	284	58	264	95	24
Alamosa	....	3	1	3	29	156	15	105	26	9
Arapahoe	4	64	54	86	78	130	44	161	76	21
Archuleta	....	1	1	17	32	147	30	47	16	8
Baca	....	....	....	4	14	96	28	641	146	25
Bent	....	1	8	59	85	193	53	289	42	6
Boulder	3	23	48	123	248	259	86	62	8	....
Chaffee	3	3	16	17	24	82	24	55	14	6
Cheyenne	....	....	....	1	1	124	9	303	92	24
Clear Creek	....	4	4	3	2	7	4	4	3	2
Conejos	....	3	15	92	110	125	43	39	13	3
Costilla	....	11	43	88	72	53	22	22	6	1
Crowley	....	1	4	64	103	131	26	125	7	....
Custer	....	....	....	3	13	68	38	131	103	25
Delta	32	67	164	513	356	232	68	34	9	....
Dolores	....	....	....	....	13	94	10	155	5	....
Douglas	....	....	1	10	19	52	36	124	106	68
Eagle	....	....	1	8	20	79	27	64	10	4
Elbert	....	....	1	3	18	187	77	492	208	111
El Paso	....	1	1	24	34	187	73	515	179	61
Fremont	193	348	128	160	47	54	15	35	17	1
Garfield	5	20	27	122	130	217	64	82	23	8
Gilpin	1	....	2	4	3	9	3	12	3	3
Grand	....	5	12	4	15	207	18	125	60	23
Gunnison	....	....	....	4	12	124	43	99	41	10
Hinsdale	....	....	....	....	3	21	2	12	4	1
Huerfano	1	4	7	34	39	124	43	136	65	31
Jackson	....	1	....	....	2	65	11	58	70	54
Jefferson	29	143	168	125	74	93	19	117	35	11
Kiowa	....	....	....	....	2	39	4	403	81	22
Kit Carson	....	....	....	4	26	250	76	628	204	60
Lake	....	....	....	....	1	26	5	23	22	6
La Plata	....	....	5	40	97	186	72	105	25	4
Larimer	2	32	42	130	224	333	66	79	25	13
Las Animas	9	32	43	145	170	286	68	713	251	50
Lincoln	....	....	1	2	11	135	45	639	207	42
Logan	....	5	1	4	57	222	62	328	86	24
Mesa	22	240	456	753	444	371	105	108	46	11
Mineral	....	....	....	....	1	14	....	4	3	7
Moffat	....	....	1	20	40	219	57	824	454	36
Montezuma	....	1	5	40	84	106	42	36	9	1
Montrose	2	20	53	286	315	232	61	71	17	2
Morgan	....	1	4	39	266	462	123	442	83	29
Otero	4	32	83	258	293	182	53	34	18	2
Ouray	....	....	....	10	25	82	15	33	2	1
Park	....	....	2	2	7	54	15	68	103	45
Phillips	....	....	....	3	6	109	59	354	131	32
Pitkin	....	....	1	6	17	47	26	38	16	4
Prowers	....	....	1	51	130	335	111	414	106	16
Pueblo	2	25	104	228	202	297	106	410	140	64
Rio Blanco	....	....	....	1	2	43	20	93	42	12
Rio Grande	....	....	....	2	16	126	30	106	16	5
Routt	....	2	....	12	25	206	60	225	71	11
Saguache	....	....	1	4	8	101	14	107	18	6
San Miguel	....	....	....	7	37	215	36	234	96	18
Sedgwick	1	1	1	12	92	154	102	128	38	3
Summit	....	....	....	....	1	20	3	16	7	3
Teller	2	1	....	10	27	220	47	77	30	15
Washington	....	....	1	16	69	319	99	910	336	75
Weld	5	18	27	163	864	1,267	353	675	154	27
Yuma	....	2	....	1	19	194	101	777	372	89
State	326	1,253	1,683	3,986	5,344	10,452	3,025	13,410	4,691	1,275

NUMBER OF FARMS AND AVERAGE NUMBER OF ACRES IN CULTIVATION PER FARM AS REPORTED BY COUNTY ASSESSORS

COUNTY	Total Number of Farms				Average Acreage in Cultivation per Farm			
	1923	1922	1921	1920	1923	1922	1921	1920
Adams	1,535	1,485	1,450	1,326	107.65	117.35	102.28	109.30
Alamosa	359	333	255	161	128.19	137.01	157.55	178.61
Arapahoe	624	650	375	803	128.87	107.54	115.06	98.05
Archuleta	301	199	293	288	37.97	50.77	50.11	53.52
Baca	1,266	1,559	1,532	755	154.82	157.73	128.81	113.56
Bent	859	915	931	753	92.34	97.48	87.29	82.78
Boulder	796	967	745	1,083	87.63	79.39	77.14	76.43
Chaffee	246	258	251	189	68.09	61.55	65.23	76.91
Cheyenne	559	660	638	557	155.12	175.00	139.03	98.91
Clear Creek	36	36	33	25	22.33	24.03	29.24	38.72
Conejos	549	563	504	340	107.93	116.74	112.67	113.92
Costilla	419	483	462	368	73.59	95.35	83.70	74.28
Crowley	531	655	671	658	69.50	67.64	71.82	77.33
Custer	383	387	370	224	61.52	63.94	70.12	92.42
Delta	1,500	1,395	1,533	1,518	30.03	38.51	34.77	33.09
Dolores	277	277	238	217	33.66	39.57	36.43	30.17
Douglas	426	436	491	430	107.86	105.08	104.30	104.88
Eagle	217	269	266	236	73.22	82.52	79.79	70.02
Elbert	1,125	1,205	1,190	1.198	130.16	124.03	119.74	112.78
El Paso	1,189	1,260	1,110	1,269	104.38	94.15	101.46	104.94
Fremont	1,031	833	799	833	15.89	20.82	19.61	21.08
Garfield	844	919	851	799	56.87	58.98	61.17	65.26
Gilpin	39	43	41	36	36.56	29.23	32.90	35.64
Grand	475	514	378	306	59.01	58.90	73.14	81.66
Gunnison	337	349	347	299	93.93	94.75	93.93	114.43
Hinsdale	43	75	67	40	65.04	28.55	32.28	57.33
Huerfano	685	676	688	987	32.09	40.18	31.57	48.93
Jackson	276	336	385	159	251.35	164.88	185.86	460.50
Jefferson	1,029	1,202	1,160	748	34.69	40.71	34.74	41.01
Kiowa	564	615	550	427	155.60	146.22	123.95	78.58
Kit Carson	1,353	1,486	1,588	1,263	244.15	199.37	196.81	166.92
Lake	25	33	34	24	132.64	87.94	135.44	151.79
La Plata	759	863	857	649	48.77	48.01	53.33	61.67
Larimer	1,088	1,207	1,258	1,140	96.33	90.79	92.11	90.76
Las Animas	1,820	1,763	1,779	1,759	46.96	57.05	51.27	46.06
Lincoln	1,131	1,254	1,251	1,241	165.21	142.72	141.07	125.76
Logan	2,216	2,488	2,526	2,295	181.26	170.84	171.06	175.78
Mesa	2,662	3,018	3,004	1,705	22.61	20.99	20.81	27.44
Mineral	29	31	28	32	96.41	95.38	102.25	97.06
Moffat	2,195	1,916	1,120	891	24.11	31.40	46.52	60.25
Montezuma	605	620	588	833	40.37	54.38	56.32	54.55
Montrose	1,216	1,185	1,104	1,275	54.08	52.61	56.92	53.18
Morgan	1,432	1,473	1,498	1,494	132.73	123.53	120.04	113.78
Otero	1,187	1,273	1,290	1,601	62.65	66.26	61.22	55.52
Ouray	170	178	148	124	60.84	63.87	64.24	77.96
Park	297	306	305	247	121.22	125.25	135.50	125.87
Phillips	710	755	682	677	296.42	281.12	279.32	268.93
Pitkin	156	201	199	147	78.15	67.16	74.47	86.87
Prowers	1,197	1,359	1,408	1,322	132.13	126.43	106.24	96.76
Pueblo	1,538	1,758	1,732	1,346	57.56	63.28	52.15	69.17
Rio Blanco	458	469	480	381	52.13	64.68	69.87	81.12
Rio Grande	483	483	450	398	129.23	150.53	169.98	172.21
Routt	691	769	688	780	74.75	73.83	86.84	83.09
Saguache	232	231	228	162	207.02	213.67	231.10	224.61
San Miguel	645	518	516	414	30.24	24.93	34.13	42.86
Sedgwick	534	641	643	600	218.44	182.59	178.64	170.12
Summit	50	104	69	90	106.76	64.65	74.84	64.91
Teller	387	270	169	222	55.66	59.13	41.88	37.05
Washington	1,905	2,090	1,888	2,040	232.90	187.36	180.72	176.99
Weld	4,176	4,617	4,177	5,273	121.00	123.28	127.07	119.60
Yuma	1,722	1,867	1,774	1,732	207.64	220.45	211.01	202.74
State	51,589	54,667	52,245	49,117	105.10	104.52	102.55	101.99

PERCENT OF CULTIVATED LAND IN TOTAL AREA BY COUNTIES, 1923

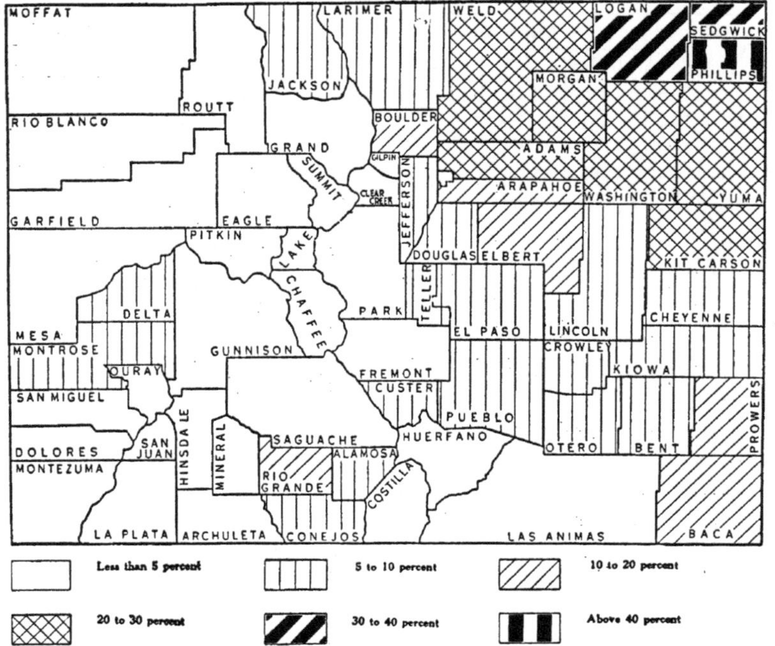

PERCENT OF PATENTED LAND IN TOTAL AREA BY COUNTIES, 1923

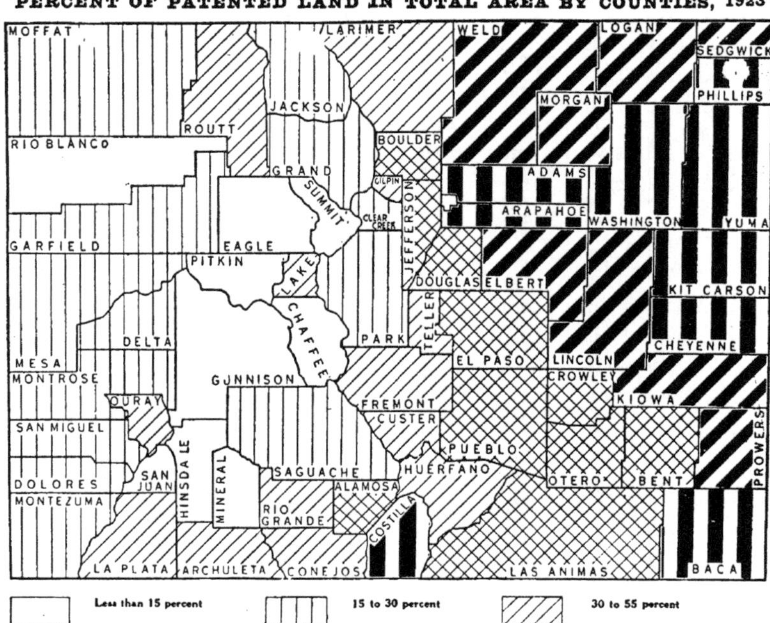

SILOS AND FARM TRACTORS

COUNTY	NUMBER OF SILOS					NUMBER OF FARM TRACTORS				
	1923	1922	1921	1920	1919	1923	1922	1921	1920	1919
Adams	250	363	363	363	363	107	109	135	132	131
Alamosa	....	....	....	....	....	22	35	24	6	1
Arapahoe	107	145	145	123	43	66	47	126	126	126
Archuleta	....	....	....	....	....	6	2	2	....	....
Baca	12	86	86	3	....	20	83	89	8	....
Bent	52	76	76	76	76	48	60	68	50	13
Boulder	211	267	261	261	189	41	91	97	97	70
Chaffee	6	16	16	6	....	15	12	16	16	14
Cheyenne	50	86	86	86	86	111	90	78	56	14
Clear Creek	1	1	....	....	....	....	....	....	....	....
Conejos	8	5	3	3	3	28	29	47	22	19
Costilla	10	10	10	6	6	30	44	52	51	18
Crowley	26	26	26	26	6	2	20	36	36	20
Custer	7	7	7	1	1	23	19	18	8	....
Delta	122	91	91	91	91	26	12	15	12	....
Dolores	1	....	....	....	....	....	1	3	1	....
Douglas	192	179	171	153	116	71	58	68	65	35
Eagle	....	....	....	....	....	14	9	11	2	2
Elbert	137	190	190	144	113	110	136	131	131	71
El Paso	237	237	237	120	116	134	16	57	57	44
Fremont	17	33	33	14	13	11	16	11	8	....
Garfield	12	9	5	5	3	21	23	28	28	6
Gilpin	....	....	....	....	....	....	....	....	....	....
Grand	....	....	....	....	....	11	8	3	3	1
Gunnison	....	....	....	....	....	5	3	5	3	....
Hinsdale	....	....	....	....	....	2	1	....	....	....
Huerfano	27	27	27	27	27	25	42	79	39	31
Jackson	....	....	....	....	....	....	1	1	1	....
Jefferson	64	51	51	35	35	35	46	54	36	23
Kiowa	44	44	44	44	44	60	65	35	28	11
Kit Carson	121	121	121	121	76	232	226	226	124	26
Lake	....	....	....	....	....	....	....	....	....	....
La Plata	16	92	92	16	7	13	10	27	18	5
Larimer	146	146	146	118	94	67	80	101	86	50
Las Animas	48	60	60	60	58	37	39	55	55	16
Lincoln	80	112	112	112	78	147	123	145	107	49
Logan	39	39	39	39	9	278	409	431	369	225
Mesa	64	59	59	59	32	27	20	34	34	34
Mineral	....	....	....	....	....	....	....	....	....	....
Moffat	40	40	40	37	31	27	41	47	38	14
Montezuma	8	59	59	59	6	13	4	15	12	4
Montrose	61	61	61	61	61	31	25	40	28	1
Morgan	29	29	23	23	....	105	130	139	54	38
Otero	155	169	169	154	77	49	39	66	57	21
Ouray	....	....	....	....	....	4	2	2	2	....
Park	2	....	....	....	....	7	4	9	2	1
Phillips	5	11	5	4	4	230	279	315	224	146
Pitkin	....	....	....	....	....	9	4	10	10	10
Prowers	102	102	102	102	93	103	118	85	85	27
Pueblo	150	146	146	146	96	97	102	83	63	15
Rio Blanco	1	1	....	....	....	17	17	27	19	1
Rio Grande	4	....	....	....	....	15	12	8	3	3
Routt	4	2	2	1	....	19	31	28	27	20
Saguache	1	2	2	2	....	26	19	10	7	....
San Miguel	3	3	2	2	....	11	13	24	17	5
Sedgwick	11	43	43	43	4	185	191	223	170	107
Summit	....	....	....	....	....	....	....	....	....	....
Teller	....	....	....	....	....	7	5	2	1	....
Washington	31	31	31	31	31	305	201	338	338	338
Weld	554	523	523	523	431	258	473	504	504	365
Yuma	31	9	9	9	9	149	157	214	137	79
State	3,299	3,809	3,774	3,309	2,528	3,512	3,856	4,497	3,613	2,253

BROOD SOWS, HENS, HOGS SLAUGHTERED AND MILCH COWS

COUNTY	Brood Sows		Hens		Hogs Slaughtered		Heifers Broken for Milch Cows	
	1923	1922	1923	1922	1923	1922	1923	1922
Adams	1,408	1,339	56,271	39,447	1,442	993	1,032	443
Alamosa	1,167	1,337	9,302	9,737	1,500	....	1,113	35
Arapahoe	759	709	31,059	24,061	511	437	315	338
Archuleta	266	125	5,847	2,251	387	291	109	75
Baca	1,836	2,112	51,891	58,331	2,250	420	....	3
Bent	1,516	1,520	30,537	43,188	1,204	1,121	439	340
Boulder	523	667	42,090	44,200	892	1,066	1,659	1,923
Chaffee	518	625	6,578	7,515	956	1,295	81	110
Cheyenne	1,857	1,599	31,464	23,103	714	....	186	4
Clear Creek	1	2	661	761	11	17	1	12
Conejos	2,209	2,121	10,637	15,693	1,379	1,177	100	99
Costilla	1,330	1,247	8,524	9,105	565	557	95	101
Crowley	1,101	1,196	22,133	23,341	511	537	177	201
Custer	176	161	10,568	9,348	833	554	44	52
Delta	1,168	855	45,541	38,626	2,365	2,490	455	490
Dolores	143	245	3,476	4,023	320	410	23	25
Douglas	758	712	23,262	20,526	662	718	373	699
Eagle	235	214	4,395	4,912	540	420	61	27
Elbert	2,612	2,876	54,456	48,998	1,907	2,147	942	1,099
El Paso	1,999	2,149	48,037	51,468	1,694	1,338	323	492
Fremont	204	186	40,810	28,683	838	681	529	285
Garfield	1,142	991	28,629	28,686	1,709	1,842	328	356
Gilpin	7	6	1,225	111	24	9	17	19
Grand	21	48	3,832	3,533	147	156	130	131
Gunnison	64	40	4,577	4,740	279	195	57	52
Hinsdale	6	1	249	250	37	33	15	....
Huerfano	632	762	12,318	13,596	624	1,104	1,203	375
Jackson	13	35	3,390	2,848	95	58	14	7
Jefferson	227	319	39,593	44,315	152	278	1,717	475
Kiowa	1,238	1,324	26,427	27,468	507	540	292	207
Kit Carson	5,146	4,326	84,016	87,695	2,313	2,303	783	986
Lake	....	1	512	538	....	....	16	17
La Plata	1,214	1,233	21,529	21,900	1,274	981	276	180
Larimer	1,206	1,109	53,364	54,663	1,187	1,324	275	365
Las Animas	647	1,088	51,441	51,846	1,612	1,875	646	478
Lincoln	3,591	3,172	66,454	62,143	1,780	1,454	1,123	687
Logan	5,403	4,143	101,197	101,597	2,431	2,421	828	845
Mesa	1,184	1,033	55,729	52,818	2,949	2,583	1,073	868
Mineral	5	2	324	236	5	9	5	5
Moffat	521	785	17,136	20,775	1,415	1,391	205	300
Montezuma	1,825	2,084	18,644	18,629	1,056	1,086	124	221
Montrose	1,724	1,081	46,577	40,200	2,411	1,895	360	348
Morgan	3,392	2,742	56,378	48,850	1,693	1,608	609	409
Otero	1,775	2,136	54,079	44,832	1,920	1,588	414	386
Ouray	138	118	2,735	2,868	101	171	37	67
Park	44	56	5,400	5,136	168	184	75	117
Phillips	3,515	3,097	46,872	42,815	1,420	1,515	329	364
Pitkin	208	201	3,779	3,917	383	361	....	15
Prowers	2,110	2,366	66,414	70,269	2,150	2,103	794	940
Pueblo	1,613	1,994	57,266	59,163	1,781	2,177	656	752
Rio Blanco	465	462	10,035	9,645	808	803	153	184
Rio Grande	1,012	495	27,440	27,146	850	500	250	150
Routt	554	660	21,589	20,181	1,909	1,289	425	407
Saguache	916	851	7,234	7,140	209	407	....	....
San Miguel	256	227	6,290	4,746	659	527	51	51
Sedgwick	2,194	1,852	30,100	29,554	1,036	1,038	413	265
Summit	36	60	1,776	1,408	110	....	212	426
Teller	76	44	9,243	4,543	54	3	47	40
Washington	5,581	4,205	101,488	93,867	2,724	2,075	2,577	1,523
Weld	4,868	5,557	167,977	123,827	5,486	4,689	3,727	5,621
Yuma	7,469	7,048	89,570	98,481	3,200	3,254	2,489	2,917
State	83,824	79,769	1,940,367	1,844,362	70,149	62,498	30,802	28,428

LIVESTOCK IN COLORADO AS REPORTED BY COUNTY ASSESSORS FOR 1923

COUNTY	Horses	Mules	Range Cattle	Milch Cows	Sheep	Swine	Goats	Poultry Doz.	Bee Stands
Adams	8,312	420	8,418	6,065	4,005	12,937	....	7,278	1,500
Alamosa	2,449	196	11,228	1,097	10,293	2,244	....	892	130
Arapahoe	3,320	204	8,592	4,247	6,393	3,181	42	5,574	1,220
Archuleta	1,461	39	11,825	651	21,880	1,081	1,316	586	420
Baca	10,060	2,240	26,549	155	2,177	8,456	....	5,710	....
Bent	5,921	1,002	15,311	1,275	16,204	4,718	....	3,175	1,434
Boulder	4,577	365	6,315	5,536	2,158	2,506	....	....	4,170
Chaffee	1,452	35	6,850	1,150	2,710	1,436	19	848	57
Cheyenne	4,537	694	19,968	2,634	9,614	6,174	....	3,177	....
Clear Creek	303	14	335	113	2,500	9	....	102	....
Conejos	2,467	154	11,955	697	68,636	3,868	....	1,200	244
Costilla	1,781	153	4,603	508	13,804	2,918	235	892	5
Crowley	3,363	533	15,261	175	490	5,367	....	2,892	1,519
Custer	1,526	63	10,492	599	1,719	303	....	633	64
Delta	5,508	455	24,240	4,886	30,187	3,493	....	5,022	5,555
Denver	1,602	83	......	1,117	....	....	....	2,225	....
Dolores	710	81	5,371	286	7,958	258	....	301	....
Douglas	2,232	104	12,639	5,050	2,911	2,301	130	2,133	263
Eagle	2,019	49	17,520	778	2,375	527	....	534	....
Elbert	6,068	1,078	18,381	5,872	21,230	8,838	....	5,144	199
El Paso	5,465	1,298	22,505	6,155	100	....	225	6,156	246
Fremont	2,779	350	13,959	1,526	3,907	1,017	179	5,105	659
Garfield	6,104	244	34,278	3,493	19,328	4,349	....	3,362	3,734
Gilpin	198	7	559	103	47	18	58	....	....
Grand	2,400	27	15,409	1,473	10,818	151	....	448	....
Gunnison	3,063	128	31,108	846	18,207	322	....	556	6
Hinsdale	298	22	2,020	51	2,208	14	....	....	....
Huerfano	2,994	560	15,703	1,137	17,168	1,150	400	1,010	252
Jackson	3,650	36	39,830	573	2,054	114	....	334	....
Jefferson	4,041	158	10,702	4,415	844	1,132	289	7,603	3,872
Kiowa	2,030	358	14,801	630	6,275	1,209	....	2,861	....
Kit Carson	11,468	2,000	22,825	3,320	3,870	15,166	66	8,283	....
Lake	363	....	596	226	....	25	....	....	....
La Plata	4,335	199	18,792	1,680	25,718	3,851	1,247	2,661	2,277
Larimer	9,677	573	22,393	5,764	16,361	5,479	....	8,018	4,620
Las Animas	10,276	1,440	40,180	1,885	36,079	3,343	6,600	4,032	135
Lincoln	7,589	1,171	38,850	2,872	8,404	11,176	....	6,500	....
Logan	11,840	1,021	20,460	7,020	290	14,714	....	10,000	1,080
Mesa	6,675	444	39,250	5,338	28,885	....	2,500	7,900	4,116
Mineral	299	12	1,738	72	4,460	16	....	64	....
Moffat	8,126	218	25,003	1,389	24,855	1,209	....	1,611	32
Montezuma	3,378	340	15,343	2,247	31,283	5,446	151	2,101	1,897
Montrose	6,217	330	24,775	2,796	27,300	4,537	....	4,545	3,993
Morgan	10,408	758	15,873	3,999	1,500	10,898	....	6,623	659
Otero	7,943	1,414	12,728	3,480	12,123	9,731	139	9,094	3,961
Ouray	950	51	5,911	285	5,505	250	....	165	63
Park	2,281	88	15,525	610	42,907	277	21	610	....
Phillips	4,572	647	5,865	1,343	16	10,518	....	4,256	....
Pitkin	1,319	29	6,740	665	3,252	738	56	432	74
Prowers	9,946	1,940	21,429	2,813	7,212	6,696	....	7,162	2,021
Pueblo	5,285	553	17,333	4,481	1,424	6,449	135	6,430	1,436
Rio Blanco	3,580	154	35,661	928	2,120	746	....	934	....
Rio Grande	3,081	562	12,193	1,953	45,613	3,502	50	....	....
Routt	8,318	121	45,565	3,245	36,204	2,416	....	2,981	....
Saguache	3,426	319	35,843	570	77,026	2,106	792	1,119	52
San Juan	58	52	52	44	8,297	....	....	....	....
San Miguel	1,441	61	14,987	794	4,498	665	....	669	....
Sedgwick	3,980	269	7,144	857	585	6,080	....	2,776	263
Summit	627	5	3,766	449	....	63	....	93	....
Teller	1,341	112	7,192	906	149	205	....	167	....
Washington	13,706	1,340	26,710	378	11,403	14,201	....	10,018	248
Weld	26,679	2,477	34,034	15,785	12,479	16,730	....	19,125	6,846
Yuma	12,382	2,678	28,706	1,676	170	19,357	....	9,802	12
State	304,256	32,528	1,060,189	143,163	788,188	256,681	14,650	213,924	59,334

NUMBER OF BEEF CATTLE PER SQUARE MILE OF AREA AS REPORTED BY COUNTY ASSESSORS FOR 1923

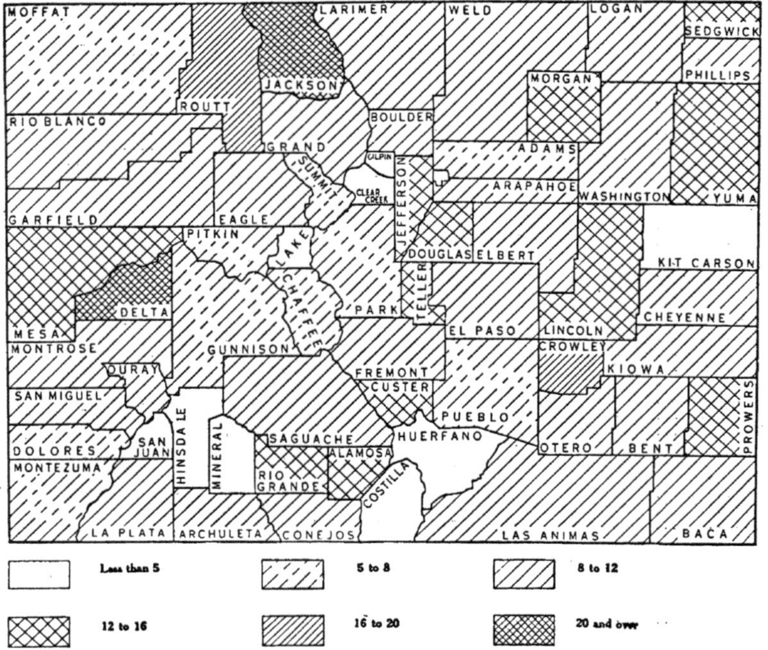

NUMBER OF DAIRY CATTLE PER SQUARE MILE OF AREA AS REPORTED BY COUNTY ASSESSORS FOR 1923

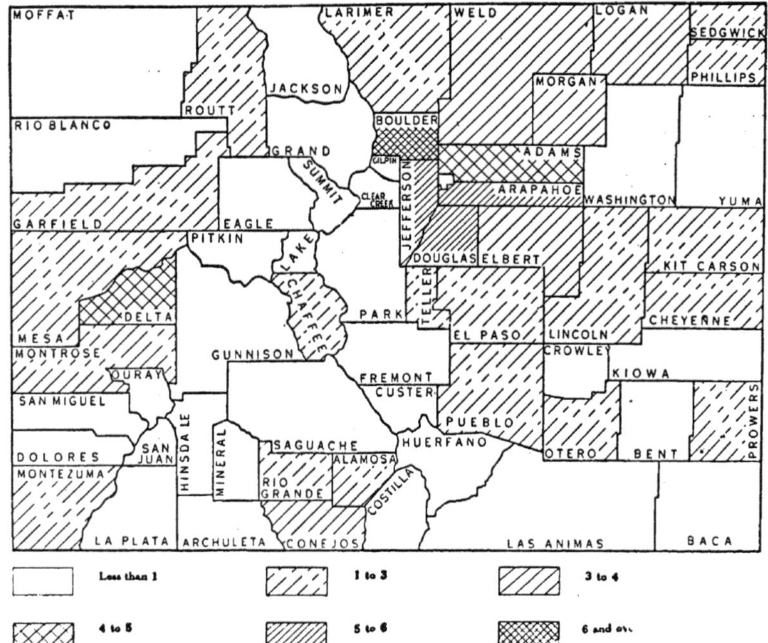

NUMBER OF SHEEP PER SQUARE MILE OF AREA AS REPORTED BY COUNTY ASSESSORS FOR 1923

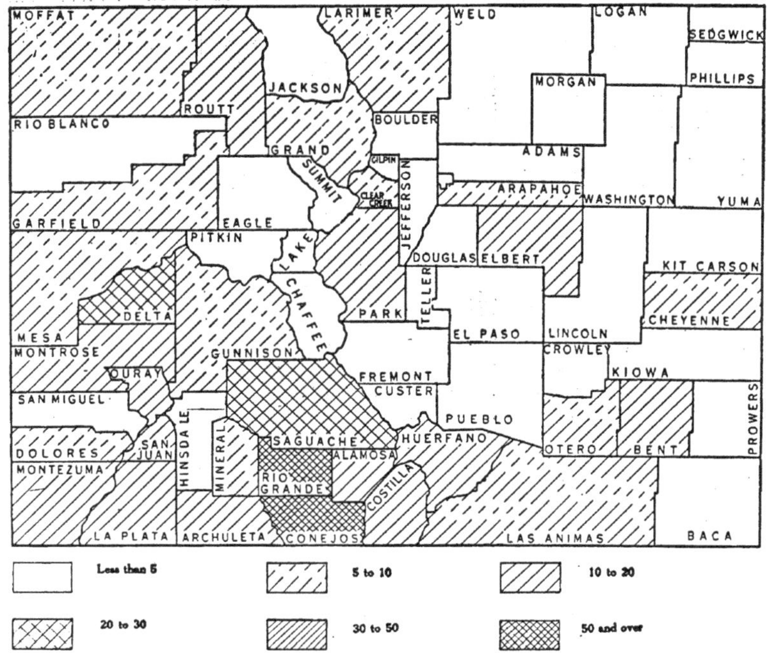

NUMBER OF SWINE PER SQUARE MILE OF AREA AS REPORTED BY COUNTY ASSESSORS FOR 1923

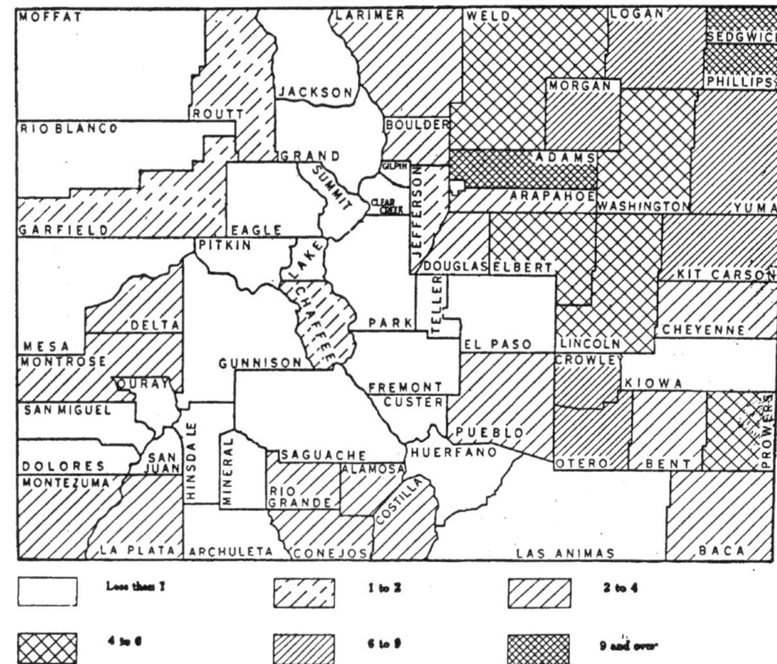

LIVESTOCK IN COLORADO AS REPORTED BY COUNTY ASSESSORS

COUNTY	HORSES				MULES			
	1923	1922	1921	1920	1923	1922	1921	1920
Adams	8,312	6,608	6,755	6,816	420	357	361	297
Alamosa	2,449	2,716	2,511	2,521	196	178	164	166
Arapahoe	3,320	3,797	4,898	3,561	204	240	342	306
Archuleta	1,461	1,468	1,772	1,798	39	49	45	58
Baca	10,060	9,318	9,557	9,601	2,240	2,428	1,948	2,236
Bent	5,921	6,061	6,446	6,540	1,002	1,009	771	816
Boulder	4,577	4,613	4,669	5,128	365	424	464	443
Chaffee	1,452	1,380	1,461	1,427	35	29	19	16
Cheyenne	4,537	4,699	5,021	4,429	694	498	478	419
Clear Creek	303	271	283	292	14	3	3	4
Conejos	2,467	2,803	3,090	3,780	154	179	248	169
Costilla	1,781	1,859	1,725	1,827	153	160	147	169
Crowley	3,363	3,778	4,093	4,106	533	562	538	402
Custer	1,526	1,556	1,507	1,159	63	51	65	66
Delta	5,508	5,730	5,984	6,036	455	557	397	408
Denver	1,602	1,670	1,869	2,724	83	63	61	120
Dolores	710	765	914	1,027	81	93	108	70
Douglas	2,232	2,308	2,194	2,319	104	93	83	63
Eagle	2,019	2,010	2,152	2,387	49	55	48	43
Elbert	6,068	5,996	6,106	6,594	1,078	1,024	1,002	1,200
El Paso	5,465	5,748	5,383	5,814	1,298	1,294	1,131	1,131
Fremont	2,779	2,521	2,752	2,831	350	452	302	262
Garfield	6,104	5,415	5,561	5,853	244	213	199	202
Gilpin	198	189	181	181	7	2	1	1
Grand	2,400	2,585	2,427	2,588	27	55	31	38
Gunnison	3,063	3,292	3,675	3,458	128	109	135	122
Hinsdale	298	328	349	337	22	28	31	20
Huerfano	2,994	2,964	2,933	2,410	560	561	542	540
Jackson	3,650	3,982	3,569	3,471	36	58	74	45
Jefferson	4,041	4,353	4,595	5,076	158	148	150	180
Kiowa	2,030	2,332	3,300	3,433	358	399	457	444
Kit Carson	11,468	12,240	13,243	14,367	2,000	1,764	1,401	1,087
Lake	363	399	402	503	......	3	3	19
La Plata	4,335	4,438	4,494	4,379	199	175	157	141
Larimer	9,677	10,026	11,090	9,371	573	520	511	629
Las Animas	10,276	10,426	13,558	10,861	1,440	1,592	1,543	1,554
Lincoln	7,589	8,785	7,994	8,199	1,171	1,079	901	792
Logan	11,840	12,020	12,000	11,661	1,021	950	1,000	948
Mesa	6,675	6,878	7,434	7,333	444	471	518	421
Mineral	299	368	438	446	12	6	5	7
Moffat	8,126	8,479	7,904	10,092	218	227	168	179
Montezuma	3,378	3,626	3,664	3,681	340	333	327	302
Montrose	6,217	7,405	6,922	7,569	330	286	329	305
Morgan	10,408	10,753	10,950	10,195	758	801	754	739
Otero	7,949	8,787	9,319	9,614	1,414	1,642	1,502	1,514
Ouray	950	1,020	1,059	1,339	51	52	34	46
Park	2,281	2,314	2,363	2,445	88	86	75	89
Phillips	4,572	4,687	4,855	4,608	647	471	424	403
Pitkin	1,319	1,374	1,386	1,418	29	31	16	12
Prowers	9,946	10,289	10,299	9,869	1,940	1,801	1,603	1,434
Pueblo	5,285	6,012	5,544	6,459	553	604	413	511
Rio Blanco	3,580	4,604	5,167	5,170	154	179	165	195
Rio Grande	3,081	3,489	3,636	3,336	562	486	501	515
Routt	8,318	9,282	9,306	8,434	121	146	171	126
Saguache	3,426	3,457	3,542	4,047	319	288	241	210
San Juan	58	62	78	73	52	56	59	49
San Miguel	1,441	1,578	1,693	1,820	61	107	68	95
Sedgwick	3,980	4,596	4,765	4,656	269	210	170	151
Summit	627	711	695	773	5	6	6	6
Teller	1,341	1,351	1,261	1,381	112	76	67	76
Washington	13,706	14,865	16,451	17,142	1,340	1,130	1,083	1,086
Weld	26,679	29,249	29,693	31,964	2,477	3,061	2,929	2,459
Yuma	12,382	12,104	14,732	15,174	2,678	1,731	2,050	2,126
State	304,262	318,798	333,669	337,903	32,528	31,741	29,539	28,682

LIVESTOCK IN COLORADO AS REPORTED BY COUNTY ASSESSORS

COUNTY	RANGE CATTLE				MILCH COWS			
	1923	1922	1921	1920	1923	1922	1921	1920
Adams	8,418	8,121	8,743	9,399	6,065	5,884	6,398	4,783
Alamosa	11,228	11,524	11,226	11,071	1,097	1,073	1,052	884
Arapahoe	8,510	7,523	9,828	9,096	4,247	5,742	5,800	3,743
Archuleta	11,542	12,402	11,053	11,038	651	750	819	838
Baca	26,549	29,168	32,775	33,585	155	116	258	383
Bent	15,311	18,515	22,132	21,691	1,275	1,432	1,302	1,445
Boulder	6,315	6,145	7,188	7,375	5,536	5,686	4,763	4,851
Chaffee	6,850	7,185	7,850	7,763	1,150	1,291	952	706
Cheyenne	19,968	25,246	26,437	29,242	2,634	491	485	1,451
Clear Creek	335	598	648	679	113	144	129	160
Conejos	11,955	12,491	12,895	13,201	697	763	549	854
Costilla	4,603	6,771	4,151	4,111	508	398	400	448
Crowley	15,261	13,160	10,229	8,738	175	536	1,043	2,162
Custer	10,492	10,283	11,063	8,735	599	764	793	358
Delta	24,240	25,626	21,990	22,970	4,886	4,208	5,031	4,852
Denver	......	......	......	......	1,117	1,081	1,080	1,600
Dolores	5,371	6,320	7,588	9,200	286	286	239	193
Douglas	12,229	14,536	14,061	15,681	5,050	5,544	5,157	4,630
Eagle	17,520	18,138	18,808	18,966	778	1,075	1,017	1,070
Elbert	17,691	18,948	22,260	25,067	5,872	6,155	6,418	7,388
El Paso	22,505	23,896	21,634	25,790	6,155	6,405	6,655	7,709
Fremont	13,793	15,500	17,113	15,770	1,526	1,778	1,535	1,136
Garfield	34,278	32,334	32,567	35,602	3,493	2,924	2,861	2,838
Gilpin	559	485	451	612	103	112	77	67
Grand	15,409	16,229	12,823	15,005	1,473	1,264	1,093	1,067
Gunnison	31,108	33,278	40,087	39,705	846	750	686	158
Hinsdale	202	1,869	2,152	2,312	51	38	71	69
Huerfano	15,303	17,518	15,646	14,010	975	1,092	833	655
Jackson	39,830	41,600	38,073	36,719	573	538	529	575
Jefferson	9,776	11,726	13,389	13,730	4,415	4,862	4,640	4,800
Kiowa	14,801	15,304	17,918	19,179	630	923	1,274	1,731
Kit Carson	2,285	20,618	26,784	24,073	3,320	4,835	5,775	7,398
Lake	596	694	546	647	226	219	232	267
La Plata	18,792	19,110	19,774	18,092	1,680	2,011	2,073	1,935
Larimer	22,393	23,974	21,454	23,539	5,764	5,814	5,738	5,508
Las Animas	40,180	50,170	50,860	55,545	1,885	2,720	3,136	2,839
Lincoln	38,850	38,186	34,775	39,701	2,872	2,954	3,469	3,055
Logan	20,460	18,700	18,400	23,820	7,020	6,060	5,700	5,485
Mesa	39,250	43,135	41,321	43,550	5,338	5,000	4,883	4,618
Mineral	1,738	2,002	1,891	2,148	72	78	71	89
Moffat	25,003	19,262	18,574	26,889	1,389	1,749	1,190	998
Montezuma	15,343	16,283	16,157	14,882	2,247	2,480	2,111	2,137
Montrose	24,775	26,789	25,405	26,234	2,796	2,733	2,701	2,774
Morgan	15,873	16,153	15,046	16,671	3,999	4,099	4,069	3,972
Otero	13,537	14,965	16,297	16,072	3,481	2,761	2,595	3,829
Ouray	5,911	7,170	6,524	8,335	285	319	356	388
Park	15,525	17,702	19,381	20,083	610	750	651	742
Phillips	5,865	4,893	5,671	6,172	1,343	1,537	1,601	2,091
Pitkin	6,740	7,498	6,310	6,399	665	706	728	642
Prowers	21,429	26,148	26,099	30,811	2,813	2,466	2,802	2,833
Pueblo	17,333	19,063	17,964	24,346	4,481	4,443	3,784	3,913
Rio Blanco	35,661	38,694	41,787	44,546	928	1,194	1,160	855
Rio Grande	12,193	12,447	11,353	12,157	1,953	1,806	1,843	1,741
Routt	45,565	45,860	41,619	43,538	3,245	3,201	3,010	2,770
Saguache	35,843	34,819	35,686	33,319	570	570	595	490
San Juan	52	147	68	59	44	43	46	46
San Miguel	14,987	16,585	16,531	15,746	794	793	685	816
Sedgwick	7,144	6,868	7,465	8,941	857	1,045	1,145	1,001
Summit	3,766	3,984	3,599	4,165	449	443	342	337
Teller	7,192	7,041	7,108	6,796	906	758	651	562
Washington	26,710	27,732	30,432	31,066	378	.....	115	216
Weld	34,034	33,365	32,956	36,843	15,785	16,837	14,625	12,778
Yuma	28,706	29,820	32,889	36,253	1,676	2,590	3,249	3,147
State	1,035,683	1,112,325	1,123,594	1,187,480	143,002	147,119	145,070	143,981

LIVESTOCK IN COLORADO AS REPORTED BY COUNTY ASSESSORS

COUNTY	SHEEP				SWINE			
	1923	1922	1921	1920	1923	1922	1921	1920
Adams	4,005	2,840	2,911	5,137	12,937	9,578	9,360	10,191
Alamosa	10,293	7,278	6,969	6,177	2,244	2,075	2,397	2,846
Arapahoe	6,393	6,803	12,048	9,029	3,181	2,904	2,450	2,909
Archuleta	21,880	27,157	38,281	40,561	1,081	984	1,449	1,454
Baca	2,177	2,770	2,336	2,416	8,456	8,873	7,141	5,122
Bent	16,204	14,818	18,782	22,728	4,718	2,889	1,482	1,229
Boulder	2,158	548	259	355	2,506	2,124	1,459	2,530
Chaffee	2,710	4,215	2,500	6,758	1,436	1,284	1,717	1,605
Cheyenne	9,614	8,393	8,519	8,453	6,174	4,105	2,931	2,082
Clear Creek	2,500	844	1,903	2,468	9	3	14	15
Conejos	68,636	66,667	93,604	87,028	3,868	2,898	3,157	4,290
Costilla	13,804	9,828	10,157	16,307	2,918	2,956	2,638	3,640
Crowley	490	87	182	247	5,367	3,702	3,088	2,835
Custer	1,719	219	126	28	303	346	376	264
Delta	30,187	34,839	24,230	19,850	3,493	3,019	3,973	4,960
Denver	......	......	......	......	......	......	......	......
Dolores	7,958	9,020	10,832	10,931	258	340	297	164
Douglas	2,911	610	530	1,261	2,301	2,002	1,464	1,345
Eagle	2,375	13,402	11,294	10,321	527	574	542	917
Elbert	21,230	16,584	19,498	22,401	8,838	7,029	5,390	4,506
El Paso	100	1,449	1,996	2,738	......	4,602	3,626	3,425
Fremont	3,907	165	229	......	1,017	1,064	1,276	1,712
Garfield	19,328	19,026	18,054	18,090	4,349	3,034	3,043	4,057
Gilpin	47	13	16	2	18	10	13	16
Grand	10,818	5,985	6,172	5,364	151	142	131	184
Gunnison	18,207	12,254	27,593	29,354	322	260	393	427
Hinsdale	2,208	1,165	4,275	277	14	6	24	23
Huerfano	17,168	21,056	20,327	16,000	1,150	1,326	1,267	810
Jackson	2,054	1,035	888	531	114	128	105	95
Jefferson	844	3,400	4,652	4,376	1,132	1,312	2,328	3,401
Kiowa	6,275	5,555	5,600	6,000	1,209	1,211	1,185	749
Kit Carson	3,870	3,418	2,774	1,410	15,166	10,123	6,056	4,767
Lake	......	32	2,600	9,153	25	2	......	......
La Plata	25,718	34,084	36,609	38,887	3,851	3,410	3,867	4,561
Larimer	16,361	15,071	12,111	12,387	5,479	4,032	3,928	5,787
Las Animas	36,079	39,639	41,377	44,937	3,343	3,278	2,546	2,370
Lincoln	8,404	7,324	4,893	6,553	11,176	7,750	4,322	3,868
Logan	290	166	271	393	14,714	9,746	7,000	7,754
Mesa	28,885	30,607	17,262	24,472	......	......	......	......
Mineral	4,460	4,923	8,115	6,185	16	9	8	9
Moffat	24,855	28,552	21,173	29,707	1,209	1,668	782	1,180
Montezuma	31,283	32,925	33,618	35,500	5,446	5,151	6,625	5,779
Montrose	27,300	32,583	37,146	48,127	4,537	2,971	3,471	4,568
Morgan	1,500	1,500	1,400	3,000	10,898	8,826	5,469	5,710
Otero	12,123	8,752	10,444	14,655	9,681	7,138	5,566	5,437
Ouray	5,505	8,206	8,200	9,000	250	211	250	356
Park	42,907	41,966	43,083	44,780	277	162	141	213
Phillips	16	39	......	......	10,518	6,750	5,970	4,284
Pitkin	3,252	3,773	5,454	7,532	738	674	592	634
Prowers	7,212	6,615	5,962	8,720	6,696	5,765	4,347	3,857
Pueblo	1,424	1,616	1,783	6,697	6,449	5,685	3,140	3,467
Rio Blanco	2,120	6,072	1,800	3,505	746	926	580	1,114
Rio Grande	45,613	46,651	46,139	43,918	3,502	3,226	4,073	4,999
Routt	36,204	35,855	36,440	30,077	2,416	2,121	1,659	2,110
Saguache	77,026	79,438	84,936	93,125	2,106	2,090	1,841	2,662
San Juan	8,297	10,171	10,494	10,922	......	......	......	......
San Miguel	4,498	4,921	5,461	6,521	665	582	547	747
Sedgwick	585	163	......	686	6,080	4,796	3,484	2,643
Summit	......	......	2	2	63	60	64	74
Teller	149	......	......	......	205	207	183	180
Washington	11,403	7,571	10,183	6,635	14,201	9,623	7,490	6,020
Weld	12,479	10,566	11,330	12,698	16,730	14,295	10,918	12,362
Yuma	......	90	50	22	19,357	14,000	13,209	12,182
State	788,018	801,314	855,973	915,394	256,631	206,057	172,844	177,497

AVERAGE VALUE OF MULES PER HEAD AS RETURNED BY COUNTY ASSESSORS ANNUALLY FOR PAST TEN YEARS

COUNTY	1923	1922	1921	1920	1919	1918	1917	1916	1915	1914
Adams	$38.10	$71.20	$73.16	$89.40	$113.50	$105.00	$103.68	$121.08	$95.21	$93.64
Alamosa	65.30	84.15	92.53	129.39	111.90	118.77	87.80	87.01	89.86	81.57
Arapahoe	42.32	54.38	64.03	75.33	84.73	90.00	95.00	92.00	86.20	82.05
Archuleta	42.57	62.95	86.70	77.67	60.00	79.50	65.53	87.42	49.90	63.71
Baca	41.58	40.00	57.53	73.00	60.00	74.90	78.49	72.81	57.32	45.97
Bent	45.80	54.09	69.00	79.17	70.25	102.11	99.91	99.98	72.30	68.11
Boulder	73.67	85.97	90.04	98.62	114.81	113.52	113.68	103.40	103.05	88.59
Chaffee	50.57	56.20	67.85	91.25	85.00	86.62	75.83	84.11	82.50	100.00
Cheyenne	32.28	49.88	59.03	78.01	81.56	89.17	80.50	69.46	58.44	73.34
Clear Creek	30.00	50.00	60.00	52.50	62.50	61.43	85.00	82.85	65.65	112.50
Conejos	36.15	60.00	65.85	99.42	87.00	162.00	160.00	173.00	95.00	98.53
Costilla	49.87	61.63	71.36	78.20	76.68	102.00	100.00	100.00	89.62	100.73
Crowley	45.13	49.36	55.10	79.71	84.74	90.00	93.48	92.16	94.72	94.80
Custer	42.38	46.26	66.30	85.92	67.80	65.00	53.75	59.00	48.84	53.21
Delta	58.00	53.75	69.31	93.27	95.20	88.19	80.67	81.40	109.00	102.97
Denver	100.84	114.60	117.50	115.34	100.00	100.00	95.00	76.92	77.20	77.16
Dolores	58.39	71.93	81.48	105.21	105.78	108.75	109.06	106.58	90.61	80.83
Douglas	54.71	65.64	75.95	88.17	97.10	83.17	96.94	92.32	76.00	63.15
Eagle	85.20	87.10	94.60	92.68	78.30	97.70	65.29	65.56	93.60	96.15
Elbert	44.13	53.23	62.00	73.66	87.89	97.77	90.05	76.40	72.00	72.37
El Paso	38.76	51.05	61.63	83.50	89.00	94.00	96.00	96.57	82.51	82.92
Fremont	58.27	52.65	68.67	70.13	78.00	88.00	82.50	80.24	72.47	72.75
Garfield	66.37	84.32	87.01	87.48	96.42	95.37	88.02	78.86	95.00	78.77
Gilpin	37.20	62.50	75.00	75.00	75.00	80.00	83.00	58.00	75.00	56.00
Grand	33.00	29.45	48.22	65.48	62.66	56.81	68.84	47.62	55.45	67.27
Gunnison	74.65	82.71	83.00	108.90	104.89	102.00	70.00	37.16	76.94	100.48
Hinsdale	48.64	53.22	46.80	50.00	53.00	46.00	35.00	75.00	58.33	66.66
Huerfano	88.89	96.15	108.40	120.00	122.00	120.00	133.00	101.20	91.15	97.91
Jackson	34.40	44.30	50.87	73.89	84.68	72.81	76.00	70.00	66.00	72.76
Jefferson	48.74	81.66	76.63	74.92	102.45	100.00	120.00	121.00	120.00	110.00
Kiowa	41.76	47.29	60.63	94.62	95.04	98.16	90.06	86.96	92.42	93.09
Kit Carson	27.34	33.21	47.16	56.68	58.04	77.00	76.09	68.27	68.61	66.02
Lake	....	41.33	35.00	30.80	73.20	....	....	....	....	....
La Plata	43.41	51.28	66.21	89.18	72.28	75.27	65.55	65.40	63.31	64.73
Larimer	67.29	91.05	110.32	118.21	123.40	123.00	122.50	116.00	119.27	111.74
Las Animas	72.00	72.19	84.82	86.00	103.00	100.00	100.00	107.48	100.00	93.16
Lincoln	34.56	44.75	55.96	82.60	89.52	103.75	103.00	79.27	71.80	67.20
Logan	52.50	62.61	78.36	100.00	106.98	104.47	96.88	89.82	111.01	87.25
Mesa	61.75	68.30	69.66	86.72	87.82	84.71	85.91	73.74	77.50	86.92
Mineral	50.00	71.84	75.00	77.10	84.00	70.62	77.35	80.32	55.30	35.00
Moffat	43.67	50.01	76.48	86.69	85.40	88.88	100.94	94.71	94.60	105.84
Montezuma	48.68	51.48	58.85	87.59	82.60	83.17	86.00	89.79	90.41	100.00
Montrose	33.51	57.06	72.84	91.97	98.89	90.00	95.00	91.85	98.00	94.19
Morgan	43.82	52.00	70.03	95.61	95.56	135.87	118.20	112.55	102.30	105.34
Otero	45.99	57.61	77.25	97.98	98.78	93.27	90.29	92.77	91.54	103.63
Ouray	50.00	61.15	66.61	72.93	62.04	69.48	85.00	72.60	68.71	71.71
Park	66.87	71.80	76.07	76.18	81.80	86.29	93.06	82.92	77.70	117.20
Phillips	44.59	53.68	59.60	92.59	83.87	79.80	99.11	78.00	66.82	74.07
Pitkin	68.00	60.16	100.00	166.66	101.33	109.50	96.00	72.00	55.67	50.00
Prowers	34.09	46.00	65.92	85.08	80.00	82.00	77.00	81.00	81.00	78.79
Pueblo	69.70	78.96	88.18	100.00	100.89	100.82	100.66	104.18	86.80	83.09
Rio Blanco	62.53	75.80	88.00	93.48	92.30	92.31	95.60	106.51	89.62	93.57
Rio Grande	98.00	101.71	105.31	110.89	113.08	114.20	106.30	110.77	117.76	107.43
Routt	59.50	67.12	77.00	84.69	93.00	93.46	89.86	89.06	87.97	90.27
Saguache	44.20	48.95	61.07	71.70	80.00	80.20	75.00	84.07	70.74	62.76
San Juan	50.96	57.14	64.23	76.12	76.81	90.71	100.00	99.64	74.20	74.25
San Miguel	57.00	61.82	70.60	84.63	79.59	83.55	77.81	81.70	74.90	81.00
Sedgwick	38.56	58.47	84.30	97.64	88.10	90.60	93.95	82.50	83.59	81.10
Summit	67.00	66.66	75.00	75.00	75.00	75.00	73.50	73.75	75.00	77.14
Teller	57.81	71.45	104.48	94.86	83.20	85.86	92.38	115.67	88.82	74.03
Washington	32.12	39.15	47.39	71.29	79.02	82.60	81.25	74.40	72.83	84.53
Weld	46.64	58.36	74.66	97.76	100.26	104.79	101.34	101.76	113.60	101.33
Yuma	32.17	53.41	60.10	71.00	72.00	78.48	75.32	62.90	56.80	67.58
State	$46.10	$56.31	$69.56	$86.33	$ 88.56	$ 95.31	$ 92.80	$ 87.66	$85.54	$85.03

AVERAGE VALUE OF HORSES PER HEAD AS RETURNED BY COUNTY ASSESSORS ANNUALLY FOR PAST TEN YEARS

COUNTY	1923	1922	1921	1920	1919	1918	1917	1916	1915	1914
Adams	$34.57	$66.70	$65.94	$80.32	$87.30	$80.00	$89.49	$82.17	$78.66	$73.58
Alamosa	44.92	48.89	54.37	73.28	73.33	74.18	64.60	63.10	48.26	43.74
Arapahoe	36.35	44.81	47.96	68.03	68.36	73.50	72.00	69.50	63.60	62.86
Archuleta	43.50	60.07	63.21	66.89	61.72	62.10	61.51	55.25	51.16	44.12
Baca	23.10	34.00	37.89	45.00	45.00	46.59	49.36	54.18	36.86	34.20
Bent	35.02	43.16	45.39	60.00	57.71	60.42	59.96	57.24	60.00	58.20
Boulder	54.73	71.29	90.18	95.11	113.04	109.71	108.20	85.53	86.02	83.55
Chaffee	52.45	61.13	65.86	71.23	62.88	59.03	58.40	51.40	57.77	55.67
Cheyenne	25.82	34.42	34.45	52.70	59.09	70.61	68.83	60.58	51.00	40.61
Clear Creek	54.76	62.77	63.35	63.50	66.39	66.34	64.00	62.04	61.00	70.03
Conejos	39.35	57.60	64.76	79.85	75.40	75.00	75.00	76.00	78.00	66.50
Costilla	39.63	44.03	55.13	76.30	74.50	67.00	61.00	56.23	49.61	46.12
Crowley	38.58	42.79	50.34	66.79	67.61	74.00	72.00	72.80	63.41	70.03
Custer	36.82	39.65	52.15	79.65	67.51	60.50	57.96	64.32	62.50	60.36
Delta	52.90	59.58	68.78	89.31	85.01	91.27	81.56	78.90	81.00	75.17
Denver	72.01	72.72	83.50	99.00	100.00	100.00	86.00	85.87	64.35	63.79
Dolores	45.58	62.20	58.16	77.64	78.72	76.58	81.52	76.89	70.50	67.70
Douglas	49.08	46.35	57.59	66.22	68.79	65.73	69.80	56.00	73.00	64.17
Eagle	80.89	87.21	85.41	83.46	81.94	88.17	71.70	70.64	69.62	66.91
Elbert	37.18	42.46	52.21	67.09	68.20	72.89	70.87	61.91	57.73	56.00
El Paso	34.00	41.19	49.38	62.48	67.00	65.42	68.00	66.29	61.15	60.19
Fremont	39.10	44.50	49.29	51.20	53.72	61.40	59.70	58.10	57.11	56.64
Garfield	52.94	66.08	67.59	72.87	72.03	71.43	68.59	65.33	68.92	65.20
Gilpin	55.03	56.06	58.00	59.22	60.48	60.00	61.00	60.00	59.00	58.22
Grand	36.86	37.29	57.65	64.33	64.08	63.77	62.28	63.00	61.37	55.01
Gunnison	48.62	54.00	57.50	68.22	70.06	75.00	72.00	64.01	57.61	61.99
Hinsdale	35.80	38.95	40.40	59.78	58.00	53.00	64.00	50.00	53.45	52.09
Huerfano	42.39	47.10	59.27	62.80	64.50	65.70	64.00	68.58	74.10	74.11
Jackson	17.70	30.07	33.98	45.71	48.88	61.18	57.89	56.43	59.58	61.53
Jefferson	36.94	43.88	57.89	65.00	71.19	67.89	70.05	79.00	78.00	75.13
Kiowa	38.90	39.74	39.60	55.34	59.65	63.28	58.93	59.17	58.40	45.57
Kit Carson	31.42	33.72	43.68	47.09	52.13	78.00	79.10	68.08	70.15	58.58
Lake	57.72	64.52	67.37	77.84	73.95	88.26	88.00	87.96	87.86	88.15
La Plata	37.76	44.40	58.83	69.92	69.20	77.53	68.27	69.02	68.75	67.54
Larimer	51.11	64.10	74.37	111.13	112.00	112.00	101.00	98.50	88.00	87.30
Las Animas	27.38	38.38	35.26	46.00	49.70	43.20	55.18	60.95	50.00	61.00
Lincoln	28.71	28.80	36.92	47.95	54.83	68.05	59.76	59.82	55.57	52.33
Logan	45.95	56.77	62.54	77.77	93.29	95.24	88.49	85.88	81.84	66.24
Mesa	48.75	59.70	61.08	73.50	73.29	74.61	69.24	64.92	65.36	60.26
Mineral	26.35	37.41	38.35	47.36	54.71	50.55	45.50	49.82	49.10	48.72
Moffat	21.70	30.22	39.42	42.15	63.00	65.03	66.83	57.74	54.03	50.60
Montezuma	43.54	47.08	51.26	61.84	71.20	63.60	65.49	66.12	73.91	90.00
Montrose	39.61	50.46	68.20	80.14	81.39	83.82	80.00	69.50	73.00	71.77
Morgan	40.08	47.36	60.86	85.34	87.84	109.44	96.90	90.40	83.50	80.40
Otero	37.56	48.69	61.64	76.99	74.41	81.44	78.26	82.87	75.79	75.82
Ouray	47.49	54.48	64.14	63.40	55.95	80.55	52.17	53.29	56.63	68.87
Park	52.78	56.66	59.53	68.77	71.14	71.28	69.06	61.21	58.14	60.99
Phillips	43.18	43.83	52.20	68.52	66.40	62.05	64.37	62.26	61.93	58.09
Pitkin	60.72	66.80	73.13	71.82	71.29	77.23	71.50	65.74	68.00	64.98
Prowers	28.93	38.00	50.77	60.00	62.00	65.00	62.00	65.00	60.00	61.15
Pueblo	52.25	56.55	60.57	67.57	68.70	69.84	68.65	67.32	67.66	60.07
Rio Blanco	46.70	47.20	54.00	57.08	57.94	58.86	57.67	52.95	55.36	55.86
Rio Grande	70.30	66.58	64.65	73.60	75.70	76.55	74.19	75.03	73.86	72.30
Routt	39.01	48.85	57.42	69.64	75.58	80.33	75.38	72.23	72.66	68.79
Saguache	36.62	41.07	47.30	50.90	51.00	50.11	50.00	49.75	47.67	36.94
San Juan	62.50	57.82	66.41	75.34	68.25	65.08	66.07	64.61	70.70	72.57
San Miguel	53.94	60.93	67.32	86.00	81.00	81.91	73.00	71.98	71.41	70.99
Sedgwick	41.64	50.46	56.40	63.94	62.05	83.25	86.30	78.68	75.87	68.45
Summit	51.24	62.90	64.21	79.84	80.24	95.80	79.05	73.50	83.40	64.78
Teller	48.63	54.16	53.60	57.03	57.06	54.58	54.59	60.14	56.56	54.38
Washington	28.01	31.98	35.82	48.66	59.19	66.55	66.47	72.71	67.62	62.47
Weld	45.23	63.43	76.57	86.96	89.34	95.00	85.45	87.18	83.02	80.86
Yuma	28.59	38.12	42.17	56.00	60.00	68.20	63.32	55.20	57.43	58.03
State	$39.12	$48.15	$55.42	$67.65	$71.16	$76.05	$73.12	$70.53	$67.59	$65.08

AVERAGE VALUE OF RANGE CATTLE PER HEAD AS RETURNED BY COUNTY ASSESSORS ANNUALLY FOR PAST TEN YEARS

COUNTY	1923	1922	1921	1920	1919	1918	1917	1916	1915	1914
Adams	$24.75	$32.80	$30.85	$41.44	$43.00	$46.90	$40.02	$37.50	$35.32	$32.01
Alamosa	23.29	27.36	27.43	42.74	44.24	46.10	36.30	39.13	31.41	35.05
Arapahoe	23.35	33.92	30.58	40.00	41.29	40.00	39.00	39.60	35.00	30.79
Archuleta	24.83	26.47	29.59	46.39	45.00	46.12	46.39	38.18	35.06	25.40
Baca	23.00	25.09	25.01	42.14	41.00	41.76	38.07	42.70	35.00	26.56
Bent	24.18	25.06	26.69	39.88	41.88	42.69	40.43	39.14	38.93	35.45
Boulder	25.31	30.74	32.68	49.68	52.08	49.90	43.72	36.19	35.08	28.67
Chaffee	24.58	28.42	27.94	41.77	42.47	40.16	37.96	37.81	35.16	32.49
Cheyenne	23.10	26.05	25.65	45.87	45.87	45.64	43.29	41.51	39.14	39.85
Clear Creek	23.73	25.00	25.05	40.00	41.44	40.72	40.00	40.00	40.00	40.39
Conejos	23.17	25.51	25.64	41.45	42.00	42.25	41.00	41.00	40.00	37.46
Costilla	25.32	27.77	27.80	51.00	43.00	43.00	40.16	40.00	38.69	36.62
Crowley	27.23	27.42	25.10	47.66	44.85	44.00	43.05	40.33	39.39	34.70
Custer	24.43	26.94	28.31	40.54	41.85	40.00	38.35	37.55	35.06	35.06
Delta	24.68	25.26	26.14	42.84	45.05	44.22	40.91	38.10	36.00	35.42
Denver	....	....	....	....	....	....	....	....	....	....
Dolores	25.01	27.10	27.30	48.71	45.57	44.19	39.82	39.04	37.46	33.67
Douglas	28.51	26.89	29.86	44.87	47.50	49.94	44.39	43.70	34.00	32.34
Eagle	26.79	31.17	30.62	46.53	44.87	46.04	41.86	40.08	35.93	33.50
Elbert	25.33	28.37	27.57	40.33	43.66	43.26	38.20	38.69	35.00	26.27
El Paso	24.00	25.00	29.12	42.50	42.71	42.00	38.00	37.86	32.83	31.96
Fremont	24.95	25.28	27.46	44.05	42.70	41.48	37.05	36.70	35.00	30.26
Garfield	24.28	25.69	26.40	43.24	42.61	43.13	40.22	37.50	37.36	34.50
Gilpin	25.48	26.68	28.57	40.89	40.00	40.00	39.50	38.00	35.00	30.14
Grand	23.94	30.08	31.94	43.17	45.27	41.14	38.96	39.21	39.20	37.24
Gunnison	24.29	26.06	26.66	44.51	47.97	45.00	40.00	38.69	39.25	36.66
Hinsdale	24.00	26.54	25.70	41.13	42.00	40.00	39.00	37.00	32.50	30.29
Huerfano	26.15	27.34	29.12	40.00	42.00	41.93	42.35	38.87	35.02	36.61
Jackson	25.84	26.06	30.81	43.41	44.99	44.09	41.31	40.96	40.39	39.99
Jefferson	31.66	28.55	34.14	47.73	46.17	43.27	40.12	45.00	37.00	35.91
Kiowa	25.00	25.00	26.10	43.18	44.92	46.12	42.39	42.15	43.43	35.25
Kit Carson	23.26	27.89	26.23	41.72	42.95	43.00	40.60	38.10	35.22	29.53
Lake	25.24	30.19	30.42	43.34	42.53	39.99	41.43	40.00	35.03	34.60
La Plata	23.13	25.00	25.00	40.66	40.40	41.18	38.75	37.53	34.82	30.26
Larimer	42.59	25.00	30.36	41.26	42.25	40.00	40.00	39.00	40.00	31.83
Las Animas	23.00	25.52	33.91	43.90	44.00	48.60	37.50	40.00	35.00	32.50
Lincoln	23.28	25.57	26.50	43.12	44.13	43.25	39.33	37.58	35.03	33.15
Logan	23.50	26.27	28.32	42.41	48.21	49.30	43.83	41.18	41.28	35.14
Mesa	24.21	25.15	26.25	42.56	43.20	43.08	38.25	37.36	37.53	36.66
Mineral	23.90	25.60	26.54	40.00	40.00	40.10	40.40	37.48	35.24	29.98
Moffat	23.00	31.98	26.64	47.72	42.50	41.42	48.88	44.18	42.72	39.01
Montezuma	23.08	27.21	29.58	42.84	42.33	40.24	38.05	37.19	35.23	32.71
Montrose	24.70	24.96	27.42	42.75	46.44	45.61	41.85	39.40	36.40	35.42
Morgan	24.72	25.10	27.90	40.60	41.71	45.16	40.84	40.60	34.75	41.77
Otero	23.10	26.45	27.60	42.64	43.22	42.19	39.60	45.35	42.92	42.35
Ouray	24.52	27.00	26.90	43.63	42.26	40.73	38.28	37.78	36.54	35.07
Park	26.70	28.26	28.27	44.18	44.09	43.82	41.24	40.55	40.64	35.00
Phillips	25.73	26.27	26.26	40.28	45.26	43.45	35.00	37.37	35.00	35.01
Pitkin	26.82	30.07	27.65	45.00	48.20	41.75	37.76	37.15	45.58	30.60
Prowers	23.00	25.00	28.56	40.44	41.70	41.00	40.00	38.00	38.26	32.23
Pueblo	29.00	29.50	31.00	46.29	45.73	46.69	42.81	39.99	39.66	36.02
Rio Blanco	25.02	25.96	27.91	44.12	44.00	41.60	41.38	41.51	41.13	35.73
Rio Grande	23.83	25.77	25.93	40.64	40.61	40.05	37.50	37.84	35.85	34.78
Routt	25.59	30.46	34.24	43.25	58.65	48.79	42.82	41.31	38.37	36.65
Saguache	23.64	26.03	26.27	40.38	39.55	40.03	38.10	39.07	38.95	33.67
San Juan	25.00	26.43	25.00	45.22	47.21	40.00	....	....	....	....
San Miguel	25.75	28.91	32.60	48.00	47.96	46.75	41.10	41.21	41.94	38.00
Sedgwick	23.31	25.00	28.45	41.28	41.60	40.00	39.75	37.96	36.75	35.21
Summit	28.68	29.42	29.60	56.38	54.66	49.50	40.05	38.15	35.51	35.16
Teller	26.27	27.10	27.20	44.91	40.17	40.01	38.33	36.36	36.45	33.41
Washington	24.20	25.06	27.20	43.46	41.88	41.18	39.56	39.75	37.31	35.23
Weld	23.47	28.91	31.00	43.59	44.38	44.13	41.59	39.60	37.46	35.35
Yuma	26.17	25.92	25.47	40.50	41.25	43.46	38.09	31.28	34.72	35.23
State	$24.60	$26.72	$28.35	$42.38	$44.30	$43.75	$40.56	$39.36	$37.63	$34.74

AVERAGE VALUE OF DAIRY CATTLE PER HEAD AS RETURNED BY COUNTY ASSESSORS ANNUALLY FOR PAST TEN YEARS

COUNTY	1923	1922	1921	1920	1919	1918	1917	1916	1915	1914
Adams	$45.12	$64.40	$50.35	$78.75	$78.28	$75.00	$66.12	$71.29	$62.76	$52.17
Alamosa	44.74	56.44	59.37	76.38	75.14	....	63.10	63.44	51.40	53.00
Arapahoe ...	48.65	50.85	61.93	81.25	78.30	69.00	64.00	62.40	62.30	55.40
Archuleta ...	40.16	43.83	54.64	69.68	67.20	74.00	60.00	50.53	....	42.31
Baca	35.55	41.00	53.46	65.90	66.00	61.25	55.16	56.79	....	....
Bent	40.35	45.83	50.03	60.03	62.26	62.44	61.72	60.13	59.09	58.25
Boulder	43.28	50.85	59.50	71.57	74.60	69.10	65.42	58.30	60.21	50.84
Chaffee	46.81	50.60	58.42	70.04	68.29	60.63	57.69	60.08	51.36	48.62
Cheyenne	40.05	41.14	51.38	65.25	65.27	60.21	62.60	....	....	....
Clear Creek ..	52.39	60.50	60.00	66.00	65.10	64.85	59.50	60.00	50.00	50.00
Conejos	41.95	44.47	52.77	66.27	65.00	71.00	61.00	60.00	58.00	45.00
Costilla	40.34	54.36	52.00	70.00	76.23	67.00	61.00	65.00	70.00	50.27
Crowley	36.91	43.67	82.67	62.11	66.77	64.00	66.93	60.71	48.72	48.29
Custer	40.00	40.08	52.97	63.23	60.13	59.00	55.86	60.00	60.23	43.98
Delta	40.82	51.10	52.98	68.38	78.66	73.53	66.39	62.40	64.00	63.00
Denver	60.16	59.50	75.50	100.57	80.00	100.00	80.00	60.00	55.36	47.95
Dolores	40.29	47.72	50.00	73.10	69.86	64.51	61.35	60.58	45.00	44.59
Douglas	51.62	51.33	58.23	81.28	77.62	69.78	63.03	62.66	55.00	50.52
Eagle	53.07	55.57	63.23	69.50	71.75	67.41	60.00	60.13	46.71	46.53
Elbert	40.70	43.27	53.41	67.88	68.47	66.03	60.00	60.23	46.04	43.16
El Paso	41.32	50.00	50.67	66.09	61.00	61.00	61.00	60.00	49.53	52.74
Fremont	41.88	43.96	53.95	73.44	72.00	74.50	63.50	63.00	60.09	44.71
Garfield	43.60	52.50	56.16	69.06	68.39	66.15	61.15	61.78	60.05	48.25
Gilpin	40.00	40.00	50.00	60.00	60.00	60.00	60.00	60.00	50.00	....
Grand	46.86	58.98	60.10	66.79	66.38	65.60	60.63	60.00	60.00	50.00
Gunnison	52.05	54.88	53.40	73.00	71.00	71.00	70.00	60.00	60.00	....
Hinsdale	50.00	50.00	50.36	64.14	64.00	64.00	62.00	60.00	50.00	50.16
Huerfano	43.34	47.18	51.94	82.00	95.00	94.80	94.86	69.50	....	....
Jackson	40.00	50.00	65.00	75.00	65.00	65.00	60.00	60.00	55.00	55.00
Jefferson	40.93	49.10	62.61	80.77	80.00	72.00	68.00	65.00	60.00	60.13
Kiowa	40.50	40.00	50.90	65.74	64.75	64.94	60.00	60.00	....	....
Kit Carson...	40.27	39.64	50.02	59.31	61.14	60.00	60.00	60.00	60.00	42.63
Lake	52.30	50.07	57.20	67.10	64.92	63.00	61.94	60.91	60.64	58.24
La Plata	40.23	40.58	50.58	66.70	69.77	67.39	60.25	60.78	60.00	50.49
Larimer	52.00	53.16	52.51	70.60	77.00	72.00	63.60	60.00	60.00	51.30
Las Animas ..	40.26	50.68	61.56	75.20	74.00	70.70	65.20	66.31	60.00	56.89
Lincoln	39.89	41.80	50.32	62.29	65.06	65.60	60.00	50.00	....	....
Logan	40.00	45.61	50.00	68.76	72.61	70.45	60.54	60.68	58.53	50.25
Mesa	44.24	52.40	55.11	74.50	70.16	69.88	61.85	61.50	56.27	48.67
Mineral	43.40	62.37	65.00	65.00	65.77	65.00	60.00	53.87	45.55	46.40
Moffat	40.42	44.33	53.24	76.30	65.00	68.96	68.65	....	....	....
Montezuma ..	39.58	44.99	53.52	67.93	66.81	65.35	61.50	60.52	48.47	45.02
Montrose ...	40.35	45.83	54.37	73.50	72.54	74.33	67.60	63.90	59.50	58.26
Morgan	42.73	47.35	51.88	67.02	65.38	64.62	62.32	62.10	53.25	48.14
Otero	38.74	45.98	55.41	68.58	71.36	70.58	61.99	60.48	60.47	58.50
Ouray	45.00	50.00	55.42	62.13	64.83	69.50	60.37	60.28	60.00	44.88
Park	50.00	52.47	54.50	65.00	65.00	65.00	60.00	60.00	60.00	55.00
Phillips	42.46	44.81	50.95	65.61	62.85	60.96	60.00	60.00	47.35	48.69
Pitkin	50.00	50.56	50.00	75.00	75.00	70.00	60.00	60.00	....	55.00
Prowers	46.15	55.00	57.28	66.76	73.50	73.00	73.00	62.00	62.10	59.26
Pueblo	49.01	55.69	55.43	72.77	72.52	73.20	62.89	62.24	60.05	51.39
Rio Blanco...	50.40	51.42	53.27	70.30	70.23	70.50	60.40	60.08	52.70	53.57
Rio Grande ..	47.70	50.23	58.37	70.11	70.00	70.10	62.50	60.05	50.00	50.64
Routt	42.54	49.98	58.32	71.60	72.45	77.09	74.44	62.70	61.08	50.50
Saguache	42.05	56.18	55.15	65.63	60.00	60.00	60.48	60.04	50.62	....
San Juan	45.56	45.58	53.58	66.63	65.16	64.57	61.50	60.93	56.58	57.10
San Miguel ..	50.78	52.44	60.32	75.60	76.90	72.00	61.83	64.21	60.70	63.86
Sedgwick ...	41.84	51.06	50.00	70.35	69.13	66.66	65.00	60.11	60.00	49.58
Summit	50.00	60.00	60.13	75.00	75.00	75.00	73.32	68.74	....	....
Teller	42.15	56.51	56.53	70.00	60.09	60.04	60.00	60.18	48.51	46.05
Washington ..	40.63	....	62.43	75.41	75.30	66.00	60.54	60.25	....	61.76
Weld	41.78	50.10	55.36	73.77	75.18	67.49	66.12	62.46	56.09	51.87
Yuma	41.61	42.63	50.00	65.00	65.37	67.59	60.00	46.23	....	....
State....	$43.62	$48.92	$55.01	$70.63	$71.06	$68.91	$63.70	$60.99	$57.27	$51.10

AVERAGE VALUE OF SHEEP PER HEAD AS RETURNED BY COUNTY ASSESSORS ANNUALLY FOR PAST TEN YEARS

COUNTY	1923	1922	1921	1920	1919	1918	1917	1916	1915	1914
Adams	$ 5.61	$ 4.98	$ 4.10	$ 9.40	$ 7.39	$10.17	$ 6.45	$ 4.36	$ 2.60	$ 3.02
Alamosa	5.46	4.57	3.67	10.19	10.20	10.00	7.00	4.50	2.99	2.47
Arapahoe	5.48	4.08	3.57	9.00	10.00	10.00	6.20	4.70	4.00	3.50
Archuleta ...	5.55	4.07	3.77	9.00	10.00	10.00	8.81	5.00	3.00	3.00
Baca	5.50	4.00	3.54	10.05	9.00	10.00	6.47	4.00	3.00	2.50
Bent	5.35	4.03	3.83	9.20	9.40	10.02	6.83	3.02	3.00	2.64
Boulder	5.44	5.31	6.70	17.35	9.34	10.00	7.55	4.31	3.27	3.33
Chaffee	6.23	4.70	3.54	9.55	10.00	10.00	6.23	4.69	3.01	3.88
Cheyenne ...	5.48	4.03	3.53	10.00	10.01	10.00	6.81	5.00	3.52	3.00
Clear Creek ..	5.66	4.23	3.50	9.00	10.00	10.00	6.00	....	....	....
Conejos	5.52	4.04	3.60	10.10	10.00	10.00	7.10	5.35	3.14	2.74
Costilla	5.56	4.05	3.56	9.01	10.27	10.00	6.00	3.50	3.03	3.00
Crowley	5.00	5.00	5.85	10.28	8.23	10.00	7.44	4.00	2.39	3.06
Custer	5.48	5.59	3.57	10.00	10.00	10.00	4.00	2.00	....	2.62
Delta	5.80	4.34	3.83	10.51	11.16	11.35	8.41	5.27	4.20	3.99
Denver	....	....	....	....	....	....	....	....	....	....
Dolores	5.31	4.35	3.92	11.38	10.53	10.80	6.48	5.00	3.94	4.00
Douglas	6.03	5.00	4.23	14.46	10.00	10.00	5.00	5.48	3.00	....
Eagle	5.50	4.23	3.86	9.06	9.80	11.98	5.99	5.00	3.50	2.99
Elbert	5.40	4.22	3.56	9.36	9.55	10.46	6.37	4.90	3.50	2.39
El Paso	5.00	4.25	4.09	9.00	10.00	10.00	6.00	4.08	2.78	2.49
Fremont	5.50	4.20	3.71	....	....	....	6.00	5.00	....	....
Garfield	5.64	4.25	4.00	10.55	10.00	11.02	7.00	5.00	4.00	3.96
Gilpin	5.00	5.00	5.00	10.00	10.00	....	....	....	....	....
Grand	5.89	4.43	3.99	10.00	10.00	10.00	5.00	5.00	3.50	2.51
Gunnison ...	6.88	6.10	4.00	11.08	11.91	14.50	10.00	6.14	4.01	4.00
Hinsdale	7.00	4.00	3.55	10.62	10.00	16.00	6.00	5.50	3.50	3.64
Huerfano	5.50	4.10	3.52	10.00	10.00	10.00	6.00	5.10	3.32	3.04
Jackson	6.00	4.00	4.00	9.15	10.07	10.11	6.00	5.00	4.00	2.70
Jefferson	5.00	4.91	4.74	10.00	10.00	10.00	9.00	5.00	4.00	4.02
Kiowa	5.00	4.00	3.50	10.00	10.00	10.00	7.45	5.00	3.56	3.00
Kit Carson...	5.00	4.85	3.64	9.03	10.88	10.00	7.40	5.00	3.63	3.03
Lake	....	85	3.51	10.12	11.60	10.61	....	....	2.50	2.55
La Plata	5.47	00	3.50	10.43	10.15	10.38	6.62	5.21	3.45	2.74
Larimer	5.	55	3.51	10.79	10.26	10.00	8.20	5.00	4.00	2.48
Las Animas ..	5.	.00	3.99	9.00	10.00	10.00	6.00	5.00	3.50	3.49
Lincoln	5.	4.13	4.00	9.93	10.07	10.00	6.00	4.00	3.50	2.49
Logan	5.50	4.56	5.81	10.83	10.81	10.00	6.02	5.34	3.13	4.06
Mesa	5.50	.65	4.10	10.20	10.85	13.51	8.16	5.05	4.09	3.93
Mineral	5.50	11	3.56	10.00	10.00	10.00	6.00	5.00	3.50	3.49
Moffat	5.76	.47	3.69	9.99	11.20	10.91	6.91	4.93	4.00	3.99
Montezuma ..	5.49	.38	3.96	10.04	10.35	10.48	6.49	4.76	3.91	4.00
Montrose	6.08	4.01	3.99	12.09	13.03	14.26	8.00	6.04	4.00	3.57
Morgan	5.47	4.00	3.50	10.00	10.00	....	....	....	....	2.65
Otero	5.05	4.31	3.78	9.25	9.72	10.00	6.71	3.04	2.68	2.71
Ouray	6.03	3.97	3.87	12.50	15.70	13.12	8.79	5.25	3.72	3.96
Park	5.35	4.24	3.73	9.80	9.47	11.90	7.50	5.00	4.00	2.75
Phillips	6.56	4.35	....	....	....	....	....	....	....	....
Pitkin	5.00	4.00	3.49	9.71	10.00	10.22	5.06	5.00	2.51	1.84
Prowers	5.00	4.00	3.81	8.50	8.16	10.00	5.78	3.79	2.76	2.35
Pueblo	5.55	4.77	4.00	10.13	12.75	11.36	6.27	5.00	3.88	3.71
Rio Blanco...	5.00	4.51	4.50	11.02	12.02	12.09	8.00	5.00	4.09	....
Rio Grande...	5.50	4.23	3.71	10.01	10.03	10.00	7.01	5.05	4.10	3.56
Routt	5.60	5.00	4.00	10.00	12.50	12.06	7.96	5.00	3.69	3.50
Saguache	5.60	4.17	3.61	10.00	10.00	10.00	7.00	5.00	4.08	2.47
San Juan	5.82	4.36	3.69	10.25	10.01	10.07	6.16	5.00	4.00	3.97
San Miguel ..	5.25	4.46	3.72	10.50	10.72	11.24	7.90	5.00	3.88	2.09
Sedgwick	5.99	5.00	....	9.00	5.97	....	5.00	5.00	3.16	2.79
Summit	....	....	10.00	10.00	12.00	10.00	5.00	4.00	3.87	4.00
Teller	6.31	....	....	....	....	....	....	....	....	....
Washington ..	5.50	4.00	3.51	9.25	9.05	10.93	5.42	3.98	4.21	3.39
Weld	5.20	5.05	3.68	10.54	11.14	12.35	6.04	5.32	3.78	2.67
Yuma	6.11	6.00	4.00	15.00	10.10	10.00	5.00	4.00	3.22	2.88
State....	$ 5.57	$ 4.22	$ 3.76	$10.08	$10.46	$10.87	$ 7.16	$ 4.77	$ 3.48	$ 3.12

AVERAGE VALUE OF SWINE PER HEAD AS RETURNED BY COUNTY ASSESSORS ANNUALLY FOR PAST TEN YEARS

COUNTY	1923	1922	1921	1920	1919	1918	1917	1916	1915	1914
Adams	$ 9.49	$11.44	$ 9.67	$10.21	$15.06	$12.00	$12.43	$ 6.05	$ 7.60	$ 9.03
Alamosa	8.46	7.67	8.42	10.70	16.96	16.26	9.30	7.30	8.13	8.30
Arapahoe ...	8.00	8.94	10.25	12.52	15.00	14.00	9.40	8.70	7.90	9.31
Archuleta ...	6.11	6.83	6.43	8.46	10.50	11.24	8.04	5.00	5.33	5.89
Baca	6.00	6.00	6.59	9.95	12.00	8.00	7.05	7.25	5.83	4.45
Bent	6.96	9.57	7.88	10.00	9.77	9.52	6.32	6.37	7.30	5.89
Boulder	8.70	12.14	12.53	13.44	16.47	20.10	13.27	8.08	7.50	10.29
Chaffee	7.27	8.10	8.16	10.56	11.19	9.98	8.84	7.10	6.42	6.21
Cheyenne	8.27	10.07	10.28	20.01	20.67	21.04	12.54	9.44	7.05	7.58
Clear Creek...	9.00	11.66	9.64	19.66	18.12	12.50	12.50	....	....	....
Conejos	6.72	8.36	7.90	11.42	13.00	12.00	9.00	8.38	7.30	6.48
Costilla	8.43	8.18	8.27	10.73	14.00	13.00	9.28	8.31	8.79	7.17
Crowley	6.94	7.85	9.89	10.41	12.95	15.00	....	5.81	6.14	5.94
Custer	6.93	6.79	8.02	14.70	13.48	8.29	9.47	5.00	5.11	5.10
Delta	8.54	8.54	7.00	12.33	12.53	12.34	8.88	6.60	9.00	7.66
Denver	....	....	....	....	....	....	....	....	....	....
Dolores	8.23	11.47	10.27	17.43	12.90	12.72	7.60	6.84	6.93	7.33
Douglas	9.68	12.98	11.41	18.26	15.04	18.40	11.80	9.22	9.00	7.90
Eagle	9.3	9.06	9.84	12.14	12.16	13.74	5.67	4.53	5.33	5.41
Elbert	7.65	8.32	10.12	12.68	16.35	15.67	10.38	7.42	6.54	7.09
El Paso.....	....	12.00	10.80	14.36	16.47	14.00	8.00	7.71	9.00	7.44
Fremont	6.86	8.65	8.20	9.63	13.80	11.70	8.41	5.69	7.15	6.59
Garfield	6.73	7.11	7.61	10.16	10.70	11.13	7.62	5.57	5.59	5.17
Gilpin	8.61	8.80	9.50	11.50	20.00	....	....	....	....	....
Grand	9.50	10.31	9.88	11.58	13.96	14.92	7.47	7.37	5.00	5.00
Gunnison	6.17	8.44	7.90	11.46	13.59	12.00	8.00	4.23	6.24	7.61
Hinsdale	5.43	6.00	5.00	9.79	7.00	10.50	10.00	5.00	5.00	5.00
Huerfano	7.50	7.68	8.98	16.00	15.00	12.00	11.62	6.30	6.24	6.23
Jackson	8.00	5.63	7.38	9.73	12.24	12.50	6.41	6.38	5.00	10.00
Jefferson	10.75	12.14	10.10	11.89	17.00	15.80	12.00	....	9.00	9.00
Kiowa	14.30	16.13	12.64	21.79	17.75	17.15	11.33	10.27	10.35	7.54
Kit Carson...	8.50	9.73	11.15	12.19	15.94	16.00	11.13	10.79	8.63	7.88
Lake	4.40	12.50	....	....	....	....	6.50	7.86	....	....
La Plata	7.06	7.70	7.37	10.48	11.47	9.85	7.43	6.19	5.99	6.26
Larimer	8.66	9.85	9.05	10.50	19.00	16.00	14.00	8.50	9.00	8.12
Las Animas ..	6.45	7.42	8.21	9.09	9.00	....	10.00	10.00	10.00	12.65
Lincoln	8.25	8.95	11.11	12.59	15.35	15.58	14.64	6.68	7.68	6.77
Logan	8.70	8.27	10.44	11.31	15.63	15.34	10.51	8.45	7.62	9.11
Mesa	....	....	....	....	....	12.51	9.91	5.55	7.70	6.82
Mineral	7.81	8.90	8.75	13.65	11.25	10.00	5.00	3.34	3.43	....
Moffat	7.21	8.12	8.52	9.88	12.00	13.27	10.04	8.08	8.34	5.93
Montezuma ..	5.34	7.38	5.88	10.12	11.21	10.70	7.43	6.79	7.07	10.00
Montrose	8.00	8.58	7.61	10.25	12.86	13.70	7.68	5.20	6.00	5.71
Morgan	8.58	8.16	9.35	11.15	14.14	14.40	9.05	7.50	7.20	8.08
Otero	7.34	8.45	8.55	10.36	13.57	13.79	9.15	6.44	5.97	7.26
Ouray	7.22	7.06	10.02	10.88	10.52	9.29	6.32	6.73	5.47	6.24
Park	6.07	9.66	9.18	14.39	15.40	14.77	11.29	7.35	7.70	11.78
Phillips	9.16	10.11	8.77	13.67	16.56	14.75	10.31	10.00	10.00	9.90
Pitkin	7.00	8.20	8.92	10.74	14.00	13.65	6.53	5.90	5.52	5.51
Prowers	8.19	8.40	9.84	11.01	14.20	9.35	9.45	7.50	6.78	6.13
Pueblo	6.75	7.42	9.42	14.48	14.19	13.08	8.87	6.12	6.05	6.17
Rio Blanco...	8.63	9.57	12.70	12.09	13.27	12.00	7.57	7.23	6.76	7.59
Rio Grande ..	8.75	8.83	8.90	14.38	16.10	12.00	9.32	7.98	7.95	8.41
Routt	7.95	9.04	9.00	12.00	17.95	14.93	9.63	6.70	8.49	8.20
Saguache	9.94	9.49	11.10	12.40	15.52	12.23	10.12	7.55	8.43	8.30
San Juan	....	....	....	....	....	....	....	....	....	....
San Miguel...	7.21	7.66	7.89	11.62	14.25	12.00	4.92	7.54	8.22	7.44
Sedgwick	8.69	8.97	9.82	14.94	18.23	16.00	10.10	12.00	8.66	10.65
Summit	15.00	15.00	14.77	15.00	15.00	10.00	10.00	10.00	10.00	10.00
Teller	10.63	10.60	10.55	11.05	10.93	11.28	9.65	5.02	5.43	5.90
Washington ..	8.97	9.20	10.29	12.54	15.79	16.01	9.69	7.65	7.12	8.83
Weld	8.51	9.17	9.07	10.05	14.90	19.63	9.43	7.41	6.13	8.44
Yuma	10.00	10.27	10.50	13.00	18.90	17.42	12.00	8.81	6.90	8.24
State....	$ 8.61	$ 9.14	$ 9.37	$12.00	$15.14	$14.23	$ 9.86	$ 7.50	$ 7.25	$ 7.86

AVERAGE VALUE OF ALL LIVESTOCK PER HEAD AS RETURNED ANNUALLY BY COUNTY ASSESSORS FOR THE PAST TEN YEARS

COUNTY	1923	1922	1921	1920	1919	1918	1917	1916	1915	1914
Adams	$23.33	$37.22	$34.20	$41.80	$43.55	$46.53	$44.87	$36.98	$32.28	$32.01
Alamosa	18.49	23.05	23.35	35.51	27.82	32.48	30.41	33.95	30.81	25.78
Arapahoe	23.03	26.79	28.00	37.44	37.11	37.65	36.00	33.11	29.52	27.11
Archuleta	13.46	12.96	11.70	18.70	16.60	16.58	16.48	11.63	9.87	8.42
Baca	20.23	23.11	25.23	39.94	40.14	40.14	38.39	34.20	16.87	12.37
Bent	17.88	20.91	21.37	30.05	29.60	26.45	27.29	14.93	15.59	10.80
Boulder	31.96	40.15	47.80	55.86	58.27	58.93	58.70	54.34	56.74	45.09
Chaffee	23.79	25.32	27.23	30.60	28.09	28.82	26.23	39.76	26.22	36.20
Cheyenne	18.57	21.65	21.98	39.68	40.30	40.85	38.53	33.89	29.26	26.30
Clear Creek	13.91	23.84	16.51	22.05	22.96	50.36	49.33	47.87	47.60	50.83
Conejos	9.26	9.53	8.24	16.88	17.23	17.52	13.98	11.94	10.79	8.88
Costilla	13.21	16.44	15.33	21.78	18.97	19.45	13.70	11.08	13.97	10.05
Crowley	24.50	27.77	31.99	48.33	48.10	47.27	48.83	33.30	23.42	17.85
Custer	23.84	28.38	31.71	44.11	42.49	41.58	38.99	39.23	36.62	36.88
Delta	19.08	19.06	22.74	36.56	34.63	32.36	30.82	28.02	34.78	36.61
Denver	72.48	73.01	86.03	105.22	84.31	97.69	85.88	66.79	54.79	45.03
Dolores	15.50	16.78	16.35	31.35	29.92	27.26	29.25	26.75	23.23	21.43
Douglas	30.56	32.44	36.71	51.06	51.43	54.13	48.63	46.75	41.85	38.88
Eagle	29.93	24.59	25.92	37.49	42.62	35.52	35.43	37.83	30.07	29.56
Elbert	18.90	22.31	24.07	34.67	34.76	35.26	33.12	29.40	23.95	19.44
El Paso	30.77	28.94	34.12	47.05	44.87	44.52	40.51	39.01	31.74	27.65
Fremont	24.05	28.46	30.68	44.12	43.72	42.86	39.90	38.88	37.54	35.24
Garfield	21.52	23.17	24.16	36.09	33.41	30.43	31.92	32.41	32.26	31.84
Gilpin	30.35	32.52	34.28	43.77	34.97	46.82	48.33	53.74	49.39	43.82
Grand	19.56	26.22	28.34	38.92	42.59	40.13	42.71	42.49	42.62	40.39
Gunnison	20.16	23.39	19.80	32.48	23.25	30.40	25.24	23.95	23.70	19.97
Hinsdale	17.00	20.48	13.03	40.23	41.61	36.30	41.46	39.61	35.20	11.82
Huerfano	18.93	18.29	19.42	29.12	30.03	30.46	26.43	22.93	16.89	17.58
Jackson	24.46	26.19	30.95	43.63	43.20	43.16	42.51	42.30	41.88	42.21
Jefferson	32.15	34.69	37.62	47.96	42.57	41.92	47.75	58.59	45.51	47.27
Kiowa	21.32	22.35	24.55	39.79	37.62	42.36	39.70	36.07	32.59	25.21
Kit Carson	20.95	25.56	30.63	42.46	44.47	51.69	50.99	46.51	44.23	35.64
Lake	39.35	42.96	18.46	16.84	17.20	18.40	56.87	62.94	5.70	7.17
La Plata	15.12	14.42	15.09	23.18	22.40	21.95	18.74	17.53	16.39	15.20
Larimer	25.35	28.78	34.86	46.66	46.88	44.84	45.54	49.80	49.07	9.53
Las Animas	16.38	18.39	22.14	27.98	27.13	28.27	16.92	16.59	12.82	11.02
Lincoln	20.17	22.71	26.78	39.80	39.69	41.13	38.30	33.55	27.28	21.67
Logan	26.91	33.40	39.16	50.87	56.78	57.28	52.41	52.38	50.65	41.27
Mesa	20.85	22.37	26.47	37.17	37.81	33.53	31.26	27.01	28.51	28.67
Mineral	11.91	12.27	9.58	19.71	21.18	29.75	23.97	14.01	37.32	18.23
Moffat	15.96	18.34	19.46	30.55	35.67	34.35	36.24	36.60	35.48	32.05
Montezuma	13.89	15.18	15.52	23.29	22.62	21.99	18.12	19.15	20.07	20.58
Montrose	17.95	18.42	19.92	28.89	30.11	31.18	25.84	19.88	21.80	23.39
Morgan	25.98	29.55	37.72	49.43	50.77	59.60	51.43	54.36	47.88	24.15
Otero	19.56	25.81	29.83	39.57	39.00	36.60	36.88	29.63	19.70	13.73
Ouray	18.57	17.82	18.38	30.43	31.64	27.15	24.84	25.83	25.17	23.44
Park	13.00	13.59	13.56	22.69	21.60	24.28	21.69	20.16	20.75	17.94
Phillips	23.31	27.24	30.49	45.55	48.45	46.19	45.42	45.28	41.86	41.14
Pitkin	24.87	26.64	23.29	31.20	33.30	30.65	29.40	21.63	18.78	11.58
Prowers	21.49	25.48	31.53	39.65	37.23	38.21	33.16	25.88	19.23	18.17
Pueblo	30.81	33.56	36.42	44.60	49.19	51.02	43.44	37.91	36.68	34.30
Rio Blanco	26.23	25.80	30.34	43.29	43.45	42.71	42.18	42.90	42.28	38.18
Rio Grande	14.02	13.46	13.27	21.39	19.12	15.86	13.47	13.05	12.43	12.60
Routt	19.35	22.95	25.01	34.50	38.41	35.18	31.69	30.07	19.28	17.39
Saguache	12.19	11.90	11.61	19.06	19.09	18.67	16.46	14.83	15.83	12.27
San Juan	6.82	5.43	4.82	11.38	10.91	12.22	8.34	7.48	7.47	9.10
San Miguel	24.06	26.59	29.06	40.86	40.67	43.24	39.37	44.54	41.10	41.27
Sedgwick	22.99	29.02	34.46	44.13	43.16	49.48	46.93	46.32	40.20	40.47
Summit	33.38	36.50	36.76	60.20	58.11	55.35	47.71	45.00	40.96	39.79
Teller	30.60	32.90	32.57	47.03	42.78	43.27	42.15	42.15	39.01	38.46
Washington	18.89	21.91	24.19	38.90	38.77	42.60	41.17	39.85	34.05	32.17
Weld	27.81	37.55	43.84	53.60	54.39	56.10	47.49	49.40	13.51	21.09
Yuma	22.49	26.32	28.95	41.44	43.99	46.00	42.00	34.56	34.53	36.10
State	$20.20	$22.68	$24.46	$35.02	$34.86	$34.76	$31.81	$29.18	$25.99	$20.49

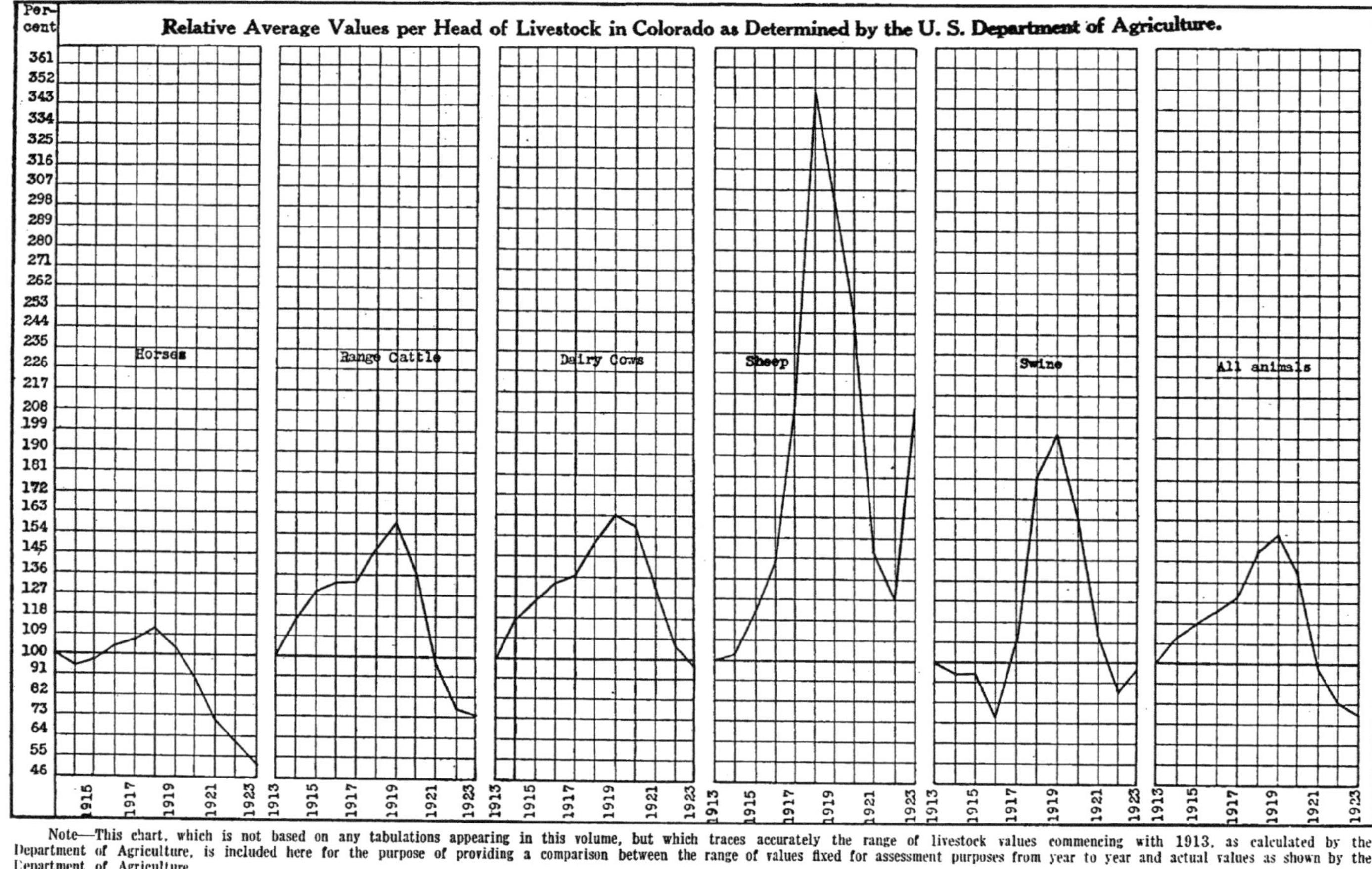

Note—This chart, which is not based on any tabulations appearing in this volume, but which traces accurately the range of livestock values commencing with 1913, as calculated by the Department of Agriculture, is included here for the purpose of providing a comparison between the range of values fixed for assessment purposes from year to year and actual values as shown by the Department of Agriculture.

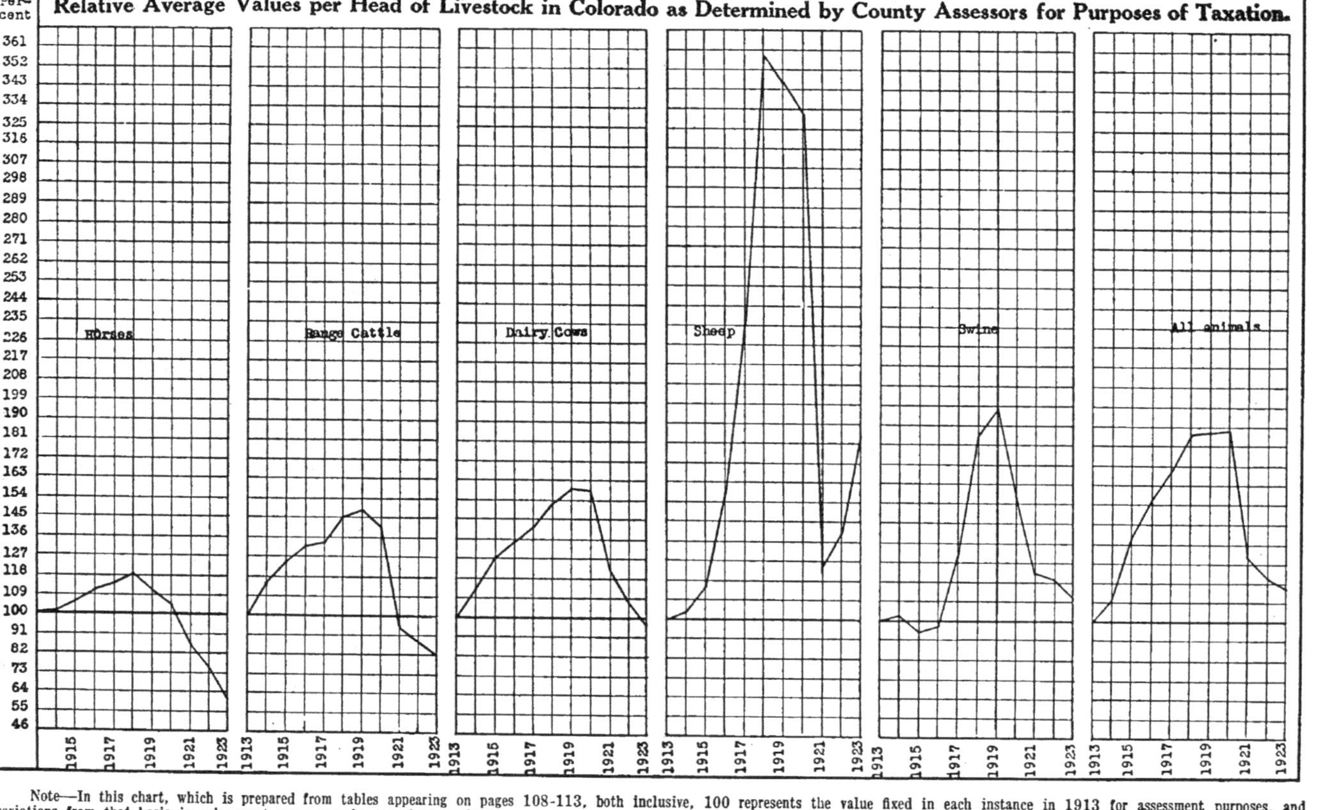

Note—In this chart, which is prepared from tables appearing on pages 108-113, both inclusive, 100 represents the value fixed in each instance in 1913 for assessment purposes, and variations from that basis in subsequent years may be traced at a glance.

ASSESSED VALUE OF LIVESTOCK IN COLORADO, 1923

(Compiled from Records of State Tax Commission)

COUNTY	Horses	Mules	Range Cattle	Dairy Cattle	Sheep	Swine	All Other Animals	Total
Adams	$ 287,390	$ 16,030	$ 216,070	$ 273,690	$ 23,960	$ 122 820	$ 6 150	$ 946,110
Alamosa	110,015	12 800	261,557	49,080	56,223	18,989	......	508,664
Arapahoe	120,700	8,635	200,650	206,615	35,035	25,450	1,230	598,315
Archuleta	63,565	1,660	293,530	26,145	120,550	6,605	3,285	515,340
Baca	232,381	93,145	610,625	5,510	11,978	50,737	......	1,004 376
Bent	207,350	45,895	371,060	51,440	183,305	32,815	......	891,865
Boulder	250,530	26,890	210,890	239,620	15,280	21,810	69,990	835,010
Chaffee	76,160	1,770	168,395	53,835	16,885	10,450	4,020	331,515
Cheyenne	117,145	22,405	461,425	105,485	52,735	51,075	......	810 270
Clear Creek	16,595	430	7,950	5,920	14,150	80	700	45,825
Conejos	97,060	5,565	277,000	29,240	378,650	26,000	......	813,515
Costilla	70,575	7,630	116,535	20,490	76,820	24,600	720	317,370
Crowley	129,760	24,050	417,555	6,460	2,450	37,225	4,135	621,635
Custer	56,195	2,670	256,270	23,970	9,420	2,100	......	350,625
Delta	291,485	26,395	598,120	199,445	175,275	29,845	1,690	1,322,255
Denver	115,360	8,370	....	67,200	....	....	12,180	203,110
Dolores	32,363	4,730	134,357	11,525	42,312	2,125	130	227,542
Douglas	109,545	5,690	360,345	260,665	17,555	22,275	5,970	782,045
Eagle	163,320	4,175	469,330	41,385	79,312	4,930	1,207	763,659
Elbert	225,649	47,575	465,678	239,023	114,804	67,476	6,770	1,166,975
El Paso	185,850	50,310	540,120	254,330	500	57,060	32,680	1,120,850
Fremont	108,660	20,395	348,340	63,930	21,490	6,985	715	570,515
Garfield	323,155	16,195	832,295	152,255	109,120	29,270	1,000	1,463 290
Gilpin	10,895	260	14,240	4,120	235	155	179	30,084
Grand	88,465	890	368,970	69,025	63,720	1,435	......	592,505
Gunnison	148,920	9,550	755,625	44,035	125,195	1,985	3,510	1,088,820
Hinsdale	10,670	1,070	48,481	2,550	15,456	76	775	79,078
Huerfano	126,930	49,780	410,575	49,275	94,424	8,625	1,235	740,844
Jackson	64,610	1,240	1,029,600	22,920	12,320	920	......	1,131,610
Jefferson	149,270	7,700	338,875	180,700	4,230	12,175	910	693,860
Kiowa	78,962	14,950	370,030	25,120	31,375	17,391	2,080	539,908
Kit Carson	360,331	54,690	530,910	133,726	19,377	127,975	5,014	1,232,023
Lake	20,950	......	15,040	11,820	33,930	110	95	81,945
La Plata	163,695	8,640	434,485	67,590	140,765	27,210	2,750	845,135
Larimer	494,625	38,560	635,920	299,780	434,570	47,455	8,310	1,959,220
Las Animas	281,400	103,680	924,140	75,890	198,440	21,560	30,525	1 635,635
Lincoln	217,900	40,475	904,505	114,590	43,750	92,305	......	1,413 525
Logan	544,055	53,600	581,920	280,970	6,300	128,130	450	1,595,425
Mesa	325,406	27,417	950,243	236,153	158,868	27,230	7,750	1,733,067
Mineral	7,880	600	41,550	3,125	24,550	125	980	78,810
Moffat	176,355	9,520	575 260	56,720	143,400	8,730	2,200	972,185
Montezuma	147,095	16,550	354,225	88,950	171,815	29,105	605	808,345
Montrose	246,275	11,060	611,950	112,845	166,065	36,280	......	1 184,475
Morgan	417,080	33,210	476,470	170,860	84,700	93,585	16,260	1,292,165
Otero	298,355	65,040	401,340	134 825	98,635	71,440	9,570	1,079,205
Ouray	45,110	2,550	144,960	12,825	33,195	1,880	......	240,520
Park	120,400	5,885	414,460	30,555	229,865	1,680	1,015	803,860
Phillips	197,490	28,855	150,935	57,025	105	96,395	8,030	538,835
Pitkin	80,095	1,970	180,775	33,400	16,310	5,175	740	318,465
Prowers	287,750	66,140	499,675	129,825	121,795	54,850	14 915	1,174,950
Pueblo	276,150	38,520	502,690	219,625	7,910	43,440	20,030	1,108,365
Rio Blanco	167,210	9,630	892,190	46,780	10,600	6,440	......	1,132,850
Rio Grande	217,190	55 040	290,570	93,130	250,870	30,680	2,020	939,500
Routt	324,510	7,200	1,166,400	138,050	202,655	19,225	645	1,858,685
Saguache	125,487	14 101	847,342	23,972	431,562	20,939	1,683	1,465,086
San Juan	3,625	2,650	1,300	2,005	48,448	....	40	58,068
San Miguel	77,735	3,480	385,870	40,325	23,635	4,895	4,185	540,125
Sedgwick	165,705	10,370	166,511	35,858	3,502	52 817	375	435,138
Summit	32,125	335	108,045	22,450	....	945	......	163,900
Teller	65,205	6 475	188,955	38,195	940	2,180	6,525	308,475
Washington	383,930	43,055	646,240	15,360	62,745	127,395	3,040	1,281,765
Weld	1,206,940	115 530	934,530	663,320	430,860	143,830	65,620	3,560,630
Yuma	354,000	86,140	751,360	69 740	1,040	193,570	6 500	1,462,350
State........	$11,901,589	$1,499,818	$26,665,259	$6,245,287	$5,505,966	$2,211,060	$381,133	$54,410,112

NORMAL MONTHLY AND ANNUAL PRECIPITATION IN INCHES

(From the records of the U. S. Weather Bureau)

PLACE	COUNTY	Normal Monthly and Annual Precipitation												
		Jan.	Feb.	Mar.	Apr.	May	June	July	Aug.	Sept.	Oct.	Nov.	Dec.	Annual
Akron	Washington	0.24	0.58	1.28	2.44	2.78	2.58	2.50	1.93	1.43	1.14	0.50	0.57	17.97
Auldhurst	Teller	0.40	0.89	1.04	2.29	1.76	1.88	3.96	2.88	1.96	0.91	0.59	0.89	19.45
Boulder	Boulder	0.40	0.78	1.44	2.72	3.06	1.36	2.20	1.46	1.61	1.54	0.68	0.81	18.06
Burlington	Kit Carson	0.26	0.46	0.83	2.06	2.21	2.77	2.84	2.54	1.39	0.93	0.43	0.63	17.35
Calhan	El Paso	0.36	0.74	0.69	2.12	2.00	1.50	3.00	2.74	1.39	0.87	0.53	0.82	16.76
Cathedral*	Hinsdale	0.44	0.69	1.09	2.26	2.49	2.80	2.70	1.11	1.20	1.21	0.50	0.83	17.32
Cheesman	Jefferson	0.57	0.48	0.84	1.14	1.58	2.45	2.07	3.33	0.38	0.70	0.50	0.23	13.82
Cheyenne Wells	Cheyenne	0.27	0.55	0.78	1.93	1.87	2.61	3.02	2.53	1.31	0.87	0.46	0.59	16.79
Colorado Springs	El Paso	0.21	0.40	0.69	1.64	2.24	1.83	2.82	2.09	1.08	0.65	0.34	0.33	14.32
Columbine	Routt	1.95	2.72	2.35	2.19	1.86	1.01	1.81	1.30	2.08	1.62	1.45	2.17	22.51
Cuchara Camps	Huerfano	1.41	2.09	2.21	3.40	2.14	1.57	3.46	2.35	1.39	2.40	1.45	1.72	25.59
Cumbres	Conejos	4.31	5.07	4.13	2.14	1.45	1.04	2.69	2.40	2.14	2.46	1.65	3.71	33.19
Del Norte	Rio Grande	0.14	0.29	0.19	0.20	0.39	2.00	1.21	3.05	0.08	T	0.02	0.10	7.67
Delta	Delta	0.60	0.53	0.68	1.63	0.85	0.30	0.84	0.88	0.91	0.79	0.55	0.58	8.14
Denver	Denver	0.42	0.49	1.00	2.17	2.54	1.47	1.62	1.34	0.89	0.96	0.52	0.60	14.02
Dillon	Summit	1.41	1.89	1.61	1.70	1.38	0.88	2.40	1.34	1.36	1.39	1.29	1.59	18.24
Dolores	Montezuma	0.97	0.61	1.91	2.09	2.06	1.54	2.35	5.05	0.11	1.43	0.85	2.68	21.65
Durango	La Plata	1.28	1.39	1.46	1.14	1.14	0.78	1.55	1.79	1.85	1.75	1.14	1.40	16.67
Eads	Kiowa	0.15	0.52	0.36	1.29	2.07	1.80	2.35	1.04	0.82	1.27	0.19	0.31	12.17
Edgewater	Jefferson	0.38	0.83	1.11	2.25	2.36	1.50	2.18	2.18	1.77	1.46	0.72	0.85	17.59
Elk Creek*	Park	0.66	0.03	0.65	4.27	0.75	7.20	4.64	4.87	0.33	0.76	0.58	1.27	26.01
Estes Park	Larimer	0.59	0.91	1.20	2.40	2.38	1.29	3.04	2.07	1.94	0.64	0.92	0.74	18.12
Flagler	Kit Carson	0.56	0.26	0.35	4.53	1.60	2.28	1.98	2.89	2.31	1.35	0.20	0.80	19.11
Fort Collins	Larimer	0.43	0.62	0.96	2.12	2.91	1.45	1.87	1.21	1.32	1.09	0.45	0.46	14.89
Fort Lewis	La Plata	1.61	1.76	1.37	1.28	0.90	0.78	2.38	2.19	1.56	1.99	1.20	1.76	18.78
Fort Lupton	Weld	0.15	0.44	0.51	1.63	2.44	0.81	1.85	1.40	1.32	1.28	0.46	0.64	12.93
Fort Morgan	Morgan	0.24	0.42	0.71	1.76	2.38	1.85	2.55	1.67	0.96	0.87	0.30	0.39	14.10
Fraser	Grand	1.62	1.68	1.69	2.20	1.60	1.05	2.33	1.47	1.84	1.38	1.09	1.68	19.63
Fruita (near)	Mesa	0.97	0.86	1.10	0.78	0.89	0.38	0.89	1.06	1.10	1.23	0.73	0.74	10.73
Fry's Ranch	Larimer	0.68	0.98	1.11	2.31	2.14	1.28	2.20	1.44	1.80	1.62	0.73	1.17	17.46
Garnett	Alamosa	0.14	0.22	0.25	0.51	0.69	0.65	1.27	1.18	0.80	0.57	0.27	0.24	6.79
Georgetown	Clear Creek	0.49	0.62	0.87	1.60	1.74	1.19	2.51	1.97	1.39	1.11	0.69	0.70	14.88
Glenwood Springs	Garfield	1.26	0.87	1.16	1.20	1.04	0.64	1.29	1.43	1.15	1.07	0.93	1.15	13.19
Grand Junction	Mesa	0.49	0.63	0.71	0.76	0.92	0.40	0.50	1.04	0.95	0.91	0.55	0.44	8.30
Greeley	Weld	0.29	0.42	0.76	1.72	2.50	1.40	1.87	1.06	1.02	0.96	0.33	0.41	12.74
Gunnison	Gunnison	0.83	0.71	0.61	0.86	0.79	0.63	1.46	1.31	0.85	0.64	0.55	0.64	9.88
Hartsel	Park	0.18	0.27	0.32	0.85	0.90	1.33	3.80	1.93	1.49	0.46	0.33	0.29	12.15
Hayden	Routt	1.26	1.71	1.83	2.49	1.75	2.34	1.02	1.98	0.70	0.85	0.71	1.75	18.39
Hermit	Hinsdale	1.37	1.16	1.41	1.60	1.35	1.33	3.01	2.54	1.78	2.28	0.76	1.23	19.82
Huerfano*	Huerfano	0.22	0.23	1.02	1.33	1.34	2.16	1.97	2.68	0.55	0.34	0.45	1.15	12.44
Idaho Springs	Clear Creek	0.38	0.53	1.03	2.07	2.21	1.31	2.75	2.01	1.32	1.33	0.52	0.63	16.09
Ignacio*	La Plata	0.81	0.60	1.08	0.32	1.93	2.52	4.20	4.94	0.29	1.28	0.50	1.68	20.15
Julesburg	Sedgwick	0.33	0.53	0.65	2.44	2.82	2.81	2.27	2.08	0.82	0.97	0.18	0.45	16.35
Kassler	Jefferson	0.50	0.71	1.12	2.76	2.25	1.69	1.94	1.76	1.59	1.28	0.57	0.86	17.03
Lake Moraine	El Paso	0.75	1.01	1.80	3.25	2.52	2.41	4.41	3.52	1.59	1.64	0.76	0.93	24.59
Lamar	Prowers	0.28	0.61	0.82	1.85	2.04	2.09	2.68	2.00	1.25	0.91	0.42	0.69	15.64
La Porte	Larimer	0.39	0.72	1.06	2.20	2.97	1.38	1.83	1.43	1.32	1.10	0.52	0.51	15.43
Las Animas	Bent	0.19	0.44	0.52	1.52	1.90	1.42	2.05	1.72	1.02	0.70	0.31	0.43	12.22
Lay	Moffat	1.16	1.23	1.44	1.22	1.27	1.26	0.98	0.97	1.37	1.13	0.85	0.87	13.75
Leadville	Lake	1.21	1.52	1.64	1.68	1.19	0.97	2.05	1.60	1.19	1.12	0.81	1.12	16.10
Le Roy (near)	Logan	0.34	0.62	0.94	2.57	2.54	2.42	2.12	2.34	1.17	1.06	0.40	0.63	17.15
Limon (near)	Lincoln	0.19	0.40	0.41	1.63	2.05	1.82	2.83	1.80	1.16	0.83	0.28	0.62	14.02
Long Branch*	Lincoln	0.64	0.25	0.32	3.33	1.31	3.18	3.45	2.57	0.10	0.67	0.14	0.30	16.26
Longmont	Boulder	0.36	0.67	0.89	2.09	2.98	1.41	1.84	1.19	1.15	1.38	0.57	0.59	15.12
Madrid	Las Animas	0.23	0.71	0.86	2.05	1.27	1.44	3.04	1.98	1.04	1.44	0.38	0.52	14.96
Meeker (near)	Rio Blanco	1.10	1.01	1.41	1.55	1.39	0.88	1.46	1.58	1.72	1.51	1.11	1.09	15.81
Montrose	Montrose	0.71	0.65	0.78	1.05	0.83	0.40	0.82	1.31	0.99	1.00	0.57	0.74	9.85
Monument	El Paso	0.51	0.95	1.04	2.97	2.38	1.94	3.18	2.43	1.54	1.14	0.54	1.07	19.69
Nast*	Pitkin	1.64	1.64	1.83	1.63	0.83	2.43	1.98	3.78	0.62	1.13	1.59	3.13	22.23
Ordway*	Crowley	0.51	0.09	0.62	1.40	1.64	3.00	3.06	2.21	0	0.57	0.16	0.59	13.85
Palisades*	Mesa	0.56	0.09	0.92	1.77	1.28	1.78	1.84	1.82	0.34	0.67	0.60	1.06	12.73
Paonia	Delta	1.33	1.24	1.44	1.38	1.45	0.54	1.03	1.25	1.33	1.48	0.96	1.03	14.46
Pueblo	Pueblo	0.35	0.47	0.86	1.43	1.68	1.47	1.97	1.57	0.62	0.70	0.37	0.46	11.95
Redvale*	Montrose	0.47	0.66	1.86	1.59	0.82	2.08	3.79	4.99	T	0.95	0.99	1.31	19.51
Rico	Dolores	3.03	3.17	2.98	1.40	1.56	1.08	2.84	2.00	2.47	1.44	1.41	2.11	25.52
Rifle	Garfield	0.81	0.85	1.32	1.11	1.26	1.33	1.04	1.18	1.30	1.26	0.82	0.85	12.57
Sapinero (near)	Gunnison	1.88	1.96	1.92	2.14	1.67	0.91	1.42	1.84	1.62	1.51	1.11	1.48	19.46
Sedgwick	Sedgwick	0.38	0.67	0.75	2.34	1.31	2.70	2.22	2.53	1.47	1.10	0.30	0.51	17.24
Silverton (near)	San Juan	2.62	2.09	2.73	1.49	1.03	1.50	2.97	3.05	2.87	2.92	1.56	2.04	26.87
Spicer (near)	Jackson	0.74	0.78	0.53	0.82	0.93	0.80	1.25	1.05	1.25	1.03	0.85	0.62	10.65
Steamboat Springs	Routt	2.61	2.56	1.81	1.99	1.91	1.24	1.42	1.51	1.57	1.85	1.57	2.54	22.58
Sterling	Logan	0.32	0.38	0.50	1.86	2.51	1.87	1.43	2.46	1.35	1.16	0.27	0.57	14.68
Tacoma	La Plata	2.28	1.93	1.87	1.77	1.11	1.16	2.71	2.48	2.25	2.39	1.56	1.74	23.25
Telluride	San Miguel	1.87	1.50	2.60	2.56	1.72	1.02	2.84	3.43	1.75	1.92	1.53	1.13	23.87
Trinidad	Las Animas	0.53	0.98	0.84	2.16	1.62	2.05	2.35	2.36	1.25	1.37	0.77	0.76	17.04
Victor	Teller	0.34	0.52	1.12	1.43	1.82	1.75	4.65	3.68	1.75	0.89	0.46	0.56	18.97
Wagon Wheel Gap	Mineral	1.10	1.14	1.36	1.56	1.13	1.22	3.38	2.01	1.64	1.84	1.34	1.26	18.98
Yuma	Yuma	0.35	0.59	1.04	2.24	2.33	2.76	2.53	2.46	1.06	0.97	0.43	0.54	17.30

*Precipitation for 1921 alone.

NORMAL MONTHLY AND ANNUAL MEAN TEMPERATURES IN DEGREES FAHRENHEIT

(From the records of the U. S. Weather Bureau)

PLACE	COUNTY	Jan.	Feb.	Mar.	Apr.	May	June	July	Aug.	Sept.	Oct.	Nov.	Dec.	Annual
Akron	Washington	...	...	...	...	...	...	...	...	...	...	...	...	...
Auldhurst	Teller	33.1	32.5	36.1	48.4	56.3	65.2	70.9	70.6	63.2	52.2	42.7	33.6	50.4
Boulder	Boulder	...	...	...	...	...	...	...	...	...	...	...	...	...
Burlington	Kit Carson	...	...	...	...	...	...	...	...	...	...	...	...	...
Calhan	El Paso	27.2	27.4	35.3	42.2	50.7	61.6	67.1	65.9	58.9	40.7	36.4	25.7	45.4
Cathedral†	Hinsdale	15.5	17.8	29.8	32.1	43.8	51.6	57.4	54.9	48.5	46.0	28.4	24.4	37.1
Cheesman	Jefferson	30.4	29.8	36.5	42.7	50.8	61.0	66.0	64.8	58.1	47.7	39.0	29.8	46.4
Cheyenne Wells	Cheyenne	28.3	29.7	38.7	48.4	57.9	68.4	73.9	72.6	64.5	52.0	39.8	29.4	50.3
Colorado Springs	El Paso	28.5	29.7	37.2	44.6	53.7	61.9	67.7	66.2	59.3	48.3	37.8	30.1	47.1
Columbine	Routt	...	...	...	...	...	...	...	...	...	...	...	...	...
Cuchara Camps	Huerfano	...	...	...	...	...	...	...	...	...	...	...	...	...
Cumbres	Conejos	...	...	...	...	...	...	...	...	...	...	...	...	...
Del Norte	Rio Grande	24.7	28.5	38.9	38.7	49.6	58.0	62.2	60.6	56.2	49.4	36.8	30.6	44.5
Delta	Delta	23.9	31.2	42.3	46.5	58.8	67.7	74.0	71.6	62.5	50.1	37.6	25.1	49.5
Denver	Denver	29.1	31.1	38.7	47.7	56.7	66.4	71.8	70.0	62.7	51.0	39.2	32.2	51.8
Dillon†	Summit	14.2	13.6	26.6	28.6	42.0	50.1	54.1	52.9	45.6	36.8	27.2	21.6	34.4
Dolores†	Montezuma	29.0	32.8	40.4	41.1	51.8	58.4	66.0	64.6	58.9	51.2	39.8	33.7	47.3
Durango	La Plata	24.5	29.9	37.5	46.4	55.0	62.7	68.7	66.3	58.2	48.9	37.2	28.3	47.0
Eads†	Kiowa	32.7	37.6	46.4	49.8	61.8	69.8	75.4	74.0	68.7	57.6	42.9	31.6	54.0
Edgewater	Jefferson	30.0	31.4	39.1	41.9	53.6	65.5	69.9	68.2	60.9	48.9	42.6	30.1	48.7
Elk Creek†	Park	25.0	26.2	34.6	32.8	46.1	52.4	57.0	56.4	50.9	44.6	35.0	30.3	40.9
Estes Park†	Larimer	27.1	29.0	36.4	36.0	49.6	57.1	62.5	59.4	53.7	47.8	37.8	33.1	44.1
Flagler†	Kit Carson	30.7	33.4	42.2	43.2	56.3	65.2	71.6	70.4	62.8	53.8	40.3	31.8	50.1
Fort Collins	Larimer	26.4	26.9	35.9	45.3	54.2	63.6	68.4	67.6	59.2	37.9	35.5	28.1	46.6
Fort Lewis	La Plata	20.5	24.6	32.2	38.2	50.9	60.4	67.0	63.6	55.9	45.6	32.8	26.7	43.2
Fort Lupton†	Weld	29.7	32.6	43.8	44.8	56.8	67.7	72.5	70.1	62.2	54.1	40.0	31.6	50.5
Fort Morgan	Morgan	24.3	28.6	37.8	47.1	56.7	66.9	73.2	71.8	62.3	49.5	36.8	25.7	48.4
Fraser	Grand	11.1	13.6	20.7	30.8	39.5	48.5	53.1	51.7	45.0	34.2	21.8	11.7	31.4
Fruita (near)	Mesa	20.9	30.5	42.2	50.7	58.7	68.3	73.9	72.9	63.5	49.8	37.5	24.1	49.4
Fry's Ranch	Larimer	25.6	26.1	32.1	38.1	46.3	56.0	60.8	59.1	...	43.2	34.5	25.2	...
Garnett	Alamosa	17.1	23.8	32.8	41.5	49.3	58.4	62.5	61.2	54.4	42.9	30.7	16.7	40.9
Georgetown	Clear Creek	...	...	...	...	...	...	...	...	...	...	...	...	...
Glenwood Springs	Garfield	22.2	27.0	37.3	45.8	53.3	60.7	66.6	65.4	58.1	46.8	35.6	25.3	45.3
Grand Junction	Mesa	24.7	31.5	43.5	53.2	61.6	72.6	79.2	76.1	66.4	53.3	39.9	28.2	52.5
Greeley	Weld	25.6	28.0	37.9	47.8	56.9	66.6	71.1	70.2	61.1	49.3	36.4	26.8	48.9
Gunnison	Gunnison	7.6	12.8	25.8	39.2	47.7	55.7	61.3	59.5	52.0	41.0	27.3	11.2	36.8
Hartsel	Park	...	...	...	...	...	...	...	...	...	...	...	...	...
Hayden†	Routt	20.2	21.7	35.0	40.9	51.5	60.6	65.6	63.6	55.6	48.4	36.6	29.8	44.1
Hermit	Hinsdale	11.6	13.9	20.9	30.1	38.8	47.8	53.1	51.9	45.4	36.5	25.2	12.9	32.3
Huerfano†	Huerfano	35.3	35.2	45.3	45.2	57.4	63.0	68.8	67.9	65.2	54.2	43.0	37.3	51.5
Idaho Springs	Clear Creek	28.0	29.4	34.3	41.3	48.5	57.9	63.1	62.0	55.5	44.5	35.3	28.0	43.9
Ignacio†	La Plata	27.6	31.4	40.4	41.4	51.7	60.7	66.8	64.2	57.0	49.2	36.2	31.4	46.5
Julesburg†	Sedgwick	29.8	34.1	43.1	47.0	58.6	69.2	74.7	72.4	63.2	53.7	38.6	27.0	51.0
Kassler	Jefferson	35.6	38.3	45.4	46.4	57.7	67.2	73.0	70.9	65.4	57.2	44.6	36.3	53.2
Lake Moraine	El Paso	21.8	21.0	25.6	31.9	40.1	49.7	54.0	52.9	47.2	37.4	30.0	21.2	36.0
Lamar	Prowers	30.6	33.4	43.9	53.3	62.7	73.2	77.9	76.8	70.0	54.9	42.0	31.3	54.2
La Porte	Larimer	...	...	...	...	...	...	...	...	...	...	...	...	...
Las Animas	Bent	26.8	31.8	41.2	51.2	61.6	72.1	76.8	74.7	65.8	52.9	38.7	29.1	51.9
Lay	Moffat	18.0	20.3	31.4	41.7	49.7	59.2	66.6	65.1	55.9	43.6	31.1	19.0	41.8
Leadville	Lake	16.8	18.2	23.3	31.5	39.9	49.5	55.2	54.1	47.7	36.8	26.9	18.8	34.9
Le Roy (near)	Logan	26.3	27.1	35.8	43.6	55.5	65.3	71.7	70.9	62.8	50.3	37.0	28.5	48.1
Limon (near)	Lincoln	26.4	29.0	36.8	44.2	53.1	63.3	69.3	67.7	60.1	48.7	37.7	25.6	46.8
Long Branch†	Lincoln	30.4	33.1	42.4	42.4	57.3	64.7	71.5	69.6	54.0	54.0	40.2	32.6	50.2
Longmont	Boulder	25.9	38.4	37.6	47.3	60.0	65.4	70.1	68.2	62.2	47.7	35.4	26.4	47.4
Madrid	Las Animas	...	...	...	...	...	...	...	...	...	...	...	...	...
Meeker (near)	Rio Blanco	20.3	24.1	34.2	43.3	47.6	59.1	65.0	63.6	55.3	43.8	33.0	20.0	42.4
Montrose	Montrose	23.8	31.1	39.8	47.6	55.9	65.0	70.2	68.1	60.7	48.7	33.9	23.9	47.4
Monument	El Paso	27.3	27.8	32.8	39.6	49.3	58.5	64.3	62.4	55.6	44.7	35.0	26.5	43.6
Nast†	Pitkin	17.1	17.7	28.8	31.6	45.3	54.6	59.2	57.6	51.5	38.8	29.2	23.4	37.0
Ordway	Crowley	...	...	...	...	...	...	...	...	...	...	...	...	...
Palisades†	Mesa	31.6	38.4	47.	50.4	62.3	73.0	76.4	73.8	66.2	56.8	43.0	36.6	54.7
Paonia	Delta	25.2	31.1	39.	48.3	56.3	65.7	71.5	69.8	61.5	55.4	39.2	26.2	49.2
Pueblo	Pueblo	29.1	31.8	40.	50.5	59.5	69.0	74.2	72.1	64.4	52.3	39.3	31.7	51.2
Redvale†	Montrose	29.7	34.8	42.8	43.4	55.4	64.6	69.6	66.6	63.5	55.0	41.2	34.8	50.1
Rico	Dolores	...	...	...	...	...	...	...	...	...	...	...	...	...
Rifle	Garfield	23.2	27.9	37.6	47.6	55.6	65.1	70.8	69.2	60.8	48.8	36.7	24.7	47.3
Sapinero (near)	Gunnison	14.6	18.3	27.7	37.3	46.5	53.3	59.0	57.9	50.8	40.2	29.5	15.9	37.5
Sedgwick	Sedgwick	25.2	28.3	38.6	...	57.0	67.6	73.5	70.7	62.4	49.9	37.2	23.4	...
Silverton (near)	San Juan	16.6	17.8	23.8	31.4	39.8	48.6	54.8	52.5	46.3	27.0	26.6	16.3	34.3
Spicer (near)†	Jackson	20.2	31.3	41.2	36.2	42.0	56.2	58.4	56.0	50.2	44.7	31.4	25.8	41.1
Steamboat Springs	Routt	14.5	17.9	26.7	38.7	48.6	55.5	61.1	59.1	53.0	41.9	29.8	15.5	38.5
Sterling	Logan	24.1	28.9	37.9	47.2	56.5	66.9	72.1	69.7	60.5	49.5	37.5	23.6	48.0
Tacoma	La Plata	...	...	...	...	...	...	...	...	...	...	...	...	...
Telluride	San Miguel	21.4	23.6	27.9	36.4	45.3	53.8	58.5	56.7	50.9	40.8	31.3	21.7	39.0
Trinidad	Las Animas	33.8	35.4	42.0	48.6	57.8	66.3	70.9	69.5	62.6	53.2	42.2	33.7	51.3
Victor	Teller	25.6	26.0	30.5	35.9	43.8	54.5	58.1	57.2	51.5	41.4	33.3	25.1	40.2
Wagon Wheel Gap	Mineral	16.0	18.3	24.8	33.0	42.5	51.9	56.0	54.2	47.5	36.5	25.6	15.2	35.1
Yuma	Yuma	...	...	...	...	...	...	...	...	...	...	...	...	...

†Normal Temperature for 1921 alone.

LENGTH OF GROWING SEASON

(From the Records of the U. S. Weather Bureau)

STATION	COUNTY	Number of days between killing frosts			Range of dates of last killing frost in spring and first in fall	
		Average	Shortest	Longest	Spring	Fall
Akron	Washington	142	117	165	May 12 to June 5	Sept. 15 to Oct. 8
Arriba	Lincoln	133	119	146	May 12 to June 7	Sept. 28 to Oct. 12
Blanca	Costilla	110	81	126	May 28 to June 23	Sept. 12 to Oct. 1
Boulder	Boulder	159	137	182	Apr. 19 to June 2	Sept. 27 to Oct. 19
Buena Vista	Chaffee	102	78	142	June 1 to June 21	Sept. 5 to Oct. 23
Burlington	Kit Carson	148	111	168	Apr. 28 to June 4	Sept. 23 to Oct. 14
Calhan	El Paso	136	108	164	Apr. 29 to June 6	Sept. 14 to Oct. 8
Canon City	Fremont	161	130	194	Apr. 28 to June 2	Sept. 29 to Nov. 8
Castle Rock	Douglas	129	99	144	May 6 to June 7	Sept. 14 to Oct. 8
Cedaredge	Delta	149	134	164	Apr. 22 to June 6	Sept. 14 to Oct. 19
Cheyenne Wells	Cheyenne	151	128	169	Apr. 19 to June 4	Sept. 28 to Oct. 11
Collbran	Mesa	127	78	165	Apr. 28 to July 3	Sept. 14 to Oct. 24
Colorado Springs	El Paso	142	112	160	Apr. 30 to June 3	Sept. 12 to Oct. 14
Crawford	Montrose	140	111	171	May 3 to June 12	Sept. 14 to Oct. 26
Delta	Delta	144	111	166	Apr. 24 to June 3	Sept. 27 to Oct. 26
Denver	Denver	168	131	193	Apr. 19 to June 2	Sept. 30 to Oct. 28
Dolores	Montezuma	122	109	138	May 19 to June 5	Sept. 21 to Oct. 7
Durango	La Plata	127	110	142	Apr. 28 to June 3	Sept. 14 to Oct. 16
Eads	Kiowa	165	128	184	Apr. 8 to June 2	Sept. 30 to Oct. 19
Fort Collins	Larimer	138	124	155	Apr. 12 to June 3	Sept. 14 to Oct. 10
Fort Morgan	Morgan	144	112	169	Apr. 19 to June 3	Sept. 19 to Oct. 10
Fruita	Mesa	156	139	184	Apr. 18 to June 1	Oct. 5 to Oct. 28
Garnet	Alamosa	111	97	134	May 24 to June 6	Sept. 14 to Oct. 8
Glenwood Springs	Garfield	110	81	134	Apr. 25 to June 23	Sept. 12 to Oct. 6
Grand Junction	Mesa	183	163	231	Mch. 23 to May 12	Oct. 5 to Nov. 9
Greeley	Weld	131	112	141	May 2 to June 3	Sept. 14 to Oct. 7
Grover	Weld	113	90	131	May 13 to June 30	Sept. 14 to Oct. 27
Hamps	Elbert	137	112	163	Apr. 25 to June 3	Sept. 15 to Nov. 23
Hayden	Routt	85	63	98	June 9 to July 3	Sept. 4 to Sept. 30
Hoehne	Las Animas	154	138	169	Apr. 19 to June 2	Sept. 30 to Oct. 26
Holly	Prowers	164	145	189	Apr. 2 to June 1	Sept. 20 to Oct. 14
Holyoke	Phillips	140	112	167	Apr. 25 to June 2	Sept. 15 to Oct. 24
Huerfano	Huerfano	140	110	165	May 20 to June 2	Sept. 12 to Oct. 6
Ignacio	La Plata	112	93	134	May 3 to June 13	Sept. 1 to Oct. 2
Julesburg	Sedgwick	140	111	167	May 10 to May 31	Sept. 19 to Oct. 24
Lamar	Prowers	171	150	182	Apr. 12 to June 2	Sept. 4 to Oct. 29
Las Animas	Bent	154	131	171	Apr. 25 to June 1	Sept. 21 to Oct. 25
Lay	Moffat	81	53	113	Apr. 28 to July 2	Aug. 19 to Sept. 22
Le Roy	Logan	151	125	163	Apr. 29 to June 2	Sept. 24 to Oct. 28
Limon	Lincoln	142	121	169	Apr. 19 to June 5	Sept. 28 to Oct. 25
Longmont	Boulder	138	112	169	Apr. 18 to June 2	Sept. 14 to Oct. 11
Manassa	Conejos	107	89	127	May 19 to June 19	Sept. 12 to Sept. 25
Mancos	Montezuma	120	112	127	May 31 to June 7	Sept. 14 to Oct. 12
Meeker	Rio Blanco	97	76	106	June 2 to July 3	Sept. 5 to Sept. 22
Montrose	Montrose	134	112	151	Apr. 28 to June 2	Sept. 14 to Oct. 23
Monument	El Paso	118	101	137	May 10 to June 7	Sept. 9 to Oct. 3
Pagosa Springs	Archuleta	91	82	97	June 9 to July 11	Sept. 1 to Sept. 25
Palisades	Mesa	157	117	183	Apr. 27 to May 26	Sept. 8 to Oct. 27
Paonia	Delta	151	117	220	Mar. 25 to June 2	Sept. 22 to Nov. 8
Platte Canon	Jefferson	159	137	164	Apr. 11 to June 2	Sept. 14 to Oct. 26
Pueblo	Pueblo	168	131	193	Apr. 19 to June 2	Oct. 1 to Oct. 26
Redvale	Montrose	129	93	163	May 1 to June 13	Sept. 12 to Oct. 26
Rifle	Garfield	143	124	167	Apr. 24 to June 2	Sept. 14 to Oct. 26
Rocky Ford	Otero	157	120	181	Apr. 20 to June 2	Sept. 23 to Oct. 27
Saguache	Saguache	110	93	123	May 20 to June 26	Sept. 14 to Oct. 6
Salida	Chaffee	113	93	148	Apr. 28 to June 15	Sept. 12 to Sept. 30
San Luis	Costilla	108	97	118	May 28 to June 7	Sept. 11 to Sept. 28
Sapinero	Gunnison	91	63	117	June 2 to July 5	Sept. 6 to Sept. 27
Sedgwick	Sedgwick	147	131	167	Apr. 25 to May 27	Sept. 12 to Oct. 24
Sterling	Logan	144	111	177	Apr. 28 to June 3	Sept. 22 to Oct. 24
Trinidad	Las Animas	160	130	180	Apr. 19 to June 3	Sept. 30 to Oct. 26
Two Buttes	Baca	157	130	178	Apr. 19 to June 2	Oct. 9 to Oct. 26
Victor	Teller	91	59	121	May 31 to July 7	Aug. 17 to Sept. 21
Wagon Wheel Gap	Mineral	105	84	120	May 15 to June 14	Sept. 5 to Sept. 25
Westcliffe	Custer	97	81	131	May 6 to June 23	Aug. 31 to Sept. 28
Wiggins	Morgan	130	114	149	May 11 to June 2	Sept. 14 to Oct. 7
Wray	Yuma	148	135	168	Apr. 11 to June 2	Sept. 28 to Oct. 25

These records include the unusually late frosts which occurred in almost all parts of the state June 1-3, 1919.

DISTRIBUTION OF AGRICULTURAL LAND

(From County Assessors' Report 1923)

COUNTY	Area Acres	Agricultural Land	Percentage of Total Area	Irrigated Land	Percent Agricultural Land	Grazing Land	Percent Agricultural Land	Dry Farming Land	Percent Agricultural Land
Adams	807,680	740,459	91.67	99,677	13.46	152,000	20.52	488,782	66.01
Alamosa ...	465,280	322,606	69.33	64,700	20.05	156,356	48.46	101,550	31.47
Arapahoe ...	538,880	493,830	91.64	30,680	6.21	83,210	16.84	379,940	76.93
Archuleta ..	780,800	298,265	38.19	10,600	3.55	276,337	92.64	11,328	3.79
Baca	1,633,280	1,483,750	90.84	5,008	.33	552,449	37.23	926,293	62.42
Bent	975,360	610,937	62.63	47,232	7.73	558,575	91.42	5,130	.83
Boulder	488,960	260,564	53.28	87,669	33.64	149,588	57.40	23,307	8.94
Chaffee	693 120	86,388	12.46	23,478	27.17	62,910	72.82	....	....
Cheyenne ...	1,137,280	1,066,768	93.79	....	....	....	....	1,066,768	100.00
Clear Creek..	249,600	34,280	13.73	....	....	34,280	100.00	....	....
Conejos	801,280	241,454	30.13	97,100	40.21	144,354	59.78	....	....
Costilla	758,400	174,860	23.05	87,860	50.24	77,000	44.03	10,000	5.71
Crowley	517,120	385,288	74.50	48,800	12.66	326,613	84.77	9,875	2.56
Custer	478,080	192,657	40.29	23,265	12.07	167,046	86.70	2,346	1.21
Delta	768,640	129,427	16.83	71,327	55.10	30,187	23.32	27,913	21.56
Denver	37,120	7,184	19.35	7,184	100.00	....	....	....	....
Dolores	667,520	102,645	15.37	865	.84	53,121	51.75	48,659	47.40
Douglas	540,800	378,479	69.98	13,300	3.51	278,258	73.52	86,921	22.96
Eagle	1,036,800	108,970	10.51	23,159	21.25	85,811	78.74	....	....
Elbert	1,188,480	1,056,948	88.93	10,737	1.01	650,549	61.54	395,662	37.43
El Paso.....	1,357,440	976,652	71.94	22,530	2.30	736,122	75.37	218,000	22.32
Fremont	996,480	282,482	28.34	28,525	10.09	205,836	72.86	48,121	17.03
Garfield	1,988 480	298,378	15.00	65,901	22.08	203,197	68.10	29,280	9.81
Gilpin	84,480	19 601	23.20	....	....	19,601	100.00	....	....
Grand	1,194,240	196,290	16.43	31,220	15.90	165,070	84.09	....	....
Gunnison ...	2 034,560	199,298	9.79	37,154	18.64	162,144	81.35	....	....
Hinsdale ...	621,440	15,607	2.51	2,212	14.17	13,049	83.60	346	2.21
Huerfano ...	960,000	501,158	52.20	23,758	4.74	446,380	89.06	31,020	6.18
Jackson	1,044,480	232,187	22.22	71,645	30.85	160,542	69.14	....	....
Jefferson ...	517,120	307,908	59.54	48,262	15.67	233,355	75.78	26,291	8.53
Kiowa	1,150,720	1,023,856	88.97	....	....	1,023,856	100.00	....	....
Kit Carson ..	1,381,760	1,306,144	94.67	3,514	.26	233,218	17.82	1,071,412	81.90
Lake	237,440	27,110	11.41	....	....	27,110	100.00	....	....
La Plata....	1,184,640	381 556	32.20	62,932	16.49	299,800	78.49	18,824	4.93
Larimer	1,682,560	678,511	40.32	123,331	18.17	532,660	78.50	22 520	3.31
Las Animas..	3,077,760	1,935,750	62.89	30,601	1.58	1,800,020	92.98	105,129	5.43
Lincoln	1,644,800	1,472,710	89.53	3,199	.21	639,029	43.39	830,482	56.39
Logan	1,166,080	982,015	84.21	77,900	7.93	320,900	32.67	583,215	59.38
Mesa	2,024 320	382,355	18.88	87,490	22.88	294,865	77.11	....	....
Mineral	554,240	21,199	3.82	3,211	15.14	17,988	84.85	....	....
Moffat	2 981,120	584,079	19.59	17,173	2.94	421,182	72.11	145,724	24.94
Montezuma ..	1,312,640	256,313	19.52	36,156	14.10	184,546	72.00	35,611	13.89
Montrose ...	1,448,960	330,963	22.84	73,727	22.27	223,843	67.63	33,393	10.08
Morgan	823,040	716,348	87.03	80,515	11.23	385,691	53.84	250,142	34.91
Otero	805 760	503,011	62.42	80,916	16.08	400,498	79.62	21,597	4.29
Ouray	332,160	134,153	40.38	16,943	12.62	113,310	84.46	3,900	2.90
Park	1,434,880	289,876	20.20	23,346	8.05	259,787	89.62	6,743	2.32
Phillips	440,320	411,932	93.55	....	....	46,428	11.27	365,504	88.72
Pitkin	652,160	60,810	9.32	15,937	26.20	44,573	73.29	300	.49
Prowers	1,043,200	920 545	88.24	99,222	10.77	221,203	24.02	600,120	65.19
Pueblo	1,557,720	1,076,594	69.11	47,039	4.36	950,372	88.27	79,183	7.35
Rio Blanco ..	2,062,720	234,009	11.34	22,188	9.48	195,346	83.47	16,475	7.04
Rio Grande ..	574,720	198,938	34.61	47,840	24.04	114,978	57.79	36,120	18.15
Routt	1,477,760	412,756	27.92	45,664	11.06	317,975	77.03	49,117	11.89
Saguache ...	2,005,120	483,269	24.10	86,640	17.92	396,629	82.07	....	....
San Juan....	289,920	200	.06	....	....	200	100.00	....	....
San Miguel..	824,320	164,668	19.97	8,861	5.38	147,670	89.67	8,137	4.94
Sedgwick ...	339,840	300,317	88.37	24,805	8.25	96,509	32.13	179,003	59.60
Summit	415,360	30,308	7.29	6,133	20.23	24,175	79.76	....	....
Teller	350,080	133,144	38.03	2,485	1.86	109,107	81.94	21,552	16.18
Washington ..	1,613,440	1,472,439	91.26	7,007	.47	242,700	16.48	1,222,732	83.04
Weld	2,574,080	2,226,697	86.50	362,346	16.27	1,014,101	45.54	850,250	38.18
Yuma	1,514,880	1,404,093	92.68	7,740	.55	724,140	51.57	672,213	47.87
State....	66,341,120	31,763,988	47.87	2 588,709	8.14	18,008,349	56.69	11,166,930	35.15

Colorado Land Classification

COUNTY	Area Acres	Fruit Land	Irrigated Land	Natural Hay Land	Dry Farming Land	Grazing Land	Productive Coal Land	Non-Productive Coal Land	Timber Land	Metalliferous Mining Claims Non-Productive	Producing Mineral Land	Other Mineral Land	Railroad Rights-of-Way	Town and City Lots	Total Patented Land	
Adams	807,880		99,877		488,782	152,090							2,798	3,200	746 457	
Alamosa	465,280		27,500	37,200	101,550	156,356							1,287	980	324,873	
Arapahoe	538,880		30,080		379,940	83,216							1,577	3,200	498,607	
Archuleta	780,800		10,200	310	11,328	276,337[2]			11,325				1,583	850	312,023	
Baca	1,633,280		5,008		926,293	552,449								440	1,484,190	
Bent	975,360		47,232		5,130	558 575							1 941	1,625	614,503	
Boulder	488,960		83,251	4,418[4]	23,307	149,588	2,090				575		3,840	8,250	275,910	
Chaffee	693,120		23,478			62,910					395		3,670	2,910	93,363	
Cheyenne	1,137,280				1,066,788								1,579	960	1,069,307	
Clear Creek	249,600					34,280				23,398	391		1,040	806	59,915	
Conejos	801,280		87,250	9,850		144,354					15		1,352	1,250	244,071	
Costilla	758,400		82,260	5,600	10,000	77,000			579,440[9]	840	12		1,589	675	757,416	
Crowley	517,120	321	48,479[3]		9,875	326,613							785	785	386 858	
Custer	478,080		10,810	12,455	2,346	167,046				3,861	50		447	485	197,500	
Delta	768,640	10,466	60,861		27,913	30,187	519	1,806	86,000[10]				750	1,100	220,268	
Denver	37,120		7,184[1]										2,750	26,401	30 335	
Dolores	667,520		865		48,659	53,121		601	4,742	2,877	300		420	160	111,805	
Douglas	540,800		7,941	5,359	86,921	278,258							2,468	675	381,622	
Eagle	1,036,800		23,159			85,811				4,569	320		2 568	375	116,800	
Elbert	1,188,480		585	10,152	395 862	650,549[7]							2 810	440	1,060,198	
El Paso	1,357,440	220	20,400	1,910	218,000	736,122	250	1,080					6,375	15,250	999,607	
Fremont	996,480	1,879	25,446	1,200	48,121	205,836	13,181	4,200	6,850[10]	6 474			2,931	1,275	316,393	
Garfield	1,988,480	923	64,978		29 280	203,197	2,100	2,500				9 128	4,075	895	317,176	
Gilpin	84,480					19,001					295	12 539	1,002	485	23,932	
Grand	1,194,240		31,220			105,070			48,000	1,303			2,243	425	248 270	
Gunnison	2,034,560		37,154			102,144	12,886[6]			21,269	250	7,043	2,250	1,880	244,876	
Hinsdale	621,440		2,212		346[3]	13,048				5,264	195	884	237	175	22,362	
Huerfano	960,000	44	6,769	16,945	31,020	446,380	2,585	19,362[8]					2,945	1,250	527,310	
Jackson	1,044,480		71,645			160 542	30	2,609	5,195	942			1,100	144	242,207	
Jefferson	517,120		48,262[3]		26,291	233,355	2,027[7]						2,520	5,750	318,199	
Kiowa	1,150,720					1,023,856							2,196	220	1,028 266	
Kit Carson	1,381,760		55	3,450	1,071,412	233,218							1,499	975	1,310,618	
Lake	237 440					27,110				41,702	1,100		2,328	1,250	73,488	
La Plata	1,184,640	06	57,354	5 512	18,824	299,800	998	5,037			375		3,030	1,525	392,521	
Larimer	1,682,560		107,931	15,400	22,520	532,660							3,020	4,400	685,931	
Las Animas	3,077,760		27,677	2,924	105 129	1,800 020	3,893	44,847					5,845	7 250	1,997,585	
Lincoln	1,644,800			3,199	830,482	639,029							1,822	1,350	1,475,882	
Logan	1,166,080		64 500	13,400	583,215	320,900							3,334	2,010	987,359	
Mesa	2,024,320	7,315	80,175			294 865	3,961[8]				400		3,105	4,000	393,821	
Mineral	554,240		579	2,632		17,988			6,055[9]	2,842	320		435	425	31,276	
Moffat	2,981,120		14,036	3,137	145,724	421,182		6,789		598		5	140	675	592,288	
Montezuma	1,312,640	850	35,306		35,611	184,546	133		5,434	798	15		1,568	730	264 991	
Montrose	1,448,960	1,410	72,311		33,393	223,843[2]				534	438		1 310	1,090	334,335	
Morgan	823,040		78,315	2 200	250,142	385 691							2,271	2,010	720,629	
Otero	805,760	774	80,142		21,597	400,498							2,300	2,150	507,521	
Ouray	332 160		10,100	6,843[4]	3,900	113,310		447		14,305	1 262		1,060	910	152 137	
Park	1,434,880			23,346	6,743	259,787		2,869		36 803	325		3,854	785	334,512	
Phillips	440,320				365 504	46 428							908	895	413 735	
Pitkin	652 160		15,937		300	44,573		11,157		13,210	375	319	2,165	450	88,486	
Prowers	1,043,200		96,394	2,828	600,120	221 203							2 021	1,080	923,026	
Pueblo	1,557,120	5,821[1]	41,218		79,183	950,372							6,132	17,250	1,099,976	
Rio Blanco	2,062,720		21 311	877	14,475	185,346		4,644	11,571[10]			169	195	400	250,988	
Rio Grande	574,720		39,600	8,150	36 120[4]	114,978					50	1 694	1,313	985	202,980	
Routt	1,477,760	34	43,110	2,520[4]	49,117	317,975	55,463[8]		18,767			2,739	2,437	800	492,962	
Saguache	2,005,120		37,640	49 000		396,629					50		2,680	1,150	487,149	
San Juan	289,920					200			195	24,273	673		913	560	26,814	
San Miguel	824,320		8 861		8,137	147,670		580		8,439	225		1,193	240	175,345	
Sedgwick	339,840		19,080	5,145	179 003	96,509							802	875	301,994	
Summit	415,360		5,933	200		24,175			520		450		1,718	450	33,446	
Teller	350,080			2,486	21,552	109,107				33,003	1,250		2,562	1,250	172,109	
Washington	1,613,440		7 007		1,222,732	242,700							1,090	1,100	1,474,029	
Weld	2,574,080		354,084	8,262	850,250	1,014,101	2,190	5,500					9,830	8,850	2,253,376	
Yuma	1,514 880		2,670	5 070	672,213	724,140							1,013	1,250	1,406,356	
State	66,341,120	30,129	2,286,592	271,988	11,166,930	18,008 349	103,219	114,088	784,709	247,204	10,166	34 520	137,071	152 526	33,347,491	8.

1 Suburban land.
2 Includes waste land.
3 Includes fruit land.
4 Includes seep land.
5 Fish lakes.

6 Includes non-productive coal land.
7 Includes hay land.
8 Includes grazing land in coal belt.
9 Desert land.
10 Oil land.

11 This column is mostly homestead land that has been filed on but not yet patented. It includes about 750,000 acres of state land sold but not yet fully paid for and about 1,400 000 acres of government land temporarily withdrawn from entry.
12 On account of errors in surveys and errors from other sources the combined areas of patented and non-patented land in this county exceed the total area by the amount here given.
13 Includes about 20,327 acres of the Rocky Mountain National Park.

B
B
B

C
C
C
C
C
C
C

D
D
D
D

E
E
E

F

G
G
G
G

H
H

Ja
Jo

K
K

L.
La
La
La
L.
L

M
M
M
M
M
M

O
O

P
Pl
P
Pr
P

R.
R
R

Sa
Sa
Sa
Sc
St

T

W
W

Y

COLORADO LAND CLASSIFICATION BY PERCENTAGES

COUNTY	Area Acres	Patented Land Pct.	Patented Agricultural Land Pct.	Homestead Land Pct.	National Forests Pct.	State Land Pct.
Adams	807,680	92.41	91.67	.004	....	2.94
Alamosa	465,280	69.82	69.33	8.75	6.75	9.32
Arapahoe	538,880	92.52	91.64	.007	....	2.54
Archuleta	780,800	39.96	38.19	15.21	50.28	2.25
Baca	1,633,280	90.87	90.84	.06	....	3.87
Bent	975,360	63.00	62.63	.20	....	13.99
Boulder	488,960	56.42	53.28	.17	26.14	1.41
Chaffee	693,120	13.46	12.46	9.34	61.09	2.71
Cheyenne	1,137,280	94.02	93.79	.006	....	3.87
Clear Creek	249,600	24.00	13.73	5.58	67.37	1.17
Conejos	801,280	30.46	30.13	16.93	34.31	7.25
Costilla	758,400	99.87	23.05	....	....	....
Crowley	517,120	74.81	74.50	1.54	....	11.25
Custer	478,080	41.31	40.29	1.29	33.63	2.74
Delta	768,640	28.65	16.83	21.22	24.73	.0002
Denver	37,120	97.88	19.35	....	....	1.70
Dolores	667,520	16.74	15.37	7.70	46.63	1.37
Douglas	540,800	70.56	69.98	.12	25.04	1.56
Eagle	1,036,800	11.26	10.51	24.17	57.12	1.74
Elbert	1,188,480	89.20	88.93	....	....	6.04
El Paso	1,357,440	73.63	71.94	.24	7.44	13.71
Fremont	996,480	31.75	28.34	29.91	6.64	5.86
Garfield	1,988,480	15.95	15.00	35.39	26.36	.0004
Gilpin	84,480	40.16	23.20	4.78	47.86	2.03
Grand	1,194,240	20.78	16.43	9.96	44.84	5.22
Gunnison	2,034,560	12.03	9.79	20.10	55.23	.87
Hinsdale	621,440	3.59	2.51	17.65	82.69	1.40
Huerfano	960,000	54.92	52.20	3.79	12.29	4.55
Jackson	1,044,480	23.18	22.22	16.41	37.86	4.33
Jefferson	517,120	61.53	59.54	.42	18.42	2.99
Kiowa	1,150,720	89.18	88.97	.23	....	6.06
Kit Carson	1,381,760	94.85	94.67	.01	....	3.83
Lake	237,440	30.95	11.41	3.04	67.05	.91
La Plata	1,184,640	33.13	32.20	4.87	31.96	1.28
Larimer	1,682,560	40.76	40.32	1.93	37.80	4.10
Las Animas	3,077,760	64.90	62.89	1.77	.89	4.86
Lincoln	1,644,800	89.73	89.53	.46	....	7.22
Logan	1,166,080	84.67	84.21	.08	....	11.46
Mesa	2,024,320	19.45	18.88	41.12	28.83	
Mineral	554,240	5.64	3.82	....	93.20	.11
Moffat	2,981,120	19.86	19.59	43.71	1.42	6.78
Montezuma	1,312,640	20.18	19.52	16.31	17.06	2.59
Montrose	1,448,960	23.07	22.84	37.41	21.60	.013
Morgan	823,040	87.55	87.03	.18	....	6.73
Otero	805,760	62.98	62.42	.20	....	14.53
Ouray	332,160	45.80	40.38	4.00	40.34	.75
Park	1,434,880	23.31	20.20	4.65	43.66	6.50
Phillips	440,320	93.96	93.55	.03	....	3.75
Pitkin	652,160	13.56	9.32	4.97	74.99	.13
Prowers	1,043,200	88.53	88.24	.01	....	4.68
Pueblo	1,557,120	70.64	69.11	.25	2.27	13.97
Rio Blanco	2,062,720	12.16	11.34	53.50	16.80	.06
Rio Grande	574,720	35.31	34.61	9.47	40.87	2.27
Routt	1,477,760	33.35	27.92	8.71	38.21	4.66
Saguache	2,005,120	24.29	24.10	17.20	43.99	4.83
San Juan	289,920	9.24	.06	....	69.47	2.55
San Miguel	824,320	21.27	19.97	21.95	20.55	2.16
Sedgwick	339,840	88.86	88.37	.03	....	6.81
Summit	415,360	8.05	7.29	2.58	68.97	.07
Teller	350,080	49.16	38.03	9.26	29.27	3.02
Washington	1,613,440	91.39	91.26	.02	....	5.50
Weld	2,574,080	87.54	86.50	.16	....	6.48
Yuma	1 514,880	92.83	92.68	.06	....	3.09
State	66,341,120	50.26	47.87	11.68	20.01	4.50

ASSESSED VALUATION OF AGRICULTURAL LAND FOR 1923

(From Records of the State Tax Commission)

COUNTY	Improved Fruit Land	Irrigated Land	Natural Hay Land	Dry Farming Land	Grazing Land	Total
Adams	$	$ 8,634,300	$	$ 6,138,650	$ 1,058,430	$ 15,831,380
Alamosa	....	1,045,000	1,116,000	1,624,800	681,116	4,466,916
Arapahoe	....	4,261,560	....	4,422,930	591,300	9,275,790
Archuleta	....	454,355	10,150	114,235	861,950	1,440,690
Baca	....	60,237	....	5,820,464	2,316,582	8,197,283
Bent	....	3,893,700	....	71,880	2,548,120	6,513,700
Boulder	....	9,350,250	48,040	814,050	1,334,610	11,546,950
Chaffee	....	1,173,790	....	....	263,195	1,436,985
Cheyenne	....	....	....	13,990,105	....	13,990,105
Clear Creek	....	....	....	....	396,965	396,965
Conejos	....	3,926,250	197,000	....	277,950	4,401,200
Costilla	....	2,486,745	112,000	30,000	231,000	2,859,745
Crowley	25,125	3,327,385	....	87,290	1,482,805	4 922,605
Custer	....	310,440	497,420	23,460	681,750	1,513 070
Delta	1,211,090	4,787,235	....	639,325	229,275	6,866,925
Denver	....	3,417,970	....	....	....	3,417,970
Dolores	....	17,300	....	534,940	212,484	764,724
Douglas	....	621,740	276,540	1,563,710	1,689,725	4,151,715
Eagle	....	1,591,832	....	....	384,840	1 976,672
Elbert	....	28,950	432,765	6,105,898	4,794,076	11,361 689
El Paso	33,000	1,530,000	88,820	3,679,460	5,152,850	10,484,130
Fremont	712,750	1,637,320	42,000	346,935	775,859	3,514,864
Garfield	101,050	4,159,555	....	451,985	557,725	5,270,315
Gilpin	....	....	....	....	60,274	60,274
Grand	....	1,120,890	....	....	587,280	1,708,170
Gunnison	....	1,738,820	....	....	602,525	2,341,345
Hinsdale	....	33,180	....	3,460	48,188	84,828
Huerfano	4,400	270,760	704,625	217,140	1,562,337	2,759,262
Jackson	....	1,432,900	....	....	613,740	2,046,640
Jefferson	....	7,110,465	....	1,183,100	1,633,490	9,927,055
Kiowa	....	....	....	....	9,581,729	9 581,729
Kit Carson	....	1,925	123 420	16,262,407	1,862,302	18,250,054
Lake	....	....	....	....	176,620	176,620
La Plata	9,855	2,543,125	38,570	288,390	1,155,120	4,035,060
Larimer	....	13,922,970	385,000	563,090	2,214,140	17,085,200
Las Animas	....	1,503,055	93,010	1,051,290	8,123,668	10,771,023
Lincoln	....	....	92,890	10,492,180	5,113,450	15,698,520
Logan	....	5,162,000	302,000	11,650,100	1,605,500	18,719,600
Mesa	1,636 732	6,661,809	....	....	1,607,014	9,905,555
Mineral	....	7,955	65,800	....	89,940	163,695
Moffat	....	589,580	83,400	1,036,780	1,372,255	3,082,015
Montezuma	42 565	1,406,620	....	721,590	546,995	2,717,770
Montrose	127,845	4,519,470	....	636,835	826,265	6,110,415
Morgan	....	6,419,910	51,700	3,289,250	2,271,995	12,032,855
Otero	145,705	9,458,115	....	343,985	1,589,695	11,537,500
Ouray	....	606,150	28,380	40,600	437,845	1,112,975
Park	....	....	872,320	101,145	846,590	1,820,055
Phillips	....	....	....	11,292,800	299,690	11,592 490
Pitkin	....	942,100	....	6,000	141,260	1,089,360
Prowers	....	6,994,170	71,920	4,174,815	1,076,130	12,317,035
Pueblo	883,470	3,918,013	....	1,281,247	3,849,010	9,931,740
Rio Blanco	....	1,269,160	28,320	358,900	795,220	2,451,600
Rio Grande	....	3,373,650	264,870	939,120	695,560	5,273,200
Routt	3,450	2,135,620	6,190	1,025,365	1,422,825	4,593,450
Saguache	....	1,656,160	1,225,000	....	1,671,787	4,552 947
San Juan	....	....	....	....	1,280	1,280
San Miguel	....	357,290	....	193,685	673,745	1,224,720
Sedgwick	....	1,248,385	78,075	5,199,245	483,335	7,009,040
Summit	....	207,655	7,000	....	90,656	305,311
Teller	....	....	44,375	226,680	287,945	559,000
Washington	....	678,580	....	17,685,080	1,755,210	20,118,870
Weld	....	38,325,860	177,360	10,504,220	5,614,740	54,622,180
Yuma	....	150,200	142,610	13,620,970	2,742,460	16,656 240
State	$4 937,037	$182,464,456	$7,707,570	$160,849,586	$92,652,417	$448,629,066

AVERAGE VALUE OF ALL FARM LAND PER ACRE AS RETURNED ANNUALLY BY COUNTY ASSESSORS FOR THE PAST TEN YEARS

COUNTY	1923	1922	1921	1920	1919	1918	1917	1916	1915	1914
Adams	$ 21.38	$ 20.92	$ 23.01	$ 23.53	$ 20.68	$ 20.49	$ 22.38	$ 17.14	$ 18.62	$ 19.93
Alamosa	13.84	11.65	14.44	14.64	15.06	13.68	10.43	8.19	6.80	7.48
Arapahoe	18.78	18.74	20.47	20.21	16.27	16.04	15.79	14.29	14.66	14.56
Archuleta	4.83	4.90	4.99	5.37	4.98	4.96	3.83	3.69	3.63	3.32
Baca	5.52	5.73	6.00	5.47	6.40	5.33	5.43	3.12	3.12	3.12
Bent	10.66	12.47	14.19	16.12	18.57	18.91	19.43	19.85	20.82	21.44
Boulder	44.31	45.47	45.95	47.54	46.60	40.20	40.26	38.01	37.40	36.23
Chaffee	16.63	17.82	17.54	17.13	17.06	16.34	14.90	16.02	15.80	15.82
Cheyenne	13.11	14.12	13.98	12.66	10.25	6.25	6.00	5.00	5.00	5.00
Clear Creek ...	11.58	11.34	10.87	9.15	5.19	4.53	4.72	3.89	3.48	4.04
Conejos	18.22	19.16	19.78	20.08	18.40	19.42	19.41	19.60	19.60	21.35
Costilla	16.35	16.27	13.40	13.53	8.86	8.32	7.90	3.99	4.09	4.31
Crowley	12.77	17.80	19.87	19.86	15.53	24.77	28.67	31.29	35.52	38.98
Custer	7.85	8.42	9.35	8.71	8.58	8.64	8.61	8.97	9.24	9.13
Delta	53.05	34.51	26.95	37.37	26.12	31.94	32.73	32.66	35.51	36.15
Denver	475.77	472.47	464.43	481.09	485.45	482.83	484.47	487.94	491.97	481.77
Dolores	7.45	7.65	7.49	7.49	7.76	7.47	7.34	7.31	7.00	6.85
Douglas	10.96	10.98	11.04	11.12	10.98	8.29	8.16	7.94	7.15	7.17
Eagle	18.13	29.14	18.96	19.04	18.10	18.67	18.42	18.43	18.76	19.31
Elbert	10.74	11.10	11.40	11.31	11.22	7.79	7.31	5.96	5.83	5.76
El Paso......	10.73	10.55	10.89	11.65	10.29	9.07	8.91	8.61	7.66	9.46
Fremont	12.44	14.78	15.46	15.17	16.12	16.29	17.54	17.03	17.63	17.48
Garfield	17.66	18.72	19.81	20.19	20.35	20.87	21.13	21.53	23.87	24.11
Gilpin	3.07	3.11	1.84	3.00	3.00	3.00	3.00	3.00	3.06	3.00
Grand	8.70	8.89	9.33	9.28	9.65	9.12	8.52	8.64	8.59	7.78
Gunnison	11.74	12.19	12.73	14.22	15.12	14.02	14.16	14.79	16.42	12.06
Hinsdale	5.43	5.31	5.28	5.38	5.43	5.27	5.10	5.51	3.15	3.27
Huerfano	5.50	6.00	6.66	6.08	5.98	5.52	4.82	4.96	4.99	4.78
Jackson	8.81	8.85	10.39	12.74	12.18	12.82	12.83	12.92	7.57	6.28
Jefferson	32.24	31.60	31.59	31.06	26.65	26.86	28.09	27.73	27.24	27.64
Kiowa	9.35	10.24	10.51	10.59	7.33	6.25	5.00	5.00	5.01	4.37
Kit Carson....	13.95	15.86	15.82	16.15	15.72	11.47	6.52	5.53	5.03	3.51
Lake	6.51	6.48	6.87	7.16	7.13	7.25	7.32	6.48	6.48	6.41
La Plata	10.57	11.39	11.97	11.94	11.72	12.16	12.52	12.56	12.40	13.50
Larimer	25.18	25.70	26.02	25.45	24.95	21.65	21.03	19.71	19.18	17.35
Las Animas ...	5.56	5.69	6.42	6.33	6.13	5.85	6.49	6.55	6.55	6.41
Lincoln	10.65	10.58	11.20	11.59	10.01	8.95	5.98	5.03	5.02	5.01
Logan	19.06	20.43	23.19	23.67	21.00	19.93	13.16	10.84	11.59	10.64
Mesa	25.90	27.00	28.78	29.50	29.89	29.56	31.13	31.76	35.39	41.60
Mineral	7.72	7.73	5.92	7.92	7.89	8.02	7.70	7.03	7.19	6.03
Moffat	5.27	6.91	9.15	10.55	9.87	10.87	10.46	10.01	9.24	10.35
Montezuma ...	10.60	10.39	10.84	11.00	10.49	10.85	11.34	11.45	12.18	15.26
Montrose	18.46	22.18	23.82	24.84	25.08	23.09	22.90	24.50	25.49	23.53
Morgan	16.79	17.54	18.58	19.50	16.82	18.57	16.44	14.70	14.46	16.99
Otero	22.93	24.61	30.36	34.42	32.30	31.31	33.48	34.75	36.34	37.58
Ouray	8.29	9.11	9.70	8.49	8.13	9.13	9.24	8.04	8.65	8.97
Park	6.27	6.56	6.93	8.17	6.73	7.01	7.01	7.01	7.04	6.95
Phillips	28.14	29.08	29.36	29.65	38.38	26.98	11.50	9.83	9.79	7.49
Pitkin	17.91	17.82	17.98	17.88	17.57	17.64	17.05	17.59	18.42	16.84
Prowers	13.38	13.56	14.51	14.54	14.22	15.05	15.90	15.52	16.67	16.34
Pueblo	9.22	9.48	9.87	10.57	10.89	10.95	11.10	11.14	11.24	11.54
Rio Blanco ...	10.47	10.67	13.24	13.92	13.47	13.65	14.20	14.03	15.07	15.92
Rio Grande ..	26.50	27.22	28.19	28.84	29.35	23.85	21.52	21.05	20.96	21.65
Routt	11.12	13.05	13.50	13.54	13.36	13.16	11.78	11.90	11.52	11.49
Saguache	9.42	10.01	10.94	10.41	10.47	10.68	10.79	10.83	10.98	9.01
San Juan.....	6.40	6.40	6.40	6.40	6.40	6.40	6.40	6.40	6.40	6.40
San Miguel....	7.43	7.84	8.39	8.74	7.88	7.99	7.99	8.01	8.44	8.76
Sedgwick	23.33	23.35	23.52	23.67	23.41	23.54	12.54	10.63	10.71	9.65
Summit	10.07	10.20	10.51	10.47	10.63	10.64	8.47	8.17	8.32	8.57
Teller	4.19	3.99	3.94	3.74	3.70	3.69	3.21	2.74	2.75	2.77
Washington ...	13.66	15.16	17.19	17.35	12.55	10.45	10.23	6.85	6.89	7.27
Weld	24.53	25.77	26.00	25.85	23.14	20.90	19.00	18.51	19.66	17.19
Yuma	11.86	12.93	14.32	13.15	9.97	8.39	7.95	4.91	5.02	5.12
State....	$ 14.12	$ 15.02	$ 15.71	$ 16.45	$ 15.13	$ 13.90	$ 12.75	$ 11.58	$ 11.78	$ 11.67

AVERAGE VALUE OF IRRIGATED LAND PER ACRE AS RETURNED ANNUALLY BY COUNTY ASSESSORS FOR PAST TEN YEARS

COUNTY	1923	1922	1921	1920	1919	1918	1917	1916	1915	1914
Adams	$ 87.00	$ 93.48	$ 91.58	$ 92.94	$ 88.20	$ 84.09	$ 81.49	$ 74.98	$ 82.62	$ 77.78
Alamosa	38.00	42.00	48.00	48.00	45.00	38.00	32.00	19.95	14.51	13.44
Arapahoe	139.00	138.64	139.62	126.09	97.00	97.00	97.00	98.90	99.40	99.52
Archuleta	44.15	40.93	39.88	41.35	42.63	42.42	27.62	27.77	25.00	24.74
Baca	12.03	12.50	15.00	25.00	25.00	....	....	....	....	....
Bent	82.44	91.32	97.58	110.96	89.45	70.16	69.92	66.61	65.01	65.04
Boulder	112.31	112.40	112.79	113.09	109.75	92.72	95.41	73.41	72.28	71.42
Chaffee	50.00	55.50	50.15	56.93	53.54	52.23	49.72	50.36	53.49	52.31
Cheyenne	....	....	....	....	....	....	....	....	....	....
Clear Creek	....	....	....	....	....	....	....	....	....	....
Conejos	45.00	45.00	44.97	45.00	40.00	40.00	40.00	40.00	40.00	36.22
Costilla	30.23	29.86	28.65	30.00	22.81	24.00	22.26	22.44	22.70	21.69
Crowley	68.63	102.72	112.08	89.32	73.14	72.00	86.35	100.49	104.85	87.77
Custer	28.72	28.56	28.12	40.00	39.94	....	27.60	33.31	32.63	34.16
Delta	78.66	83.43	83.41	89.09	85.23	75.59	75.70	77.00	80.00	76.00
Denver*	475.74	472.44	468.81	481.10	485.43	482.89	484.47	487.96	491.97	481.77
Dolores	20.00	20.00	20.00	20.00	20.00	20.00	20.00	20.00	18.00	18.00
Douglas	78.29	79.12	78.97	79.03	78.37	58.33	53.26	45.30	43.00	45.70
Eagle	68.74	105.70	69.63	69.89	68.26	69.10	69.97	68.27	70.13	71.33
Elbert	49.48	50.00	46.06	46.06	40.00	40.00	40.00	40.00	40.00	40.00
El Paso	75.00	75.00	75.00	75.00	75.00	75.00	91.26	75.00	79.86	78.00
Fremont	64.34	101.19	100.47	66.94	73.28	100.50	74.96	82.75	82.10	76.68
Garfield	64.01	70.29	70.38	70.73	66.78	67.02	67.17	67.00	70.93	71.70
Gilpin	....	....	....	....	....	....	....	....	....	....
Grand	35.32	36.82	36.45	35.67	36.26	33.15	29.79	29.63	29.25	20.00
Gunnison	46.80	47.12	48.53	46.76	46.57	46.00	45.50	45.34	47.43	34.07
Hinsdale	15.00	15.00	15.21	14.00	14.00	14.00	13.00	13.39	10.85	10.94
Huerfano	40.00	40.00	41.22	38.20	35.00	35.00	30.00	30.00	30.00	31.94
Jackson	20.00	20.00	24.79	29.77	27.68	29.59	29.17	29.94	17.00	15.00
Jefferson	147.33	146.02	145.83	148.00	149.00	150.00	152.00	152.00	151.38	150.32
Kiowa	....	....	....	....	....	....	....	....	....	....
Kit Carson	35.00	38.50	75.00	75.00	75.31	50.00	18.00	17.00	17.00	20.00
Lake	....	....	....	....	....	....	....	....	....	....
La Plata	44.34	46.73	47.39	45.95	44.84	46.31	47.19	47.37	49.32	49.40
Larimer	129.00	131.31	133.20	131.00	121.00	96.42	94.98	88.09	85.58	72.06
Las Animas	54.00	55.40	55.63	59.00	51.50	50.00	50.00	50.00	50.00	48.22
Lincoln	....	....	....	....	....	....	....	....	....	....
Logan	80.00	83.00	82.70	82.79	60.11	60.85	60.85	52.26	52.31	45.65
Mesa	83.09	83.11	84.08	77.93	81.69	76.83	78.53	80.42	85.31	94.53
Mineral	13.74	13.67	11.03	11.35	10.96	10.61	10.71	9.81	10.58	17.78
Moffat	42.00	43.72	49.07	49.54	37.00	37.55	36.39	40.99	40.45	37.55
Montezuma	39.84	37.25	37.08	37.70	33.45	33.80	33.89	32.64	33.09	37.00
Montrose	62.50	72.53	73.93	71.51	71.39	60.02	60.33	60.50	60.00	55.08
Morgan	81.98	87.00	94.00	93.02	76.14	69.07	58.55	53.00	50.10	49.54
Otero	118.02	117.98	118.60	122.48	102.47	92.80	97.16	94.30	99.80	100.47
Ouray	60.00	63.67	59.47	68.29	54.28	54.80	54.93	41.00	41.51	40.15
Park	....	....	....	....	....	....	....	....	....	....
Phillips	....	....	....	....	....	....	....	....	....	....
Pitkin	59.11	57.40	57.95	58.08	56.65	55.91	55.12	57.56	55.25	53.97
Prowers	72.56	72.00	77.02	86.78	77.50	72.00	70.00	66.00	65.00	59.75
Pueblo	95.05	93.62	95.02	98.82	96.63	96.58	96.59	96.54	98.25	102.49
Rio Blanco	60.07	60.10	65.79	67.45	63.90	64.89	64.02	63.88	64.21	64.95
Rio Grande	84.99	85.78	85.41	87.40	81.20	63.03	50.17	40.17	39.53	39.18
Routt	49.53	49.43	48.95	41.58	35.98	43.69	39.36	39.34	39.39	38.01
Saguache	44.00	44.00	43.45	39.53	38.00	38.00	38.00	38.00	37.85	42.00
San Juan	....	....	....	....	....	....	....	....	....	....
San Miguel	40.32	40.00	39.51	40.00	36.75	35.92	30.20	31.14	32.70	34.50
Sedgwick	63.50	62.71	62.92	63.61	55.33	55.00	46.00	46.08	48.32	43.06
Summit	35.00	35.00	35.06	35.00	35.02	35.00	30.00	25.00	25.00	24.92
Teller	....	....	....	....	....	....	....	....	....	....
Washington	96.83	101.65	117.28	117.94	74.70	69.00	75.42	65.00	77.95	70.00
Weld	108.24	108.92	110.14	110.64	97.18	90.15	86.14	83.22	91.09	72.20
Yuma	56.25	61.00	71.30	61.00	45.00	41.00	37.75	....	18.25	22.21
State	$ 79.80	$ 82.76	$ 83.45	$ 83.52	$ 76.04	$ 71.21	$ 69.38	$ 65.10	$ 66.58	$ 62.11

*Mostly suburban land.

AVERAGE VALUE OF DRY FARMING LAND PER ACRE AS RETURNED ANNUALLY BY COUNTY ASSESSORS FOR PAST TEN YEARS

COUNTY	1923	1922	1921	1920	1919	1918	1917	1916	1915	1914
Adams	$ 12.56	$ 10.57	$ 12.82	$ 13.76	$ 12.62	$ 12.24	$ 13.26	$ 14.02	$ 32.57	$ 15.67
Alamosa	16.00	18.00	15.00	15.00	15.00	15.00	15.00	....	....	....
Arapahoe	11.64	11.12	13.56	13.50	9.50	9.50	9.50	....	....	12.74
Archuleta	10.00	10.10	10.11	10.21	10.00	10.47	7.12	7.00	6.00	7.44
Baca	6.28	6.00	5.82	5.42	6.00	5.39	5.46	....	....	....
Bent	14.01	15.00	15.00	15.00	15.11	14.21	14.22	14.01	....	....
Boulder	34.92	35.65	36.12	36.05	35.34	30.88	30.00	....	....	....
Chaffee	....	....	....	....	....	....	....	....	....	....
Cheyenne	13.11	14.12	13.99	12.67	10.25	6.25	6.00	....	....	....
Clear Creek	....	....	....	....	....	....	....	....	....	....
Conejos	....	....	....	....	....	....	....	....	....	....
Costilla	3.00	3.00	3.00	10.00	10.00	12.00	12.00	....	12.00	....
Crowley	8.84	8.89	10.19	20.53	22.32	30.00	13.25	11.05	12.41	18.93
Custer	10.00	10.00	10.00	20.88	25.56	26.00	....	....	....	....
Delta	22.90	24.80	24.58	24.74	22.17	21.91	22.18	20.42	24.00	....
Denver	....	....	....	....	....	....	....	....	....	....
Dolores	11.00	10.94	10.00	10.01	10.03	11.28	9.65	....	....	....
Douglas	18.00	18.01	18.04	18.09	18.12	10.45	10.37	10.54	10.00	10.22
Eagle	....	....	....	....	....	....	....	....	....	....
Elbert	15.43	16.36	16.44	16.54	16.97	10.35	9.73	7.62	6.10	6.01
El Paso	16.88	16.03	14.00	13.96	13.00	11.23	11.00	10.75	11.50	12.00
Fremont	7.20	7.96	9.10	8.74	9.05	10.00	9.75	10.50	10.47	9.46
Garfield	15.44	14.88	16.47	15.89	16.50	16.73	17.10	17.17	18.61	17.22
Gilpin	....	....	....	....	....	....	....	....	....	....
Grand	....	....	....	....	....	....	20.00	20.00	10.00	....
Gunnison	....	....	....	....	....	....	3.00	20.00	....	....
Hinsdale	10.00	10.00	....	....	....	....	....	....	....	....
Huerfano	7.00	6.98	10.02	7.00	7.00	5.10	5.00	4.88	....	....
Jackson	....	....	....	....	....	....	....	....	....	....
Jefferson	45.00	44.50	44.88	33.00	27.00	25.00	25.00	25.00	25.00	25.00
Kiowa	....	....	....	....	....	....	....	....	....	....
Kit Carson	15.18	17.48	17.56	17.78	17.65	15.09	6.97	5.97	5.50	4.00
Lake	....	....	....	....	....	....	....	....	....	....
La Plata	15.32	15.44	17.74	16.83	13.61	16.21	17.44	20.66	19.62	18.28
Larimer	25.00	25.00	24.99	24.96	25.00	20.00	18.00	13.34	12.11	13.83
Las Animas	10.00	10.00	20.02	20.00	19.80	19.60	18.80	20.95	18.63	16.38
Lincoln	12.63	12.61	12.63	13.11	10.94	9.82	5.98	....	....	....
Logan	20.00	22.00	25.60	26.01	22.53	21.03	12.42	10.40	10.43	9.92
Mesa	....	....	....	....	....	....	....	....	....	....
Mineral	....	....	....	....	....	....	....	....	....	....
Moffat	7.11	8.26	12.69	12.04	10.80	11.90	10.74	15.49	15.49	15.40
Montezuma	20.26	15.01	15.21	15.04	15.09	15.10	15.21	14.86	14.70	17.00
Montrose	19.10	19.02	20.70	18.07	18.24	18.17	18.33	17.40	18.00	15.14
Morgan	13.14	13.28	13.38	13.84	13.90	16.01	12.12	11.97	12.70	14.47
Otero	15.92	16.02	14.36	15.82	15.46	15.91	15.89	16.20	12.00	14.48
Ouray	10.40	12.00	12.03	12.50	13.29	14.61	12.17	12.78	11.80	16.23
Park	15.00	15.00	15.00	15.00	15.00	15.00	15.00	15.00	15.00	15.00
Phillips	30.89	31.41	31.55	31.30	30.30	26.98	11.50	9.84	9.80	7.49
Pitkin	20.00	20.00	20.00	22.92	23.00	23.00	24.00	24.00	24.00	24.00
Prowers	6.96	6.90	7.30	26.65	23.70	24.00	....	....	....	....
Pueblo	16.18	16.21	16.55	16.81	16.56	16.53	15.82	15.44	15.45	15.56
Rio Blanco	21.78	16.21	[illegible]	22.43	18.48	18.04	16.08	25.51	27.48	27.63
Rio Grande	26.00	26.12	24.00	24.00	30.00	28.25	29.64	....	....	....
Routt	20.85	28.98	28.24	27.22	27.00	24.93	18.97	19.74	19.78	19.90
Saguache	....	....	....	....	....	....	....	....	....	....
San Juan	....	....	....	....	....	....	....	....	....	....
San Miguel	23.60	23.86	24.07	24.00	20.51	20.97	19.00	20.24	19.50	21.00
Sedgwick	29.04	29.12	29.18	29.16	29.20	28.80	12.50	9.40	9.00	8.00
Summit	....	....	....	....	....	....	....	....	....	....
Teller	10.50	10.40	10.25	10.18	10.00	10.00	10.00	10.00	10.00	10.00
Washington	14.46	16.85	18.54	17.86	12.96	10.55	10.15	6.59	6.33	6.74
Weld	12.35	14.14	15.85	13.75	14.40	13.24	8.36	17.78	14.55	11.05
Yuma	20.26	26.00	24.50	21.00	15.00	13.00	11.89	6.22	5.27	6.12
State	$ 14.40	$ 15.26	$ 15.91	$ 16.16	$ 14.59	$ 12.48	$ 9.52	$ 9.58	$ 9.16	$ 8.91

AVERAGE VALUE OF NATURAL HAY LAND PER ACRE AS RETURNED ANNUALLY BY COUNTY ASSESSORS FOR PAST TEN YEARS

COUNTY	1923	1922	1921	1920	1919	1918	1917	1916	1915	1914
Adams	$	$	$	$	$	$	$	$	$	$ ....
Alamosa	30.00	26.00	30.00	30.00	30.00	25.00	25.00	19.66	19.30	18.00
Arapahoe	....	....	....	....	....	....	....	16.90	16.90	....
Archuleta	32.74	32.91	34.90	....	....	....	....	....	....	....
Baca	....	....	....	....	....	....	....	....	....	....
Bent	....	....	....	....	....	....	....	....	....	....
Boulder	10.87	14.46	16.00	17.71	17.57	15.26	12.72	....	....	....
Chaffee	....	....	....	....	....	....	....	....	....	....
Cheyenne	....	....	....	....	....	....	....	....	....	....
Clear Creek	....	....	....	....	....	....	....	....	....	....
Conejos	20.00	20.00	20.00	22.06	20.00	25.00	25.00	25.00	25.00	25.00
Costilla	20.00	20.00	20.00	20.00	20.00	20.00	20.00	20.00	20.00	20.00
Crowley	....	....	....	....	....	....	....	....	....	....
Custer	39.93	39.70	40.00	....	....	40.00	40.00	40.25	40.48	41.17
Delta	....	....	....	....	....	....	....	....	....	....
Denver	....	....	....	....	....	....	....	....	....	....
Dolores	....	....	....	....	....	....	....	....	....	10.00
Douglas	51.60	50.49	50.99	50.04	49.61	35.70	33.06	31.30	26.00	28.02
Eagle	....	....	....	....	....	....	....	....	....	....
Elbert	42.62	42.19	29.47	37.30	35.00	25.07	24.64	24.90	24.80	24.90
El Paso	46.50	46.50	46.50	46.50	47.00	42.43	42.65	35.00	30.00	35.00
Fremont	35.00	35.00	35.00	35.00	35.00	35.50	35.50	35.00	30.54	28.00
Garfield	....	....	....	....	....	....	....	....	....	....
Gilpin	....	....	....	....	....	....	....	....	....	....
Grand	....	....	....	....	....	....	....	....	....	....
Gunnison	....	....	....	....	....	....	....	....	....	....
Hinsdale	....	....	....	....	....	....	....	....	....	....
Huerfano	41.58	44.06	....	....	....	....	....	....	....	....
Jackson	....	....	....	....	....	....	....	....	....	....
Jefferson	....	....	....	....	....	....	....	....	....	....
Kiowa	....	....	....	....	....	....	....	....	....	....
Kit Carson	35.68	36.91	35.50	37.08	34.94	35.00	8.00	7.02	12.00	10.00
Lake	....	....	....	....	....	....	....	....	....	....
La Plata	6.99	....	....	....	....	....	....	6.08	6.00	....
Larimer	25.00	25.00	25.00	25.00	25.00	25.00	25.00	25.00	25.18	26.00
Las Animas	31.81	30.70	29.48	31.00	30.70	22.20	22.20	21.74	21.74	28.23
Lincoln	29.03	27.50	30.00	29.01	25.41	24.33	....	....	....	....
Logan	22.50	22.50	25.00	25.54	24.55	18.09	16.86	14.41	15.56	....
Mesa	....	....	....	....	....	....	....	....	....	....
Mineral	25.00	25.00	25.00	25.00	25.00	25.46	25.00	25.00	25.00	25.00
Moffat	26.58	29.10	31.10	....	30.00	20.17	7.25	30.04	30.00	....
Montezuma	....	....	....	....	....	....	....	....	....	....
Montrose	....	....	....	....	....	....	....	....	....	....
Morgan	23.50	23.50	23.50	23.51	22.85	23.09	9.87	21.38	19.60	16.16
Otero	....	....	....	....	....	....	....	....	....	....
Ouray	4.15	6.61	2.12	10.35	13.50	15.86	15.82	11.69	10.00	....
Park	37.36	37.45	36.66	37.16	36.71	36.20	36.49	36.61	36.27	36.36
Phillips	....	....	....	....	....	....	....	....	....	....
Pitkin	....	....	....	....	....	....	....	....	....	....
Prowers	25.43	26.00	29.62	30.32	30.00	29.00	29.00	28.00	28.85	27.72
Pueblo	....	....	....	....	....	....	....	....	....	....
Rio Blanco	32.29	38.80	40.17	38.96	39.73	39.71	43.00	45.52	49.56	48.95
Rio Grande	32.50	32.50	32.50	32.50	32.50	32.50	32.50	32.50	32.50	....
Routt	2.45	....	....	....	....	....	....	....	....	28.88
Saguache	25.00	28.00	28.00	28.10	28.10	28.10	28.10	28.10	28.15	18.00
San Juan	....	....	....	....	....	....	....	....	....	....
San Miguel	....	....	....	....	....	....	....	....	....	....
Sedgwick	15.17	15.32	15.00	15.25	15.31	15.00	16.03	15.40	15.92	15.18
Summit	35.00	35.00	....	....	....	....	....	....	....	....
Teller	17.85	15.45	15.40	15.38	15.00	15.00	15.00	14.99	15.16	14.95
Washington	....	....	....	....	10.75	10.22	11.93	....	....	16.00
Weld	21.46	23.12	22.56	24.50	26.20	22.95	21.50	21.80	19.91	18.47
Yuma	28.12	30.00	30.50	29.00	27.50	21.00	7.16	....	....	....
State	$ 28.34	$ 28.60	$ 27.88	$ 29.25	$ 29.55	$ 27.08	$ 26.30	$ 25.88	$ 25.67	$ 23.78

Note—In some of the counties the assessors do not list any land as natural hay land, including it under other classifications.

AVERAGE VALUE OF IMPROVED FRUIT LAND PER ACRE AS RETURNED ANNUALLY BY COUNTY ASSESSORS FOR PAST TEN YEARS

COUNTY	1923	1922	1921	1920	1919	1918	1917	1916	1915	1914
Adams	$	$	$	$	$	$	$	$	$	$ ....
Alamosa	....	....	....	....	....	....	....	....	....	....
Arapahoe	....	....	....	....	....	....	....	....	....	....
Archuleta	....	....	....	....	....	....	....	....	....	....
Baca	....	....	....	....	....	....	....	....	....	....
Bent	....	....	....	....	....	....	....	....	....	....
Boulder	....	....	....	....	....	....	....	....	....	....
Chaffee	....	....	....	....	....	....	....	....	....	200.00
Cheyenne	....	....	....	....	....	....	....	....	....	....
Clear Creek	....	....	....	....	....	....	....	....	....	....
Conejos	....	....	....	....	....	....	....	....	....	....
Costilla	....	....	....	....	....	....	....	....	....	....
Crowley	78.27	92.74	83.00	120.00	100.00	100.00	100.45	99.91	98.35	97.34
Custer	....	....	....	....	....	....	....	....	....	....
Delta	115.72	109.30	103.72	107.60	103.33	100.00	123.74	163.47	180.00	227.00
Denver	....	....	....	....	....	....	....	....	....	....
Dolores	....	....	....	....	....	....	....	....	....	....
Douglas	....	....	....	....	....	....	....	....	....	....
Eagle	....	....	....	....	....	....	....	....	....	....
Elbert	....	....	....	....	....	....	....	....	....	....
El Paso	150.00	150.00	150.00	150.00	145.30	145.30	150.00	145.00	150.00	200.00
Fremont	379.34	398.70	396.07	397.80	414.60	406.00	413.05	372.20	373.67	382.39
Garfield	109.48	106.31	102.82	108.49	108.31	106.48	107.23	120.00	98.21	109.76
Gilpin	....	....	....	....	....	....	....	....	....	....
Grand	....	....	....	....	....	....	....	....	....	....
Gunnison	....	....	....	....	....	....	....	....	....	....
Hinsdale	....	....	....	....	....	....	....	....	....	....
Huerfano	100.00	100.00	150.00	150.00	150.00	....	....	....	....	....
Jackson	....	....	....	....	....	....	....	....	....	....
Jefferson	....	....	....	....	....	....	....	....	....	....
Kiowa	....	....	....	....	....	....	....	....	....	....
Kit Carson	....	....	....	....	....	....	....	....	....	....
Lake	....	....	....	....	....	....	....	....	....	....
La Plata	149.32	154.35	136.37	150.90	150.00	150.00	138.28	150.00	150.00	150.00
Larimer	....	....	....	....	....	....	179.00	179.00	175.00	157.00
Las Animas	....	....	....	....	....	....	....	....	....	....
Lincoln	....	....	....	....	....	....	....	....	....	....
Logan	....	....	....	....	....	....	....	....	....	....
Mesa	223.75	224.01	225.53	225.04	226.92	223.29	251.22	250.99	275.24	341.48
Mineral	....	....	....	....	....	....	....	....	....	....
Moffat	....	....	....	....	....	....	....	....	....	....
Montezuma	50.07	50.00	50.60	50.70	49.09	49.67	55.42	60.52	64.17	74.98
Montrose	90.28	97.20	99.15	103.50	103.26	93.85	90.00	91.10	230.00	230.31
Morgan	....	....	....	....	....	....	....	....	....	....
Otero	188.28	190.68	184.41	191.69	161.31	154.18	149.59	150.88	150.14	166.30
Ouray	....	....	....	....	....	....	....	....	....	....
Park	....	....	....	....	....	....	....	....	....	....
Phillips	....	....	....	....	....	....	....	....	....	....
Pitkin	....	....	....	....	....	....	....	....	....	100.00
Prowers	....	....	....	....	....	....	....	....	....	....
Pueblo	149.38	149.19	146.07	151.63	148.14	140.61	148.87	144.45	143.65	....
Rio Blanco	....	....	....	....	....	....	....	....	....	....
Rio Grande	....	....	....	....	....	....	....	....	....	....
Routt	100.00	92.19	93.50	97.27	76.00	100.00	100.00	100.00	120.60	172.29
Saguache	....	....	....	....	....	....	....	....	....	....
San Juan	....	....	....	....	....	....	....	....	....	....
San Miguel	....	....	....	....	....	....	....	....	....	....
Sedgwick	....	....	....	....	....	....	....	....	....	....
Summit	....	....	....	....	....	....	....	....	....	....
Teller	....	....	....	....	....	....	....	....	....	....
Washington	....	....	....	....	....	....	....	....	....	....
Weld	....	....	....	....	....	....	....	....	....	....
Yuma	....	....	....	....	....	....	....	....	....	....
State	$163.86	$168.59	$163.76	$168.47	$169.08	$167.92	$188.05	$190.69	$209.36	$251.03

AVERAGE VALUE OF GRAZING LAND PER ACRE AS RETURNED ANNUALLY BY COUNTY ASSESSORS FOR PAST TEN YEARS

COUNTY	1923	1922	1921	1920	1919	1918	1917	1916	1915	1914
Adams	$ 6.96	$ 8.09	$ 9.77	$ 9.20	$ 7.52	$ 7.84	$ 7.80	$ 5.71	$ 7.08	$ 5.33
Alamosa	4.36	4.24	4.16	4.35	5.37	6.00	6.50	3.95	4.63	5.08
Arapahoe	7.10	7.04	8.10	8.10	5.30	5.30	5.30	5.80	5.80	4.91
Archuleta	3.12	3.19	3.16	3.42	3.20	3.16	3.09	2.64	2.72	2.41
Baca	4.19	3.00	3.33	3.25	3.00	3.00	3.00	3.13	3.13	3.12
Bent	4.56	5.00	5.08	5.05	5.49	5.51	5.49	5.58	6.54	6.81
Boulder	8.92	9.41	9.49	9.49	9.57	9.54	9.69	12.06	12.04	10.37
Chaffee	4.18	4.50	3.93	4.53	3.77	4.00	3.87	3.98	4.13	4.05
Cheyenne	....	....	....	....	....	....	....	5.00	4.98	5.00
Clear Creek	11.58	11.34	10.87	9.15	5.38	4.53	4.76	3.89	3.48	4.04
Conejos	1.92	2.02	2.31	3.07	2.77	4.45	4.45	4.80	3.40	5.00
Costilla	3.00	3.00	3.00	3.00	3.00	3.00	3.00	1.56	1.51	1.80
Crowley	4.54	4.50	4.56	4.66	3.62	5.62	6.30	6.73	7.25	9.71
Custer	4.08	4.25	4.69	4.23	3.95	3.90	3.90	4.31	4.50	4.45
Delta	7.60	6.53	2.88	3.09	2.72	2.47	2.51	2.24	2.15	11.65
Denver	....	....	....	....	....	....	....	....	....	....
Dolores	4.00	4.04	5.63	4.50	4.35	4.04	4.45	5.48	5.26	4.96
Douglas	6.07	6.08	6.12	6.16	6.06	6.22	6.21	6.64	6.00	5.94
Eagle	4.48	7.04	4.16	4.18	3.65	3.36	3.20	3.22	2.75	2.79
Elbert	7.37	7.41	7.48	7.03	6.82	5.69	5.63	5.69	5.66	5.59
El Paso	7.00	7.00	8.00	8.99	7.37	6.24	6.22	5.60	5.50	5.95
Fremont	3.76	4.01	3.98	4.15	4.37	4.76	4.51	4.51	4.26	4.10
Garfield	2.74	2.76	2.54	2.52	2.61	2.62	2.64	2.53	2.68	1.30
Gilpin	3.08	3.12	3.00	3.00	3.00	3.00	3.00	3.00	3.00	3.00
Grand	3.56	3.56	3.57	3.47	3.55	3.56	3.55	3.57	3.55	4.92
Gunnison	3.71	3.68	3.72	4.13	5.16	3.87	3.73	4.21	4.76	3.34
Hinsdale	3.69	3.57	3.56	3.71	3.70	3.88	3.00	4.09	2.10	2.15
Huerfano	3.50	3.86	4.61	4.00	4.00	3.49	3.08	3.26	3.30	3.01
Jackson	3.82	3.78	3.78	4.86	4.80	4.83	4.85	4.84	3.50	2.02
Jefferson	7.00	7.26	7.25	7.07	6.00	6.00	6.00	6.00	5.50	6.00
Kiowa	9.35	10.24	10.50	10.60	7.34	6.25	5.00	5.00	5.01	4.37
Kit Carson	7.98	8.53	7.87	8.45	8.03	11.12	6.49	5.49	4.99	3.47
Lake	6.52	6.48	6.87	7.16	7.14	7.25	7.33	6.49	6.48	6.41
La Plata	3.85	3.91	4.06	3.90	4.07	4.10	4.34	4.45	4.37	4.60
Larimer	4.15	3.97	3.91	3.81	3.65	4.63	3.67	3.58	3.50	3.66
Las Animas	4.51	4.54	4.61	4.60	4.70	4.38	4.77	4.81	4.81	4.74
Lincoln	8.00	7.81	8.11	8.65	6.76	6.45	....	5.04	5.02	5.01
Logan	5.00	5.45	7.20	7.84	8.84	8.46	6.62	5.05	5.05	4.46
Mesa	5.45	5.70	5.69	5.82	6.49	6.37	6.43	6.36	6.38	6.22
Mineral	5.00	5.00	5.00	5.00	5.00	5.00	5.00	4.71	5.00	4.02
Moffat	3.25	4.07	4.49	4.76	5.44	5.76	5.13	5.34	4.05	5.98
Montezuma	2.95	3.00	3.02	3.01	3.06	3.06	3.14	3.11	3.18	3.99
Montrose	3.69	4.17	5.08	4.04	4.24	4.22	4.20	4.00	4.14	3.84
Morgan	5.89	5.97	5.83	6.09	6.54	7.26	6.90	4.95	3.60	4.04
Otero	3.96	3.96	4.13	4.22	4.29	4.21	4.35	4.36	5.00	4.74
Ouray	3.86	4.00	4.05	4.00	3.58	3.60	3.61	3.53	3.75	3.85
Park	3.26	3.27	3.30	3.42	3.09	3.25	3.21	3.22	3.23	3.18
Phillips	6.43	7.65	7.21	9.14	8.00	....	....	....	....	....
Pitkin	3.16	3.16	3.16	3.15	3.22	3.01	2.53	2.57	2.76	2.51
Prowers	4.86	4.70	4.97	5.26	4.29	4.37	4.63	3.97	4.28	3.15
Pueblo	4.05	4.05	4.02	4.03	4.07	3.81	3.60	3.35	3.31	3.35
Rio Blanco	4.07	4.27	4.62	4.60	4.50	4.37	4.42	4.03	4.13	4.33
Rio Grande	6.04	6.43	6.20	6.08	5.50	5.34	6.20	6.24	6.20	5.46
Routt	4.50	5.47	5.76	6.00	6.00	5.86	5.73	5.85	5.16	5.15
Saguache	4.21	4.37	5.00	5.10	5.10	5.16	5.25	5.12	5.27	2.32
San Juan	6.40	6.40	6.40	6.40	6.40	6.40	6.40	6.40	6.40	6.40
San Miguel	4.56	4.71	4.87	4.96	4.33	4.24	4.70	5.03	5.41	5.49
Sedgwick	5.01	5.00	5.00	5.00	5.00	5.00	4.00	3.50	3.50	4.00
Summit	3.75	3.75	3.76	3.75	3.75	3.75	3.75	3.75	3.75	3.76
Teller	2.64	2.50	2.49	2.16	2.14	2.15	2.00	2.00	2.01	2.01
Washington	7.23	8.37	9.33	9.80	7.95	6.49	6.23	4.00	4.69	....
Weld	5.54	5.98	5.83	5.93	5.72	5.22	5.16	5.05	5.00	4.45
Yuma	3.78	3.71	4.60	5.50	5.00	4.50	4.10	2.70	3.00	2.71
State	$ 5.14	$ 5.42	$ 5.66	$ 5.87	$ 5.34	$ 5.52	$ 5.01	$ 4.66	$ 4.66	$ 4.41

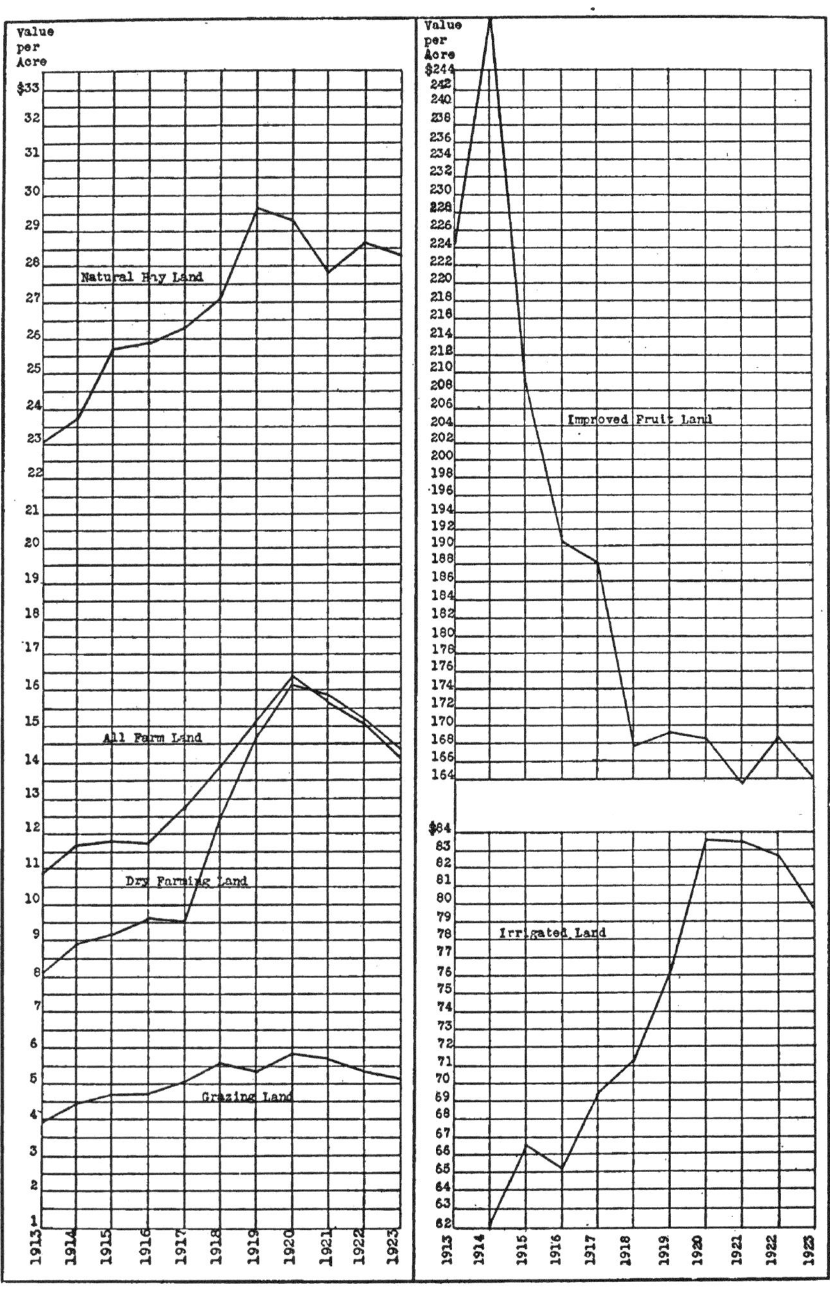

Note—This chart is prepared from the tabluations appearing on pages 123 to 128, both inclusive, and shows the range in average assessed valuations of different classes of land for the entire state for the period from 1913 to 1923.

ACREAGE OF IRRIGATED LAND AS RETURNED BY COUNTY ASSESSORS FOR ASSESSMENT FOR PAST ELEVEN YEARS

COUNTY	1923	1922	1921	1920	1919	1918	1917	1916	1915	1914	1913
Adams	99,677	99,403	100,970	102,073	88,330	89,341	86,594	96,799	76,932	100,381	140,864
Alamosa	27,500	26,450	26,000	26,000	24,000	21,000	20,000	64,310	63,110	65,900	28,550
Arapahoe	30,680	30,680	30,680	33,180	41,770	39,240	37,177	40,830	40,830	38,625	39,991
Archuleta	10,290	11,128	11,395	11,826	10,295	10,370	10,879	9,753	9,553	8,918	8,105
Baca	5,008	5,470	9,000	9,000	10,312	....	....	....	....	....	....
Bent	47,232	45,320	46,887	46,732	47,414	47,894	46,559	46,652	46,242	46,234	39,302
Boulder	83,251	83,251	83,907	86,407	86,354	82,621	82,189	98,327	98,346	98,323	98,432
Chaffee	23,478	21,301	24,217	20,045	22,424	20,271	21,446	20,939	19,110	19,037	20,053
Cheyenne	....	....	....	....	....	....	....	....	....	....	....
Clear Creek	....	....	....	....	....	....	....	....	....	....	....
Conejos	87,250	87,250	87,400	87,300	87,200	85,300	85,000	85,000	90,000	97,656	140,120
Costilla	82,260	84,060	83,200	83,000	83,000	81,000	80,150	81,700	85,701	92,239	88,714
Crowley	48,479	51,020	49,372	54,050	53,911	53,529	45,399	39,493	37,434	45,336	37,132
Custer	10,810	11,521	9,994	11,965	11,260	....	7,951	6,865	7,299	7,083	7,206
Delta	60,861	60,498	63,711	64,849	64,552	64,840	62,353	60,975	59,533	56,123	55,741
Denver	7,184	7,319	7,398	7,519	7,539	7,779	7,829	7,833	7,843	7,724	....
Dolores	865	1,310	2,065	2,065	1,728	1,595	1,517	1,460	1,399	1,358	1,080
Douglas	7,941	7,638	7,769	7,715	7,554	6,643	7,394	7,035	7,175	7,075	6,794
Eagle	23,159	15,195	22,927	22,259	21,708	21,830	20,451	20,854	20,296	19,778	19,823
Elbert	585	415	330	330	340	340	530	290	290	220	163
El Paso	20,400	20,400	20,500	20,500	20,500	20,500	14,281	21,050	20,092	19,120	18,230
Fremont	25,446	14,360	14,320	20,633	19,023	13,363	21,170	15,615	15,546	15,337	16,634
Garfield	64,978	59,802	59,382	59,278	58,666	56,868	55,478	54,029	52,899	53,278	48,783
Gilpin	....	....	....	....	....	....	....	....	....	....	....
Grand	31,220	30,146	30,138	31,097	29,943	28,668	27,170	25,902	25,156	25,111	23,261
Gunnison	37,154	37,153	36,782	35,955	34,322	33,742	33,015	32,932	33,542	32,497	33,378
Hinsdale	2,212	2,173	2,304	2,233	2,248	1,942	2,179	1,831	1,495	1,445	1,488
Huerfano	6,769	6,803	23,493	21,802	21,720	21,720	21,633	21,550	21,548	19,037	17,887
Jackson	71,645	70,188	68,036	67,685	66,725	66,039	65,257	61,641	58,524	59,710	59,181
Jefferson	48,262	48,011	48,190	49,397	41,051	40,840	40,390	40,120	40,000	40,200	40,545
Kiowa	....	....	....	....	....	....	....	....	....	....	....
Kit Carson	55	50	245	180	352	200	450	450	450	750	....

Lake	....	....	....	....	....	....	....	....	....	....	....
La Plata	57,354	57,427	54,927	57,881	50,398	50,318	48,110	47,050	44,270	44,995	43,703
Larimer	107,931	108,707	107,134	106,921	114,269	111,267	110,767	110,767	110,567	111,278	111,278
Las Animas	27,677	26,893	27,668	22,931	22,059	23,541	23,541	23,541	23,541	23,876	23,595
Lincoln	....	....	....	....	....	....	....	....	....	....	....
Logan	64,500	60,112	60,112	59,472	57,056	50,967	50,930	52,401	54,595	63,344	62,647
Mesa	80,175	80,360	80,095	89,452	78,519	78,450	77,339	77,518	80,099	82,589	82,449
Mineral	579	565	390	370	440	605	635	800	695	1,309	2,739
Moffat	14,036	15,456	15,432	16,247	16,619	16,558	18,110	14,108	14,945	15,168	14,273
Montezuma	35,306	38,429	38,627	37,077	36,510	36,277	36,276	36,602	35,766	38,660	35,622
Montrose	72,311	72,712	74,418	79,240	76,664	76,296	75,259	73,691	73,553	73,129	80,380
Morgan	78,315	78,312	77,800	76,269	74,582	74,369	72,545	72,124	74,471	74,580	73,074
Otero	80,142	80,102	80,694	79,015	77,379	79,852	76,269	79,466	76,317	70,201	80,930
Ouray	10,100	10,400	10,532	11,655	10,327	10,228	10,263	10,390	10,272	10,143	9,633
Park	....	....	....	....	....	....	....	....	....	....	....
Phillips	....	....	....	....	....	....	....	....	....	....	....
Pitkin	15,937	15,950	15,854	15,407	14,999	15,283	15,125	14,277	14,942	14,081	14,122
Prowers	96,394	97,330	95,882	89,851	89,585	88,461	87,848	88,065	89,154	96,585	99,897
Pueblo	41,218	41,489	41,310	40,788	39,939	39,746	40,379	40,436	40,054	47,641	46,318
Rio Blanco	21,311	22,725	23,494	22,990	22,470	22,100	21,846	19,825	19,815	19,973	21,359
Rio Grande	39,690	39,370	42,830	42,721	45,869	39,050	39,906	68,526	68,526	80,861	78,055
Routt	43,110	42,831	43,095	47,864	42,935	40,025	39,401	38,438	37,085	36,159	36,837
Saguache	37,640	37,640	37,480	37,480	37,480	37,480	37,480	37,480	37,449	26,496	....
San Juan	....	....	....	....	....	....	....	....	....	....	....
San Miguel	8,861	9,483	9,477	9,390	9,200	9,438	8,709	7,291	7,291	6,631	6,863
Sedgwick	19,660	19,957	19,966	20,054	20,364	20,474	20,670	20,790	20,659	20,396	21,251
Summit	5,933	6,243	6,418	6,225	6,020	5,620	5,200	5,015	4,947	4,970	3,062
Teller	....	....	....	....	....	....	....	....	....	....	....
Washington	7,007	6,758	6,728	6,682	7,163	7,028	6,687	6,981	7,341	7,050	7,093
Weld	354,084	353,718	348,399	343,808	327,920	292,262	284,687	263,518	263,211	283,058	305,612
Yuma	2,670	2,670	3,327	3,550	3,469	1,447	2,494	....	4,258	4,332	3,036
State	2,286,592	2,263,954	2,292,701	2,308,415	2,246,476	2,144,617	2,114,917	2,173,335	2,154,168	2,236,000	2,255,286

ACREAGE OF DRY FARMING LAND AS RETURNED BY COUNTY ASSESSORS FOR ASSESSMENT FOR THE PAST ELEVEN YEARS

COUNTY	1923	1922	1921	1920	1919	1918	1917	1916	1915	1914	1913
Adams	488,782	507,905	497,929	442,385	460,820	434,769	428,084	150,869	57,345	135,930	....
Alamosa	101,550	101,550	102,000	102,000	102,000	105,000	110,000	....	....	....	....
Arapahoe	379,940	379,940	379,940	375,440	383,140	374,900	369,902	....	....	42,760	42,760
Archuleta	11,328	11,214	11,022	10,876	8,850	8,343	7,350	5,929	4,708	3,938	3,860
Baca	926,293	1,167,482	1,218,770	1,080,212	829,745	804,020	704,428	....	....	....	....
Bent	5,130	5,440	6,035	6,435	6,390	6,415	6,857	6,762	....	....	....
Boulder	23,307	23,156	23,609	22,838	22,521	23,512	24,214	....	....	....	....
Chaffee	....	....	....	....	....	....	....	....	....	....	....
Cheyenne	1,066,768	1,061,593	1,060,679	1,044,149	1,015,080	988,364	952,806	....	....	....	....
Clear Creek	....	....	....	....	....	....	....	....	....	....	....
Conejos	....	....	....	....	....	....	....	....	....	....	....
Costilla	10,000	10,000	10,000	1,000	2,800	2,400	2,700	....	6,538	....	....
Crowley	9,875	10,001	6,181	2,351	3,462	4,007	6,378	5,295	2,861	1,751	....
Custer	2,346	2,378	1,954	12,101	9,223	9,399	....	....	....	....	....
Delta	27,913	31,502	31,277	38,075	38,479	36,490	37,371	36,385	37,007	....	52,835
Denver	....	....	....	....	....	....	....	....	....	....	....
Dolores	48,659	38,088	16,560	14,292	12,422	6,504	4,350	....	....	....	....
Douglas	86,921	88,416	88,118	89,217	89,154	64,513	62,599	27,633	23,690	23,666	23,473
Eagle	....	....	....	....	....	....	....	....	....	....	....
Elbert	395,662	391,093	406,840	407,190	416,091	419,894	368,396	72,114	63,303	65,512	46,584
El Paso	218,000	217,560	214,920	213,520	208,640	198,890	198,250	196,280	193,280	193,150	188,150
Fremont	48,121	27,585	20,085	21,366	20,493	18,495	15,096	20,203	25,777	17,510	17,429
Garfield	29,280	30,826	30,571	32,961	28,966	29,724	29,122	27,934	33,047	39,602	34,196
Gilpin	....	....	....	....	....	....	....	....	....	....	....
Grand	....	....	....	....	....	....	416	416	80	....	....
Gunnison	....	....	....	....	....	....	200	320	....	....	....
Hinsdale	346	342	....	....	....	....	....	....	....	....	....
Huerfano	31,020	20,983	29,238	5,012	4,852	3,840	3,500	2,984	....	....	....
Jackson	....	....	....	....	....	....	....	....	....	....	....
Jefferson	26,291	29,514	29,064	29,029	34,301	34,200	34,193	31,290	31,000	30,970	30,469
Kiowa	....	....	....	....	....	....	....	....	....	....	3,100
Kit Carson	1,071,412	1,060,633	1,062,603	1,033,286	1,073,996	100,455	75,807	70,807	50,000	59,947	50,000

Lake	....	....	....	....	....	....	....	....	....	....	....
La Plata	18,824	17,840	18.728	15.289	18,371	13,446	8,823	8,908	8,721	6,045	6,900
Larimer	22,520	22,520	22,520	22,520	22,425	23,552	25,412	25,363	25,336	20,004	22,004
Las Animas	105,129	96,319	64,155	27,293	10,880	10,149	11,495	11,495	11,325	12,507	17,787
Lincoln	830,482	840,021	976,633	914,318	1,012,783	890,895	1,183,240	....	....	....	....
Logan	583,215	584,400	584,482	584,019	579,608	551,608	402,022	361,832	339,691	252,429	232,777
Mesa	....	....	....	....	....	....	....	....	....	....	....
Mineral	....	....	....	....	....	....	....	....	....	....	....
Moffat	145,724	141,456	94,720	79,808	64,999	48,219	42,617	8,863	6,601	4,936	3,603
Montezuma	35,611	33,878	31,690	23,468	26,893	26,134	24,734	24,653	28,023	30,413	30,574
Montrose	33,393	43,505	42,823	37,621	38,097	37,203	35,195	24,053	28,169	25,261	....
Morgan	250,142	244,773	246,445	236,392	232,857	143,077	98,212	66,274	50,064	41,578	43,759
Otero	21,597	22,547	21,199	20,316	19,813	21,031	19,174	19,155	18,550	19,550	10,250
Ouray	3,900	3,805	5,876	2,986	3,118	2,713	2,575	2,524	2,024	1,778	1,784
Park	6,743	6,480	6,235	6,021	5,125	4,614	4,383	3,933	3,647	3,483	2,828
Phillips	365,504	364,783	364,562	366,420	366,298	393,292	391,112	387,843	385,671	426,161	375,763
Pitkin	300	480	480	480	480	480	480	480	480	480	480
Prowers	600,120	590,050	569,931	5,090	5,483	4,907	....	....	....	....	....
Pueblo	79,183	78,243	75,589	72,942	62,928	63,245	65,361	64,898	62,993	62,485	60,836
Rio Blanco	16,475	22,846	18,992	18,684	17,484	15,882	14,626	7,794	7,056	5,076	4,149
Rio Grande	36,120	34,600	30,000	28,400	27,000	31,040	29,420	....	....	....	....
Routt	49,117	47,548	45,103	42,015	37,662	38,048	34,174	28,333	25,309	22,376	21,637
Saguache	....	....	....	....	....	....	....	....	....	....	383,592
San Juan	....	....	....	....	....	....	....	....	....	....	....
San Miguel	8,137	8,116	7,399	7,452	6,895	6,460	5,677	5,045	4,632	4,500	4,477
Sedgwick	179,003	178,429	178,634	179,121	178,971	178,151	178,894	183,657	187,033	177,345	178,749
Summit	....	....	....	....	....	....	....	....	....	....	....
Teller	21,552	20,262	19,180	18,281	18,616	18,184	13,360	6,956	7,050	6,749	8,018
Washington	1,222,732	1,081,592	1,126,039	1,215,046	1,099,478	1,085,728	1,023,452	978,176	902,474	859,538	697,219
Weld	850,250	804,749	739,23[illegible]	806,842	754,843	785,507	745,550	128,521	112,947	62,564	49,430
Yuma	672,213	531,120	622,430	620,238	620,170	516,300	464,500	640,042	856,224	617,925	703,610
State	11,166,930	11,037,563	11,161,376	10,339,797	10,002,192	8,583,999	8,266,507	3,644,019	3,602,656	3,277,919	3,353,082

ACREAGE OF NATURAL HAY LAND AS RETURNED BY COUNTY ASSESSORS FOR ASSESSMENT FOR PAST ELEVEN YEARS

COUNTY	1923	1922	1921	1920	1919	1918	1917	1916	1915	1914	1913
Adams	....	....	....	....	....	....	....	....	....	....	....
Alamosa	37,200	37,000	37,000	37,000	37,000	37,000	40,000	12 500	12,500	12,368	6,500
Arapahoe	....	....	....	....	....	....	....	9,514	9,514	....	....
Archuleta	310	326	487	....	....	....	....	....	....	....	....
Baca	....	....	....	....	....	....	....	....	....	....	....
Bent	....	....	....	....	....	....	....	....	....	....	....
Boulder	4,418	3,166	3,129	2,904	2,927	4,649	5,742	....	....	....	....
Chaffee	....	....	....	....	....	....	....	....	....	....	....
Cheyenne	....	....	....	....	....	....	....	....	....	....	....
Clear Creek	....	....	....	....	....	....	....	....	....	....	....
Conejos	9,850	9,450	9,300	9,400	9,300	9,600	9,500	9,593	9,575	10,000	10,040
Costilla	5,600	5,000	5,000	5,200	5,200	5,500	6,135	5,280	5,300	5,300	5,300
Crowley	....	....	....	....	....	....	....	....	....	....	....
Custer	12,455	12,554	13,059	....	....	10,577	10,876	10,195	9,847	9,306	9,629
Delta	....	....	....	....	....	....	....	....	....	....	....
Denver	....	....	....	....	....	....	....	....	....	....	....
Dolores	....	....	....	....	....	....	....	....	....	142	142
Douglas	5,359	5,327	5,310	5,453	5,082	5,257	4,340	3,985	3,085	3,388	3,246
Eagle	....	....	....	....	....	....	....	....	....	....	....
Elbert	10,152	10,541	19,939	11,587	9,445	8,148	6,925	6,138	6,222	6,454	5,597
El Paso	1,910	1,910	1,910	1,910	3,800	3,800	3,780	1,130	1,200	1,240	450
Fremont	1,200	1,200	1,200	1,200	1,200	900	900	920	1,320	1,910	1,844
Garfield	....	....	....	....	....	....	....	....	....	....	....
Gilpin	....	....	....	....	....	....	....	....	....	....	....
Grand	....	....	....	....	....	....	....	....	....	....	....
Gunnison	....	....	....	....	....	....	....	....	....	....	....
Hinsdale	....	....	....	....	....	....	....	....	....	....	....
Huerfano	16,945	15,877	....	....	....	....	....	....	....	....	....
Jackson	....	....	....	....	....	....	....	....	....	....	....
Jefferson	....	....	....	....	....	....	....	....	....	....	....
Kiowa	....	....	....	....	....	....	....	....	....	....	....
Kit Carson	3,459	3,571	2,875	3,666	3,290	900	1 800	1,888	2,681	600	....

Lake	....	....	....	....	....	....	....	....	....	....	....
La Plata	5,512	....	....	....	....	....	....	10,464	9,098	....	....
Larimer	15,400	15,400	15,400	15,400	15,400	15,400	15,400	15,340	15,329	15,025	15,025
Las Animas	2,924	3,189	3,431	4,016	4,440	6,815	6,815	6,815	6,815	3,436	5,021
Lincoln	3,199	3,560	3,290	3,310	4,382	5,155	....	....	....	....	....
Logan	13,400	13,400	13,410	13,424	6,175	6,012	9,934	945	4,371	....	....
Mesa	....	....	....	....	....	....	....	....	....	....	....
Mineral	2,632	2,629	2,629	2,885	2,765	2,798	2,365	2,040	2,000	1,400	....
Moffat	3,137	2,761	2,542	....	1,710	6,242	5,149	2,462	2,078	....	....
Montezuma	....	....	....	....	....	....	....	....	....	....	....
Montrose	....	....	....	....	....	....	....	....	....	....	....
Morgan	2,200	2,200	2,200	2,700	3,018	3,142	5,603	4,506	4,165	4,064	5,038
Otero	....	....	....	....	....	....	....	....	....	....	....
Ouray	6,843	6,200	14,225	1,424	1,127	1,040	864	1,048	1,000	....	....
Park	23,346	23,328	24,026	22,662	22,066	22,187	21,675	21,242	21,313	21,311	21,220
Phillips	....	....	....	....	....	....	....	....	....	....	....
Pitkin	....	....	....	....	....	....	....	....	....	....	....
Prowers	2,828	3,134	3,777	3,647	4,435	4,128	3,792	3,532	5,914	5,973	5,892
Pueblo	....	....	....	....	....	....	....	....	....	....	....
Rio Blanco	877	9,188	1.018	1,010	1,117	1,100	1,723	3,381	3,846	3,599	2,018
Rio Grande	8.150	8,850	8,870	8,870	8,840	8,840	9,000	8,764	8,931	....	....
Routt	2,520	....	....	....	....	....	....	....	....	90	....
Saguache	49,000	48,750	48,750	48,750	48,750	48,750	48,750	48,750	48,392	71,124	....
San Juan	....	....	....	....	....	....	....	....	....	....	....
San Miguel	....	....	....	....	....	....	....	....	....	....	....
Sedgwick	5,145	5,051	5,321	5,469	5,509	5,280	5,173	5,162	5,781	5,165	4,738
Summit	200	215	....	....	....	....	....	....	....	....	....
Teller	2,485	2,470	2,441	2,322	2,309	1,722	1,440	1,469	1,448	1,580	1,633
Washington	....	....	....	....	320	88	1,530	....	....	1,755	1,105
Weld	8,262	8,651	9,666	9,631	7,199	14,074	13,419	14,384	12,517	5,635	11,167
Yuma	5,070	3,030	3,191	4,490	3,933	3,522	4,757	....	....	....	....
State	271,988	267,928	263,396	228,330	220,739	242,626	247,467	211,447	214,242	190,865	115,605

ACREAGE OF IMPROVED FRUIT LAND AS RETURNED BY COUNTY ASSESSORS FOR ASSESSMENT FOR PAST ELEVEN YEARS

COUNTY	1923	1922	1921	1920	1919	1918	1917	1916	1915	1914	1913
Adams	......	......	......	......	......	......	......	......	......	......	......
Alamosa	......	......	......	......	......	......	......	......	......	......	......
Arapahoe	......	......	......	......	......	......	......	......	......	......	......
Archuleta	......	......	......	......	......	......	......	......	......	......	......
Baca	......	......	......	......	......	......	......	......	......	......	......
Bent	......	......	......	......	......	......	......	......	......	......	......
Boulder	......	......	......	......	......	......	......	......	......	......	......
Chaffee	......	......	......	......	......	......	......	......	......	150	150
Cheyenne	......	......	......	......	......	......	......	......	......	......	......
Clear Creek	......	......	......	......	......	......	......	......	......	......	......
Conejos	......	......	......	......	......	......	......	......	......	......	......
Costilla	......	......	......	......	......	......	......	......	......	......	......
Crowley	321	349	572	535	594	588	555	546	525	540	263
Custer	......	......	......	......	......	......	......	......	......	......	......
Delta	10,466	9,189	10,506	10,303	9,159	6,966	5,876	5,387	5,032	4,630	4,933
Denver	......	......	......	......	......	......	......	......	......	......	......
Dolores	......	......	......	......	......	......	......	......	......	......	......
Douglas	......	......	......	......	......	......	......	......	......	......	......
Eagle	......	......	......	......	......	......	......	......	......	......	......
Elbert	......	......	......	......	......	......	......	......	......	......	......
El Paso	220	220	320	320	320	320	350	330	320	380	......
Fremont	1,879	2,368	2,408	2,371	2,422	2,265	2,521	2,760	2,800	2,803	2,808
Garfield	923	794	1,041	898	938	1,142	1,147	1,381	2,087	1,509	1.821
Gilpin	......	......	......	......	......	......	......	......	......	......	......
Grand	......	......	......	......	......	......	......	......	......	......	......
Gunnison	......	......	......	......	......	......	......	......	......	......	......
Hinsdale	......	......	......	......	......	......	......	......	......	......	......
Huerfano	44	42	38	20	20	......	......	......	......	......	......
Jackson	......	......	......	......	......	......	......	......	......	......	......
Jefferson	......	......	......	......	......	......	......	......	......	......	......
Kiowa	......	......	......	......	......	......	......	......	......	......	......
Kit Carson	......	......	......	......	......	......	......	......	......	......	......

Lake	....	....	....	....	....	....	....	....	....	....	....
La Plata	66	62	11	88	61	55	96	83	83	83	78
Larimer	....	....	....	....	....	....	500	500	500	2,011	2,011
Las Animas	....	....	....	....	....	....	....	....	....	....	....
Lincoln	....	....	....	....	....	....	....	....	....	....	....
Logan	....	....	....	....	....	....	....	....	....	....	....
Mesa	7,315	7,359	7.628	8,070	7,961	8,199	8,302	7,385	7,455	7,024	7,497
Mineral	....	....	....	....	....	....	....	....	....	....	....
Moffat	....	....	....	....	....	....	....	....	....	....	....
Montezuma	850	848	838	806	813	751	739	821	843	1.017	832
Montrose	1,416	1,775	1,697	1,743	1,623	1,636	1,653	1,699	1,462	1,450	1,096
Morgan	....	....	....	....	....	....	....	....	....	....	....
Otero	774	933	1,163	1,051	1,240	1,039	1,193	1,137	1,148	1,553	1.956
Ouray	....	....	....	....	....	....	....	....	....	....	....
Park	....	....	....	....	....	....	....	....	....	....	....
Phillips	....	....	....	....	....	....	....	....	....	....	....
Pitkin	....	....	....	....	....	....	....	....	....	45	45
Prowers	....	....	....	....	....	....	....	....	....	....	....
Pueblo*	5.821	5,888	5,824	5.910	6,037	6,402	6,101	6,361	6,361	....	....
Rio Blanco	....	....	....	....	....	....	....	....	....	....	....
Rio Grande	....	....	....	....	....	....	....	....	....	....	....
Routt	34	32	38	33	59	31	43	83	197	305	346
Saguache	....	....	....	....	....	....	....	....	....	....	....
San Juan	....	....	....	....	....	....	....	....	....	....	....
San Miguel	....	....	....	....	....	....	....	....	....	....	....
Sedgwick	....	....	....	....	....	....	....	....	....	....	....
Summit	....	....	....	....	....	....	....	....	....	....	....
Teller	....	....	....	....	....	....	....	....	....	....	....
Washington	....	....	....	....	....	....	....	....	....	....	....
Weld	....	....	....	....	....	....	....	....	....	....	....
Yuma	....	....	....	....	....	....	....	....	....	....	....
State	30,129	29,859	32,084	32,148	31,247	29,394	29,076	28,473	28,813	23,500	23,836

*Suburban land.

ACREAGE OF GRAZING LAND AS RETURNED BY COUNTY ASSESSORS FOR ASSESSMENT FOR PAST ELEVEN YEARS

COUNTY	1923	1922	1921	1920	1919	1918	1917	1916	1915	1914	1913
Adams	152,000	151,855	139,264	192,665	171,082	165,390	152,036	448,530	495,430	355,512	408,264
Alamosa	156,356	145,183	146,381	142,800	130,499	139,131	132,712	212,537	258,890	218,392	149,030
Arapahoe	83,210	83,850	83,210	81,930	70,580	67,400	66,383	403,153	391,103	331,884	320,742
Archuleta	276,337	273,150	256,075	234,439	241,625	240,755	239,664	241,180	235,316	226,948	214,573
Baca	552,449	230,525	117,418	48,684	32,801	24,787	8,993	609,432	540,620	474,067	401,060
Bent	558,575	480,221	429,733	393,620	254,893	180,840	166,020	149,205	143,083	137,772	....
Boulder	149,558	145,470	144,808	139,641	137,944	137,801	135,029	134,120	134,420	133,820	138,277
Chaffee	62,910	60,234	57,993	63,318	61,503	59,049	66,237	59,712	61,577	61,359	59,865
Cheyenne	....	....	....	....	....	....	....	928,282	888,535	821,560	728,279
Clear Creek	34,280	34,524	34,057	33,857	33,186	32,804	32,576	31,006	30,828	30,828	29,800
Conejos	144,354	131,862	126,094	128,904	121,495	120,750	120,520	120,585	116,688	91,054	154,217
Costilla	77,000	77,430	130,000	130,000	225,000	252,000	252,018	666,956	671,917	674,084	671,883
Crowley	326,613	320,862	292,537	250,603	266,886	136,232	114,412	108,386	90,623	75,500	68,481
Custer	167,046	150,372	126,404	116,339	109,881	104,196	104,630	103,886	100,507	101,572	100,263
Delta	30,187	106,962	106,492	104,940	101,307	99,694	93,309	97,362	87,667	127,328	72,072
Denver	....	....	....	....	....	....	....	....	....	....	....
Dolores	53,121	39,206	36,035	20,678	14,457	13,060	10,175	10,007	8,858	8,237	7,119
Douglas	278,258	275,965	275,802	273,199	272,441	296,539	298,093	330,303	333,320	338,854	339,790
Eagle	85,811	52,634	78,472	76,135	75,349	71,923	69,240	68,288	65,096	62,290	62,007
Elbert	650,549	650,186	618,070	615,324	595,613	583,425	614,325	892,878	882,276	843,349	800,560
El Paso	736,122	732,010	724,016	715,708	697,200	688,188	657,243	629,410	584,264	542,483	547,043
Fremont	205,836	184,192	176,692	168,838	164,270	165,864	162,097	150,926	136,887	135,289	135,582
Garfield	203,197	189,992	172,848	165,985	151,786	142,367	136,991	130,916	116,487	104 888	107,108
Gilpin	19,601	19,752	19,265	18,091	17,771	16,399	16,239	16,840	15,936	16 754	31,600
Grand	165,070	156,026	141,625	141,172	130,414	123,911	117,387	107,991	103,010	107,020	100,641
Gunnison	162,144	152,466	146,122	115,972	105,506	106,249	101,098	95,292	89,159	82,036	78,244
Hinsdale	13,049	12,940	13,288	12,526	12,201	12,132	11,334	10,202	10,586	9,882	9,642
Huerfano	446,380	401,919	378,349	340,125	320,776	315,101	314,706	316,492	318,663	291,720	276,566
Jackson	160,542	154,295	148,074	146,359	141,365	138,806	133,534	129,032	135,416	122,151	120,675
Jefferson	233,355	241,200	242,079	243,917	245,164	240,217	223,006	226,520	225,175	224,048	222,997
Kiowa	1,023,856	996,035	975,525	960,670	908,969	850,612	792,298	724,725	680,986	607,114	485,232
Kit Carson	233,218	243,610	242,141	228,829	285,423	1,130,129	1,124,674	1,100,521	1,075,027	998,347	842,690

Lake	27,110	27,739	26,772	27,011	26,407	25,459	25,459	26,796	26,658	26,652	26,431
La Plata	299,800	282,190	259,704	255,585	223,900	220,879	210,884	199,743	203,662	186,040	173,448
Larimer	532,660	526,965	517,491	521,332	516,587	462,410	475,000	469,820	469,636	469,678	469,678
Las Animas	1,800,020	1,583,540	1,275,158	1,024,029	913,058	883,700	739,429	726,629	723,629	716,102	874,823
Lincoln	639,029	622,411	471,612	491,790	307,484	341,949	....	1,109,059	1,058,771	993,743	859,527
Logan	320,900	314,100	313,012	309,715	257,596	233,080	330,725	346,499	281,379	329,042	298,609
Mesa	294,865	279,669	256,762	240,762	240,816	228,386	222,326	212,091	199,501	183,083	168,062
Mineral	17,988	17,844	17,635	17,296	16,784	16,214	15,887	16,700	16,561	20,891	20,407
Moffat	421,182	302,304	215,819	133,655	124,482	107,509	98,674	116,559	106,130	100,246	92,001
Montezuma	184,546	165,334	151,507	143,551	133,890	124,768	115,261	107,786	95,472	84,736	72,530
Montrose	223,843	202,417	190,157	175,089	163,860	155,221	147,927	135,324	127,145	121,579	122,077
Morgan	385,691	380,998	360,282	318,919	275,952	304,645	277,924	267,714	238,545	179,079	156,875
Otero	400,498	360,131	265,285	221,636	187,602	173,936	159,846	148,293	144,260	126,795	119,553
Ouray	113,310	110,150	92,764	118,137	109,216	88,650	85,638	79,541	70,497	64,273	64,031
Park	259,789	235,928	210,470	186,171	193,390	181,534	177,111	173,940	171,172	173,917	166,621
Phillips	46,428	39,649	35,871	29,360	28,910	....	....	....	....	....	....
Pitkin	44,573	43,124	42,808	42,191	41,020	40,131	39,880	38,192	35,279	36,988	36,225
Prowers	221,203	209,228	203,424	712,576	583,005	484,990	427,012	388,612	353,857	322,898	280,695
Pueblo	950,372	891,310	821,546	749,407	676,015	641,767	614,350	587,970	579,033	559,892	546,544
Rio Blanco	195,346	185,136	166,237	151,782	139,315	132,434	119,218	118,321	109,097	99,872	91,792
Rio Grande	114,978	111,230	107,400	105,294	101,576	98,370	96,630	95,193	93,223	87,613	89,342
Routt	317,975	305,856	283,520	255,707	239,242	228,996	220,626	212,266	198,456	188,763	171,175
Saguache	396,629	382,414	357,932	367,643	351,529	339,205	333,225	325,671	321,482	226,221	....
San Juan	200	200	200	200	200	200	200	200	200	200	200
San Miguel	147,670	140,569	116,473	108,427	98,644	92,243	85,102	77,249	75,175	69,054	69,413
Sedgwick	95,509	96,649	94,509	93,008	98,109	88,241	82,274	74,817	67,500	73,794	63,006
Summit	24,175	24,801	23,336	22,720	21,374	19,697	22,202	19,083	17,663	16,922	17,930
Teller	109,107	105,736	102,518	91,867	91,763	87,327	88,680	92,460	91,309	88,437	87,777
Washington	242,700	354,669	278,663	171,281	193,111	130,047	97,590	50,000	4,800	....	....
Weld	1,014,101	1,011,219	1,079,487	1,011,289	1,016,035	908,568	810,906	1,262,924	1,242,646	1,192,886	1,002,684
Yuma	724,140	773,180	676,560	668,467	664,290	633,000	503,787	376,066	133,134	285,540	50,464
State	18,008,349	16,981,618	15,593,783	15,071,165	14,132,527	14,129,307	13,090,752	17,110,263	16,284,222	15,381,078	13,876,229

ACRES OF FARM LAND RETURNED ANNUALLY FOR ASSESSMENT IN COLORADO FOR THE PAST TEN YEARS

COUNTY	1923	1922	1921	1920	1919	1918	1917	1916	1915	1914
Adams	740,459	759,163	738,163	737,123	720,232	689,500	666,714	696,198	629,707	591,823
Alamosa	322,606	310,183	311,381	307,800	293,499	302,131	302,712	289,347	334,500	296,640
Arapahoe	493,830	494,470	493,830	490,550	495,490	481,540	473,462	453,497	441,447	413,269
Archuleta	298,265	295,818	278,979	257,141	260,770	259,468	257,893	256,862	249,577	239,804
Baca	1,483,750	1,403,477	1,355,188	1,137,896	872,858	828,807	713,421	609,432	540,620	474,067
Bent	610,937	530,981	482,655	446,787	308,697	235,149	219,436	202,619	189,325	184,006
Boulder	260,564	255,043	255,453	251,790	249,746	248,583	247,174	232,447	232,766	232,143
Chaffee	86,388	81,535	82,210	83,363	83,927	79,320	87,683	80,651	80,687	80,546
Cheyenne	1,066,768	1,061,593	1,060,679	1,044,149	1,015,080	988,364	952,806	928,282	888,535	821,560
Clear Creek	34,280	34,524	34,057	33,857	33,186	32,804	32,576	31,006	30,828	30,828
Conejos	241,454	228,562	222,794	225,604	217,995	215,650	215,020	215,178	216,263	198,710
Costilla	174,860	176,490	228,200	219,200	316,000	340,900	341,003	*753,936	*769,456	*771,623
Crowley	385,288	382,232	348,662	307,539	324,853	194,356	166,744	153,720	131,443	123,127
Custer	192,657	176,825	151,411	140,405	130,372	124,172	123,457	120,946	117,653	117,961
Delta	1,129,427	208,151	277,560	218,167	213,497	207,990	198,908	200,109	189,239	188,081
Denver	7,184	7,319	7,468	7,519	7,539	7,779	7,829	7,833	7,843	7,724
Dolores	102,645	78,604	54,660	37,035	28,587	21,159	16,042	11,537	10,257	9,737
Douglas	378,479	377,346	376,999	375,584	374,231	372,952	372,426	368,956	367,270	372,983
Eagle	108,970	67,829	101,399	98,394	97,057	93,753	89,691	89,142	85,392	82,068
Elbert	1,056,948	1,052,235	1,045,189	1,034,431	1,021,489	1,011,807	990,176	971,420	952,091	915,535
El Paso	976,652	972,100	961,666	951,958	930,460	911,698	873,904	848,200	799,156	756,373
Fremont	282,482	229,705	214,705	214,408	207,408	200,887	201,784	190,424	182,330	172,849
Garfield	298,378	281,414	263,842	259,122	240,356	230,101	222,738	214,260	204,520	199,277
Gilpin	19,601	19,752	31,491	18,091	17,771	16,399	16,239	16,840	15,936	16,754
Grand	196,290	186,172	171,763	172,269	160,357	152,579	144,973	134,309	128,246	132,131
Gunnison	199,298	189,619	182,904	151,927	139,828	139,991	134,313	128,544	122,701	114,533
Hinsdale	15,607	15,455	15,592	14,759	14,449	14,074	13,513	12,033	12,081	11,327
Huerfano	501,158	445,624	451,928	366,959	347,368	340,661	339,839	341,026	340,211	310,757
Jackson	232,187	224,483	216,110	214,044	208,090	204,845	198,791	190,673	193,940	181,861
Jefferson	307,908	318,725	319,333	322,343	320,516	315,257	297,589	297,930	296,175	295,218
Kiowa	1,023,856	996,035	975,525	960,670	908,969	850,612	792,298	724 725	680,986	607,114
Kit Carson	1,308,144	1,307,864	1,307,864	1,265,961	1,359,781	1,231,684	1,202,811	1,173,666	1,128,158	1,059,644

Lake	27,110	27,739	26,772	27,011	26,407	25,459	25,459	26,796	26,658	26,652
La Plata	381,556	357,519	333,370	328,843	292,730	284,698	267,913	266,248	265,834	237,163
Larimer	678,511	673,592	662,545	666,173	668,681	612,629	627,079	621,790	621,368	617,996
Las Animas	1,935,750	1,709,941	1,370,412	1,078,269	950,437	924,205	781,280	768,480	765,310	755,921
Lincoln	1,472,710	1,465,992	1,451,535	1,409,418	1,324,739	1,237,999	1,183,240	1,109,059	1,058,771	993,743
Logan	982,015	972,012	971,016	966,630	899,835	841,739	793,611	761,677	680,036	644,815
Mesa	382,355	367,388	344,485	338,284	327,296	315,035	307,967	296,994	287,055	272,696
Mineral	21,199	21,038	26,683	20,551	19,989	19,617	18,887	19,540	19,256	23,600
Moffat	584,079	461,977	328,513	229,710	207,810	178,528	164,550	141,992	129,754	120,350
Montezuma	256,313	238,489	222,662	209,902	198,106	187,930	177,010	169,862	160,104	154,826
Montrose	330,963	320,409	309,095	293,693	280,244	270,356	260,034	234,767	230,329	221,419
Morgan	716,348	706,283	686,727	634,280	586,409	525,233	454,284	410,618	367,245	299,301
Otero	503,011	463,713	368,341	323,442	286,034	275,858	256,482	248,051	240,275	218,099
Ouray	134,153	130,555	113,639	155,440	123,788	102,631	99,340	93,503	83,793	76,194
Park	289,876	265,736	240,731	192,192	220,581	208,335	203,169	199,115	196,132	198,711
Phillips	411,932	404,432	400,433	395,780	295,208	393,292	391,112	387,843	385,671	426,161
Pitkin	60,810	59,554	59,142	58,078	56,499	55,894	55,485	52,949	50,701	51,594
Prowers	920,545	899,742	873,014	811,164	682,508	582,486	518,652	480,209	448,925	425,456
Pueblo	1,076,594	1,016,930	944,269	867,047	784,919	751,160	726,191	699,665	688,441	670,018
Rio Blanco	234,009	239,895	209,741	194,466	180,386	171,516	157,413	149,321	139,814	128,520
Rio Grande	198,938	194,050	189,100	185,285	183,285	177,300	174,956	172,483	170,680	168,474
Routt	412,756	396,267	371,757	345,619	319,898	307,100	294,244	279,120	261,047	247,693
Saguache	483,269	468,804	437,162	453,873	437,759	425,435	419,455	411,901	407,323	323,841
San Juan	200	200	200	200	200	200	200	200	200	200
San Miguel	164,668	158,168	133,349	125,269	114,739	108,141	99,488	89,585	87,098	80,185
Sedgwick	300,317	300,086	298,510	297,652	293,953	292,146	287,011	284,426	280,973	276,700
Summit	30,308	31,259	29,753	28,945	27,394	25,317	27,402	24,098	22,610	21,892
Teller	133,144	128,468	124,139	112,470	112,688	107,233	103,480	100,885	99,807	96,766
Washington	1,472,439	1,443,019	1,412,329	1,393,009	1,300,072	1,222,891	1,129,259	1,035,157	914,615	868,343
Weld	2,226,697	2,178,337	2,176,788	2,171,570	2,105,997	2,000,411	1,854,562	1,669,347	1,631,321	1,544,143
Yuma	1,404,093	1,310,000	1,305,508	1,296,745	1,291,862	1,154,269	975,538	1,016,102	993,616	907,797
State	31,763,988	30,580,922	29,963,248	27,979,855	26,620,911	25,130,015	23,748,718	23,167,531	22,284,101	21,109,362

ASSESSED VALUE OF ALL FARM LAND IN COLORADO AS RETURNED BY COUNTY ASSESSORS ANNUALLY FOR THE PAST TEN YEARS

COUNTY	1923	1922	1921	1920	1919	1918	1917	1916	1915	1914
Adams	$ 15,831,380	$ 15,889,250	$ 16,988,410	$ 17,346,280	$ 14,894,670	$ 14,128,480	$ 14,921,510	$ 11,938,043	$ 11,731,350	$ 11,799,115
A[illegible]sa	4,466,916	3,616,546	4,497,326	4,509,139	4,421,966	4,133,279	3,157,935	2,369,860	2,275,990	2,219,823
[illegible]hoe	9,275,790	9,268,660	10,109,400	9,915,770	8,065,590	7,725,050	7,479,880	6,482,250	6,473,900	6,020,790
Archuleta	1,44[illegible]0	1,450,850	1,392,295	1,382,773	1,300,575	1,287,972	989,780	949,776	907,132	797,160
Baca	8,197,283	8,050,285	8,143,655	6,233,251	5,593,818	4,422,451	3,875,333	1,904,474	1,689,437	1,481,459
Bent	6,[illegible]0	6,624,550	6,849,435	7,206,575	5,734,985	4,448,110	4,265,360	4,023,875	3,942,210	3,945,835
Boulder	11,546,950	11,597,220	11,738,720	11,971,220	11,644,970	9,995,400	9,951,930	8,835,820	8,726,800	8,410,915
[illegible]ee	1,436,985	1,453,350	1,442,280	1,428,500	1,432,610	1,296,325	1,307,215	1,292,505	1,275,335	1,274,885
Cheyenne	13,990,105	14,993,345	14,836,555	13,228,595	10,413,080	6,177,275	5,716,836	4,641,474	4,442,677	4,107,800
C[illegible]ar Creek	396,965	391,515	370,535	309,815	172,305	148,725	153,785	120,830	107,510	124,850
Conejos	4,401,200	4,381,185	4,408,630	4,532,364	4,011,463	4,189,338	4,173,814	4,219,118	4,240,655	4,243,145
Costilla	2,859,745	2,871,931	3,057,846	2,966,242	2,800,473	2,838,800	2,695,404	3,011,322	3,150,750	3,325,821
[illegible]ey	4,922,605	6,806,715	6,930,881	6,108,970	5,045,445	4,814,240	4,781,630	4,810,940	4,669,539	4,800,553
[illegible]er	1,513,070	1,489,920	1,416,150	1,223,170	1,119,746	1,073,820	1,064,161	1,085,600	1,088,200	1,077,450
Delta	6,866,925	7,184,315	7,480,935	8,152,925	5,577,031	6,644,590	6,510,365	6,538,365	6,721,485	6,800,395
[illegible]er	3,[illegible]70	3,458,070	3,468,390	3,617,390	3,659,820	3,755,980	3,792,930	3,822,050	3,858,530	3,721,250
[illegible]es	[illegible]24	601,343	409,841	277,415	221,995	158,150	117,805	84,449	71,848	66,762
Douglas	4,151,715	4,145,060	4,163,905	4,179,510	4,112,040	3,091,940	3,039,870	2,930,375	2,628,305	2,675,[illegible]0
Eagle	1,976,672	1,976,579	1,923,102	1,873,775	1,756,988	1,750,458	1,652,421	1,643,616	1,602,427	1,585,069
Elbert	11,361,689	11,685,064	11,915,675	11,706,966	11,468,378	7,882,500	7,241,245	5,793,375	5,551,416	5,281,674
El Paso	10,484,130	10,265,010	10,475,330	11,096,370	9,577,620	8,274,130	7,789,830	7,303,360	6,124,770	7,161,750
Fremont	3,514,864	3,397,175	3,320,616	3,254,630	3,344,100	3,273,030	3,540,030	3,244,535	3,215,976	3,021,915
Garfield	5,270,315	5,270,855	5,228,630	5,232,570	4,893,375	4,803,460	4,707,715	4,614,920	4,883,820	4,805,150
Gilpin	0,2[illegible]4	61,555	58,137	54,273	53,313	49,197	48,717	50,625	47,808	50,262
Grand	1,7[illegible]8,17[illegible]	1,655,965	1,603,400	1,599,980	1,549,015	1,392,660	1,235,832	1,161,190	1,102,450	1,028,885
Gunnison	2,341,345	2,311,835	2,328,665	2,160,525	2,115,425	1,963,972	1,902,348	1,901,297	2,014,878	1,381,900
Hinsdale	84,828	82,190	82,386	79,425	78,563	74,255	68,994	66,352	38,083	37,145
Huerfano	2,759,262	2,674,353	3,010,766	2,231,420	2,080,268	1,882,637	1,638,416	1,694,155	1,699,296	1,488,466
Jackson	2,046,640	1,986,950	2,246,920	2,727,695	2,536,125	2,627,885	2,552,195	2,463,925	1,468,864	1,142,420
Jefferson	9,927,055	10,074,470	10,087,925	10,013,595	8,542,375	8,468,930	8,361,990	8,263,495	8,069,735	8,161,500
Kiowa	[illegible]9	10,204,256	10,258,424	10,179,094	6,671,770	5,316,650	3,962,090	3,625,010	3,413,286	2,656,500
Kit Carson	18,250,054	20,754,320	20,690,700	20,453,265	21,385,842	14,133,047	7,850,901	6,493,642	5,679,205	3,728,964

Lake	176,620	179,780	184,020	193,530	188,545	184,645	186,540	173,830	172,825	170,920
La Plata	4,035,060	4,075,050	3,991,125	3,927,655	3,431,783	3,462,560	3,355,645	3,345,674	3,298,920	3,203,540
Larimer	17,085,200	17,315,785	17,241,155	16,959,870	16,689,895	13,263,520	13,191,725	12,258,295	11,923,983	10,725,495
Las Animas	10,771,023	9,740,132	8,806,229	6,835,416	5,830,507	5,412,130	5,071,525	5,036,813	5,017,713	4,851,947
Lincoln	15,698,520	15,555,550	16,266,860	16,343,285	13,273,270	11,080,545	7,085,550	5,589,010	5,315,710	4,984,215
Logan	18,719,600	19,860,575	22,523,955	22,884,010	18,905,500	16,784,720	10,448,760	8,258,336	7,885,974	6,864,605
Mesa	9,905,555	9,921,420	9,917,620	9,979,585	9,783,870	9,312,700	9,589,205	9,432,995	10,159,695	11,345,430
Mineral	163,695	162,670	158,215	162,875	157,885	157,445	145,480	137,430	138,635	142,470
Moffat	3,082,015	3,193,615	3,008,370	2,424,190	2,052,267	1,942,084	1,722,360	1,422,120	1,198,940	1,245,640
Montezuma	2,717,770	2,479,955	2,415,235	2,310,452	2,078,818	2,040,292	2,008,233	1,945,433	1,951,590	2,362,670
Montrose	6,110,415	7,106,960	7,364,560	7,298,220	7,029,230	6,242,955	5,955,925	5,753,010	5,872,205	5,212,190
Morgan	12,032,855	12,394,210	12,761,855	12,371,500	9,867,395	9,757,840	7,468,580	6,039,790	5,313,540	5,086,370
Otero	11,537,500	11,414,680	11,184,315	11,136,010	9,241,075	8,637,865	8,589,065	8,621,880	8,733,185	8,196,170
Ouray	1,112,975	1,189,440	1,103,307	1,320,604	1,007,530	937,529	917,930	751,765	724,900	684,190
Park	1,820,055	1,744,320	1,670,175	1,570,285	1,484,885	1,462,270	1,425,948	1,397,497	1,381,540	1,381,920
Phillips	11,592,490	11,761,980	11,759,195	11,735,765	11,332,450	10,613,441	4,497,788	3,813,455	3,776,655	3,196,121
Pitkin	1,089,360	1,061,585	1,063,790	1,038,980	993,065	986,470	946,370	931,420	934,290	869,165
Prowers	12,317,035	12,208,015	12,670,460	11,796,415	9,708,635	8,771,815	8,250,800	7,455,575	7,483,880	6,955,325
Pueblo	9,931,740	9,641,252	9,328,835	9,169,292	8,551,363	8,230,238	8,066,328	7,795,678	7,739,328	7,736,463
Rio Blanco	2,451,600	2,561,530	2,777,345	2,707,495	2,430,590	2,342,200	2,235,590	2,095,700	2,107,221	2,046,312
Rio Grande	5,273,200	5,283,940	5,332,330	5,344,250	5,380,200	4,229,350	3,766,300	3,632,355	3,577,850	3,647,575
Routt	4,593,450	5,172,360	5,020,520	4,682,835	4,274,930	4,041,835	3,466,795	3,322,442	3,009,790	2,847,040
Saguache	4,552,947	4,693,999	4,783,263	4,726,651	4,586,488	4,545,055	4,528,566	4,462,301	4,473,019	2,919,803
San Juan	1,280	1,280	1,280	1,280	1,280	1,280	1,280	1,280	1,280	1,280
San Miguel	1,224,720	1,240,095	1,119,620	1,094,880	904,390	864,965	795,720	717,933	735,710	703,110
Sedgwick	7,009,040	7,008,801	7,022,058	7,047,526	6,883,747	6,878,946	3,599,258	3,025,904	3,009,920	2,670,649
Summit	305,311	319,127	312,829	303,300	291,224	269,558	232,120	196,939	188,232	187,642
Teller	559,000	513,125	489,705	420,900	416,950	396,110	332,560	276,510	275,100	268,880
Washington	20,118,870	21,889,655	24,285,630	24,176,680	16,324,600	12,781,700	11,557,319	7,100,770	6,306,191	6,316,625
Weld	54,622,180	56,156,130	56,609,690	56,135,660	48,738,000	41,813,280	35,239,830	30,912,350	32,081,740	26,545,040
Yuma	16,656,240	16,941,550	18,696,465	17,065,095	12,888,280	9,693,850	7,764,855	4,997,555	4,990,032	4,654,975
State	$448,629,066	$459,463,253	$470,805,876	$460,438,978	$402,833,386	$349,361,629	$302,992,217	$268,282,668	$262,693,260	$246,448,385

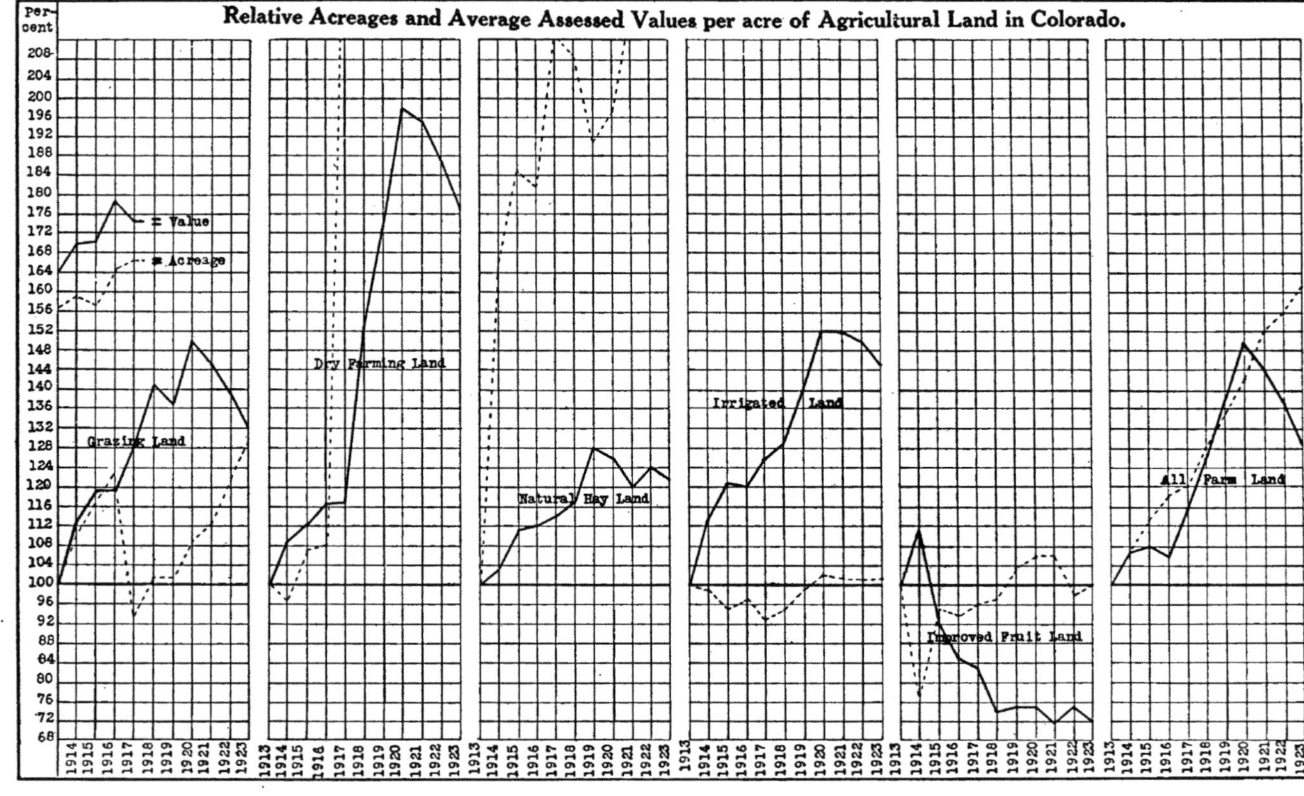

Note—The tabulations showing the acreages of the various classes of farm land reported by the assessors each year from 1913 to 1923, indicated by the dotted lines in this chart, appear on pages 130-141, both inclusive, while the tabulation showing range in average assessed value from year to year for the same period, indicated by the solid lines, appears on pages 142 and 143. It will be noted that the increase in acreage of dry farming and natural hay land was so great that the lines go entirely out of the chart. The values fixed in 1913 and the acreages reported for that year are the basic figures and are indicated by 100.

ASSESSED VALUE OF FARM PROPERTY IN COLORADO, 1923

(Compiled from Records of State Tax Commission)

COUNTY	Farm Land	Livestock	Poultry and Bees	Equities in State Land	Improvements on Patented Land	Improvements on Public Land	Agricultural Implements	Total
Adams	$ 15,831,380	$ 946,110	$ 42,390	$ 100,070	$ 2,077,300	$ 36,660	$ 339,670	$ 19,373,580
Alamosa ...	4,466,916	508,664	5,142	39,955	280,005	7,780	81,410	5,389,872
Arapahoe ..	9,275,790	598,315	32,770	55,365	1,644,660	17,700	113,155	11,737,755
Archuleta ..	1,440,690	515,340	4,690	4,250	158,105	1,450	34,185	2,158,710
Baca	8,197,283	1,004,376	28,550	71,148	445,340	45,120	15,540	9,947,218
Bent	6,513,700	891,865	21,610	36,990	694,265	70,440	77,705	8,306,575
Boulder ...	11,546,950	835,010	41,580	....	2,047,440	....	234,840	14,705,820
Chaffee	1,436,985	331,515	5,325	....	406,905	40,210	104,565	2,325,505
Cheyenne ..	13,990,105	810,270	15,885	127,555	423,655	7,250	143,575	15,518,295
Clear Creek..	396,965	45,825	1,020	13,750	98,120	5,180	2,285	563,145
Conejos ...	4,401,200	813,515	7,235	96,250	460,030	11,695	40,840	5,830,765
Costilla ...	2,859,745	317,370	4,690	....	264,635	7,385	59,860	3,513,685
Crowley ...	4,922,605	621,635	23,110	27,985	481,305	27,760	101,920	6,206,320
Custer	1,513,070	350,625	3,485	....	297,200	19,070	36,255	2,219,705
Delta	6,866,925	1,322,255	47,545	....	1,155,085	15,815	292,585	9,700,210
Denver	3,417,970	203,110	13,350	....	4,130,980	....	20,390	7,785,800
Dolores	764,724	227,542	1,505	360	59,760	28,690	11,600	1,094,181
Douglas ...	4,151,715	782,045	12,900	....	856,285	18,885	145,935	5,967,765
Eagle	1,976,672	763,659	4,219	1,891	276,280	11,190	68,055	3,101,966
Elbert	11,361,689	1,166,975	26,880	335,501	1,059,355	72,258	217,740	14,240,398
El Paso	10,484,130	1,120,850	32,010	91,610	1,800,900	31,900	91,960	13,653,360
Fremont ...	3,514,864	570,515	28,440	12,090	1,505,300	22,890	52,335	5,706,434
Garfield ...	5,270,315	1,463,290	33,255	....	809,850	42,590	270,920	7,890,220
Gilpin	60,274	30,084	....	1,275	11,453	....	2,412	105,498
Grand	1,708,170	592,505	2,290	19,190	265,600	42,000	27,975	2,657,730
Gunnison ..	2,341,345	1,088,820	2,890	4,440	780,150	27,350	24,785	4,269,780
Hinsdale ...	84,828	79,078	....	....	10,025	10,810	2,240	186,981
Huerfano ..	2,759,262	740,844	6,058	26,768	516,105	15,115	52,771	4,116,923
Jackson ...	2,046,640	1,131,610	1,670	20,530	255,270	19,170	37,640	3,512,530
Jefferson ...	9,927,055	693,860	54,195	23,680	3,401,235	106,650	239,470	14,446,145
Kiowa	9,581,729	539,908	14,350	75,994	310,900	2,500	43,490	10,568,871
Kit Carson..	18,250,054	1,232,023	41,415	119,959	1,527,965	108,905	320,252	21,600,573
Lake	176,620	81,945	....	....	199,490	....	4,715	462,770
La Plata ...	4,035,060	845,135	22,575	....	971,200	12,960	93,430	5,980,360
Larimer ...	17,085,200	1,959,220	58,570	41,690	3,910,020	30,820	501,825	23,587,345
Las Animas.	10,771,023	1,635,635	20,835	39,850	1,018,570	176,060	115,180	13,777,153
Lincoln ...	15,698,520	1,413,525	32,950	181,680	665,720	73,580	154,545	18,220,520
Logan	18,719,600	1,595,425	54,610	222,660	1,948,360	80,255	500,070	23,120,980
Mesa	9,905,555	1,733,067	55,964	....	1,847,295	28,700	257,880	13,828,461
Mineral ...	163,695	78,810	320	....	76,465	4,510	3,990	327,790
Moffat	3,082,015	972,185	7,920	74,720	626,895	118,040	135,805	5,017,580
Montezuma ..	2,717,770	808,345	19,165	53,250	521,900	28,290	67,940	4,216,660
Montrose ..	6,110,415	1,184,475	38,755	....	1,033,435	49,645	182,410	8,599,135
Morgan ...	12,032,855	1,292,165	35,750	74,090	1,502,640	78,450	325,260	15,341,210
Otero	11,537,500	1,079,205	65,140	34,400	2,046,975	186,005	255,735	15,204,960
Ouray	1,112,975	240,520	1,140	....	153,020	7,710	33,110	1,548,475
Park	1,820,055	803,860	3,660	12,195	511,170	56,230	91,630	3,298,800
Phillips ...	11,592,490	538,835	22,940	63,555	669,715	93,810	179,140	13,160,485
Pitkin	1,089,360	318,465	3,200	2,810	211,380	8,080	82,040	1,715,335
Prowers ...	12,317,035	1,174,950	44,605	50,840	1,342,380	51,790	186,865	15,168,465
Pueblo	9,931,740	1,108,365	37,990	263,957	11,284,261	59,735	168,125	22,854,173
Rio Blanco..	2,451,600	1,132,850	4,740	....	413,035	25,415	53,900	4,081,540
Rio Grande .	5,273,200	939,500	....	265,130	633,050	142,300	82,320	7,335,500
Routt	4,593,450	1,858,685	15,765	149,510	1,088,580	126,030	253,045	8,085,065
Saguache ..	4,552,947	1,465,086	5,803	135,668	462,316	56,810	86,898	6,765,528
San Juan...	1,280	58,068	....	....	....	....	385	59,733
San Miguel .	1,224,720	540,125	3,605	19,740	253,280	43,830	35,260	2,120,560
Sedgwick ..	7,009,040	435,138	14,932	88,477	396,740	48,330	181,726	8,174,383
Summit ...	305,311	163,900	465	1,344	48,100	500	11,075	530,695
Teller	559,000	308,475	835	....	101,180	32,500	33,205	1,035,195
Washington..	20,118,870	1,281,765	51,250	219,610	878,830	9,225	295,410	22,854,960
Weld	54,622,180	3,560,630	124,890	353,230	6,318,910	268,060	975,430	66,223,330
Yuma	16,656,240	1,462,350	49,070	197,490	1,106,480	10,400	278,100	19,760,130
State...	$448,629,066	$54,410,112	$1,357,898	$3,852,502	$70,752,855	$2,782,488	$9,074,670	$590,859,591

DETAILED STATEMENT OF ASSESSMENT FOR 1923

(Fom the Records of the State Tax Commission)

COUNTY	Valuation by County Assessor	Valuation by Tax Commission								Total Assessment
		Railroad Companies	Telephone Companies	Telegraph Companies	Express Companies	Pullman Company	Private Car Lines	Self-Winding Clocks	Local Utility Companies	Total Valuation by Tax Commission	
Adams	$ 27,526,712	$ 4,449,000	$ 147,890	$ 118,070	$ 19,050	$ 43,160	$ 28,540	$ 580	$ 160,980	$ 4,967,270	$ 32,493,982
Alamosa	7,630,877	1,419,530	45,780	8,450	7,880	5,690	7,290	300	180,480	1,603,400	9,234,277
Arapahoe	17,595,445	2,408,130	179,250	70,850	13,620	33,350	19,060	......	527,460	3,251,720	20,847,165
Archuleta	2,922,710	1,740,960	9,240	9,360	9,670	....	......	......	9,500	1,778,730	4,701,440
Baca	10,455,102	....	9,910	....	....	....	......	......	....	9,910	10,465,012
Bent	10,743,470	3,015,220	73,020	35,580	11,890	16,690	12,200	370	37,270	3,202,240	13,945,710
Boulder	40,132,839	3,492,520	584,530	27,450	15,380	16,620	28,090	980	2,469,420	6,634,990	46,767,829
Chaffee	6,575,470	3,557,570	73,860	35,490	9,490	21,350	16,010	650	277,100	3,991,520	10,566,990
Cheyenne	17,032,588	2,717,320	6,740	59,350	9,670	28,530	19,530	......	....	2,841,140	19,873,728
Clear Creek	4,239,515	818,850	43,570	3,390	3,990	....	......	......	424,410	1,294,210	5,533,725
Conejos	7,147,535	1,491,270	34,730	15,350	8,280	....	......	......	20,350	1,569,980	8,717,515
Costilla	4,486,670	1,106,370	32,960	6,380	9,750	14,510	10,000	......	....	1,179,970	5,666,640
Crowley	8,290,858	1,037,690	43,570	6,750	4,800	14,160	9,210	400	140,210	1,256,790	9,547,648
Custer	2,734,885	357,300	10,570	2,620	1,980	....	4,150	......	460	377,080	3,111,965
Delta	14,856,822	1,917,540	138,480	11,080	10,650	....	22,610	350	51,570	2,152,280	17,009,102
Denver	353,103,760	3,533,220	6,298,780	56,620	9,750	18,800	18,610	25,750	25,104,720	35,066,250	388,170,010
Dolores	1,536,818	196,900	1,200	1,740	2,720	....	......	......	5,850	208,410	1,745,228
Douglas	7,992,430	3,107,810	83,470	144,030	14,470	50,170	27,090	......	144,960	3,572,000	11,564,430
Eagle	4,276,544	2,000,340	32,160	50,220	12,600	28,990	24,150	......	126,250	2,274,710	6,551,254
Elbert	15,461,214	3,189,370	17,810	50,070	17,110	38,350	24,080	......	....	3,336,790	18,798,004
El Paso	58,764,840	6,254,850	1,030,200	194,010	32,670	86,650	53,430	3,470	3,636,610	11,291,890	70,056,730
Fremont	16,711,241	3,327,700	154,740	43,200	12,800	32,090	35,860	430	1,260,100	4,866,920	21,578,161
Garfield	12,283,140	3,437,910	114,790	58,540	17,720	30,350	28,440	500	1,500,780	5,189,030	17,472,170
Gilpin	2,105,230	592,690	29,890	7,960	5,660	....	3,600	......	75,690	715,490	2,820,720
Grand	3,867,110	732,410	34,320	15,920	11,740	....	10,850	......	3,100	808,340	4,675,450
Gunnison	10,494,185	5,379,060	45,770	16,960	17,910	....	......	400	50,760	5,510,860	16,005,045
Hinsdale	651,389	260,730	1,990	....	1,450	....	......	......	16,920	281,090	932,479
Huerfano	11,467,440	3,892,750	72,820	79,100	19,810	41,320	34,760	......	297,870	4,438,430	15,905,870
Jackson	4,016,870	207,750	6,710	....	6,690	....	......	......	....	221,150	4,238,020
Jefferson	20,324,975	2,770,080	214,920	43,610	14,510	2,580	8,590	......	779,080	3,833,370	24,158,345
Kiowa	11,401,167	2,895,920	6,130	18,280	13,410	39,540	27,400	......	....	3,000,680	14,401,847
Kit Carson	24,945,124	2,156,130	25,370	31,410	9,220	27,200	16,820	470	5,950	2,272,570	27,217,694

Lake	5,419,970	1,924,340	76,540	25,170	7,120	14,120	9,400	480	610,060	2,667,230	8,087,200
La Plata	11,285,763	2,846,820	76,180	16,890	18,540	....	......	370	831,830	3,790,630	15,076,393
Larimer	46,968,099	3,991,820	362,130	21,680	15,170	23,520	20,610	1,280	634,720	5,070,930	52,039,029
Las Animas	33,438,018	8,531,080	233,390	135,230	30,520	63,130	64,000	820	1,082,060	10,140,260	43,578,278
Lincoln	20,361,070	2,941,080	23,690	56,100	11,460	33,790	21,030	......	....	3,087,150	23,448,220
Logan	33,322,690	6,315,040	155,200	58,340	23,190	44,770	38,580	970	283,590	6,919,680	40,242,370
Mesa	24,936,131	3,778,190	269,950	62,410	19,650	31,760	35,340	1,080	488,760	4,687,140	29,623,271
Mineral	821,615	480,070	8,340	1,820	2,670	....	5,290	......	47,330	545,520	1,367,135
Moffat	6,078,615	71,640	11,940	....	1,150	....	1,040	......	17,000	102,770	6,181,385
Montezuma	5,569,085	696,590	22,380	6,220	9,610	....	......	......	7,000	741,800	6,310,885
Montrose	12,624,010	1,444,360	125,280	12,400	8,020	....	5,520	370	140,800	1,736,750	14,360,760
Morgan	24,392,998	4,194,600	157,240	88,790	14,400	42,450	27,560	......	....	4,525,040	28,918,038
Otero	29,377,970	3,596,710	201,740	61,660	14,190	33,850	23,910	900	391,860	4,324,820	33,702,790
Ouray	3,484,149	814,960	39,030	7,700	5,730	....	......	150	184,130	1,051,700	4,535,849
Park	5,029,285	3,375,110	42,710	61,840	12,360	....	......	......	313,400	3,805,420	8,834,705
Phillips	15,488,775	1,754,510	24,350	3,340	5,560	....	9,960	......	....	1,797,720	17,286,495
Pitkin	3,770,660	656,040	27,160	2,840	3,120	....	5,900	......	158,380	853,440	4,624,100
Prowers	19,820,620	3,131,410	123,210	38,070	12,350	17,400	12,570	630	....	3,335,640	23,156,260
Pueblo	61,483,883	7,274,220	797,780	167,700	33,600	89,590	58,110	2,300	2,810,170	11,233,470	72,717,353
Rio Blanco	4,995,990	129,900	20,780	....	1,200	....	......	......	....	151,880	5,147,870
Rio Grande	10,025,320	1,227,170	70,180	4,470	6,250	....	13,350	950	141,310	1,463,680	11,489,000
Routt	13,912,780	869,750	59,600	11,590	13,940	....	12,790	......	37,000	1,004,670	14,917,450
Saguache	8,248,895	2,945,420	50,620	14,840	13,740	....	......	......	59,210	3,083,830	11,332,725
San Juan	2,650,525	434,940	28,190	1,350	2,010	....	......	......	142,970	609,460	3,259,985
San Miguel	6,297,390	530,020	34,880	5,670	7,120	....	......	320	829,030	1,407,040	7,704,430
Sedgick	9,701,495	1,360,080	37,010	27,350	4,830	13,830	9,560	......	....	1,452,660	11,154,155
Summit	2,767,841	2,031,190	30,440	12,030	6,890	....	......	......	391,680	2,472,230	5,240,071
Teller	5,484,180	516,100	174,730	1,130	....	....	3,520	......	756,830	1,452,310	6,936,490
Washington	25,141,825	1,956,830	28,630	41,550	6,610	19,480	11,340	......	25,030	2,089,470	27,231,295
Weld	97,237,200	15,450,860	575,740	271,760	56,860	65,200	101,610	1,350	751,960	17,275,340	114,512,540
Yuma	23,333,590	1,957,990	50,290	42,320	6,210	18,310	11,920	......	550	2,087,590	25,421,180
State	$1,315,245,412	$160,693,730	$ 13,544,500	$ 2,484,100	$ 730,410	$ 1,101,300	$993,280	$ 46,650	$ 48,372,510	$227,966,480	$1,543,211,892

MILEAGE AND VALUE OF RAILROADS, TELEGRAPH AND TELEPHONE LINES AS RETURNED BY STATE TAX COMMISSION FOR 1923

COUNTY	Miles of Railroad	Value	Miles of Telephone	Value	Miles of Telegraph	Value
Adams	97.05	$ 4,449,000	3,996.06	$ 147,890	1,270.11	$ 118,070
Alamosa	51.45	1,419,530	1,290.50	45,780	80.92	8,450
Arapahoe	62.93	2,408,130	4,929.06	179,250	735.29	70,850
Archuleta	63.10	1,740,960	190.50	9,240	89.65	9,360
Baca	......	....	270.50	9,910	....	....
Bent	77.59	3,015,220	1,875.50	73,020	519.20	35,580
Boulder	102.15	3,492,520	16,114.00	584,530	262.80	27,450
Chaffee	122.55	3,557,570	2,036.00	73,860	350.75	35,490
Cheyenne	63.13	2,717,320	160.00	6,740	568.17	59,350
Clear Creek	26.03	818,850	1,201.00	43,570	32.42	3,390
Conejos	54.05	1,491,270	982.00	34,730	146.93	15,350
Costilla	63.63	1,106,370	880.00	32,960	61.08	6,380
Crowley	31.35	1,037,690	1,133.52	43,570	64.58	6,750
Custer	12.95	357,300	295.00	10,570	25.06	2,620
Delta	69.50	1,917,540	3,987.34	138,480	106.04	11,080
Denver	62.62	3,533,220	173,594.36	6,298,780	641.07	56,620
Dolores	17.72	196,900	31.00	1,200	16.67	1,740
Douglas	94.39	3,107,810	2,226.92	83,470	1,688.83	144,030
Eagle	82.21	2,000,340	949.00	32,160	480.82	50,220
Elbert	83.24	3,189,370	491.00	17,810	479.35	50,070
El Paso	190.57	6,254,850	28,204.82	1,030,200	2,236.45	194,010
Fremont	110.79	3,327,700	4,282.18	154,740	488.04	43,200
Garfield	118.37	3,437,910	3,183.45	114,790	561.72	58,540
Gilpin	36.95	592,690	824.00	29,890	76.23	7,960
Grand	76.58	732,410	956.00	34,320	152.37	15,920
Gunnison	195.24	5,379,060	1,178.66	45,770	227.24	16,960
Hinsdale	9.45	260,730	83.00	1,990	....	....
Huerfano	130.96	3,892,750	2,175.00	72,820	837.16	79,100
Jackson	43.88	207,750	185.00	6,710	....	....
Jefferson	99.44	2,770,080	5,964.00	214,920	417.51	43,610
Kiowa	87.49	2,895,920	169.00	6,130	175.00	18,280
Kit Carson	60.18	2,156,130	735.00	25,370	300.70	31,410
Lake	67.61	1,924,340	2,110.00	76,540	240.99	25,170
La Plata	120.95	2,846,820	2,128.25	76,180	161.68	16,890
Larimer	119.11	3,991,820	9,977.50	362,130	207.52	21,680
Las Animas	233.34	8,531,080	6,434.00	233,390	1,747.01	135,230
Lincoln	73.71	2,941,080	660.60	23,690	537.05	56,100
Logan	133.56	6,315,040	3,845.13	155,200	788.84	58,340
Mesa	123.75	3,778,190	7,449.87	269,950	597.49	62,410
Mineral	17.40	480,070	230.00	8,340	17.41	1,820
Moffat	7.49	71,640	324.00	11,940	....	....
Montezuma	62.69	696,590	698.00	22,380	59.59	6,220
Montrose	52.35	1,444,360	3,429.00	125,280	118.75	12,400
Morgan	90.84	4,194,600	4,144.34	157,240	1,032.06	88,790
Otero	92.58	3,596,710	5,475.92	201,740	970.95	61,660
Ouray	38.90	814,960	1,076.00	39,030	73.69	7,700
Park	107.29	3,375,110	1,174.00	42,710	592.00	61,840
Phillips	36.30	1,754,510	507.47	24,350	32.00	3,340
Pitkin	38.99	656,040	743.00	27,160	38.64	2,840
Prowers	80.58	3,131,410	3,179.24	123,210	551.40	38,070
Pueblo	229.65	7,724,220	21,787.82	797,780	1,990.11	167,700
Rio Blanco	7.80	129,900	585.50	20,780	....	....
Rio Grande	52.51	1,227,170	1,908.00	70,180	42.80	4,470
Routt	90.94	869,750	1,621.25	59,600	111.00	11,590
Saguache	107.10	2,945,420	1,415.00	50,620	163.23	14,840
San Juan	37.40	434,840	777.00	28,190	12.92	1,350
San Miguel	47.70	530,020	973.00	34,880	54.26	5,670
Sedgwick	31.49	1,360,080	943.08	37,010	361.66	27,350
Summit	67.32	2,031,190	876.00	30,440	115.20	12,030
Teller	39.70	516,100	4,817.00	174,730	10.80	1,130
Washington	40.33	1,956,830	723.08	28,630	409.76	41,550
Weld	401.66	15,450,860	15,753.83	575,740	3,187.52	271,760
Yuma	40.51	1,957,990	1,361.27	50,290	405.10	42,320
State	5,088.69	$160,693,730	371,700.52	$13,544,500	27,723.59	$2,484,100

COMPARATIVE ASSESSED VALUATION AS REPORTED BY TAX COMMISSION, 1918, 1919, 1920, 1921, 1922 AND 1923

COUNTY	1918	1919	1920	1921	1922	1923
Adams	$ 28,473,925	$ 30,907,320	$ 34,538,052	$ 33,254,170	$ 32,629,150	$ 32,493.982
Alamosa	8,544,005	9,177,851	9,665,940	9,459,506	9,352 503	9,234,277
Arapahoe	19,420,432	19,104,920	22,169,954	22,219,980	20,642,355	20,847,165
Archuleta	5,276,277	5,241,174	5,236,668	4,894,225	4,804,155	4,701,440
Baca	7,512,356	8,836,711	9,690,710	10,964,227	10,673,091	10,465,012
Bent	12,127,275	13,702,090	15,890,600	15,022,630	14,381,325	13,945,710
Boulder	44,153,000	47,601,740	48,022,880	47,458,410	46,558,760	46,767,829
Chaffee	11,088,055	11,531,295	11,116,340	10,894,300	10,747,740	10,566,990
Cheyenne	11,614,995	16,426,644	19,663,542	20,512,832	20,646,818	19,873,728
Clear Creek	5,561,650	5,582,355	5,714,245	5,664,960	5,533,315	5,533,725
Conejos	9,741,958	9,453,242	10 224,879	8,967,647	8,668,297	8,717,515
Costilla	5,700,687	5,842,969	6,248,810	5,967,383	5,796,913	5,666,640
Crowley	9,532,360	10,008,365	11,314,450	11,957,186	11,671,185	9,547,648
Custer	2,552,531	2,707,615	2,859,323	3,118,705	3,093,315	3,111,965
Delta	16,535,150	17,760,135	19,071,185	17,962,485	17,348,495	17,009,102
Denver	348,055,410	351,111,890	371,684,900	377,607,720	376,855,210	388,170,010
Dolores	1,774,125	1,836,670	1,881,575	1,634,189	1,635,178	1,745,228
Douglas	11,486,720	11,923,620	12,014,525	11,659,435	11,515,915	11,564,430
Eagle	7,610,319	7,106,952	6,941,409	6,664,316	6,738,291	6,551,254
Elbert	15,246,642	19,480,385	20,584,695	19,843,218	19,055,031	18,798,004
El Paso	67,066,460	67,666,710	69,639,190	69,400,050	69,679,460	70,056,730
Fremont	20,001,690	20,425,395	20,975,781	21,692,996	21,177,214	21,578,161
Garfield	19,341,985	19,129,815	18,794,145	17,685,460	17,294,610	17,472,170
Gilpin	3,103,270	3,064,197	2,839,748	2,812,403	2,791,167	2,820,720
Grand	5,035,455	5,317,640	4,751,760	4,568,515	4,723,340	4,675.450
Gunnison	16,082,935	16,559,550	16,695,950	16,301,160	15,874,805	16,005,045
Hinsdale	1,010,547	1,031,303	1,010,784	983,964	936,771	932,479
Huerfano	13,792,111	14,317,448	14,664,113	16,067,641	15,774,914	15,905,870
Jackson	5,645,665	5,755,450	5,541,780	4,694,930	4,236,350	4,238,020
Jefferson	23,348,880	21,046,955	23,369,030	23,706,820	24,081,450	24,158,345
Kiowa	10,866,530	12,274,695	16 078,585	15,422,565	15,079,719	14,401,847
Kit Carson	21,182,783	31,934,400	30,763,511	30,581,436	29,995,756	27,217,694
Lake	10,857,295	10,476,345	9,517,735	8,931,975	8,237,205	8,087,200
La Plata	15,877,705	15,560,084	16,134,025	15 625 510	15,206,515	15,076,393
Larimer	43,181,550	49,281,350	50,884,485	52,684,240	52,302,225	52,039,029
Las Animas	39,701,754	40,761,282	41,992,707	43,747,875	43,668,935	43,578,278
Lincoln	19,147,025	21,543,495	25,358,775	24,384,500	23,431,115	23,448,220
Logan	37,746,887	40,509,670	46,720,410	45,419,320	42,147,070	40,242,370
Mesa	28,897,603	30,036,455	30,647,930	29,903,290	29,505,850	29,623,271
Mineral	1,531,625	1,684,735	1.563,310	1,486,395	1,446,223	1,367,135
Moffat	6,714,199	6,824,961	6,979,680	6,469,430	6,601,500	6,181,385
Montezuma	6,463,107	6,364,015	6,637,292	6 269,080	6,215,725	6,310,885
Montrose	16,839,360	18,043,680	18,582,530	17,273,219	16,232,115	14,360,760
Morgan	25,825,480	27,291,581	29,935,300	30,272,050	28,793,390	28,918,038
Otero	28,863,930	30,914,825	34,704,985	34.122,890	33,200,020	33,702,790
Ouray	5,493,696	4,962,365	5,587,955	4,384,092	4,532,989	4,535,849
Park	9,041,250	9,006,865	9,416,535	8,914,275	8,924,485	8,834,705
Phillips	15 840,788	17,171,450	17,856,045	17,896,920	17,501,050	17,286,495
Pitkin	5,750,370	5,385,880	5.180,360	4,803,690	4,732,110	4,624,100
Prowers	20,104,700	21,034,610	23,773,515	24.106,140	23,228,850	23,156,260
Pueblo	70,178,990	71,270,908	72,942,562	71,143,117	71,848,870	72,717,353
Rio Blanco	6,198,010	6 591,040	6.865,720	6,194,745	5,527,170	5,147,870
Rio Grande	11,072,250	12,433,210	12,396,780	11,853,170	11,544,300	11,489,000
Routt	15,766,550	16,506,590	16,111,740	15,769,860	15,745,050	14,917,450
Saguache	12,518,707	12,452,021	12,775,709	11,662,493	11,477,063	11,332.725
San Juan	4,578,081	4,458,845	4,216,747	3,847,064	3,421,701	3,259,985
San Miguel	9,151,725	9,068,345	8,926,835	8,089,040	7,974,665	7,704,430
Sedgwick	10,783,172	10,917,523	11,650,330	11 624,630	11,320.137	11,154,155
Summit	6,499,040	6,303,868	6,054,146	5,714,385	5,225,848	5,240,071
Teller	13,876,890	10,405,250	8,932,890	7,574,520	7,333,790	6,936,490
Washington	20 208,310	24.000,380	32,661,225	32,230,685	29,106,815	27,231.295
Weld	96,306,880	107,742,580	117,816,500	117,713,680	116,160,220	114,512,540
Yuma	18,610,210	22,341,950	27,783,850	28,498,745	26,032,280	25,421,180
State	$1,422,113,275	$1,495,213,659	$1,590,267,667	$1,578,256,499	$1,548,617,879	$1,543,211,892

DISTRIBUTION OF GENERAL TAX LEVIES IN COLORADO FOR 1922

(From the Records of the State Tax Commission)

COUNTY	Revenue of State	Revenue of County	Revenue of Schools	Revenue of Towns	Total Revenue
Adams	$ 145,552.29	$ 205,332.72	$ 269,139.36	$ 68,410.19	$ 688,434.56
Alamosa	41,907.28	53,449.42	135,999.39	32,182.04	263,538.13
Arapahoe	92,834.81	120,602.36	282 153.88	76,357.80	571,948.85
Archuleta	21,596.62	39,047.46	48,040.18	7,691.29	116,375.55
Baca	47,815.44	68,521.24	128,396.11	2,096.97	246,829.76
Bent	64,394.24	72,874.74	170,421.03	29,356.05	337,046.06
Boulder	208,920.86	287,965.72	647,884.44	221 374.79	1,366.145.81
Chaffee	47,947.77	92,577.75	117,021.92	39,303.67	296,851.11
Cheyenne	92,497.74	54,094.66	191,127.54	11,254.23	348,974.17
Clear Creek	24,769.16	43,677.75	47,217.72	22,750.35	138,414.98
Conejos	38,833.97	73,680.52	99 017.24	8 064.55	219,596.28
Costilla	25,970.17	90,895.61	87,726.20	3,762.06	208,354.04
Crowley	52,200.24	65,716.57	172,769.78	28,562.05	319,248.64
Custer	13,905.90	29,488.25	30,898.31	2,285.39	76.577.85
Delta	77,723.36	110,339.41	255,748.26	47.251.78	491,062.81
Denver	1,689,073.34	946,333.50	4,445,128.29	3,336,673.91	10,417,209.04
Dolores	7,325.60	29,760.24	18,311.00	2,191.09	57,587.93
Douglas	51,598.96	65,650.86	81,441.85	9,073.18	207,764.85
Eagle	30,187.87	108,555.07	88,175.58	13,011.16	239,929.68
Elbert	85,413.00	122,209.21	173,562.55	2,395.72	383,580.48
El Paso	312,939.11	440,070.62	1,090,434.05	627,107.89	2,470,551.67
Fremont	94,400.72	146,447.54	342,922.83	97,954.38	681,725.47
Garfield	77,744.52	179,853.00	320,260.08	48,806.72	626,664.32
Gilpin	12,662.72	40,984.24	34,494.79	8,799.21	96 940.96
Grand	21,157.72	51,713.62	35,874.15	4.083.82	112,829.31
Gunnison	71,067.84	129,286.34	102,923.42	24,565.26	327,842.86
Hinsdale	4,199.44	19.223.13	13,360.06	2,221.03	39,003.66
Huerfano	70,674.85	134,092.72	248,099.48	39,950.32	492,817.37
Jackson	19,215.25	25,624.20	29,730.10	3,873.80	78,443.35
Jefferson	107,780.67	108,261.84	278,314.33	43,952.88	538,309.72
Kiowa	67.561.64	52,179.30	158,639.00	9,259.95	287.639.89
Kit Carson	134,382.73	134,982.66	269,769.28	44,807.34	583,942.01
Lake	36,921.98	75,162.61	102,728.32	71,185.12	285,998.03
La Plata	68,003.98	118,855.10	201,415.74	57,026.18	445,301.00
Larimer	234,187.61	313 644.11	624,916.47	177,581.18	1,350 329.37
Las Animas	197,891.71	314,064.74	656,809.47	222,327.29	1,391,093.21
Lincoln	105,071.02	105,071.02	215,338.98	33,879.66	459,360.68
Logan	189,000.72	203,566.40	502,986.21	122,076.35	1,017,629.68
Mesa	132,189.12	222,183.94	386,575.17	152,498.97	893,447.20
Mineral	6,529.08	16,570.45	12,135.95	5,499.53	40,735.01
Moffat	30.285.11	60,164.62	81,815.28	17,880.60	190,145.61
Montezuma	27,833.50	73.125.07	104 883.16	20,469.85	226,311.58
Montrose	72,781.02	140,688.32	246.433.62	50.407.91	510.310.87
Morgan	130,697.96	109,051.40	367,068.27	58,755.60	665,573.23
Otero	148,734.39	173,302.12	498,643.61	146,602.38	967,282.50
Ouray	20,249.55	74,805.82	48,706.28	15 571.18	159 332.83
Park	39,983.30	71,398.74	44,265.53	1,365.87	157,013.44
Phillips	78,405.78	58,191.79	160,745.51	30,451.74	327,794.82
Pitkin	21,200.26	63,884.70	47,020.94	18,913.12	151,019.02
Prowers	104,108.52	127,811 80	287.218.74	60.034.66	579,173.72
Pueblo	323,648.37	422,621.19	1,088,580.75	705,742.09	2.540,592.40
Rio Blanco	25,389.95	48,286.25	61,535.35	9,507.53	144 719.08
Rio Grande	51.815.27	85,009.44	245,256.00	32,788.05	414,868.76
Routt	70,475.01	114,049.97	214,970.18	38,918.28	438,413.44
Saguache	51,520.70	71,070.97	121,245.86	19,805.66	263,643.19
San Juan	15,329.22	42,189.57	24,602.03	8,446.82	90,567.64
San Miguel	36,233.86	95,599.16	85,461.84	20,183.41	237,478.27
Sedgwick	50,779.04	73,168.92	114,033.14	24,943.98	262,925.08
Summit	23,912.05	43,367.28	47,428.55	7,365.14	122,073.02
Teller	32,855.38	88,738.85	97,865.45	76,905.22	296,364.90
Washington	130,398.53	130,980.66	271,538.80	27.073.80	559,991.79
Weld	520,416.76	585,468.88	1,366,470.36	286,603.34	2,758 959.34
Yuma	116,624.61	151,247.55	356,850.24	50,968.81	675,691.21
State	$ 6,947,729.19	$ 8,416,833.71	$19,100,548.00	$ 7,491,210.19	$41 956,321.09

DISTRIBUTION OF GENERAL TAX IN COLORADO FOR 1923

(From the Records of the State Tax Commission)

COUNTY	Revenue of State	Revenue of County	Revenue of Schools	Revenue of Towns	Total Revenue
Adams	$ 127,698.55	$ 184,236.84	$ 295,723.80	$ 69,992.27	$ 677,651.46
Alamosa	36,330.01	57,499.41	132,739.67	38,305.88	264,874.97
Arapahoe	82,593.79	104,450.67	285,968.77	80,015.69	553,028.92
Archuleta	18,688.92	41,134.65	48,537.68	7,844.92	116,206.17
Baca	41,127.50	56,511.03	135,362.83	2,084.20	235,085.56
Bent	55,058.90	74,013.30	160,331.62	29,178.88	318,582.70
Boulder	184,971.64	276,515.97	663,397.85	228,392.98	1,353,278.44
Chaffee	41,559.02	81,426.07	115,727.86	39,414.66	278,127.61
Cheyenne	78,137.84	49,706.01	168,107.84	11,112.19	307,063.88
Clear Creek	21,805.27	54,929.30	43,314.70	21,373.32	141,422.59
Conejos	34,259.83	85,867.53	112,260.45	11,170.05	243,557.86
Costilla	22,269.90	90,099.58	71,711.19	3,085.55	187,166.22
Crowley	38,708.24	75,153.14	176,442.19	25,668.04	315,971.61
Custer	12,219.11	26,433.09	32,746.67	2,956.19	74,355.06
Delta	66,843.74	115,318.20	284,983.02	57,025.12	524,170.08
Denver	1,527,237.97	1,321,274.58	4,523,422.38	3,727,548.75	11,099,483.68
Dolores	6,858.75	32,894.81	17,769.86	2,431.95	59,955.37
Douglas	45,450.76	80,377.35	88,525.75	11,587.16	225,941.02
Eagle	25,746.43	98,923.93	99,304.47	13,053.81	237,028.64
Elbert	73,754.76	100,967.08	139,229.05	9,210.49	323,161.38
El Paso	276,980.62	387,631.92	1,147,602.39	637,642.15	2,449,857.08
Fremont	84,794.97	159,017.53	358,403.57	100,961.31	703,177.38
Garfield	68,886.60	184,048.16	333,606.60	56,212.78	642,754.14
Gilpin	11,144.76	35,533.83	34,696.74	11,440.82	92,816.15
Grand	18,371.79	55,162.11	43,782.84	3,951.63	121,268.37
Gunnison	62,893.66	123,866.90	112,865.11	26,562.13	326,187.80
Hinsdale	3,663.75	19,625.56	12,564.02	2,206.15	38,059.48
Huerfano	62,510.07	135,199.89	257,286.64	43,529.34	498,525.94
Jackson	16,718.97	19,994.70	22,944.02	3,470.61	63,128.30
Jefferson	96,637.21	119,751.45	306,537.60	49,672.06	572,598.32
Kiowa	56,599.26	52,566.71	169,117.67	9,467.26	287,750.90
Kit Carson	111,590.39	113,578.00	246,025.42	51,426.76	522,620.57
Lake	31,787.39	78,214.77	96,978.23	68,947.74	275,928.13
La Plata	59,665.88	119,028.14	198,959.81	56,106.24	433,760.07
Larimer	206,198.22	327,924.86	598,334.26	194,752.91	1,327,210.25
Las Animas	171,311.79	343,059.49	715,877.35	211,325.24	1,441,573.87
Lincoln	92,397.42	109,559.82	248,435.61	33,928.94	484,321.79
Logan	158,172.83	169,844.63	498,847.43	115,297.26	942,162.15
Mesa	116,419.45	254,760.14	422,973.76	159,535.69	953,689.04
Mineral	5,372.84	15,544.33	10,970.88	4,893.25	36,781.30
Moffat	24,729.60	64,498.30	75,002.60	16,687.40	180,917.90
Montezuma	24,825.69	85,152.75	106,852.21	19,022.60	235,853.25
Montrose	56,765.69	123,642.33	236,103.79	48,396.01	464,907.82
Morgan	115,040.42	86,060.76	362,999.39	57,996.03	622,096.60
Otero	132,447.05	168,507.70	516,712.21	149,978.05	967,645.01
Ouray	17,810.95	76,365.03	52,752.66	14,193.64	161,122.28
Park	34,816.85	61,956.48	47,121.24	1,439.68	145,334.25
Phillips	67,935.93	58,946.95	165,225.18	27,021.94	319,130.00
Pitkin	18,168.54	82,753.72	46,243.21	18,935.71	166,101.18
Prowers	91,138.23	113,864.81	283,610.78	56,465.45	545,079.27
Pueblo	286,913.61	463,588.14	1,205,052.42	701,412.23	2,656,966.40
Rio Blanco	21,363.48	45,499.32	65,695.93	9,120.37	141,679.10
Rio Grande	45,278.32	86,410.75	255,860.94	40,026.09	427,576.10
Routt	58,446.61	130,129.21	218,012.97	36,932.98	443,521.77
Saguache	44,870.59	82,662.34	131,204.55	20,294.78	279,032.26
San Juan	12,811.74	40,032.62	25,395.29	7,631.14	85,870.79
San Miguel	30,267.88	91,034.69	85,370.03	18,154.65	224,827.25
Sedgwick	43,811.19	52,060.44	126,786.27	24,193.33	246,851.23
Summit	20,697.80	42,791.28	49,289.51	7,405.90	120,184.49
Teller	27,260.41	92,255.32	91,033.18	79,533.43	290,082.34
Washington	105,686.60	120,985.20	271,180.35	24,788.00	522,640.15
Weld	446,848.35	565,098.29	1,270,370.67	287,222.84	2,569,540.15
Yuma	99,424.56	144,203.56	373,419.00	54,533.49	671,580.61
State	$ 6,080,798.89	$ 8,710,145.47	$19,493,711.98	$ 7,954,168.11	$42,238,824.45

Figures for two or three counties in this table are subject to revision.

VALUATION, TOTAL TAXES LEVIED, COUNTY LEVY, AVERAGE TOWN AND SCHOOL LEVIES AND AVERAGE TOTAL LEVY FOR 1922. STATE LEVY, 4.48 MILLS

(From Records of the State Tax Commission)

COUNTY	Valuation*	Revenue	County Levy, Mills	Average Town Levy, Mills	Average School Levy, Mills	Average Total Levy, Mills
Adams	$ 32,489,350	$ 688,434.56	6.32	20.17	8.28	19.65
Alamosa	9,344,303	263,538.13	5.72	14.42	14.55	28.20
Arapahoe	20,722,055	571,948.85	5.82	15.10	13.62	27.60
Archuleta	4,820,675	116,375.55	8.10	12.60	9.97	24.14
Baca	10,673,091	246,829.76	6.42	5.07	12.03	23.13
Bent	14,373,715	337,046.06	5.07	17.25	11.86	23.45
Boulder	46,634,130	1,366,145.81	6.175	11.34	13.89	29.29
Chaffee	10,702,630	296,851.11	8.65	10.06	10.93	27.74
Cheyenne	20,646,818	348,974.17	2.62	15.00	9.26	16.90
Clear Creek	5,528,830	138,414.98	7.90	11.64	8.54	25.03
Conejos	8,668,297	219,596.28	8.50	6.91	11.42	25.33
Costilla	5,796,913	208,354.04	15.68	12.00	15.13	35.94
Crowley	11,651,915	319,248.64	5.64	14.47	14.83	27.40
Custer	3,103,995	76,577.85	9.50	8.44	9.95	24.67
Delta	17,348,965	491,062.81	6.36	9.34	14.74	28.30
Denver	377,025,300	10,417,209.04	2.51	8.85	11.79	27.63
Dolores	1,635,178	57,587.93	18.20	12.50	11.20	35.22
Douglas	11,517,670	207,764.85	5.70	19.30	7.07	18.04
Eagle	6,738,366	239,929.68	16.11	17.58	13.09	35.61
Elbert	19,065,401	383,580.48	6.41	3.76	9.10	20.12
El Paso	69,852,480	2,470,551.67	6.30	14.28	15.61	35.37
Fremont	21,071,589	681,752.47	6.95	12.00	16.27	32.35
Garfield	17,293,420	626,664.32	10.40	13.90	18.52	36.24
Gilpin	2,826,499	96,940.96	14.50	15.65	12.20	34.43
Grand	4,722,705	112,829.31	10.95	17.98	7.60	23.89
Gunnison	15,863,355	327,842.86	8.15	11.00	6.49	20.67
Hinsdale	937,436	39,003.66	20.50	18.00	14.25	41.61
Huerfano	15,775,614	492,817.37	8.50	12.33	15.73	31.24
Jackson	4,289,120	78,443.35	6.00	14.00	6.93	18.29
Jefferson	24,058,185	538,309.72	4.50	13.18	11.57	22.37
Kiowa	15,080,732	287,639.89	3.46	17.47	10.52	19.07
Kit Carson	29,996,146	583,942.01	4.50	13.88	8.99	19.47
Lake	8,241,515	285,998.03	9.12	34.00	12.46	34.70
La Plata	15,179,450	445,301.00	7.83	12.13	13.27	29.33
Larimer	52,274,020	1,350,329.37	6.00	11.09	11.95	25.83
Las Animas	44,172,257	1,391,093.21	7.11	18.42	14.87	31.49
Lincoln	23,453,355	459,360.68	4.48	19.29	9.18	19.58
Logan	42,187,660	1,017,629.68	4.83	15.75	11.92	24.12
Mesa	29,506,500	893,447.20	7.53	15.30	13.10	30.28
Mineral	1,457,383	40,735.01	11.37	18.57	8.33	27.95
Moffat	6,760,070	190,145.61	8.90	20.00	12.10	28.13
Montezuma	6,212,835	226,311.58	11.77	16.77	16.88	36.43
Montrose	16,245,764	510,310.87	8.66	13.14	15.17	31.41
Morgan	29,173,650	665,573.23	3.738	11.67	12.58	22.81
Otero	33,199,640	967,282.50	5.22	15.22	15.02	29.14
Ouray	4,519,989	159,332.83	16.55	16.50	10.78	35.25
Park	8,924,845	157,013.44	8.00	4.96	4.96	17.59
Phillips	17,501,290	327,794.82	3.325	13.28	9.18	18.73
Pitkin	4,732,200	151,019.02	13.50	43.00	9.94	31.91
Prowers	23,238,510	579,173.72	5.50	16.41	12.36	24.92
Pueblo	72,242,939	2,540,592.40	5.85	20.81	15.07	35.17
Rio Blanco	5,667,400	144,719.08	8.52	13.00	10.86	25.54
Rio Grande	11,565,910	414,868.76	7.35	13.06	21.21	35.87
Routt	15,731,030	438,413.44	7.25	17.34	13.67	27.87
Saguache	11,500,157	263,643.19	6.18	16.28	10.54	22.88
San Juan	3,421,701	90,567.64	12.33	10.25	7.19	26.47
San Miguel	8,087,915	237,478.27	11.82	11.65	10.57	29.36
Sedgwick	11,334 607	262 925.08	6.455	15.27	10.06	23.20
Summit	5,337,511	122,073.02	8.125	12.48	8.89	22.87
Teller	7,333,790	296,364.90	12.10	46.19	13.34	14.41
Washington	29,106,815	559,991.79	4.50	13.04	9.33	19.24
Weld	116,164,460	2,758,959.34	5.04	13.48	11.76	23.75
Yuma	26,032,280	675,691.21	5.81	15.69	13.71	25.95
Totals	$1,550,762,317	$41,956,321.09				27.06

*Final valuations as corrected by county treasurers.

DISTRIBUTION OF POPULATION AND PER CAPITA STATISTICS

COUNTY	Estimated Population Jan. 1, 1924	Area Square Miles	Population Per Square Mile	Assessed Valuation Per Capita 1923	Taxes Assessed Per Capita* 1922	Bank Deposits Per Capita
Adams	14 825	1,262	11.74	$2.191.80	$ 46.83	$117.17
Alamosa	5.680	727	7.81	1,625.75	47.06	244.41
Arapahoe	14,275	842	16.95	1,460.39	40.56	155.67
Archuleta	3,725	1,220	3.05	1,262.13	31.45	85.35
Baca	9.500	2.552	3.72	1,101.58	26.25	44.97
Bent	10.250	1,524	6.72	1,360.55	33.04	98.54
Boulder	33.600	764	43.97	1,391.89	41.52	233.94
Chaffee	7,900	1,083	7.29	1.337.59	38.05	197.59
Cheyenne	4.700	1,777	2.64	4,228.45	75.86	76.74
Clear Creek	2,500	390	6.41	2,213.49	55.36	266.70
Conejos	8.700	1,252	6.94	1.002.01	25.38	70.16
Costilla	5.150	1,185	4.34	1,100.31	40.85	36.32
Crowley	6.450	808	7.98	1,480.25	49.11	110.14
Custer	2,600	747	3.48	1.196.90	30.63	76.08
Delta	14,050	1,201	11.69	1 210.61	35.07	176.10
Denver	277.215	58	4,779.56	1,400.24	38.29	591.66
Dolores	1,365	1,043	1.30	1,278.55	42.65	No Banks
Douglas	3,610	845	4.27	3,203.44	57.71	156.04
Eagle	3.550	1,620	2.19	1.845.42	68.55	127.71
Elbert	7,810	1,857	4.20	2.406.91	49.17	114.39
El Paso	46.600	2,121	21.97	1.503.36	53.70	380.76
Fremont	18,225	1,557	11.10	1,183.98	37.45	227.70
Garfield	9,360	3,107	3.01	1,866.68	67.02	277.33
Gilpin	1.250	132	9.46	2,256.57	74.56	210.15
Grand	2.820	1,866	1.51	1,657.96	40.29	97.92
Gunnison	5,750	3,179	1.80	2,783.48	56.52	247.40
Hinsdale	600	971	61	1,554.13	65.00	No Banks
Huerfano	17,300	1,500	11.53	919.41	28.98	136.88
Jackson	1.385	1,632	84	3,059.94	56.03	227.10
Jefferson	15,580	808	19.28	1,550.59	34.72	88.35
Kiowa	4.680	1,798	2.60	3.077.31	61.19	105.79
Kit Carson	9.860	2.159	4.56	2,760.41	59.28	85.75
Lake	5.600	371	15.09	1.444.14	57.19	291.92
La Plata	12.150	1,851	6.56	1.240.85	36.80	215.69
Larimer	29,925	2.629	11.38	1.738.98	46.64	237.14
Las Animas	40.100	4.809	8.33	1.086.74	34.77	206.85
Lincoln	8.700	2.570	3.38	2.695.19	53.41	101.81
Logan	18,850	1,822	10.34	2,134.87	54.41	138.02
Mesa	23.100	3.163	7.30	1.282.39	38.84	184.33
Mineral	780	866	.90	1.752.73	52.22	127.16
Moffat	5 480	4.658	1.17	1.127.98	36.92	97.50
Montezuma	6.550	2.051	3.19	963.49	34.81	181.24
Montrose	12.500	2.264	5.52	1,148.86	40.82	155.58
Morgan	16.600	1,286	12.90	1,742.05	40.52	204.14
Otero	23.350	1.259	18.54	1.443.37	42.05	133.96
Ouray	2,710	519	5.22	1.673.74	59.45	126.55
Park	2.100	2.242	.93	4,207.00	78.70	91.28
Phillips	5.725	688	8.32	3.019.47	58.52	213.06
Pitkin	2.650	1,019	2.60	1.744.94	60.40	164.78
Prowers	14.500	1.630	8.89	1.596.98	40.50	111.44
Pueblo	62.500	2.433	25.68	1,161.47	40.97	292.08
Rio Blanco	3.150	3.223	.97	1.634.24	46.08	227.45
Rio Grande	8.625	898	9.60	1,332.05	48.80	152.46
Routt	9.100	2,309	3.94	1.639.28	48.98	172.15
Saguache	4.875	3.133	1.55	2.324.66	55.50	115.03
San Juan	1.750	453	3.86	1.862.84	53.27	247.64
San Miguel	5.510	1.288	4.27	1.398.26	44.80	232.87
Sedgwick	4 650	531	8.75	2.398.74	57.15	160.21
Summit	1.715	649	2.64	3,055.43	70.76	123.90
Teller	6.650	547	12.15	1,043.08	45.59	397.45
Washington	12 850	2.521	5.09	2.119.16	44.79	66.61
Weld	55.850	4.022	13.88	2.050.35	49.71	153.99
Yuma	14.600	2.367	6.16	1,741.17	46.76	109.79
State	994.060	103.658	9.45	$1.552.43	$ 42.79	$301.57

* Includes municipal and school district taxes.

MILEAGE OF HIGHWAYS IN COLORADO AT THE BEGINNING OF 1924

(Supplied by the U. S. Bureau of Roads)

COUNTY	Total Mileage	State Roads	County Roads	STATE ROADS				COUNTY ROADS		
				Hard Surfaced	Gravel and Sand Clay	Graded	Projected*	Gravel and Sand Clay	Graded	Unimproved
Adams	1,557	100	1,457	27.0	61.5	11.5	....	150	750	557
Alamosa	605	59	546	....	39.0	20.5	....	150	370	26
Arapahoe	596	96	500	9.0	56.5	30.5	....	100	400	....
Archuleta	610	102	508	....	12.0	90.0	....	10	303	195
Baca	600	229	371	....	23.5	205.5	....	56	220	95
Bent	802	73	729	0.5	34.5	38.0	....	36	400	293
Boulder	834	120	714	11.5	72.0	36.5	....	146	537	31
Chaffee	350	98	252	....	64.0	34.0	....	17	190	45
Cheyenne	968	131	837	....	78.0	53.0	....	9	330	498
Clear Creek	136	95	41	....	27.0	59.0	9.0	....	41	....
Conejos	692	106	586	....	10.0	88.0	8.0	71	411	104
Costilla	241	126	115	....	22.0	104.0	....	46	49	20
Crowley	854	68	786	....	22.0	46.0	....	9	700	77
Custer	700	96	604	....	......	96.0	....	5	279	320
Delta	596	120	476	....	42.0	78.0	....	2	474	....
Dolores	285	78	207	....	......	78.0	....	....	206	1
Douglas	655	155	500	5.2	108.8	40.0	....	110	295	95
Eagle	369	124	245	....	10.0	107.5	6.5	9	116	120
Elbert	1,801	109	1,692	....	54.0	55.0	....	....	473	1,219
El Paso	2,800	260	2,540	10.2	177.4	64.0	8.4	173	356	2,011
Fremont	431	172	259	1.3	69.7	101.0	....	74	185	....
Garfield	1,407	150	1,257	....	26.0	113.0	11.0	10	597	650
Gilpin	173	27	146	....	4.0	23.0	....	11	135	....
Grand	412	185	227	....	10.0	175.0	....	83	34	110
Gunnison	607	226	381	....	28.0	192.0	6.0	19	327	35
Hinsdale	129	37	92	....	......	37.0	....	....	26	66
Huerfano	628	126	502	....	34.8	91.2	....	95	407	....
Jackson	396	140	256	....	......	140.0	....	....	134	122
Jefferson	1,298	208	1,090	20.7	93.6	80.7	13.0	180	402	508
Kiowa	811	148	663	....	28.0	120.0	....	48	391	224
Kit Carson	2,170	174	1,996	....	93.0	81.0	....	90	351	1,555

Lake	150	80	70	....	57.0	6.0	17.0	....	63	7
La Plata	1,605	105	1,500	....	40.0	65.0	....	15	920	565
Larimer	1,106	257	849	15.2	114.3	123.0	4.5	117	527	205
Las Animas	6,000	254	5,746	3.0	100.0	151.0	....	42	1,040	4,664
Lincoln	1,300	321	979	....	64.5	256.5	....	274	220	485
Logan	3,300	158	3,142	10.0	148.0	......	....	152	1,500	1,490
Mesa	2,689	220	2,469	5.8	20.2	177.0	17.0	91	2,362	16
Mineral	111	71	40	....	......	71.0	....	3	37	....
Moffat	1,295	188	1,107	....	14.0	174.0	....	12	188	907
Montezuma	520	124	396	....	12.0	112.0	....	5	350	41
Montrose	1,380	208	1,172	....	63.3	111.7	33.0	108	707	357
Morgan	993	137	856	5.9	99.6	31.5	....	187	600	69
Otero	1,584	86	1,498	7.9	32.5	45.6	....	45	600	853
Ouray	261	53	208	....	10.0	43.0	....	50	52	106
Park	504	229	275	....	80.0	134.0	15.0	39	224	12
Phillips	820	84	736	....	84.0	......	....	60	145	531
Pitkin	215	142	73	....	......	119.0	23.0	10	50	13
Prowers	930	203	727	1.4	71.6	130.0	....	92	500	135
Pueblo	2,108	199	1,909	7.7	114.5	76.8	....	200	800	909
Rio Blanco	720	150	570	....	36.0	114.0	....	32	320	218
Rio Grande	404	91	313	....	32.5	46.5	12.0	20	263	30
Routt	1,876	175	1,701	....	24.0	151.0	....	10	1,671	20
Saguache	1,272	173	1,099	....	65.0	108.0	....	61	629	409
San Juan	140	44	96	....	9.0	35.0	....	5	76	15
San Miguel	560	150	410	....	......	138.0	12.0	6	404	....
Sedgwick	675	66	609	....	47.5	18.5	....	10	365	234
Summit	243	93	150	....	8.0	65.0	20.0	62	49	39
Teller	261	107	154	....	64.0	21.0	22.0	122	32	....
Washington	2,816	262	2,554	....	166.0	96.0	....	488	1,000	1,066
Weld	4,837	330	4,507	25.0	176.0	125.0	4.0	920	2,098	1,489
Yuma	2,420	225	2,195	....	155.7	69.3	....	66	925	1,204
Totals	67,608	8,923	58,685	167.3	3,211.5	5,303.3	241.4	5,013	28,606	25,066

*The mileage included in this column is all a part of various state highways, but none of it has yet been improved.

COUNTY DISBURSEMENTS FOR HIGHWAY PURPOSES, CONSTRUCTION, 1923

(Supplied by the U. S. Bureau of Roads)

COUNTY	Roads	Bridges	Engi-neering	Machinery and Equipment	Repair Mach. and Equipm't	Rental Mach. and Equipm't	Purchase R. O. W.	Admin. Expense	Miscellaneous Expense	Total
Adams	$ 8,616.76	$	$ 1,311.19	$	$	$	$ 306.00	$	$	$ 10,233.95
Alamosa	....	....	....	....	....	....	....	....	....	....
Arapahoe	7,908.00	8,250.00	....	2,000.00	1,000.00	....	....	750.00	....	19,908.00
Archuleta	....	....	....	....	....	....	....	....	....	....
Baca	....	....	....	....	....	....	....	....	....	....
Boulder	19,024.00	16,500.00	200.00	....	....	....	573.00	400.00	....	36,697.00
Bent	....	....	....	....	....	....	....	....	....	....
Chaffee	....	240.00	....	....	....	....	....	....	....	240.00
Cheyenne	3,960.89	9,011.12	133.84	2,245.14	756.00	....	752.00	14.00	700.76	17,573.75
[illegible]	15,543.46	....	....	....	200.00	....	....	....	....	15,743.46
Clear Creek	6,193.37	1,647.00	....	....	....	....	....	....	....	7,840.37
Conejos	....	....	....	....	....	....	300.00	....	....	300.00
Crowley	3,450.00	10,000.00	....	6,475.00	2,000.00	....	....	2,700.00	889.68	25,514.68
Custer	4,301.52	523.17	....	122.38	622.47	....	500.00	276.18	366.67	6,712.39
Delta	....	....	....	....	....	....	....	....	....	....
Dolores	661.60	....	....	....	....	....	....	....	....	661.60
Douglas	....	....	....	....	....	....	....	....	....	....
Eagle	1,490.88	4,943.14	....	....	....	....	....	....	....	6,434.02
Elbert	19,000.00	19,000.00	....	2,520.00	....	10.00	40.00	....	....	40,570.00
El Paso	....	....	....	....	....	....	....	....	....	....
Fremont	1,500.00	7,500.00	....	....	....	....	....	....	....	9,000.00
Garfield	7,164.00	5,691.00	1,051.80	6,643.60	....	....	50.00	....	....	20,600.40
Gilpin	....	....	....	....	....	....	....	....	....	....
Grand	....	....	....	....	....	....	....	....	....	....
Gunnison	20,556.57	2,871.69	....	....	....	....	....	....	....	23,428.26
Hinsdale	5,000.00	....	1,533.27	....	....	....	....	....	....	6,533.27
Huerfano	13,676.02	12,256.85	1,171.72	2,917.73	1,641.54	90.00	652.00	1,112.32	1,030.38	34,548.56
Jackson	14,744.37	....	....	....	....	....	....	1,107.65	....	15,852.02
Jefferson	....	....	....	....	....	....	....	....	....	....
Kiowa	....	....	....	....	....	....	....	....	....	....
Kit Carson	6,000.00	9,900.00	800.00	4,000.00	....	....	800.00	....	8,000.00	29,500.00

Lake	....	....	....	....	....	....	....	....	....	....
La Plata	....	....	....	....	....	....	....	....	....	....
Larimer	....	....	....	....	....	....	....	....	....	....
Las Animas	5,795.37	5,000.00	....	....	....	....	....	....	....	10,795.37
Lincoln	57,963.15	3,805.60	....	....	....	....	....	....	....	61,768.75
Logan	....	....	....	....	....	....	....	....	....	....
Mesa	....	....	....	....	....	....	....	....	....	....
Mineral	15,741.17	....	....	....	....	....	....	200.00	240.00	16,181.17
Moffat	4,752.97	4,610.73	....	....	....	....	....	....	....	9,363.70
Montezuma	18,069.36	4,277.92	600.00	4,303.66	1,337.57	105.00	360.00	....	....	29,053.51
Montrose	42,821.37	10,558.44	3,022.57	900.00	600.00	4,500.00	1,367.40	....	....	63,769.78
Morgan	....	14,381.83	140.12	....	....	....	502.04	....	....	15,023.99
Otero	....	....	....	....	....	....	....	....	....	....
Ouray	....	....	....	....	....	....	....	....	....	....
Park	7,064.59	4,409.03	141.25	2,644.42	750.31	....	....	....	....	15,009.60
Phillips	....	....	....	....	....	....	....	....	....	....
Pitkin	1,200.00	....	....	....	286.50	....	1,200.00	....	....	2,686.50
Prowers	7,325.48	3,299.19	....	....	....	....	....	....	....	10,624.67
Pueblo	9,527.09	77,428.05	....	....	....	....	....	....	....	86,955.14
Rio Blanco	5,832.50	....	....	....	....	....	....	....	....	5,832.50
Rio Grande	8,075.00	3,600.00	250.00	600.00	350.00	....	....	900.00	....	....
Routt	....	....	....	....	....	....	....	....	....	....
Saguache	17,920.00	....	....	....	....	....	....	....	....	17,920.00
San Juan	2,677.40	1,758.99	....	....	....	....	....	....	....	4,436.39
San Miguel	....	....	....	....	....	....	....	....	....	....
Sedgwick	....	....	....	....	....	....	....	....	....	....
Summit	....	....	....	....	....	....	....	....	....	....
Teller	....	....	....	....	....	....	....	....	....	....
Washington	25,237.23	39,891.37	....	7,138.50	1,737.24	....	....	....	....	74,004.34
Weld	41,514.81	58,081.18	....	13,790.75	....	....	14,547.29	16,859.46	90,944.81	235,738.30
Yuma	15,800.00	5,400.00	....	1,900.00	10,000.00	....	....	2,400.00	6,000.00	41,500.00
State	$ 446,108.93	$344,836.30	$ 10,355.76	$ 58,201.18	$ 21,281.63	$ 4,705.00	$ 21,949.73	$ 26,719.61	$108,172.30	$1,042,330.44

COUNTY DISBURSEMENTS FOR HIGHWAY PURPOSES, MAINTENANCE, 1923

(Supplied by the U. S. Bureau of Roads)

COUNTY	Roads	Bridges	Engineering	Machinery and Equipment	Repair Mach. and Equipm't	Rental Mach. and Equipm't	Purchase R. O. W.	Admin. Expense	Miscellaneous Expense	Total
Adams	$ 58,000.19	$ 50,712.83	$	$	$ 2,788.22	$	$	$	$ 61,621.45	$ 173,122.[illegible]
Alamosa	14,500.00	600.00	....	875.00	625.00	....	....	....	....	16,600.00
Arapahoe	18,000.00	8,000.00	....	12,350.00	3,600.00	....	....	750.00	....	42,700.00
Archuleta	21,000.00	....	....	2,025.00	950.00	....	....	50.00	....	24,025.00
Baca	109,176.66	....	....	500.00	300.00	....	....	600.00	1,000.00	[illegible]66
Boulder	114,326.00	5,174.00	....	6,349.00	13,625.00	100.00	....	2,600.00	....	142,174.00
Bent	24,141.58	3,364.91	210.10	6,447.61	5,932.24	....	803.50	2,665.39	843.91	44,409.24
Chaffee	38,626.94	208.00	82.50	....	....	281.25	....	....	491.23	39,689.92
Cheyenne	12,680.90	3,003.71	133.81	4,570.18	1,349.38	60.00	....	19.00	901.00	22,716.98
Costilla	18,334.02	382.31	....	....	....	....	....	898.00	....	19,614.33
Clear Creek	22,031.98	1,065.27	....	2,154.49	1,926.17	....	....	....	172.04	27,349.95
Conejos	20,000.00	1,500.00	....	....	850.00	100.00	....	520.00	....	22,970.00
Crowley	4,000.00	....	....	....	....	....	....	....	....	4,[illegible]
Custer	12,301.61	4,146.65	....	....	1,244.94	....	....	276.17	....	17,969.37
Delta	54,402.87	7,552.42	231.95	12,935.83	2,518.32	218.32	607.50	1,596.00	1,423.23	81,486.44
Dolores	3,186.53	....	....	....	....	....	....	....	....	3,186.55
Douglas	90,508.86	....	....	....	....	....	....	2,013.48	....	92,522.34
Eagle	56,425.22	20,779.33	....	....	....	....	....	....	....	77,204.55
Elbert	31,000.00	31,000.00	....	....	....	....	....	....	....	62,000.00
El Paso	228,770.28	....	1,143.70	29,434.96	30,414.33	....	710.9[illegible]	2,400.[illegible]	....	292,874.26
Fremont	35,106.62	2,500.00	100.00	10,000.00	5,500.00	1,150.00	....	5,000.[illegible]	....	59,356.62
Garfield	63,925.86	16,343.54	....	....	461.60	....	....	....	....	80,731.00
Gilpin	5,000.00	....	....	....	....	....	....	....	....	5,[illegible]
Grand	30,000.00	....	....	8,500.00	2,500.00	....	917.00	....	13,335.36	55,252.36
Gunnison	30,305.95	....	....	1,000.00	....	....	978.20	....	....	32,284.15
Hinsdale	2,000.00	....	....	....	....	....	....	....	....	2,000.00
Huerfano	29,768.25	12,910.19	....	2,917.74	3,283.10	....	....	2,224.67	1,030.38	52,134.33
Jackson	10,892.35	....	....	....	....	....	....	600.00	....	11,492.35
Jefferson	99,240.67	....	....	....	....	....	....	....	....	99,240.67
Kiowa	....	....	....	....	....	....	....	....	....	....
Kit Carson	....	1,000.00	2,100.00	5,000.00	25,000.00	....	....	....	....	33,100.00

Lake	7,500.00	....	....	....	....	....	....	....	....	7,500.00
La Plata	84,332.79	....	....	....	....	....	....	3,200.00	....	87,532.79
[illegible]	137,500.00	....	4,500.00	12,000.00	4,000.00	....	2,000.00	....	20,000.00	1 8 ,000.00
Las Animas	121,965.30	3,243.55	....	26,360.02	7,438.10	....	....	....	....	159,006.97
Lincoln	91,050.27	....	....	....	....	....	....	....	....	91,050.27
Logan	157,885.74	....	....	....	....	....	....	....	....	157,885.74
Mesa	116,805.77	39,679.30	....	....	....	....	2,250.75	....	....	158,843.[illegible]
Mineral	4,915.00	54.00	245.91	1,753.50	273.42	....	....	100.00	209.41	7,551.24
Moffat	12,091.25	11,390.66	....	1,222.50	2,623.94	....	....	1,600.00	965.72	29,894.07
Montezuma	9,554.00	856.50	200.00	720.00	145.30	....	....	....	8,000.00	19,475.80
Montrose	36,280.75	7,974.06	....	931.11	373.85	2,085.94	....	3,774.85	1,009.47	52,430.03
Morgan	58,067.29	1,412.48	....	2,448.00	2,903.82	....	....	4,812.38	....	69,643.97
[illegible]ro	39,209.71	11,536.55	....	45,262.32	....	....	....	....	....	96,008.58
Ouray	22,562.46	6,000.00	1,000.00	1,000.00	1,800.00	1.00	400.00	....	....	3 ,763.40
Park	25,279.55	....	....	....	....	....	....	....	3,953.53	29,233.08
Phillips	45,181.44	....	....	....	....	....	....	....	....	45,181.44
Pitkin	11,552.14	....	....	....	....	....	....	....	....	11,552.14
Prowers	81,590.75	4,751.31	224.10	6,735.87	10,140.09	....	835.50	3,000.00	2,776.11	110,053.73
Pueblo	118,708.42	19,842.02	....	8 647.21	29,821.90	....	2,540.00	4,732.06	609.86	184,891.47
Rio Blanco	15,6 0 .34	....	....	3,571. 8	....	....	....	983.91	1,071.23	21,226.81
Rio [illegible]	2,107.28	1,500.00	....	....	500.00	....	....	900.00	....	5,007.28
Routt	49,520.23	....	....	....	....	....	834.50	....	14,010.86	64,365.59
[illegible]ache	39,396.14	....	2,400.00	21,836.76	....	....	....	1,585.92	....	65,218.82
San Juan	7,[illegible]87.07	....	....	1,734.68	....	460.50	....	....	....	10,162.25
San Miguel	37,868.20	....	....	....	....	....	....	....	....	37,868.20
Sedgwick	18,[illegible]97.06	36,076.09	....	....	611.14	....	....	....	5,222.21	60,406.50
[illegible]mit	12,903.90	....	....	3,656.59	1,128.73	....	....	1,800.00	4,810.43	24,299.65
Teller	55,286.08	....	....	....	....	....	....	....	....	55,286.08
Washington	2,476.05	320.00	....	....	....	....	....	....	....	2,796.85
[illegible]	122,544.91	5,230.64	....	....	97 422.63	....	....	....	....	225,198.18
Yuma	40,000. 0	....	....	....	....	....	....	....	....	40,000.00
State	$2,84[illegible]043.23	$320,120.12	$ 12,572.07	$242,939.70	$262,050.22	$ 4,457.01	$ 12,877.94	$ 48,691.83	$143,457.43	$3,891,118.55

COUNTY REVENUES FOR HIGHWAY PURPOSES, 1923

(Supplied by the U. S. Bureau of Roads)

COUNTY	Bonds	Taxes or Appropriations	Motor Vehicle Tax	Gas Tax	Miscel-laneous	Total
Alamosa	....	16,711.79	3,413.00	2,283.77	....	22.408.56
Arapahoe	....	45,613.46	9,576.10	3,242.85	287.00	58.719.41
Archuleta	....	25,000.00	....	....	....	25 000.00
Baca	....	31 043.59	4,038.12	8,135.26	62,669.64	105.886.61
Bent	....	28,747.43	3,963.85	3,019.02	17,039.60	52,769.99
Boulder	....	156,700.00	21,469.00	3,850.00	3,948.00	185,967.00
Chaffee	....	15,705.60	1,922.20	3,523.27	25,337.36	46 488.43
Cheyenne	....	25,602.05	2,288.19	4,532.42	5,056.58	37.479.24
Costilla	7.163.83	10,732.37	892.86	3,656.02	13,847.14	36.292.22
Clear Creek	....	18,000.00	826.55	2,708.75	13,631.26	35,166.56
Conejos	....	26,152.00	1,954.62	3,266.48	....	31,373.10
Crowley	....	24,032.60	2,982.08	2,600.00	....	29,614 68
Custer	....	20,505.43	919.27	3,664.72	169.08	25,258.50
Delta	3,075.54	60,721.37	6,073.55	4,691.52	20,945.88	95 507.86
Dolores	....	....	....	....	3,848.13	3,848.13
Douglas	....	28,794.17	2,519.39	7,914.66	12,500.00	51,728.22
Eagle	6,434.02	55,292.54	862.87	4,755.32	13,009.98	80.354.73
Elbert	....	100,000.00	3,500.00	3 565.55	....	107 065.55
El Paso	....	174,631.20	30 828.07	9,492.28	89,074.30	304.025.85
Fremont	....	37,762.22	5,058.69	2,868.08	22.667.63	68,356.62
Garfield	....	102,716.40	....	....	....	102 716.40
Gilpin	....	5,000.00	....	....	....	5.000.00
Grand	....	20,774.14	800.00	9,400.00	12.500.00	43 474.14
Gunnison	4 261.29	32,567.70	1,581.38	7,984.79	63,852.96	110,248.12
Hinsdale	....	6.000.00	408.68	2,124.59	....	8,533.27
Huerfano	30,398.14	42,523.13	6,777.69	4,461.52	1,100.54	85,261.02
Jackson	....	11,563.64	676.94	4.744.74	20.201.86	37.187.18
Jefferson	....	66,008.06	14,000.00	7,363.33	11,869.28	99,240.67
Kiowa	....	No record	....	....	....	....
Kit Carson	....	63,887.62	6,135.06	6,139.06	....	76,161.74
Lake	....	7,500.00	....	....	....	7 500.00
La Plata	11,859.48	57,593.66	3,331.96	3,672.09	21,833.88	98,291.07
Larimer	....	140,000.00	18.000.00	16,000.00	6,000.00	180,000.00
Las Animas	....	124,951.59	14,865.46	8,250.29	42.781.93	190,849.27
Lincoln	....	135 229.80	4,765.45	11,649.52	172.72	151,817.49
Logan	....	95,704.56	10,384.75	5,452.49	33,999.44	145,541.24
Mesa	....	104,588.55	11,355.00	11,000.00	31,900.27	158,843.82
Mineral	16,537.13	4,827.16	210.88	2.407.82	4,181.62	28,164.61
Moffat	....	26,406.00	1,051.29	6,391.19	21,052.73	54,901.21
Montrose	....	43,024.99	4,759.18	9,073.52	68,212.43	125,070.12
Montezuma	....	40.383.42	1,660.59	3.514.25	2,971.05	48,529.31
Morgan	....	161,918.98	8,687.73	6,995.53	3,882.38	181,484.62
Otero	....	66,278.95	12,756.11	3.032.07	6.325.48	88,392.61
Ouray	399.53	16,730.68	684.62	2,080.14	11,649.69	31,544.65
Park	....	35.699.38	1 138.28	6,993.07	10.083.57	53,914.30
Phillips	....	17,000.00	4,680.88	2,726.47	13.085.19	37,492.54
Pitkin	....	7,707.05	336.56	2,797.35	2,249.47	13,170.43
Prowers	....	126,205.88	6.716.11	6,709.85	854.63	140.486.47
Pueblo	....	124,000.00	22,000.00	8,000.00	46.000.00	200,000.00
Rio Blanco	....	19,715.71	675.50	5,771.61	1,495.89	27.658.71
Rio Grande	56,000.00	....	11,132.00	4,646.67	....	71,778.67
Routt	21,468.57	38,118.13	2 287.68	5,983.93	6,232.11	74,090.42
Saguache	....	37,600.87	2 862.51	7,347.17	40,372.65	88,183.20
San Juan	4,376.64	5,027.99	165.96	1,699.92	4,689.59	15.960.10
San Miguel	....	32,373.76	908.87	4,585.57	....	37,868.20
Sedgwick	....	47,000.00	3,600.00	2.572.00	....	53 172.00
Summit	....	12,810.00	402.47	3,664.72	7,422.46	24,299.65
Teller	....	25,323.28	2,031.48	3,965.66	32 381.58	63.702.00
Washington	....	43,660.23	....	....	46,539.57	90.199.80
Weld	....	288,491.17	....	11,295.42	116,317.53	416,104.12
Yuma	....	65.000.00	7.967.00	8,621.00	....	81.588.00
Adams	$	$ 97,058.04	$ 9,202.12	$ 3,832.92	$ 69,976.57	$ 180,069.65
State....	$ 161,974.16	$3,300,798.34	$ 302,088.60	$ 300,720.24	$1,066,220.74	$5,131,802.08

COLORADO BANK STATISTICS

COUNTY	December 31, 1922		December 31, 1923		
	Loans and Discounts	Deposits	Loans and Discounts	Deposits	Total Assets
Adams	$ 1,227,159.91	$ 1,539,131.23	$ 1,336,186.08	$ 1,737,073.65	$ 1,996,053.45
Alamosa	1,016,755.91	1,324,294.22	844,090.35	1,388,293.40	1,627 201.25
Arapahoe	1,502,381.87	1,985,174.83	1,542,996.00	2,222,234.05	2,584,255.45
Archuleta	383,568.80	334,981.65	363,589.19	317,930.20	484,125.45
Baca	416,826.67	514,890.77	380,643.35	427,277.56	593,199.70
Bent	1,142,403.70	1,118,331.71	980,187.55	1,010,137.24	1,331,982.75
Boulder	5,843,978.93	7,009,081.60	5,998,017.89	7,860,638.94	10,347,858.80
Chaffee	701,005.44	1,521,109.14	723,636.50	1,560,980.07	1,841,644.07
Cheyenne	499,163.27	475,890.17	366,596.21	360,680.31	496,442.51
Clear Creek	435,198.06	724,685.51	403,126.20	666,767.08	860,951.14
Conejos	434,500.82	590,868.07	423,443.92	610,410.53	737 572.50
Costilla	186,812.65	237,226.66	178,178.83	187,050.40	255,465.15
Crowley	456,684.50	640,091.29	403,830.02	710,412.66	930,680.94
Custer	105,196.20	190,192.74	111,200.98	197,821.77	252,948.27
Delta	2,122 942.19	3,001,529.68	1,764,505.40	2,474,330.34	3,113,116.34
Denver	92,998,754.07	166,476,278.28	94,599,196.08	164,019,652.40	184,986,006.48
Dolores (No Banks)	....	....	....	....	....
Douglas	527,063.41	545,393.72	573,462.03	563,332.96	814,596.04
Eagle	381,469.61	417,513.74	308,838.12	453,405.72	609 263.41
Elbert	828,824.38	909,511.45	776 846.92	893,391.81	1,109,768.51
El Paso	12,366,050.43	18,153,173.53	12,011,590.19	17,743,615.81	20,922,687.35
Fremont	2,275,163.37	3,767,088.60	2,336,896.06	4,149,849.27	4,664,986.30
Garfield	1,745,705.64	2,447,050.29	1,927,359.28	2,595,829.15	3,261,140.90
Gilpin	46,540.00	262,566.18	35 416.00	262,688.26	322,647.16
Grand	158,751.56	266,310.05	163 048.35	276,158.20	322,522.50
Gunnison	685,826.48	1,314,040.57	665,153.81	1,422,592.72	1,720,075.29
Hinsdale (No Banks)	....	....	....	....	....
Huerfano	1,418,151.90	2,433,065.97	1,338,449.56	2,368,091.53	2,608,939.71
Jackson	280,379.67	318,288.30	311,316.41	314,540.83	401,884.94
Jefferson	984,815.77	1,404,161.69	959,896.26	1,376 600.85	1,582,182.23
Kiowa	700,176.39	562,467.63	708 802.56	495,132.82	891,518.70
Kit Carson	1,306,808.70	1,402,847.30	799,856.10	845,564.22	1,157 321.94
Lake	244,296.30	1,687,445.75	247,936.04	1,634,762.44	2,103,937.84
La Plata	1,893,416.90	2 565,581.30	1,655 836.44	2,620,684.25	3,265,168.05
Larimer	8,043,928.37	8,605,531.20	6,633,623.47	7,096,632.91	9 931,838.82
Las Animas	5,362,776.38	8,087,087.19	5,054,147.93	8,295,069.81	9 594,440.95
Lincoln	1,057,351.90	1,091,461.80	924,043.60	885,763.65	1,348,397.63
Logan	2,610,966.72	2,493,426.69	2,476,511.84	2,601,718.98	3,898,352.06
Mesa	3,070,773.04	4,249,239.89	2,774,729.82	4,258,132.60	5 070,400.98
Mineral	60,653.40	95,252.58	73,245.24	99,190.98	119,190.98
Moffat	546,377.56	553 209.96	437,975.46	534,304.80	696,825.43
Montezuma	919,074.99	1,178,069.56	841,082.50	1,187,158.22	1,531,925.14
Montrose	1,389,298.35	1,751,792.29	1,296,420.92	1,944,803.96	2,463,875.15
Morgan	2,953,073.34	3,069,857.48	2,804,079.63	3,388,726.05	4 336,991.82
Otero	2,628,804.66	3,315,767.03	2,482,322.77	3,128,167.56	4,138,783.10
Ouray	261,490.04	410,294.74	254,391.66	342,966.25	425,648.47
Park	52,796.33	201,757.28	63,791.43	191,704.96	243 065.98
Phillips	1,496,527.11	1,293,176.56	1,296,606.26	1,219,818.98	1,917,381.74
Pitkin	237,485.03	486,333.37	206,615.05	436,680.81	479,503.83
Prowers	1,328,856.34	1,951,186.31	1,379,618.87	1,615,972.12	2,116,603.21
Pueblo	8,533,837.10	19,556,238.31	8,394,972.82	18,255,465.39	22 359,472.25
Rio Blanco	609,734.40	696,765.81	629,624.43	716,481.82	827,236.02
Rio Grande	1,381,982.24	1,293,512.19	1,432 299.34	1,315 012.78	1,870,364.12
Routt	1,264,609.05	1,408,150.83	1,312,767.56	1,566,586.18	1,885,277.17
Saguache	809,651.06	524,359.69	654,249.48	560 804.64	975,232.96
San Juan	195 007.11	355,348.57	258,422.17	433,374.37	574,264.27
San Miguel	1,149,020.00	1,381,699.03	947,397.01	1,283,139.56	1 805,824.85
Sedgwick	895,671.49	809,528.54	825,751.66	744 999.52	1,219,505.83
Summit	119,713.47	186,776.35	123,772.69	212,492.82	252,832.17
Teller	983 516.05	2,453 624.73	987,240.31	2,643,052.89	2,846,656.98
Washington	1,016,849.75	1,001,929.50	981 789.98	855,994.82	1,326,477.95
Weld	7,525,926.75	8,203,046.52	6,764,356.33	8,600,871.97	11,206,699.78
Yuma	1,471,017.06	1,741,308.95	1,442,742.01	1,602,993.38	2,299,481.05
State	$193,293,542.59	$304,585,996.57	$188,994,720.92	$299,786,014.22	$355,960,695.81

COLORADO LIBRARIES

City	Library	No. of Volumes	Registered Borrowers	Circulation	Appropriation
Boulder	Public	13,800	3,582	55,096	$ 4,466
Boulder	University of Colorado	151,295	1,900	258,628	34,000
Brighton	Public	4,700	2,171	27,945	2,131
Brush	Carnegie	4,053	1,628	17,244	....
Burlington	Public	1,194	147	2,593	....
Canon City	Public	8,222	......	23,134	2,000
Cheyenne Wells	High School	1,200	93	....	....
Colorado Springs	Public	41,725	15,000	150 546	16,652
Colorado Springs	West End Branch	7,536	508	22,073	....
Craig	Public	2,800	600	400	800
Cripple Creek	Public	3,089	1,033	14,502	492
Del Norte	Private Kings Daughters	......	......	....	....
Delta	Public	6,105	1,506	29,902	1,396
Denver	Colorado State (Ref.)	90,000	......	....	2,300
Denver	Colorado Traveling Library	10,500	......	15,000	2,000
Denver	Public	228,676	......	1,199,323	140 000
Denver	State Historical and Natural History Society	2,782	......	....	500
Denver	Supreme Court Law	24,747	......	....	....
Durango	Public	12,035	3,163	31,767	3,500
Eaton	Public	5,000	300	10,050	900
Estes Park	Estes Park Library	2,746	370	4,954	65
Evergreen	Public	5,100	528	5,648	....
Florence	Public	3,638	......	9,000	1,000
Fort Collins	Public	14 343	4,411	58,340	5,000
Fort Collins	State Agricultural College	50,986	......	36,651	....
Fort Lupton	Public	1,500	840	3,274	1,100
Fort Morgan	Carnegie	6,500	4,080	18,874	2,861
Golden	Golden Library	4 600	......	4,000	500
Golden	Colorado School of Mines	17,450	......	2,580	....
Grand Junction	Carnegie	8,436	2,614	44,029	3,000
Greeley	Public	10,958	......	....	....
Greeley	Colorado State Teachers College	56,000	......	49,000	5,400
Gunnison	Western State College of Colorado	12,000	300	....	....
Hotchkiss	Public	1,000	100	600	30
Idaho Springs	Carnegie	5,384	506	12,340	1,000
La Junta	Woodruff Memorial	30,533	3,948	24,303	2,500
Lamar	Carnegie	4,850	1,500	12,784	1,200
Las Animas	Public	2,000	850	9,007	....
Longmont	Public	7,742	3,324	30,341	3 070
Loveland	Public	4,964	2,932	35,237	3 700
Manitou	Public	4,400	367	8,277	1,000
Meeker	Public	2,138	854	1,862	716
Monte Vista	Carnegie	5,000	1,200	20,556	2 000
Montrose	Public	2,600	1,066	5,345	1,480
Platteville	Public	1,924	90	2,160	....
Pueblo	McClelland	34,000	10 000	120,000	9,000
Rocky Ford	Public	5,888	1,328	15,863	1,560
Saguache	Saguache County High School	3,271	178	1,948	420
Salida	Public	7 554	2,247	7,318	....
Sterling	Public	7,000	3,055	34,922	....
Swink	Public	852	495	1,597	120
Telluride	School and Public	7,000	800	14,000	....
Trinidad	Carnegie	24,000	9,900	61,227	4,760
Victor	Public	7,000	1,700	6,660	....
Wellington	Public	600	700	....	50
Windsor	Public	1,704	461	....	....
Wray	Public	1,500	200	10,400	....

Data compiled by the State Board of Library Commissioners; Chalmers Hadley, Denver, president; Elfreda Stebbins, Fort Collins, secretary.

COLORADO COUNTIES AND COUNTY SEATS

COUNTY	COUNTY SEAT	Railway Distance from Denver, Miles	Population of County Seat	
			1910	1920
Adams	Brighton	19	850	2,715
Alamosa	Alamosa	252	3,013	3,171
Arapahoe	Littleton	10	1,373	1,636
Archuleta	Pagosa Springs	421	669	1,032
Baca	Springfield*	285	......	295
Bent	Las Animas	201	2,008	2 252
Boulder	Boulder	27	9,539	10,006
Chaffee	Buena Vista	176	1,041	903
Cheyenne	Cheyenne Wells	177	270	508
Clear Creek	Georgetown	50	950	703
Conejos	Conejos	281	......	350
Costilla	San Luis*	248	......	550
Crowley	Ordway	169	705	1,186
Custer	Silver Cliff	210	250	241
Delta	Delta	273	2,388	2,623
Denver	Denver	...	213,381	256,491
Dolores	Rico	443	368	326
Douglas	Castle Rock	32	365	461
Eagle	Eagle	329	186	358
Elbert	Kiowa*	46	......	148
El Paso	Colorado Springs	75	29,078	30,105
Fremont	Canon City	160	5,162	†6,386
Garfield	Glenwood Springs	284	2,019	2,073
Gilpin	Central City	45	1,782	552
Grand	Sulphur Springs	109	182	123
Gunnison	Gunnison	288	1 026	1,329
Hinsdale	Lake City	351	405	317
Huerfano	Walsenburg	171	2,323	3,565
Jackson	Walden	256	162	260
Jefferson	Golden	16	2,477	2,484
Kiowa	Eads	230	......	406
Kit Carson	Burlington	166	368	991
Lake	Leadville	212	1 508	4,959
La Plata	Durango	451	4,686	4,116
Larimer	Fort Collins	68	8,210	8,755
Las Animas	Trinidad	210	10,204	10,906
Lincoln	Hugo	115	343	838
Logan	Sterling	123	3,044	6,415
Mesa	Grand Junction	373	7,754	8,665
Mineral	Creede	321	741	500
Moffat	Craig	255	392	1,297
Montezuma	Cortez	506	565	541
Montrose	Montrose	351	3,254	3,581
Morgan	Fort Morgan	78	2,800	3 818
Otero	La Junta	182	4,154	4,964
Ouray	Ouray	387	1,644	1,165
Park	Fairplay	115	265	183
Phillips	Holyoke	173	659	1,205
Pitkin	Aspen	203	1 834	1,265
Prowers	Lamar	235	2,977	2,512
Pueblo	Pueblo	119	44,395	40,050
Rio Blanco	Meeker	355	807	935
Rio Grande	Del Norte	283	840	1,007
Routt	Steamboat Springs	214	1,227	1,249
Saguache	Saguache*	265	620	948
San Juan	Silverton	497	2,153	1,150
San Miguel	Telluride	422	1,756	1,618
Sedgwick	Julesburg	197	962	1,320
Summit	Breckenridge	110	834	796
Teller	Cripple Creek	126	6,206	2,325
Washington	Akron	112	647	1,041
Weld	Greeley	52	8,179	10,958
Yuma	Wray	165	1,000	1,538

*Not directly on railroad. †Greater Canon City.

PUBLIC SCHOOLS, TEACHERS AND SCHOOL POPULATION, 1922

COUNTY	Total Number			Teachers			School Population		
	School Districts	Schools	School Bldgs.	Male	Female	Total	Persons of School Age	Enrollm't in Public Schools	Average Daily Attendance
Adams	40	81	76	19	134	153	4,439	3,821	2,691
Alamosa	14	24	36	14	56	70	1,805	1,651	1,158
Arapahoe	28	52	59	4	40	44	1,264	1,117	660
Archuleta	20	35	41	19	122	141	4,311	3,543	2,720
Baca	63	94	94	45	73	118	2,716	2,619	1,720
Bent	37	55	54	17	61	78	2,622	2,177	1,686
Boulder	55	64	62	50	239	289	9,338	7,814	5,895
Chaffee	25	30	31	10	58	68	2,325	1 681	1,287
Cheyenne	11	44	50	9	48	57	1,269	1,201	1,005
Clear Creek	9	12	14	4	25	29	619	531	430
Conejos	28	38	32	16	74	90	3,382	2 736	1,924
Costilla	14	25	20	15	25	40	1,971	1,356	902
Crowley	9	35	34	18	73	91	2,222	2,203	1,529
Custer	21	23	23	4	25	29	581	482	327
Delta	22	51	50	21	127	148	5,132	4,340	3,403
Denver	1	125	120	118	1,173	1,291	66,551	57,595	35,102
Dolores	7	13	13	7	9	16	464	......	......
Douglas	34	30	31	7	39	46	946	854	602
Eagle	23	34	40	7	48	55	970	907	786
Elbert	41	93	95	20	94	114	2 009	2,022	1 542
El Paso	39	106	89	71	336	407	12,632	10,759	8,171
Fremont	34	55	47	32	155	187	5,986	5,367	4,190
Garfield	40	58	54	21	93	114	3,030	2,782	2,052
Gilpin	12	10	19	2	18	20	246	222	189
Grand	18	25	21	7	23	30	571	443	369
Gunnison	26	35	29	7	49	56	1,610	1,483	1,113
Hinsdale	4	8	9	1	11	12	158	131	110
Huerfano	45	76	73	15	113	128	6 554	4,539	3,655
Jackson	6	11	11	1	13	14	255	227	158
Jefferson	48	61	62	18	131	149	4,480	3,911	2,972
Kiowa	18	40	32	19	48	67	1 312	1,228	977
Kit Carson	74	97	100	38	112	150	3,361	2,961	2,168
Lake	9	19	23	10	41	51	1,793	1,085	986
La Plata	36	64	90	16	113	129	4,131	3,336	2,089
Larimer	46	85	100	33	257	290	9,503	8,004	6,090
Las Ainmas	121	....	203	69	310	379	14,149	12,273	8,511
Lincoln	42	99	122	22	115	137	2,857	2 710	2,018
Logan	56	107	217	29	172	201	6,452	5,855	3,769
Mesa	35	65	60	34	176	210	7 464	6 715	5,076
Mineral	4	6	2	1	4	5	158	139	123
Moffat	27	....	....	22	58	80	1,576	1,165	......
Montezuma	28	45	55	14	60	74	2,138	2,098	1,407
Montrose	27	44	47	13	92	105	4,089	3,921	2,802
Morgan	19	85	116	32	158	190	5,335	5,352	3,481
Otero	22	60	55	41	187	228	7,526	7,065	5 222
Ouray	13	23	18	2	23	25	613	564	440
Park	19	33	33	4	34	38	517	349	267
Phillips	38	38	42	10	54	64	1,910	1,732	1,395
Pitkin	15	16	34	7	28	35	781	656	521
Prowers	48	75	73	30	130	160	4,516	4,325	2 971
Pueblo	44	116	79	58	419	477	18,642	14,672	10,058
Rio Blanco	15	34	33	8	33	41	966	731	573
Rio Grande	9	12	13	6	57	63	2,570	2,184	1,708
Routt	41	77	104	16	102	118	2,463	2,209	1,547
Saguache	18	25	20	12	47	59	1,991	1,523	1,091
San Juan	1	5	5	2	6	8	281	192	168
San Miguel	12	32	30	6	44	50	1,231	1,063	798
Sedgwick	23	29	27	5	38	43	1,456	1,424	828
Summit	10	10	10	6	13	19	304	250	191
Teller	11	20	24	12	36	48	1,479	1,165	975
Washington	78	127	136	30	135	165	3 453	3,408	2,644
Weld	105	220	219	91	519	610	17,165	16,622	11 937
Yuma	106	132	134	39	157	196	4,678	4,323	3,307
State	1,944	3,243	3 635	1,336	7,263	8,599	287,318	249,813	174 484

AVERAGE ANNUAL PER CAPITA COST OF EDUCATION IN PUBLIC SCHOOLS

(From Records of the State Superintendent of Schools)

COUNTY	1920		1921		1922		1923	
	Based on Enrollment	Based on Average Attendance	Based on Enrollment	Based on Average Attendance	Based on Enrollment	Based on Average Attendance	Based on Enrollment	Based on Average Attendance
Adams	$87.92	$145.81	$64.93	$100.22	$90.91	$135.15	$75.61	$107.37
Alamosa	59.16	94.83	71.27	102.31	71.46	102.26	83.10	118.49
Arapahoe	51.83	81.36	68.10	97.59	78.57	103.30	81.43	106.07
Archuleta	32.34	58.79	41.69	134.62	49.60	88.49	42.22	71.46
Baca	18.77	.....	58.46	125.70	58.43	79.29	61.10	93.07
Bent	41.98	68.85	49.23	101.67	56.90	83.72	75.34	97.28
Boulder	55.93	75.83	56.85	80.71	80.69	102.11	81.58	108.13
Chaffee	43.66	60.29	55.17	64.11	53.40	70.88	132.04	172.47
Cheyenne	65.61	94.08	89.95	127.08	213.36	268.33	190.22	227.32
Clear Creek	98.75	133.71	83.22	113.96	124.81	159.18	93.93	115.99
Conejos	26.16	46.10	37.97	55.05	37.55	54.07	51.03	72.57
Costilla	45.92	74.91	42.76	75.27	35.93	60.12	45.39	68.24
Crowley	68.57	115.99	87.77	133.45	88.92	131.43	84.65	121.97
Custer	35.80	45.03	47.56	75.30	41.75	67.75	59.03	76.00
Delta	45.68	64.86	49.92	78.11	60.52	106.30	60.24	76.82
Denver	57.98	77.93	82.60	117.74	92.24	140.96	90.43	148.38
Dolores	30.85	48.39	39.92	73.14	.....	......	.....	......
Douglas	79.10	119.05	67.64	77.15	80.03	118.83	99.99	141.85
Eagle	61.41	64.06	85.20	99.17	70.51	94.19	96.93	111.85
Elbert	58.77	91.01	61.21	92.51	110.73	144.72	78.00	102.28
El Paso	65.16	76.19	85.88	139.44	92.46	129.56	121.97	160.60
Fremont	51.09	71.43	55.72	72.28	64.91	84.55	70.32	90.07
Garfield	32.12	53.01	50.89	107.03	73.62	116.57	83.01	112.54
Gilpin	112.45	150.15	121.55	251.78	106.02	136.78	161.80	190.06
Grand	57.25	82.92	70.40	106.07	64.64	78.87	71.45	85.78
Gunnison	49.50	74.61	56.37	82.78	76.01	97.77	70.34	93.72
Hinsdale	81.93	105.79	118.03	127.48	84.22	156.09	83.84	99.85
Huerfano	40.64	64.34	52.75	90.22	62.64	98.60	62.24	77.29
Jackson	72.02	119.80	93.63	126.45	114.34	144.96	114.26	164.16
Jefferson	63.42	89.75	56.47	68.54	62.84	81.07	65.01	85.55
Kiowa	52.07	75.32	131.76	224.23	117.56	154.13	140.69	176.83
Kit Carson	61.29	79.30	70.72	85.60	105.81	151.20	95.67	130.66
Lake	72.21	93.48	82.20	100.70	82.21	99.03	87.48	96.27
La Plata	61.96	98.14	59.56	74.92	68.06	96.61	80.07	127.87
Larimer	57.64	84.96	67.89	91.38	83.64	112.80	81.11	106.60
Las Animas	35.16	59.58	46.45	72.51	44.93	65.39	62.23	89.74
Lincoln	62.99	83.96	91.44	118.53	78.52	105.40	86.34	116.23
Logan	73.61	133.04	68.32	104.19	86.04	126.34	98.58	153.15
Mesa	48.78	69.03	67.78	89.65	56.25	73.81	66.54	88.03
Mineral	40.43	58.16	105.37	112.84	62.13	76.63	86.95	98.26
Moffat	64.66	94.98	83.02	121.06	77.91	101.04	83.42	......
Montezuma	43.64	72.52	57.13	82.36	73.75	97.78	60.22	89.79
Montrose	41.21	70.92	53.15	91.99	55.60	79.63	81.28	113.74
Morgan	50.23	80.09	79.17	115.77	66.09	82.11	68.54	105.38
Otero	49.94	74.37	56.59	76.54	70.56	93.91	76.36	103.31
Ouray	57.25	73.78	48.71	74.45	48.44	79.03	51.14	65.55
Park	88.39	112.52	96.63	127.06	128.98	208.31	118.45	154.83
Phillips	157.43	234.81	66.55	113.36	87.23	95.50	109.87	136.41
Pitkin	71.77	85.88	57.51	65.59	58.04	67.37	72.00	90.66
Prowers	56.46	96.94	55.76	81.20	63.94	133.16	70.49	102.51
Pueblo	52.04	79.54	69.94	102.46	76.43	106.53	83.73	122.14
Rio Blanco	69.12	108.56	70.65	114.71	56.40	76.74	93.90	119.80
Rio Grande	57.08	87.44	76.91	95.85	117.65	169.73	106.86	136.65
Routt	72.60	111.88	91.01	122.06	82.44	114.78	92.22	131.68
Saguache	143.09	217.35	85.76	121.63	96.51	142.69	88.08	122.97
San Juan	106.65	149.00	105.55	135.37	113.16	161.15	120.41	137.61
San Miguel	72.00	102.15	76.61	125.36	101.48	128.76	81.19	108.15
Sedgwick	51.34	73.62	69.40	184.20	78.85	139.20	96.76	166.41
Summit	106.63	150.77	114.47	171.89	132.95	168.26	130.18	170.40
Teller	90.69	113.12	95.43	127.33	83.34	92.71	76.04	90.86
Washington	64.04	96.42	46.15	64.72	82.78	116.38	102.45	132.05
Weld	75.94	111.83	96.06	139.46	87.09	125.19	76.76	106.89
Yuma	44.28	72.68	48.22	76.79	62.79	88.90	77.60	101.44
State	$57.85	$88.48	$70.56	$97.97	$80.57	$114.88	$83.53	$119.59

AVERAGE MONTHLY SALARIES OF TEACHERS IN PUBLIC SCHOOLS

(From Records of State Superintendent of Schools)

COUNTY	MEN					WOMEN				
	In High Schools	In One Teacher Schools	In Two Teacher Schools	In Three Teacher Schools	In Junior High Schools	In High Schools	In One Teacher Schools	In Two Teacher Schools	In Three Teacher Schools	In Junior High Schools
Adams	$162.88	$102.05	$123.06	$160.00	$160.00	$127.69	$ 98.10	$108.85	$105.05	$155.55
Alamosa	157.71	75.00	100.00	130.67	......	122.92	104.00	117.69	99.93	108.33
Arapahoe	171.94	93.00	127.77	122.91	175.00	131.81	96.60	107.35	112.02	123.60
Archuleta	181.11	85.00	......	......	125.00	140.00	90.00	100.00	117.50	......
Baca	162.50	103.38	128.50	126.66	......	150.00	101.93	116.62	96.58	......
Bent	172.67	98.75	144.43	112.50	......	137.92	98.10	120.66	95.78	......
Boulder	193.66	113.33	105.00	140.76	244.45	152.81	102.30	104.86	115.88	141.32
Chaffee	216.50	93.00	......	......	......	132.16	90.25	......	130.50	......
Cheyenne	......	105.86	125.00	100.00	......	......	103.14	110.37	110.68	......
Clear Creek	157.03	......	......	......	......	119.00	93.96	120.00	109.37	......
Conejos	200.47	90.00	95.00	106.90	115.00	139.50	90.00	97.50	98.30	125.00
Costilla	175.54	80.00	86.50	144.29	......	122.22	85.00	92.44	96.25	......
Crowley	193.88	111.66	......	75.00	194.44	137.06	97.50	......	110.27	134.66
Custer	166.66	......	112.50	......	......	137.50	83.77	87.50	......	......
Delta	190.91	100.00	......	150.00	187.50	128.19	97.90	102.42	109.50	121.60
Denver	188.33	......	125.06	139.91	141.91	186.50	......	156.00	160.00	159.00
Dolores	......	......	......	......	......	......	......	......	......	......
Douglas	......	89.03	......	194.44	......	......	86.80	120.00	122.96	......
Eagle	176.04	100.00	100.00	106.25	......	110.56	89.80	108.75	101.03	......
Elbert	186.80	88.95	......	155.00	......	139.58	87.27	......	115.13	......
El Paso	190.50	117.03	137.46	126.95	188.29	169.65	97.03	126.62	133.43	154.20
Fremont	169.20	......	90.00	138.00	172.00	138.60	95.00	105.00	113.00	134.00
Garfield	176.10	90.00	111.80	143.75	93.75	120.56	94.60	98.14	109.31	130.00
Gilpin	......	......	140.00	88.89	......	......	86.67	104.13	101.22	......
Grand	200.00	92.50	140.00	125.00	......	125.00	87.60	121.66	111.11	......
Gunnison	157.49	93.00	113.00	150.00	125.00	130.00	80.00	103.75	116.00	135.00
Hinsdale	200.00	......	......	......	......	150.00	91.66	......	125.00	......
Huerfano	......	120.00	127.11	236.66	......	......	97.15	125.28	130.50	......
Jackson	......	......	125.00	......	......	......	97.40	87.50	......	......
Jefferson	160.00	93.00	......	104.04	150.00	116.00	90.00	90.00	95.00	104.50

Kiowa	167.20	111.22	......	105.55	......	121.40	103.73	94.38	105.90	......
Kit Carson	189.56	102.40	120.00	143.75	166.85	140.93	97.16	116.00	113.24	139.09
Lake	163.92	......	......	150.21	......	132.41	94.37	75.00	106.25	......
La Plata	210.00	100.00	......	160.00	210.00	112.57	97.75	109.84	111.45	146.21
Larimer	214.10	139.16	108.33	138.77	......	164.16	87.21	106.16	124.16	......
Las Animas	175.47	102.45	129.44	148.36	155.20	126.87	100.06	105.75	112.95	110.87
Lincoln	164.81	95.00	107.50	133.33	133.33	128.80	95.80	95.00	118.07	120.00
Logan	146.96	100.00	133.33	125.00	......	125.14	98.77	120.00	112.56	......
Mesa	162.98	85.00	112.50	145.04	168.70	132.92	89.00	99.23	101.25	130.12
Mineral	......	......	......	160.00	......	......	100.00	......	111.11	......
Moffat	122.22	100.00	95.00	95.00	......	100.00	87.50	95.00	95.00	......
Montezuma	206.33	110.00	107.50	142.71	......	135.78	100.22	102.50	115.73	130.60
Montrose	......	156.09	112.50	145.83	......	......	100.04	111.50	117.13	......
Morgan	165.59	80.42	85.00	108.33	142.00	114.93	73.00	76.01	86.46	100.69
Otero	198.29	106.85	130.00	152.77	186.11	155.09	100.51	115.00	118.43	143.98
Ouray	......	90.00	......	177.77	......	......	88.75	......	113.51	......
Park	185.00	......	180.00	195.00	......	125.00	85.00	120.00	125.00	......
Phillips	143.48	111.31	105.00	147.45	......	119.48	103.00	102.50	110.00	......
Pitkin	191.60	......	105.00	......	105.00	150.00	90.00	95.00	96.66	105.00
Prowers	159.72	97.22	120.92	155.00	144.44	123.39	95.00	101.66	102.27	119.97
Pueblo	176.79	105.66	125.00	112.50	186.00	144.87	103.33	125.00	115.81	155.55
Rio Blanco	158.33	100.04	......	104.16	......	116.66	85.00	......	87.99	......
Rio Grande	246.30	......	......	......	155.55	135.78	112.50	......	137.50	162.22
Routt	182.22	105.00	175.00	112.50	175.00	138.33	95.43	115.85	108.66	118.75
Saguache	166.66	107.36	......	110.83	200.00	141.88	86.00	111.25	99.67	112.50
San Juan	175.00	......	......	......	......	130.00	115.00	......	87.50	......
San Miguel	168.60	100.00	......	......	......	118.89	82.45	......	100.68	......
Sedgwick	......	......	90.00	175.00	......	......	95.55	110.00	110.00	......
Summit	192.50	91.66	125.00	......	......	127.50	103.50	100.00	125.00	......
Teller	125.00	......	100.00	121.87	......	116.00	85.57	94.22	88.58	107.00
Washington	......	99.73	......	174.30	......	......	101.74	110.00	106.93	......
Weld	212.50	97.08	140.47	137.39	171.56	151.62	102.37	114.90	118.31	143.55
Yuma	216.66	102.17	113.76	204.16	......	173.15	85.07	98.25	110.69	163.33
State	$177.87	$100.63	$118.53	$138.46	$161.93	$136.11	$ 94.32	$106.79	$110.60	$130.87

SCHOOL DISTRICT BONDS ISSUED AND OUTSTANDING JANUARY 1, 1924

COUNTY	Number of Dist's Having School Bonds Outstanding	Total Number of Issues	Amount Issued	Amount Redeemed	Amount Outstanding
Adams	17	27	$ 359,000	$ 7,000	$ 352 000
Alamosa	5	9	196,700	2,000	194,700
Arapahoe	11	13	328,800	2,000	326,800
Archuleta	5	7	11,400	500	10,900
Baca	15	17	62,350	11,500	50,850
Bent	12	13	80,700	6 000	74,700
Boulder	26	43	646,100	12,200	633,900
Chaffee	2	3	136,200	......	136,200
Cheyenne	3	4	253,000	......	253,000
Clear Creek	...	...	....	......	....
Conejos	15	21	127,800	......	127,000
Costilla	13	19	95,300	......	95,300
Crowley	9	15	416,000	13,500	402,500
Custer	...	...	....	......	....
Delta	14	24	335,650	15,000	320,650
Denver	1	3	4,350,000	......	4,350,000
Dolores	1	1	2,500	......	2,500
Douglas	2	2	11,500	3,000	8,500
Eagle	4	5	43,800	1,250	42,550
Elbert	7	24	138,100	3,500	134,600
El Paso	12	20	1,067,500	224,000	843,500
Fremont	11	15	300,600	21,500	279,100
Garfield	18	26	458,820	......	458,820
Gilpin	...	...	....	......	....
Grand	4	4	29,300	......	29,300
Gunnison	4	4	61,800	3,000	58 800
Hinsdale	...	...	....	......	....
Huerfano	7	8	40,800	......	40,800
Jackson	...	...	....	......	....
Jefferson	11	15	421,200	3,000	418,200
Kiowa	6	6	93,600	......	93,600
Kit Carson	22	30	289,000	......	289,000
Lake	...	...	....	......	....
La Plata	17	21	254,900	2,400	252,500
Larimer	17	31	760 000	......	760,000
Las Animas	30	37	544 800	24,000	520,800
Lincoln	10	22	225,600	......	225 600
Logan	29	53	574,800	11,800	563,000
Mesa	22	33	477,650	......	477,650
Mineral	...	...	....	......	....
Moffat	3	4	81,000	......	81,000
Montezuma	8	14	86,500	1,500	85 000
Montrose	19	28	171,200	500	170,700
Morgan	11	26	386,900	12,000	374,900
Otero	18	29	700 900	32,500	668,400
Ouray	2	2	4,700	500	4 200
Park	1	1	12,000	......	12,000
Phillips	21	27	216,200	......	216,200
Pitkin	1	1	1,500	......	1 500
Prowers	21	32	395,600	1,200	394,400
Pueblo	22	43	1,284,400	57,500	1,226,900
Rio Blanco	4	6	55,500	......	55,500
Rio Grande	8	13	486 300	......	486 300
Routt	10	19	266,200	......	266,200
Saguache	3	3	68,000	......	68,000
San Juan	1	1	60,000	5,000	55,000
San Miguel	8	8	61,800	3,500	58,300
Sedgwick	14	21	116,000	......	116,000
Summit	1	1	35,000	......	35,000
Teller	...	...	....	......	....
Washington	19	27	199,100	......	199,100
Weld	72	72	2,610,400	......	2,610,400
Yuma	21	28	360,000	......	360,000
State	670	981	$20 854,470	$481,350	$20,373,120

COUNTY	COUNTY BONDS Total Issued	COUNTY BONDS Amount Redeemed	COUNTY BONDS Amount Outstanding	MUNICIPAL BONDS Total Issued	MUNICIPAL BONDS Amount Redeemed	MUNICIPAL BONDS Amount Outstanding	SCHOOL DISTRICT BONDS Total Issued	SCHOOL DISTRICT BONDS Amount Redeemed	SCHOOL DISTRICT BONDS Amount Outstanding	TOTAL BONDS Total Issued	TOTAL BONDS Amount Redeemed	TOTAL BONDS Amount Outstanding
Adams	$	$	$	$ 825,000.00	$	$ 825,000.00	$ 359,000.00	$ 7,000.00	$ 352,000.00	$ 1,184,000.00	$ 7,000.00	$ 1,177,000.00
Alamosa	61,700	4,500	57,200	133,000.00	....	133,000.00	196,700.00	2,000.00	194,700.00	391,400.00	6 500.00	384 900.00
Arapahoe	....	....	....	483,466.98	47,500.00	435,966.98	328,800.00	2,000.00	326,800.00	812,266.98	49,500.00	762,766.98
Archuleta	....	....	....	17,500.00	....	17,500.00	11,400.00	500.00	10,900.00	28,900.00	500.00	28,400.00
Baca	29,500	3,000	26,500	....	....	....	62,350.00	11,500.00	50,850.00	91,850.00	14,500.00	77,350.00
Bent	35,000	7,000	28,000	125,000.00	48,500.00	76 500.00	80,700.00	6,000.00	74,700.00	240,700.00	61,500.00	179,200.00
Boulder	....	....	....	2,463,880.00	240,780.00	2,223,100.00	646,100.00	12,200.00	633,900.00	3,109,980.00	252,980.00	2,857,000.00
Chaffee	221,000	....	221,000	70 000.00	57,500.00	12,500.00	136,200.00	....	136,200.00	427,200.00	57,500.00	369,700.00
Cheyenne	....	....	....	94 000.00	....	94 000.00	253 000.00	....	253,000.00	347,000.00	....	347 000.00
Clear Creek	....	....	....	51,500.00	10,000.00	41,500.00	....	....	....	51,500.00	10,000.00	41,500.00
Conejos	35,800	3,300	32,500	88,000.00	....	88,000.00	127,800.00	....	127,800.00	251,600.00	3,300.00	248,300.00
Costilla	26,000	24 500	1,500	....	....	....	95,300.00	....	95,300.00	121,300.00	24,500.00	96,800.00
Crowley	....	....	....	123,981.41	23,281.41	100,700.00	416,000.00	13,500.00	402,500.00	539,981.41	36,781.41	503,200.00
Custer	25,000	....	25,000	....	....	....	....	....	....	25,000.00	....	25,000.00
Delta	27,000	....	27,000	507,200.00	1,500.00	505,700.00	335,650.00	15,000.00	320,650.00	869,850.00	16 500.00	853 350.00
Denver	....	....	....	18,695,600.00	....	18,695,600.00	4,350,000.00	....	4,350 000.00	23,045 600.00	....	23,045,600.00
Dolores	87,000	....	87,000	10,000.00	4 00 .0	6 000.00	2,500.00	....	2,500.00	99,500.00	4,000.00	95,500.00
Douglas	....	....	....	75 000.00	300 0.0	72,000.00	11,500.00	3,000.00	8,500.00	86,500.00	6,000.00	80,500.00
Eagle	....	....	....	84,000.00	12,500.00	71,500.00	43 800.00	1,250.00	42,550.00	127,800.00	13,750.00	114,050.00
Elbert	....	....	....	66,100.00	3,000.00	63,100.00	138,100.00	3,500.00	134,600.00	204,200.00	6,500.00	197,700.00
El Paso	....	....	....	3,273,600.00	15,000.00	3,258,600.00	1,067,500.00	224,000.00	843,500.00	4,341 100.00	239,000.00	4,102,100.00
Fremont	....	....	....	642,227.65	146,777.65	495,450.00	300,600.00	21,500.00	279,100.00	942,827.65	168 277.65	774,550.00
Garfield	218,500	....	218,500	523 088.00	45 000.00	478,088.00	458,820.00	....	458,820.00	1,200,408.00	45,000.00	1,155,408.00
Gilpin	....	....	....	98 500.00	10 50 .0	88,000.00	....	....	....	98,500.00	10,500.00	88,000.00
Grand	....	....	....	10,500.00	1,500.00	9,000.00	29,300.00	....	29,300.00	39,800.00	1,500.00	38,300.00
Gunnison	402,000	24,000	378,000	160,000.00	4,100.00	155,900.00	61,800.00	3,000.00	58,800.00	623,800.00	31,100.00	592,700.00
Hinsdale	*173,030	....	*173,030	24,000.00	1,000.00	23,000.00	....	....	....	197,030.00	1 000.00	196 030.00
Huerfano	114,000	12,000	102,000	878,000.00	61,500.00	816,500.00	40,800.00	....	40,800.00	1,032,800.00	73,500.00	959,300.00
Jackson	14,000	....	14,000	20 000.00	900.00	19 100.00	....	....	....	34,000.00	900.00	33,100.00
Jefferson	....	....	....	711,015.00	98,700.00	612,315.00	421 200.00	3,000.00	418,200.00	1,132,215.00	101,700.00	1,030,515.00
Kiowa	....	....	....	76,000.00	....	76,000.00	93,600.00	....	93,600.00	169,600.00	....	169,600.00
Kit Carson	....	....	....	484,200.00	....	484,200.00	289,000.00	....	289,000.00	773,200.00	....	773,200.00
Lake	....	....	....	....	....	....	....	....	....	....	....	....
La Plata	120,000	20,000	100,000	283 700.00	31,400.00	252,300.00	254,900.00	2 400.00	252 500.00	658,600.00	53,800.00	604,800.00
Larimer	....	....	....	1 522 667.83	438,110.80	1,084 557.03	760,000.00	....	760,000.00	2 282,667.83	438,110.80	1 844,557.03
Las Animas	155,000	63,000	92,000	2,347,700.00	283,800.00	2 063,900.00	544,800.00	24,000.00	520,800.00	3,047,500.00	370,800.00	2,676,700.00
Lincoln	90 000	....	90,000	260,700.00	800 0.0	252,700.00	225,600.00	....	225,600.00	576,300.00	8,000.00	568,300.00
Logan	125,000	16,000	109,000	1,413,000.00	80,500.00	1,332,500.00	574,800.00	11,800.00	563,000.00	2,112,800.00	108,300.00	2,004 500.00
Mesa	150,000	....	150,000	2,227,200.00	194 5500	2,032,650.00	477,650.00	....	477,650.00	2,854,850.00	194,550.00	2,660,300.00
Mineral	2,000	....	2000	....	....	....	....	....	....	2,000.00	....	2 000.00
Moffat	40,000	....	40,000	90,000.00	16 000.00	74,000.00	81 000.00	....	81,000.00	211,000.00	16,000.00	195,000.00
Montezuma	....	....	....	136 300.00	32 500.00	103,800.00	86,500.00	1,500.00	85,000.00	222,800.00	34,000.00	188,800.00
Montrose	280,000	22,000	258,000	449,782.20	53,482.20	396,300.00	171 200.00	500.00	170 700.00	900,982.20	75,982.20	825 000.00
Morgan	....	....	....	1,030,230.61	221,612.00	808,618.61	386,900.00	12,000.00	374,900.00	1,417,130.61	233,612.00	1,183,518.61
Otero	....	....	....	834,994.40	114,000.00	720,994.40	700,900.00	32,500.00	668,400.00	1 535,894.40	146,500.00	1,389 394.40
Ouray	140,000	10,000	1300 (	59,880.00	35 00 .00	24,880.00	4,700.00	500.00	4,200.00	204,580.00	45,500.00	159,080.00
Park	....	....	....	....	....	....	12,000.00	....	12,000.00	12,000.00	....	12,000.00
Phillips	102,000	....	102,000	397 500.00	12,000.00	385 500.00	216,200.00	....	216,200.00	715,700.00	12,000.00	703,700.00
Pitkin	330,000	105 000	225 000	85 800.00	....	85,800.00	1 500.00	....	1,500.00	417,300.00	105,000.00	312,300.00
Prowers	....	....	....	836,700.00	11,500.00	825,200.00	395 600.00	1,200.00	394,400.00	1,232,300.00	12 700.00	1,219,600.00
Pueblo	350,000	100,000	250,000	4,358,300.00	....	4,358,300.00	1,284 400.00	57,500.00	1,226,900.00	5,992,700.00	157,500.00	5,835,200.00
Rio Blanco	85,000	5,000	80,000	74,200.00	7,500.00	66 700.00	55 500.00	....	55,500.00	214,700.00	12,500.00	202,200.00
Rio Grande	175,000	24,000	151,000	111 800.00	1,500.00	110 300.00	486,300.00	....	486,300.00	773,100.00	25 500.00	747,600.00
Routt	94,000	....	94,000	318,625.54	68,700.00	249,925.54	266,200.00	....	266,200.00	678,825.54	68,700.00	610,125.54
Saguache	....	....	....	52 100.00	....	52,100.00	68,000.00	....	68,000.00	120,100.00	....	120,100.00
San Juan	168,000	24,000	140( )	20,000.00	4,000.00	16,000.00	60,000.00	5,000.00	55,000.00	248,000.00	33 000.00	215,000.00
San Miguel	90 000	48,600	41,400	26,000.00	8,000.00	18,000.00	61,800.00	3,500.00	58,300.00	177,800.00	60,100.00	117,700.00
Sedgwick	213,000	....	213,000	242 500.00	6,000.00	236 500.00	116 000.00	....	116,000.00	571,500.00	6,000.00	565 500.00
Summit	....	....	....	17,000.00	....	17,000.00	35,000.00	....	35,000.00	52,000.00	....	52,000.00
Teller	....	....	....	652,100.00	60,500.00	591,600.00	....	....	....	652,100.00	60 500.00	591,600.00
Washington	....	....	....	135 000.00	9 500.00	125 500.00	199 100.00	....	199,100.00	334 100.00	9 500.00	324 600.00
Weld	....	....	....	1,316,454.50	153,500.00	1,162,954.50	2,610,400.00	....	2,610,400.00	3,926,854.50	153,500.00	3,773,354.50
Yuma	....	....	....	486,700.00	18,000.00	468,700.00	360,000.00	....	360,000.00	846,700.00	18,000.00	828,700.00
State	$4,178,530	$ 515,900	$3,662,630	$50,601,294.12	$ 2,706,194.06	$47,895,100.06	$20,854,470.00	$ 481,350.00	$20,373,120.00	$75,634,294.12	$ 3,703,444.06	$71,930,850.06

NOTE—This table, which constitutes the first tabulation of the bonded public debt of all of the tax-levying subdivisions of Colorado, was prepared by the State Board of Immigration with the co-operation of county and city and town clerks and treasurers, and is believed to be complete in all respects. The outstanding bonded debt of the state as of June 1, 1924, which is not included in the above total, was $10,536,500, and at the same time there were large amounts outstanding in two large legally created districts—the Moffat Tunnel district and the Pueblo Conservancy district. In the former district, which was formed for the purpose of financing construction of a railroad tunnel to improve transportation facilities in northwestern Colorado, the total authorized issue of $6,700,000 has been sold and is outstanding, and in the latter district the authorized issue of $3,600,000, floated for the purpose of financing flood protection works and bearing date of January 1, 1924, is outstanding. The tabulation does not include irrigation and drainage district bonds for the reason that these are not general public debts but are more in the nature of business debts. Municipals, by which is meant city and town bonds, do not include floating debt such as outstanding warrants and the like, but do include bonds issued by local improvement districts.

COUNTY BONDS OUTSTANDING JANUARY 1, 1924

COUNTY	Funding and Refunding	Schools	Public Building	Miscellaneous	Tot'l Bonds Issued	Amount Redeemed	Amount Outstanding
Adams	$	$	$	$	$	$	$
Alamosa	61,700				61,700	4,500	57,200
Arapahoe							
Archuleta							
Baca	29,500				29,500	3,000	26,500
Bent		35,000			35,000	7,000	28,000
Boulder							
Chaffee	221,000				221,000		221,000
Cheyenne							
Clear Creek							
Conejos	35,800				35,800	3,300	32,500
Costilla	26,000				26,000	24,500	1,500
Crowley							
Custer		25,000			25,000		25,000
Delta	24,000			3,000	27,000		27,000
Denver*							
Dolores	87,000				87,000		87,000
Douglas							
Eagle							
Elbert							
El Paso							
Fremont							
Garfield	218,500				218,500		218,500
Gilpin							
Grand							
Gunnison	252,000	150,000			402,000	24,000	378,000
Hinsdale	173,030				173,030		173,030
Huerfano	24,000	90,000			114,000	12,000	102,000
Jackson			14,000		14,000		14,000
Jefferson							
Kiowa							
Kit Carson							
Lake							
La Plata	120,000				120,000	20,000	100,000
Larimer							
Las Animas	155,000				155,000	63,000	92,000
Lincoln			90,000		90,000		90,000
Logan		85,000	40,000		125,000	16,000	109,000
Mesa			150,000		150,000		150,000
Mineral		2,000			2,000		2,000
Moffat			40,000		40,000		40,000
Montezuma							
Montrose	144,000	38,000	98,000		280,000	22,000	258,000
Morgan							
Otero							
Ouray	140,000				140,000	10,000	130,000
Park							
Phillips	42,000	60,000			102,000		102,000
Pitkin	330,000				330,000	105,000	225,000
Prowers							
Pueblo	350,000				350,000	100,000	250,000
Rio Blanco		85,000			85,000	5,000	80,000
Rio Grande	80,000	95,000			175,000	24,000	151,000
Routt			94,000		94,000		94,000
Saguache							
San Juan	168,000				168,000	24,000	144,000
San Miguel	90,000				90,000	48,600	41,400
Sedgwick	213,000				213 000		213,000
Summit							
Teller							
Washington							
Weld							
Yuma							
State	$2,984,530	$665,000	$526,000	$ 3,000	$4,178,530	$ 515,900	$3,662,630

*Although Denver is a county by itself, its bond issues are municipal rather than county and are so listed on page 168A.

MINE PRODUCTION OF GOLD, SILVER, COPPER, LEAD AND ZINC IN COLORADO IN 1922

(U. S. Geological Survey)

COUNTY	Gold		Silver		Copper		Lead		Zinc		Total Value
	Fine Ounces	Value	Fine Ounces	Value	Pounds	Value,	Pounds	Value	Pounds	Value	
Boulder	2,276	$ 47,049	120,687	$ 120,687	......	$	87,000	$ 4,785	....	$	$ 172,521
Chaffee	969	20,031	26,187	26,187	20,000	2,700	652,000	35,860	177,000	10,089	94,867
Clear Creek	1,789	36,982	196,222	196,222	14,000	1,890	957,000	52,635	800,000	45,600	333,329
Custer	9	186	14,520	14,520	32,000	4,320	397,509	21,863	....	....	40,889
Dolores	79	1,633	28,994	28,994	24,000	3,240	85,600	4,708	....	....	38,575
Eagle	3,489	72,124	583,737	583,737	1,600,000	216,000	308,000	16,940	11,000,000	627,000	1,515,801
Fremont	30	620	177	177	......	......	....	....	....	....	797
Gilpin	2,514	51,969	43,910	43,910	24,000	3,240	240,000	13,200	....	....	112,319
Gunnison	448	9,261	3,808	3,808	......	......	13,291	731	....	....	13,800
Hinsdale	64	1,323	50,100	50,100	14,000	1,890	112,000	6,160	....	....	59,473
Lake	19,734	407,938	952,000	952,000	870,000	117,450	5,000,000	275,000	9,000,000	513,000	2,265,388
La Plata	1,563	32,310	10,700	10,700	......	......	....	....	....	....	43,010
Mineral	79	1,633	119,000	119,000	......	......	167,000	9,185	....	....	129,818
Montrose	......	......	17,000	17,000	62,304	8,411	....	....	....	....	25,411
Ouray	3,340	69,044	533,300	533,300	55,000	7,425	1,450,000	79,750	....	....	689,519
Park	6,853	141,664	15,530	15,530	......	......	153,000	8,415	....	....	165,609
Pitkin	......	......	525,200	525,200	......	......	3,500,000	192,500	....	....	717,700
Routt	......	......	82	82	......	......	....	....	....	....	82
Saguache	238	4,920	63,500	63,500	42,000	5,670	110,000	6,050	....	....	80,140
San Juan	1,243	25,695	77,634	77,634	110,000	14,850	1,600,000	88,000	1,300,000	74,100	280,279
San Miguel	55,658	1,150,553	2,283,000	2,283,000	660,000	89,100	6,900,000	379,500	....	....	3,902,153
Summit	13,609	281,323	118,000	118,000	94,000	12,690	415,000	22,825	677,000	38,589	473,427
Teller	195,999	4,051,659	25,900	25,900	......	......	....	....	....	....	4,077,559
Total, 1922	309,983	$6,407,917	5,809,188	$5,809,188	3,621,304	$ 488,876	22,147,400	$ 1,218,107	22,954,000	$ 1,308,378	$15,232,466
Total, 1921	330,659	6,835,328	5,631,657	5,631,657	4,153,442	535,794	19,660,466	884,721	2,360,000	118,000	14,005,500
Increase or decrease, 1922	—20,676	—427,411	+177,531	+177,531	—532,138	—46,918	+2,486,934	+333,386	+20,594,000	+1,190,378	+1,226,966

TOTAL PRODUCTION OF GOLD, SILVER, LEAD, COPPER AND ZINC IN COLORADO TO THE END OF 1922

(U. S. Geological Survey)

COUNTY	Gold	Silver		Lead		Copper		Zinc		TOTAL
	Value	Fine Ounces	Value	Pounds	Value	Pounds	Value	Pounds	Value	
[illegible]oe, [illegible]8-1904	$ 8,101	101	$ 64	....	$	....	$	....	$	$ 8,165
Archuleta, [illegible]-1904	1,489	505	302	....	....	....	....	....	....	1,791
[illegible]a, [illegible]0-1919	295	413	273	....	....	....	....	....	....	568
[illegible]r, [illegible]8-1922	15,991,149	8,266,791	7,755,289	7,092,809	399,670	1,004,215	157,885	....	....	24,303,993
[illegible]ee, [illegible]9-1922	7,523,564	5,348,642	4,338,782	132,054,040	5,894,327	398,894	1,947,116	29,600,020	2,612,601	22,316,390
[illegible] [illegible]ek, [illegible]9-1922	22,955,719	58,133,723	52,828,140	181,890,569	8,450,973	2,608,905	2,107,591	33,424,833	2,521,500	88,863,923
Conejos, [illegible]-1915	38,445	55,823	33,278	3,400	149	4,815	797	....	....	72,669
[illegible]la, [illegible]-1914; [illegible]	43,468	2,715	1,592	50,048	1,802	1,827	239	....	....	47,101
[illegible]ter, [illegible]-1922	2,190,768	4,601,036	4,593,690	31,643,847	1,392,611	625,662	129,884	217,227	14,787	8,[illegible]
e[illegible]a, [illegible]-1915	4,273	306	175	....	....	....	....	....	....	4,449
[illegible]es, [illegible]-1922	1,979,596	11,719,244	9,238,923	38,659,701	1,806,621	6,657,887	1,274,394	12,282,642	887,371	15,[illegible]
[illegible]s, [illegible]-1915; 1921	4,497	161	128	....	....	....	....	....	....	[illegible]
[illegible]a, [illegible]-1922	2,404,028	7,430,399	6,375,103	89,246,649	4,060,705	6,542,244	996,968	154,770,791	14,604,000	28,440,804
El [illegible]o, [illegible]-1914	....	....	....	....	....	13,276	2,000	....	....	2,000
Fremont, [illegible]-1922	82,300	90,992	85,897	678,713	28,479	726,663	136,751	1,432,769	104,333	437,760
[illegible]ld, [illegible]8-1919	16,924	528	327	....	....	1,044	153	....	....	17,404
[illegible]in, [illegible]-1922	84,356,434	10,595,866	8,608,923	35,931,783	2,605,958	25,740,616	4,279,074	626,956	52,656	99,903,045
[illegible]d, [illegible]-1896; [illegible]-1920	13,265	3,305	2,449	18,078	1,019	5,171	805	....	....	17,538
[illegible]n, [illegible]- [illegible]8; 1922	1,212,126	5,450,935	4,916,773	1,074,981	82,716	15,333	997	3,739,555	278,606	6,491,218
[illegible]le, [illegible]- [illegible]8; [illegible]	1,444,856	5,628,942	4,560,609	97,442,735	4,010,598	2,858,411	403,283	1,108,151	58,348	10,477,694
Huerfano, [illegible]- 185; 1907	3,474	1,176	698	1,067	38	92	11	....	....	4,221
[illegible]n, [illegible]8-1885; [illegible]	62,296	7,049	4,622	10,863	398	19,695	3,100	....	....	70 416
Lake, [illegible]-1922	52,094,569	232,073,874	190,726,524	1,938,084,095	86,700,478	101,725,288	14,842,562	1,299,972,574	91,843,498	436,207,631
La Plata and Montezuma, 1878-1922	3,600,986	1,753,596	1,129,052	261,833	248,873	306,511	52,727	....	....	5,031,638
Larimer and Jackson, 1895-1919	24,891	3,104	2,231	....	....	259,053	45,124	30,722	1,659	73,905
Las Animas, [illegible]-1887; 1899	2,094	20	15	....	....	....	....	....	....	2,109
[illegible]a, [illegible]-1919	5,040	4,934	2,970	20	1	35,280	5,222	....	....	13,233
[illegible]l, [illegible]-1922	2,731,275	44,692,069	29,286,080	199,421,576	8,851,128	27,534,453	1,511,036	382,779	55,055	42,434,574
Montrose, [illegible]-1922	47,504	202,117	128,286	64	3	537,193	97,242	....	....	[illegible]
Ouray, [illegible]8-1922	35,115,968	40,743,740	31,210,959	160,411,507	7,092,655	24,421,887	3,413,975	1,725,061	154,814	76,988,371
Park, [illegible]-1922	10,948,112	6,945,321	6,900,745	41,373,167	1,851,442	2,044,788	389,413	2,971,532	195,512	20,285,224
[illegible]in, [illegible]-1922	578,035	73,516,341	73,516,341	576,761,832	26,824,706	1,155,866	204,924	16,948,684	1,086,327	102,210,333
[illegible]o, [illegible]-1896; [illegible]-1901	793	90	55	....	....	210	35	....	....	883
Rio [illegible]de, [illegible]-1919	2,263,279	182,328	175,303	49,453	2,283	124,447	20,006	....	....	2,460,871
Routt ard [illegible]at, 1[illegible]6; 1873-1921	392,226	30,285	20,792	139 536	5,205	82,896	17,885	....	....	[illegible]
[illegible]e, [illegible]-1922	272,207	1,549,664	1,549,664	7,900,259	367,483	1,045,104	181,190	1,191,822	76,458	2,[illegible]
San Juan, [illegible]8- [illegible]	22,808,183	28,814,394	28,814,394	320,761,661	15,507,029	50,566,766	8,011,620	45,993,470	3,812,434	78,953,660
San [illegible]. 1875-1922	60,178,638	31,840,035	31,840,035	44,739,022	8 876,830	16,075,039	2,766,086	20,008,096	1,510,853	105,172,442
S[illegible]it, [illegible]-1922	19,484,994	11,720,177	11,720,177	150,528,524	6,610,826	1,184,124	177,055	150,222,646	12,781,170	50,[illegible]
[illegible]er, [illegible]-1922	330,181,668	1,180,571	1,180,571	612	49	451	83	....	....	331,362,371
Miscellaneous [illegible]ll Counties	8,785	1,124	1,141	....	....	....	....	....	....	9,926
State Total	$681,076,314	592,592,436	$511,551,373	4,056,232,444	$191,675,055	274,324,106	$ 43,177,233	1,776,650,330	$132,651,982	$1,560,131,957

NUMBERS ALLOTTED FOR MOTOR VEHICLE LICENSES IN COLORADO IN 1924

(From the Records of the Secretary of State)

COUNTY	Owners	Trucks	Trailers	Dealers	Truck Dealers	Motor Cycles	M. C. Dealers	Drivers	Replacements	Permits	Non-Residents
Adams	100001—104500	6751—7250	156—165	1651—1695	251—255	2501—2575	71—72	6401—6525	4401—4500	13526—13625	11901—12100
Alamosa	105001—106500	7251—7350	166—170	1696—1730	256—260	2576—2595	73—74	6526—6565	4501—4550	13626—13645	12101—12150
Arapahoe	107001—111200	7351—7650	171—180	1731—1780	261—265	2596—2670	75—76	6566—6740	4551—4650	13646—13795	12151—12250
Archuleta	111501—112000	7651—7680	181—185	1781—1790	266—270	2671—2680	77—	6741—6755	4651—4665	13796—13805	12251—12275
Baca	112501—114500	7681—7930	186—190	1791—1805	271—275	2681—2695	78—	6756—6770	4666—4695	13806—13815	12276—12325
Bent	115001—117600	7931—8030	191—195	1806—1835	276—280	2696—2715	79—80	6771—6800	4696—4725	13816—13840	12326—12350
Boulder	118001—125800	8031—8480	196—210	1836—1960	281—285	2716—2890	81—95	6801—7100	4726—4875	13841—14040	12351—12750
Chaffee	127001—128500	8481—8540	211—215	1961—1995	286—290	2891—2915	96—	7101—7125	4876—4905	14041—14090	12751—12800
Cheyenne	129001—130400	8541—8640	216—220	1996—2010	291—295	2916—2925	97—98	7126—7140	4906—4930	14091—14110	12801—12900
Clear Creek	131001—131500	8641—8680	221—225	2011—2015	296—300	2926—2940	99—	7141—7170	4931—4945	14111—14125	12901—12915
Conejos	131801—132800	8681—8740	226—230	2016—2030	301—305	2941—2950	100—	7171—7195	4946—4965	14126—14135	12916—12940
Costilla	132801—133500	8741—8780	231—235	2031—2040	306—310	2951—2960	101—	7196—7215	4966—4985	14136—14145	12941—12960
Crowley	133801—135800	8781—8880	236—240	2041—2065	311—315	2961—2980	102—	7216—7245	4986—5025	14146—14185	12961—12985
Custer	136001—136500	8881—8945	241—245	2066—2070	316—320	2981—2985	103—	7246—7255	5026—5035	14186—14195	12986—13005
Delta	136801—139500	8946—9245	246—255	2071—2145	321—325	2986—3015	104—107	7256—7330	5036—5085	14196—14215	13006—13055
Denver	1—55000	101—4100	1—100	1—1000	101—200	201—1500	1—30	1—4700	1001—3500	1—12500	1001—6000
Dolores	140501—140600	9246—9260	256—260	2146—2150	326—330	3016—3020	108—	7331—7335	5086—5095	14216—14225	13056—13065
Douglas	140701—142100	9261—9335	261—265	2151—2165	331—335	3021—3030	109—	7336—7375	5096—5120	14226—14255	13066—13140
Eagle	142401—143000	9336—9385	266—270	2166—2170	336—340	3031—3040	110—	7376—7400	5121—5130	14256—14265	13141—13160
Elbert	143101—145100	9386—9465	271—275	2171—2205	341—345	3041—3050	111—	7401—7420	5131—5150	14266—14280	[illegible]185
El Paso	55001—65500	4101—4750	101—115	1001—1200	201—215	1501—1775	31—40	4701—5500	3501—3700	12501—12700	6001—11000
Fremont	145501—149700	9466—9790	276—285	2206—2280	346—350	3051—3110	112—113	7421—7495	5151—5225	14281—14340	13186—13285
Garfield	150201—152200	9791—9890	286—295	2281—2315	351—355	3111—3130	114—	7496—7545	5226—5255	14341—14360	13286—13315
Gilpin	153001—153200	9891—9910	296—300	2316—2320	356—360	3131—3135	115—	7546—7555	5256—5270	14361—14370	13316—13325
Grand	153501—154000	9911—9930	301—305	2321—2330	361—365	3136—3140	116—	7556—7575	5271—5290	14371—14380	13326—13365
Gunnison	[illegible]5300	9931—9960	306—310	2331—2345	366—370	3141—3155	117—	7576—7615	5291—5315	14381—14390	13366—13390
Hinsdale	155401—155500	9961—9975	311—315	2346—2350	371—375	3156—3165	118—	7616—7635	5316—5325	14391—14400	13391—13400
Huerfano	155601—158900	9976—10150	316—325	2351—2425	376—380	3166—3190	119—120	7636—7735	5326—5450	14401—14525	13401—13600
Jackson	159601—160100	10151—10180	326—330	2426—2430	381—385	3191—3200	121—	7736—7745	5451—5460	14526—14535	13601—13615
Jefferson	160501—165000	10181—10630	331—340	2431—2480	386—390	3201—3260	122—123	7746—7945	5461—5585	14536—14575	[illegible]5
Kiowa	166001—167300	10631—10715	341—345	2481—2490	391—395	3261—3270	124—	7946—7955	5586—5610	14576—14585	13666—13680
Kit Carson	[illegible]40	10716—11015	346—355	2491—2540	396—400	3271—3300	125—126	7956—8030	5611—5660	14586—14635	13681—13780

Lake	170801—171400	11016—11030	356—360	2541—2565	401—405	33 10—3315	127—128	8031—8070	5661—5675	14636—14650	13781—13795
La Plata	171701—173400	11031—11130	361—365	2566—2630	406—410	3316—3335	129—	8071—8135	5 76—5700	14651—14665	13796—13820
Lnier	91001— 98500	6251— 6750	146—155	1551—1650	241—250	2301—2500	6 —6 70	6201—6400	4301—4400	13451—13525	11651—11900
Las Animas	- 940	11131—11530	366—375	2631—2755	411—415	3336—3460	130—139	8136—8360	5701—5950	14666—14865	13821—14020
Leln	181001—183300	11531—11780	376—380	2756—2795	416—420	3461—3475	140—141	8— 90	5951—5980	14866—14880	14021—14050
Lgan	184001—188600	11781—12155	381—390	2796—2895	421—425	3476—3575	142—146	8391—8465	5981—6130	14881—14955	4414200
Msa	189501—194000	12156—12505	391—400	2896—2995	426—435	3576—3700	147—151	8466—8665	6131—6230	45	14201—14300
Mal	9400	12506—12525	( )4405	2996—3000	436—440	3701—3705	152—	8666—8675	6231—6240	15106—15115	14301—14315
Moffat	194401—195300	12526—12565	406—410	3001—3020	441—445	3706—3715	153—	8676—8700	6241—6265	5— 35	14316—14340
Mzuma	195801—196700	12566—12640	411—415	3021—3045	446—450	3716—3725	154—	8701—8725	6266—6285	15136—15145	14341—14355
Mrose	197001—199500	12641—12840	416—425	3046—3085	451—455	3726—3750	155—	8726—8775	6286—6335	15146—15160	14356—14380
Man	200501—204900	12841— 85	426—435	3086—3145	456—460	3751—3825	156—158	8776—8875	6336—6435	4— 20	14381—14480
ro	206001—211000	13066—13365	436—445	3146—3245	461—465	3826—3925	159—163	8876—8975	6436—6535	15211—15240	14481—14530
Ouray	211801—212200	13366—13385	446—450	3246—3265	466—470	3926—3940	164—	8976—9005	6536—6555	15241—15250	14531—14540
Park	212301—212900	13386—13425	451—455	3266—3275	471—475	3941—3955	165—	9006—9015	6556—6570	15251—15260	14541—14550
Phillips	213101—215500	13426—13700	456—460	3276—3305	476—480	3956—3975	16 0—	9016—9035	6571—6645	15261—15280	14551—14575
Pkin	21 001—2163 0	13701—13710	461—465	3306—3310	481—485	3976—3990	67—	9036—9055	6646—6660	15281—15290	14576—14585
Prowers	216401—219600	13711—13935	466—475	3311—3385	486—490	3991—4010	168—	9056—9115	6661—6735	15291—15320	14586—14685
Pblo	66001— 75100	4751— 5450	116—130	1201—1350	216—230	1776—2025	41— 55	5501—5800	3701—4050	12701—13200	11001— 1100
Rio Bco	220301—220900	13936—13970	476—480	3386—3395	491—495	4011—4015	169—	9116—9135	6736- 6760	15321—15330	14686—14700
Rio Grande	221501—223700	13971—14245	481—485	3396—3435	496—500	4016—4035	170—	9136—9210	6761—6835	15331—15350	14701—14725
Routt	224001—225500	14246—14285	486—490	3436—3475	501—505	4036—4050	17—	9211—9260	8360 860	15351—15365	14726—14750
Sche	225901—227100	14286—14435	491—495	3476—3490	506—510	4051—4065	172—	9261—9300	6861—6890	15366—15380	14751—14775
San Juan	227601—227750	14436—14450	496—500	3491—3495	511—515	4066—4070	173—	9301—9330	6891—6905	15381—15399	14776—14790
San Miguel	227801—228300	14451—14500	501—505	3496—3510	516—520	4071—4110	174—	9331—9380	6906—6930	15391—15400	91—14800
Sedgwick	228801—230300	14501—14650	506—510	3511—3530	521—525	4111—4120	175—	9381—9405	6931—6955	15401—15425	14801—14900
Smit	231001—231300	14651—14665	511—515	3531—3535	526—530	4135	176—	9406—9415	6956- 6970	15426—15435	14901—14915
Teller	231601—232800	14666—14740	516—520	3536—3550	531—535	4136—4160	17—	9416—9465	971—6995	15436—15475	14916—14940
Washington	233001—236200	14741—15190	521—530	3551—3590	536—540	45	178—179	9466—9490	6996—7045	45	14941—14965
Wld	77001— 89600	5451— 6250	131—145	1351—1550	231—240	2026—2300	56— 65	4— 00	4051—4300	13201—13450	11401— 1650
Yuma	237301—240800	15191—15740	531—540	3591—3640	4— 55	4186—4210	180—	94-9540	7046—7120	15536—15560	14966—15015

MOTOR VEHICLE REGISTRATION AND FEES COLLECTED FOR 1923

(From the Records of the Secretary of State)

COUNTY	Owners	Trucks and Trailers	Dealers	Truck Deal's	Motor Cycles	M. C. Deal's	Drivers	Re-Issues	Re-place-ments	Permits	Spc. Eng. No.	Fees Collected
Adams	3 558	489	26	...	43	...	119	406	79	90	19	$ 23,693.3
Alamosa	1,237	75	25	...	11	...	21	95	28	10	2	7,377.9
Arapahoe	3,471	272	39	1	49	...	138	365	84	157	7	21,056.7
Archuleta	283	17	4	...	3	...	7	21	1	....	...	1,471.9
Baca	1,275	203	3	...	5	...	2	64	21	4	22	8 202.1
Bent	1,605	55	9	...	6	...	10	112	25	5	3	8,615.8
Boulder	7,348	376	98	...	112	6	296	834	148	169	26	45,223.1
Chaffee	1,176	47	27	...	15	...	18	125	23	41	3	6,868.6
Cheyenne	405	79	9	...	2	...	12	52	3	13	4	5,002.4
Clear Creek	302	25	....	...	5	...	24	26	3	7	...	1,929.7
Conejos	780	37	5	...	2	...	11	38	5	....	1	4,255.8
Costilla	412	22	2	...	6	...	7	23	8	....	...	2,307.9
Crowley	1,064	82	10	...	9	...	13	87	18	38	2	6,278.0
Custer	314	48	....	...	2	...	1	22	2	4	...	1,988.0
Delta	2,169	261	42	2	16	...	48	160	34	7	13	14,014.9
Denver	52,174	3,868	730	30	1,037	17	4,361	7,384	1,651	10,872	336	363,525.6
Dolores	64	6	....	...	...	...	1	4	....	....	...	298.1
Douglas	904	53	7	...	6	...	24	74	17	29	1	5,449.3
Eagle	345	34	....	...	4	...	11	12	1	4	...	1,869.6
Elbert	1,273	57	23	...	3	...	10	87	19	5	8	7,339.5
El Paso	10,008	611	142	2	149	5	669	1,144	107	150	64	68,018.3
Fremont	3,749	271	59	2	47	...	55	443	61	39	3	22,491.2
Garfield	1,234	71	12	...	9	...	22	60	9	9	2	7,062.4
Gilpin	101	6	....	...	...	...	2	8	3	3	...	591.2
Grand	361	23	6	...	3	...	11	13	2	6	1	1,746.3
Gunnison	703	16	7	1	5	...	18	37	14	7	...	3,331.0
Hinsdale	62	9	2	...	4	...	13	6	....	1	...	408.6
Huerfano	2,549	123	60	...	15	...	71	284	111	100	3	14,939.3
Jackson	296	17	3	...	5	...	2	23	2	3	...	1,481.9
Jefferson	4,033	401	36	...	46	...	159	376	93	27	7	25,516.8
Kiowa	829	64	2	...	3	...	5	44	7	....	9	4,766.8
Kit Carson	1,921	249	31	...	6	...	50	126	28	28	3	13,623.3
Lake	438	4	13	...	4	...	25	22	6	9	...	2,497.1
La Plata	1 246	61	39	...	12	...	48	106	10	6	4	7,310.3
Larimer	6 830	348	82	...	129	...	155	576	76	46	10	41 800.
Las Animas	5,436	334	91	...	75	3	172	649	161	194	29	33,169.5
Lincoln	1,633	186	22	...	5	...	9	89	20	6	6	10.334.
Logan	3,578	275	54	1	37	...	46	307	100	80	33	21,871.1
Mesa	4,022	298	76	4	63	1	168	445	66	89	21	23.910.
Mineral	84	8	....	...	1	...	3	5	1	....	...	443.
Moffat	515	15	3	...	3	...	12	13	1	5	2	2.359.
Montezuma	618	60	11	...	1	...	13	26	1	1	4	3,726.
Montrose	1 670	155	18	...	12	...	28	85	12	8	...	10.357.
Morgan	3,384	159	35	...	34	...	40	387	53	33	1	19,153.
Otero	4,402	257	50	...	62	3	64	350	86	16	13	25,889.
Ouray	261	8	4	...	5	...	19	6	4	....	...	1.482.
Park	398	30	5	...	6	...	1	20	2	2	...	2.225.
Phillips	1,570	214	14	...	7	...	3	79	33	5	2	10.186.
Pitkin	169	1	....	...	4	...	4	7	1	2	...	745.
Prowers	2,555	185	40	...	7	...	84	238	76	25	20	
Pueblo	8,911	591	128	2	176	6	194	916	167	485	30	
Rio Blanco	307	17	4	...	1	...	4	7	1	2	...	1,515.
Rio Grande	1,557	245	25	...	8	...	43	89	18	4	1	11,063.
Routt	1,020	25	24	...	8	...	21	52	4	2	3	4,990.
Saguache	900	105	5	...	2	...	18	68	14	6	11	5,680.
San Juan	58	8	....	...	1	...	15	4	....	....	...	.
San Miguel	336	21	5	...	15	...	22	23	3	1	2	1,991.
Sedgwick	918	87	8	1	...	...	3	62	4	13	4	.
Summit	184	4	3	...	4	...	...	16	....	....	...	.
Teller	781	43	3	...	10	...	29	81	1	14	3	689.
Washington	1,966	428	15	2	11	...	8	141	20	79	3	316.
Weld	11,174	736	108	2	131	2	246	1,278	177	222	29	069.
Yuma	2,743	476	22	...	11	...	28	192	34	7	9	141.
Total	175,669	13,351	2,326	50	2,473	43	7,736	18,894	3,759	13,190	779	$1,126,218.

Rank of Counties in Area

County	Rank	Area
Las Animas	1	3,077,760
Moffat	2	2,981,120
Weld	3	2,574,080
Rio Blanco	4	2,062,720
Gunnison	5	2,034,560
Mesa	6	2,024,320
Saguache	7	2,005,120
Garfield	8	1,988,480
Larimer	9	1,682,560
Lincoln	10	1,644,800
Baca	11	1,633,280
Washington	12	1,613,440
Pueblo	13	1,557,120
Yuma	14	1,514,880
Routt	15	1,477,760
Montrose	16	1,448,960
Park	17	1,434,880
Kit Carson	18	1,381,760
El Paso	19	1,357,440
Montezuma	20	1,312,640
Grand	21	1,194,240
Elbert	22	1,188,480
La Plata	23	1,184,540
Logan	24	1,166,080
Kiowa	25	1,150,720
Cheyenne	26	1,137,280
Jackson	27	1,044,480
Prowers	28	1,043,200
Eagle	29	1,036,800
Fremont	30	996,480
Bent	31	975,360
Huerfano	32	960,000
San Miguel	33	824,320
Morgan	34	823,040
Adams	35	807,680
Otero	36	805,760
Conejos	37	801,280
Archuleta	38	780,800
Delta	39	768,640
Costilla	40	758,400
Chaffee	41	693,120
Dolores	42	667,520
Pitkin	43	652,160
Hinsdale	44	621,440
Rio Grande	45	574,720
Mineral	46	554,240
Douglas	47	540,800
Arapahoe	48	538,880
Jefferson	49	517,120
Crowley	50	517,120
Boulder	51	488,960
Custer	52	478,080
Alamosa	53	465,280
Phillips	54	440,320
Summit	55	415,360
Teller	56	350,080
Sedgwick	57	339,840
Ouray	58	332,160
San Juan	59	289,920
Clear Creek	60	249,600
Lake	61	237,440
Gilpin	62	84,480
Denver	63	37,120

Rank of Counties According to Population

County	Rank 1910	Rank 1920	Population 1920
Denver	1	1	256,491
Pueblo	2	2	57,638
Weld	4	3	54,059
El Paso	3	4	44,027
Las Animas	5	5	38,975
Boulder	6	6	31,861
Larimer	7	7	27,872
Otero	9	8	22,623
Mesa	8	9	22,281
Logan	22	10	18,427
Fremont	10	11	17,883
Huerfano	14	12	16,879
Morgan	21	13	16,124
Adams	24	14	14,430
Jefferson	12	15	14,400
Yuma	25	16	13,897
Prowers	23	17	13,845
Arapahoe	19	18	13,766
Delta	13	19	13,668
Montrose	18	20	11,852
La Plata	17	21	11,218
Washington	30	22	11,208
Bent	35	23	9,705
Garfield	20	24	9,304
Routt	27	25	8,948
Kit Carson	28	26	8,915
Baca	51	27	8,721
Conejos	15	28	8,416
Lincoln	31	29	8,273
Rio Grande	29	30	7,855
Chaffee	26	31	7,753
Elbert	34	32	6 980
Teller	11	33	6,696
Lake	16	34	6,630
Crowley	*	35	6,383
Montezuma	36	36	6,260
Gunnison	32	37	5,590
Phillips	46	38	5,499
San Miguel	38	39	5,381
Alamosa	*	40	5,148
Moffat	*	41	5,129
Costilla	33	42	5,032
Saguache	40	43	4,638
Sedgwick	48	44	4,207
Kiowa	50	45	3,755
Cheyenne	42	46	3,746
Archuleta	44	47	3,590
Douglas	45	48	3,517
Eagle	49	49	3,385
Rio Blanco	53	50	3,135
Clear Creek	37	51	2,891
Pitkin	39	52	2,707
Grand	56	53	2,659
Ouray	43	54	2,620
Custer	55	55	2,172
Park	52	56	1,977
Summit	54	57	1,724
San Juan	47	58	1,700
Gilpin	41	59	1,364
Jackson	58	60	1,340
Dolores	60	61	1,234
Mineral	57	62	779
Hinsdale	59	63	538
State			939,629

*Crowley county was created in 1911, Alamosa county in 1913, and Moffat county in 1911.

Colorado Cities and Towns

INCORPORATED municipalities in Colorado include towns, cities of the second class and cities of the first class. All incorporated places with populations not exceeding 2,000 are towns. When a town achieves a population of 2,000 or more and furnishes satisfactory proof of same, such as a state or federal census report or the findings of a special census authorized by its board of trustees, it may become a city of the second class; and when its population reaches the 15,000 mark it is entitled to the dignity of rank as a city of the first class.

The following list includes municipalities against which taxes were assessed for municipal purposes in 1924. It is made up of three cities of the first class, 28 cities of the second class and 184 towns. But the classification is by no means constant. Leadville, now a comparatively small city of the second class, was once an ambitious and growing city of the first class, and Creede, now a town of 500, was once a thriving city of the second class. All over the state, but more numerous in the metal mining districts, are the sites of ghost towns, once incorporated places, but now only postoffices and in some cases barren land only, with no trace of the buildings that once housed their populations. The list here given includes only active municipal corporations.

The date of incorporation given is the date on which the people of the community voted to make it a municipal corporation, this being the only process by which a municipal corporation could be established in Colorado after statehood was conferred, in 1876. Previous to that towns were incorporated in several ways. Data have not yet been completed showing the dates of incorporation for the cities and towns organized before Colorado became a state.

Only municipal utilities are mentioned here. It may be said, however, that almost every municipality in this list has an electric light system and electric current available for power, though it is not mentioned specifically unless it is operated by the municipality. It is also possible that a few municipalities have privately owned water systems, though the number is very small. Bank deposits here given are as of January 1, 1924, and assessed valuations and tax levies are for 1923, fixing taxes to be paid in 1924. Bonds are given as of January 1, 1924.

Key to pronunciation—The simplest possible system of pronunciation has been adopted here, with full realization that it fails in indicating certain shades of sound and stress.

āte, ăt, ärm, dāta, saw.
mē, met, mẽrge.
mīte, mit.
nōte, not, nôrth.
tōō, look.
hūe, hŭt.
out, thin, the.

Aguilar (ă' gwă lär)—Town in Las Animas county; on D. & R. G. W. railroad; incorporated 11-13-1893; population—1920 census, 1,236; 1924 estimate, 1,520; altitude, 6.700 feet; assessed valuation, $640,426; municipal tax levy, 22.5 mills; has municipal water system; bank deposits, $206,420. Bonds issued—Water works, $81,000; all outstanding.

Akron (ăk' rŭn)—Town, countyseat of Washington county; on Burlington railroad; incorporated 8-2-1887; population—1920 census, 1,401; 1924 estimate, 1,480; altitude, 4,300 feet; assessed valuation, $1,425,512; municipal tax levy, 11 mills; has municipal water system, sanitary sewer system and light system; bank deposits, $500,180. Bonds issued—Water works, $60,000; sanitary sewer, $50,000. Total bonds issued, $110,000; redeemed, $9,500; outstanding, $100,500.

Alamosa (ăl' a mō' sa)—City of second class, countyseat of Alamosa county; on D. & R. G. W. railroad; incorporated, 7-20-1878; population—1920 census, 3,171; 1924 estimate, 3,550; altitude, 7,500 feet; assessed valuation, $2,177,-690; municipal tax levy, 17.5 mills; has municipal water system and light system; bank deposits, $1,324,230. Bonds issued—Water works, $120,000; sanitary sewers, $13,000. Total bonds issued, $133,000, all outstanding.

Animas City (ăn' i măs)—Town in La Plata county; on D. & R. G. W. railroad; incorporated, 9-5-1878; population—1920 census, 250; 1924 estimate, 210; altitude, 6.500 feet; assessed valuation, $166.065; municipal tax levy, 17 mills. Bonds issued—Water works, $25,000; redeemed, $3,000; outstanding, $22.000.

Antonito (ăn tō nē' tō)—Town in Conejos county; on D. & R. G. W. railroad; incorporated, 11-2-1889; population—1920 census, 946; 1924 estimate, 1,050; altitude, 7,888 feet; assessed valuation, $524,610; municipal tax levy, 11 mills; has municipal water system and sanitary sewer system; bank deposits, $278-946. Bonds issued—Refunding warrants, $15,000; water works, $65,000; sanitary sewer, $3,000. Total bonds issued, $83,-000, all outstanding.

Arvada (är vă' da)—Town in Jefferson county; on C. & S., Denver & Salt Lake railroads and Interurban electric; incorporated, 7-26-1904; population—1920 census, 915; 1924 estimate, 1,150; altitude, 5,300 feet; assessed valuation, $916,375; municipal tax levy, 14 mills; has municipal water system and sanitary sewer system; bank deposits, $485,960. Bonds issued—Water works, $56,000; sanitary sewer, $68,000; streets and alleys, $32,-715. Total bonds issued, $156,715; redeemed, $17,500; outstanding, $139,215.

Aspen (ăs' pen)—Town, countyseat of Pitkin county; on D. & R. G. W. railroad; incorporated, 2-5-1881; population—1920 census, 1,265; 1924 estimate, 1,330; altitude, 7,850 feet; assessed valuation, $440,365; municipal tax levy, 20.23 mills; bank deposits, $436,681. Bonds issued—Miscellaneous, $85,800, all outstanding.

Ault (awlt)—Town in Weld county; on U. P. railroad; incorporated, 3-21-1904; population—1920 census, 769; 1924 estimate, 820; altitude, 4,940 feet; assessed valuation, $557,860; municipal tax levy, 16.5 mills; has municipal water system; bank deposits, $411,974. Bonds issued—Water works, $44,000; parks, $5,000. Total bonds issued, $49,000; redeemed, $6,000; outstanding, $43,000.

Aurora (aw rō' ra)—Town in Adams and Arapahoe counties; incorporated, under name of Fletcher, 4-21-1891; name changed to Aurora, 2-25-1907; population—1920 census, 983; 1924 estimate, 1,050; altitude, 5,400 feet; assessed valuation, $1,245,230; municipal tax levy, 45 mills; has municipal water system; bank deposits, $527,219. Bonds issued—Water works, $400,000, all outstanding.

Basalt (bă' sawlt or bă sawlt')—Town in Eagle county; on D. & R. G. railroad; incorporated, 8-12-1901; population—1920 census, 185; 1924 estimate, 205; altitude, 6,600 feet; assessed valuation, $50,102; municipal tax levy, 4.4 mills. No bonded debt.

Bayfield (bā' fēld)—Town in La Plata county; on D. & R. G. W. railroad; incorporated, 7-13-1906; population—1920 census, 267; 1924 estimate, 310; altitude, 6,500 feet; assessed valuation, $115,630; municipal tax levy, 11 mills. Bonds issued—Miscellaneous, $17,000, all outstanding.

Berthoud (bẽr' thōōd)—Town in Larimer county; on C. & S. railroad; incorporated, 7-17-1888; population—1920 census, 852; 1924 estimate, 900; altitude, 5,240 feet; assessed valuation, $969,140; municipal tax levy, 8.8 mills; has municipal water and light systems; bank deposits, $446,019. Bonds issued—Water works, $30,000; redeemed, $24,000; outstanding, $6,000.

Blanca (blăn' ka)—Town in Costilla county; on D. & R. G. W. railroad; incorporated, 10-25-1909; population—1920 census, 380; 1924 estimate, 365; altitude, 7,870 feet; assessed valuation, $308,555; municipal tax levy, 10 mills; bank deposits, $53,606. No bonded debt.

Bonanza (bō năn' za)—Town in Saguache county; incorporated, 1-3-1881; population—1920 census, 91; 1924 estimate, 130; altitude, 8,000 feet; assessed valuation, $28,967; municipal tax levy, 10 mills. No bonded debt.

Boulder (bōl' dẽr)—City of second class, countyseat of Boulder county; on C. & S. railroad and Interurban electric; incorporated, ...; population—1920 census, 11,006; 1924 estimate, 12,400; altitude, 5,350 feet; assessed valuation, $12,338,274; municipal tax levy, 10.3 mills; has municipal water and light systems and sanitary sewer system; bank deposits, $4,785,085. Bonds issued—Water works, $640,000; bridges and viaducts, $75,000; sanitary sewer, $114,700; storm sewer, $147,100; streets and alleys, $793,700; miscellaneous, $4,000. Total bonds issued, $1,774,500; redeemed, $49,-000; outstanding, $1,725,500.

Breckenridge (brek' en rij) — Town, countyseat of Summit county; on C. & S. railroad; incorporated, 2-4-1880; population—1920 census, 796; 1924 estimate, 580; altitude, 9,579; assessed valuation, $477,261; municipal tax levy, 13 mills; has municipal water and light systems; bank deposits, $212,493. Bonds issued—Water works, $17,000, all outstanding.

Brighton (brī' tŭn) — City of second class, countyseat of Adams county; on U. P. railroad; incorporated 6-11-1887; population—1920 census, 2,715; 1924 estimate, 3,350; altitude, 4,979; assessed valuation, $2,446,930; municipal tax levy, 12.5 mills; has municipal water and light systems; bank deposits, $1,048,022. Bonds issued—Water works, $200,000; sanitary sewer $80,000; streets and alleys, $117,000. Total bonds issued, $397,-000, all outstanding.

Branson (brăn sŭn)—Town in Las Animas county; on C. & S. railroad; incorporated, 6-3-1920; population—1924 estimate, 400; altitude, 6,000 feet; assessed valuation, $183,871; municipal tax levy, 23 mills; has municipal light plant; bank deposits, $50,127. Bonds issued—Water works, $35,000, all outstanding.

Brush (brŭsh)—Town in Morgan county; on Burlington railroad; incorporated, 10-18-1884; population—1920 census, 2,103; 1924 estimate, 2,560; altitude, 4,280 feet; assessed valuation, $1,535,684; municipal tax levy, 15.5 mills; has municipal water system, sanitary sewer system, municipal light system; bank deposits, $1,153,470. Bonds issued—Water works, $183,000; sanitary sewers, $23,-500; storm sewers, $39,000; streets and alleys, $125,500. Total bonds issued, $371,000; redeemed, $50,112; outstanding, $320,888.

Buena Vista (bū' na vis' ta) — Town, countyseat of Chaffee county; on D. & R. G. W. railroad; incorporated, 10-28-1879; population—1920 census, 903; 1924 estimate, 1,085; altitude, 7,800 feet; assessed valuation, $517,551; municipal tax levy, 11 mills; has municipal water system; bank deposits, $159,246. Bonds issued—Water works, $30,000; redeemed, $18,500; outstanding, $11,500.

Burlington (bẽr' ling tŭn) — Town, countyseat of Kit Carson county; on Rock Island railroad; incorporated, 5-15-1888; population—1920 census, 991; 1924 estimate, 1,200; altitude, 4,250 feet; assessed valuation, $1,353,934; municipal tax levy, 20.45 mills; has municipal water system, sanitary sewer system; bank deposits, $363,248. Bond issue — Water works, $170,000; miscellaneous, $63,200. Total bonds issued, $233,200, all outstanding.

Calhan (kăl' hăn) — Town in El Paso county; on Rock Island railroad; incorporated, 4-22-1919; population—1924 estimate, 400; altitude, 6,508 feet; assessed valuation, $315,130; municipal tax levy, 6 mills; bank deposits, $308,856. No bonded debt.

Canon City (kăn'yŭn)—City of second class, countyseat of Fremont county; on D. & R. G. W. railroad; incorporated, ...; population—1920 census, 4,551; 1924 estimate, 5,000; altitude, 5,333 feet; assessed valuation, $4,425,498; municipal tax levy, 11 mills; has municipal water system, sanitary sewer system, and electric light system; bank deposits, $2,752,-

394. Bonds issued—General municipal, $40,000; water works, $350,000; electric lights, $30,000; streets and alleys, $80,-050. Total bonds issued, $500,050; redeemed, $57,600; outstanding, $442,450.

Carbondale (kăr' bŭn dāl) — Town in Garfield county; on D. & R. G. W. railroad; incorporated, 1-30-1888; population 1920 census, 310; 1924 estimate, 360; altitude, 6,000 feet; assessed valuation, $386,621; municipal tax levy, 14.2 mills; has municipal water system; bank deposits, $213,360. Bonds issued — Water works, $37,500; redeemed, $7,500; outstanding, $30,000.

Castle Rock (kăsl)—Town, countyseat of Douglas county; on A. T. & S. F. and D. & R. G. W. railroads; incorporated, 4-14-1881; population—1920 census, 461; 1924 estimate, 500; altitude, 6,000 feet; assessed valuation, $565,225; municipal tax levy, 20.5 mills; has municipal water system, sanitary sewer system; bank deposits, $530,753. Bonds issued—Water works, $75,000; redeemed, $3,000; outstanding, $72,000.

Cedaredge (sē' dēr ej)—Town in Delta county; incorporated, 2-12-1907; population—1920 census, 455; 1924 estimate, 485; altitude, 6,100 feet; assessed valuation, $275,730; municipal tax levy, 13 mills; has municipal water system; bank deposits, $165,732. Bonds issued—Miscellaneous, $43,700; redeemed, $500; outstanding, $43,200.

Center (sen tēr) — Town in Saguache county; on San Luis Central railroad; incorporated, 9-1-1906; population—1920 census, 547; 1924 estimate, 680; altitude, 7,641 feet; assessed valuation, $47,369; municipal tax levy, 11.55 mills; has municipal water system; bank deposits, $141,566. Bonds issued—Water works, $35,000, all outstanding.

Central City (sen' trăl)—Town, county seat of Gilpin county; on C. & S. railroad; incorporated, ...; population, 1920 census, 552; 1924 estimate, 490; altitude, 8,560 feet; assessed valuation, $486,465; municipal tax levy, 23 mills; has municipal water system; bank deposits, $262,-688. Bonds issued—Water works, $95,-000; redeemed, $10,500; outstanding, $84,500.

Cheraw (chē raw') — Town in Otero county; on A. T. & S. F. railroad; incorporated, 3-12-1917; population—1920 census, 186; 1924 estimate, 250, altitude, 4,500 feet; assessed valuation, $177,483; municipal tax levy, 13.5 mills; has municipal water system; bank deposits, $84,476. Bonds issued—Water works, $12,000, all oustanding.

Cheyenne Wells (shī' en) — Town, countyseat of Cheyenne county; on U. P. railroad; incorporated, 5-3-1890; population—1920 census, 508; 1924 estimate, 690; altitude, 4,282 feet; assessed valuation, $868,140; municipal tax levy, 12.8 mills; has municipal water system, sanitary sewer system; bank deposits, $182,-905. Bonds issued—Water works, $94,-000, all outstanding.

Coal Creek (kōl) — Town in Fremont county; incorporated, 1-10-1882; population—1920 census, 618; 1924 estimate, 615; altitude, 5,600 feet; assessed valuation, $79,111; municipal tax levy, 26 mills. No bonded debt.

Collbran (kōl' brăn) — Town in Mesa county; incorporated, 6-23-1908; population—1920 census, 286; 1924 estimate, 295; altitude, 6,000 feet; assessed valuation, $157,959; municipal tax levy, 16 mills; has municipal water system; bank deposits, $166,147. Bonds issued—Water works, $14,500, all outstanding.

Colorado Springs—City of first class, countyseat of El Paso county; on four railroads; incorporated, ...; population —1920 census, 30,105; 1924 estimate, 33,600; altitude, 5,900 feet; assessed valuation, $39,929,430; municipal tax levy, 14.5 mills; has municipal water system, sanitary sewer system, and municipal light system; bank deposits, $16,643,314. Bonds issued—Public building, $500,000; water works, $1,145,000; sanitary sewers, $16,000; storm sewers, $111,000; streets and alleys, $1,104,000. Total bonds issued, $2,876,000, all outstanding.

Cortez (kôr tez')—Town, countyseat of Montezuma county; incorporated, 9-27-1902; population—1920 census, 541; 1924 estimate, 670; altitude, 6,198 feet; assessed valuation, $424,045; municipal tax levy, 19 mills; has municipal water system; bank deposits, $305,503. Bonds issued—Water works, $61,000, all outstanding.

Craig (krāg) — Town, county seat of Moffat county; on Denver & Salt Lake railroad; incorporated, 4-21-1908; population—1920 census, 1,297; 1924 estimate, 1,500; altitude, 6,200 feet; assessed valuation, $834,370; municipal tax levy, 20 mills; has municipal water system, sanitary sewer system; bank deposits, $534,-305. Bonds issued—Water works, $52,-000; sanitary sewer, $38,000. Total bonds issued, $90,000; redeemed, $16,000; outstanding, $74,000.

Crawford (kraw' fōrd)—Town in Delta county; incorporated, 10-11-1910; population—1920 census, 149; 1924 estimate, 150; altitude, 6,800 feet; assessed valuation, $61,335; municipal tax levy, 6 mills; bank deposits, $86,807. No bonded debt.

Creed (krēd) — Town, countyseat of Mineral county; on D. & R. G. W. railroad; incorporated, 3-19-1892; population—1920 census, 500; 1924 estimate, 515; altitude, 8,854 feet; assessed valuation, $265,400; municipal tax levy, 25 mills; has municipal water system, sanitary sewer system; bank deposits, $99,-191. No bonded debt.

Crested Butte (krest' ed būt)—Town in Gunnison county; on D. & R. G. W. railroad; incorporated, 6-24-1880; population—1920 census, 1,213; 1924 estimate, 1,225; altitude, 9,000 feet; assessed valuation, $408,545; municipal tax levy, 13.5 mills; bank deposits, $219,475. Bonds issued—Miscellaneous, $10,000; redeemed, $600; outstanding, $9,400.

Crestone (kres' tōn)—Town in Saguache county; on D. & R. G. W. railroad; incorporated, 3-29-1901; population—1920 census, 74; 1924 estimate, 90; altitude 7,500 feet; assessed valuation, $32,410, municipal tax levy, 11 mills. No bonded debt.

Cripple Creek (kripl)—City of second class, countyseat of Teller county; incorporated, 5-28-1892; population—1920 census, 2,325; 1924 estimate, 2,350; altitude, 9,375 feet; assessed valuation, $748,150; municipal tax levy, 50 mills; bank deposits, $1,415,865. Bonds issued —General municipal, $123,000; redeemed, $42,000; outstanding, $81,000.

Crook (krook)—Town in Logan county; on U. P. railroad; incorporated, 9-3-1918; population—1920 census, 232; 1924 estimate, 260; altitude, 3,700 feet; assessed valuation, $185,238; municipal tax levy, 23 mills; has municipal water system, municipal light system; bank deposits, $85,649. Bonds issued — Water works, $28,000, electric lights, $6,000. Total bonds issued, $34,000, all outstanding.

Crowley (krou'li)—Town in Crowley county; on Missouri Pacific railroad; incorporated, 9-20-21; population — 1920 census, 224; 1924 estimate, 290; altitude, 4,275 feet; assessed valuation, $196,380; municipal tax levy, 10.7 mills; bank deposits, $32,761. No bonded debt.

Dacono (dā ko' no) — Town in Weld county; on U. P. railroad; incorporated, 1-8-1908; population—1920 census, 172; 1924 estimate, 275; altitude, 4,500 feet; assessed valuation, $61,490; municipal tax levy, 15.8 mills; has municipal water system. No bonded debt.

DeBeque (dē bek')—Town in Mesa county; on D. & R. G. W. railroad; incorporated, 11-13-1889; population — 1920 census, 292; 1924 estimate, 385; altitude, 4,800 feet; assessed valuation, $217,452; municipal tax levy, 17.7 mills; has municipal water system; bank deposits, $89,443. Bonds issued—Water works, $77,000, all outstanding.

Deer Trail (dēr trāl)—Town in Arapahoe county; on U. P. railroad; incorporated, 1-5-1920; population—1924 estimate, 330; altitude 5,183 feet; assessed valuation, $276,685; municipal tax levy, 23 mills; has municipal water system; bank deposits, $227,247. Bonds issued—Water works, $40,000, all outstanding.

Del Norte (del nôrt) — Town, countyseat of Rio Grande county; on D. & R. G. W. railroad; incorporated, ...; population—1920 census, 1,007; 1924 estimate, 995; altitude, 7,778 feet; assessed valuation, $509,550; municipal tax levy, 16 mills; has municipal water system, sanitary sewer system, municipal light system; bank deposits, $331,827. Bonds issued—Water works, $52,500; miscellaneous, $8,500. Total bonds issued, $61,000; redeemed, $1,500; outstanding, $59,500.

Delagua (de lä' wä) — Town in Las Animas county; on C. & S. railroad; incorporated, 11-13-1889; population—1920 census, 1,035; 1924 estimate, 1,200; altitude, 6,700 feet. No bonded debt.

Delta (del' ta)—City of second class, countyseat of Delta county; on D. & R. G. W. railroad; incorporated, 10-12-1882; population—1920 census, 2,623; 1924 estimate, 2,800; altitude, 4,980 feet; assessed valuation, $2,822,155; municipal tax levy, 13.5 mills; has municipal water system and sanitary sewer system; bank deposits, $1,210,699. Bonds issued—Water works, $115,000; miscellaneous, $198,000. Total bonds issued, $313,000, all outstanding.

Denver (den' vẽr)—City of first class, countyseat of Denver county; all railroads; incorporated, ...; population—1920 census, 256,491; 1924 estimate, 277,215; altitude, 5,280 feet; assessed valuation, $388,610,170; municipal tax levy, 9.59 mills; has municipal water system and sanitary sewer system; bank deposits, $164,019,652. Bonds issued — Water works, $14,523,600; bridges and viaducts, $260,000; parks, $445,700; sanitary sewers, $242,800; storm sewers, $780,100; streets and alleys, $2,443,400. Total bonds issued, $18,695,600, all outstanding.

Dillon (dil' ŭn)—Town in Summit county; on C. & S. railroad; incorporated, 12-16-1882; population—1920 census, 126; 1924 estimate, 75; altitude, 8,600 feet; assessed valuation, $99,914; municipal tax levy, 8 mills. No bonded debt.

Dolores (dōl ō' rez)—Town in Montezuma county; on Rio Grande Southern railroad; incorporated, 7-7-1900; population—1920 census, 465; 1924 estimate, 460; altitude, 6,957 feet; assessed valuation, $381,475; municipal tax levy, 16 mills; has municipal water system; bank deposits, $400,778. Bonds issued—Water works, $45,000; redeemed, $32,500; outstanding, $12,500.

Durango (dōō răn' gō)—City of second class, countyseat of La Plata county; on D. & R. G. W. railroad; incorporated, 4-9-1881; population—1920 census, 4,116; 1924 estimate, 4,650; altitude, 6,505 feet; assessed valuation, $4,280,107; municipal tax levy, 12 mills; has municipal water system and sanitary sewer system; bank deposits, $1,668,594. Bonds issued—Water works, $230,700; miscellaneous, $11,000. Total bonds issued, $241,700; redeemed, $28,400; outstanding, $213,300.

Eads (ēdz)—Town, countyseat of Kiowa county; on Missouri Pacific railroad; incorporated, 1-4-1916; population—1920 census, 406; 1924 estimate, 450; altitude, 4,262 feet; assessed valuation, $400,460; municipal tax levy, 20 mills; has municipal water system and sanitary sewer system; bank deposits, $304,668. Bonds issued—Water works, $71,000; electric lights, $5,000. Total bonds issued, $76,000, all outstanding.

Eagle (ē' gl) — Town, countyseat of Eagle county; on D. & R. G. W. railroad; incorporated, 11-2-1920; population—1920 census, 358; 1924 estimate, 430; altitude, 6,602 feet; assessed valuation, $294,874; municipal tax levy, 17.4 mills; has municipal water system and sanitary sewer system; bank deposits, $260,780. Bonds issued—Sanitary sewer, $25,000, all outstanding.

Eaton (ē' tŭn)—Town in Weld county; on U. P. railroad; incorporated, 10-26-1892; population—1920 census, 1,289; 1924 estimate, 1,560; altitude, 4,750; assessed valuation, $1,426,280; municipal tax levy, 12 mills; has municipal water system; bank deposits, $615,104. Bonds issued—Water works, $13,000, all outstanding.

Eckley (ek' li)—Town in Yuma county; on Burlington railroad; incorporated, 3-16-1920; population — 1920 census, 332; 1924 estimate, 360; altitude, 3,890 feet; assessed valuation, $258,440; municipal tax levy, 25 mills; has municipal water and light systems; bank deposits, $67,238. Bonds issued — Water works, $40,000; electric lights, $9,500. Total bonds issued, $49,500, all outstanding.

Edgewater (ej' wä tẽr)—Town in Jefferson county; suburb of Denver; incorporated, 8-17-1901; population—1920 census, 664; 1924 estimate, 815; altitude, 5,353 feet; assessed valuation, $489,460; municipal tax levy, 15 mills; has municipal water system and sanitary sewer system. Bonds issued — Water works, $40,000; sanitary sewers, $37,500; streets and alleys, $300. Total bonds issued, $77,800; redeemed, $7,500; outstanding, $70,300.

Eldora (el dō' ra) — Town in Boulder county; incorporated, 3-9-1898; population—1920 census, 35; 1924 estimate, 60; altitude, 8,700 feet; assessed valuation,

$39,897; municipal tax levy, 20 mills. Bonds issued—General municipal, $7,880; redeemed, $3,780; outstanding, $4,100.

Elizabeth (ē liz' ā beth)—Town in Elbert county; on C. & S. railroad; incorporated, 8-30-1890; population—1920 census, 230; 1924 estimate, 250; altitude, 6,400 feet; assessed valuation, $195,492; municipal tax levy, 4.6 mills; has sanitary sewer system; bank deposits, $168,-459. Bonds issued—Sanitary sewers, $5,-500; redeemed, $3,000; outstanding, $2,-500.

Empire (em' pīr)—Town in Clear Creek county; on C. & S. railroad; incorporated pouulation—1920 census, 105; 1924 estimate, 100; altitude, 8,603 feet; assessed valuation, $49,145; municipal tax levy, 5 mills; has municipal water system. No bonded debt.

Englewood (en' gel wood)—City of second class, in Arapahoe county; suburb of Denver; incorporated, 5-12-1893; population—1920 census, 4,356; 1924 estimate, 5,500; altitude, 5,200 feet; assessed valuation, $2,800,210; municipal tax levy, 12 mills; has sanitary sewer system; bank deposits, $899,272. Bonds issued—Sanitary sewers, $271,000; streets and alleys, $103,000. Total bonds issued, $374,000; redeemed, $24,000; outstanding, $350,000.

Erie (ē' ri)—Town in Weld county; on Burlington railroad; incorporated ....; population—1920 census, 697; 1924 estimate, 780; altitude, 5,000 feet; assessed valuation, $232,930; municipal tax levy, 24 mills; has municipal water system; bank deposits, $231,952. Bonds issued—Water works, $48,000; redeemed, $8,000; outstanding, $40,000.

Estes Park (es' tēz)—Town in Larimer county; incorporated, 4-3-1917; populaiton—1924 estimate, 640; altitude, 7,500 feet; assessed valuation, $707,020; municipal tax levy, 10.5 mills; has sanitary sewer system; bank deposits, $215,426. Bonds issued—Sanitary sewers, $6,800, all outstanding.

Eureka (ū rē' ka)—Town in San Juan county; on D. & R. G. W. railroad; incorporated, 11-6-1883; population—1920 census, 160; 1924 estimate, 105; altitude, 9,800 feet; assessed valuation, $38,677; municipal tax levy, 15 mills. No bonded debt.

Evans (ev' ănz)—Town in Weld county; on U. P. railroad; incorporated ....; population—1920 census, 505; 1924 estimate, 560; altitude, 4,647 feet; assessed valuation, $269,980; municipal tax levy, 20 mills; has municipal water system; bank deposits, $36,179. No bonded debt.

Fairplay (făr' plā)—Town, countyseat of Park county; on C. & S. railroad; incorporated ....; population—1920 census, 183; 1924 estimate, 200; altitude, 9,964 feet; assessed valuation, $287,930; municipal tax levy, 5 mills; has municipal water system; bank deposits, $144,-349. No bonded debt.

Firestone (fīr' stōn) — Town in Weld county; on U. P. railroad; incorporated, 2-12-1908; population—1920 census, 214; 1924 estimate, 280; altitude, 5.280 feet; assessed valuation, $64,160; municipal tax levy, 18 mills; has municipal water and light systems. Bonds issued—Water works, $15,000, all outstanding.

Flagler (flăg' lẽr)—Town in Kit Carson county; on Rock Island railroad; incorporated, 10-17-1916; population — 1920 census, 544; 1924 estimate, 650; altitude, 4,920 feet; assessed valuation, $633,736; municipal tax levy, 20 mills; has municipal water and light systems; bank deposits, $231,397. Bonds issued—Water works, $120,000, all outstanding.

Fleming (flem' ing) — Town in Logan county; on Burlington railroad; incorporated, 4-16-1917; population—1920 census, 518; 1924 estimate, 590; altitude, 3,900 feet; assessed valuation, $425,564; municipal tax levy, 22 mills; has municipal water and light systems; bank deposits, $104,309. Bonds issued—Water works, $80,000; electric lights, $12,500. Total bonds issued, $92,500, all outstanding.

Florence (flôr' ens) — City of second class, in Fremont county; on D. & R. G. W. railroad; incorporated, 6-6-1887; population—1920 census, 2,629; 1924 estimate, 2,860; altitude, 5,187 feet; assessed valuation, $2,716,326; municipal tax levy, 14 mills; has municipal water system and sanitary sewer system; bank deposits, $1,397,455. Bonds issued—Water works, $85,000; streets and alleys, $53,677. Total bonds issued, $138,677; redeemed, $87,177; outstanding, $51,500.

Florissant (flôr' is ănt)—Town in Teller county; incorporated, 6-27-1891; population—1920 census, 48; 1924 estimate, 40; altitude, 8,193 feet. No bonded debt.

Fort Collins (kol' lins)—City of second class, county seat of Larimer county; on C. & S. and U. P. railroads; incorporated; ....; population—1920 census, 8,755; 1924 estimate, 11,500; altitude, 5,100 feet; assessed valuation, $9,053,840; municipal tax levy, 12.9 mills; has municipal water system and sanitary sewer system; bank deposits, $4,687,743. Bonds issued—Water works, $160,000; parks, $10,000; sanitary sewers, $27,844; storm sewers, $223,-059; streets and alleys, $516,531; miscellaneous, $100,000. Total bonds issued, $1,037,435; redeemed, $352,474; outstanding, $684,961.

Fort Lupton (lŭp' tŭn)—Town in Weld county; on U. P. railroad; incorporated 12-30-1889; population—1920 census, 1,-014; 1924 estimate, 1,550; altitude, 4,906 feet; assessed valuation, $1,051,420; municipal tax levy, 16 mills; has municipal water system and sanitary sewer system; bank deposits, $533,959. Bonds issued—Water works, $30,000; sanitary sewers, $11,000; miscellaneous, $15,000. Total bonds issued, $56,000, all outstanding.

Fort Morgan (môr' găn)—City of second class, countyseat of Morgan county; on Burlington and U. P.; incorporated. 5-21-1887; population—1920 census, 3,818; 1924 estimate, 4,200; altitude. 4,240 feet; assessed valuation, $3,328,327; municipal tax levy, 10 mills; has municipal water system, sanitary sewer system, municipal light system; bank deposits, $1,972,-682. Bonds issued—Water works, $235,-000; sanitary sewers, $75,230; streets and alleys, $349,000. Total bonds issued, $659,230; redeemed, $171,500; outstanding, $487,730.

Fountain (fount' en)—Town in El Paso county; on D. & R. G. W. and A. T. & S. F. railroads; incorporated, 4-7-1903; population—1920 census, 595; 1924 estimate, 590; altitude, 5,500 feet; assessed valuation, $326,180; municipal tax levy, 18 mills; has municipal water and light systems; bank deposits, $149,671. Bonds issued—Water works, $76,000, all outstanding.

Fowler (foul' ẽr) — Town in Otero county; A. T. & S. F. railroad; incorporated, 7-28-1900; population—1920 census, 1,062; 1924 estimate, 1,100; altitude, 4,300 feet; assessed valuation, $931,977; municipal tax levy, 10 mills; has municipal water system; bank deposits, $357,748. Bonds issued—Refunding warrants, $19,-500; public buildings, $10,000; water works, $41,500. Total bonds issued, $71,000, all outstanding.

Frederick (fred' ẽr ik)—Town in Weld county; on U. P. railroad; incorporated, 12-17-1907; population—1920 census, 361; 1924 estimate, 410; altitude, 5,120 feet; assessed valuation, $165,920; municipal tax levy, 32 mills; has municipal water and light systems; bank deposits, $103,-756. Bonds issued—Water works, $33,-000; redeemed, $1,000; outstanding, $32,-00.

Fruita (frōō' ta)—Town in Mesa county; on D. & R. G. W. railroad; incorporated, 3-24-1894; population—1920 census, 1,193; 1924 estimate, 1,200; altitude, 4,-512 feet; assessed valuation, $627,454; municipal tax levy, 18.5 mills; has municipal water and light systems; bank deposits, $337,553. Bonds issued—Water works, $102,000; redeemed, $18,000; outstanding, $84,000.

Frisco (fris' co) — Town in Summit county; incorporated, 9-7-1880; altitude, 9,097 feet; assessed valuation, $18,100; municipal tax levy, 10 mills. No bonded debt.

Georgetown (jôrj' town)—Town, county seat of Clear Creek county; on C. & S. railroad; incorporated, ...; population—1920 census, 703; 1924 estimate, 500; altitude, 8,640 feet; assessed valuation, $476,105; municipal tax levy, 12.5 mills; has municipal water system and sanitary sewer system; bank deposits, $222,511. No bonded debt.

Gilcrest (gil' krest) — Town in Weld county; on U. P. railroad; incorporated, 3-4-1912; population—1920 census, 222; 1924 estimate, 280; altitude, 4,752 feet; assessed valuation, $146,920; municipal tax levy, 6 mills; bank deposits, $34,461; No bonded debt.

Gillet (jil let')—Town in Teller county; incorporated, 1-31-1895; altitude, 9,-938 feet; assessed valuation, $12,390; municipal tax levy, 30 mills. No bonded debt.

Glenwood Springs (glen' wood)—City of second class, countyseat of Garfield county; on D. & R. G. W. railroad; incorporated, 8-22-1885; population—1920 census, 2,073; 1924 estimate, 2,110; altitude, 5,747 feet; assessed valuation, $2,-099,810; municipal tax levy, 16.2 mills; has municipal water and sanitary sewer systems; bank deposits, $1,496,766. Bonds issued—Water works, $250,000; miscellaneous, $60,500. Total bonds issued, $310,500; redeemed, $12,500; outstanding, $298,000.

Golden (gōld' en) — City of second class, countyseat of Jefferson county; on C. & S. railroad and interurban electric; incorporated, ...; population—1920 census, 2,484; 1924 estimate, 2,800; altitude, 5,680 feet; assessed valuation, $1,737,865; muncipal tax levy, 14.5 mills; has municipal water system and sanitary sewer system; bank deposits, $890,-641. Bonds issued—Water works, $275,-000; sanitary sewers, $5,000; streets and alleys, $135,000; miscellaneous, $40,000. Total bonds issued, $455,000; redeemed, $73,700; outstanding, $381,300.

Goldfield (gōld' fēld)—Town in Teller county; incorporated, 1-8-1895; population—1920 census, 633; 1924 estimate, 400; altitude, 9,996 feet; assessed valuation, $172,710; municipal tax levy, 87 mills. No bonded debt.

Granada (grȧ nä' da)—Town in Prowers county; on A. T. & S. F. railroad; incorporated, 1-5-1887; population — 1920 census, 308; 1924 estimate, 380; altitude, 3,479 feet; assessed valuation, $249,215; municipal tax levy, 20 mills; has municipal water system; bank deposits, $80,-978. Bonds issued—Water works, $50,-000, all outstanding.

Grand Junction (jŭnk' shŭn)—City of second class, county seat of Mesa county; on D. & R. G. W. and Grand River Valley railroads; incorporated, 6-22-1882; population—1920 census, 8,665; 1924 estimate, 9,680; altitude, 4,587 feet; assessed valuation, $8,828,094; municipal tax levy, 14.5 mills; has municipal water and sanitary sewer systems; bank deposits, $3,233,414. Bonds issued — Refunding warrants, $20,000; water works, $671,250; sanitary sewers, $133,750; streets and alleys, $406,500; miscellaneous, $91,000. Total bonds issued, $1,-322,500; redeemed, $160,100; outstanding, $1,162,400.

Grand Valley—Town in Garfield county; on D. & R. G. W. railroad; incorporated, 3-7-1908; population—1920 census, 228; 1924 estimate, 335; altitude, 5,095 feet; assessed valuation, $180,033; municipal tax levy, 26.1 mills; has municipal water system; bank deposits, $89,649. Bonds issued—Water works, $44,000, all outstanding.

Greeley (grē' li)—City of second class, countyseat of Weld county; on U. P. railroad; incorporated, ...; population—1920 census, 10,958; 1924 estimate, 12,150; altitude, 4,637 feet; assessed valuation, $12,939,440; municipal tax levy, 11 5 mills; has municipal water and sanitary sewer systems; bank deposits, $4,952,099 Bonds issued—Water works, $515,000; redeemed, $126,000; outstanding, $389,000.

Green Mountain Falls — Town in El Paso and Teller counties; incorporated, 7-19-1890; population—1920 census, 100; 1924 estimate, 100; altitude, 7,694 feet; assessed valuation, $150,110; municipal tax levy, 26.5 mills; has municipal water system. Bonds issued—Water works, $16,000, all outstanding.

Grover (grōv' ẽr)—Town in Weld county; on Burlington railroad; incorporated, 8-8-1916; population—1920 census, 195; 1924 estimate, 160; altitude, 5,000 feet; assessed valuation, $203,690; municipal tax levy, 20 mills; has municipal water and light systems; bank deposits, $34,-632. Bonds issued—Water works, $35,-272, all outstanding.

Gunnison (gŭn' ni sŭn)—Town, countyseat of Gunnison county; on D. & R. G. W. railroad; incorporated, 2-7-1880; population—1920 census, 1,329; 1924 estimate, 1,560; altitude, 7,683 feet; assessed valuation, $1,579,945; municipal tax levy, 12 mills; has municipal water system, sanitary sewer system; municipal light system; bank deposits, $1,203,118. Bonds issued—Water works, $45,000; sanitary sewer, $41,500; miscellaneous, $63,500. Total bonds issued, $150,000; redeemed, $3,500; outstanding, $146,500.

Gypsum (jip' sŭm) — Town in Eagle county; on D. & R. G. W. railroad; incorporated, 1-17-1911; population—1920 census, 164; 1924 estimate, 165; altitude,

6,325 feet; assessed valuation, $141,377; municipal tax levy, 13 mills; has municipal water and sanitary sewer systems; bank deposits, $71,628. Bonds issued—Water works, $15,000; sanitary sewer, $4,000. Total bonds issued, $19,000, all outstanding.

Hartman (härt' măn)—Town in Prowers county; on A. T. & S. F. railroad; incorporated, 3-11-1910; population—1920 census, 175; 1924 estimate, 205; altitude, 3,500 feet; assessed valuation, $123,162; municipal tax levy, 20 mills; has municipal water system; bank deposits, $42,709. Bonds issued—Water works, $13,000; redeemed, $5,500; outstanding, $7,500.

Haswell (hăs' wel) — Town in Kiowa county; on Missouri Pacific railroad; incorporated, 7-30-1920; population—1924 estimate, 200; altitude, 4,528 feet; assessed valuation, $145,896; municipal tax levy, 10 mills; bank deposits, $127,077. No bonded debt.

Haxtun (hăx' tŭn)—Town in Phillips county; on Burlington railroad; incorporated, 6-1-1909; population—1920 census, 1,118; 1924 estimate, 1,210; altitude, 4,000 feet; assessed valuation, $863,790; municipal tax levy, 12.5 mills; has municipal water system, sanitary sewer system, municipal light system; bank deposits, $392,786. Bonds issued—Water works, $20,000; electric lights, $80,000; sanitary sewers, $74,500. Total bonds issued, $174,500; redeemed, $1,000; outstanding, $173,500.

Hayden (hā' den) — Town in Routt county; on Denver & Salt Lake railroad; incorporated, 3-13-1906; population—1920 census, 455; 1924 estimate, 585; altitude, 6,350 feet; assessed valuation, $431.500; municipal tax levy, 20 mills; has municipal water system and sanitary sewer system; bank deposits, $414.875. Bonds issued—Water works, $35,000; sanitary sewers, $27,500. Total bonds issued, $62,500; redeemed, $3,000; outstanding, $59,500.

Hillrose (hil' rōz)—Town in Morgan county; on U. P. railroad, incorporated, 4-21-1919; population — 1924 estimate, 190; altitude, 4,900 feet; assessed valuation, $181,932; municipal tax levy, 5 mills; bank deposits, $101,262. No bonded debt.

Holly (hol' li)—Town in Prowers county; an A. T. & S. F. railroad; incorporated, 7-28-1903; population—1920 census, 940; 1924 estimate, 1,100; altitude, 3,400 feet; assessed valuation, $694,421; municipal tax levy, 18 mills; has municipal water system, sanitary sewer system, municipal light system; bank deposits, $273,323. Bonds issued—Water works, $90,000; sanitary sewers, $20,500. Total bonds issued, $110,500; redeemed, $5,000; outstanding, $105,500.

Holyoke (hōl' yōk)—Town, countyseat of Phillips county; on Burlington railroad; incorporated, 4-24-1888; population —1920 census, 1,205; 1924 estimate, 1,450; altitude, 3,745 feet; assessed valuation, $1,201,820; municipal tax levy, 13.5 mills; has municipal water system, sanitary sewer system municipal light system; bank deposits, $760,407. Bonds issued—Water works, $178,000; sanitary sewers, $45,000. Total bonds issued, $223,000; redeemed, $11,000; outstanding, $212,000.

Hooper (hōōp' er)—Town in Alamosa county; on D. & R. G. W. railroad; incorporated, 4-11-1898; population—1920 census, 156; 1924 estimate, 160; altitude, 7,500 feet; assessed valuation, $98,150; municipal tax levy, 2 mills; bank deposits, $64,063. No bonded debt.

Hotchkiss (hotch' kis)—Town in Delta county; on D. & R. G. W. railroad; incorporated, 4-24-1900; population — 1920 census, 572; 1924 estimate, 605; altitude, 5,369 feet; assessed valuation, $435,925; municipal tax levy, 14.4 mills, has municipal water system and sanitary sewer system; bank deposits, $340,578. Bonds issued—Water works, $48,000, all outstanding.

Hot Sulphur Springs (sŭl' fẽr)—Town, countyseat of Grand county; on Denver & Salt Lake railroad; incorporated, 3-7-1903; population—1920 census, 123; 1924 estimate, 170; altitude, 7,655 feet; assessed valuation, $117,995; municipal tax levy, 15 mills; has municipal water system; bank deposits, $127,979. Bonds issued—Water works, $10,500; redeemed, $1,500; outstanding, $9,000.

Hudson (hŭd' sŭn) — Town in Weld county; on Burlington railroad; incorporated, 2-17-1914; population—1920 census, 322; 1924 estimate, 310; altitude, 5,000 feet; assessed valuation, $302,720; municipal tax levy, 13 mills; has municipal water system. Bonds issued—Water works, $48,000, all outstanding.

Hugo (hū' gō) — Town, countyseat of Lincoln county; on U. P. railroad; incorporated, 4-20-1909; population — 1920 census, 838; 1924 estimate, 980; altitude, 4,970 feet; assessed valuation, $694,535; municipal tax levy, 17 mills; has municipal water system, sanitary sewer system, municipal light system; bank deposits, $464,953. Bonds issued—Water works, $61,000; electric lights, $15,000; sanitary sewers, $7,000; miscellaneous, $19,000. Total bonds issued, $102,000; redeemed, $6,000; outstanding, $96,000.

Idaho Springs (ī dā hō) — Town in Clear Creek county; on C. & S. railroad; incorporated, ...; population—1920 census, 1,192; 1924 estimate, 1,340; altitude, 7,500 feet; assessed valuation, $1,205,420; municipal tax levy, 11 mills; has municipal water system and sanitary sewer system; bank deposits, $444,255. Bonds issued—Water works, $51,000; redeemed, $10,000; outstanding, $41,000.

Ignacio (ig nash' i ō) — Town in La Plata county; near D. & R. G. W. railroad; incorporated, 6-10-1913; population —1920 census, 290; 1924 estimate, 340; altitude, 6,432 feet; assessed valuation, $162,605; municipal tax levy, 4 mills; bank deposits, $85,536. No bonded debt.

Iliff (ī' lif)—Town in Logan county; on U. P. railroad; incorporated, 3-17-1914; population—1920 census, 238; 1924 estimate, 370; altitude, 3,998 feet; assessed valuation, $199,610; municipal tax levy, 22 mills; has municipal water system: bank deposits, $88.594. Bonds issued—Water works, $24,500, all outstanding.

Jamestown (jāmz' toun) — Town in Boulder county; incorporated, 4-3-1883; population—1920 census, 150; 1924 estimate, 140; altitude, 7,000 feet; assessed valuation, $30,305; municipal tax levy, 12.5 mills. No bonded debt.

Johnstown (jonz' toun)—Town in Weld county; on Great Western railroad; incorporated, 5-7-1907; population — 1920 census, 274; 1924 estimate, 370; altitude, 4,820 feet; assessed valuation, $614,310; municipal tax levy, 11 mills; has municipal water system; bank deposits, $386,849. Bonds issued—Water works, $40,000; redeemed, $5,000; outstanding, $35,000.

Julesburg (jōōlz' bẽrg)—Town, county seat of Sedgwick county; on U. P. railroad; incorporated; population—1920 census, 1,320; 1924 estimate, 1,420; altitude, 3,500 feet; assessed valuation, $1,297,-242; municipal tax levy, 13 mills; has municipal water system, sanitary sewer system, municipal light system; bank deposits, $481,383. Bonds issued—Water works, $130,000; sanitary sewers, $11,-500; miscellaneous, $30,000. Total bonds issued, $171,500; redeemed, $6,000; outstanding, $165,500.

Keenesburg (kēnz' bẽrg) — Town in Weld county; on Burlington railroad; incorporated, 4-30-1919; population—1920 census, 164; 1924 estimate, 175; altitude, 4,951 feet; assessed valuation, $238,790; municipal tax levy, 18 mills; has municipal water system; bank deposits, $35,432. Bonds issued—Water works, $26,000; all outstanding.

Kersey (ker' zi)—Town in Weld county; on U. P. railroad; incorporated, 11-10-1908; population — 1920 census, 319; 1924 estimate, 380; altitude, 4,614 feet; assessed valuation, $281,050; municipal tax levy, 27 mills; has municipal water system and sanitary sewer system. Bonds issued — Water works, $50,000; sanitary sewer, $35,682. Total bonds issued, $85,682; redeemed, $2,000; outstanding, $83,682.

Keota (kē ō' ta) — Town in Weld county; on Burlington railroad; incorporated, 3-25-1919; population—1920 census, 129; 1924 estimate, 150; altitude, 5,000 feet; assessed valuation, $907,000; municipal tax levy, 18 mills; has municipal water system. Bonds issued—water works, $23,000, all outstanding.

Kiowa (kī' ō wa)—Town, countyseat of Elbert county; 7 miles from railroad; incorporated, 8-20-1912; population — 1920 census, 148; 1924 estimate, 170; altitude, 6,400 feet; assessed valuation, $143,664; municipal tax levy, 1.57 mills; bank deposits, $218,149. No bonded debt.

Kokomo (kō' kō mō)—Town in Summit county; on C. & S. railroad; incorporated, 5-16-1879; population—1920 census, 93; 1924 estimate, 80; altitude, 10,618 feet; No bonded debt.

Kremmling (krem' ling) — Town in Grand county; on Denver & Salt Lake railroad; incorporated, 4-30-1904; population—1920 census, 254; 1924 estimate, 305; altitude, 7,322 feet; assessed valuation, $117,605; municipal tax levy, 7.16 mills; bank deposits, $148,178.

Lafayette (lă fā et')—Town in Boulder county; on Burlington railroad and Interurban electric; incorporated, 4-2-1889; population—1920 census, 1,815; 1924 estimate, 1,835; altitude, 5,176 feet; assessed valuation, $695,683; municipal tax levy, 25 mills; has municipal water system; bank deposits, $141,938. Bonds issued—Water works, $135,000; redeemed, $38,500; outstanding, $96,500.

La Jara (la hä' ra)—Town in Conejos county; on D. & R. G. W. railroad; incorporated, 2-21-1902; population—1920 census, 521; 1924 estimate, 565; altitude, 7,600 feet; assessed valuation, $314,425; municipal tax levy, 8 mills; bank deposits, $257,407. No bonded debt.

La Junta (la hūn' ta)—City of second class, countyseat of Otero county; on A. T. & S. F. railroad; incorporated, 4-5-1881; population—1920 census, 4,964; 1924 estimate, 5,710; altitude, 4,100 feet; assessed valuation, $5,088,788; municipal tax levy, 14 mills; has municipal water system and sanitary sewer system; bank deposits, $1,437,242. Bonds issued—Water works, $204,000; redeemed, $14,000; outstanding, $190,000.

Lake City—Town, countyseat of Hinsdale county; on D. & R. G. W. railroad; incorporated, ...; population—1920 census, 317; 1924 estimate, 325; altitude, 8,500 feet; assessed valuation, $122,564; municipal tax levy, 18 mills; has municipal water system. Bonds issued—Water works, $24,000; redeemed, $1,000; outstanding, $23,000.

Lamar (la mär')—City of second class, countyseat of Prowers county; on A. T. & S. F. railroad; incorporated 11-13-1886; population—1920 census, 2,512; 1924 estimate, 3,980; altitude, 3,500 feet; assessed valuation, $2,477,244; municipal tax levy, 13 mills; has municipal water and light systems and sanitary sewer system; bank deposits, $1,218,960. Bonds issued—Water works, $395,000; electric lights, $45,000; sanitary sewers, $48,000; streets and alleys, $122,500; miscellaneous, $20,700. Total bonds issued, $631,-200, all outstanding.

La Salle (la săl')—Town in Weld county; on U. P. railroad; incorporated, 4-18-1910; population—1920 census, 460; 1924 estimate, 550; altitude, 4,700 feet; assessed valuation, $416,780; municipal tax levy, 18 mills; has municipal water system and sanitary sewer system; bank deposits, $70,860. Bonds issued—Water works, $25,000; sanitary sewers, $32,500. Total bonds issued, $57,500, all outstanding.

Las Animas (läs ăn' ī mäs)—City of second class, countyseat of Bent county; on A. T. & S. F. railroad; incorporated, ...; population—1920 census, 2,252; 1924 estimate, 2,710; altitude, 4,100 feet; assessed valuation, $1,667,365; municipal tax levy, 17.5 mills; has municipal water system, sanitary sewer system, electric light system; bank deposits, $972,064. Bonds issued—Water works, $20,000; sanitary sewer, $38,500; streets and alleys, $66,500. Total bonds issued, $125,-000; redeemed, $48,500; outstanding, $76,500.

La Veta (lä vē' ta)—Town in Huerfano county; on D. & R. G. W. railroad; incorporated, ...; population—1920 census, 737; 1924 estimate, 880; altitude, 7,024 feet; assessed valuation, $435,794; municipal tax levy, 10 mills; has municipal water system. Bonds issued—Water works, $31,500; sanitary sewers, $28,-000. Total bonds issued—$59,500; redeemed, $22,000; outstanding, $37,500.

Leadville (led' vil)—City of second class, countyseat of Lake county; on D. & R. G. W. railroad; incorporated, 2-4-1878; population—1920 census, 4,-959; 1924 estimate, 5,050; altitude, 10,190 feet; assessed valuation, $2,027,575; municipal tax levy, 34 mills; has municipal sanitary sewer system; bank deposits, $1,634,762. No bonded debt.

Limon (lī' mŭn)—Town in Lincoln coln county; on Rock Island and U. P. railroads; incorporated 10-24-1909; population—1920 census, 1,047; 1924 estimate, 1,390; altitude, 5,280 feet; assessed valuation, $766,265; municipal tax levy, 24.5 mills; has municipal water system, sanitary sewer system, municipal light system; bank deposits, $285,589. Bonds issued—Public buildings, $7,500; water works, $109,000; sanitary sewers, $32,500. Total bonds issued, $149,000; redeemed, $2,000; outstanding, $147,000.

Littleton (lit' el tŭn)—Town, countyseat of Arapahoe county; on A. T. & S. F. and D. & R. G. W. railroads; incorporated, 3-8-1890; population—1920 census, 1,636;- 1924 estimate, 1,820; altitude, 5,362 feet; assessed valuation, $1,438,515; municipal tax levy, 11 mills; has municipal water system and sanitary sewer system; bank deposits, $909,724. Bonds issued—Public buildings, $25,000; sanitary sewers, $32,000; streets and alleys, $12,466. Total bonds issued, $69,466; redeemed, $23,500; outstanding, $45,966.

Longmont (lông' mont)—City of second class, in Boulder county; on C. & S. and Burlington railroads; incorporated, ...; population—1920 census, 5,848; 1924 estimate, 6,110; altitude, 5,000 feet; assessed valuation, $6,020,039; municipal tax levy, 11.5 mills; has municipal water system, sanitary sewer system, municipal light system; bank deposits, $2,677,-497. Bonds issued—Public buildings, $55,000; water works, $200,000; parks, $65,000; sanitary sewers, $5,000; streets and alleys, $162,500. Total bonds issued, $487,500; redeemed, $130,500; outstanding, $357,000.

Louisville (lōō' is vil)—Town in Boulder county; on Burlington railroad; incorporated, 5-24-1882; population—1920 census, 1,799; 1924 estimate, 1,950; altitude, 5,350; assessed valuation, $562,621; municipal tax levy, 11 mills; has municipal water system; bank deposits, $114,-595. Bonds issued — Water works, $17,000, all outstanding.

Loveland (lŭv lănd)—City of second class, in Larimer county; on C. & S. railroad; incorporated, 4-11-1881; population—1920 census, 5,065; 1924 estimate, 5,850; altitude, 4,982 feet; assessed valuation, $4,535,870; municipal tax levy, 12.4 mills; has municipal water system and sanitary sewer system; bank deposits, $1,554,623. Bonds issued—Water works, $200,000; storm sewers, $39,455; streets and alleys, $152,077. Total bonds issued, $391,532; redeemed, $61,636; outstanding, $329,896.

Lyons (lī' ŭnz) — Town in Boulder county; on Burlington railroad; incorporated, 3-31-1891; population—1920 census, 570; 1924 estimate, 625; altitude, 5,375 feet; assessed valuation, $251,674; municipal tax levy, 12 mills; has municipal water system and electric light system; bank deposits, $87,582. Bonds issued—Water works, $20,000; electric lights, $2,000. Total bonds issued, $22,-000; redeemed, $10,000; outstanding, $12,000.

Manassa (ma năs' sa)—Town in Conejos county; incorporated, 4-22-1889; population—1920 census, 906; 1924 estimate, 1,010; altitude, 7,700 feet; assessed valuation, $185,667; municipal tax levy, 8.5 mills; has municipal light system; bank deposits, $74,856. Bonds issued—Electric lights, $5,000, all outstanding.

Mancos (măn' kos)—Town in Montezuma county; on D. & R. G. W. railroad; incorporated, 6-12-1894; population—1920 census, 682; 1924 estimate, 715; altitude, 7,035 feet; assessed valuation, $429,270; municipal tax levy, 12 mills; has municipal water system; bank deposits, $480,-876. Bonds issued—Water works, $25,-000; miscellaneous, $5,300. Total bonds issued, $30,300, all outstanding.

Manitou Springs (măn' i tōō)—Town in El Paso county; incorporated under name of Manitou, ...; name changed to Manitou Springs, 7-9-1912; population—1920 census, 1,129; 1924 estimate, 1,340; altitude, 6,336 feet; assessed valuation, $3,151,500; municipal tax levy, 13.25 mills; has municipal water system and sanitary sewer system; bank deposits, $371,440. Bonds issued—Water works, $198,000; parks, $36,000; streets and alleys, $40,600. Total bonds issued, $274,600; redeemed, $15,000; outstanding, $259,600.

Manzanola (măn zăn ō' la)—Town in Otero county; on A. T. & S. F. railroad; incorporated, 6-16-1900; population—1920 census, 562; 1924 estimate, 660; altitude, 4,250 feet; assessed valuation, $480,361; municipal tax levy, 13.6 mills; has municipal water system; bank deposits, $227,492. Bonds issued—Water works, $27,500, all outstanding.

Marble (mär' bel)—Town in Gunnison county; incorporated, 6-20-1899; population—1920 census, 81; 1924 estimate, 160; altitude, 7,800 feet; assessed valuation, $324,850; municipal tax levy, 4 mills. No bonded debt.

Mead (mēd)—Town in Weld county; on Great Western railroad; incorporated, 3-2-1908; population—1920 census, 145; 1924 estimate, 205; altitude, 5,280 feet; assessed valuation, $213,730; municipal tax levy, 15 mills; has municipal water system; bank deposits, $65,718. Bonds issued—Water works, $42,000, all outstanding.

Meeker (mēk' ẽr)—Town, countyseat of Rio Blanco county; incorporated, 10-12-1885; population—1920 census, 935; 1924 estimate, 990; altitude, 6,240 feet; assessed valuation, $729,630; municipal tax levy, 12.5 mills; has municipal water system, sanitary sewer system, municipal light system; bank deposits, $716,-481. Bonds issued—Water works, $50,-000; electric lights, $24,200. Total bonds issued, $74,200; redeemed, $7,500; outstanding, $66,700.

Merino (me rē' nō)—Town in Logan county; on U. P. railroad; incorporated, 12-2-1916; population—1920 census, 263; 1924 estimate, 280; altitude, 4,042 feet; assessed valuation, $222,379; municipal tax levy, 16.5 mills; has municipal water system and sanitary sewer system; bank deposits, $90,487. Bonds issued—Water works, $40,000; sanitary sewer, $15,000. Total bonds issued, $55,000, all outstanding.

Milliken (mil' i ken)—Town in Weld county; on U. P. railroad; incorporated, 9-19-1910; population—1920 census, 372; 1924 estimate, 380; altitude, 4,760 feet; assessed valuation, $298,080; municipal tax levy, 12 mills; bank deposits, $42,697. Bonds issued—Water works, $32,000; redeemed, $3,000; outstanding, $29,000.

Minturn (min' turn)—Town in Eagle county; on D. & R. G. W. railroad; incorporated, 10-12-1904; population—1920 census, 298; 1924 estimate, 305; altitude, 7,825 feet; assessed valuation, $61,672; municipal tax levy, 24 mills; has municipal water system. Bonds issued—Water works, $20,000; redeemed, $10,000; outstanding, $10,000.

Moffat (mof' ăt)—Town in Saguache county; on D. & R. G. W. railroad; incorporated, 3-24-1911; population—1924 estimate, 150; altitude, 7,564 feet; assessed valuation, $149,006; municipal tax levy, 5 mills; has municipal water system; bank deposits, $23,043. No bonded debt.

Monte Vista (mon′ ta vis′ ta)—City of second class, in Rio Grande county; on D. & R. G. W. railroad; incorporated, 6-21-1886; population — 1920 census, 2,484; 1924 estimate, 2,870; altitude, 7,500 feet; assessed valuation, $1,992,100; municipal tax levy, 16 mills; has municipal sanitary sewer system; bank deposits, $983,185. Bonds issued—Sanitary sewers, $200; miscellaneous, $50,600. Total bonds issued, $50,800, all outstanding.

Montrose (mont rōz′)—City of second class, countyseat of Montrose county; on D. & R. G. W. railroad; incorporated, 4-3-1882; population—1920 census, 3,581; 1924 estimate, 3,890; altitude, 5,820 feet; assessed valuation, $2,999,021; municipal tax levy 13.5 mills; has municipal water system and sanitary sewer system; bank deposits, $1,566,060. Bonds issued—Water works, $135,000; streets and alleys, $57,782; miscellaneous, $100,000. Total bonds issued, $292,782; redeemed, $39,282; outstanding, $253,500.

Monument (mon′ ū ment)—Town in El Paso county; on A. T. & S. F. and D. & R. G. W. railroads; incorporated, 6-2-1879; population—1920 census, 192; 1924 estimate, 240; altitude, 6,895 feet; assessed valuation, $88,560; municipal tax levy, 17 mills; has municipal water system; bank deposits, $79,150. Bonds issued—Water works, $10,500, all outstanding.

Morrison (môr′ ri sŭn)—Town in Jefferson county; on C. & S. railroad; incorporated, 1-9-1906; population—1920 census, 195; 1924 estimate, 240; altitude, 5,669 feet; assessed valuation, $128,330; municipal tax levy, 22 mills; has municipal water system. Bonds issued—Water works, $21,500, all outstanding.

Nederland (ned′ ẽr lănd) — Town in Boulder county; incorporated, ...; population—1920 census, 291; 1924 estimate, 230; altitude, 8,200 feet; assessed valuation, $129,506; municipal tax levy, 21 mills; has municipal water system. Bonds issued—Water works, $20,000; redeemed, $9,000; outstanding, $11,000.

New Castle (kăs′ el)—Town in Garfield county; on D. & R. G. W. railroad; incorporated, 2-24-1888; population—1920 census, 447; 1924 estimate, 440; altitude, 5,552 feet; assessed valuation, $159,268; municipal tax levy, 7 mills; has municipal water system; bank deposits, $132,-191. Bonds issued—Refunding warrants, $6,000; redeemed, $4,000; outstanding, $2,000.

Norwood (nôr′ wood)—Town in San Miguel county; incorporated, 3-7-1905; population—1920 census, 365; 1924 estimate, 420; altitude, 7,017 feet; assessed valuation, $304,020; municipal tax levy, 23 mills; has municipal water system; bank deposits, $171,504. Bonds issued—Water works, $26,000; redeemed, $8,000; outstanding, $18,000.

Nucla (nū′ kla)—Town in Montrose county; incorporated, 1-18-1915; population—1920 census, 217; 1924 estimate, 210; altitude, 7,017 feet; assessed valuation, $146,325; municipal tax levy, 20 mills; has municipal water system. Bonds issued—Refunding warrants, $40,-000; water works, $12,000. Total bonds issued, $52,000; redeemed, $2,700; outstanding, $49,300.

Nunn (nŭn)—Town in Weld county; on U. P. railroad; incorporated, 3-5-1908; population—1920 census, 149; 1924 estimate, 205; altitude, 5,186 feet; assessed valuation, $246,560; municipal tax levy, 21 mills; has municipal water system; bank deposits, $56,145. Bonds issued—Water works, $40,000, all outstanding.

Oak Creek—Town in Routt county; on Denver & Salt Lake railroad; incorporated, 11-25-1907; population—1920 census, 967; 1924 estimate, 1,060; altitude, 7,401 feet; assessed valuation, $407,950; municipal tax levy, 22 mills; has municipal water system; bank deposits, $243,-657. Bonds issued—Water works, $5,000; sanitary sewers, $12,873.16; miscellaneous, $40,700. Total bonds issued, $58-573.16; redeemed, $10,700; outstanding, $47,873.16.

Olathe (ō lā′ thē)—Town in Montrose county; on D. & R. G. W. railroad; incorporated, 9-3-1907; population—1920 census, 491; 1924 estimate, 540; altitude, 5,346 feet; assessed valuation, $535,776; municipal tax levy, 9.3 mills; has municipal water system and sanitary sewer system; bank deposits, $378,743. Bonds issued—Public buildings, $3,500; water works, $83,000; sanitary sewers, $18,500. Total bonds issued, $105,000; redeemed, $11,500; outstanding, $93,500.

Olney Springs (ol′ ni)—Town in Crowley county; on Missouri Pacific railroad; incorporated, 4-6-1912; population—1920 census, 240; 1924 estimate, 285; altitude, 4,400 feet; assessed valuation, $155,665; municipal tax levy, 8 mills; has municipal light system; bank deposits, $107,-889. Bonds issued—Water works, $10,-000, all outstanding.

Ophir (ō fẽr)—Town in San Miguel county; incorporated, 7-5-1881; population—1920 census, 29; 1924 estimate, 35; altitude, 9,800 feet; assessed valuation, $23,170; municipal tax levy, 15 mills; has municipal water system. No bonded debt.

Orchard—Town in Delta county; incorporated, 5-2-1912; population—1920 census, 531; 1924 estimate, 550; altitude, 5,300 feet; assessed valuation, $625,135; municipal tax levy, 1.5 mills. No bonded debt.

Ordway (ôrd′ wā)—Town, countyseat of Crowley county; on Missouri Pacific railroad; incorporated, 6-8-1900; population—1920 census, 1,186; 1924 estimate, 1,220; altitude, 4,300 feet; assessed valuation, $1,066,920; municipal tax levy, 15 mills; has municipal water system; bank deposits, $466,026. Bonds issued—Water works, $55,000; public buildings, $10,000. Total bonds issued, $65,000; redeemed, $8,500; outstanding, $56,500.

Otis (ō′ tis)—Town in Washington county; on Burlington railroad; incorporated, 1-30-1917; population—1920 census, 467; 1924 estimate, 565; altitude, 4,000 feet; assessed valuation, $650,478; municipal tax levy, 14 mills; has municipal water system and electric light system; bank deposits, $294,293. Bonds issued—Water works, $25,000; all outstanding.

Ouray (ū rā′)—Town, countyseat of Ouray county; on D. & R. G. W. railroad; incorporated, ...; population—1920 census, 1,165; 1924 estimate, 1,105; altitude, 7,800 feet; assessed valuation, $684,900; municipal tax levy, 15.3 mills; has municipal water system and sanitary sewer system; bank deposits, $219,-208. Bonds issued—Water works, $20,-000; miscellaneous, $9,880. Total bonds issued, $29,880; redeemed, $15,000; outstanding, $14,880.

Pagosa Springs (pā gō' sa) — Town, countyseat of Archuleta county; on D. & R. G. W. railroad; incorporated, 2-28-1891; population—1920 census, 1,032; 1924 estimate, 1,120; altitude, 7,077 feet; assessed valuation, $581,105; municipal tax levy, 13.5 mills; has municipal water system; bank deposits, $317,930. Bonds issued—Water works, $17,500; all outstanding.

Palisades (păl i sādz')—Town in Mesa county; on D. & R. G. W. railroad; incorporated, 4-4-1904; population—1920 census, 855; 1924 estimate, 965; altitude, 4,740; assessed valuation, $615,648; municipal tax levy, 22 mills; has municipal water system; bank deposits, $431,572. Bonds issued—Water works, $75,000; parks, $5,000. Total bonds issued, $80,-000; redeemed, $11,250; outstanding, $68,750.

Palmer Lake (päm' ĕr)—Town in El Paso county; on D. & R. G. and A. T. & S. F. railroads; incorporated, 2-23-1889; population—1920 census, 160; 1924 estimate, 160; altitude, 6,237; assessed valuation, $478,260; municipal tax levy, 8 mills; has municipal water system. Bonds issued—Water works, $20,500, all outstanding.

Paonia (pā ōn' ya)—Town in Delta county; on D. & R. G. W. railroad; incorporated, 7-14-1902; population—1920 census, 925; 1924 estimate, 1,020; altitude, 5,696 feet; assessed valuation, $710,910; municipal tax levy, 10.9 mills; has municipal water and light systems and sanitary sewer system; bank deposits, $596,786. Bonds issued—Water works, $45,000; electric lights, $4,500; sanitary sewers, $53,000. Total bonds issued, $102,500; redeemed, $1,000; outstanding, $101,500.

Peetz (pētz)—Town in Logan county; on Burlington railroad; incorporated, 4-9-1917; population—1920 census, 322; 1924 estimate, 350; altitude, 4,300 feet; assessed valuation, $316,998; municipal tax levy, 21.2 mills; has municipal water and light systems; bank deposits, $103,-195. Bonds issued—Water works, $93,-500, all outstanding.

Pierce—Town in Weld county; on U. P. railroad; incorporated, 5-10-1918; population—1920 census, 327; 1924 estimate, 350; altitude, 5,041 feet; assessed valuation, $205,660; municipal tax levy, 17.5 mills; has municipal water system. Bonds issued—Water works, $43,000, all outstanding.

Pitkin (pit' kin)—Town in Gunnison county; on D. & R. G. W. railroad; incorporated, 8-11-1879; population—1920 census, 165; 1924 estimate, 160; altitude, 9,200 feet; assessed valuation, $98,505; municipal tax levy, 8 mills. No bonded debt.

Platteville (plăt' vil)—Town in Weld county; on U. P. railroad; incorporated by reorganization under the general incorporation laws, 3-21-1885; population—1920 census, 479; 1924 estimate, 500; altitude, 4,820 feet; assessed valuation, $380,980; municipal tax levy, 17 mills; has municipal water system and sanitary sewer system; bank deposits, $258,826. Bonds issued—Water works, $35,000, all outstanding.

Poncha Springs (pon' cha)—Town in Chaffee county; on D. & R. G. W. railroad; incorporated, 12-31-1880; population—1920 census, 37; 1924 estimate, 50; altitude, 7,500 feet; assessed valuation, $71,616; municipal tax levy, 4.5 mills. No bonded debt.

Pueblo (pweb' lō)—City of first class, county seat of Pueblo county; on D. & R. G. W. and A. T. & S. F. railroads; incorporated, ...; population—1920 census, 43,050; 1924 estimate, 45,000; altitude, 4,700 feet; assessed valuation, $69,829,451; municipal tax levy, 24.6 mills; has municipal water system and sanitary sewer system; bank deposits, $18,154,576. Bonds issued—Public buildings, $300,000; water works, $1,216,000; parks, $334,000; streets and alleys, $1,-948,300; miscellaneous, $560,000. Total bonds issued, $4,358,300, all outstanding.

Raymer (rā' mĕr)—Town in Weld county; on Burlington railroad; incorporated, 3-14-1919; population—1920 census, 267; 1924 estimate, 250; altitude, 4,779 feet; assessed valuation, $229,790; municipal tax levy, 9.5 mills; has municipal water system. Bonds issued—Water works, $20,000, all outstanding.

Red Cliff—Town in Eagle county; on D. & R. G. W. railroad; incorporated, 7-29-1880; population—1920 census, 347; 1924 estimate, 350; altitude, 9,608 feet; assessed valuation, $158,860; municipal tax levy, 27.6 mills; has municipal water system; bank deposits, $120,996. Bonds issued—Water works, $20,000; redeemed, $2,500; outstanding, $17,500.

Rico (rē' kō)—Town, countyseat of Dolores county; on Rio Grande Southern; incorporated, 7-29-1880; population—1920 census, 326; 1924 estimate, 245; altitude, 8,900 feet; assessed valuation, $143,056; municipal tax levy, 17 mills; has municipal water system. Bonds issued—Water works, $10,000; redeemed, $4,000; outstanding, $6,000.

Ridgway (rij' wā)—Town in Ouray county; on D. & R. G. W. railroad; incorporated, 2-28-1891; population—1920 census, 400; 1924 estimate, 425; altitude, 6,770 feet; assessed valuation, $218,510; municipal tax levy, 17 mills; has municipal water system; bank deposits, $123,-758. Bonds issued—Water works, $30,-000; redeemed, $20,000; outstanding, $10,000.

Rifle—Town in Garfield county; on D. & R. G. W. railroad; incorporated, 8-7-1905; population—1920 census, 885; 1924 estimate, 980; altitude, 5,332 feet; assessed valuation, $725,652; municipal tax levy, 12.5 mills; has municipal water and sanitary sewer systems; bank deposits, $545,192. Bonds issued—Water works, $60,000; sanitary sewers, $7,088; streets and alleys, $52,000. Total bonds issued, $119,088; redeemed, $21,000; outstanding, $98,088.

Rockvale (rok' vāl)—Town in Fremont county; on D. & R. G. W. railroad; incorporated, 8-28-1886; population—1920 census, 1,249; 1924 estimate, 1,350; altitude, 5,260 feet; assessed valuation, $181,654; municipal tax levy, 13 mills; has municipal water system. No bonded debt.

Rocky Ford—City of second class, in Otero county; on A. T. & S. F. railroad; incorporated, 8-6-1887; population—1920 census, 3,746; 1924 estimate, 4,280; altitude, 4,250 feet; assessed valuation, $2,987,040; municipal tax levy, 19.1 mills; has municipal water and sanitary sewer systems; bank deposits, $900,600. Bonds issued—Water works, $165,000; storm sewers, $143,543; streets and alleys, $201,950. Total bonds issued, $510,494; redeemed, $100,000; outstanding, $410,494.

Saguache (sa wäch')—Town, countyseat of Saguache county; incorporated, ...; population—1920 census, 948; 1924 estimate, 1,030; altitude, 7,800 feet; assessed valuation, $552,427; municipal tax levy, 24.4 mills; has municipal light system; bank deposits, $396,196. Bonds issued—Public buildings, $3,900; electric lights, $10,000; miscellaneous, $3,200. Total bonds issued, $17,100, all outstanding.

Salida (sā lī' da)—City of second class, in Chaffee county; on D. & R. G. W. railroad; incorporated, 10-4-1880; population—1920 census, 4,689; 1924 estimate, 4,750; altitude, 7,050 feet; assessed valuation, $3,317,344; municipal tax levy, 10 mills; has muncipal water and sanitary sewer systems; bank deposits, $1,401,733. Bonds issued—Water works, $40,000; redeemed, $39,000; outstanding, $1,000.

Sanford (săn' fōrd)—Town in Conejos county; incorporated, ...; population—1920 census, 555; 1924 estimate, 580; altitude, 7,560 feet; assessed valuation, $132,155; municipal tax levy, 4 mills. No bonded debt.

Sawpit (saw' pit)—Town in San Miguel county; on D. & R. G. W. railroad; incorporated 5-5-1896; population, 121; 1924 estimate, 90; altitude, 7,400 feet. No bonded debt.

Sedgwick (sej' wik)—Town in Sedgwick county; on U. P. railroad; incorporated, 1-15-1918; population—1920 census, 380; 1924 estimate, 450; altitude, 3,500 feet; assessed valuation, $333,145; municipal tax levy, 22 mills; has municipal water and light systems; bank deposits, $218,365. Bonds issued—Water works, $71,000; all outstanding.

Seibert (sē' bĕrt)—Town in Kit Carson county; on Rock Island railroad; incorporated, 3-16-1917; population—1920 census, 311; 1924 estimate, 360; altitude, 4,705 feet; assessed valuation, $356,050; municipal tax levy, 15 mills; has municipal water and light systems; bank deposits, $88,931. Bonds issued—Water works, $50,000; electric lights, $6,000. Total bonds issued, $56,000, all outstanding.

Sheridan (shĕr' i dăn)—Town in Arapahoe county; on A. T. & S. F. and D. & R. G. W. railroads; incorporated, 2-18-1890; population—1920 census, 455; 1924 estimate, 610; altitude, 5,394 feet; assessed valuation, $493,640; municipal tax levy, 6 mills. No bonded debt.

Silt (silt)—Town in Garfield county; on D. & R. G. W. railroad; incorporated, ...; population—1920 census, 165; 1924 estimate, 170; altitude, 5,338 feet; assessed valuation, $119,588; municipal tax levy, 15.2 mills; has municipal water system; bank deposits, $118,669. Bonds issued—Refunding warrants, $3,000; water works, $3,000. Total bonds issued, $6,000, all outstanding.

Silver Cliff—Town, countyseat of Custer county; on D. & R. G. W. railroad; incorporated, 12-30-1878; population—1920 census, 241; 1924 estimate, 270; altitude, 8,000 feet; assessed valuation, $25,594; municipal tax levy, 12.5 mills; has municipal water system. No bonded debt.

Silver Plume (plōōm)—Town in Clear Creek county; on C. & S. railroad; incorporated, 8-16-1880; population—1920 census, 272; 1924 estimate, 230; altitude, 9,175 feet; assessed valuation, $150,415; municipal tax levy, 12.75 mills; has municipal water system. Bonds issued—Water works, $500, all outstanding.

Silverton (sil' vĕr tŭn)—Town, countyseat of San Juan county; on D. & R. G. W. railroad; incorporated, ...; population—1920 census, 1,150; 1924 estimate, 1,015; altitude, 9,302 feet; assessed valuation, $705,106; municipal tax levy, 10 mills; has municipal water and light systems; bank deposits, $433,374. Bonds issued—Water works, $20,000; redeemed, $4,000; outstanding, $16,000.

Simla (sim' la) — Town in Elbert county; on Rock Island railroad; incorporated, 12-28-1911; population—1920 census, 387; 1924 estimate, 495; altitude, 6,090 feet; assessed valuation, $284,934; municipal tax levy, 28.37 mills; has municipal water and light systems; bank deposits, $90,565. Bonds issued—Water works, $41,000; electric lights, $19,600. Total bonds issued, $60,600, all outstanding.

Springfield—Town, countyseat of Baca county; incorporated, 1-7-1890; population—1920 census, 295; 1924 estimate, 580; altitude, 4,400 feet; assessed valuation, $315,500; municipal tax levy, 6 mills; bank deposits, $240,388. No bonded debt.

Steamboat Springs—Town, countyseat of Routt county; on Denver & Salt Lake railroad; incorporated, 7-17-1900; population—1920 census, 1,249; 1924 estimate, 1,490; altitude, 6,762 feet; assessed valuation, $1,171,100; municipal tax levy, 14.5 mills; has municipal water and sanitary sewer systems; bank deposits, $734,506. Bonds issued—Water works, $84,000; sanitary sewers, $70,552.38; streets and alleys, $32,500. Total bonds issued, $187,052.38; redeemed, $53,000; outstanding, $134,052.38.

St. Elmo (el' mō)—Town in Chaffee county; on C. & S. railroad; incorporated, 10-30-1880; population—1920 census, 37; 1924 estimate, 25; altitude, 10,000 feet; assessed valuation, $11,295; municipal tav levy, 20 mills; has municipal water system. No bonded debt.

Sterling (stĕr' ling)—City of second class, countyseat of Logan county; on U. P. railroad; incorporated, 11-8-1884; population—1920 census, 6,415; 1924 estimate, 7,250; altitude, 3,947 feet; assessed valuation, $6,206,642; municipal tax levy, 14 mills; has municipal water and sanitary sewer systems; bank deposits, $2,010,899. Bonds issued—Water works, $520,000; sanitary sewers, $114,000; streets and alleys, $479,500. Total bonds issued, $1,113,500; redeemed, $80,500; outstanding, $1,033,000.

Stratton (străt' ŭn)—Town in Kit Carson county; on Rock Island railroad; incorporated, 3-18-1919; population—1920 census, 421; 1924 estimate, 530; altitude, 4,404 feet; assessed valuation, $677,026; municipal tax levy, 10 mills; has municipal water and light systems; bank deposits, $97,260. Bonds issued—Water works, $75,000, all outstanding.

Sugar City—Town in Crowley county; on Missouri Pacific railroad; incorporated, 5-31-1900; population—1920 census, 836; 1924 estimate, 840; altitude, 4,325 feet; assessed valuation, $350,435; municipal tax levy, 18 mills; has municipal water and sanitary sewer systems; bank deposits, $103,735. Bonds issued—Water works, $20,000; sanitary sewers, $12,981; miscellaneous, $16,000. Total bonds issued, $48,981; redeemed, $14,781; outstanding, $34,200.

Superior (sōō pē' ri or)—Town in Boulder county; on C. & S. railroad; incorporated, 4-5-1904; population—1920 census, 233; 1924 estimate, 295; altitude, 5,512 feet; assessed valuation, $49,680; municipal tax levy, 22 mills. No bonded debt.

Swink (swink)—Town in Otero county; on A. T. & S. F. railroad; incorporated, 5-19-1906; population—1920 census, 465; 1924 estimate, 425; altitude, 4,000 feet; assessed valuation, $252,490; municipal tax levy, 13.6 mills; has municipal water system; bank deposits, $103,154. Bonds issued—Water works, $10,000, all outstanding.

Telluride (tel' ū rīd)—Town, countyseat of San Miguel county; on D. & R. G. W. railroad; incorporated, ...; population—1920 census, 1,618; 1924 estimate, 1,510; altitude, 8,500 feet; assessed valuation, $1,351,830; municipal tax levy, 8 mills; has municipal water system and sanitary sewer system; bank deposits, $1,111,635. No bonded debt.

Timnath (tim' năth)—Town in Larimer county; on C. & S. railroad; incorporated, 6-22-1920; population—1924 estimate, 215; altitude, 4,875; assessed valuation, $158,380; municipal tax levy, 8 mills; has municipal water system; bank deposits, $37,766. Bonds issued—Water works, $14,000, all outstanding.

Trinidad (trin' i dăd)—City of second class, county seat of Las Animas county; on four railroads; incorporated, ...; population—1920 census, 10,906; 1924 estimate, 12,100; altitude, 5,999 feet; assessed valuation, $10,704,813; municipal tax levy, 18 mills; has municipal water system and sanitary sewer system; bank deposits, $8,009,104. Bonds issued—Water works, $1,171,000; bridges and viaducts, $69,700; sanitary sewers, $30,000; streets and alleys, $961,000. Total bonds issued, $2,231,700; redeemed, $283,800; outstanding, $1,947,900.

Two Buttes (būtz)—Town in Baca county; incorporated, 8-1-1911; population—1920 census, 93; 1924 estimate, 100; altitude, 4,075 feet; assessed valuation, $95,600; municipal tax levy, 2 mills; has municipal water system; bank deposits, $59,264. No bonded debt.

Victor (vik' tĕr) — Town in Teller county; incorporated, 5-15-1894; population—1920 census, 1,777; 1924 estimate, 1,450; altitude, 9,900 feet; assessed valuation, $507,680; municipal tax levy, 50 mills; bank deposits, $1,227,187. Bonds issued—Water works refunding, $384,000; warrant refunding, $139,100. Total bonds issued, $523,100; redeemed, $17,500; outstanding, $505,600.

Vona (vō' na)—Town in Kit Carson county; on Rock Island railroad; incorporated, 6-9-1919; population—1920 census, 268; 1924 estimate, 215; altitude, 4,494; assessed valuation, $209,761; municipal tax levy, 5.37 mills; has municipal water system; bank deposits, $45,086. No bonded debt.

Walden (wäl' den)—Town, countyseat of Jackson county; on Colorado & Wyoming railroad; incorporated, 8-6-1890; population—1920 census, 260; 1924 estimate, 265; altitude, 8,300 feet; assessed valuation, $266,970; municipal tax levy, 13 mills; has municipal water system and light system; bank deposits, $314,541. Bonds issued—Water works, $20,000; redeemed, $900.00; outstanding, $19,100.

Walsenburg (wäl' sen bĕrg)—City of second class, countyseat of Huerfano county; on D. & R. G. W. and C. & S. railroads; incorporated, ...; population—1920 census, 3,565; 1924 estimate, 4,054; altitude, 6,200 feet; assessed valuation, $2,797,957; municipal tax levy, 14 mills; has municipal water and sanitary sewer systems; bank deposits, $2,368,091. Bonds issued—Water works, $353,500; streets and alleys, $465,000. Total bonds issued, $818,500; redeemed, $39,500; outstanding, $779,000.

Ward—Town in Boulder county; incorporated, 5-20-1896; population—1920 census, 74; 1924 estimate, 35; altitude, 9,350; assessed valuation, $27,966; municipal tax levy, 15 mills; has municipal water and light systems. No bonded debt.

Wellington (wel' ing tŭn)—Town in Larimer county; on C. & S. railroad; incorporated, 10-24-1905; population—1920 census, 439; 1924 estimate, 950; altitude, 5,000 feet; assessed valuation, $431,410; municipal tax levy, 10 mills; has municipal water system; bank deposits, $155,055. Bonds issued—Public buildings, $2,900; water works, $40,000. Total bonds issued, $42,900; all outstanding.

Westcliffe (west' klif)—Town in Custer county; on D. & R. G. W. railroad; incorporated, 6-2-1887; population—1920 census, 338; 1924 estimate, 350; altitude, 7,800 feet; assessed valuation, $263,627; municipal tax levy, 10 mills; has municipal water system; bank deposits, $197,821. No bonded debt.

Westminister (west' min stĕr) — Town in Adams county; on C. & S. railroad; incorporated, 4-4-1911; population—1920 census, 235; 1924 estimate, 360; altitude, 5,280 feet; assessed valuation, $392,940; municipal tax levy, 14.25 mills; has municipal water system. Bonds issued—Water works, $28,000, all outstanding.

Wiley (wī' li) — Town in Prowers county; on A. T. & S. F. railroad; incorporated, 6-3-1908; population—1920 census, 565; 1924 estimate, 570; altitude, 3,100 feet; assessed valuation, $303,815; municipal tax levy, 14.2 mills; has municipal water system; bank deposits, $109,851. Bonds issued—Water works, $32,000; redeemed, $1,000; outstanding, $31,000.

Williamsburg (wil' yămz bĕrg—Town in Fremont county; on D. & R. G. W. railroad; incorporated, 3-29-1888; population—1920 census, 402; 1924 estimate, 305; altitude, 5,250 feet; assessed valuation, $66,262; municipal tax levy, 21 mills; has municipal water system. Bonds issued—Water works, $3,500; redeemed, $2,000; outstanding, $1,500.

Windsor (wind' sĕr)—Town in Weld county; on C. & S. railroad; incorporated, 4-1-1890; population—1920 census, 1,290; 1924 estimate, 1,350; altitude, 4,900 feet; assessed valuation, $1,149,220; municipal tax levy, 13.5 mills; has municipal water and sanitary sewer systems; bank deposits, $515,465. Bonds issued—Public buildings, $3,500; water works, $32,500; streets and alleys, $24,000. Total bonds issued, $60,000; redeemed, $2,500; outstanding, $57,500.

Wray (rā)—Town, countyseat of Yuma county; on Burlington railroad; incorporated, 12-29-1888; population—1920 census, 1,538; 1924 estimate, 1,795; altitude, 3,500 feet; assessed valuation, $1,510,040; municipal tax levy, 19.5 mills; has municipal water system, sanitary sewer system, municipal light system; bank deposits, $682,153. Bonds issued—Water works, $110,000; electric lights,

$27,000; sanitary sewers, $71,300. Total bonds issued, $208,300; redeemed, $10,000; outstanding, $198,300.

Yampa (yăm′ pa) — Town in Routt county; on Denver & Salt Lake railroad; incorporated, 4-17-1906; population—1920 census, 200; 1924 estimate, 285; altitude, 7,884 feet; assessed valuation, $142,250; municipal tax levy, 16.5 mills; has municipal water system; bank deposits, $173,547. Bonds issued—Water works, $10,000; redeemed, $2,000; outstanding, $8,000.

Yuma (ū′ ma)—Town in Yuma county; on Burlington railroad; incorporated, 2-19-1887; population — 1920 census, 1,177; 1924 estimate, 1,260; altitude, 4,128 feet; assessed valuation, $1,194,020; muncipal tax levy, 15.6 mills; has municipal water and light systems and sanitary sewer system; bank deposits, $596,005. Bonds issued—Water works, $141,000; electric lights, $2,900; sanitary sewers, $85,000. Total bonds issued, $228,900; redeemed, $8,000; outstanding, $220,900.

Railway Distances From Denver

IN the accompanying list only incorporated towns are given, and only distances from Denver, but by reference to the map accompanying this volume, it will not be difficult to determine the railroad distances between nearly all important places in the state. The railroad given is the road on which the town is located or the nearest road. If it is on more than one road, only one is named in most cases, being that over which the distance from Denver is the shortest. Which of these towns are countyseats may be determined from the table on page 163. The following abbreviations are used:

Burlington, Chicago, Burlington & Quincy; C. & S., Colorado & Southern; C. C. Short Line, Colorado Springs & Cripple Creek District; D. & R. G., Denver & Rio Grande Western; D. & S. L., Denver & Salt Lake; Midland, Colorado Midland; M. P., Missouri Pacific; R. I., Chicago, Rock Island & Pacific; Santa Fe, Atchison, Topeka & Santa Fe; U. P., Union Pacific; C. W. & E.; Colorado, Wyoming and Eastern.

Portions of the Colorado Midland railroad have been temporarily abandoned, and several points formerly reached over this road now must be reached over the Denver & Rio Grande Western, the distance being somewhat greater.

Town—	Railroad	Distance, Miles
Aguilar	C. & S.	195
Akron	Burlington	112
Alamosa	D. & R. G.	252
Alma	C. & S.	121
Antonito	D. & R. G.	280
Aspen	D. & R. G.	401
Ault	U. P.	63
Bayfield	D. & R. G.*	450
Berthoud	C. & S.	54
Blackhawk	C. & S.	39
Blanca	D. & R. G.	232
Bonanza	D. & R. G.	245
Boulder	U. P., C. & S.	27
Breckenridge	C. & S.	110
Brighton	U. P.	19
Brush	Burlington	88
Buena Vista	D. & R. G.	240
Burlington	R. I.	166
Canon City	D. & R. G.	160
Carbondale	D. & R. G.	373
Castle Rock†		32
Cedaredge	D. & R. G.*	385
Central City	C. & S.	45
Center	San Luis Central	277
Cheyenne Wells	U. P.	177
Collbran	D. & R. G.*	428
Colorado Springs†		75
Cortez	D. & R. G.*	506
Craig	D. & S. L.	255
Crawford	D. & R. G.*	390
Creede	D. & R. G.	321
Crested Butte	D. & R. G.	316
Creston	D. & R. G.	273
Cripple Creek	C. C. Short Line	126
Dacono	U. P.	25
DeBeque	D. & R. G.	417
Del Norte	D. & R. G.	283
Delta	D. & R. G.	373
Dillon	C. & S.	1[illegible]
Dolores	D. & R. G.	478
Durango	D. & R. G.	451
Eads	M. P.	230
Eagle	D. & R. G.	329
Eaton	U. P.	59
Elizabeth	C. & S.	39
Empire	C. & S.*	55
Erie	Burlington	26
Estes Park‡		70
Eureka	Silverton Nor.	525
Evans	U. P.	48
Fairplay	C. & S.	115
Firestone	U. P.	27
Flagler	R. I.	123
Fleming	Burlington	144
Florence	D. & R. G.	152
Fort Collins	U. P., C. & S.	68
Fort Lupton	U. P.	26
Fort Morgan	Burlington, U. P.	78
Fountain†		88
Fowler	Santa Fe	154
Frederick	U. P.	26
Fruita	D. & R. G.	384
Georgetown	C. & S.	50
Gilcrest	U. P.	40
Glenwood Springs	D. & R. G.	360
Golden	C. & S.	16
Goldfield	C. C. Short Line	119
Granada	Santa Fe	252
Granby	D. & S. L.	99
Grand Junction	D. & R. G.	450
Grand Valley	D. & R. G.	404
Greeley	U. P.	52
Green Mountain Falls	Midland	90
Grover	Burlington	147
Gunnison	D. & R. G.	288
Gypsum	D. & R. G.	336

Town—	Railroad	Distance, Miles
Hartman	Santa Fe	272
Haxtun	Burlington	156
Hayden	D. & S. L.	238
Holly	Santa Fe	262
Holyoke	Burlington	173
Hooper	D. & R. G.	280
Hotchkiss	D. & R. G.	398
Hot Sulphur Springs	D. & S. L.	109
Hudson	Burlington	29
Hugo	U. P.	115
Idaho Springs	C. & S.	37
Ignacio	D. & R. G.	426
Iliff	U. P.	151
Johnstown	U. P.	46
Julesburg	U. P.	197
Kersey	U. P.	54
Kiowa	C. & S.*	46
Kremmling	D. & S. L.	126
Lafayette	Burlington	22
La Jara	D. & R. G.	266
La Junta	Santa Fe	182
Lake City	D. & R. G.	351
Lamar	Santa Fe	235
LaSalle	U. P.	46
Las Animas	Santa Fe	201
LaVeta	D. & R. G.	190
Leadville	D. & R. G.	276
Limon	U. P., R. I.	90
Littleton†		10
Longmont	C. & S.	37
Louisville	C. & S.	19
Loveland	C. & S.	60
Lyons	Burlington	48
Manassa	D. & R. G.*	276
Mancos	D. & R. G.	491
Manitou	Midland	81
Manzanola	Santa Fe	163
Marble	Crystal River	299
Meeker	D. & R. G.*	428
Merino	U. P.	127
Milliken	U. P.	44
Minturn	D. & R. G.	302
Moffat	D. & R. G.	263
Monte Vista	D. & R. G.	269
Montrose	D. & R. G.	351
Monument†		60
Morrison	C. & S.	17
New Castle	D. & R. G.	373
Norwood	D. & R. G.*	424
Nucla	D. & R. G.*	450
Nunn	U. P.	72
Oak Creek	D. & S. L.	194
Olathe	D. & R. G.	362
Olney Springs	M. P.	158
Ophir	D. & R. G.	422
Ordway	M. P.	169
Otis	Burlington	126
Ouray	D. & R. G.	387
Pagosa Springs	D. & R. G.	421
Palisades	D. & R. G.	437
Palmer Lake†		52
Paonia	D. & R. G.	406
Peetz	Burlington	148
Pitkin	D. & R. G.	315
Platteville	U. P.	35
Poncha Springs	D. & R. G.	220
Pueblo†		119
Red Cliff	D. & R. G.	294
Rico	D. & R. G.	443
Ridgway	D. & R. G.	377
Rifle	D. & R. G.	387
Rocky Ford	Santa Fe	172
Saguache	D. & R. G.*	265
Salida	D. & R. G.	215
Sanford	D. & R. G.*	271
Seibert	R. I.	134
Silt	D. & R. G.	375
Silver Cliff	D. & R. G*	210
Silver Plume	C. & S.	54
Silverton	D. & R. G.	497
Simla	R. I.	115
Springfield	Santa Fe*	285
Steamboat Springs	D. & S. L.	214
St. Elmo	C. & S.	153
Sterling	Burlington, U. P.	123
Sugar City	M. P.	174
Superior	C. & S.	20
Swink	Santa Fe	177
Telluride	D. & R. G.	422
Trinidad†		210
Two Buttes	Santa Fe*	285
Victor	C. C. Short Line	119
Walden	C. W. & E.	256
Walsenburg	C. & S., D. & R. G.	171
Wellington	C. & S.	85
Westcliffe	D. & R. G.	209
Wiley	Santa Fe	233
Windsor	C. & S.	65
Wray	Burlington	138
Yampa	D. & S. L.	185
Yuma	Burlington	138

* Not directly on a railroad. The road given is the nearest.

† The Colorado & Southern, Denver & Rio Grande Western and Santa Fe railroads serve towns between Denver and Pueblo, and the distance is about the same by all lines. The two first named roads have direct lines from Denver to Trinidad, and the Santa Fe route is by way of La Junta.

‡ No railroad approaches nearer than 22 miles of Estes Park, which lies near the east entrance to the Rocky Mountain national park. The distance given is by way of Lyons.

Altitudes of Colorado Mountains

Name	County	Elevation, Feet
Achonee Mountain	Grand	12,656
Adams Mountain	Grand	12,115
Aetna Mountain	Chaffee	13,800
Albion Mountain	Boulder	12,596
Alpine Peak	Clear Creek	11,525
Alps Mountain	Clear Creek	10,508
Anchor Mountain	Dolores	12,325
Andrews Peak	Grand	12,564
Antero, Mount	Chaffee	14,245
Apache Peak	Boulder-Grand	12,873
Apiatan Mountain	Grand	10,888
Arapahoe Peak	Boulder-Grand	13,506
Arkansas Mountain	Lake	13,797
Arrow Peak	San Juan	13,803
Arthur Mountain	El Paso	10,805
Audubon Mountain	Boulder	13,223
Augusta Mountain	Gunnison	12,615
Avery Peak	Gunnison	12 652
Axtel Mountain	Gunnison	12,013
Baker Mountain	Grand	12,406
Bald Mountain	Boulder	11,470

Name	County	Elevation, Feet
Bald Mountain	Summit	13,964
Bald Mountain	Teller	12,365
Baldy Mountain	Gunnison	12,809
Baldy Peak	Ouray	10,615
Banded Peak	Archuleta	12,376
Baxter Mountain	Costilla	10,629
Bear Mountain	San Juan	12,950
Beautiful Mountain	Mineral	12,746
Beckwith Mountain	Gunnison	12,371
Belleview	Rio Grande	12,727
Bierstadt Mountain	Clear Creek	14,046
Big Bull Mountain	Teller	10,826
Big Chief Mountain	Teller	11,220
Bison Peak	Park	12,400
Blackhawk Peak	Gilpin	10,323
Blackhawk Peak	Dolores	12,687
Blanca Peak	Costilla-Huerfano-Alamosa	14,390
Bowen Mountain	Grand	12 541
Bross Mountain	Park	14,163
Buck Mountain	Routt-Jackson	11,375
Buckeye Peak	Lake	12,863
Buckskin Mountain	Costilla	10,512
Buffalo Peak	Summit	13,541
Calico Peak	Dolores	12,035
Cameron Cone	El Paso	10,705
Cameron Mountain	Park	14,233
Capitol Mountain	Pitkin	13,997
Cascade Mountain	Gunnison	11,707
Cascade Mountain	Grand	12,320
Castle Peak	Gunnison-Pitkin	14,259
Cement Mountain	Gunnison	12,212
Chama Peak	Archuleta	12,027
Chapin Mountain	Larimer	13,052
Chicago Peak	Huerfano-Costilla	10,960
Chief Mountain	Clear Creek	11,710
Chimney Peak	Hinsdale-Ouray	11,785
Chiquita Mountain	Larimer	12,458
Cinnamon Mountain	Gunnison	12 270
Cirrus Mountain	Grand	12,804
Clarence King Mountain	Boulder	13,176
Clover Mountain	Chaffee	13,000
Colorado Mountain	Gilpin	10,884
Columbia Peak	Clear Creek	14,030
Comanche Peak	Boulder	13,491
Cone Mountain	Clear Creek	12,230
Conejos Peak	Conejos	13,180
Copper Mountain	Summit	12,475
Copper Mountain	Teller	10,226
Courthouse Mountain	Hinsdale-Ouray	12,165
Cover Mountain	Park	10,165
Coxcomb Peak	Hinsdale-Ouray	13,663
Craig Mountain	Grand	12,005
Crested Butte	Gunnison	12,172
Crestone Needle	Custer-Saguache	14,130
Crestone Peak	Saguache	14,233
Crystal Peak	Hinsdale	12,927
Culebra Peak	Costilla-Las Animas	14,069
Cumulus Mountain	Grand	12,724
Dakota Hill	Gilpin	10,930
Del Norte Peak	Rio Grande	12,378
Democrat Mountain	Park-Lake	14,000
Dickenson Mountain	Larimer	11,874
Double Top Mountain	Gunnison	12,192 12,178
Dump Mountain	Costilla	10,310
Dunraven Mountain	Larimer	12,548
Eagle Peak	Dolores	12,105
Echo Mountain	La Plata	13,305
Elbert Mountain	Lake	14,419
Electric Peak	Grand	11,943
Elephant Mountain	Rio Grande	11,790
Elk Mountain	Mineral	11,030
Elk Mountain	Eagle-Summit	12,718
Elliott Mountain	Dolores	12,337
Emerson Mountain	La Plata	13,147
Emmons Mountain	Gunnison	12,414
Engineer Mountain	Hinsdale-Ouray-San Juan	13,190
Engineer Mountain	San Juan	12,972
Eolus Mountain	La Plata	14,079
Estes Cone	Larimer	11,017
Ethel Mountain	Routt-Jackson	11,940
Evans Mountain	Park-Lake	13,580
Evans Mountain	Clear Creek	14,260
Expectation Mountain	Dolores	12,071
Fairchild Mountain	Larimer	13,502
Fisher Mountain	Mineral	12,855
Fisher Mountain	Grand	12,280
Fletcher Mountain	Summit	13,917
Flora Mountain	Clear Creek-Grand	13,122
Florida Mountain	La Plata	13,076
Fox Mountain	Mineral	11,520
Freeman Peak	Jefferson	11,627
Garfield Mountain	El Paso	10,925
Garfield Mountain	San Juan	13,065
Garfield Peak	Gunnison	12,136
Gilpin Peak	Ouray-San Miguel	13,682
Glacier Peak	Summit	12,654
Gothic Mountain	Gunnison	12,646
Grant Peak	San Juan-San Miguel	13,692
Gray Head	San Miguel	10,994
Grayback Mountain	Costilla	10,575
Grayrock Peak	San Juan	12,488
Grays Peak	Clear Creek-Summit	14,341
Graystone Peak	San Juan	13,489
Greenhorn Mountain	Huerfano-Pueblo	12,334
Green Mountain	Jefferson	10 530
Greylock Mountain	La Plata	13,571
Grizzly Mountain	Pitkin-Chaffee	14,020
Grizzly Peak	La Plata	13,695
Grizzly Peak	Dolores-San Juan	13,738
Hague Peak	Larimer	13,562
Hale Mountain	Grand	11,747
Hallet Peak	Grand-Larimer	12,723
Handies Peak	Hinsdale	14,008
Harvard, Mount	Chaffee	14,375
Helmet Peak	Montezuma	11,976
Hermosa Mountain	Dolores-San Juan	12,574
Hesperus Peak	Montezuma	13,225
Holy Cross Mountain	Eagle	13,978
Homestake Peak	Eagle	13,217
Hope Mountain	Mineral	12,841
Horseshoe Mountain	Park-Lake	13,902
Howard Mountain	Grand	12,814
Humboldt Peak	Custer-Saguache	14,044
Hunchback Mountain	San Juan	13,133
Ida Mountain	Grand-Larimer	12,868
Irving Peak	La Plata	13,210
Jacque Mountain	Summit	13,235
Jacque Peak	Summit	13,205
Jugged Mountain	San Juan	13,829
James Peak	Clear Creek-Grand-Gilpin	13,260
Johnny Bull Mountain	Dolores	12,018
Jura Knob	San Juan	12,617
Kendall	San Juan	13,480
Kingston Peak	Clear Creek-Gilpin	12,137
Kit Carson Peak	Saguache-Custer	14,100
Klondike Mountain	Boulder	10,802
La Garita	Mineral-Saguache	13,725
La Plata Peak	Chaffee	14,332
Lead Mountain	Grand	12,532
Leviathan Peak	San Juan	13,528
Lillie	Larimer	11,384
Lincoln Mountain	Park	14,287
Lizard Head	Dolores-San Miguel	13,156
London Mountain	Park	13,161
Lone Cone	San Miguel-Dolores	12,761
Lonesome Peak	Grand	10,588
Longs Peak	Boulder	14 255
Lookout Mountain	Grand	10,155
Lookout Mountain	Larimer	10,633
Lookout Peak	San Juan-San Miguel	13,674
Lulu Mountain	Grand	11,720
McCauley Peak	La Plata	13,551
McGregor Mountain	Larimer	10,482
Madden Peak	Montezuma-La Plata	11,980
Mahana Peak	Boulder	12,629
Marcellina Mountain	Gunnison	11,349
Maroon Peak	Pitkin	14,126

Name	County	Elevation, Feet
Martha Washington Mtn.	Larimer	13,269
Massive, Mount	Lake	14,404
Matterhorn Peak	Hinsdale	13,589
McClellan, Mount	Clear Creek-Summit.	13,423
Meadow Mountain	Boulder	11,634
Meeker Mountain	Boulder	13,911
Metroz Mountain	Mineral	11,900
Mineral Hill	Summit	10,885
Mineral Point	Gunnison	12,541
Missouri Hill	Chaffee	12,700
Monitor Peak	La Plata	13,703
Monument Hill	La Plata	10,830
Monument Peak	Mineral	10,641
Mosquito Peak	Park-Lake	13,784
Mummy Mountain	Larimer	13,413
Naki Peak	Grand	12,221
Navajo Peak	Boulder-Grand	13,406
Nebo Mountain	San Juan	13,192
Nebraska Hill	Gilpin	11,548
Nigger Hill	Summit	10,171
Nimbus Mountain	Grand	12,730
Nipple Mountain	Fremont	10,068
North Italian Mountain	Gunnison	13,225
North Maroon	Pitkin	14,000
Ohio Peak	Gunnison	12,251
Old Baldy	Costilla-Huerfano	14,176
Old Baldy Mountain	Rio Grande	12,602
Oregon Hill	Gilpin	10,884
Orton Mountain	Boulder	11,662
Oso Mountain	La Platte	13,706
Otis Peak	Grand-Larimer	12,478
Ouray, Mount	Chaffee	13,956
Overlook Point	La Plata	12,995
Owen Mountain	Gunnison	13,102
Park Mountain	Costilla	10,396
Parrott Peak	La Plata	11,876
Parry Peak	Clear Creek-Grand	13,345
Pearl Mountain	Gunnison	13,484
Peeler Peak	Gunnison	12,219
Pigeon Peak	La Plata	13,961
Pikes Peak	El Paso	14,410
Pilot Knob	San Juan-San Miguel	13,375
Pisgah Mountain	Clear Creek-Gilpin	10,085
Pole Creek Mountain	Hinsdale	13,740
Pool Table Mountain	Mineral	12,142
Porphyry Peaks	Grand	11,155 11,355
Potato Hill	San Juan	11,876
Potosi Peak	Ouray	13,763
Princeton, Mount	Chaffee	14,196
Prospect Mountain	Lake	12,608
Ptarmigan Hill	Eagle	12,174
Ptarmigan Peak	Park-Lake	13,736
Purple Peak	Gunnison	12,989
Pyramid Peak	Pitkin	14,000
Quandary Peak	Summit	14,256
Red Cloud Peak	Hinsdale	14,050
Red Hill	La Plata	10,670
Red Mountain	Grand	11,505
Republican Mountain	Clear Creek	12,393
Rhyolite Mountain	Teller	10,771
Richmond Mountain	Gunnison	12,543
Richhtofen Mountain	Grand	12,953
Rio Grande Pyramid	Hinsdale	13,830
Rolling Mountain	San Juan	13,694
Rosalie Peak	Park	13,575
Rosa Mountain	Teller	11,495
Ruby Peak	Gunnison	12,749
Rudoplh Hill	Gunnison	10,130
Saddle Mountain	Park	10,815
Saddle Mountain	Mineral	12,033
St. Vrain Mountain	Boulder	12,162
San Bernardo Mountain	San Miguel	11,845
San Luis Mountain	Teller	10,490
San Luis Mountain	Saguache	14,149
Satanta Peak	Grand	11,885
Sawtooth Mountain	Mineral	12,590
Sawtooth Mountain	Boulder-Grand	12,304
Saxon Mountain	Clear Creek	11,535
Schuylkill Mountain	Gunnison	12,188
Shavano Peak	Chaffee	14,239
Sheep Mountain	Gunnison	13,180
Sheep Mountain	Mineral	12,374
Sheep Mountain	Eagle-Summit	12,380
Sheep Mountain, North	Eagle-Summit	12,429
Sheridan Mountain	La Plata	12,785
Sherman Mountain	Park	14,039
Shoshone Peak	Boulder	13,579
Silex Mountain	San Juan	13,627
Silverheels Mountain	Park	13,825
Sioux Mountain	Boulder-Grand	13,310
Sneffels, Mount	Ouray	14,158
Snowdon Peak	San Juan	13,070
Snowmass Mountain	Pitkin-Gunnison	13,970
Sopris, Mount	Pitkin	12 823
Spanish Peak, West	Huerfano-Las Animas	13,623
Spanish Peak, East	Huerfano-Las Animas	12,708
Specimen Mountain	Grand-Larimer	12 482
Star Peak	Gunnison	13,562
Stearns Mountain	Huerfano-Costilla	11 409
Stewart Peak	Saguache	14,032
Stoll Mountain	Park	10,915
Stones Peak	Larimer	12,928
Stony Mountain	Ouray	12,677
Storm King Peak	San Juan	13,742
Storm Peak	Larimer	13,336
Storm Ridge	Gunnison	11,859
Stormy Peak	Park	11,748
Sugarloaf	Eagle-Summit	12,556
Sugarloaf Peak	Clear Creek	12 513
Sugarloaf Rock	Hinsdale	10,831
Sultan Mountain	San Juan	13,336
Summit Peak	Archuleta	13,272
Sunlight Peak	La Plata	14 084
Sunshine Mountain	San Miguel	12,945
Sunshine Peak	Hinsdale	14 018
Tanima Peak	Boulder-Grand	12,417
Tarryall Peak	Park	11,300
Taylor Mountain	Chaffee	13 600
Taylor Peak	Gunnison	13,419
Taylor Peak	Grand-Larimer	13,150
Telescope Mountain	Dolores	12,210
Teocalli Mountain	Gunnison	13,220
Terra Tomah Peak	Larimer	12,686
The Guardian	San Juan	13,617
Tilton Mountain	Gunnison	12,633
Torrey Peak	Clear Creek-Summit.	14,336
Trachyte Mountain	Teller	10,863
Trinchera Mountain	Costilla-Huerfano	13 546
Trinity Peak	San Juan	13,752 13,804 13,745
Turret Peak	La Plata	13 819
Twilight Peak	San Juan	13,153
Twin Sisters	Larimer	11,435
Twin Sisters	San Juan	13,438
Uncompahgre Peak	Hinsdale	14 306
Union Mountain	Summit	12,336
Vermillion Peak	San Juan-San Miguel	13,870
Vestal Peak	San Juan	13 846
Vigil Peak	El Paso	10,075
Wasatch Mountain	San Miguel	13 551
West Needle Mountain	San Juan	13,050
Wetterhorn Peak	Hinsdale-Ouray	14,020
Wheatstone Mountain	Gunnison	12,543
Whitecross Mountain	Hinsdale	13,550
White Dome	San Juan	13,607
Whitehouse Mountain	Ouray	13,496
White Pine Mountain	Larimer	10,250
White Rock Mountain	Gunnison	13,532
Wildhorse Peak	Ouray	13,271
Wilson Mountain	Dolores	14,250
Wilson Peak	San Miguel	14,026
Windom Mountain	La Plata	14,084
Witter Peak	Clear Creek	12,856
Yale, Mount	Chaffee	14,187
Ypsilon Mountain	Larimer	13,507
Zirkel Mountain	Jackson-Routt	11,815

Lakes and Reservoirs

Name	County	Altitude
Arapahoe	Gilpin	11,165
Antero Res.	Park	8,934
Adams Res.	Adams	.....
Adobe Creek Res.	Bent-Kiowa	4,150
Bradford	Huerfano	5,850
Black Hollow Res.	Weld	5,065
Bee	Larimer	5,175
Bolles	Boulder	5,040
Boedecker	Larimer	5,075
Bison Res.	Teller	10,400
Blue	Conejos	11,937
Burch's	Boulder	5,145
Beasley Res.	Boulder	5,195
Boulder	Boulder	5,228
Boyd Lakes	Larimer	4,960
Bent County Res.	Bent	4,300
Barr	Adams	.....
Badger Res.	Morgan	.....
Big Creek Lakes	Jackson	9,010
Boetcher	Jackson	8,160
Breman	Gunnison	10,325
Balsam	San Juan	11,435
Big Nile	Adams	.....
Clear	Clear Creek	9,870
Chicago	Clear Creek	11,350
Crater	Jefferson	8,877
Chinn	Clear Creek	11,020
Chasm	Boulder	11,800
Caroline	Clear Creek	11,853
Castlewood Res.	Douglas	6,475
Calkins	Weld	4,975
Curtis	Larimer	5,080
Cheesman	Jefferson	6,856
Clear Lake	San Juan	11,875
Devils	Hinsdale	11,968
Duck	Clear Creek	11,070
Diamond	Boulder	10,960
Dorothy	Boulder	12,050
Douglas	Larimer	5,200
Demmel	Larimer	5,250
Dead	Teller	10,900
Dye Res.	Otero	4,150
Emerald	Hinsdale	10,020
Eldora	Boulder	9,245
Edith	Clear Creek	10,117
Eileen	La Plata	8,924
Erdman	Pueblo	4,610
Empire Res.	Morgan-Weld	.....
Fossil Creek Res.	Larimer	4,890
Fountain Valley Res.	El Paso	5,800
Grand	Grand	8,369
Gold	Boulder	8,600
Gerard Res.	Prowers	4,050
George	Park	6,915
Hoffman	Boulder	5,120
Hazel	San Juan	11,420
Hazel	La Plata	12,420
Head	Alamosa	7,527
Hermit Lakes	Hinsdale	9,975
Horse Creek Res.	Bent-Otero	4,950
Hungerford	Pueblo	4,520
Huerfano	Pueblo	4,725
Hayden Res.	Pueblo	.....
Ice	Clear Creek	12,188
Ignacio Res.	La Plata	8,375
Isabelle	Boulder	10,852
Irish	Larimer-Boulder	5,090
Jasper	Boulder	10,733
Julesburg Res.	Sedgwick-Logan	.....
Jackson	Morgan	.....
Jim Crowe Res.	Weld	.....
King Res.	Kiowa-Prowers	3,860
Lost	Boulder	9,980
Lower Crater	Gilpin	10,580
Los Lagos	Boulder-Gilpin	8,930
Loch Lomond	Clear Creek	11,140
Lena	Routt	9,980
Lorland	Larimer	5,022
Loch Ivanho	Pitkin	10,930
Long	Boulder	10,499
McIntosh	Boulder	5,060
Moraine	El Paso	10,215
Monarch	Grand	8,340
Mills	Larimer	11,496
Maroon	Pitkin	9,700
Molas	San Juan	10,488
Margareta	Routt	10,450
Milton	Weld	.....
Middle Plum Res.	Prowers	4,100
Meredith	Crowley	4,308
Minnequa	Pueblo	4,740
Naylor	Clear Creek	11,348
New Windsor Res.	Weld	4 920
North Plum Res.	Prowers	4,100
North Butte Res.	Prowers	4 200
Nee Noshee Res. No. 3	Kiowa	3,870
Nee Sopa Res. No. 5	Kiowa	3,860
Nee Gronda Res. No. 4	Kiowa	3,840
Nee Skah Res.	Kiowa	3,885
Owens	Boulder	5,220
Otanawanda	Ouray	8,800
Palmer	Douglas	9,210
Peterson	Boulder	9,245
Point of Rocks Res.	Logan	3,800
Price Res.	Prowers	3,850
Prewitt Res.	Logan	3,900
Pisgah	Gilpin	9,656
Powderhorn	Hinsdale	11,830
Res. No. 2	El Paso	11,270
Res. No. 4	Teller	10,900
Res. No. 5	Teller	10,900
Res. No. 7	El Paso	12,080
Res. No. 8	El Paso-Teller	11,675
Riverside Res.	Weld	.....
Res. No. 1, No. 2	Kiowa	3,770
Res. No. 4	Kiowa	4,025
Res. No. 1	Otero	4,750
Res. No. 4	Otero	4,750
Res. No. 5	Otero	4,750
Shaw	Mineral	9,830
Spruce Lakes	Mineral	11,263
Silver	San Juan	11,675
Seeley	Weld	4,175
San Cristobal	Hinsdale	8,997
Santa Maria	Mineral	9,475
San Luis	Alamosa	7,525
Strawberry	Grand	8,340
Summit	Clear Creek	12,740
Slater	Clear Creek	11,385
Silver	Boulder	10,190
Swedes	Boulder	5,095
Snowden	Otero	4,820
Seven Lakes	Teller	10 900
Sanchez Res.	Costilla	8,500
Stanley Res.	Jefferson	.....
Twin Lakes	Lake	9,012
Trout	San Miguel	9,750
Terry	Boulder	5,095
Timnath	Weld	4,900
Two Buttes Res.	Baca-Prowers	4 230
Turkey Creek Res.	Pueblo	5,580
Thatcher	Pueblo-El Paso	5 395
Upper Crater	Gilpin	10,997
Upper Nile	Adams	.....
Wellington	Jefferson	9,863
Warren	Larimer	4,985
Woods	Weld	4,860
Woods	Eagle	9,405
Webster Park Res.	Fremont	5,950
Williams-McGreery	Morgan	.....

This list includes only some of the more important lakes and reservoirs in the state. There are hundreds of small lakes in the mountains, many of which have no names. On Battlement mesa and Grand mesa, in Delta and Mesa counties there are more than a hundred comparatively small lakes lying at an altitude above 8,000 feet, all well stocked with trout.

Altitudes and Location of Mountain Passes

Name of Pass	County	Elevation
Alpine Tunnel	Chaffee-Gunnison	11,606
Antelope	Gilpin	8,050
Argentine	Summit	13,286
Arapahoe	Boulder-Grand	11,906
Beckwith	Gunnison	9,890
Berthoud	Clear Creek-Grand	11,306
Boreas	Park-Summit	11,489
Breckenridge	Summit-Park	11,503
Buchanan	Boulder-Grand	12,304
Buffalo	Jackson-Routt	10,180
Cameron	Larimer-Jackson	10,285
Cebolla	Hinsdale	10,394
Corona	Gilpin-Grand	11,660
Cumbres	Conejos	10,003
Cochetopa	Saguache	10,032
Cinnamon	Hinsdale-San Juan	12,300
Devil's Thumb	Boulder-Grand	11,900
East River	Gunnison	11,163
Elwood	Conejos-Archuleta	11,678
Eagle	La Plata	10,750
Fall River	Larimer	11,797
Fremont	Lake-Summit	11,320
Fawn Creek	Grand	9,430
Georgia	Park-Summit	11,476
Hagerman	Lake	11,495
Halfmoon	Saguache	12,712
Hoosier	Park-Summit	10,313
Hancock	Gunnison-Chaffee	12,263
Hayden	Fremont	10,780
Hunter	Lake-Pitkin	12,226
Independence	Lake-Pitkin	12,095
Lake Creek	Lake-Gunnison	12,226
La Veta	Huerfano-Costilla	9,378
Loveland	Clear Creek-Summit	11,876
Medanos	Saguache-Huerfano	10,150
Mosquito	Park-Lake	13,188
Mosca	Huerfano-Saguache	9,713
Marshall	Saguache	10,950
Monarch	Chaffee-Gunnison	11,650
Muddy	Jackson-Grand	8,772
Music	Custer-Saguache	11,800
Meadow	Rio Grande-Mineral	10,300
Milnero	Grand-Larimer	10,759
Ohio	Gunnison	10,033
Ophir	San Juan-San Miguel	11,350
Poudre Lakes	Grand-Larimer	10,192
Pearl	Pitkin-Gunnison	12 715
Poncha	Chaffee-Saguache	8,945
Rabbit Ears	Grand-Jackson-Routt	9,680
Red Mountain	San Juan-Ouray	11,018
Rollins	Boulder-Grand	11,680
Raton	Las Animas	7,893
San Francisco	Las Animas	8,560
Sangre de Cristo	Huerfano-Costilla	9,459
Slumgullion	Hinsdale	11 025
Swampy	Gunnison	10,365
Stony	San Juan	12,594
Tarryall	Park	12,456
Tennessee	Lake	10,276
Trout Lake	Chaffee-Park	9,346
Trimble	La Plata	13,076
Ute	Jackson-Routt	10,900
Victor	Teller	10,202
Weminuche	Hinsdale	10,622
Weston	Lake-Park	12,109
Willow Creek	Park-Summit	9,683
Wolf Creek	Mineral-Archuleta	10,850

Colorado Banks

Adams County

First National Bank.... Aurora
Bennett State Bank.... Bennett
American State Bank.... Brighton
Farmers State Bank.... Brighton
First National Bank.... Brighton
East Lake State Bank.... East Lake

Alamosa County

Alamosa National Bank.... Alamosa
American National Bank.... Alamosa
First State Bank of Alamosa.... Alamosa
Hooper State Bank.... Hooper

Arapahoe County

Byers State Bank.... Byers
Deertrail State Bank.... Deertrail
First National Bank.... Deertrail
First National Bank.... Englewood
Englewood State Bank.... Englewood
First National Bank.... Littleton
Littleton National Bank.... Littleton
First National Bank.... Strasburg

Archuleta County

First National Bank.... Pagosa Springs
Citizens Bank of Pagosa Springs.... Pagosa Springs

Baca County

Campo State Bank.... Campo
First National Bank.... Springfield
Colorado State Bank.... Stonington
Bank of Baca County.... Two Buttes

Bent County

Bent County Bank.... Las Animas
Farmers State Bank.... Las Animas
First National Bank.... Las Animas
McClave State Bank.... McClave

Boulder County

Boulder National Bank.... Boulder
Citizens National Bank.... Boulder
First National Bank.... Boulder
Mercantile Bank & Trust Co.... Boulder
National State Bank.... Boulder
Broomfield State Bank.... Broomfield
Farmers State Bank.... Lafayette
First National Bank.... Lafayette
American National Bank.... Longmont
Colorado Bank & Trust Co.... Longmont
Farmers National Bank.... Longmont
Longmont National Bank.... Longmont
First State Bank of Louisville.... Louisville
State Bank of Lyons.... Lyons
First State Bank.... Nederland
Niwot State Bank.... Niwot

Chaffee County

First National Bank.... Buena Vista
First National Bank.... Salida
Commercial National Bank.... Salida

Cheyenne County

Arapahoe State Bank.... Arapahoe
Cheyenne County State Bank.... Cheyenne Wells
Kit Carson State Bank.... Kit Carson

Clear Creek County

Bank of Clear Creek County..............Georgetown
Bank of Georgetown.......................Georgetown
Bank of Idaho Springs..................Idaho Springs
First National Bank ....Idaho Springs

Conejos County

Commercial State Bank.....................Antonito
First National Bank........................La Jara
Colonial State Bank........................Manassa

Costilla County

Blanca State Bank..........................Blanca
Costilla County Bank.....................San Acacio
San Luis State Bank.......................San Luis

Crowley County

Crowley State Bank.........................Crowley
First National Bank.........................Ordway
Olney Springs State Bank...............Olney Springs
State Bank of Sugar City..................Sugar City

Custer County

The Westcliffe State Bank..................Westcliffe

Delta County

State Bank of Austin........................Austin
First National Bank ....Cedaredge
Crawford State Bank........................Crawford
First National Bank ....Delta
Delta National Bank.........................Delta
First National Bank.......................Hotchkiss
North Fork State Bank.....................Hotchkiss
First National Bank.........................Paonia
Fruita Exchange Bank........................Paonia

Denver County

American Bank & Trust Co....................Denver
American National Bank......................Denver
Broadway National Bank......................Denver
Capitol Hill State Bank......................Denver
Central Savings Bank & Trust Co..............Denver
Colorado National Bank......................Denver
Colorado State & Savings Co..................Denver
Commercial State & Savings Co................Denver
Continental Trust Co.........................Denver
Denver National Bank........................Denver
Drovers National Bank.......................Denver
First National Bank.........................Denver
Globe National Bank.........................Denver
Guardian Trust Co...........................Denver
Home Savings & Trust Co......................Denver
International Trust Co. ....Denver
Italian-American Bank.......................Denver
Metropolitan State Bank.....................Denver
Motor Bank ....Denver
North Denver Bank...........................Denver
Pioneer State Bank ....Denver
Stockyards National Bank ....Denver
South Denver Bank...........................Denver
Union Deposit & Trust Co.....................Denver
United States National Bank.................Denver
West Side State Bank ....Denver

Dolores County

No Banks.

Douglas County

Castle Rock State Bank...................Castle Rock
First National Bank......................Castle Rock
Parker State Bank...........................Parker
Douglas County Bank of Parker................Parker

Eagle County

First National Bank ....Eagle
Bank of Gypsum..............................Gypsum
Red Cliff State Bank......................Red Cliff

Elbert County

Agate State Bank............................Agate
Elbert County State Bank....................Elbert
First National Bank.........................Elbert
Elizabeth State Bank.....................Elizabeth
Kiowa State Bank ....Kiowa
Stockgrowers State Bank.....................Kiowa
Matheson State Bank.......................Matheson
First National Bank.........................Simla

El Paso County

Farmers State & Savings Bank.................Calhan
First State Bank of Calhan...................Calhan
City National Bank.................Colorado Springs
Colorado Savings Bank ....Colorado Springs
Colorado Springs National Bank.......Colorado Springs
Colorado Title & Trust Co...........Colorado Springs
Exchange National Bank.............Colorado Springs
First National Bank................Colorado Springs
State Savings Bank.................Colorado Springs
First National Bank.......................Fountain
Bank of Manitou............................Manitou
Monument State Bank.......................Monument
Farmers State Bank..........................Peyton
State Bank of Ramah..........................Ramah

Fremont County

First National Bank ....Canon City
Fremont County National Bank.............Canon City
Arkansas Valley National Bank..............Florence
First National Bank ....Florence

Garfield County

First National Bank......................Carbondale
Citizens National Bank.............Glenwood Springs
First National Bank................Glenwood Springs
Garfield County State Bank ....Glenwood Springs
New Castle State Bank....................New Castle
First National Bank..........................Rifle
Union State Bank of Rifle....................Rifle
First State Bank..............................Silt

Gilpin County

First National Bank....................Central City

Grand County

First State Bank of Sulphur Springs..Hot Sulphur Springs
Bank of Kremmling........................Kremmling

Gunnison County

Bank of Crested Butte................Crested Butte
First National Bank.......................Gunnison
Gunnison Bank & Trust Co..................Gunnison

Hinsdale County

No Banks.

Huerfano County

First Natioanl Bank.........................La Veta
First National Bank ....Walsenburg
Guarantee State Bank.....................Walsenburg

Jackson County

First National Bank.........................Walden
North Park Bank.............................Walden

Jefferson County

First National Bank.........................Arvada
First State Bank............................Arvada
Rubey National Bank.........................Golden

Kiowa County

First State Bank of Brandon................Brandon
First National Bank...........................Eads
Eads State Bank...............................Eads
Colorado State Bank........................Haswell
Peoples State Bank of Towner................Towner

Kit Carson County

Bethune State Bank.........................Bethune
First National Bank.....................Burlington
Stockgrowers State Bank.................Burlington
Farmers State Bank.........................Flagler
First National Bank ....Flagler
Seibert State Bank.........................Seibert
First National Bank.......................Stratton
Vona State Bank ....Vona

Lake County

American National Bank....................Leadville
Carbonate National Bank ....Leadville

La Plata County

Burns National Bank........................Durango
Durango Trust Co...........................Durango
First National Bank........................Durango
Ignacio State Bank.........................Ignacio
Marvel State Bank............................Kline

Larimer County

Berthoud National Bank....................Berthoud
First National Bank.......................Berthoud
Estes Park Bank...........................Estes Park
Farmers Bank & Trust Co...................Fort Collins
First National Bank.......................Fort Collins
Fort Collins National Bank................Fort Collins
Poudre Valley National Bank...............Fort Collins
Larimer County Bank & Trust Co............Loveland
Loveland National Bank....................Loveland
First National Bank.......................Loveland
Liberty State Bank........................Timnath
First National Bank.......................Wellington

Las Animas County

First State Bank..........................Aguilar
Farmers State Bank........................Branson
Farmers State Bank........................Kim
Commercial Savings Bank...................Trinidad
First National Bank.......................Trinidad
International Bank........................Trinidad
Trinidad National Bank....................Trinidad

Lincoln County

Lincoln State Bank........................Arriba
Genoa State Bank..........................Genoa
First National Bank.......................Hugo
Hugo National Bank........................Hugo
First National Bank.......................Limon
Limon National Bank.......................Limon

Logan County

First State Bank..........................Crook
Dailey State Bank.........................Dailey
First National Bank.......................Fleming
Iliff State Bank..........................Iliff
Merino State Bank.........................Merino
Padroni State Bank........................Padroni
Farmers State Bank........................Peetz
First National Bank.......................Peetz
Proctor State Bank........................Proctor
Commercial Savings Bank...................Sterling
Logan County National Bank................Sterling

Mesa County

Stockmans Bank............................Collbran
Bank of De Beque..........................De Beque
First Bank of Fruita......................Fruita
First National Bank.......................Fruita
Grand Valley National Bank................Grand Junction
United States Bank & Trust Co.............Grand Junction
Bank of Grand Junction....................Grand Junction
Palisades National Bank...................Palisades

Mineral County

Tomkins Brothers, Bankers.................Creede

Moffat County

Craig National Bank.......................Craig
First National Bank.......................Craig

Montezuma County

Montezuma Valley National Bank............Cortez
First National Bank.......................Dolores
J. J. Harris & Co., Bankers...............Dolores
First National Bank.......................Mancos

Montrose County

First National Bank.......................Montrose
Montrose National Bank....................Montrose
Nucla State Bank..........................Nucla
First National Bank.......................Olathe
Olathe State Bank.........................Olathe

Morgan County

Farmers State Bank........................Brush
First National Bank.......................Brush
Stockmens National Bank...................Brush
Farmers State Bank........................Fort Morgan
First National Bank.......................Fort Morgan
Morgan County National Bank...............Fort Morgan
First State Bank of Hillrose..............Hillrose
First State Bank..........................Wiggins
Weldon Valley State Bank..................Weldona

Otero County

First State Bank..........................Cheraw
Farmers State Bank........................Fowler
First National Bank.......................Fowler
Colorado Savings & Trust Co...............La Junta
First National Bank.......................La Junta
La Junta State Bank.......................La Junta
J. N. Beaty & Co., Bankers................Manzanola
Peoples Home Bank.........................Rocky Ford
Rocky Ford National Bank..................Rocky Ford
First State Bank..........................Swink
Timpas State Bank.........................Timpas

Ouray County

Citizens State Bank.......................Ouray
Miners & Merchants Bank...................Ouray
Bank of Ridgeway..........................Ridgeway

Park County

Bank of Alma..............................Alma
Bank of Fairplay..........................Fairplay

Phillips County

American State Bank.......................Amherst
Farmers State Bank........................Haxtun
First National Bank.......................Haxtun
Haxtun State Bank.........................Haxtun
Citizens State Bank.......................Holyoke
First National Bank.......................Holyoke
Phillips County State Bank................Holyoke
Paoli State Bank..........................Paoli

Pitkin County

Aspen State Bank..........................Aspen

Prowers County

American State Bank.......................Granada
Hartman State Bank........................Hartman
First National Bank.......................Holly
Holly State Bank..........................Holly
First National Bank.......................Lamar
Lamar National Bank.......................Lamar
Valley State Bank.........................Lamar
Bank of Wiley.............................Wiley

Pueblo County

Citizens State & Savings Bank.............Boone
First National Bank.......................Pueblo
Minnequa Bank of Pueblo...................Pueblo
Pueblo Savings Bank & Trust Co............Pueblo
Southern Colorado Bank....................Pueblo
Western National Bank.....................Pueblo
Bank of Rye...............................Rye

Rio Blanco County

First National Bank.......................Meeker
First State Bank..........................Meeker

Rio Grande County

Bank of Del Norte.........................Del Norte
Rio Grande State Bank.....................Del Norte
First National Bank.......................Monte Vista
Monte Vista Bank & Trust Co...............Monte Vista
The Wallace State Bank....................Monte Vista

Routt County

First National Bank.......................Hayden
Yampa Valley Bank.........................Hayden
Routt County Bank.........................Oak Creek
Bank of Steamboat Springs.................Steamboat Springs
First National Bank.......................Steamboat Springs
Bank of Yampa.............................Yampa

Saguache County

First National Bank.......................Center
Peoples State Bank........................Center
Rank of Moffat............................Moffat
First National Bank.......................Saguache
Saguache County Bank......................Saguache

San Juan County

First National Bank.......................Silverton

San Miguel County

Norwood State Bank........................Norwood
Bank of Telluride.........................Telluride
First National Bank.......................Telluride

Sedgwick County

Bank	Town
Citizens National Bank	Julesburg
First National Bank	Julesburg
State Bank of Ovid	Ovid
Farmers State Bank	Sedgwick
First National Bank	Sedgwick

Summit County

Bank	Town
Engle Brothers Exchange Bank	Breckenridge

Teller County

Bank	Town
First National Bank	Cripple Creek
Bank of Victor	Victor

Washington County

Bank	Town
Bank of Akron	Akron
Citizens National Bank	Akron
First National Bank	Akron
Farmers State Bank	Cope
Farmers State Bank	Otis
First National Bank	Otis

Weld County

Bank	Town
Farmers National Bank	Ault
First National Bank	Ault
Briggsdale State Bank	Briggsdale
Eaton National Bank	Eaton
First National Bank	Eaton
Erie Bank	Erie
Fort Lupton State Bank	Fort Lupton
Platte Valley State Bank	Fort Lupton
First State Bank	Frederick
Gilcrest State Bank	Gilcrest
Farmers State Bank	Gill
First National Bank	Greeley
Greeley National Bank	Greeley
Union National Bank	Greeley
Weld County Savings Bank	Greeley
Grover State Bank	Grover
Hereford State Bank	Hereford
First State Bank of Hudson	Hudson
First National Bank	Johnstown
First State Bank	Keenesburg
La Salle State Bank	La Salle
First State Bank	Milliken
First National Bank	Mead
First State Bank	Nunn
Farmers State Bank	Platteville
Platteville National Bank	Platteville
State Bank of Raymer	Raymer
Roggen State Bank	Roggen
Farmers Bank of Severance	Severance
First National Bank	Windsor

Yuma County

Bank	Town
Eckley State Bank	Eckley
First State Bank	Idalia
First State Bank	Joes
First State Bank	Kirk
Laird State Bank	Laird
Farmers State Bank	Yuma
First National Bank	Yuma
Union State Bank	Yuma
Vernon State Bank	Vernon
First National Bank	Wray
Peoples State Bank	Wray

Colorado Post Offices

POST OFFICE	COUNTY
Abarr	Yuma
Abbott*	Washington
Ackmen*	Montezuma
Adena*	Morgan
Agate*	Elbert
Aguilar†	Las Animas
§Akron†	Washington
Alamo	Huerfano
§Alamosa†	Alamosa
Alcott, Sta.	Denver
Alcreek*	Las Animas
Alder*	Saguache
Alfalfa	Las Animas
Alice*	Clear Creek
Allenspark*	Boulder
Allison*	La Plata
Alma*	Park
§Almont*	Gunnison
Alvin*	Yuma
Amherst*	Phillips
Amity†	Prowers
Amy*	Lincoln
Andrix*	Las Animas
Antlers*	Garfield
Antonito†	Conejos
Apache*	Huerfano
Apex*	Gilpin
Arapahoe*	Cheyenne
Arboles*	Archuleta
Arickaree*	Washington
Arlington*	Kiowa
Armel*	Yuma
Aroya*	Cheyenne
Arriba†	Lincoln
Arriola*	Montezuma
§Arvada†	Jefferson
§Aspen†	Pitkin
Association Camp‡	Larimer
Atchee*	Garfield
Atwood*	Logan
Augusta*	Las Animas
§Ault†	Weld
Aurora†	Adams
Austin†	Delta
Avalo*	Weld
Avon*	Eagle
Avondale*	Pueblo
Axial*	Moffat
Ayer	Otero
Bailey*	Park
Baldwin*	Gunnison
Bardeen*	El Paso
Barela*	Las Animas
Barnesville*	Weld
Barr Lake*	Adams
§Basalt†	Eagle
Battle Creek*	Routt
§Bayfield†	La Plata
Bear River*	Routt
Bedrock*	Montrose
Bellvue*	Larimer
Bennett†	Adams
Berthoud†	Larimer
Berwind*	Las Animas
Bessemer, Stat. A	Pueblo
Bethune*	Kit Carson
Beulah*	Pueblo
Bijouview*	Morgan
Blackhawk†	Gilpin
Blaine*	Baca
Blanca†	Costilla
Bloom*	Otero
Bonanza†	Saguache
Boncarbo*	Las Animas
Bonny	Kit Carson
Boone†	Pueblo
§Boulder†	Boulder
Bovina*	Lincoln
Bowen*	Las Animas
Bowie*	Delta
Boyero*	Lincoln
Brandon*	Kiowa
Branson†	Las Animas
§Breckenridge†	Summit
Breen*	La Plata
Briggsdale†	Weld
§Brighton†	Adams
Bristol†	Prowers
Brodhead*	Las Animas
Bronquist	Pueblo
Brook Forest	Jefferson
Brookston	Routt
Brookvale*	Clear Creek

POST OFFICE	COUNTY
Broomfield*	Boulder
§Brush†	Morgan
Buckingham*	Weld
§Buena Vista†	Chaffee
Buffalo Creek*	Jefferson
Buford*	Rio Blanco
Buick*	Elbert
Burdett*	Washington
§Burlington†	Kit Carson
Burns*	Eagle
Buster*	Las Animas
§Byers†	Arapahoe
Caddoa†	Bent
Cahone*	Dolores
Caisson	Moffat
Calcite*	Fremont
Calhan†	El Paso
Cameo*	Mesa
Campo†	Baca
Camp Shumway*	Huerfano
§Canon City†	Fremont
Capitol Hill, Sta.	Denver
§Carbondale†	Garfield
Carlton*	Prowers
Carr*	Weld
Carr Crossing*	Lincoln
Cary Ranch*	Routt
Cascade*	El Paso
Cassells*	Park
Castle Rock†	Douglas
Cebolla	Gunnison
Cedar*	San Miguel
Cedar Creek*	Montrose
§Cedaredge†	Delta
Cedarwood*	Pueflo
Center†	Saguache
Centerville	Chaffee
§Central City†	Gilpin
Champa*	Costilla
Chandler*	Fremont
Cheneycenter*	Prowers
Cheraw*	Otero
Cherokee Park	Larimer
§Cheyenne Wells†	Cheyenne
Chivington*	Kiowa
Chromo*	Archuleta
Cimarron*	Montrose
Clanda	Las Animas
Clark*	Routt
Cliffdale*	Jefferson
§Clifton†	Mesa
Climax*	Lake
Coalcreek†	Freemont
Coaldale*	Fremont
Coalmont*	Jackson
Cokedale*	Las Animas
§Collbran†	Mesa
Colona*	Ouray
§Colorado Springs†	El Paso
Columbine*	Routt
Comanche*	Adams
Como†	Park
Concrete*	Fremont
Conejos*	Conejos
Conifer*	Jefferson
Cope†	Washington
Coppertown	Eagle
Cornish*	Weld
Cortez†	Montezuma
Cory*	Delta
Cotopaxi*	Fremont
Cowans*	Lincoln
Cowdrey*	Jackson
§Craig†	Moffat
Crawford†	Delta
§Creede†	Mineral
Crest*	Weld
§Crested Butte†	Gunnison
Crestone*	Saguache
§Cripple Creek†	Teller
Critchell*	Jefferson
Crook*	Logan
Cross Mountain*	Moffat
Crossons	Jefferson
Crowley*	Crowley
Cuchara Camps	Huerfano

POST OFFICE	COUNTY
Dacono*	Weld
Dailey*	Logan
Dalerose*	Las Animas
§DeBeque†	Mesa
Debs	Hinsdale
Deckers*	Douglas
Deep Channel	Moffat
Deepcreek*	Routt
Deertrail†	Arapahoe
Delagua†	Las Animas
Delcarbon*	Huerfano
Delhi*	Las Animas
§Del Norte†	Rio Grande
§Delta†	Delta
De Nova*	Washington
§Denver†	Denver
Deora*	Baca
Derby*	Adams
Dillon*	Summit
Divide*	Teller
Dolores†	Montezuma
Dove Creek*	Dolores
Dover*	Weld
Doyleville*	Gunnison
Drake*	Larimer
Drennan, R. Sta., Colorado Springs	El Paso
Dumont*	Clear Creek
Dunkley*	Routt
Dunton*	Dolores
§Durango†	La Plata
Dyke*	Archuleta
Eads†	Kiowa
§Eagle†	Eagle
Earl*	Las Animas
Eastlake*	Adams
Eastonville*	El Paso
§Eaton†	Weld
Eckert†	Delta
Eckley†	Yuma
§Edgewater†	Jefferson
Edler*	Baca
Edwards*	Eagle
Egnar*	San Miguel
Elba*	Washington
Elbert†	Elbert
Eldora*	Boulder
Elizabeth†	Elbert
Elkdale*	Grand
Elk Head	Routt
Elkton*	Teller
El Moro*	Las Animas
Elphis	Kit Carson
Empire†	Clear Creek
Engleburg	Las Animas
Englewood†	Arapahoe
Erie†	Weld
Escalante Forks	Mesa
Eskdale*	Adams
Espinoza*	Conejos
Estabrook*	Park
Estelene*	Baca
Estes Park†	Larimer
Eureka†	San Juan
Evans*	Weld
Evergreen†	Jefferson
Fairplay†	Park
Falcon*	El Paso
Farisita	Huerfano
Farr*	Huerfano
Firestone*	Weld
Firstview*	Cheyenne
Fitzsimmons†	Adams
Flagler†	Kit Carson
Fleming†	Logan
§Florence†	Fremont
Florissant*	Teller
Floyd Hill	Clear Creek
Flues*	Las Animas
Focus*	Custer
Fondis*	Elbert
Foothills	Pueblo
Forbes*	Las Animas
Forder*	Lincoln
Forestdale	Custer
Fordscreek*	Jefferson
§Fort Collins†	Larimer

POST OFFICE	COUNTY
Fort Garland*	Costilla
Fort Logan†	Arapahoe
Fort Lupton†	Weld
Fort Lyon†	Bent
§Fort Morgan†	Morgan
Fosston*	Weld
Fountain†	El Paso
§Fowler†	Otero
Foxton*	Jefferson
Franktown*	Douglas
Fraser†	Grand
Frederick†	Weld
Frisco*	Summit
§Fruita†	Mesa
Galatea*	Kiowa
Galeton*	Weld
Garcia*	Costilla
Gardner*	Huerfano
Garfield	Chaffee
Garo*	Park
Gary*	Morgan
Gateway*	Mesa
Genoa†	Lincoln
§Georgetown†	Clear Creek
Gibson*	Saguache
Gilcrest*	Weld
Gill*	Weld
Gilman*	Eagle
Gladel	San Miguel
Glade Park*	Mesa
Glendevey	Larimer
Glen Haven	Larimer
Glentivar	Park
§Glenwood Springs†	Garfield
§Golden†	Jefferson
§Goldfield†	Teller
Goodrich*	Morgan
Gorham*	Boulder
Gowanda*	Weld
Graft*	Baca
§Granada†	Prowers
Granby*	Grand
§Grand Junction†	Mesa
Grandlake*	Grand
§Grand Valley†	Garfield
Graneros*	Pueblo
Granite*	Chaffee
Great Divide*	Moffat
§Greeley†	Weld
Green Knoll*	Lincoln
Greenland*	Douglas
Green Mountain Falls*	El Paso
Greystone*	Moffat
Griffith*	La Plata
Grover†	Weld
Guffey*	Park
Gulnare*	Las Animas
§Gunnison†	Gunnison
Gurney	Yuma
Gypsum†	Eagle
Hahn's Peak*	Routt
Hale*	Yuma
Hamilton*	Moffat
Harbourdale	Bent
Hardin*	Weld
Harrisburg*	Washington
Hartman†	Prowers
Hartsel*	Park
Hastings†	Las Animas
Hasty*	Bent
Haswell†	Kiowa
Hawthorne*	Boulder
Haxtun†	Phillips
Haybro	Routt
Hayden†	Routt
Heartstrong*	Yuma
Heiberger*	Mesa
Henderson*	Adams
Hereford*	Weld
Hesperus*	La Plata
Higbee*	Otero
Highlands Sta.	Denver
Highmore*	Garfield
Higho*	Jackson
Hillrose†	Morgan
Hillside*	Fremont
Hill Top*	Douglas
Hoehne*	Las Animas
§Holly†	Prowers
Holyoke†	Phillips
Home*	Larimer
Homelake*	Rio Grande
Hooper*	Alamosa
Hoopup*	Las Animas
§Hotchkiss†	Delta
Hot Sulphur Springs†	Grand
Howard*	Fremont
Howardsville*	San Juan
Howbert*	Park
Hoyt*	Morgan
Hudson†	Weld
Huerfano*	Huerfano
Hughes*	Yuma
§Hugo†	Lincoln
Hygiene*	Boulder
Hyde*	Washington
Hydrate	Routt
§Idaho Springs†	Clear Creek
Idalia*	Yuma
Ideal*	Huerfano
Ignacio†	La Plata
Iliff*	Logan
Ilse*	Custer
Independence†	Teller
Iola*	Gunnison
Irwin Canyon	Las Animas
Jamestown†	Boulder
Jaroso*	Costilla
Jasper	Rio Grande
Jefferson*	Park
Joes*	Yuma
Johnstown*	Weld
Joycoy*	Baca
§Julesburg†	Sedgwick
Juniper Springs	Moffat
Kalous	Weld
Kant	Las Animas
Karval*	Lincoln
Kauffman*	Weld
Kazan*	Las Animas
Kearns	Archuleta
Keating*	Custer
Keenesburg†	Weld
Kelim	Larimer
Kendrick*	Lincoln
Keota*	Weld
Kersey†	Weld
Keysor*	Elbert
Kim*	Las Animas
§Kiowa†	Elbert
Kirk†	Yuma
Kit Carson†	Cheyenne
Kittredge	Jefferson
Kline*	La Plata
Koenig	Weld
Kokomo†	Summit
Kremmling†	Grand
Kutch*	Elbert
LaBoca	La Plata
Ladore*	Moffat
§Lafayette†	Boulder
La Garita*	Saguache
Laird*	Yuma
La Jara†	Conejos
§La Junta†	Otero
Lake City†	Hinsdale
Lake George*	Park
§Lamar†	Prowers
Lamport*	Baca
Laplata*	La Plata
Laporte*	Larimer
Larkspur*	Douglas
La Salle†	Weld
§Las Animas†	Bent
Lascar*	Huerfano
La Veta†	Huerfano
Lawson*	Clear Creek
Lay*	Moffat
Lazear†	Delta
Leader*	Adams

POST OFFICE	COUNTY
§Leadville†	Lake
Leal*	Grand
Lebanon*	Montezuma
Leonard*	San Miguel
Lester*	Huerfano
Lewis*	Montezuma
Lily	Moffat
Lime*	Pueblo
§Limon†	Lincoln
Lindon*	Washington
Little Beaver	Rio Blanco
§Littleton†	Arapahoe
Livermore*	Larimer
Logcabin*	Larimer
Loma*	Mesa
Lone Oak*	Las Animas
§Longmont†	Boulder
Longs Peak*	Larimer
Longview‡*	Jefferson
Loretto*	Arapahoe
§Louisville†	Boulder
Louviers*	Douglas
§Loveland†	Larimer
Lucerne*	Weld
Ludlow†	Las Animas
Lycan*	Baca
§Lyons†	Boulder
McClave*	Bent
McCoy*	Eagle
McElmo	Montezuma
McGregor*	Routt
§Mack†	Mesa
Maher*	Montrose
Maitland*	Huerfano
Malta*	Lake
Manassa†	Conejos
§Mancos†	Montezuma
§Manitou†	El Paso
§Manzanola†	Otero
Marble*	Gunnison
Marnel	Pueblo
Marshall Pass	Saguache
Martin*	Grand
Marvine*	Rio Blanco
Masonville*	Larimer
Massadona	Moffat
Masters*	Weld
Matheson†	Elbert
Maxey*	Baca
Maybell*	Moffat
Mead*	Weld
§Meeker†	Rio Blanco
Meredith*	Pitkin
Merino†	Logan
Mesa†	Mesa
Mesita*	Costilla
Messex*	Washington
Micanite*	Fremont
Mildred*	Yuma
Milliken*	Weld
Milner*	Routt
Mindeman*	Otero
Mineral Hot Springs*	Saguache
Minturn†	Eagle
Mirage*	Saguache
Model*	Las Animas
Moffat*	Saguache
Molding*	Dolores
Molina*	Mesa
§Monte Vitsa†	Rio Grande
Montezuma*	Summit
§Montrose†	Montrose
Monument*	El Paso
Morapos	Moffat
Morley*	Las Animas
Mosca*	Alamosa
Mount Harris†	Routt
Mount Morrison†	Jefferson
Mustang*	Huerfano
Mystic*	Routt
Nathrop*	Chaffee
Naturita†	Montrose
§Nederland†	Boulder
Nepesta*	Pueblo
§New Castle†	Garfield
New Raymer†	Weld
Ninaview*	Bent
Niwot*	Boulder
Noel*	San Miguel
North Avondale*	Pueblo
Northdale*	Dolores
Norwood†	San Miguel
Nucla†	Montrose
Nunn†	Weld
§Oak Creek†	Routt
Oakview*	Huerfano
Officer*	Las Animas
Ohio*	Gunnison
Ojo*	Huerfano
Oklarado*	Baca
§Olathe†	Montrose
Oleson*	Adams
Olney Springs†	Crowley
Opal*	Bent
Ophir*	San Miguel
Orchard†	Morgan
Ordway†	Crowley
Ortiz*	Conejos
Osgood*	Weld
Osier*	Conejos
Otis†	Washington
§Ouray†	Ouray
Ovid*	Sedgwick
Oxford*	La Plata
Padroni*	Logan
Pagoda*	Routt
Pagosa Junction*	Archuleta
§Pagosa Springs†	Archuleta
§Palisades†	Mesa
Pallas*	Routt
Palmer Lake*	El Paso
Pando*	Eagle
Paoli*	Phillips
§Paonia†	Delta
Paradox*	Montrose
Parkdale*	Fremont
Parker*	Douglas
Parlin*	Gunnison
Parshall*	Grand
Patches	Las Animas
Patt*	Las Animas
Pauley	Huerfano
Paulus	Jackson
Pawnee*	Morgan
Peaceful Valley	Boulder
Peckham*	Weld
Peetz†	Logan
Penrose*	Fremont
Pershing*	Routt
Peyton*	El Paso
Phippsburg*	Routt
Piceance*	Rio Blanco
Picotu*	Huerfano
Piedra	Archuleta
Pierce*	Weld
Pikeview*	El Paso
Pine*	Jefferson
Pinecliffe*	Boulder
Pinnacle	Routt
Pinneo*	Washington
Pitkin*	Gunnison
Placerville*	San Miguel
Plainview*	Jefferson
Plateau City*	Mesa
Planter*	Washington
§Platteville†	Weld
Plum Valley*	Las Animas
Poncha Springs†	Chaffee
Portland*	Fremont
Powderhorn*	Gunnison
Price Creek*	Moffat
Primero	Las Animas
Proctor*	Logan
Prowers*	Bent
Pryor*	Huerfano
§Pueblo†	Pueblo
Purcell*	Weld
Pyramid	Rio Blanco
Pyrolite*	Fremont
Radium*	Grand
Ragged Mountain	Gunnison

POST OFFICE	COUNTY
Rago*	Washington
Ramah†	El Paso
Rand*	Jackson
Rangely*	Rio Blanco
Rapson	Las Animas
Rattlesnake Buttes	Huerfano
Raven*	Garfield
Ravenwood*	Huerfano
Read*	Delta
§Redcliff†	Eagle
Red Lion*	Logan
Redmesa*	La Plata
Redvale*	Montrose
Redwing*	Huerfano
Renaraye*	Montezuma
Richards*	Baca
Rico†	Dolores
Ridge*	Jefferson
§Ridgway†	Ouray
§Rifle†	Garfield
Riland	Eagle
Rioblanco*	Rio Blanco
Riverbend*	Elbert
Rockvale†	Fremont
Rockwood*	La Plata
§Rocky Ford†	Otero
Rodley*	Baca
Roggen*	Weld
Rollinsville*	Gilpin
Romeo*	Conejos
Romley*	Chaffee
Rosemont*	Teller
Rosita*	Custer
Rouse*	Huerfano
Ruedi*	Eagle
Rugby*	Las Animas
Ruin Canon*	Montezuma
Rush*	El Paso
Russell	Costilla
Russell Gulch†	Gilpin
§Rye*	Pueblo
Sago*	Montezuma
Saguache†	Saguache
Saint Elmo*	Chaffee
§Salida†	Chaffee
Salina*	Boulder
San Acacio*	Costilla
Sanatorium*	Jefferson
Sanford*	Conejos
San Luis†	Costilla
San Pablo*	Costilla
Sapinero*	Conejos
Sargents*	Saguache
Sawpit*	San Miguel
Scholl*	Grand
Schramm*	Yuma
Sedalia*	Douglas
Sedgwick†	Sedgwick
Segundo*	Las Animas
§Seibert†	Kit Carson
Serene	Weld
Severance*	Weld
Sharpsdale	Huerfano
Shaw*	Lincoln
Shawnee*	Park
Sheephorn*	Eagle
Sheridan Lake*	Kiowa
Sidney*	Routt
Siloam*	Pueblo
Silt†	Garfield
Silver Cliff*	Custer
Silver Plume†	Clear Creek
§Silverton†	San Juan
Simla*	Elbert
Simpson*	Washington
Sinbad	Montrose
Slater*	Moffat
Sligo*	Weld
Sloss	Eagle
Smuggler†	San Miguel
Sneffels*	Ouray
Snowmass*	Pitkin
Snyder*	Morgan
Solar	Huerfano
Somerset*	Gunnison
Sopris†	Las Animas
South Denver, Sta.	Denver
South Fork*	Rio Grande
South Platte*	Jefferson
Spargo*	Montezuma
Spicer*	Jackson
§Springfield†	Baca
Spurgin*	Weld
Squaw Point	Dolores
Starbuck*	Jefferson
Starkville†	Las Animas
§Steamboat Springs†	Routt
§Sterling†	Logan
Stillwater*	Grand
Stockyards, Sta.	Denver
Stone City*	Pueblo
Stoneham†	Weld
Stoner*	Montezuma
Stonington†	Baca
Strasburg†	Arapahoe
§Stratton†	Kit Carson
Strong*	Huerfano
Strontia Springs	Douglas
Sugar City†	Crowley
Sugarloaf*	Boulder
Sulphur	Rio Blanco
Sunbeam*	Moffat
Superior*	Boulder
Swallows*	Pueblo
Swink†	Otero
Tabasco*	Las Animas
Tabernash†	Grand
Tacoma*	La Plata
Tacony*	Pueblo
Tarryall*	Park
§Telluride†	San Miguel
Tennessee Pass*	Lake
Tercio*	Las Animas
Texas Creek*	Fremont
Thatcher*	Las Animas
Thedalund*	Adams
Thornburg*	Rio Blanco
Thurman*	Washington
Tiffany*	La Plata
Tiger*	Summit
Timnath*	Larimer
Timpas*	Otero
Tioga*	Huerfano
Tobe*	Las Animas
Tolland*	Gilpin
Tollerburg*	Las Animas
Toltec*	Huerfano
Toponas*	Routt
Towaoc*	Montezuma
Towner*	Kiowa
Trinchera*	Las Animas
§Trinidad†	Las Animas
Troublesome*	Grand
Troutville*‡	Eagle
Troy*	Las Animas
Tungsten†	Boulder
Turret*	Chaffee
Twin Lakes*	Lake
Two Buttes†	Baca
Undercliffe*	Pueblo
Ute*	Montrose
Utleyville*	Baca
Valdez*	Las Animas
Vallorso	Las Animas
Vanadium*	San Miguel
Vega Ranch*	Las Animas
Vernon*	Yuma
Veta Pass*	Costilla
§Victor†	Teller
Vilas*	Baca
Villagrove*	Saguache
Villegreen*	Las Animas
Virginia Dale*	Larimer
Vona†	Kit Carson
Vroman*	Otero
Wages*	Yuma
Wagon Wheel Gap*‡	Mineral
Waitley	Washington
Walden†	Jackson
Walsen†	Huerfano
§Walsenburg†	Huerfano
Ward†	Boulder

POST OFFICE	COUNTY
Watkins*	Adams
Waunita Hot Springs	Gunnison
Weldona†*	Morgan
Wellington†	Larmier
§Westcliffe†	Custer
West End Sta., Colorado Springs	El Paso
Westminster*	Adams
Weston†	Las Animas
Westplains*	Logan
Wetmore*	Custer
Wheatridge†	Jefferson
Whitepine*	Gunnison
Whiterock	Pueblo
Whitewater*	Mesa
§Wiggins†	Morgan
Wild Horse†	Cheyenne
Wiley†	Prowers
Willard*	Logan
Willow Creek	Routt
§Windsor†	Weld
Wolcott*	Eagle
Woodland Park*	Teller
Woodmen†	El Paso
Woodrow*	Washington
Woody Creek	Pitkin
Wornington	Las Animas
Wray†	Yuma
Yampa†	Routt
Yeiser	Las Animas
Yellow Jacket*	Montezuma
Yetta*	Las Animas
Yoder*	El Paso
Youghal	Moffat
Yuma†	Yuma

*Money order offices.
†International money order offices.
‡Summer offices.
§Postal savings depositories.

Colorado Commercial Organizations

ACTIVE commercial organizations in all parts of the state are doing excellent work toward building up their respective communities and developing the rich resources of the entire state. There is now scarcely a county in Colorado without one or more active commercial organizations and the aggregate number is increasing steadily. A number of state commercial organizations have been in operation in Colorado from time to time, through which it has generally been intended that all local commercial bodies should co-operate in movements of general state development. There is such an organization in existence at present, but its activities so far are very limited. Greater Colorado, Incorporated, with headquarters at Colorado Springs, was organized for the purpose of coordinating the efforts of the business and professional men of the state, through the regular weekly luncheon clubs of the various cities and towns, in further advertising the resources of Colorado and developing its resources. One special object undertaken by this organization is the preparation and publication of school text books on the history, geography, geology, natural resources, etc., of the state. A text book on history has been prepared and is now in process of publication. Harry L. McGinnis of Buena Vista is president, Earl C. Romine of Colorado Springs is secretary and treasurer, and A. W. Luce of Colorado Springs is field representative and organizer. The Colorado Manufacturers' association, with headquarters in Denver, was organized to represent the manufacturing interests of the entire state and its membership comes from all parts of the state. W. J. H. Doran of Denver is president and E. C. Dawson is executive secretary. Its headquarters is in Denver. There are numerous organizations of statewide scope that concern themselves with furthering the interests of special industries, but this volume makes no effort to catalogue them. Since new local commercial bodies are being formed at frequent intervals it is more than possible that a few active organizations have not reported to this department and are therefore not included in the following list.

ADAMS COUNTY

Aurora—Aurora Improvement association; president, John McMillan; secretary, L. J. Mehl; covers Aurora and vicinity.

Bennett—Commercial Club of Bennett; president, J. H. Skinner; secretary, A. O. Westerman; covers Bennett and vicinity.

Brighton—Brighton Commercial club; president, H. A. Harbeck, Jr.; secretary, B. Galen Gaunt; covers Brighton and vicinity.

ALAMOSA COUNTY

Alamosa—Alamosa County Chamber of Commerce; president, Albert L. Moses; secretary, A. F. Bethman; covers San Luis valley.

ARAPAHOE COUNTY

Deer Trail—Deer Trail Chamber of Commerce; president, Hugh Anderson; secretary, George Crowe; covers Deer Trail and vicinity.

Englewood—Englewood Chamber of Commerce; president, A. E. Ferguson; secretary, J. J. Mackin; covers city of Englewood.

BACA COUNTY

Two Buttes—Two Buttes Commercial club; president, H. D. Gaither; secretary, R. C. Best; covers Two Buttes and vicinity.

Grand Junction — Grand Junction Chamber of Commerce; president, F. C. Hogue; secretary, W. M. Wood; covers Mesa county.

Palisades—Palisades Chamber of Commerce; president, A. G. Tilton; secretary, F. P. Weyandt; covers Palisades and vicinity.

MINERAL COUNTY

Creede — Mineral County Business Men's association; president, A. H. Wasson; secretary, A. H. Major; covers Mineral county.

MOFFAT COUNTY

Craig—Craig Commercial club; president, Lee H. Jones; secretary, F. R. Cowan; corresponding secretary, W. P. Finley; covers Moffat county.

MONTEZUMA COUNTY

Cortez—Cortez Chamber of Commerce; president, F. L. Miller; secretary, George B. Bowra; covers Montezuma county.

Dolores—Dolores Commercial club; president, R. S. S. Fox; secretary, Chas. Bear; covers Dolores and northern part of Montezuma county.

Mancos — Mancos-Mesa Verde club; president, W. E. Faris; secretary, F. M. Shideler; covers Mancos and Mesa Verde National Park.

MONTROSE COUNTY

Montrose—Montrose Chamber of Commerce; president, William L. Knous; secretary, H. D. Reeves; covers Montrose and vicinity.

MORGAN COUNTY

Brush—Brush Commercial club; president, Dr. W. E. Turner; secretary, C. P. Schmidt; covers eastern part of Morgan county.

Fort Morgan—Fort Morgan Commercial club; president, U. J. Warren; secretary, Willard Reid; covers Fort Morgan and vicinity.

Hillrose—Hillrose Commercial club; president, R. A. Towne; secretary, R. E. Tebon; covers Hillrose and vicinity.

Wiggins—Wiggins Commercial club; secretary, Fred Hamilton; covers town of Wiggins.

OTERO COUNTY

Cheraw—Cheraw Commercial club; president, Rev. Geo. F. Gordon; secretary, N. N. Basinger; covers Cheraw.

La Junta—La Junta Chamber of Commerce; president, Chas. E. Sabin; secretary, W. C. Sporleder; covers La Junta and Otero county.

Rocky Ford—Arkansas Valley Fair association; president, Lewis Swink; secretary, J. L. Miller; covers Otero county.

Swink—Swink Commercial club; secretary, J. M. Powers; covers Swink and vicinity.

OURAY COUNTY

Ouray—Ouray Recreation association; president, W. F. Wheeler; secretary, Earnest Miller; covers Ouray county.

Ridgway — Ridgway Commercial association; president, C. A. McLean; secretary, G. C. Huffnagle; covers Ridgway and vicinity.

PARK COUNTY

Fairplay—Fairplay Commercial club; president, L. M. Gwinn; covers Park county.

PHILLIPS COUNTY

Haxtun—Haxtun Chamber of Commerce; president, E. A. Reagan; secretary, T. C. Christ; covers Haxtun and vicinity.

PITKIN COUNTY

Aspen—Pitkin County Chamber of Commerce; president, Fred Light; secretary, F. D. Willoughby; covers Pitkin county.

PROWERS COUNTY

Holly—Holly Commercial club; president, E. G. Thayer; secretary, R. E. Wood; covers Holly and vicinity.

Lamar—Lamar Chamber of Commerce; president, M. R. Sunday; secretary, J. R. Mayfield; covers Lamar and vicinity.

Wiley—Wiley Commercial club; president, Guy Hudsen; secretary, L. H. Minehouse; covers Wiley and vicinity.

PUEBLO COUNTY

Pueblo—Pueblo Commerce club; president, F. S. Hoag; secretary, P. A. Gray; covers Pueblo county.

RIO BLANCO COUNTY

Meeker—Rio Blanco Commercial club; president, L. B. Walbridge; secretary, F. A. Carstens; covers Rio Blanco county

RIO GRANDE COUNTY

Monte Vista—Monte Vista Commercial club; president, W. R. Wilson; secretary, M. T. Hancock; covers Rio Grande county.

ROUTT COUNTY

Hayden — Hayden Commercial club; president, J. B. Sibley; secretary, Chas. M. Birkett; covers Hayden and vicinity.

Oak Creek—Oak Creek Commercial club; president, R. I. Gwillam; secretary, Edward Bell; covers Oak Creek and vicinity.

Steamboat Springs—Steamboat Commercial club; president, C. H. Leckenby; secretary, G. E. Steele; covers Steamboat Springs and northwestern Colorado.

Yampa — Yampa Commercial club; president, E. H. Godfrey; covers southern part of Routt county.

SAGUACHE COUNTY

Saguache—Saguache Commercial club; president, O. P. Shippey; secretary, William Fellers; covers Saguache county.

SAN JUAN COUNTY

Silverton—Silverton Commercial club; president, E. W. Walter; secretary, James Pilling; covers San Juan county.

SAN MIGUEL COUNTY

Telluride—Telluride Lions club; president, E. B. Adams; secretary, A. C. Elskamp; covers San Miguel county.

SEDGWICK COUNTY

Julesburg—Julesburg Community club; president, P. R. McDowell; secretary, B. H. Achenbach; covers Sedgwick county.

SUMMIT COUNTY

Breckenridge—Breckenridge Commercial club; president, George Robinson; secretary, O. N. Brlbach; covers Summit county.

TELLER COUNTY

Cripple Creek—Cripple Creek Motor and Commercial club; president. C. W. Searles; secretary, E. F. Nickel; covers western part of Teller county.

Victor—Victor Commercial club; president, Erick Johnson, Jr.; secretary, Wm. F. Jones, Jr.; covers Victor and vicinity.

WASHINGTON COUNTY

Akron—Washington County Chamber of Commerce; president, E. P. Cooley; secretary, C. M. Cockrum; covers Washington county.

Otis—Lion Tamers club; president, Frank Vanderhoof; secretary, T. F. Musson; covers Otis and vicinity.

WELD COUNTY

Ault—Ault Agricultural and Commercial club; president, J. W. Campbell; secretary, C. L. Neisler; covers Ault and vicinity.

Eaton—Business Men's Luncheon club; president, A. A. Tinn; secretary, W. W. Watson; covers Eaton and vicinity.

Erie—Erie Consolidated Commercial association; president, Wm. Nicholson; secretary, C. R. Hunt; covers Erie and vicinity.

Fort Lupton—Fort Lupton Community association; president, C. G. Philip; secretary, Edna N. Wolling; covers Fort Lupton and vicinity.

Greeley—Greeley Chamber of Commerce; president, Fred Norcross; secretary, W. M. Williams; covers Weld county.

Johnstown—Johnstown Commercial club; president, W. T. Porter; secretary, Edward E. Engberg; covers town of Johnstown.

Keenesburg—Keenesburg Community club; president, O. J. Vallicott; secretary, F. E. O'Dell; covers Keenesburg and vicinity.

La Salle—La Salle Commercial club; president, C. C. Wheeler; secretary, Thos. Connell; covers La Salle and vicinity.

New Raymer—New Raymer Community club; president, John R. Wood; secretary, R. H. Pinkerton; covers New Raymer and vicinity.

Nunn—Nunn Commercial club; president, C. G. Wilson; secretary, G. A. Turner; covers Nunn and vicinity.

Windsor—Windsor Community association; president, Geo. E. Nelson; secretary, W. H. Evans; covers Windsor and vicinity.

YUMA COUNTY

Eckley—Eckley Chamber of Commerce and Agriculture; president, M. R. Tillotson; secretary, G. D. Hoschouer; covers Eckley and vicinity.

Wray—Wray Commercial club; president, J. M. Boggs; secretary, F. N. Hayes; covers Wray and vicinity.

Yuma—Yuma Chamber of Commerce; president, J. O. Adams; covers Yuma and vicinity.

Elected State Officials

THE accompanying list gives the names of all governors of Colorado since the creation of Colorado territory in 1861. The lists of other state officials include only the names of those elected to the various offices since the admission of Colorado into the Union as a state, in 1876, and the time each served.

Territorial Governor

William Gilpin	1861-1862
John Evans	1862-1865
Alexander Cummings	1865-1867
A. C. Hunt	1867-1869
Edward McCook	1869-1873
Samuel H. Elbert	1873-1875
John L. Routt	1875-1876

State Governor

John L. Routt	1876-1879
Frederick R. Pitkin	1879-1883
James B. Grant	1883-1885
Benjamin H. Eaton	1885-1887
Alva Adams	1887-1889
Job A. Cooper	1889-1891
John L. Routt	1891-1893
Davis H. Waite	1893-1895
Albert W. McIntire	1895-1897
Alva Adams	1897-1899
Charles S. Thomas	1899-1901
James B. Orman	1901-1903
James H. Peabody	1903-1905
Alva Adams	1905——
James H. Peabody	1905——
Jesse F. McDonald	1905-1907
Henry A. Buchtel	1907-1909
John F. Shafroth	1909-1913
Elias M. Ammons	1913-1915
George A. Carlson	1915-1917
Julius C. Gunter	1917-1919
Oliver H. Shoup	1919-1921
Oliver H. Shoup	1921-1923
William E. Sweet	1923——

Lieutenant Governor

Lafayette Head	1877-1879
Horace A. W. Tabor	1879-1881
Horace A. W. Tabor	1881-1883
William H. Meyers	1883-1885
Peter W. Breene	1885-1887
Norman H. Meldrum	1887-1889
William G. Smith	1889-1891
William Story	1891-1893
David H. Nichols	1893-1895
Jared L. Brush	1895-1897
Jared L. Brush	1897-1899
Francis Carney	1899-1901
David C. Coates	1901-1903
Warren A. Haggott	1903-1905
Arthur Cornforth	1905-1907
E. R. Harper	1907-1909
Stephen R. Fitzgerald	1909-1911
Stephen R. Fitzgerald	1911-1913
Stephen R. Fitzgerald	1913-1915
Moses E. Lewis	1915-1917
James E. Pulliam	1917-1919
George Stephan	1919-1921
Earl Cooley	1921-1923
Robert F. Rockwell	1923——

Secretary of State

William M. Clark	1877-1879
Norman H. Meldrum	1879-1881
Norman H. Meldrum	1881-1883
Melvin Edwards	1883-1885
Melvin Edwards	1885-1887
James Rice	1887-1889
James Rice	1889-1891
Edwin J. Eaton	1891-1893
Nelson O. McClees	1893-1895
Albert B. McGaffey	1895-1897
Charles H. S. Whipple	1897-1899
Elmer F. Beckwith	1899-1901
David F. Mills	1901-1903
James Cowie	1903-1905
James Cowie	1905-1907
Timothy O'Connor	1907-1909
James B. Pearce	1909-1911
James B. Pearce	1911-1913
James B. Pearce	1913-1915
John E. Ramer	1915-1917

James R. Noland	1917-1919
James R. Noland	1919-1921
Carl S. Milliken	1921-1923
Carl S. Milliken	1923——

State Treasurer

George C. Corning	1877-1879
Nathan S. Culver	1879-1881
W. S. Sanders	1881-1883
Fred Walsen	1883-1885
George R. Swallow	1885-1887
Peter W. Breene	1887-1889
W. H. Brisbane	1889-1891
James N. Carlile	1891-1893
Albert Nance	1893-1895
Harry E. Mulnix	1895-1897
George W. Kephart	1897-1899
John H. Fesler	1899-1901
James N. Chipley	1901-1903
Witney Newton	1903-1905
John A. Holmberg	1905-1907
Alfred E. Bent	1907-1909
William J. Galligan	1909-1911
Roady Kenehan	1911-1913
Michael A. Leddy	1913-1915
Allison E. Stocker	1915-1917
Robert H. Higgins	1917-1919
Harry E. Mulnix	1919-1921
Arthur M. Stong	1921-1923
Harry E. Mulnix	1923——

Auditor of State

David C. Crawford	1877-1879
Eugene K. Stimson	1879-1881
Joseph A. Davis	1881-1883
J. C. Abbott	1883-1885
Hiram A. Spurance	1885-1887
Darwin P. Kingsley	1887-1889
L. B. Schwanbeck	1889-1891
John M. Henderson	1891-1893
F. M. Goodykoontz	1893-1895
Clifford C. Parks	1895-1897
John W. Lowell	1897-1899
George W. Temple	1899-1901
Charles W. Crowter	1901-1903
John A. Holmberg	1903-1905
Alfred E. Bent	1905-1907
George D. Statler	1907-1909
Roady Kenehan	1909-1911
Michael A. Leddy	1911-1913
Roady Kenehan	1913-1915
Harry A. Mulnix	1915-1917
Charles H. Leckenby	1917-1919
Arthur M. Stong	1919-1921
Harry E. Mulnix	1921-1923
Arthur M. Stong	1923——

Attorney General

A. J. Sampson	1877-1879
Charles W. Wright	1879-1881
Charles Toll	1881-1883
D. C. Urmy	1883-1885
Theodore H. Thomas	1885-1887
Alvin Marsh	1887-1889
Samuel W. Jones	1889-1891
Joseph H. Maupin	1891-1893
Eugene Engley	1893-1895
Byron L. Carr	1895-1897
Byron L. Carr	1897-1899
David M. Campbell	1899-1901
Charles C. Post	1901-1903
Nathan C. Miller	1903-1905
Nathan C. Miller	1905-1907
William H. Dickson	1907-1909
John T. Barnett	1909-1911
Benjamin J. Griffith	1911-1913
Fred Farrar	1913-1915
Fred Farrar	1915-1917
Leslie E. Hubbard	1917-1919
Victor E. Keyes	1919-1921
Victor E. Keyes	1921-1923
Russell W. Fleming	1923——*
Wayne C. Williams	1924——

Superintendent of Public Instruction

Joseph C. Shattuck	1877-1879
Joseph C. Shattuck	1879-1881
Leonidas S. Cornell	1881-1883
Joseph C. Shattuck	1883-1885
Leonidas S. Cornell	1885-1887
Leonidas S. Cornell	1887-1889
Fred Dick	1889-1891
Nathan Coy	1891-1893
John F. Murray	1893-1895
Angenette J. Peavey	1895-1897
Grace Espey Patton	1897-1899
Helen L. Grenfell	1899-1901
Helen L. Grenfell	1901-1903
Helen L. Grenfell	1903-1905
Katherine L. Craig	1905-1907
Katherine L. Craig	1907-1909
Katherine M. Cook	1909-1911
Helen M. Wixon	1911-1913
Mary C. C. Bradford	1913-1915
Mary C. C. Bradford	1915-1917
Mary C. C. Bradford	1917-1919
Mary C. C. Bradford	1919-1921
Katherine L. Craig	1921-1923
Mary C. C. Bradford	1923——

* Attorney General Fleming died December 25, 1923.

Town and City Officials

THE following is a list of the incorporated cities and towns in Colorado, with the names of their mayors and clerks for the current year. The first name in each case is that of the mayor and the second that of the clerk. Blanks occur after the names of those towns from which the Immigration Department received no report.

Aguilar—A. I. Lindsay, Jos. I. McGinn.

Akron—Raymond R. Hayes, D. H. Sisson.

Alamosa—Herman Emperius, George E. Lake.

Alma—G. F. Galloway, J. F. Singleton.

Animas City—

Antonito—Lute Reidel, W. D. Carroll.

Arriba—Chas. J. Stahl, W. E. Kliewer.

Arvada—F. C. Murchison, Hazel M. Garlick.

Aspen — Charles Wagner, Charles Dailey.

Ault—M. E. Smith, Ralph R. Bowman.

Aurora—John McMillan, G. E. Ballard.

Basalt—E. H. Gray, M. P. Sloss.

Bayfield—Andrew F. Hopper, Mrs. Cecil B. Van Dusen.

Berthoud—M. L. Fairbairn, Ruth Peterson.

Blackhawk—Charles R. Niccum, Zack T. MacNey.

Blanca—Freda E. Weaver, A. M. Weaver.

Bonanza—Ralph Gray (Geo. R. Gray), C. M. Buck.

Boulder—J. O. Billig, Mayme Graham.

Breckenridge — Trevor B. Thomas, Thomas Tarkington.

Branson—Frank W. Roddy, L. M. Readshaw.

Brighton—H. H. Johnston, D. G. Woodard.

Brookside—

Brush—Harry T. Carroll, A. C. Harness.

Buena Vista—George M. Pyle, H. C. McLean.
Burlington—F. W. Kukuk, H. G. Hoskin.

Calhan—J. A. Lamb, Fred C. Wagoner.
Canon City—A. J. Turner, H. C. Webster.
Carbondale—W. D. Moore, E. W. Hampton.
Castle Rock—C. M. Hulbert, Caniel N. Ball.
Cedaredge—Frank J. Stewart, G. W, Hall.
Central City—H. H. Lake, G. F. Moody.
Center—M. M. Lutley, R. A. Allison.
Cheraw—Ray B. Hoskins, N. N. Basinger.
Cheyenne Wells—J. E. Hayes, D. H. Zuck.
Coal Creek—Frank Falciglie, Anton Morganstein.
Collbran—E. F. Collins, Elsie D. Walkup.
Colorado Springs—Ira Harris, S. E. Nichols.
Cortez—G. O. Harrison, May Clark.
Craig—J. G. Clayton, P. R. Keiser.
Crawford—Frank M. Drexel, W. C. Simmons.
Creede—Wm. C. Sloan, H. D. Barnhart.
Crested Butte—Fred Gulliford, John L. Byouk.
Crestone—C. S. Bonham, W. J. Hutchinson.
Cripple Creek—E. P. Arthur, Jr., W. C. McKelvey.
Crook—L. R. Gillett, Fred Stake.
Crowley—A. W. Green, O. P. Adkinson.

Dacono—Don Ball, F. G. Gerhard.
DeBeque—Volney W. Derush, Arthur Holmes.
Deer Trail—J. F. Coleman, R. L. Bloss.
Delegua — James Struthers, Ralph Gagliardi.
Del Norte—Barclay E. Newlin, C. D. Voris.
Delta—A. E. Penley, N. J. Bradley.
Denver—B. F. Stapleton.
Dillon—Norman Ashlock, Joseph Arduser.
Dolores—A. S. Miller, C. L. Flanders.
Durango—Chas. Stillwell, W. W. Parshall.

Eads—F. L. Pyles, J. R. Wood.
Eagle—Carl Mayer, L. R. Thomas.
Eaton—R. C. Wykert, W. F. Willis.
Eckley—Harvey C. Catchpole, Elmer Smith.
Edgewater—Wm. W. Cormack, Stephen Higgs.
Eldora—W. T. Harpel, Sr., Evalyn Lilly.
Elizabeth — Frank Garland, Peter Blumer.
Empire—Fred Nelson, E. E. Koch.
Englewood—Aven Aldridge, E. E. Anderson.
Erie — William Whiles, Charles Knowles.
Estes Park—A. D. Lewis, Chas. F. Hix.
Eureka — A. B. Marquard, H. B. Wagerchieffer.
Evans—

Fairplay—A. F. Willmarth, Harold C. Moyer.
Firestone — Daniel McHugh, Luther King.
Flagler—Dr. H. L. Williams, Wm. Knies.
Fleming—Dr. R. C. McCormick, Hugh Boyd.
Florence—George Wilson, Leona Dexter.
Florissant—Wm. C. Allen, S. M. Allen.
Fort Collins—Frank R. Montgomery, A. J. Rosenow.
Fort Lupton—Ora N. Putnam, Herman Funk.
Fort Morgan—Mark B. Gill, J. B. Farnsworth.
Fountain—R. E. Love, George I. Phillips.
Fowler—Andrew Waddington, W. T. Barnard.
Frederick—Newton Nicholson, Alice La Roche.
Fruita—Frank C. Merriell, Jennie Phillips.
Frisco—Gus Levene, L. A. Wildhack.

Georgetown—Edward Butts, M. S. McFarland.
Gilcrest—W. K. Gilcrest, R. H. P. Keller.
Glenwood Springs—W. G. McDonald, May McReavy.
Golden—Dr. D. E. Garvin, H. T. Curry.
Goldfield—John S. Beckman, Gertrude M. Tucker.
Granada—F. A. Barge, L. H. Kelso.
Granby—C. H. Nuckolls, L. G. Davis.
Grand Junction—W. G. Hirons, Fred A. Peck.
Grand Valley—J. E. Sipprelle, Phil Waterman.
Greeley—Walter S. Hayden, W. A. Hotchkiss.
Green Mountain Falls—Rex Brown, R. F. Balthis.
Grover—D. H. Williamson, H. L. Peterson.
Gunnison—F. W. Zugelder, Carlton T. Sills.
Gypsum — O. F. Tracy, Mayme Stremme.

Hartman—H. M. Lowe, W. J. Dicklebower.
Hastings—W. E. Miller, J. H. Helm.
Haswell—George W. Robinson, W. P. Lawrence.
Haxtun—J. A. Brooks, Floyd W. Gipple.
Hayden—John I. Birkett, A. Anderson.
Hillrose—B. P. Wind, D. E. Wind.
Holly—G. W. Smeltzer, T. G. Demaray.
Holyoke—Dr. P. S. Struble, W. E. Heginbotham.
Hooper, M. B. Chrisman, D. E. McIntosh.
Hot Sulphur Springs—J. N. Pettingell, Harriet A. M. Huntington.
Hotchkiss—D. L. Blakley, Wilson L. Allen.
Hudson—E. R. Ensor, Dr. J. E. Hotchkiss.
Hugo—W. D. Owen, J. C. Piburn.

Idaho Springs—Chas. L. Harrington, John R. White.
Ignacio—Wm. Bryan, H. C. Biggs.
Iliff—H. L. Oldfather, George B. Holmes.

Jamestown—E. O. Kemptner, Asa C. Hempsted.
Johnstown—H. A. Clingenpeel, Fred A. Harsh.
Julesburg—C. W. White, C. P. Greene.

Keenesburg—Virgil M. Porter, Ernestine V. L. Beggs.
Keota—E. M. Singer, C. L. Stanley.
Kersey—L. R. Mondt, E. J. Meikel.
Kiowa—Ed. P. Wott, Carl Nache.

Kokomo—H. A. Recena, J. M. Armstrong.
Kremmling—F. A. McQueary, C. C. Eastin.

Lafayette—Lee Baker, Ruth A. Richards.
La Jara—Franklin D. Calkins, J. C. Jensik.
La Junta—John G. Washburn, Robert B. Miller.
Lake City—
Lamar—Charles Maxwell, C. A. Lacy.
La Salle—Charles Hall, J. T. Kidd.
Las Animas—C. N. Troup, Lizzie C. Collett.
La Veta—Dr. L. W. Lee, J. P. Stranger.
Leadville—Joseph E. Cummings, Louise T. Stewart.
Limon—J. T. Osborne, A. C. Moschel.
Littleton—Dr. W. C. Crysler, J. Clyde Hoskin.
Longmont—J. F. Hays, George H. Stonex.
Louisville—Wm. McColloch, N. E. Rockley.
Loveland—W. E. Banks, J. B. Sella.
Lyons—R. W. Epley, Henry Bohn.

Manassa—A. E. Mortensen, James A. Holman.
Mancos—J. L. Martin, E. E. Humiston.
Manitou—L. K. Van Horne, W. H. Williams.
Manzanola—H. B. Dyer, A. R. Stover.
Marble—Edward C. Hanley, John A. Williams.
Mead—T. H. Hill, C. N. Brust.
Meeker—W. B. McWilliams, Herbert Gordon.
Merino—D. W. B. Lutes, S. J. Neely.
Milliken—E. J. Elam, L. W. Defenbaugh.
Minturn—Chas. A. Wilcox, Walter Guire.
Moffat—D. W. Crabtree, J. F. DeVinna.
Monte Vista—H. E. Lague, George B. Boutwell.
Montrose—J. J. Gatschet, Doris Wittmeyer.
Monument—W. E. Higby, Andrew Curry.
Morrison—William J. Lukens, Otis A. Pike.

Nederland—William T. Todd, Edward G. Lawrence.
Nevadaville — No Mayor; John B. Doran, Clerk.
New Castle—J. Ritter, A. E. Westley.
New Raymer—C. L. Snyder, E. W. Schweizer.
Norwood—R. M. White, F. E. Rice.
Nucla — G. Chrisman, Albrecht Schroeder.
Nunn—A. P. Hart, U. E. Madden.

Oak Creek—G. F. Watt, B. F. Snyder.
Olathe—Chas. E. Lockwood, G. C. Hoadley.
Olney Springs—S. T. Hussen, R. B. Milhollin.
Ophir—
Ordway—D. J. Mooney, John B. Estes.
Otis—Lon Felkey, Alice Clement.
Ouray—Thomas V. Canavan, Mary S. Powell.

Pagosa Springs—S. H. Dickerson, J. L. Giger.
Palisade—J. D. Secor, J. W. Hoke.
Palmer Lake—N. E. Medlock, Alice A. Wills.
Paonia—Abner S. McKee, W. R. Osboldstone.
Peetz—C. M. Kitchell, M. A. Shipman, Jr.
Pierce—Jesse Ogden, R. M. Jones.
Pitkin—W. S. Henderson, R. T. Hefftner.
Platteville—L. S. Birkle, J. F. Gleason.
Poncha Springs—E. G. Holman, Mary T. Smith.
Pueblo—John M. Jackson, J. W. Carpenter.

Raymer—
Red Cliff—J. M. Dismant, Mrs. J. May Hart.
Rico—Robert L. Pellet, G. M. Mullins.
Ridgway—R. E. Israel, C. M. Stanwood.
Rifle—R. F. Magor, John I. Buckles.
Rockvale—Fred C. Dyer, James Williams.
Rocky Ford—A. S. Kitch, J. A. Johnson.

Saguache—Horace B. Means, W. L. Hammond.
Salida—W. S. Buchanan, Bertie Roney.
Sanford—James P. Jensen, Fred Bentley.
Sawpit—J. H. Hughes, J. W. Osborn.
Sedgwick—C. R. Stockham, J. C. Davis.
Seibert—S. W. Abbott, M. D. Haynes.
Silt—Roy Howard, C. W. Hamilton.
Silver Cliff—J. T. Stroehlke, A. H. Henning.
Silver Plume—Fred M. Coughlin, C. E. Stanton.
Silverton—B. B. Allen, Wm. Brayden.
Simla—N. S. Eddy, John L. Bartsch.
Springfield—Earl C. Denney, Charles L. Doughty.
Steamboat Springs—F. E. Willet, T. W. Poulson.
St. Elmo—Daniel Clark, S. L. Taber.
Sterling—H. B. Swedlund, H. M. Krull.
Sugar City—J. M. Cravens, F. M. Putnam.
Superior—Jerry Meevis, James J. Kerr.
Stratton—Roy T. Wingfield, W. M. Long.
Swink—O. I. Blake, F. H. Farless.

Telluride—James F. Quine, Clara J. Rogers.
Timnath—E. W. Stevens, E. A. Russell.
Trinidad—George Mason, Mrs. Mattie H. Butler.
Two Buttes—A. M. Lucas, Gaither.

Victor—Dr. C. E. Elliott, Violet Bluette.
Vona—E. B. Wilson, L. N. Scheidegger.

Walden—K. J. MacCallum, W. E. Viner.
Walsenburg—H. D. Mustain, C. Victor Mazzone.
Ward—William T. Schmoll, George B. Holden.
Wellington—Arthur J. Piatt, I. H. Wallen.
Westcliffe — George B. Beardsley, Grover Falkenberg.
Westminster—J. W. Martin, H. T. Buswell.
Wiley—F. E. Durham, Carl H. Davis.
Williamsburg—Arthur McShane, John Frew, Sr.
Windsor—Roy Ray, U. L. Carleton.
Woodland Park—H. D. Hackman, Mrs. S. E. Mulnix.
Wray—J. G. Jones, Sam Williams.

Yampa—Chas. J. Wheeler, Charles R. Simon.
Yuma—C. H. Hatcher, Lulu P. Miller.

COUNTY OFFICIALS

COUNTY	SHERIFF	TREASURER	CLERK	SURVEYOR	ASSESSOR	CORONER	COUNTY JUDGE	SUPERINTENDENT OF SCHOOLS
[illegible]s	L. H. Miller	Ben Shearston	Fred O. Pearce	Pete O'Brien, Jr.	L[illegible] W. [illegible]	E. G. Jones	[illegible] A. Garard	E. G. Baker
[illegible]	John Baumaster	A. C. [illegible]	Robt. [illegible]	Chas M. Johnston	[illegible] Bergman	J. F. Wenz	Geo. H. Shone	Harriet Dalzel
[illegible]	John F. Bennett	Claude Cartwright	[illegible] H. [illegible]	Arthur F. Goddard	C. E. Watlington	Arthur O. Tiedt	Geo. W. [illegible]	[illegible] Ruth B. Vertrees
Archuleta	[illegible] A. Dutton	[illegible] Hayden	[illegible] R. Johnson	J. O. Sullivan	[illegible] R. [illegible]	A. J. [illegible]	John I. Vermillion	M. R. Thomas
Baca	[illegible] E. Dunivan	Jesse L. H[illegible]	Victor G. Baker	John R. [illegible]	Roy D. [illegible]	W. P. [illegible]	T. Eldon [illegible]	Cora B. Mordica
Bent	Richard Thaxton	C. E. Stuart	Mary S. Bell	H. W. Alexander	E. J. Wallinger	Dr. J. O. Hardy	Leroy M. Campbell	Minnie L. Rimmer
Boulder	Robert V. [illegible]	Francis Beckwith	J. Etta Coons	Geo. E. Wilson	John M. Jones	Leslie [illegible]	[illegible] J. Ingram	Anna J. Ewing Bittner
Chaffee	J. M. Hutchinson	John H. Owen	F. A. Bromley	H[illegible] [illegible]	F. M. Tomlin	L. B. [illegible]	Joseph Newitt	Marion B. Wallace
Cheyenne	Art Brown	R. A. Pfost	E. H. Akerly	Adolph Froelich	C. S. Woodrow	C. A. Badsell	V. H. [illegible]	Ester B. Weir
Clear Creek	William J. Harvey	Mary E. Devany	Kenneth E. Moscript	Percy P. Barbour	A. H. J. Horstmann	Dr. Alan D. Fraser	Royal R. [illegible]	Elizabeth J. [illegible]
Conejos	J. Parley Hayme	Reginaldo Garcia	Severiano [illegible]	J. F. [illegible]	A. M. Richardson	F. D. Potthoff	C. A. [illegible]	Mable [illegible]
Costilla	J. D. [illegible]	J. E. Lucero	Daniel Sanchez	A. H. Martin	C. Sanchez	J. N. [illegible]	A. I. Vigil	[illegible] M. Corporon
Crowley	Geo. E. Herman	[illegible] A. Walker	B. D. Bradley	Geo. E. [illegible]	H. K. Smedley	E. O. McCleary	[illegible] C. Wooldridge	Harriet W. [illegible]
Custer	Mel H. Manning	W. H. Funderburk	Ralph Callaghan	[illegible] Koppe	E. C. [illegible]	R. H. Ray	Edward L. [illegible]	Lou C. Beaman
Delta	W. A. [illegible]	[illegible]	Paul K. Osborne	Homer D. Graham	[illegible] H. Merchant	T. E. Remley	Frank M. Goddard	Alice Burnett
[illegible]	Clifford Wright	[illegible] [illegible]	Lyla K. Drommond	A. E. Armes	J. A. [illegible]	Dr. F. A. McNeill	Geo. E. Hicks	Mittie Sitton
[illegible]	Roy [illegible]	Fred Bean	Harry [illegible]	[illegible] N. Stewart	H. G. Johnson	[illegible] E. Alexander, M.D	John Anderson	[illegible] I. [illegible]
Eagle	W. M. Wilson	A. F. Carlson	[illegible] M. Cave	W. H. [illegible]	[illegible] S. Fuller	Dr. F. H. Harrison	Lydia B. [illegible]	Mrs. Dora [illegible]
Elbert	G. R. Brown	C. W. Elsner	F. D. Hart	D. M. Sultz	James F. Mauldin	Dr. E. K. Shelton	Frank S. [illegible]	N. N. Bailey
El Paso	Sam Berl[illegible]	A. H. [illegible]	C. R. Furrow	H. R. Wright	F. A. Perkins	Howard Swan	James F. Sanford	Inez Johnson [illegible]
Fremont	[illegible] R. Glasson	[illegible] P. Owens	Blake Rogers	A. B. [illegible]	Willis A. [illegible]	Dr. V. A. Hutton	Kent L. Eldred	Carrie T. Anthony
Garfield	George L. [illegible]	Chas. H. King	Walter J. Frost	W. H. Trumbor	Alex S. [illegible]	Dr. L. G. Clark	J. W. Bell	Gretta C. Pottenger
Gilpin	Oscar Williams	[illegible] P. [illegible]	Clifford I. Parsons	S. A. Rank	[illegible] O. Ziegs	Geo. L. Hamilik	William C. Fullerton	[illegible] Frey
Grand	R. L. West	H. F. Adams	Hugh J. Harrison	Roy F. Polhamus	R. O. Throckmorton	W. S. [illegible]	J. N. Pettingell	[illegible] D. Schnoor
Gunnison	Pat [illegible]	M. B. Herrick	C. C. [illegible]	J. H. Robinson	J. W. Haymaker	N. J. Hyatt	J. M. McDougal	[illegible] M. [illegible]
[illegible]	[illegible] A. [illegible]	William F. Green	Frank B. Hough	H. G. [illegible]	[illegible]	Dr. B. F. Cummings	Eugene Otis	Mabel B. Rawson
Huerfano	[illegible] Cornwall	[illegible]	Frank [illegible]	Ross H[illegible]	Damaso [illegible]	Gabe Furphy	Jos[illegible] H. Patterson	Martha M. Thorne
[illegible]	H. R. Riddle	Florence A. Wilkins	C. E. Mitchell	M. C. Ward	Wm. H. Winscom	C. E. Mosman	H. C. Chedsey	Minnie A. [illegible]
[illegible]	[illegible] C. [illegible]	S. B. Fleming	[illegible] B. [illegible]	C. E. Lytle	J. A. Hogan	Wm. [illegible]	Cha[illegible] McCall	Evangeline Cummings
Kiowa	W. P. Mayne	J. R. Proctor	Ithal Jenkin[illegible]	Ed Immer	J. C. Miller	C. L. [illegible]	A. T. [illegible]	Effie Matthews
Kit Carson	John G. [illegible]	Anna E. Adkisson	Bessie Guth[illegible]	D. D. Buck	C. G. McConnell	Orin P. [illegible]	Wyatt Boger	Della Hendricks

Lake	[illegible] Schrader	Frank E. Kendrick	John Gregory	Fred J. [illegible]	William A. [illegible]	[illegible]rt W. Walsh	[illegible] D. Bonner	[illegible]
La [illegible]	[illegible]ge A. [illegible]	W. E. [illegible]	Clara C. Goeglein	Allison L. Kroeger	Ellis M. Hampton	Grover [illegible]	Ira J. Bradford	Nell B. McCartey
Larimer	Frank Smith	William J. [illegible]	Matthew Auld	James G. Edwards	H. B. Hammond	W. T. Hollowell	Jay H. [illegible]	Alice C. Fuller
Las Animas	John J. [illegible]	Frank R. Dunlavy	[illegible]an B. Romero	B. I. [illegible]er	William J. [illegible]leton	Thomas Bradley	[illegible]vid M. [illegible]	S. J. Shadel
Lincoln	A. G. Loss	Wm. M. Jones	Claude [illegible]	Charles Musser	[illegible]nk [illegible]	F. W. [illegible]	P. O. Hedlund	Della Winder
Logan	Ray R. [illegible]ll	R. E. [illegible]	Mrs. Edyth C. Wheele[illegible]	J. E. Youngquist	[illegible]bert Swinney	A. D. [illegible]	Norris C. [illegible]	Flora Allison
[illegible]	Jeff [illegible]	Mark R. Bunting	Ella M. Gallupe	Frank Sleeper	Ocee O. Fellows	E. A. Krohn	N. C. M[illegible]	Elizabeth Hinton
Mineral	E. S. Pollock	[illegible] A. Wheeler	H. D. Barnhart	Don C. LaFonte	Jno. J. [illegible]er	Royal I. Fisher	C. Y. Butler	Mary N. [illegible]
Moffat	Tom G. Blevins	Clyde M. Downs	David E. [illegible]	R. G. [illegible]	N. F. [illegible]	Jas. G. Clayton	J. F. Meador	Blanche B. Chivington
[illegible]	Frank Philley	[illegible]on D. [illegible]	Samuel M. Burke	....	[illegible]rk R. [illegible]	E. E. [illegible]	J. M. Brumley	Mrs. Nora S. Hutchings
Montrose	Samuel Phillips	J. W. [illegible]	T. W. [illegible]ell	W. H. Fleming	L. E. [illegible]	Dr. Fred Schermerhorn	S. S. Sherman	Mrs. Sarah L. [illegible]
[illegible]	[illegible]e A. [illegible]se	[illegible] H. [illegible]	A. H. Asmus	Robert F. [illegible]er	[illegible]m S. Lee	L. H. [illegible]	Clayton C. Rickel	Laura N. [illegible]
Otero	D. N. Houghton	C. R. [illegible]	C. M. Wilson	J. C. [illegible]	J. E. Lawson	H. H. King	E. C. [illegible]	R. R. [illegible]
Ouray	Roy Laird	J. P. [illegible]	[illegible] F. Kiesel	Rich [illegible]	Patricio [illegible]	C. V. [illegible]	Eliza C. [illegible]	Minnie M. Rathmell
Park	D. W. Denny	Frank H. [illegible]	[illegible] L. [illegible]er	G. F. Galloway	Harry C. Bishop	L. M. Gwinn	[illegible]ge W. Shema	Ruth [illegible]
Phillips	W. B. [illegible]	Thomas H. [illegible]	Rex C. Evans	C. A. [illegible]	W. H. [illegible]	O. J. Colver	G. B. Weir	Walter V. Riffenburg
[illegible]	[illegible]nk [illegible]	[illegible]bert S. Killey	Jennie E. Sanders	Chas. Armstrong	Earl McPhee	Frank Hamilton	Wm. R. [illegible]	Anna Short
Prowers	Alonzo [illegible]	Hinton H. Hunter	J. R. Mayfield	[illegible] W. Smith	H. G. Lawson	A. C. Davis	J. C. Horn	Pauline Gilbert
Pueblo	S. E. Thon[illegible]	A. H. [illegible]	William Barber	Cl[illegible] B. Clark	[illegible] N. Bright	Dr. M. S. Middlekamp	F. G. [illegible]	Mrs. Ella Crow Cowles
Rio Blanco	E. L. Manaugh	J. W. C. Shepherd	Claude J. Wilson	D. Kirk [illegible]	E. L. Davis	Chas. H. [illegible]	Herbert Gordon	Lillian Baker
Rio [illegible]	Earl P. [illegible]	B. F. Ayers	H. G. Trapp	W. W. Reilly	[illegible] J. [illegible]	Dr. R. J. Day	[illegible] M. Howard	Edna L. [illegible]uire
[illegible]	Charles W. Neiman	[illegible]rd W. Davis	John D. [illegible]	Wilbur I. [illegible]	Roy P. Hofstetter	William E. Hosking	Charles A. Morning	Nan B. Scales
Saguache	Ed Paul	[illegible] Ellis	[illegible] K. Slane	W. W. [illegible]	Homer Holland	J. A. Keys	M. N. Jordan	J[illegible]. F. Johnson
San [illegible]	Alva [illegible]	F. J. Bawden	C. E. Dresback	Alfred W. [illegible]	Alice M. Kimball	Chas. Scheer	William Palmquist	Mrs. Anna [illegible]
San Miguel	[illegible] G. [illegible]	C. E. [illegible]	Chas. Hooks	H. C. Browning	Stockton Smith	Walter H. Balliger	J. M. Woy	Etta Hall
[illegible]	W. E. Cunningham	Victor Miller	Nellie E. Nichols	[illegible]st [illegible]	Finley [illegible]	Dr. G. F. Ewing	J. S. Labaree	Elma Schroeder
S[illegible]it	J. G. Detwiler	George Robinson	[illegible] F. [illegible]	Chas. D. Galloway	Edward Stuard	Dr. Chas. E. Condon	D. W. [illegible]	Alice W. [illegible]
Teller	Henry vonPhul	Herrick McLeod	John F. [illegible]	A. H. Bebee	J. E. Hall	J. R. Schmalzried	A. R. Jackson	Mary Myrtle [illegible]
Washi[illegible]on	J. W. [illegible]	Harley E. Barnhart	John H. Duncan	John T. Andrews	Hayward R. Rice	E. E. Dey	John G. [illegible]	Phoebe A. [illegible]er
Weld	H. L. [illegible]	Fred W. [illegible]	Claude E. [illegible]ton	H. M. Thompson	Homer F. Bedford	W. H. Wood	Frederic W. Cl[illegible]k	Arch I. Fleming
[illegible]	Wm [illegible]	Ralph Crews	John [illegible]	J. W. [illegible]	John C. [illegible]	J. M. Knowles	I. L. Barker	T. H. [illegible]

County Commissioners

Adams—H. G. Tiffany, H. C. Flanders, H. G. Nunemaker.

Alamosa—S. P. Long, John Fultz, Herman Emperius.

Arapahoe—E. F. Burden, P. Y. Ancell, Raman A. Miller.

Archuleta—C. O. Dunagan, Thos. S. Reavis, G. T. Howe.

Baca—J. M. Graft, Albert Peterson, Jno. M. Johnston.

Bent—J. L. Thompson, Dan Carl, John C. Peper.

Boulder—E. B. Hill, S. D. Buster, Guy Miller.

Chaffee—J. H. Habenicht, Mell DeWitt, G. F. Snell.

Cheyenne—Anton I. Johnson, J. W. Shy, W. C. Schultz.

Clear Creek—George H. Curnow, Louis V. Crist, John W. Green.

Conejos—Frank A. Espinoza, C. P. Jensen, Asisclo Gonzales.

Costilla—S. N. Smith, Jerry L. Morris, A. Lopez.

Crowley—W. F. Tarbox, J. E. Downey, S. S. Spillars.

Custer—Wm. Kettle, Clarence Pond, E. W. Vickerman.

Delta—J. E. Beckley, W. T. McMurray, W. G. Balch.

Dolores—George E. Moore, Edward Baer, George W. Snyder.

Douglas—C. H. Lowell, Andy Sealburg, J. T. Berry.

Eagle—C. L. Hartman, G. D. Roberts, J. H. Heyer.

Elbert—E. T. Evans, Jack Wood, W. J. Park.

El Paso—J. Oscar Cell, W. H. Bartell, Frank F. Lyons.

Fremont—Frank Stienmier, Charles A. Somerville, Sanford G. Kelso.

Garfield—Z. B. Kiggins, R. P. Coulter, John L. Heuschkel.

Gilpin—Richard I. Hughes, Thomas P. Atkinson, John L. Robins.

Grand—Simon Olson, Thos. J. Mitchell, Fount McQueary.

Gunnison—Ted Knowles, Geo. Sullivan, W. U. Mergelman.

Hinsdale—W. E. Christe, D. C. Baker, John H. Hammond.

Huerfano—G. A. Goemmer, T. A. Martinez, George S. Neibuhr.

Jackson—Harry Green, Owen S. Case, C. B. Harmon.

Jefferson—O. N. Evans, E. L. West, Fred Blackmer.

Kiowa—Wirt Bailey, John Rebel, J. O. Walker

Kit Carson—G. W. Huntley, I. D. Messenger, C. J. Buchanan.

Lake—Daniel Colahan, Morgan Walsh, George Bennett.

La Plata—Wm. E. Tyner, John A. Bell, J. H. McHolland.

Larimer—Harris Akin, J. W. McMullen, F. E. Baxter.

Las Animas—Joseph Ray, Hal Barnes, Higinio Cordova.

Lincoln—R. R. Lucore, J. D. Peyton, Chas. Giles.

Logan—C. M. Morris, S. A. Richerson, J. P. Dillon.

Mesa—Gus J. Johnson, Chas. S. Jones, Chas. A. Wallace.

Mineral—B. C. Hosselkus, L. G. Carpenter, Jas. H. Soward.

Moffat—Emery Ehret, Frank C. Barnes, Jr., Henry Phibbs.

Montezuma—H. L. Crawford, F. C. Hallar, E. S. Porter.

Montrose—H. P. Steel, F. J. Hartman, John Howell.

Morgan—James Hurley, O. B. Schooley, M. S. Richeson.

Otero—George Barr, J. E. Stubbs, J. C. Vaughn.

Ouray—Geo. B. Croft, W. H. Brown, C. H. Rowley.

Park—J. F. Rhodes, G. S. Singleton, J. T. Witcher.

Phillips—Ralph L. Anderson, Clithro Barkey, Roy E. Owens.

Pitkin—J. R. Williams, G. B. Brown, C. M. Reed.

Prowers—A. P. Knuckey, Ray McGrath, Henry Masser.

Pueblo—W. L. Rees, O. G. Smith, Hurh H. Wilson.

Rio Blanco—Dennis Murray, Fred A. Nichols, Frank M. Green.

Rio Grande—O. A. Lindstrom, R. A. Chisholm, T. J. Hawkins.

Routt—A. H. Poppen, A. H. Chivington, Alva Jones.

Saguache—D. S. Jones, Geo. Woodard, Ed Clark.

San Juan—Edw. Meyer, J. Ernest Shaw, H. Clay Johnston.

San Miguel—Fred Anderson, T. B. McMahon, A. T. Woods.

Sedgwick—Gustav Sprick, Geo. R. Sellers, John C. Wagner.

Summit—Andrew Lindstrom, Ben F. Rich, William H. Briggle.

Teller—Matt Edwards, R. Quinn, J. B. Wild.

Washington—R. M. Buckmaster, J. B. White, Terrence McAloon.

Weld—Chas. A. Hewitt, Dan C. Straight, Forrest L. Powars.

Yuma—Alex Shaw, Harry F. Strangways, H. H. Brand.

Index

D

CPSIA information can be obtained
at www.ICGtesting.com
Printed in the USA
BVHW090730081118
532427BV00011B/366/P

9 780331 322361